THE ESSENTIAL WORLD HISTORY

VOLUME I: TO 1800

SECOND EDITION

WILLIAM J. DUIKER
THE PENNSYLVANIA STATE UNIVERSITY

JACKSON J. SPIELVOGEL
THE PENNSYLVANIA STATE UNIVERSITY

THOMSON

WADSWORTH™

Australia • Canada • Mexico • Singapore • Spain
United Kingdom • United States

THOMSON

WADSWORTH

Publisher: Clark Baxter
Senior Development Editor: Sue Gleason
Assistant Editor: Paul Massicotte
Editorial Assistant: Richard Yoder
Technology Project Manager: Melinda Newfarmer
Executive Marketing Manager: Caroline Croley
Marketing Assistant: Mary Ho
Advertising Project Manager: Brian Chaffee
Project Manager, Editorial Production: Kimberly Adams
Print/Media Buyer: Doreen Suruki
Permissions Editor: Joohee Lee

Production Service: Orr Book Services
Text Designer: Diane Beasley
Photo Researcher: Sarah Evertson
Copy Editor: Mark Colucci
Illustrator: Maps.com
Cover Designer: Lisa Devenish
Cover Image: Dutch Merchants in Japan. Artist Unknown.
© Superstock, Inc.
Compositor: New England Typographic Service
Printer: Quebecor World/Dubuque

Printed in the United States of America
1 2 3 4 5 6 7 08 07 06 05 04

For more information about our products, contact us at:
Thomson Learning Academic Resource Center
1-800-423-0563
For permission to use material from this text or product, submit a request online at http://www.thomsonrights.com

Any additional questions about permissions can be submitted by email to thomsonrights@thomson.com

Library of Congress Control Number: 2003117126

Student Edition: ISBN 0-534-62713-7

Instructor's Edition: ISBN 0-534-62716-1

Wadsworth Group/Thomson Learning
10 Davis Drive
Belmont, CA 94002-3098
USA

Asia
Thomson Learning
5 Shenton Way #01-01
UIC Building
Singapore 068808

Australia/New Zealand
Thomson Learning
102 Dodds Street
Southbank, Victoria 3006
Australia

Canada
Nelson
1120 Birchmount Road
Toronto, Ontario M1K 5G4
Canada

Europe/Middle East/Africa
Thomson Learning
High Holborn House
50/51 Bedford Row
London WC1R 4LR
United Kingdom

Latin America
Thomson Learning
Seneca, 53
Colonia Polanco
11560 Mexico D.F.
Mexico

Spain/Portugal
Paraninfo
Calle Magallanes, 25
28015 Madrid, Spain

About the Authors

WILLIAM J. DUIKER is liberal arts professor emeritus of East Asian studies at The Pennsylvania State University. A former U.S. diplomat with service in Taiwan, South Vietnam, and Washington, D.C., he received his doctorate in Far Eastern history from Georgetown University in 1968, where his dissertation dealt with the Chinese educator and reformer Cai Yuanpei. At Penn State, he has written extensively on the history of Vietnam and modern China, including the widely acclaimed *The Communist Road to Power in Vietnam* (revised edition, Westview Press, 1996), which was selected for a Choice Outstanding Academic Book Award in 1982–1983 and 1996–1997. Other recent books are *China and Vietnam: The Roots of Conflict* (Berkeley, 1987), *Sacred War: Nationalism and Revolution in a Divided Vietnam* (McGraw-Hill, 1995), and *Ho Chi Minh* (Hyperion, 2000). While his research specialization is in the field of nationalism and Asian revolutions, his intellectual interests are considerably more diverse. He has traveled widely and has taught courses on the History of Communism and Non-Western Civilizations at Penn State, where he was awarded a Faculty Scholar Medal for Outstanding Achievement in the spring of 1996.

To Yvonne,
for adding sparkle to this book, and to my life
W. J. D.

JACKSON J. SPIELVOGEL is associate professor emeritus of history at The Pennsylvania State University. He received his Ph.D. from The Ohio State University, where he specialized in Reformation history under Harold J. Grimm. His articles and reviews have appeared in such journals as *Moreana*, *Journal of General Education*, *Catholic Historical Review*, *Archiv für Reformationsgeschichte*, and *American Historical Review*. He has also contributed chapters or articles to *The Social History of the Reformation*, *The Holy Roman Empire: A Dictionary Handbook*, *Simon Wiesenthal Center Annual of Holocaust Studies*, and *Utopian Studies*. His work has been supported by fellowships from the Fullbright Foundation and the Foundation for Reformation Research. At Penn State, he helped inaugurate the Western civilization courses as well as a popular course on Nazi Germany. His book *Hitler and Nazi Germany* was published in 1987 (fourth edition, 2001). He is the author of *Western Civilization*, published in 1991 (fifth edition, 2003). Professor Spielvogel has won five major university-wide teaching awards. During the year 1988–1989, he held the Penn State Teaching Fellowship, the university's most prestigious teaching award. In 1996, he won the Dean Arthur Ray Warnock Award for Outstanding Faculty Member, and in 2000, received the Schreyer Honors College Excellence in Teaching Award.

To Diane,
whose love and support made it all possible
J. J. S

BRIEF CONTENTS

DETAILED CONTENTS

Part I THE FIRST CIVILIZATIONS AND THE RISE OF EMPIRES (PREHISTORY TO 500 C.E.) 1

Part II NEW PATTERNS OF CIVILIZATION 114

Chapter 17

The West on the Eve of a New World Order   362

DOCUMENT CREDITS

CHAPTER 1

THE CODE OF HAMMURABI   10

From Pritchard, James B., ed.; *Ancient Near Eastern Texts Relating to the Old Testament*, 3rd Edition with Supplement. Copyright © 1969 by Princeton University Press. Reprinted by permission of Princeton University Press.

THE SIGNIFICANCE OF THE NILE RIVER AND THE PHARAOH   12

From Pritchard, James B., ed., *Ancient Near Eastern Texts: Relating to the Old Testament*, 3rd Edition with Supplement. Copyright 1969 by Princeton University Press. Reprinted by permission of Princeton University Press. "Hymn to the Pharaoh": Reprinted from *The Literature of the Ancient Egyptians*, Adolf Erman, copyright 1927 by E.P. Dutton.

THE COVENANT AND THE LAW: THE BOOK OF EXODUS   19

Reprinted from the Holy Bible, New International Version.

THE ASSYRIAN MILITARY MACHINE   21

"King Sennacherib (704–681 B.C.E.) Describes a Battle with the Elamites in 691": Reprinted with permission from Pan Macmillan, London, from *The Might That Was Assyria* by H. W. Saggs. Copyright © 1984 by Sidgwick & Jackson Limited. Pritchard, James B., ed.; *Ancient Near Eastern Texts Relating to the Old Testament*, 3rd Edition with Supplement. Copyright © 1969 by Princeton University Press. Reprinted by permission of Princeton University Press.

CHAPTER 2

THE DUTIES OF A KING   31

Excerpt from *Sources of Indian Tradition*, by William Theodore de Bary. Copyright © 1988 by Columbia University Press. Reprinted with the permission of the publisher.

HOW TO ACHIEVE ENLIGHTENMENT   38

From *The Teachings of the Compassionate Buddha*, E. A. Burtt, ed. Copyright 1955 by Mentor. Used by permission of the E. A. Burtt Estate.

THE VOICES OF SILENCE   39

"Sumangalamata" (A woman well set free! How free I am). Translated from Pali by Uma Chakravarti and Kumkum Roy. Reprinted by permission of The Feminist Press at the City University of New York, www.feministpress.org from *Women Writing in India: 600 B.C. to the Present*, VOL. I, edited by Susie Tharu and K. Lalita, copyright © 1991 by Susie Tharu and K. Lalita. "Venmanipputi" (What she said to her girlfriend), translated by A. K. Ramanujan from *The Interior Landscape* edited by A. K. Ramanujan, 1967. Reprinted by permission of Peter Owen Ltd, London.

RAMA AND SITA   42

From *The Ramayana* by R. K. Narayan. Viking Books, 1972.

CHAPTER 3

LIFE IN THE FIELDS   49

Reprinted from *Ancient China in Transition*, by Cho-yun Hsu, with the permission of the publishers, Stanford University Press, www.sup.org. Copyright © 1965 by the Board of Trustees of the Leland Stanford Junior University.

THE WAY OF THE GREAT LEARNING   53

Excerpt from *Sources of Indian Tradition*, by William Theodore de Bary. Copyright © 1988 by Columbia University Press. Reprinted with the permission of the publisher.

SEEKING THE ETERNAL DAO   54

Reprinted with permission of Macmillan College Publishing Company from *The Way of Lao Tso* by Wing-Tsit Chan. trans. ©1963 by Macmillan College Publishing Co., Inc.

MEMORANDUM ON THE BURNING OF BOOKS   56

Excerpt from *Sources of Chinese Tradition*, by William Theodore de Bary. Copyright © 1960 by Columbia University Press. Reprinted with the permission of the publisher.

CHAPTER 4

HOMER'S IDEAL OF EXCELLENCE   72

From *The Iliad* by Homer, translated by E. V. Rieu (Penguin Classics 1950). Copyright © the Estate of R. V. Rieu, 1946. Reproduced by permission of Penguin Books Ltd.

THE LYCURGAN REFORMS   75

From *Plutarch, The Lives of the Noble Grecians and Romans*, translated by John Dryden, and revised by Arthur Hugh Clough. (New York: Modern Library).

HOUSEHOLD MANAGEMENT AND THE ROLE OF THE ATHENIAN WIFE   82

Reprinted by permission of the publishers and the Trustees of the Loeb Classical Library from *Xenophon: Memoribilia and Oeconomicus*, Volume IV, Loeb Classical Library 168, translated by E. C. Marchant, Cambridge, Mass.: Harvard University Press, 1923. The Loeb Classical Library® is a registered trademark of the President and Fellows of Harvard College.

ALEXANDER MEETS AN INDIAN KING   84

From *The Campaigns of Alexander* by Arrian, translated by Aubrey de Selincourt. Viking Press, 1976.

CHAPTER 5

CINCINNATUS SAVES ROME: A ROMAN MORALITY TALE   92

From *The Early History of Rome By Livy*, translated by Aubrey de Selincourt. Copyright the Estate of Aubrey de Selincourt 1960.

THE ASSASSINATION OF JULIUS CAESAR   96

From *Plutarch, The Lives of the Noble Grecians and Romans*, translated by John Dryden, and revised by Arthur Hugh Clough. (New York: Modern Library).

THE ROMAN FEAR OF SLAVES   102

From *Letters of the Younger Pliny*, translated by Betty Radice (Penguin Classics, 1963). Copyright © Betty Radice, 1963. Reproduced by permission of Penguin Books Ltd. From *The Annals of Imperial Rome* by Tacitus, translated by Michael Grant (Penguin Classics, 1956, Sixth revised edition 1989). Copyright © Michael Grant Publications Ltd, 1956, 1959, 1971, 1989. Reproduced by permission of Penguin Books Ltd.

CHRONOLOGIES

Maps

MAP CREDITS

The authors wish to acknowledge their use of the following books as reference in preparing the maps listed here:

SPOT MAP, PAGE 28   Geoffrey Barraclough, ed., *Times Atlas of World History*, (Maplewood, N.J.: Hammond Inc., 1978), p. 65.

MAP 3.2   Geoffrey Barraclough, ed., *Times Atlas of World History*, (Maplewood, N.J.: Hammond Inc., 1978), p. 63.

MAP 3.3   Conrad Schirokauer, *A Brief History of Chinese and Japanese Civilizations*, 2d ed. (San Diego: Harcourt Brace Jovanovich, 1989), p. 52.

MAP 3.4   Hammond Past Worlds: *The Times Atlas of Archeology*, (Maplewood, N.J.: Hammond Inc. 1988), pp. 190–191.

MAP 6.2   Michael Coe, Dean Snow, and Elizabeth Benson, *Atlas of Ancient America* (New York: Facts on File, 1988), p. 144.

MAP 6.3   Geoffrey Barraclough, ed., *Times Atlas of World History*, (Maplewood, N.J.: Hammond Inc., 1978), p. 47.

MAP 6.4   Phillipa Fernandez-Arnesto, *Atlas of World Exploration*, (New York: Harper Collins, 1991), p. 35.

MAP 6.5   Geoffrey Barraclough, ed., *Times Atlas of World History*, (Maplewood, N.J.: Hammond Inc., 1978), p. 47.

MAP 7.3   Geoffrey Barraclough, ed., *Times Atlas of World History*, (Maplewood, N.J.: Hammond Inc., 1978), pp. 134–135.

MAP 7.4   Geoffrey Barraclough, ed., *Times Atlas of World History*, (Maplewood, N.J.: Hammond Inc., 1978), p. 135.

MAP 8.1   Geoffrey Barraclough, ed., *Times Atlas of World History*, (Maplewood, N.J.: Hammond Inc., 1978), pp. 44–45.

MAP 8.4   Geoffrey Barraclough, ed., *Times Atlas of World History*, (Maplewood, N.J.: Hammond Inc., 1978), pp. 136–137.

MAP 9.1   Michael Edwardes, *A History of India* (London: Thames and Hudson, 1961), p. 79.

MAP 10.1   John K. Fairbank, Edwin O. Reischauer, and Albert M. Craig, *East Asia: Tradition and Transformation* (Boston: Houghton Mifflin, 1973), p. 103.

SPOT MAP, PAGE 204   Albert Hermann, *An Historical Atlas of China* (Chicago: Aidine, 1966), p. 13.

MAP 11.1   John K. Fairbank, Edwin O. Reischauer, and Albert M. Craig, *East Asia: Tradition and Transformation* (Boston: Houghton Mifflin, 1973), p. 363.

MAP 14.1   Geoffrey Barraclough, ed., *Times Atlas of World History*, (Maplewood, N. J.:Hammond, Inc. 1978), p. 160.

MAP 15.3   Geoffrey Barraclough, ed., *Times Atlas of World History*, (Maplewood, N. J.: Hammond, Inc. 1978), p. 173.

MAP 16.1   Jonathan Spence, *The Search for Modern China*, (New York: W. W. Norton, 1990), p. 19.

MAP 16.2   Conrad Schirokauer, *A Brief History of Chinese and Japanese Civilizations*, 2d ed., (San Diego: Harcourt Brace Jovanovich, 1989), p. 330.

MAP 16.3   John K. Fairbank, Edwin O. Reischauer, and Albert M. Craig, *East Asia: Tradition and Transformation*, (Boston: Houghton Mifflin, 1973), pp. 402–403.

PHOTO CREDITS

PREFACE

For several million years after primates first appeared on the surface of the earth, human beings lived in small communities, seeking to survive by hunting, fishing, and foraging in a frequently hostile environment. Then suddenly, in the space of a few thousand years, there was an abrupt change of direction as human beings in a few widely scattered areas of the globe began to master the art of cultivating food crops. As food production increased, the population in those areas rose correspondingly, and people began to congregate in larger communities. Governments were formed to provide protection and other needed services to the local population. Cities appeared and became the focal point of cultural and religious development. Historians refer to this process as the beginnings of civilization.

For generations, historians in Europe and the United States have pointed to the rise of such civilizations as marking the origins of the modern world. Courses on Western civilization conventionally begin with a chapter or two on the emergence of advanced societies in Egypt and Mesopotamia and then proceed to ancient Greece and the Roman Empire. From Greece and Rome, the road leads directly to the rise of modern civilization in the West.

There is nothing inherently wrong with this approach. Important aspects of our world today can indeed be traced back to these early civilizations, and all human beings the world over owe a considerable debt to their achievements. But all too often this interpretation has been used to imply that the course of civilization has been linear in nature, leading directly from the emergence of agricultural societies in ancient Mesopotamia to the rise of advanced industrial societies in Europe and North America. Until recently, most courses on world history taught in the United States routinely focused almost exclusively on the rise of the West, with only a passing glance at other parts of the world, such as Africa, India, and East Asia. The contributions made by those societies to the culture and technology of our own time were often passed over in silence.

Several reasons have been advanced to justify this approach. Some have argued that students simply are not interested in what is unfamiliar to them. Others have said that it is more important that young minds understand the roots of their own heritage than that of peoples elsewhere in the world. In many cases, however, the motivation for this Eurocentric approach has been the belief that since the time of Socrates and Aristotle Western civilization has been the sole driving force in the evolution of human society.

Such an interpretation, however, represents a serious distortion of the process. During most of the course of human history, the most advanced civilizations have been not in the West, but in East Asia or the Middle East. A relatively brief period of European dominance culminated with the era of imperialism in the late nineteenth century, when the political, military, and economic power of the advanced nations of the West spanned the globe. During recent generations, however, that dominance has gradually eroded, partly as the result of changes taking place within Western societies and partly because new centers of development are emerging elsewhere on the globe—notably in East Asia, where the growing economic strength of Japan and many of its neighbors has led to the now familiar prediction that the twenty-first century will be known as the Pacific Century.

World history, then, is not simply a chronicle of the rise of the West to global dominance, nor is it a celebration of the superiority of the civilization of Europe and the United States over other parts of the world. The history of the world has been a complex process in which many branches of the human community have taken an active part, and the dominance of any one area of the world has been a temporary rather than a permanent phenomenon. It will be our purpose in this book to present a balanced picture of this story, with all respect for the richness and diversity of the tapestry of the human experience. Due attention must be paid to the rise of the West, of course, since that has been the most dominant aspect of world history in recent centuries. But the contributions made by other peoples must be given adequate consideration as well, not only in the period prior to 1500 when the major centers of civilization were located in Asia, but also in our own day, where a multipolar picture of development is clearly beginning to emerge.

Anyone who wishes to teach or write about world history must decide whether to present the topic as an integrated whole or as a collection of different cultures. The world that we live in today, of course, is in many respects an interdependent one in terms of economics as well as culture and communications, a reality that is often expressed by the phrase "global village." The convergence of peoples across the surface of the earth into an integrated world system began in early times and intensified after the rise of capitalism in the early modern era. In growing recognition of this trend, historians trained in global history, as well as instructors in the growing number of world history courses, have now begun to speak and write of a "global approach" that turns attention away from the study of individual civilizations and focuses instead on the "big picture" or, as the world historian Fernand Braudel termed it, interpreting world history as a river with no banks.

On the whole, this development is to be welcomed as a means of bringing the common elements of the evolution of human society to our attention. But there is a problem involved in this approach. For the vast majority of their time on earth, human beings have lived in partial or virtually total isolation from each other. Differences in climate, location, and geographical features have created human societies very different from each other in culture and historical experience. Only in relatively recent times—the commonly accepted date has long been the beginning of the age of European exploration at the end of the fifteenth century, but some would now push it back to the era of the Mongol empire or even further—have cultural interchanges begun to create a common "world system," in which events taking place in one part of the world are rapidly transmitted throughout the globe, often with momentous consequences. In recent generations, of course, the process of global interdependence has been proceeding even more rapidly. Nevertheless, even now the process is by no means complete, as ethnic and regional differences continue to exist and to shape the course of world history. The tenacity of these differences and sensitivities is reflected not only in the rise of internecine conflicts in such divergent areas as Africa, India, and Eastern Europe, but also in the emergence in recent years of such regional organizations as the Organization of African Unity, the Association for the Southeast Asian Nations, and the European Economic Community. Political leaders in various parts of the world speak routinely of "Arab unity," the "African road to socialism," and the "Confucian path to economic development."

The second problem is a practical one. College students today are all too often not well informed about the distinctive character of civilizations such as China and India and, without sufficient exposure to the historical evolution of such societies, will assume all too readily that the peoples in these countries have had historical experiences similar to ours and will respond to various stimuli in a similar fashion to those living in Western Europe or the United States. If it is a mistake to ignore those forces that link us together, it is equally a mistake to underestimate those factors that continue to divide us and to differentiate us into a world of diverse peoples.

Our response to this challenge has been to adopt a global approach to world history while at the same time attempting to do justice to the distinctive character and development of individual civilizations and regions of the world. The presentation of individual cultures will be especially important in Parts I and II, which cover a time when it is generally agreed that the process of global integration was not yet far advanced. Later chapters will begin to adopt a more comparative and thematic approach, in deference to the greater number of connections that have been established among the world's peoples since the fifteenth and sixteenth centuries. Part V will consist of a series of chapters that will center on individual regions of the world while at the same time focusing on common problems related to the Cold War and the rise of global problems such as overproduction and environmental pollution. Moreover, sections entitled "Reflection" at the close of the five major parts of the book will attempt to link events together in a broad comparative and global framework.

We have sought balance in another way as well. Many textbooks tend to simplify the content of history courses by emphasizing an intellectual or political perspective or, most recently, a social perspective, often at the expense of sufficient details in a chronological framework. This approach is confusing to students whose high school social studies programs have often neglected a systematic study of world history. We have attempted to write a well-balanced work in which political, economic, social, religious, intellectual, cultural, and military history have been integrated into a chronologically ordered synthesis.

To enliven the past and let readers see for themselves the materials that historians use to create their pictures of the past, we have included primary sources (boxed documents) in each chapter that are keyed to the discussion in the text. The documents include examples of the religious, artistic, intellectual, social, economic, and political aspects of life in different societies and reveal in a vivid fashion what civilization meant to the individual men and women who shaped it by their actions.

Each chapter has a lengthy introduction and conclusion to help maintain the continuity of the narrative and to provide a synthesis of important themes. Anecdotes in the chapter introductions convey more dramatically the major theme or themes of each chapter. Timelines at the end of each chapter enable students to see the major developments of an era at a glance and within crosscultural categories, while the more detailed chronologies reinforce the events discussed in the text. An annotated bibliography at the end of each chapter reviews the most recent literature on each period and also gives references to some of the older, "classic" works in each field.

Extensive maps and illustrations serve to deepen the reader's understanding of the text. New to the second edition are map captions, designed to enrich students' awareness of the importance of geography to history, and a large number of spot maps, which enable students to see at a glance the region or subject being discussed in the text. In addition, special globe icons indicate maps for which an interactive version appears on the Web site. The maps have also been revised where needed. To facilitate understanding of cultural movements, illustrations of artistic works discussed in the text are placed next to the discussions. Chapter outlines and focus questions, including analytical questions, at the beginning of each chapter help students with an overview and guide them to the main subjects of each chapter. A glossary of important terms and a pronunciation guide are included to enrich an understanding of the text.

After reexamining the entire book and analyzing the comments and reviews of many colleagues who have found the book to be a useful instrument for introducing their students to world history, we have also made a number of other changes for the second edition. In the first place, we have continued our effort to reduce the size of the book without affecting the quality of the material contained therein. As part of this effort, we have reorganized the material of five European chapters into three new chapters. These are Chapter 12, "The Making of Europe in the Middle Ages"; Chapter 13, "Renewal, Reform, and State Building in Europe"; and Chapter 17, "The West on the Eve of a New World Order." Moreover, Chapters 31 and 32 have been synthesized into a new Chapter 29, "Toward the Pacific Century?" We have also tried to delete excess words while retaining all essential material as well as the narrative thrust of the previous edition.

Second, we have sought to strengthen the global framework of the book, but not at the expense of reducing the attention assigned to individual regions of the world. The essays entitled "Reflection" that appear at the end of each of the five parts have been shortened slightly to accommodate the advice of many of our reviewers and to enable us to more concisely draw comparisons and contrasts across geographical, cultural, and chronological lines. Each Reflection section contains boxed essays, each highlighted with an illustration, to single out issues of particular importance to that period of history. Moreover, additional comparative material has been added to each chapter to help students be aware of similar developments globally. Among other things, this material includes new comparative sections, such as "Comparison of the Roman and Han Empires" in Chapter 5 and "Europe, China, and Scientific Revolutions" in Chapter 13, as well as comparative illustrations in each chapter. We hope that these techniques will assist instructors who wish to encourage their students to adopt a comparative approach to their understanding of the human experience.

Third, this new edition contains additional information on the role of women in world history. In conformity with our own convictions, as well as what we believe to be recent practice in the field, we have tried where possible to introduce such material at the appropriate point in the text, rather than to set aside separate sections devoted exclusively to women's issues.

Finally, a number of new illustrations, boxed documents, and maps have been added, and the bibliographies have been revised to take account of newly published material. The chronologies and maps have been fine-tuned as well, to help the reader locate in time and space the multitude of individuals and place names that appear in the book. To keep up with the ever-growing body of historical scholarship, new or revised material has been added throughout the book on many topics, including early civilizations around the world; the Aryans in India; the Zhou dynasty in China; Sparta; Alexander and the Mauryan Empire in India; Roman trade with China; comparison of Roman and Han Chinese empires; the first Americans; the Maya; first civilizations in South America; Islam; early civilizations in Africa; the spread of Buddhism; the Song dynasty in China; the Mongols; early Japan; the African slave trade; the Ottoman Empire; the Mughals; Ming China; Tokugawa Japan; the impact of Western expansion on indigenous peoples; the impact of the discovery of the Pacific Islands in the eighteenth century; the defeat of Napoleon; slave revolt in Haiti; how industrialized nations limited industrialization in their colonies; Latin America; Canada; the impact of World War I on Africa, East Asia, and the Pacific; the Russian Revolution; and the Asian theater of World War II. In addition, all of the chapters in Part V have been updated to bring our treatment of contemporary events up to the present.

Because courses in world history at American and Canadian colleges and universities follow different chronological divisions, a one-volume edition, a two-volume edition, and a volume covering events to 1400 are being made available to fit the needs of instructors. Teaching and learning ancillaries include:

Instructor's Manual and Test Bank Prepared by Eugene Larson, Los Angeles, Pierce College. Contains chapter outlines, class lecture/discussion topics, thought/discussion questions for primary sources (boxed documents), possible student projects, and examination questions (essay, identification, and multiple choice). Also available on the Instructor's Resource CD-ROM.

Instructor's Resource CD-ROM with ExamView® Includes the Instructor's Manual, Resource Integration Guide, *ExamView* computerized testing, and PowerPoint® slides with lecture outlines and images that can be used as offered or customized by importing personal lecture slides or other material. *ExamView* allows you to create, deliver, and customize tests and study guides (both print and online) in minutes with this easy-to-use assessment and tutorial system. It offers both a Quick Test Wizard and an Online Test Wizard that guide you step by step through the process of creating tests, while its "what you see is what you get" capability allows you to see the test you are creating on the screen exactly as it will print or display online. You can build tests of up to 250 questions with as many as 12 question types. Using *ExamView's* complete word-processing capabilities, you can enter an unlimited number of new questions or edit existing questions.

Map Acetates with Commentary for World History   Includes more than 100 four-color map images from the text and other sources. Map commentary for each map is prepared by James Harrison, Siena College. Three-hole punched and shrinkwrapped.

History Video Library   Includes Film For Humanities (these are available to qualified adoptions), CNN® videos, and Grade Improvement: Taking Charge of Your Learning.

CNN Videos for World History   Two- to five-minute CNN segments are easy to integrate into classroom discussions or as lecture launchers.

Sights and Sounds of History   Prepared by David Redles, Cuyahoga Community College. Short, focused video clips, photos, artwork, animations, music, and dramatic readings are used to bring life to historical topics and events which are most difficult for students to appreciate from a textbook alone. For example, students will experience the grandeur of Versailles and the defeat felt by a German soldier at Stalingrad. The video segments, each averaging 4 minutes long, make excellent lecture launchers. Available on VHS video.

Music CD-ROMs   Available to instructors on request, these CDs include music selections from the twelfth century to the present and can be used to enhance lectures. The Resource Integration Guide includes a correlation guide. Contact your local Thomson Wadsworth representative for further information.

Exploring the European Past: Text & Images   A Custom Reader for the Western Civilization coverage of the class. Written by leading educators and historians, this fully customizable reader of primary and secondary sources is enhanced with an online collection of visual sources, including maps, animations, and interactive exercises. Each reading also comes with an introduction and a series of review questions. To learn more, visit www.ThomsonCustom.com or call Thomson Custom Publishing at 1.800.355.9983.

History Interactive: A Study Tool   This valuable CD-ROM for students, prepared by Laura Wood and Michael Nichols of Tarrant County College. Includes a wealth of primary source documents; interactive maps and timelines; chapter summaries; multiple choice; essay questions; analysis of primary source documents; How to Read a Document; How to Read a Map; the World History Image Bank; simulations for World History; study tips for the narrative, maps, photographs, and documents; answers to text Focus questions and map questions; and sample H-Connect interactive modules. (Packaged for free with all new copies of the text.)

H-Connect: Interactive Explorations in World History   This CD-ROM and student guide feature interactive multimedia modules to complement any college-level world history course. The student guide provides a complete index to the interactive modules, as well as a correlation guide to *The Essential World History*. Contact your Thomson Wadsworth representative for more information.

Map Exercise Workbook   Prepared by Cynthia Kosso, Northern Arizona University. Has been thoroughly revised and improved. Contains over 20 maps and exercises, which ask students to identify important cities and countries. Also includes critical thinking questions for each unit. Available in two volumes.

World History MapTutor   This new mapping CD-ROM allows students to learn by manipulating maps through "locate and label" exercises, animations, and critical thinking exercises.

Migrations in Modern World History 1500–2000 CD-ROM   An interactive multimedia curriculum on CD-ROM by Patrick Manning and the World History Center. Includes over 400 primary source documents; analytical questions to help the student develop his/her own interpretations of history; timelines; and additional suggested resources, including books, films, and web sites.

Document Exercise Workbooks   Prepared by Donna Van Raaphorst, Cuyahoga Community College. Contains a collection of exercises based around primary source documents pertaining to world history.

The Journey of Civilization CD ROM for Windows   Prepared by David Redles, Cuyahoga Community College. This CD takes students on 18 interactive journeys through history. Enhanced with QuickTime movies, animations, sound clips, maps, and more, the journeys allow students to engage in history as active participants rather than as readers of past events.

Magellan World History Atlas   Available to bundle with any history text; contains 44 historical four-color maps in a practical 8″ × 10″ format.

Internet Guide for History, Third Edition   Prepared by John Soares. Provides newly revised and up-to-date Internet exercises by topic. Available at http://history.wadsworth.com.

Kishlansky, Sources in World History, Second and Third Editions   This reader is a collection of documents designed to supplement any world history text. Available in two volumes.

Web Tutor™ Toolbox   This content-rich, Web-based teaching and learning tool helps students succeed by taking the course beyond classroom boundaries to an anywhere, anytime environment. *Web Tutor* offers real-time access to a full array of study tools, including flashcards (with audio), practice quizzes, online tutorials, and Web links. Web Tutor also provides rich communication tools, including a course calendar, asynchronous discussion, "real-time" chat, and an integrated e-mail system. Available for Blackboard and WebCT.

InfoTrac® College Edition   An online university that lets students explore and use full-length articles from more than 900 periodicals for four months. When students log on with their personal ID, they will immediately see how easy it is to search. Students can print out the articles, which date back as far as four years.

The Wadsworth History Resource Center

http://history.wadsworth.com/

Features a career section, forum, and links to museums, historical documents, the World History Image Bank, and other fascinating sites. From the Resource Center you can access the book-specific web site, which contains the following: chapter by chapter tutorial quizzing, *InfoTrac* activities, Internet activities, interactive maps and time-lines, glossary, and hyperlinks for the student, and an online instructor's manual and downloadable PowerPoint files for the Instructor.

ACKNOWLEDGMENTS

Both authors gratefully acknowledge that without the generosity of many others, this project could not have been completed. William Duiker would like to thank Kumkum Chatterjee and On-cho Ng for their helpful comments about unfamiliar issues related to the history of India and premodern China. His long-time colleague Cyril Griffith, now deceased, was a cherished friend and a constant source of information about modern Africa. Art Goldschmidt has been of invaluable assistance in reading several chapters of the manuscript, as well as in unraveling many of the mysteries of Middle Eastern civilization. Finally, he remains profoundly grateful to his wife, Yvonne V. Duiker, Ph.D. She has not only given her usual measure of love and support when this appeared to be an insuperable task, but she has also contributed her own time and expertise to enrich the sections on art and literature, thereby adding life and sparkle to

this, as well as the earlier edition of the book. To her, and to his daughters Laura and Claire, he will be forever thankful for bringing joy to his life.

Jackson Spielvogel would like to thank Art Goldschmidt, David Redles, and Christine Colin for their time and ideas and, above all, his family for their support. The gifts of love, laughter, and patience from his daughters, Jennifer and Kathryn, his sons, Eric and Christian, and his daughters-in-law, Liz and Laurie, were invaluable. Diane, his wife and best friend, provided him with editorial assistance, wise counsel, and the loving support that made a project of this magnitude possible.

Thanks to Wadsworth's comprehensive review process, many historians were asked to evaluate our manuscript. We are grateful to the following for the innumerable suggestions that have greatly improved our work:

Henry Abramson
  Florida Atlantic University
Eric H. Ash
  Wayne State University
William Bakken
  Rochester Community College
Suzanne Balch-Lindsay
  Eastern New Mexico University
Michael E. Birdwell
  Tennessee Technological University
Eileen Brown
  Norwalk Community College
Thomas Cardoza
  University of California, San Diego
Wade Dudley
  East Carolina University
E. J. Fabyan
  Vincennes University
Janine C. Hartman
  University of Connecticut
Sanders Huguenin
  University of Science and Arts of Oklahoma
C. Barden Keeler
  Gulf Coast High School
Marilynn Fox Kokoszka
  Orchard Ridge Campus, Oakland Community College
James Krippner-Martinez
  Haverford College

David Leinweber
  Oxford College, Emory University
Daniel Miller
  Calvin College
Michael Murdock
  Brigham Young University
Elsa A. Nystrom
  Kennesaw State University
Randall L. Pouwels
  University of Central Arkansas
Pamela Sayre
  Henry Ford Community College
Philip Curtis Skaggs
  Grand Valley State University
Laura Smoller
  University of Arkansas at Little Rock
Beatrice Spade
  University of Southern Colorado
Jeremy Stahl
  Middle Tennessee State University
Kate Transchel
  California State University, Chico
Lorna VanMeter
  Ball State University
Michelle White
  University of Tennessee at Chattanooga

The authors are truly grateful to the people who have helped us produce this book. We especially want to thank Clark Baxter, whose faith in our ability to do this project was inspiring. Sue Gleason thoughtfully guided the overall development of the second edition, and Paul Massicotte orchestrated the preparation of outstanding teaching and learning ancillaries. Mark Colucci and Pat Lewis were, as usual, outstanding copy editors. Sarah Evertson provided valuable assistance in obtaining permissions for the illustrations. We are grateful to the staff of New England Typographic Service for providing their array of typesetting and page layout abilities. John Orr, of Orr Book Services, was as cooperative and cheerful as he was competent in matters of production management.

A Note to Students about Languages and the Dating of Time

One of the most difficult challenges in studying world history is coming to grips with the multitude of names, words, and phrases in unfamiliar languages. Unfortunately, this problem has no easy solution. We have tried to alleviate the difficulty, where possible, by providing an English-language translation of foreign words or phrases, a glossary, and a pronunciation guide. The issue is especially complicated in the case of Chinese, since two separate systems are commonly used to transliterate the spoken Chinese language into the Roman alphabet. The Wade-Giles system, invented in the nineteenth century, was the most frequently used until recent years, when the pinyin system was adopted by the People's Republic of China as its own official form of transliteration. We have opted to use the latter, since it appears to be gaining acceptance in the United States, but the initial use of a Chinese word is accompanied by its Wade-Giles equivalent in parentheses for the benefit of those who may encounter the term in their outside reading.

In our examination of world history, we need also to be aware of the dating of time. In recording the past, historians try to determine the exact time when events occurred. World War II in Europe, for example, began on September 1, 1939, when Adolf Hitler sent German troops into Poland, and ended on May 7, 1945, when Germany surrendered. By using dates, historians can place events in order and try to determine the development of patterns over periods of time.

If someone asked you when you were born, you would reply with a number, such as 1985. In the United States, we would all accept that number without question, because it is part of the dating system followed in the Western world (Europe and the Western Hemisphere). In this system, events are dated by counting backward or forward from the birth of Christ (assumed to be the year 1). An event that took place 400 years before the birth of Christ would most commonly be dated 400 B.C. (before Christ). Dates after the birth of Christ are labeled as A.D. These letters stand for the Latin words *anno domini*, which mean "in the year of the Lord" (or the year of the birth of Christ). Thus an event that took place 250 years after the birth of Christ is written A.D. 250, or in the year of the Lord 250. It can also be written as 250, just as you would not give your birth year as A.D. 1985, but simply 1985.

Some historians now prefer to use the abbreviations B.C.E. ("before the common era") and C.E. ("common era") instead of B.C. and A.D. This is especially true of world historians who prefer to use symbols that are not so Western or Christian oriented. The dates, of course, remain the same. Thus, 1950 B.C.E. and 1950 B.C. would be the same year, as would A.D. 40 and 40 C.E. In keeping with the current usage by many world historians, this book will use the terms B.C.E. and C.E.

Historians also make use of other terms to refer to time. A decade is 10 years; a century is 100 years; and a millennium is 1,000 years. The phrase fourth century B.C.E. refers to the fourth period of 100 years counting backward from 1, the assumed date of the birth of Christ. Since the first century B.C.E. would be the years 100 B.C.E. to 1 B.C.E., the fourth century B.C.E. would be the years 400 B.C.E. to 301 B.C.E. We could say, then, that an event in 350 B.C.E. took place in the fourth century B.C.E.

The phrase fourth century C.E. refers to the fourth period of 100 years after the birth of Christ. Since the first period of 100 years would be the years 1 to 100, the fourth period or fourth century would be the years 301 to 400. We could say, then, for example, that an event in 350 took place in the fourth century. Likewise, the first millennium B.C.E. refers to the years 1000 B.C.E. to 1 B.C.E.; the second millennium C.E. refers to the years 1001 to 2000.

The dating of events can also vary from people to people. Most people in the Western world use the Western calendar, also known as the Gregorian calendar after Pope Gregory XIII who refined it in 1582. The Hebrew calendar, on the other hand, uses a different system in which the year one is the equivalent of the Western year 3760 B.C.E., considered by Jews to be the date of the creation of the world. Thus, the Western year 2003 will be the year 5763 on the Jewish calendar. The Islamic calendar begins year 1 on the day Muhammad fled Mecca, which is the year 622 on the Western calendar.

THEMES FOR UNDERSTANDING WORLD HISTORY

*I*n examining the past, historians often organize their material on the basis of themes that enable them to ask and try to answer basic questions about the past. The following ten themes are especially important.

1. *Political systems*. The study of politics seeks to answer certain basic questions that historians have about the structure of a society: How were people governed? What was the relationship between the ruler and the ruled? What people or groups of people (the political elites) held political power? What actions did people take to change their form of government? Historians also examine the causes and results of wars in order to understand the impact of war on human development.

2. *The role of ideas*. Ideas have great power to move people to action. For example, in the twentieth century, the idea of nationalism, which is based on a belief in loyalty to one's nation, helped produce two great conflicts— World War I and World War II. Together these wars cost the lives of more than fifty million people. The spread of ideas from one society to another has also played an important role in world history. From the earliest times, trade has especially served to bring different civilizations into contact with one another, and the transmission of religious and cultural ideas soon followed.

3. *Economics and history*. A society depends for its existence on certain basic needs. How did it grow its food? How did it make its goods? How did it provide the services people needed? How did individual people and governments use their limited resources? Did they spend more money on hospitals or military forces? By answering these questions, historians examine the different economic systems that have played a role in history.

4. *Social life and gender issues*. From a study of social life, we learn about the different social classes that make up a society. But we also examine how people dressed and found shelter, how and what they ate, and what they did for fun. The nature of family life and how knowledge was passed from one generation to another through education are also part of the social life of a society. So, too, are gender issues: What different roles did men and women play in their societies? How and why were those roles different?

5. *The importance of culture*. We cannot understand a society without looking at its culture, or the common ideas,

beliefs, and patterns of behavior that are passed on from one generation to another. Culture includes both high culture and popular culture. High culture consists of the writings of a society's thinkers and the works of its artists. A society's popular culture is the world of ideas and experiences of ordinary people. Today the media have embraced the term *popular culture* to describe the most current trends and fashionable styles.

6. *Religion in history*. Throughout history, people have sought to find a deeper meaning to human life. How have the world's great religions, such as Hinduism, Buddhism, Judaism, Christianity, and Islam, influenced people's lives? How have these religions spread to create new patterns of culture?

7. *The role of individuals*. In discussing the role of politics, ideas, economics, social life, cultural developments, and religion, we have dealt with groups of people and forces that often seem beyond the control of any one person. But mentioning the names of Cleopatra, Queen Elizabeth I, Napoleon, and Hitler reminds us of the role of individuals in history. Decisive actions by powerful individuals have indeed played a crucial role in the course of history.

8. *The impact of science and technology*. For thousands of years, people around the world have made scientific discoveries and technological innovations that have changed our world. From the creation of stone tools that made farming easier to the advanced computers that guide our airplanes, science and technology have altered how humans have related to their world.

9. *The environment and history*. Throughout history, peoples and societies have been affected by the physical world in which they live. Climatic changes alone have been an important factor in human history. Peoples and societies, in turn, have also made an impact on their world. Human activities have affected the physical environment and even endangered the very existence of entire societies and species.

10. *The migration of peoples*. One characteristic of world history is an almost constant migration of peoples. Vast numbers of peoples abandoned their homelands and sought to live elsewhere. Sometimes the migration was peaceful. More often than not, however, the migration meant invasion and violent conflict.

Part I

The First Civilizations and the Rise of Empires (Prehistory to 500 C.E.)

For hundreds of thousands of years, human beings lived in small communities, seeking to survive by hunting, fishing, and foraging in an often hostile environment. Then, in the space of a few thousand years, there was an abrupt change of direction as humans in a few widely scattered areas of the globe began to master the art of cultivating food crops. As food production increased, the population in such areas grew, and people began to congregate in larger communities. Cities appeared and became centers of cultural and religious development. Historians call this process the beginnings of civilization.

The first civilizations that emerged in Mesopotamia, Egypt, India, and China all shared a number of basic characteristics. Each developed in a river valley that was able to provide the agricultural resources needed to maintain a large population. In each civilization, a part of the population lived in cities, which became the focal points for political, economic, social, cultural, and religious development. All of these early civilizations established some kind of organized government bureaucracy to meet the administrative demands of the growing population and organized armies for protection and to gain land and power. A social structure based on economic control arose. While kings and an upper class of priests, political leaders, and warriors dominated, there also existed a large group of free people (farmers, artisans, craftspeople) and, at the very bottom socially, a class of slaves. Abundant agricultural yields in these regions created opportunities for economic specialization as a surplus of goods enabled people to create new products.

The new urban civilizations were also characterized by significant religious and cultural developments. The gods were often deemed critical to a community's success, and professional priestly classes regulated relations with the gods. Rulers, priests, merchants, and artisans used writing to keep records and to preserve and

create literary expression. Monumental architectural structures and new forms of artistic activity became prominent in the new urban environments.

By and large, the early river valley civilizations developed independently, grounded in local developments related to new agricultural practices. But contacts between them did occur and facilitated the exchange of new ideas and technology. Trade was often carried out by nomadic peoples from beyond the frontiers of settled states. Though not as organized as the city dwellers, these nomadic peoples too played a major role in the human experience.

From the beginnings of the first civilizations around 3000 B.C.E., there was an ongoing movement toward the creation of larger territorial states with more sophisticated systems of control. This process reached a high point in the first millennium B.C.E. Between 1000 and 500 B.C.E., the Assyrians and Persians amassed empires that encompassed large areas of the ancient Middle East. The conquests of Alexander the Great in the fourth century B.C.E. created an even larger, if short-lived, empire that soon divided into four kingdoms. Later, the western portion of these kingdoms as well as the Mediterranean world and much of western Europe fell subject to the mighty empire of the Romans. At the same time, much of India became part of the Mauryan Empire, and in the last few centuries B.C.E., the Qin and Han dynasties of China created a unified Chinese empire.

© British Museum

THE FIRST CIVILIZATIONS: THE PEOPLES OF WESTERN ASIA AND EGYPT

FOCUS QUESTIONS
- In what areas of the world did systematic agriculture develop during the Neolithic Age, and how did this development affect the lives of men and women?
- What are the characteristics of civilization, and what are some explanations for why early civilizations emerged?
- What effects did geography have on the civilizations that arose in Mesopotamia and Egypt?
- What role did religion play in the early civilizations of western Asia and Egypt, and how did Judaism and Zoroastrianism differ from the other religions of the region?
- What methods and institutions did the Assyrians and Persians use to amass and maintain their respective empires?
- ➤ In what ways were the civilizations of Mesopotamia and Egypt alike? In what ways were they different?

*I*n 1849, a daring young Englishman made a hazardous journey into the deserts and swamps of southern Iraq. Braving high winds and temperatures that reached 120 degrees Fahrenheit, William Loftus led a small expedition southward along the banks of the Euphrates River in search of the roots of civilization. As he said, "From our childhood we have been led to regard this place as the cradle of the human race."

Guided by native Arabs into the southernmost reaches of Iraq, Loftus and his small band of explorers were soon overwhelmed by what they saw. He wrote, "I know of nothing more exciting or impressive than the first sight of one of these great piles, looming in solitary grandeur from the surrounding plains and marshes." One of these piles, known to the natives as the mound of Warka, contained the ruins of Uruk, one of the first cities in the world and part of one of the world's first civilizations.

Southern Iraq, known to ancient peoples as Mesopotamia, was one area in the world where civilization began. In the fertile valleys of large rivers—the Tigris and Euphrates in Mesopotamia, the Nile in Egypt, the Indus in India, and the Yellow River in China—intensive agriculture became capable of supporting large groups of people. In these regions, civilization was born. The first civilizations emerged in western Asia (now known as the Middle East) and Egypt, where people developed the organized societies that we associate with civilization.

Before considering the early civilizations of western Asia and Egypt, however, we must briefly examine humankind's prehistory and observe how human beings made the shift from hunting and gathering to agricultural communities and ultimately to cities. •

THE FIRST HUMANS

The earliest humanlike creatures—known as hominids—lived in Africa three to four million years ago. Called australopithecines, or "southern ape-men," by their discoverers, they flourished in eastern and southern Africa and were the first hominids to make simple stone tools. Australopithecines were also bipedal—that is, they walked upright on two legs, a trait that enabled them to move over long distances and use their arms and legs for different purposes.

In 1959, Louis and Mary Leakey discovered a new form of hominid in Africa that they labeled *Homo habilis* ("handy human"). The Leakeys believed that *Homo habilis*, which had a brain almost 50 percent larger than that of the australopithecines, was the earliest toolmaking hominid. Their larger brains and the ability to walk upright allowed these hominids to become more sophisticated in the search for meat, seeds, and nuts for nourishment.

Around 1.8 million years ago, as *Homo habilis* died out, a new phase in early human development occurred with the emergence of *Homo erectus* ("upright human"). *Homo erectus* used larger and more varied tools and was the first hominid to leave Africa and move into Europe and Asia. Around 250,000 years ago, a third and crucial stage in human development began with the emergence of *Homo*

sapiens ("wise human"). By 100,000 B.C.E., two groups of *Homo sapiens* had developed. One was the Neanderthal, whose remains were first found in the Neander River valley in Germany. Neanderthal remains have since been found in both Europe and the Middle East and have been dated to between 100,000 and 30,000 B.C.E. Neanderthals relied on a variety of stone tools and were the first early people to bury their dead.

The first anatomically modern humans, known as *Homo sapiens sapiens* ("wise, wise human"), appeared in Africa between 200,000 and 150,000 years ago. Recent evidence indicates that they began to spread outside Africa around 100,000 years ago. Map 1.1 shows probable dates for different movements, although many of these are still disputed. By 30,000 B.C.E., *Homo sapiens sapiens* had replaced the Neanderthals, who had largely become extinct, and by 10,000 B.C.E., members of the *Homo sapiens sapiens* species could be found throughout the world. By that time, it was the only human species left. All humans today, whether Europeans, Australian Aborigines, or Africans, belong to the same subspecies of human being.

The Hunter-Gatherers of the Paleolithic Age

One of the basic distinguishing features of the human species is the ability to make tools. The earliest tools were made of stone, and so the early period of human history (c. 2,500,000–10,000 B.C.E.) has been designated the Paleolithic Age (*paleolithic* is Greek for "old stone").

For hundreds of thousands of years, humans relied on hunting and gathering for their daily food. Paleolithic people had a close relationship with the world around them, and over time, they came to know what animals to hunt and what plants to eat. They gathered wild nuts, berries, fruits, and a variety of wild grains and green plants. Around the world, they captured and consumed different animals, including buffalo, horses, bison, reindeer, and fish.

The hunting of animals and the gathering of wild plants no doubt led to certain patterns of living. Paleolithic people probably lived in small bands of twenty or thirty. They

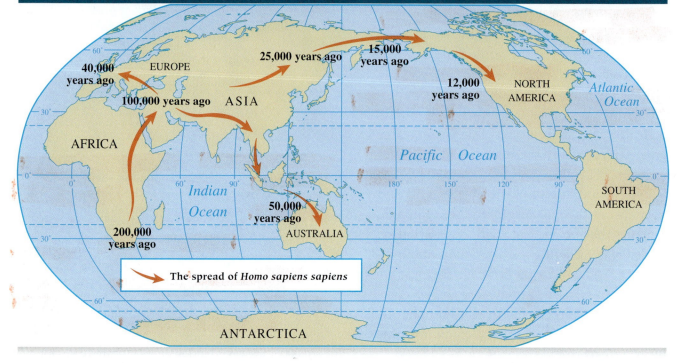

MAP 1.1   The Spread of *Homo sapiens sapiens*.   *Homo sapiens sapiens* spread from Africa beginning about 100,000 years ago. Living and traveling in small groups, these anatomically modern humans were hunter-gatherers. ➤ *Given that some diffusion of humans occurred during ice ages, how would such climate change affect humans and their movements, especially from Asia to Australia and Asia to North America?*

were nomadic, moving from place to place to follow animal migrations and vegetation cycles. Over the years, tools became more refined and more useful. The invention of the spear and later the bow and arrow made hunting considerably easier. Harpoons and fishhooks made of bone increased the catch of fish.

Both men and women were responsible for finding food—the chief work of Paleolithic people. Because women bore and raised the children, they generally stayed close to the camps, but they played an important role in acquiring food, gathering berries, nuts, and grains. Men hunted the wild animals, an activity that took them far from camp. Because both men and women played important roles in providing for the band's survival, scientists have argued that a rough equality existed between men and women.

These groups of Paleolithic people, especially those who lived in cold climates, found shelter in caves. Over time, they created new types of shelter as well. Perhaps the most common was a simple structure of wood poles or sticks covered with animal hides. The systematic use of fire, which archaeologists believe began around 500,000 years ago, made it possible for the caves and shelters to have light and heat. Fire also enabled early humans to cook their food, which made it taste better, last longer, and

in the case of some plants such as wild grain, easier to digest.

The making of tools and the use of fire—two important technological innovations of Paleolithic peoples—remind us how crucial the ability to adapt was to human survival. But Paleolithic peoples did more than just survive. The cave paintings of large animals found in southwestern France and northern Spain bear witness to the cultural activity of Paleolithic peoples. A cave discovered in southern France in 1994 contains more than three hundred paintings of lions, oxen, owls, panthers, and other animals. Most of these are animals that Paleolithic people did not hunt, which suggests that they were painted for religious or decorative purposes.

The Neolithic Revolution, c. 10,000–4000 B.C.E.

The end of the last ice age around 10,000 B.C.E. was followed by what is called the Neolithic Revolution because it ushered in the New Stone Age (*neolithic* is Greek for "new stone"). The name New Stone Age is misleading, however. Although Neolithic peoples made a new type of polished stone axes, this was not the most significant change they introduced.

A REVOLUTION IN AGRICULTURE

The biggest change was the shift from hunting animals and gathering plants for sustenance to producing food by systematic agriculture. The planting of grains and vegetables provided a regular supply of food, while the taming of animals, such as sheep, goats, cattle, and pigs, added a steady source of meat, milk, and fibers such as wool for clothing. The growing of crops and the taming of food-producing animals created a new relationship between humans and nature, which historians speak of as an agricultural revolution. Revolutionary change is dramatic and requires great effort, but the ability to acquire food on a regular basis gave humans greater control over their environment and enabled them to give up their nomadic ways of life and live in settled communities.

Systematic agriculture developed independently in different areas of the world between 8000 and 5000 B.C.E. Inhabitants of the Middle East began cultivating wheat and barley and domesticating pigs, cattle, goats, and sheep by 8000 B.C.E. From the Middle East, farming spread into the southeastern region of Europe and by 4000 B.C.E. was well established in central Europe and the coastal regions of the Mediterranean. The cultivation of wheat and barley also spread from western Asia into the Nile valley of Egypt by 6000 B.C.E. and soon spread up the Nile to other areas of Africa. In the woodlands and tropical forests of Central Africa, a separate farming system emerged with the growing of tubers or root crops such as yams and tree crops such as bananas. The cultivation of wheat and barley also moved eastward into the highlands of northwestern and central India between 7000 and 5000 B.C.E. By 5000 B.C.E., rice was being cultivated in Southeast Asia, and it soon spread into southern China. In northern China, the cultivation of millet and the domestication of pigs and dogs seem well established by 6000 B.C.E. In the Western Hemisphere, Mesoamericans (inhabitants of present-day Mexico and Central America) domesticated beans, squash, and maize (corn) as well as dogs and fowl between 7000 and 5000 B.C.E.

CONSEQUENCES OF THE NEOLITHIC REVOLUTION

The growing of crops on a regular basis gave rise to relatively permanent settlements, which historians refer to as Neolithic farming villages or towns. Although Neolithic villages appeared in Europe, India, Egypt, China, and Mesoamerica, the oldest and most extensive ones were located in the Middle East. Çatal Hüyük, located in modern Turkey, had walls that enclosed 32 acres, and its population probably reached six thousand inhabitants during its high point from 6700 to 5700 B.C.E. People lived in simple mudbrick houses that were built so close to one another that there were few streets. To get to their homes, people had to walk along the rooftops and enter the house through a hole in the roof.

The Neolithic agricultural revolution had far-reaching consequences. Once people settled in villages or towns, they built houses for protection and other structures for the storage of goods. As organized communities stored food and accumulated material goods, they began to engage in trade. People also began to specialize in certain crafts, and a division of labor developed. Pottery was made from clay and baked in a fire to make it hard. The pots were used for cooking and to store grains. Woven baskets were also used for storage. Stone tools became refined as flint blades were used to make sickles and hoes for use in the fields. Vegetable fibers from such plants as flax and cotton were used to make thread that was woven into cloth. In the course of the Neolithic Age, many of the food plants consumed today came to be cultivated.

The change to systematic agriculture in the Neolithic Age also had consequences for the relationship between men and women. Men assumed the primary responsibility for working in the fields and herding animals, jobs that kept them away from the home. Women remained behind, caring for the

➤ STATUES FROM AIN GHAZAL.
These life-size statues made of plaster and bitumen date from 6500 B.C.E. and were discovered in 1984 in Ain Ghazal, an archaeological site near Amman, Jordan. They are among the oldest statues of the human figure ever found. Archaeologists are studying the statues to try to understand their purpose and meaning.

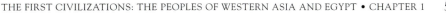

Courtesy of the Hashemite Kingdom of Jordan, Dept. of Antiquities

children, weaving clothes, and performing other household tasks that required considerable labor. In time, as work outside the home was increasingly perceived as more important than work done at home, men came to play the more dominant role in society, a pattern that persisted until our own times.

Other patterns set in the Neolithic Age also proved to be enduring elements of human history. Fixed dwellings, domesticated animals, regular farming, a division of labor, men holding power—all of these are part of the human story. For all of our scientific and technological progress, human survival still depends on the growing and storing of food, an accomplishment of people in the Neolithic Age. The Neolithic Revolution was truly a turning point in human history.

Between 4000 and 3000 B.C.E., significant technical developments began to transform the Neolithic towns. The invention of writing enabled records to be kept, and the use of metals marked a new level of human control over the environment and its resources. Already before 4000 B.C.E., artisans had discovered that metal-bearing rocks could be heated to liquefy metals, which could then be cast in molds to produce tools and weapons that were more useful than stone instruments. Copper was the first metal to be used for producing tools, but after 4000 B.C.E., metalworkers in western Asia discovered that combining copper and tin formed bronze, a much harder and more durable metal than copper alone. Its widespread use has led historians to speak of the Bronze Age from around 3000 to 1200 B.C.E., after which bronze was increasingly replaced by iron.

At first, Neolithic settlements were hardly more than villages, but as their inhabitants mastered the art of farming, more complex human societies gradually emerged. As wealth increased, these societies began to develop armies and to wall off their cities for protection. By the beginning of the Bronze Age, the concentration of larger numbers of people in river valleys was leading to a whole new pattern for human life.

THE EMERGENCE OF CIVILIZATION

As we have seen, early human beings formed small groups and developed a simple culture that enabled them to survive. As human societies grew and developed greater complexity, civilization came into being. A civilization is a complex culture in which large numbers of people share a variety of common elements. Historians have identified a number of basic characteristics of civilization, including the following:

1. *An urban focus.* Cities became the centers for political, economic, social, cultural, and religious development.

2. *A distinct religious structure.* The gods were deemed crucial to the community's success, and professional priestly classes, as stewards of the gods' property, regulated relations with the gods.
3. *New political and military structures.* An organized government bureaucracy arose to meet the administrative demands of the growing population, and armies were organized to gain land and power.
4. *A new social structure based on economic power.* While kings and an upper class of priests, political leaders, and warriors dominated, there also existed a large group of free common people (farmers, artisans, craftspeople) and, at the very bottom socially, a class of slaves.
5. *The development of writing.* Kings, priests, merchants, and artisans began to use writing to keep records.
6. *New and significant artistic and intellectual activity.* For example, monumental architectural structures, usually religious, occupied a prominent place in urban environments.

The first civilizations that developed in Mesopotamia and Egypt will be examined in detail in this chapter. But civilizations also developed independently in other parts of the world. Between 3000 and 1500 B.C.E., the valleys of the Indus River in India supported a flourishing civilization that extended hundreds of miles from the Himalayas to the coast of the Arabian Sea (see Chapter 2). Another river valley civilization emerged along the Yellow River in northern China about four thousand years ago (see Chapter 3). Under the Shang dynasty of kings, which ruled from 1750 to 1122 B.C.E., this civilization contained impressive cities with huge city walls and royal palaces.

Scholars have believed for a long time that civilization emerged only in these four areas—in the fertile river valleys of the Tigris and Euphrates, the Nile, the Indus, and the Yellow River. Recently, however, archaeologists have discovered two other early civilizations. One of these flourished in Central Asia (in what are now the republics of Turkmenistan and Uzbekistan) around four thousand years ago. People in this civilization built mudbrick buildings, raised sheep and goats, had bronze tools, used a system of irrigation to grow wheat and barley, and had a writing system.

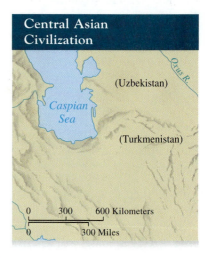

Central Asian Civilization

Oxus R.

(Uzbekistan)

Caspian Sea

(Turkmenistan)

0   300   600 Kilometers

0   300 Miles

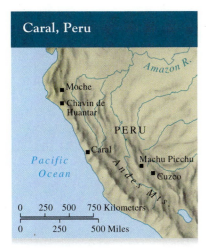

Caral, Peru

Another early civilization was discovered in the Supe River valley of Peru. At the center of this civilization was the city of Caral, which flourished around 2600 B.C.E. It contained buildings for officials, apartment buildings, and grand residences, all built of stone. The inhabitants of Caral also developed a system of irrigation by diverting a river more than a mile upstream into their fields.

CIVILIZATION IN MESOPOTAMIA

The Greeks spoke of the valley between the Tigris and Euphrates Rivers as Mesopotamia, the "land between the rivers." The region receives little rain, but the soil of the plain of southern Mesopotamia was enlarged and enriched over the years by layers of silt deposited by the two rivers. In late spring, the Tigris and Euphrates overflow their banks and deposit their fertile silt, but since this flooding depends on the melting of snows in the upland mountains where the rivers begin, it is irregular and sometimes catastrophic. In such circumstances, farming could be accomplished only with human intervention in the form of irrigation and drainage ditches. A complex system was required to control the flow of the rivers and produce the crops. Large-scale irrigation made possible the expansion of agriculture in this region, and the abundant food provided the material base for the emergence of civilization in Mesopotamia.

The City-States of Ancient Mesopotamia

The creators of the first Mesopotamian civilization were the Sumerians, a people whose origins remain unclear. By 3000 B.C.E., they had established a number of independent cities, including Eridu, Ur, Uruk, Umma, and Lagash (see Map 1.2). As the cities expanded, they came to exercise political and economic control over the surrounding countryside, forming city-states, which were the basic units of Sumerian civilization.

Sumerian cities were surrounded by walls. Uruk, for example, was encircled by a wall 6 miles long with defense towers located along it every 30 to 35 feet. City dwellings, built of sun-dried bricks, included both the small flats of peasants and the larger dwellings of the civic and priestly officials. Although Mesopotamia had little stone or wood for building purposes, it did have plenty of mud. Mudbricks, easily shaped by hand, were left to bake in the hot sun until they were hard enough to use for building. People in Mesopotamia were remarkably creative with mudbricks, inventing the arch and the dome and constructing some of the largest brick buildings in the world.

The most prominent building in a Sumerian city was the temple, which was dedicated to the chief god or goddess of the city and often built atop a massive stepped tower called a ziggurat. The Sumerians believed that gods and goddesses owned the cities, and much wealth was used to build temples to these deities and elaborate houses for the priests and priestesses who served them. Priests and priestesses, who supervised the temples and their property, had much power. The temples owned much of the city land and livestock and served not only as the physical center of the city but also as its economic and political center.

Over a period of time, ruling power in Sumerian city-states passed into the hands of kings. Sumerians viewed kingship as divine in origin—kings, they believed, derived their power from the gods and were the agents of the gods. As one person said in a petition to his king: "You in your judgment, you are the son of Anu [god of the sky]; Your commands, like the work of a god, cannot be reversed. Your words, like rain pouring down from heaven, are without number."[1] Regardless of their origins, kings had power—they led armies, supervised the building of public works, and organized workers for the irrigation projects on which Mesopotamian farming depended. The army, the government bureaucracy, and the priests and priestesses all aided the kings in their rule.

The economy of the Sumerian city-states was primarily agricultural, but commerce and industry became important as well. The people of Mesopotamia produced woolen textiles, pottery, and the metalwork for which they were especially well known. The Sumerians imported copper, tin, and timber in exchange for dried fish, wool, barley, wheat, and metal goods. Traders traveled by land to the edge of the Mediterranean in the west and by sea to India in the east. The invention of the wheel around 3000 B.C.E. led to carts that made the transport of goods easier.

Sumerian city-states contained three major social groups—nobles, commoners, and slaves. Nobles included royal and priestly officials and their families. Commoners were the nobles' clients who worked for the palace and temple estates and other free citizens who worked as farmers, merchants, fishers, and craftspeople. At least 90 percent of the population was engaged in farming. Slaves belonged to palace officials, who used them in building projects; to temple officials, who used mostly female slaves to weave cloth and grind grain; and to rich landowners, who used them for farming and domestic work.

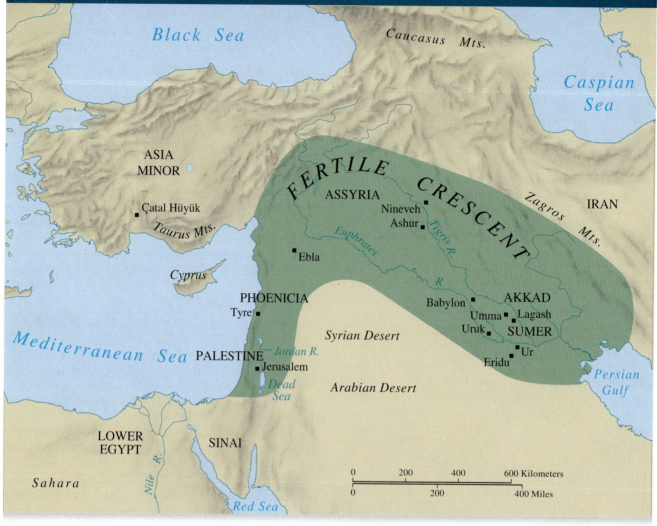

MAP 1.2 **The Ancient Near East.** The Fertile Crescent encompassed land with access to water. Employing flood management and irrigation systems, the peoples of the region established civilizations based on agriculture. These civilizations developed writing, law codes, and economic specialization. ➤ *What geographical aspects of the Mesopotamian city-states made conflict between them likely?*

Empires in Ancient Mesopotamia

As the number of Sumerian city-states grew and expanded, new conflicts arose as city-state fought city-state for control of land and water. Located in the flat land of Mesopotamia, the Sumerian city-states were also open to invasion. To the north of the Sumerian city-states were the Akkadians. We call them a Semitic people because of the language they spoke (see Table 1.1). Around 2340 B.C.E., Sargon, leader of the Akkadians, overran the Sumerian city-states and established an empire that included most of Mesopotamia as well as lands westward to the Mediterranean. Attacks from neighboring hill peoples eventually caused the Akkadian empire to fall, and its end by 2100 B.C.E. brought a return to the system of warring city-states. It was not until 1792 B.C.E. that a new empire came to control much of Mesopotamia. Leadership came from Babylon, a city-state north of Akkad, where

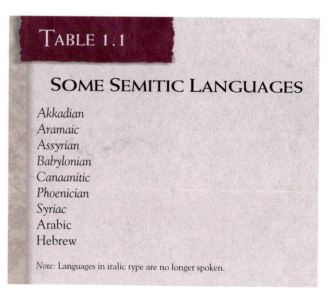

TABLE 1.1

SOME SEMITIC LANGUAGES

Akkadian
Aramaic
Assyrian
Babylonian
Canaanitic
Phoenician
Syriac
Arabic
Hebrew

Note: Languages in italic type are no longer spoken.

Hammurabi ruled over the Amorites or Old Babylonians, a large group of Semitic-speaking seminomads.

Hammurabi (1792–1750 B.C.E.) employed a well-disciplined army of foot soldiers who carried axes, spears, and copper or bronze daggers. He learned to divide his opponents and subdue them one by one. Using such methods, he gained control of Sumer and Akkad, creating a new Mesopotamian kingdom. After his conquests, he called himself "the sun of Babylon, the king who has made the four quarters of the world subservient," and established a new capital at Babylon. He also built temples, defensive walls, and irrigation canals; he encouraged trade and brought an economic revival.

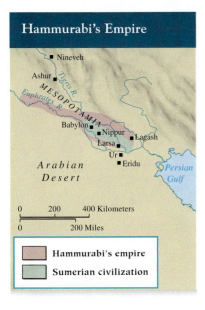

Hammurabi's Empire

Hammurabi's empire

Sumerian civilization

After his death, however, a series of weak kings were unable to keep his empire united, and it finally fell to new invaders.

THE CODE OF HAMMURABI

Hammurabi is best remembered for his law code, a collection of 282 laws. This collection provides considerable insight into almost every aspect of everyday life in Mesopotamia and gives us a priceless glimpse of the values of this early society.

The Code of Hammurabi reveals a society with a system of strict justice. Penalties for criminal offenses were severe and varied according to the social class of the victim. A crime against a member of the upper class (a noble) by a member of the lower class (a commoner) was punished more severely than the same offense against a member of a lower class (see the box on p. 10).

Hammurabi's code took the duties of public officials seriously. Officials were expected to catch burglars. If they failed to do so, officials in the district where the crime was committed had to replace the lost property. If murderers were not found, the officials had to pay a fine to the relatives of the murdered person.

The law code also furthered the proper performance of work with what amounted to consumer protection laws. Builders were held responsible for the buildings they constructed. If a house collapsed and caused the death of the owner, the builder was put to death. If the collapse caused the death of the son of the owner, the son of the builder was put to death. If goods were destroyed by the collapse, they had to be replaced and the house itself reconstructed at the builder's expense.

The largest category of laws in the Code of Hammurabi focused on marriage and the family. Parents arranged marriages for their children. After marriage, the two parties signed a marriage contract; without it, no one was considered legally married. While the husband provided a bridal payment, the woman's parents were responsible for a dowry to the new husband.

As in many patriarchal societies, women possessed fewer privileges and rights in marriage than men. A woman's place was in the home, and failure to fulfill her expected duties was grounds for divorce. If she was not able to bear children or tried to leave home to engage in business, her husband could divorce her. Furthermore, a wife who was a "gadabout, . . . neglecting her house [and] humiliating her husband," could be drowned.

Sexual relations were strictly regulated as well. Husbands, but not wives, were permitted sexual activity outside marriage. A wife caught committing adultery was pitched into the river, although her husband could ask the king to pardon her. Incest was strictly forbidden. If a father committed incestuous relations with his daughter, he would be banished. Incest between a son and mother resulted in both being burned.

Fathers ruled their children as well as their wives. Obedience was duly expected: "If a son has struck his father, he shall cut off his hand." If a son committed a serious enough offense, his father could disinherit him. Hammurabi's law code covered almost every aspect of people's lives.

The Culture of Mesopotamia

A spiritual worldview was of fundamental importance to Mesopotamian culture. To the peoples of Mesopotamia, the gods were living realities who affected all aspects of life. It was crucial, therefore, that the correct hierarchies be observed. Leaders could prepare armies for war, but success really depended on a favorable relationship with the gods. This helps explain the importance of the priestly class and the reason why even the kings took great care to dedicate offerings and monuments to the gods.

THE IMPORTANCE OF RELIGION

The physical environment had an obvious impact on the Mesopotamian view of the universe. Ferocious floods, heavy downpours, scorching winds, and oppressive humidity were all part of the Mesopotamian climate. These conditions and the resulting famines easily convinced Mesopotamians that this world was controlled by supernatural forces, which often were not kind or reliable. In the presence of nature, people in Mesopotamia could easily feel helpless, as this poem relates:

The rampant flood which no man can oppose,
Which shakes the heavens and causes earth to tremble,
In an appalling blanket folds mother and child,
Beats down the canebrake's full luxuriant greenery,
And drowns the harvest in its time of ripeness.[2]

THE CODE OF HAMMURABI

Although there were earlier Mesopotamian law codes, Hammurabi's is the most complete. The law code emphasizes the principle of retribution ("an eye for an eye") and punishments that vary according to social status. Punishments could be severe. Marriage and family affairs also play a large role in the code. The following examples illustrate these concerns.

THE CODE OF HAMMURABI

25. If fire broke out in a free man's house and a free man, who went to extinguish it, cast his eye on the goods of the owner of the house and has appropriated the goods of the owner of the house, that free man shall be thrown into that fire.

129. If the wife of a free man has been caught while lying with another man, they shall bind them and throw them into the water. If the husband of the woman wishes to spare his wife, then the king in turn may spare his subject.

131. If a free man's wife was accused by her husband, but she was not caught while lying with another man, she shall make affirmation by god and return to her house.

196. If a free man has destroyed the eye of a member of the aristocracy, they shall destroy his eye.

198. If he has destroyed the eye of a commoner or broken the bone of a commoner, he shall pay one mina of silver.

199. If he has destroyed the eye of a free man's slave or broken the bone of a free man's slave, he shall pay one-half his value.

209. If a free man struck another free man's daughter and has caused her to have a miscarriage, he shall pay ten shekels of silver for her fetus.

210. If that woman has died, they shall put his daughter to death.

211. If by a blow he has caused a commoner's daughter to have a miscarriage, he shall pay five shekels of silver.

212. If that woman has died, he shall pay one-half mina of silver.

213. If he struck a free man's female slave and has caused her to have a miscarriage, he shall pay two shekels of silver.

214. If that female slave has died, he shall pay one-third mina of silver.

The Mesopotamians discerned cosmic rhythms in the universe and accepted its order but perceived that it was not completely safe because of the presence of willful, powerful cosmic powers that they identified with gods and goddesses.

Mesopotamian religion was polytheistic, with nearly three thousand gods and goddesses animating all aspects of the universe. The four most important deities were An, god of the sky and hence the most important force in the universe; Enlil, god of wind; Enki, god of the earth, rivers, wells, and canals, as well as inventions and crafts; and Ninhursaga, a goddess associated with soil, mountains, and vegetation, who came to be worshiped as a mother goddess, the "mother of all children," who manifested her power by giving birth to kings and conferring the royal insignia on them.

THE CULTIVATION OF NEW ARTS AND SCIENCES

The realization of writing's great potential was another aspect of Mesopotamian culture. Around 3000 B.C.E., the Sumerians invented a cuneiform ("wedge-shaped") system of writing. Using a reed stylus, they made wedge-shaped impressions on clay tablets, which were then baked or dried in the sun. Once dried, these tablets were virtually indestructible, and the several hundred thousand that have been found so far have provided a valuable source of information for modern scholars. Sumerian writing began as pictures of concrete objects that evolved into simplified signs, leading eventually to a phonetic system that made possible the written expression of abstract ideas.

Mesopotamian peoples used writing primarily for record keeping, but cuneiform texts were also used in schools for scribes, which were necessary because considerable time was needed to master the cuneiform system of writing. The primary goal of scribal education was to produce professionally trained scribes for careers in the temples and palaces, the military, and government service. Pupils were male and primarily from wealthy families.

Writing was important because it enabled a society to keep records and maintain knowledge of previous practices and events. Writing also made it possible for people to communicate ideas in new ways, which is especially evident in the most famous piece of Mesopotamian literature, the *Epic of Gilgamesh,* a poem that records the exploits of a legendary king, Gilgamesh, who embarks on a search for the secret of immortality. But his efforts fail; Gilgamesh remains mortal. The desire for immortality, one of humankind's great searches, ends in complete frustration. "Everlasting life," as this Mesopotamian epic makes clear, is only for the gods.

People in Mesopotamia also made outstanding achievements in mathematics and astronomy. In math, the Sumerians devised a number system based on 60, using combinations of 6 and 10 for practical solutions. They used geometry to measure fields and erect buildings. In astronomy, the Sumerians made use of units of 60 and charted the heavenly constellations. They based their calendar on twelve lunar months and brought it into harmony with the solar year by adding an extra month from time to time.

Pictographic sign, c. 3100 B.C.E.	✳	⌣	≈	⸬		▽		⊔	
Interpretation	star	?sun over horizon	?stream	ear of barley	bull's head	bowl	head + bowl	lower leg	?shrouded body
Cuneiform sign, c. 2400 B.C.E.	✳								
Cuneiform sign c. 700 B.C.E. (turned through 90°)									
Phonetic value*	dingir, an	u_4, ud	a	še	gu_4	nig_2, ninda	ku_2	du, gin, gub	lu_2
Meaning	god, sky	day, sun	water, seed, son	barley	ox	food, bread	to eat	to walk, to stand	man

*Some signs have more than one phonetic value and some sounds are represented by more than one sign; for example, u_4 means the fourth sign with the phonetic value u.

THE DEVELOPMENT OF CUNEIFORM WRITING. This chart shows the evolution of writing from pictographic signs around 3100 B.C.E. to cuneiform signs by about 700 B.C.E. Note that the sign for *star* came to mean "god" or "sky." Pictographic signs for *head* and *bowl* came eventually to mean "to eat" in their simplified cuneiform version.

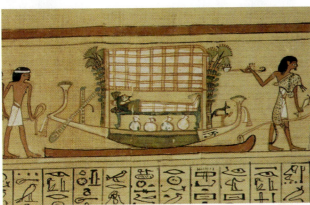

Early Writing

Pictured at left is the upper part of the cone of Uruinimgina, an example of cuneiform script from an early Sumerian dynasty. The first Egyptian writing was also pictographic, as shown in the hieroglyphs from the Book of the Dead papyrus of the Lady Anhai during the New Kingdom. In Central America, the Mayan civilization had a well-developed writing system, also based on hieroglyphs, as seen below in this text carved in 766 C.E. on the wall of Tikal's Temple of the Inscriptions.

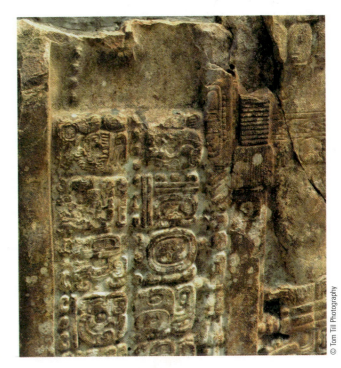

THE SIGNIFICANCE OF THE NILE RIVER AND THE PHARAOH

Two of the most important sources of life for the ancient Egyptians were the Nile River and the pharaoh. Egyptians perceived that the Nile made possible the abundant food that was a major source of their well-being. This Hymn to the Nile, probably from the nineteenth and twentieth dynasties in the New Kingdom, expresses the gratitude Egyptians felt for the Nile.

HYMN TO THE NILE

Hail to you, O Nile, that issues from the earth and comes to keep Egypt alive! . . .
He that waters the meadows which Re created, in order to keep every kid alive.
He that makes to drink the desert and the place distant from water: that is his dew coming down from heaven. . . .
The lord of fishes, he who makes the marsh-birds to go upstream. . . .
He who makes barley and brings emmer into being, that he may make the temples festive.
If he is sluggish, then nostrils are stopped up, and everybody is poor. . . .
When he rises, then the land is in jubilation, then every belly is in joy, every backbone takes on laughter, and every tooth is exposed.
The bringer of good, rich in provisions, creator of all good, lord of majesty, sweet of fragrance. . . .

He who makes every beloved tree to grow, without lack of them.

The Egyptian king, or pharaoh, was viewed as a god and the absolute ruler of Egypt. His significance and the gratitude of the Egyptian people for his existence are evident in this hymn from the reign of Sesotris III (c. 1880–1840 B.C.E.).

HYMN TO THE PHARAOH

He has come unto us that he may carry away Upper Egypt; the double diadem [crown of Upper and Lower Egypt] has rested on his head.
He has come unto us and has united the Two Lands; he has mingled the reed with the bee [symbols of Lower and Upper Egypt].
He has come unto us and has brought the Black Land under his sway; he has apportioned to himself the Red Land.
He has come unto us and has taken the Two Lands under his protection; he has given peace to the Two Riverbanks.
He has come unto us and has made Egypt to live; he has banished its suffering.
He has come unto us and has made the people to live; he has caused the throat of the subjects to breathe. . . .
He has come unto us and has done battle for his boundaries; he has delivered them that were robbed.

EGYPTIAN CIVILIZATION: "THE GIFT OF THE NILE"

"The Egyptian Nile," wrote one Arab traveler, "surpasses all the rivers of the world in sweetness of taste, in length of course and usefulness. No other river in the world can show such a continuous series of towns and villages along its banks." The Nile River was crucial to the development of Egyptian civilization (see the box above). Egypt, like Mesopotamia, was a river valley civilization.

The Importance of Geography

The Nile is a unique river, beginning in the heart of Africa and coursing northward for thousands of miles. It is the longest river in the world. The Nile was responsible for creating an area several miles wide on both banks of the river that was fertile and capable of producing abundant harvests. The "miracle" of the Nile was its annual flooding. The river rose in the summer from rains in Central Africa, crested in Egypt in September and October, and left a deposit of silt that enriched the soil. The Egyptians called this fertile land the "Black Land" because it was dark in color from the silt and the lush crops that grew on it. Beyond these narrow strips of fertile fields lay the deserts

(the "Red Land"). About 100 miles before it empties into the Mediterranean, the river splits into two major branches, forming the delta, a triangular-shaped territory called Lower Egypt to distinguish it from Upper Egypt, the land upstream to the south (see Map 1.3). Egypt's important cities developed at the apex of the delta. Even today, most of Egypt's people are crowded along the banks of the Nile River.

The Nile, unlike Mesopotamia's rivers, flooded gradually and, most often, predictably, and the river itself was seen as life-enhancing, not life-threatening. Although a system of organized irrigation was still necessary, the small villages along the Nile could make the effort without the massive state intervention that was required in Mesopotamia. Egyptian civilization consequently tended to remain more rural, with many small villages congregated along a narrow band on both sides of the Nile.

The surpluses of food that Egyptian farmers grew in the fertile Nile valley made Egypt prosperous. But the Nile also served as a unifying factor in Egyptian history. In ancient times, the Nile was the fastest way to travel through the land, making both transportation and communication easier. Winds from the north pushed sailboats south, and the current of the Nile carried them north.

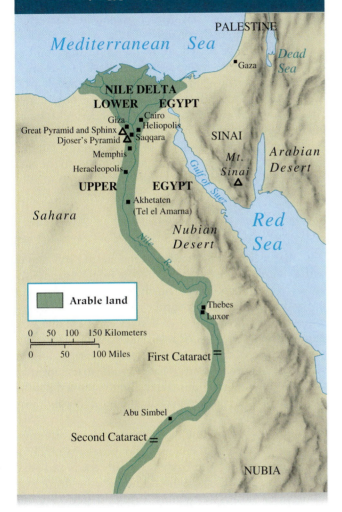

MAP 1.3 Ancient Egypt. Egyptian civilization centered on the life-giving water and flood silts of the Nile River, with most of the population living in Lower Egypt, where the river splits to form the Nile delta. Most of the pyramids, built during the Old Kingdom, are clustered south and west of Cairo. ➤ *How did the lands to the east and west of the river make invasions of Egypt difficult?*

Unlike Mesopotamia, which was subject to constant invasion, Egypt had natural barriers that gave it some protection from invasion. These barriers included deserts to the west and east; cataracts (rapids) on the southern part of the Nile, which made defense relatively easy; and the Mediterranean Sea to the north.

The regularity of the Nile floods and the relative isolation of the Egyptians created a sense of security and a feeling of changelessness. To the ancient Egyptians, when the Nile flooded each year, "the fields laugh and people's faces light up." Unlike people in Mesopotamia, Egyptians faced life with a spirit of confidence in the stability of things. Ancient Egyptian civilization was characterized by a remarkable degree of continuity for thousands of years.

The Importance of Religion

Religion, too, provided a sense of security and timelessness for the Egyptians. Actually, they had no word for religion because it was an inseparable element of the world order to which Egyptian society belonged. The Egyptians were polytheistic and had a remarkable number of gods associated with heavenly bodies and natural forces. Two groups, sun gods and land gods, came to have special importance, hardly surprising in view of the importance to Egypt's well-being of the sun, the river, and the fertile land along its banks. The sun was the source of life and hence worthy of worship. The sun god took on different forms and names, depending on his specific role. He was worshiped as Atum in human form and as Re, who had a human body but the head of a falcon. The Egyptian ruler took the title of "Son of Re," since he was seen as an earthly form of Re. River and land deities included Osiris and Isis with their child Horus, who was related to the Nile and to the sun as well. Osiris became especially important as a symbol of resurrection or rebirth.

The Course of Egyptian History: The Old, Middle, and New Kingdoms

Modern historians have divided Egyptian history into three major periods known as the Old Kingdom, the Middle Kingdom, and the New Kingdom. All were periods of long-term stability characterized by strong leadership from dynasties of kings, freedom from invasion, construction of temples and pyramids, and considerable intellectual and cultural activity. Between the periods of stability were ages of political chaos and invasion known as the Intermediate Periods.

The history of Egypt begins around 3100 B.C.E. when King Menes united the villages of both Upper and Lower Egypt into a single kingdom and created the first Egyptian royal dynasty. Henceforth the ruler would be called "king of Upper and Lower Egypt," and the royal crown would be a double diadem, signifying the unification of all Egypt. Just as the Nile united Upper and Lower Egypt physically, kingship served to unite the two areas politically (see the box on p. 12).

The Old Kingdom encompassed the third through sixth dynasties of Egyptian kings, lasting from around 2686 to 2125 B.C.E. It was an age of prosperity and splendor, made visible in the construction of the greatest and largest pyramids in Egypt's history. Unlike the kings of the Sumerian city-states, the monarchs of the Old Kingdom were very powerful rulers over a unified state.

Kingship was a divine institution in ancient Egypt and formed part of a universal scheme: "What is the king of Upper and Lower Egypt? He is a god by whose dealings one lives, the father and mother of all men, alone by himself, without an equal."[3] In obeying their king, subjects helped maintain the cosmic order. A breakdown in royal power meant that citizens were offending divinity and weakening the universal structure. Among the various titles of Egyptian kings, pharaoh (originally meaning "great house" or "palace," referring to the royal palace) eventually became the most common.

Although theoretically absolute in their power, in practice Egyptian kings did not rule alone. By the fourth dynasty, a bureaucracy with regular procedures had developed. Especially important was the office of vizier, "steward of the whole land." Directly responsible to the king, the vizier was in charge of the government bureaucracy. In time, Egypt was divided into provinces or nomes, as they were later called by the Greeks—twenty-two in Upper Egypt and twenty in Lower Egypt. A governor, called by the Greeks a nomarch, was head of each nome and was responsible to the king and vizier.

THE PYRAMIDS

One of the great achievements of Egyptian civilization, the building of pyramids, occurred in the time of the Old Kingdom. Pyramids were built as part of a larger complex of buildings dedicated to the dead—in effect, a city of the dead. The area included a large pyramid for the king's burial, smaller pyramids for his family, and several mastabas, rectangular structures with flat roofs used as tombs for the pharaoh's noble officials.

The tombs were well prepared for their residents, their rooms furnished and stocked with numerous supplies, including chairs, boats, chests, weapons, games, dishes, and a variety of food. The Egyptians believed that human beings had two bodies—a physical one and a spiritual one, which they called the *ka*. If the physical body was properly preserved (by mummification) and the tomb was furnished with all the objects of regular life, the *ka* could return, surrounded by earthly comforts, and continue to live despite the death of the physical body.

The largest and most magnificent of all the pyramids was built under King Khufu. Constructed at Giza around 2540 B.C.E., this famous Great Pyramid covers 13 acres, measures 756 feet at each side of its base, and stands 481 feet high. Its four sides are precisely oriented to the four points of the compass. The interior included a grand gallery to the burial chamber, which was built of granite and housed a lidless sarcophagus for the pharaoh's body. The Great Pyramid still stands as a visible symbol of the power of Egyptian kings of the Old Kingdom. No pyramid built later ever matched its size or splendor. The pyramid was not only the king's tomb but also an important symbol of royal power. It could be seen from miles away, reminding people of the glory, might, and wealth of the ruler who was regarded as a living god on earth.

THE MIDDLE KINGDOM

Despite the theory of divine order, the Old Kingdom eventually collapsed, ushering in a period of chaos that lasted about 150 years. Finally, a new royal dynasty managed to gain control of all Egypt and inaugurated the Middle Kingdom, a new period of stability lasting from about 2055 to 1650 B.C.E. Egyptians later portrayed the Middle Kingdom as a golden age, a clear indication of its stability.

As evidence of its newfound strength, Egypt began a period of expansion. Lower Nubia was conquered, and fortresses were built to protect the new southern frontier. The government also sent armies into Palestine and Syria, although they did not remain there. Pharaohs also sent traders to Kush, Syria, Mesopotamia, and Crete.

A new concern of the pharaohs for the people was a feature of the Middle Kingdom. In the Old Kingdom, the pharaoh had been viewed as an inaccessible god-king. Now he was portrayed as the shepherd of his people who must build public works and provide for the public welfare. Pharaohs of the Middle Kingdom undertook a number of helpful projects. The draining of swampland in the Nile delta provided thousands of acres of new farmland, and the digging of a canal to connect the Nile to the Red Sea aided trade and transportation.

CHAOS AND A NEW ORDER: THE NEW KINGDOM

The Middle Kingdom came to an end around 1650 B.C.E. with the invasion of Egypt by a people from western Asia known to the Egyptians as the Hyksos. The Hyksos used horse-drawn war chariots and overwhelmed the Egyptian soldiers, who fought from donkey carts. For almost a hundred years, the Hyksos ruled much of Egypt, but the conquered took much from their conquerors. From the Hyksos, the Egyptians learned to use bronze in making new farming tools and weapons. They also mastered the military skills of the Hyksos, especially the use of horse-drawn war chariots.

Eventually, a new line of pharaohs—the eighteenth dynasty—made use of the new weapons to throw off Hyksos domination, reunite Egypt, establish the New Kingdom (c. 1550–1085 B.C.E.), and launch the Egyptians along a new militaristic path. During the period of the New Kingdom, Egypt created an empire and became the most powerful state in the Middle East.

Massive wealth aided the power of the New Kingdom pharaohs. The Egyptian rulers showed their wealth by building new temples. Queen Hatshepsut (c. 1473–1458 B.C.E.), the first woman to become pharaoh in her own right, built a great temple at Deir el Bahri near Thebes. Hatshepsut was succeeded by her nephew, Thutmosis III (c. 1480–1450 B.C.E.), who led seventeen military campaigns into Syria and Palestine and even reached the Euphrates River. Egyptian forces occupied Palestine and Syria and also moved westward into Libya. The construction of magnificent new buildings and temples gave visible demonstration of the greatness of the empire.

The eighteenth dynasty was not without its troubles, however. Amenhotep IV (c. 1364–1347 B.C.E.) introduced

Chronology

THE EGYPTIANS

Early Dynastic Period (Dynasties 1–2)	c. 3100–2686 B.C.E.
Old Kingdom (Dynasties 3–6)	c. 2686–2125 B.C.E.
First Intermediate Period (Dynasties 7–10)	c. 2125–2055 B.C.E.
Middle Kingdom (Dynasties 11–12)	c. 2055–1650 B.C.E.
Second Intermediate Period (Dynasties 13–17)	c. 1650–1550 B.C.E.
New Kingdom (Dynasties 18–20)	c. 1550–1085 B.C.E.
Postempire (Dynasties 21–31)	c. 1085–30 B.C.E.

B.C.E.), the Egyptians regained control of Palestine, but new invasions in the thirteenth century by the Sea Peoples, as Egyptians called them, destroyed Egyptian power in Palestine and drove the Egyptians back within their old frontiers. The days of Egyptian empire were ended, and the New Kingdom itself expired with the end of the twentieth dynasty in 1085. For the next thousand years, despite periodic revivals of strength, Egypt was dominated by Libyans, Nubians, Persians, and finally Macedonians after the conquest of Alexander the Great (see Chapter 4). In the first century B.C.E., the pharaoh Cleopatra VII tried to reestablish Egypt's independence, but her involvement with Rome led to her suicide and defeat, and Egypt became a province in Rome's mighty empire.

Society and Daily Life in Ancient Egypt

For thousands of years, Egyptian society managed to maintain a simple structure, organized along hierarchical lines with the god-king at the top. The king was surrounded by an upper class of nobles and priests who participated in the elaborate rituals of life that surrounded the pharaoh. This ruling class ran the government and managed its own landed estates, which provided much of its wealth.

Below the upper classes were merchants and artisans. Merchants engaged in an active trade up and down the Nile as well as in town and village markets. Some merchants also engaged in international trade; they were sent by the king to Crete and Syria, where they obtained wood and other products. Egyptian artisans made an incredible variety of well-built and beautiful goods: stone dishes; painted boxes made of clay; wooden furniture; gold, silver, and copper tools and containers; paper and rope made of papyrus; and linen clothing.

The largest number of people in Egypt simply worked the land. In theory, the king owned all the land but

the worship of Aten, god of the sun disk, as the sole god. Amenhotep changed his own name to Akhenaten ("It is well with Aten") and closed the temples of other gods. Akhenaten's attempt at religious change failed. It was too much to ask Egyptians to abandon their traditional ways and beliefs, especially since they saw the destruction of the old gods as subversive of the very cosmic order on which Egypt's survival and continuing prosperity depended. At the same time, Akhenaten's preoccupation with his religious revolution caused him to ignore foreign affairs and led to the loss of both Syria and Palestine. Akhenaten's changes were soon undone after his death by the boy-pharaoh Tutankhamen, who restored the old gods. The eighteenth dynasty itself came to an end in 1333.

The nineteenth dynasty managed to restore Egyptian power one more time. Under Rameses II (c. 1279–1213

NUBIANS IN EGYPT. During the New Kingdom, Egypt expanded to the north, into Palestine and Syria, and to the south, into the African kingdom of Nubia. Nubia had first emerged as an African kingdom around 2300 B.C.E. (see Chapter 8). Nubians arriving in Egypt with bags and rings of gold are shown here in a fourteenth-century B.C.E. painting from an Egyptian official's tomb in Nubia. Nubia was a rich source of gold for the Egyptians.

© British Museum

granted out portions of it to his subjects. Large sections were in the possession of nobles and the temple complexes. Most of the lower classes were serfs or common people, bound to the land, who cultivated the estates. They paid taxes in the form of crops to the king, nobles, and priests, lived in small villages or towns, and provided military service and forced labor for building projects.

Ancient Egyptians had a very positive attitude toward daily life on earth. They married young (girls at twelve, boys at fourteen) and established a home and family. The husband was master in the house, but wives were respected and in charge of the household and education of the children. From a book of wise sayings (called "instructions") came this advice: "If you are a man of standing, you should found your household and love your wife at home as is fitting. Fill her belly; clothe her back. . . . Make her heart glad as long as you live."[4] Women's property and inheritance remained in their hands, even in marriage. Although most careers and public offices were closed to women, some did operate businesses. Peasant women worked long hours in the fields and at numerous domestic tasks. Upper-class women could function as priestesses, and four queens even became pharaohs in their own right.

Parents arranged marriages for their children. Their primary concerns were family and property, and clearly the chief purpose of marriage was to produce children, especially sons. From the New Kingdom came this piece of wisdom: "Take to yourself a wife while you are [still] a youth, that she may produce a son for you."[5] Only sons could carry on the family name, although daughters were not slighted. Although marriages were arranged, some of the surviving love poems from ancient Egypt would indicate an element of romance in some marriages. Marriages could and did end in divorce, which was allowed, apparently with compensation for the wife. Adultery, however, was strictly prohibited and brutally punished—adulterous women could have their noses cut off or be burned at the stake.

The Culture of Egypt: Art and Writing

Commissioned by kings or nobles for either temples or tombs, Egyptian art was largely functional. Wall paintings and statues of gods and kings in temples served a spiritual purpose. They were an integral part of the performance of ritual, which was thought necessary to preserve the cosmic order and hence the well-being of Egypt. Likewise, the mural scenes and sculptured figures found in the tombs had a specific function. They were supposed to assist the journey of the deceased into the afterworld.

Egyptian art was also formulaic. Artists and sculptors were expected to observe a strict canon of proportions that determined both form and presentation. This canon gave Egyptian art a distinctive appearance for thousands of years. Especially characteristic was the convention of combining the profile, semiprofile, and frontal views of the human body in relief work and painting in order to represent each part of the body accurately. This fashion created an art that was highly stylized yet still allowed distinctive features to be displayed.

Writing in Egypt emerged during the first two dynasties. The Greeks later labeled Egyptian writing hieroglyphics, meaning "priest carvings" or "sacred writings." Hieroglyphs were sacred characters used as picture signs that depicted objects and had a sacred value at the same time. Although hieroglyphs were later simplified for writing purposes into two scripts, they never developed into an alphabet. Egyptian hieroglyphs were initially carved in stone, but later the two simplified scripts were written on papyrus, paper made from the reeds that grew along the Nile.

NEW CENTERS OF CIVILIZATION

Our story of civilization so far has been dominated by Mesopotamia and Egypt. But significant developments were also taking place on the fringes of these civilizations. Agriculture had spread into the Balkan peninsula of Europe by 6500 B.C.E., and by 4000 B.C.E., Neolithic peoples in southern France, central Europe, and the coastal regions of the Mediterranean had domesticated animals and begun to farm largely on their own.

One outstanding feature of late Neolithic Europe was the building of megalithic structures (*megalith* is Greek for "large stone"). The first megalithic structures were built around 4000 B.C.E., more than a thousand years before the great pyramids were built in Egypt. Between 3200 and 1500 B.C.E., standing stones placed in circles or lined up in rows were erected throughout the British Isles and northwestern France. Other megalithic constructions have been found as far north as Scandinavia and as far south as the islands of Corsica, Sardinia, and Malta. Archaeologists have demonstrated that the stone circles were used as observatories not only to detect such simple astronomical phenomena as the midwinter and midsummer sunrises but also to make such sophisticated observations as the major and minor standstills of the moon.

The Role of Nomadic Peoples

On the fringes of civilization lived nomadic peoples who depended on hunting and gathering, herding, and sometimes a bit of farming for their survival. Most important were the pastoral nomads who on occasion overran civilized communities and created their own empires. Pastoral nomads domesticated animals for both food and clothing and moved along regular migratory routes to provide steady sources of nourishment for their animals.

The Indo-Europeans were among the most important nomadic peoples. These groups spoke languages derived from

❧ **STONEHENGE.** The Bronze Age in northwestern Europe is known for its megaliths, or large standing stones. Between 3200 and 1500 B.C.E., standing stones placed in circles or lined up in rows were erected throughout the British Isles and northwestern France. The most famous of these megalithic constructions is Stonehenge, in England.

TABLE 1.2

SOME INDO-EUROPEAN LANGUAGES

Subfamily	Languages
Indo-Iranian	*Sanskrit*, Persian
Balto-Slavic	Russian, Serbo-Croatian, Czech, Polish, Lithuanian
Hellenic	Greek
Italic	*Latin*, Romance languages (French, Italian, Spanish, Portuguese, Romanian)
Celtic	Irish, Gaelic
Germanic	Swedish, Danish, Norwegian, German, Dutch, English

Note: Languages in italic type are no longer spoken.

a single parent tongue. Indo-European languages include Greek, Latin, Persian, Sanskrit, and the Germanic languages (see Table 1.2). The original Indo-European-speaking peoples were probably based somewhere in the steppe region north of the Black Sea or in southwestern Asia, in modern Iran or Afghanistan, but around 2000 B.C.E., they began to move into Europe, India, and western Asia. One group of Indo-Europeans who moved into Asia Minor and Anatolia (modern Turkey) around 1750 B.C.E. coalesced with the native peoples to form the Hittite kingdom, with its capital at Hattusha (Bogazköy in modern Turkey).

Between 1600 and 1200 B.C.E., the Hittites created their own empire in western Asia and even threatened the power of the Egyptians. The Hittites were the first of the Indo-European peoples to use iron, which enabled them to construct weapons that were stronger and cheaper to make because of the widespread availability of iron ore. But around 1200 B.C.E., new waves of invading Indo-European peoples destroyed the Hittite empire. The destruction of the Hittite kingdom and the weakening of Egypt around 1200 B.C.E. temporarily left no dominant powers in western Asia, allowing a patchwork of petty kingdoms and city-states to emerge, especially in Syria and Palestine. The Phoenicians were one of these peoples.

The Phoenicians

A Semitic-speaking people, the Phoenicians lived in Palestine along the Mediterranean coast on a narrow band of land 120 miles long. Their newfound political independence after the demise of Hittite and Egyptian power helped the Phoenicians expand the trade that was already the foundation of their prosperity. The Phoenicians improved their ships and became great international sea traders. They charted new routes, not only in the Mediterranean but also in the Atlantic Ocean, where they sailed north to Britain and south along the west coast of Africa. The Phoenicians established a number of colonies in the western Mediterranean; Carthage, the most famous, was located on the North African coast.

Culturally, the Phoenicians are best known for their alphabet. They simplified their writing by using twenty-two different signs to represent the sounds of their speech. These twenty-two characters or letters could be used to spell out all the words in the Phoenician language. Although the Phoenicians were not the only people to invent an alphabet, theirs would have special significance because it was eventually passed on to the Greeks. From the ancient Greek alphabet came the modern Greek, Roman, and Cyrillic alphabets in use today.

The "Children of Israel"

To the south of the Phoenicians lived another group of Semitic-speaking people known as the Israelites. Although they were a minor factor in the politics of the region, their religion, known as Judaism, gave rise to both Christianity and Islam and flourished as a world religion. The Israelites had a tradition concerning their origins and history that was eventually written down as part of the Hebrew Bible, known to Christians as the Old Testament. Many scholars today doubt that the early books of the Hebrew Bible reflect the true history of the early Israelites. They argue that the early books of the Bible, written centuries after the events described, preserve only what the Israelites came to believe about themselves and that recent archaeological evidence often contradicts the details of the biblical account. What is generally agreed, however, is that between 1200 and 1000 B.C.E., the Israelites emerged as a distinct group of people, possibly organized in tribes or a league of tribes, who established a united kingdom known as Israel.

THE UNITED AND DIVIDED KINGDOMS

By the time of King Solomon (c. 970–930 B.C.E.), the Israelites had established control over all of Palestine (see Map 1.4) and made Jerusalem the capital of a united kingdom. Solomon did even more to strengthen royal power. He expanded the government and army and was especially active in extending the trading activities of the Israelites. Solomon is best known for his building projects, of which the most famous was the Temple in Jerusalem. The Israelites viewed the Temple as the symbolic center of their religion and hence of the kingdom of Israel itself. Under Solomon, ancient Israel was at the height of its power.

After Solomon's death, tensions between the northern and southern tribes led to the establishment of two separate kingdoms—the kingdom of Israel, composed of ten northern tribes, with its capital eventually at Samaria, and the kingdom of Judah, consisting of two southern tribes, with its capital at Jerusalem. In 722 B.C.E., the Assyrians overran the kingdom of Israel and deported many Hebrews to other parts of the Assyrian Empire. These dispersed Hebrews (the "ten lost tribes") merged with neighboring peoples and gradually lost their identity.

The southern kingdom of Judah managed for a while to retain its independence as Assyrian power declined, but a new enemy soon appeared on the horizon. The Chaldeans defeated Assyria, conquered the kingdom of Judah, and completely destroyed Jerusalem in 586 B.C.E. Many upper-class people from Judah were deported to Babylon, the memory of which is still evoked in the words of Psalm 137:

> By the rivers of Babylon, we sat and wept when we
>   remembered Zion. . . .
> How can we sing the songs of the Lord while in a foreign
>   land?

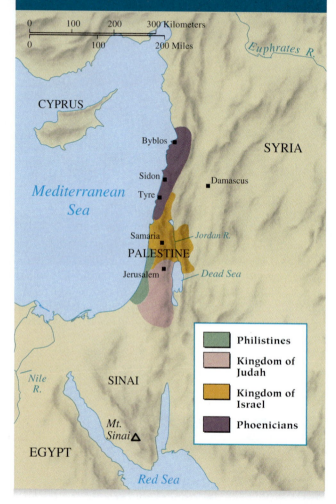

MAP 1.4 Palestine in the First Millennium B.C.E. After the death of Solomon, greater Israel split into two states—Israel and Judah. With power divided, the Israelites could not resist invasions that dispersed many of them from Palestine. Some, such as the "ten lost tribes," never returned. Others were sent to Babylon but were later allowed to return under the rule of the Persians. ➤ *Why was Israel more vulnerable to the Assyrian Empire than Judah was?*

Legend:
- Philistines
- Kingdom of Judah
- Kingdom of Israel
- Phoenicians

> If I forget you, O Jerusalem, may my right hand forget its
>   skill.
> May my tongue cling to the roof of my mouth if I do not
>   remember you,
> if I do not consider Jerusalem my highest joy.[6]

But the Babylonian captivity of the people of Judah did not last. A new set of conquerors, the Persians, destroyed the Chaldean kingdom and allowed the people of Judah to return to Jerusalem and rebuild their city and Temple. The revived kingdom of Judah remained under Persian control until the conquests of Alexander the Great in the

THE COVENANT AND THE LAW:
THE BOOK OF EXODUS

According to the biblical account, it was during the exodus from Egypt that the Israelites made their covenant with Yahweh. They agreed to obey their God and follow his law. In return, Yahweh promised to take special care of his chosen people. This selection from the Book of Exodus describes the making of the covenant and God's commandments to the Israelites.

EXODUS 19:1–8

In the third month after the Israelites left Egypt—on the very day—they came to the Desert of Sinai. After they set out from Rephidim, they entered the Desert of Sinai, and Israel camped there in the desert in front of the mountain. Then Moses went up to God, and the Lord called to him from the mountain, and said, "This is what you are to say to the house of Jacob and what you are to tell the people of Israel: 'You yourselves have seen what I did to Egypt, and how I carried you on eagles' wings and brought you to myself. Now if you obey me fully and keep my covenant, then out of all nations you will be my treasured possession. Although the whole earth is mine, you will be for me a kingdom of priests and a holy nation.' These are the words you are to speak to the Israelites." So Moses went back and summoned the elders of the people and set before them all the words the Lord had commanded him to speak. The peo-

ple all responded together, "We will do everything the Lord has said." So Moses brought their answer back to the Lord.

EXODUS 20:1–3, 7–17

And God spoke all these words, "I am the Lord your God, who brought you out of Egypt, out of the land of slavery. You shall have no other gods before me. . . . You shall not misuse the name of the Lord your God, for the Lord will not hold anyone guiltless who misuses his name. Remember the Sabbath day by keeping it holy. Six days you shall labor and do all your work, but the seventh day is a Sabbath to the Lord your God. On it you shall not do any work, neither you, nor your son or daughter, nor your manservant or maidservant, nor your animals, nor the alien within your gates. For in six days the Lord made the heavens and the earth, the sea, and all that is in them, but he rested on the seventh day. Therefore the Lord blessed the Sabbath day and made it holy. Honor your father and your mother, so that you may live long in the land the Lord your God is giving you. You shall not murder. You shall not commit adultery. You shall not steal. You shall not give false testimony against your neighbor. You shall not covet your neighbor's house. You shall not covet your neighbor's wife, or his manservant or maidservant, his ox or donkey, or anything that belongs to your neighbor."

---

fourth century B.C.E. The people of Judah survived, eventually becoming known as the Jews and giving their name to Judaism, the religion of Yahweh, the Jewish God.

THE SPIRITUAL DIMENSIONS OF ISRAEL

According to the Jewish conception, there is but one God called Yahweh, who is the creator of the world and everything in it. The Jewish God ruled the world; he was subject to nothing. This omnipotent creator, however, was not removed from the life he had created; he was a just and good God who expected goodness from his people. If they did not obey his will, they would be punished, but he was primarily a God of mercy and love: "The Lord is gracious and compassionate, slow to anger and rich in love. The Lord is good to all; he has compassion on all he has made."[7] Each person could have a personal relationship with this being.

Three aspects of the Jewish religious tradition had special significance: the covenant, law, and the prophets. The Israelites believed that during the exodus from Egypt, when Moses had supposedly led his people out of bondage toward the promised land, God made a covenant or contract with the tribes of Israel, who believed that Yahweh

had spoken to them through Moses (see the box above). The Israelites promised to obey Yahweh and follow his law. In return, Yahweh promised to take special care of his chosen people, "a peculiar treasure unto me above all people."

This covenant between Yahweh and his chosen people could be fulfilled, however, only by Hebrew obedience to the law of God. Most important were the ethical concerns that stood at the center of the law. These commandments spelled out God's ideals of behavior: "You shall not murder. You shall not commit adultery. You shall not steal."[8] True freedom consisted of following God's moral standards voluntarily. If people chose to ignore the good, then suffering and evil would follow.

The Israelites believed that certain religious teachers, called prophets, were sent by God to serve as his voice to his people. The golden age of prophecy began in the mid-eighth century B.C.E. and continued during the time when the people of Israel and Judah were threatened by Assyrian and Chaldean conquerors. These "men of God" went through the land warning the Israelites that they had failed to keep God's commandments and would be punished for breaking the covenant: "I will punish you for all your iniquities."

Out of the words of the prophets came new concepts that enriched the Jewish tradition. The prophets embraced a concern for all humanity. All nations would someday come to the God of Israel: "All the earth shall worship you." This vision encompassed the establishment of peace for all the nations of the world. In the words of the prophet Isaiah: "He will judge between the nations and will settle disputes for many people. They will beat their swords into plowshares and their spears into pruning hooks. Nation will not take up sword against nation, nor will they train for war anymore."[9]

Although the prophets developed a sense of universalism, the demands of the Jewish religion (the need to obey God) eventually encouraged a separation between the Jews and their non-Jewish neighbors. Unlike most other peoples of the Middle East, the Jews could not simply be amalgamated into a community by accepting the gods of their conquerors and their neighbors. To remain faithful to the demands of their God, they might even have to refuse loyalty to political leaders.

THE RISE OF NEW EMPIRES

A small and independent Israelite state could exist only as long as no larger state dominated western Asia. New empires soon arose, however, and conquered vast stretches of the ancient world.

The Assyrian Empire

The first of these empires was formed in Assyria, located on the upper Tigris River. The Assyrians were a Semitic-speaking people who exploited the use of iron weapons to establish an empire that by 700 B.C.E. included Mesopotamia, parts of the Iranian plateau, sections of Asia Minor, Syria, Palestine, and Egypt down to Thebes (see Map 1.5). But in less than a hundred years, internal strife and resentment of Assyrian rule led subject peoples to rebel against it. The capital city of Nineveh fell to a coalition of Chaldeans and Medes in 612 B.C.E., and seven years later, the rest of the empire was finally divided between the two powers.

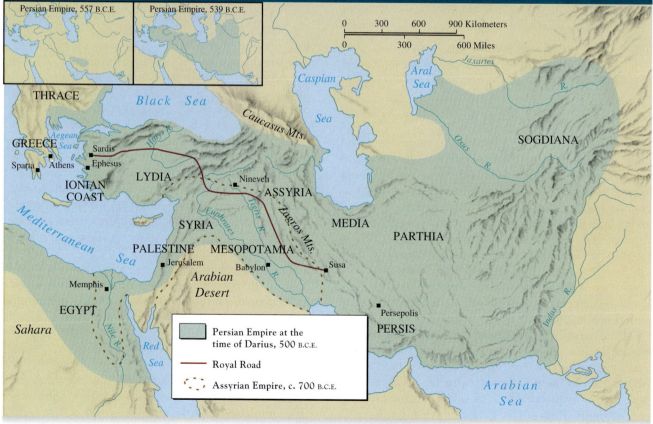

MAP 1.5   The Assyrian and Persian Empires.   Cyrus the Great united the Persians and led them in a successful conquest of much of the Near East, including most of the lands of the Assyrian Empire. By the time of Darius, the Persian Empire was the largest the world had yet seen. ➤ *How did Persian policies attempt to overcome the difficulties of governing far-flung provinces?*

THE ASSYRIAN MILITARY MACHINE

*T*he Assyrians achieved a reputation for possessing a mighty military machine. They were able to use a variety of military tactics and were successful whether they were waging guerrilla warfare, fighting set battles, or laying siege to cities. In these three selections, Assyrian kings boast of their military conquests.

KING SENNACHERIB (704–681 B.C.E.) DESCRIBES A BATTLE WITH THE ELAMITES IN 691

At the command of the god Ashur, the great Lord, I rushed upon the enemy like the approach of a hurricane. . . . I put them to rout and turned them back. I transfixed the troops of the enemy with javelins and arrows. . . . I cut their throats like sheep. . . . My prancing steeds, trained to harness, plunged into their welling blood as into a river; the wheels of my battle chariot were bespattered with blood and filth. I filled the plain with the corpses of their warriors like herbage. . . . As to the sheikhs of the Chaldeans, panic from my onslaught overwhelmed them like a demon. They abandoned their tents and fled for their lives, crushing the corpses of their troops as they went. . . . In their terror they passed scalding urine and voided their excrement into their chariots.

KING SENNACHERIB DESCRIBES HIS SIEGE OF JERUSALEM IN 701

As to Hezekiah, the Jew, he did not submit to my yoke, I laid siege to 46 of his strong cities, walled forts, and the countless small villages in their vicinity, and conquered them by means of well-stamped earth-ramps, and battering-rams brought thus near to the walls combined with the attack by foot soldiers, using mines, breeches, as well as sapper work. I drove out of them 200,150 people, young and old, male and female, horses, mules, donkeys, camels, big and small cattle beyond counting, and considered them booty. Himself I made a prisoner in Jerusalem, his royal residence, like a bird in a cage. I surrounded him with earthwork in order to molest those who were leaving his city's gate.

KING ASHURBANIPAL (669–626 B.C.E.) DESCRIBES HIS TREATMENT OF CONQUERED BABYLON

I tore out the tongues of those whose slanderous mouths had uttered blasphemies against my god Ashur and had plotted against me, his god-fearing prince; I defeated them completely. The others, I smashed alive with the very same statues of protective deities with which they had smashed my own grandfather Sennacherib—now finally as a belated burial sacrifice for his soul. I fed their corpses, cut into small pieces, to dogs, pigs, . . . vultures, the birds of the sky, and also to the fish of the ocean. After I had performed this and thus made quiet again the hearts of the great gods, my lords, I removed the corpses of those whom the pestilence had felled, whose leftovers after the dogs and pigs had fed on them were obstructing the streets, filling the places of Babylon, and of those who had lost their lives through the terrible famine.

At its height, the Assyrian Empire was ruled by kings whose power was considered absolute. Under their leadership, the empire came to be well organized. Local officials were directly responsible to the king. The Assyrians also developed an efficient system of communication to administer their empire more effectively. A network of staging posts was established throughout the empire that used relays of horses (mules or donkeys in the mountains) to carry messages. The system was so effective that a provincial governor anywhere in the empire (except Egypt) could send a question and receive an answer from the king in his palace within a week.

The Assyrians were outstanding conquerors. Over many years of practice, they developed good military leaders and fighters. The Assyrian army was large, well organized, and disciplined. A force of infantrymen was its core, accompanied by cavalrymen and horse-drawn war chariots that were used as platforms for shooting arrows. Moreover, the Assyrians had the first large armies equipped with iron weapons.

The Assyrian military machine used terror as an instrument of warfare (see the box above). As a matter of regular policy, the Assyrians laid waste the land in which they were fighting, smashing dams, looting and destroying towns, setting crops on fire, and cutting down trees, particularly fruit trees. The Assyrians were especially known for committing atrocities on their captives. King Ashurnasirpal recorded this account of his treatment of prisoners:

> 3,000 of their combat troops I felled with weapons. . . . Many of the captives taken from them I burned in a fire. Many I took alive; from some of these I cut off their hands to the wrist, from others I cut off their noses, ears and fingers; I put out the eyes of many of the soldiers. . . . I burned their young men and women to death.[10]

The Persian Empire

After the collapse of the Assyrian Empire, the Chaldeans, under their king Nebuchadnezzar II (605–562 B.C.E.), made Babylonia the leading state in western Asia.

Nebuchadnezzar rebuilt Babylon as the center of his empire, giving it a reputation as one of the great cities of the ancient world. But the splendor of Chaldean Babylonia proved to be short-lived when Babylon fell to the Persians in 539 B.C.E.

The Persians were an Indo-European-speaking people who lived in southwestern Iran. Primarily nomadic, the Persians were organized in tribes until the Achaemenid family managed to unify them. One of its members, Cyrus (559–530 B.C.E.), created a powerful Persian state that stretched from Asia Minor in the west to western India in the east. In 539, Cyrus entered Meospotamia and captured Babylon. His treatment of Babylonia showed remarkable restraint and wisdom. Babylonia was made into a Persian province, but many government officials were kept in their positions. Cyrus also issued an edict permitting the Jews, who had been brought to Babylon in the sixth century B.C.E., to return to Jerusalem with their sacred temple objects and to rebuild their Temple as well.

To his contemporaries, Cyrus the Great deserved to be called the Great. He must have been an unusual ruler for his time, a man who demonstrated considerable wisdom and compassion in the conquest and organization of his empire. Unlike the Assyrian rulers of an earlier empire, he had a reputation for mercy. Medes, Jews, Babylonians—all accepted him as their legitimate ruler. Cyrus had a genuine respect for ancient civilizations—in building his palaces, he made use of Assyrian, Babylonian, and Egyptian designs and building methods.

Cyrus' successors extended the territory of the Persian Empire. His son Cambyses (530–522 B.C.E.) undertook a successful invasion of Egypt. Darius (521–486 B.C.E.) added a new Persian province in western India that extended to the Indus River and then moved into Europe, conquering Thrace and creating the largest empire the world had yet seen. His contact with the Greeks led him to undertake an invasion of the Greek mainland (see Chapter 4).

CIVIL ADMINISTRATION AND THE MILITARY

Darius strengthened the basic structure of the Persian government by organizing more rationally the division of the empire into twenty provinces called satrapies. Each province was ruled by a governor or satrap, literally a "protector of the kingdom." Satraps collected tributes, were responsible for justice and security, raised military levies for the royal army, and normally commanded the military forces within their satrapies. In terms of real power, the satraps were miniature kings who created courts imitative of the Great King's.

An efficient system of communication was crucial to sustaining the Persian Empire. Well-maintained roads facilitated the rapid transit of military and government personnel. One in particular, the so-called Royal Road, stretched from Sardis, the center of Lydia in Asia Minor, to Susa, the chief capital of the Persian Empire. Like the Assyrians, the Persians established way stations equipped with fresh horses for the king's messengers.

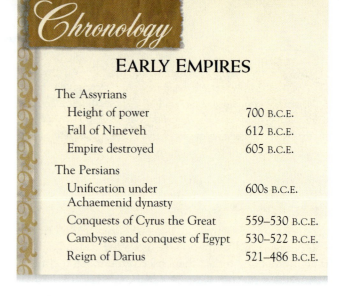

Chronology

EARLY EMPIRES

The Assyrians	
Height of power	700 B.C.E.
Fall of Nineveh	612 B.C.E.
Empire destroyed	605 B.C.E.
The Persians	
Unification under Achaemenid dynasty	600s B.C.E.
Conquests of Cyrus the Great	559–530 B.C.E.
Cambyses and conquest of Egypt	530–522 B.C.E.
Reign of Darius	521–486 B.C.E.

In this vast administrative system, the Persian king occupied an exalted position. All subjects were the king's servants, and he, the Great King, was the source of all justice, possessing the power of life and death over everyone. At its height, much of the power of the Persian Empire depended on the military. By the time of Darius, the Persian monarchs had created a standing army of professional soldiers. This army was truly international in character, composed of contingents from the various peoples who made up the empire. At its core was a cavalry force of ten thousand and an elite infantry force of the same size known as the Immortals because they were never allowed to fall below ten thousand in number. When one was killed, he was immediately replaced.

After Darius, Persian kings became more and more isolated at their courts, surrounded by luxuries provided by immense quantities of gold and silver that flowed into their treasuries, located in the capital cities. Both their hoarding of wealth and their later overtaxation of their subjects are seen as crucial factors in the ultimate weakening of the Persian Empire.

PERSIAN RELIGION

Of all the Persians' cultural contributions, the most original was their religion, Zoroastrianism. According to Persian tradition, Zoroaster was born in 660 B.C.E. After a period of wandering and solitude, he experienced revelations that caused him to be revered as a prophet of the "true religion." His teachings were eventually written down in the third century B.C.E. in the *Zend Avesta*, the sacred book of Zoroastrianism.

Like the Hebrews', Zoroaster's spiritual message was monotheistic. To Zoroaster, Ahuramazda was the only god, and the religion he preached was the only perfect one. Ahuramazda (the "Wise Lord") was the supreme deity who brought all things into being. According to Zoroaster, Ahuramazda also possessed qualities that all humans should aspire to, such as good thought, right, and piety. Although Ahuramazda was supreme, he was not unopposed. At the

© Réunion des Musées Nationaux/Art Resource, NY

tary, social, and religious structures to deal with the basic problems of human existence and organization. These first literate civilizations left detailed records that allow us to view how they grappled with three of the fundamental quandaries that humans have pondered: human relationships, the nature of the universe, and the role of divine forces in the cosmos. Although other peoples would provide different answers from those of the Mesopotamians and the Egyptians, the people of these cultures posed the questions, gave answers, and wrote them down. Human memory begins with the creation of civilizations.

By the middle of the second millennium B.C.E., the creative impulse of the Mesopotamian and Egyptian civilizations was beginning to wane. Around 1200 B.C.E., the decline of the Hittites and the Egyptians had created a power vacuum that allowed a number of small states to emerge and flourish temporarily. All of them were eventually overshadowed by the rise of the great empires of the Assyrians and the Persians. The Assyrian Empire had been the first to unite almost all of the ancient Middle East. Even larger was the empire of the Great Kings of Persia. Although it owed much to the administrative organization created by the Assyrians, the Persian Empire had its own peculiar strengths. Persian rule was tolerant as well as efficient. The many years of peace that the Persian Empire brought to the Middle East facilitated trade and the general well-being of its peoples. It is no wonder that many peoples expressed their gratitude for being subjects of the Great Kings of Persia. Among these peoples were the Israelites, who created no empire but nevertheless left an important spiritual legacy. The evolution of monotheism created in Judaism one of the world's great religions, which spurred the development of both Christianity and Islam.

beginning of the world, the good spirit of Ahuramazda was opposed by the evil spirit (later identified with Ahriman).

Humans also played a role in this cosmic struggle between good and evil. Ahuramazda, the creator, gave all humans free will and the power to choose between right and wrong. The good person chooses the right way of Ahuramazda. Zoroaster taught that there would be an end to the struggle between good and evil. Ahuramazda would eventually triumph, and at the last judgment at the end of the world, the final separation of good and evil would occur. Individuals, too, would be judged. Each soul faced a final evaluation of its actions. If a person had performed good deeds, he or she would achieve paradise; if evil deeds, the soul would be thrown into an abyss of torment.

CONCLUSION

The peoples of Mesopotamia and Egypt, like the peoples of India and China, built the first civilizations. They developed cities and struggled with the problems of organized states. They developed writing to keep records and to preserve and create literature. They constructed monumental architecture to please their gods, symbolize their power, and glorify their culture. They developed new political, mili-

The Persians had also extended their empire to the Indus River, which brought them into contact with another river valley civilization that had developed independently of the civilizations in the Middle East and Egypt. It is to India that we now turn.

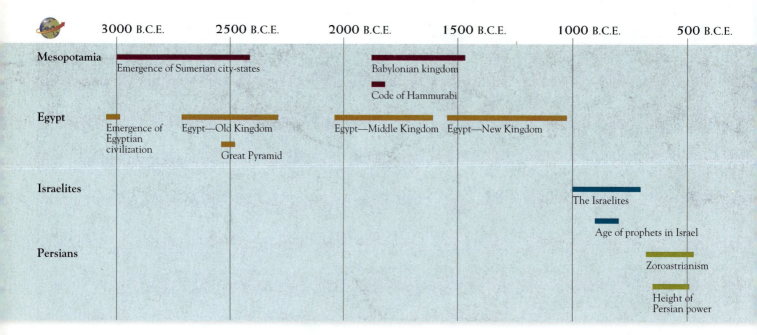

	3000 B.C.E.	2500 B.C.E.	2000 B.C.E.	1500 B.C.E.	1000 B.C.E.	500 B.C.E.

Mesopotamia
Emergence of Sumerian city-states
Babylonian kingdom
Code of Hammurabi

Egypt
Emergence of Egyptian civilization
Egypt—Old Kingdom
Great Pyramid
Egypt—Middle Kingdom
Egypt—New Kingdom

Israelites
The Israelites
Age of prophets in Israel

Persians
Zoroastrianism
Height of Persian power

CHAPTER NOTES

1. Quoted in Amélie Kuhrt, *The Ancient Near East, c. 3000–330 B.C.* (London, 1995), Vol. 1, p. 68.
2. Quoted in Thorkild Jacobsen, "Mesopotamia," in Henri Frankfort et al., *Before Philosophy* (Baltimore, 1949), p. 139.
3. Quoted in Milton Covensky, *The Ancient Near Eastern Tradition* (New York, 1966), p. 51.
4. Ibid., p. 413.
5. Ibid., p. 420.
6. Psalms 137:1, 4–6.
7. Psalms 145:8–9.
8. Exodus 20:13–15.
9. Isaiah 2:4.
10. Quoted in H. W. F. Saggs, *The Might That Was Assyria* (London, 1984), pp. 261–262.

SUGGESTED READING

For a beautifully illustrated introduction to the ancient world, see *Past Worlds: The Times Atlas of Archaeology* (Maplewood, N.J., 1988), written by an international group of scholars. The following works are of considerable value in examining the prehistory of humankind: R. Leakey, *The Making of Mankind* (London, 1981); R. J. Wenke, *Patterns in Prehistory: Humankind's First Three Million Years*, 4th ed. (New York, 1999); and P. Mellars and C. Stringer, *The Human Revolution* (Edinburgh, 1989). For a study of the role of women in early human society, see E. Barber, *Women's Work: The First 20,000 Years* (New York, 1994).

An excellent reference tool on the ancient Near East can be found in P. Bienkowski and A. Milward, eds., *Dictionary of the Ancient Near East* (Philadelphia, 2000). A very competent general survey of the political history of Mesopotamia and Egypt is W. W. Hallo and W. K. Simpson, *The Ancient Near East: A History* (New York, 1971). Also valuable are A. B. Knapp, *The History and Culture of Ancient Western Asia and Egypt* (Chicago, 1987), and W. von Soden, *The Ancient Orient: An Introduction to the Study of*

the Ancient Near East (Grand Rapids, Mich., 1994). For a detailed survey, see A. Kuhrt, *The Ancient Near East, c. 3000–330 B.C.*, 2 vols. (London, 1996). On the economic and social history of the ancient Near East, see D. C. Snell, *Life in the Ancient Near East* (New Haven, Conn., 1997).

General works on ancient Mesopotamia include J. N. Postgate, *Early Mesopotamia: Society and Economy at the Dawn of History* (London, 1992), and A. L. Oppenheim, *Ancient Mesopotamia*, 2d ed. (Chicago, 1977). A beautifully illustrated survey can be found in M. Roaf, *Cultural Atlas of Mesopotamia and the Ancient Near East* (New York, 1996). The world of the Sumerians has been well described in S. N. Kramer, *The Sumerians* (Chicago, 1963) and *History Begins at Sumer* (New York, 1959). See also the more recent summary of the historical and archaeological evidence by H. Crawford, *Sumer and the Sumerians* (Cambridge, 1991). The fundamental work on the spiritual perspective of ancient Mesopotamia is T. Jacobsen, *The Treasures of Darkness: A History of Mesopotamian Religion* (New Haven, Conn., 1976).

For a good introduction to ancient Egypt, see the beautifully illustrated works by M. Hayes, *The Egyptians* (New York, 1997); J. Baines and J. Málek, *The Cultural Atlas of the World: Ancient Egypt* (Alexandria, Va., 1991); and D. P. Silverman, ed., *Ancient Egypt* (New York, 1997). Other general surveys include N. Grant, *The Egyptians* (New York, 1996); I. Shaw, ed., *The Oxford History of Ancient Egypt* (New York, 2000); and N. Grimal, *A History of Ancient Egypt*, trans. I. Shaw (Oxford, 1992). On culture in general, see J. A. Wilson, *The Culture of Ancient Egypt* (Chicago, 1956). The leading authority on the pyramids is I. E. S. Edwards, *The Pyramids of Egypt,* rev. ed. (Harmondsworth, England, 1976). Daily life in ancient Egypt can be examined in E. Strouhal, *Life of the Ancient Egyptians* (Norman, Okla., 1992). An important new study on women is G. Robins, *Women in Ancient Egypt* (Cambridge, Mass., 1993).

There is an enormous literature on ancient Israel. Two good studies on the archaeological aspects are A. Mazar, *Archaeology of the Land of the Bible* (New York, 1992), and A. Ben-Tor, ed., *The Archaeology of Ancient Israel* (New Haven, Conn., 1992). For historical narratives, see especially J. Bright, *A History of Israel,* 3d ed. (Philadelphia, 1981), and the survey by M. Grant, *The History of Ancient Israel* (New York, 1984). For general studies on the religion of the Hebrews, see P. D. Miller, *The Religion of Ancient Israel* (Louisville, Ky., 2000), and W. J. Doorly, *The Religion of Israel* (New York, 1997).

A detailed account of Assyrian political, economic, social, military, and cultural history is H. W. F. Saggs, *The Might That Was Assyria* (London, 1984). The Chaldean Empire can be examined in H. W. F. Saggs, *Babylonians* (Norman, Okla., 1995). The classic work on the Persian Empire is A. T. Olmstead, *History of the Persian Empire* (Chicago, 1948), but a more recent work by J. M. Cook, *The Persian Empire* (New York, 1983), provides new material and fresh interpretations. Also of value is J. Curtis, *Ancient Persia* (Cambridge, Mass., 1990).

InfoTrac College Edition

Visit the source collections at infotrac.thomsonlearning.com and use the Search function with the following key terms.

Antiquities
Egypt history
Mesopotamia
Neolithic
Sumer or Sumerian

World History Resources

Visit the *Essential World History* Companion Web Site for resources specific to this textbook:

http://history.wadsworth.com/duikeressentials02/

The CD in the back of this book and the World History Resource Center at **http://history.wadsworth.com/world/** offer a variety of tools to help you succeed in this course, including access to quizzes; images; documents; interactive simulations, maps, and timelines; movie explorations; and a wealth of other sources.

Chapter 2

Freer Gallery of Art, Smithsonian Institution, Washington, D.C.

ANCIENT INDIA

FOCUS QUESTIONS

- What were the chief features of Harappan civilization, and in what ways was it similar to the civilizations that arose in Egypt and Mesopotamia?
- What roles did the caste system and the family play in Indian society?
- What are the main tenets of Hinduism and Buddhism, and how did each religion influence Indian civilization?
- Why was India unable to maintain a unified empire in the first millennium B.C.E., and how was the Mauryan Empire temporarily able to overcome the tendencies toward disunity?
- ➤ What effects did the Aryans have on Indian civilization?

A rjuna was despondent as he prepared for battle. In the opposing army were many of his friends and colleagues, some of whom he had known since childhood. In despair, he turned for advice to Krishna, his chariot driver, who, unknown to Arjuna, was in actuality an incarnation of the Indian deity Vishnu. "Do not despair of your duty," Krishna advised his friend.

> To be born is certain death,
> to the dead, birth is certain.

It is not right that you should sorrow
   for what cannot be avoided. . . .
If you do not fight this just battle
   you will fail in your own law
and in your honor,
   and you will incur sin.

Krishna's advice to Arjuna is contained in the Bhagavadgita, one of India's most sacred classical writings, and reflects one of the key tenets in Indian philosophy—the belief in reincarnation, or rebirth of the soul. It also points up the importance of doing one's duty without regard for the consequences. Arjuna was a warrior, and according to Aryan tribal tradition, he was obliged to follow the code of his class. "There is more joy in doing one's own duty badly," advised Krishna, "than in doing another man's duty well."

In advising Arjuna to fulfill his obligation as a warrior, the author of the Bhagavadgita, writing around the second century B.C.E. about a battle that took place almost a thousand years earlier, was by implication urging all readers to adhere to their own responsibility as members of one of India's major classes. Henceforth, this hierarchical vision of a society divided into groups, each with clearly distinct roles, would become a defining characteristic of Indian history.

The Bhagavadgita is part of a larger work that deals with the early history of the Aryan peoples who entered India from beyond the mountains north of the Khyber Pass between 1500 and 1000 B.C.E. When the Aryans arrived, India had already had a thriving civilization for almost two thousand years. The Indus valley civilization, although not as well known today as the civilizations of Mesopotamia and Egypt, was just as old; and its political, social, and cultural achievements were equally impressive. That civilization, known to historians by the names of its two major cities, Harappa and Mohenjo-Daro, emerged in the late fourth millennium B.C.E., flourished for over one thousand years, and then came to an abrupt end about 1500 B.C.E. It was soon replaced by a new society dominated by the Aryan peoples. The new civilization that emerged represented a rich mixture of the two cultures—Harappan and Aryan—and evolved over the next three thousand years into what we know today as India.

Thus India was and still is a land of diversity, which is evident in its languages and cultures as well as in its physical characteristics. India possesses a bewildering array of languages, few of which are mutually intelligible. It has a deserved reputation, along with the Middle East, as a cradle of religion. Two of the world's major religions, Hinduism and Buddhism, originated in India.

Although today this beautiful mosaic of peoples and cultures has been broken up into a number of separate independent states, the region still possesses a coherent history that despite its internal diversity is recognizably Indian. It is to the origins and early development of that culture that we now turn. ●

BACKGROUND TO THE EMERGENCE OF CIVILIZATION IN INDIA

In its size and diversity, India seems more like a continent than a single country. That diversity begins with the geographical environment. The Indian subcontinent, shaped like a spade hanging from the southern ridge of Asia, is composed of a number of core regions. In the far north are the Himalayan and Karakoram mountain ranges, home to the highest mountains in the world. Directly south of the Himalayas and the Karakoram range is the rich valley of the Ganges, India's "holy river" and one of the core regions of Indian culture. To the west is the Indus River valley. Today the latter is a relatively arid plateau that forms the backbone of the modern state of Pakistan, but in ancient times, it enjoyed a more balanced climate and served as the cradle of Indian civilization.

South of India's two major river valleys lies the Deccan, a region of hills and an upland plateau that extends from the Ganges valley to the southern tip of the Indian subcontinent. The interior of the plateau is relatively hilly and dry, but the eastern and western coasts are occupied by lush plains, which are historically among the most densely populated regions of India. Off the southeastern coast is the island known today as Sri Lanka. Although Sri Lanka is now a separate country quite distinct politically and culturally from India, the island's history is intimately linked with that of its larger neighbor.

In this vast region live a rich mixture of peoples: Dravidians, probably descended from the Indus River culture that flourished at the dawn of Indian civilization, over four thousand years ago; Aryans, descended from the pastoral peoples who flooded southward from Central Asia in the second millennium B.C.E.; and hill peoples, who may have lived in the region prior to the rise of organized societies and thus may have been the earliest inhabitants of all.

HARAPPAN CIVILIZATION: A FASCINATING ENIGMA

In the 1920s, archaeologists discovered agricultural settlements dating back well over six thousand years in the lower reaches of the Indus River valley in modern Pakistan. Those small mudbrick villages eventually gave rise to the sophisticated human communities that historians call Harappan civilization. Although today the area is relatively arid, during the third and fourth millennia B.C.E., it evidently received much more abundant rainfall, and the valleys of the Indus River and its tributaries supported a thriving civilization that may have covered a total area of over 600,000 square miles, from the Himalayas to the coast of the Indian Ocean. More than seventy sites have been unearthed since the area was first discovered in the 1850s, but the main sites are at the two major cities, Harappa, in the Punjab, and Mohenjo-Daro, nearly 400 miles to the south near the mouth of the Indus River (see Map 2.1).

The origin of the Harappans is still debated, but some scholars have suggested on the basis of ethnographic and linguistic analysis that the language and physical characteristics of the Harappans were similar to those of the Dravidian peoples who live in the Deccan Plateau today. If that is so, Harappa is not simply a dead civilization but a part of the living culture of the Indian subcontinent.

Political and Social Structures

In several respects, Harappan civilization closely resembled the cultures of Mesopotamia and the Nile valley. Like them, it probably began in tiny farming villages scattered throughout the river valley, some dating back to as early as 6500 or 7000 B.C.E. These villages thrived and grew until, by the middle of the third millennium B.C.E., they could support a privileged ruling elite living in walled cities of considerable magnitude and affluence. The center of power was the city of Harappa, which was surrounded by a brick wall over 40 feet thick at its base and more than $3\frac{1}{2}$ miles in circumference. The city was laid out on an essentially rectangular grid, with some streets as wide as 30 feet. Most buildings were constructed of kiln-dried mudbricks and were square in shape, reflecting

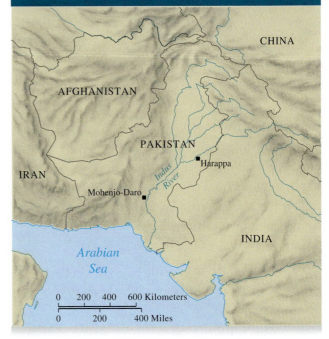

MAP 2.1 Ancient Harappan Civilization. This map shows the location of the first civilization that arose in the Indus River valley, which today is located in Pakistan. ➤ *What were the names of the two largest urban centers that have so far been excavated?*

the grid pattern. At its height, the city may have had as many as eighty thousand inhabitants, as large as some of the most populous urban centers in Sumerian civilization.

Both Harappa and Mohenjo-Daro were divided into large walled neighborhoods, with narrow lanes separating the rows of houses. Houses varied in size, with some as high as three stories, but all followed the same general plan based on a square courtyard surrounded by rooms. Bathrooms featured an advanced drainage system, which carried wastewater out to drains located under the streets and thence to sewage pits beyond the city walls.

The City of Mohenjo-Daro

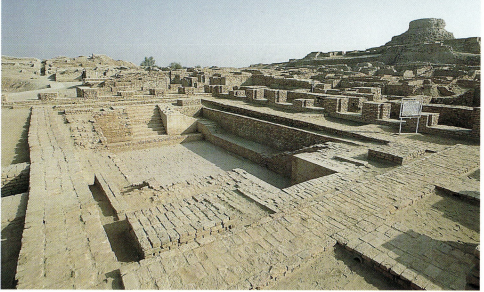

THE CITY OF THE DEAD. Mohenjo-Daro was one of the two major cities of the ancient Indus River civilization. In addition to rows on rows of residential housing, it had a ceremonial center, with a royal palace and a sacred bath that was probably used by the priests as a means of achieving ritual purity. The bath, reminiscent of water tanks in modern Hindu temples, is shown in the center of the photograph here, with the remnants of a Buddhist stupa, constructed centuries later, on the right.

Unfortunately, Harappan writing has not yet been deciphered, so historians know relatively little about the organization of the Harappan state. However, recent archaeological evidence suggests that unlike its contemporaries in Egypt and Sumer, Harappa was not a centralized monarchy with a theocratic base but a collection of over fifteen hundred towns and cities loosely connected by ties of trade and alliance and ruled by a coalition of landlords and rich merchants. There were no royal precincts or imposing burial monuments, and there are few surviving stone or terra-cotta images that might represent kings, priests, or military commanders. There are clear signs, however, that religion had advanced beyond the stage of spirit worship to belief in a single god or goddess of fertility. Presumably, priests at court prayed to this deity to maintain the fertility of the soil and guarantee the annual harvest.

As in Mesopotamia and Egypt, the Harappan economy was based primarily on agriculture. Wheat, barley, rice, and peas were apparently the primary crops. The presence of cotton seeds at various sites suggests that the Harappan peoples may have been the first to master the cultivation of this useful crop and possibly introduced it, along with rice, to other societies in the region. But Harappa also developed an extensive trading network that extended to Sumer and other civilizations to the west. Textiles and foodstuffs were apparently imported from Sumer in exchange for metals such as copper, lumber, precious stones, and various types of luxury goods. Much of this trade was conducted by ship via the Persian Gulf, although some undoubtedly went by land.

Harappan Culture

Archaeological remains indicate that the Indus valley peoples possessed a culture as sophisticated as that of the Sumerians to the west. The aesthetic quality of some Harappan pottery and sculpture is superb, rivaling equivalent work produced elsewhere. Sculpture was the Harappans' highest artistic achievement. Some artifacts possess a wonderful vitality of expression. Fired clay seals show a deft touch in carving animals such as elephants, tigers, rhinoceros, and antelope, and figures made of copper or terra-cotta show a lively sensitivity and a sense of grace and movement.

Unfortunately, the only surviving examples of Harappan writing are the pictographic symbols inscribed on the clay seals. The script contained more than four hundred characters, but most are too stylized

A HARAPPAN BUST. This four-thousand-year-old bust found at Mohenjo-Daro displays an elaborate beard, a pair of eyes originally inlaid with shell, and a toga decorated with a trefoil design. Although the trefoil had been used in Egypt and Mesopotamia as a sacred symbol representing stars and deities, little is known about the identity of this Harappan figure or whether the creative execution reflects the influence of other nearby civilizations.

to be identified by their shape, and scholars have thus far been unable to decipher them. There are no apparent links with Mesopotamian scripts. Until the script is deciphered, much about the Harappan civilization must remain, as one historian termed it, a fascinating enigma.

THE ARRIVAL OF THE ARYANS

One of the great mysteries of Harappan civilization is how it came to an end. Archaeologists working at Mohenjo-Daro have discovered signs of first a gradual decay and then a sudden destruction of the city and its inhabitants around 1500 B.C.E. Many of the surviving skeletons have been found in postures of running or hiding, reminiscent of the ruins of the Roman city of Pompeii, destroyed by the eruption of Mount Vesuvius in 79 C.E.

These tantalizing signs of flight before a sudden catastrophe have led some scholars to surmise that the city of Mohenjo-Daro (the name was applied by archaeologists and means "city of the dead") and perhaps the remnants of Harappan civilization were destroyed by the Aryans, nomads from the north, who arrived in the subcontinent around the middle of the second millennium B.C.E. Although the Aryans were almost certainly not as sophisticated culturally as the Harappans, like many nomadic peoples, they excelled at the art of war. As in Mesopotamia and the Nile valley, most contacts between pastoral and agricultural peoples proved unstable and ended in armed conflict. Nevertheless, it is doubtful that the Aryan invaders were directly responsible for the final destruction of Mohenjo-Daro. More likely, Harappan civilization had already fallen on hard times, perhaps as a result of climatic change in the Indus valley. Archaeologists have found clear signs of social decay, including evidence of trash in the streets, neglect of public services, and overcrowding in urban neighborhoods. Mohenjo-Daro itself may have been destroyed by an epidemic or by natural phenomena such as floods, an earthquake, or a shift in the course of the Indus River. If that was the case, the Aryans conquered a people whose moment of greatness had already passed.

The Early Aryans

Historians know relatively little about the origins and culture of the Aryans before they entered India, although they were part of the extensive group of Indo-European-speaking peoples who inhabited vast areas in what is now Siberia and the steppes of Central Asia. Whereas other Indo-European-speaking peoples moved westward and eventually settled in Europe, the Aryans moved south across the Hindu Kush into the plains of northern India. Between 1500 and 1000 B.C.E., they gradually advanced eastward from the Indus valley, across the fertile plain of the Ganges, and later southward into the Deccan Plateau until they had eventually extended their political mastery over the entire subcontinent and its Dravidian inhabitants, although Dravidian culture survived to remain a prominent element in the evolution of traditional Indian civilization.

After they settled in India, the Aryans gradually adapted to the geographical realities of their new homeland and abandoned the pastoral life for agricultural pursuits. They were assisted by the introduction of iron, which probably came from the Middle East, where it had first been introduced by the Hittites (see Chapter 1) about 1500 B.C.E. The invention of the iron plow, along with the development of irrigation, allowed the Aryans and their indigenous subjects to clear the dense jungle growth along the Ganges River and transform the Ganges valley into one of the richest agricultural regions in all of South Asia. The Aryans also developed their first writing system and were thus able to transcribe the legends that previously had been passed down from generation to generation by memory. Most of what is known about the early Aryans is based on oral traditions passed on in the Rigveda, an ancient work that was written down after the Aryans arrived in India (the Rigveda is one of several Vedas, or collections of sacred instructions and rituals).

As in other Indo-European societies, each of the various Aryan tribes was led by a chieftain, called a *raja* ("prince"), who was assisted by a council of elders composed of other leading members of the tribe; like them, he was normally a member of the warrior class, called the *kshatriya*. The chief derived his power from his ability to protect his tribe from rival groups, an ability that was crucial in the warring kingdoms and shifting alliances that were typical of early Aryan society. Though the *rajas* claimed to be representatives of the gods, they were not gods themselves.

As Aryan society grew in size and complexity, the chieftains began to be transformed into kings, usually called *maharajas* ("great princes"). Nevertheless, the tradition that the ruler did not possess absolute authority remained strong. Like all human beings, the ruler was required to follow the *dharma*, a set of laws that set behavioral standards for all individuals and classes in Indian society (see the box on p. 31).

While competing groups squabbled for precedence in India, powerful new empires were rising to the west. First came the Persian Empire of Cyrus and Darius. Then came the Greeks. After two centuries of sporadic rivalry and warfare,

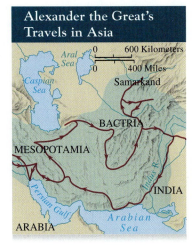

Alexander the Great's Travels in Asia

THE DUTIES OF A KING

Kautilya, India's earliest known political philosopher, was an adviser to the Mauryan rulers. The Arthasastra, though written down at a later date, very likely reflects his ideas. This passage sets forth some of the necessary characteristics of a king, including efficiency, diligence, energy, compassion, and concern for the security and welfare of the state. In emphasizing the importance of winning popular support as the means of becoming an effective ruler, the author echoes the view of the Chinese philosopher Mencius, who declared that the best way to win the empire is to win the people (see Chapter 3).

THE ARTHASASTRA

Only if a king is himself energetically active do his officers follow him energetically. If he is sluggish, they too remain sluggish. And, besides, they eat up his works. He is thereby easily overpowered by his enemies. Therefore, he should ever dedicate himself energetically to activity. . . .

A king should attend to all urgent business; he should not put it off. For what has been thus put off becomes either difficult or altogether impossible to accomplish.

The vow of the king is energetic activity; his sacrifice is constituted of the discharge of his own administrative duties; his sacrificial fee [to the officiating priests] is his impartiality of attitude toward all; his sacrificial consecration is his anointment as king.

In the happiness of the subjects lies the happiness of the king; in their welfare, his own welfare. The welfare of the king does not lie in the fulfillment of what is dear to him; whatever is dear to the subjects constitutes his welfare.

Therefore, ever energetic, a king should act up to the precepts of the science of material gain. Energetic activity is the source of material gain; its opposite, of downfall.

In the absence of energetic activity, the loss of what has already been obtained and of what still remains to be obtained is certain. The fruit of one's works is achieved through energetic activity—one obtains abundance of material prosperity.

---

the Greeks achieved a brief period of regional dominance in the late fourth century B.C.E. with the rise of Macedonia under Alexander the Great. Alexander had heard of the riches of India, and in 330 B.C.E., after conquering Persia, he launched an invasion of the east (see Chapter 4). In 326 B.C.E., his armies arrived in the plains of northwestern India. They departed almost as suddenly as they had come, leaving in their wake Greek administrators and a veneer of cultural influence that would affect the area for generations to come.

The Mauryan Empire

The Alexandrian conquest was only a brief interlude in the history of the Indian subcontinent, but it played a formative role, for on the heels of Alexander's departure came the rise of the first dynasty to control much of the region. The founder of the new state, who took the royal title Chandragupta Maurya (324–301 B.C.E.), drove out the Greek occupation forces after the departure of Alexander and solidified his control over the northern Indian plain. He established the capital of his new Mauryan Empire at Pataliputra (modern Patna) in the Ganges valley (see the map on p. 40).

Little is known of Chandragupta Maurya's empire. Most accounts of his reign rely on a lost work written by Megasthenes, a Greek ambassador to the Mauryan court, in about 302 B.C.E. Chandragupta Maurya was apparently advised by a brilliant court official named Kautilya, whose name has been attached to a treatise on politics called the *Arthasastra*. The work actually dates from a later time, but it may well reflect Kautilya's ideas.

Although the author of the *Arthasastra* follows Aryan tradition in stating that the happiness of the king lies in the happiness of his subjects, the treatise also asserts that when the sacred law of the *dharma* and practical politics collide, the latter must take precedence: "Whenever there is disagreement between history and sacred law or between evidence and sacred law, then the matter should be settled in accordance with sacred law. But whenever sacred law is in conflict with rational law, then reason shall be held authoritative."[1] The *Arthasastra* also emphasizes ends rather than means, achieved results rather than the methods employed. For this reason, it has often been compared to Machiavelli's famous political treatise of the Italian Renaissance, *The Prince*, written more than a thousand years later.

As described in the *Arthasastra*, Chandragupta Maurya's government was highly centralized and even despotic: "It is power and power alone which, only when exercised by the king with impartiality, and in proportion to guilt, over his son or his enemy, maintains both this world and the next."[2] The king possessed a large army and a secret police responsible to his orders (according to the Greek ambassador Megasthenes, Chandragupta Maurya was chronically fearful of assassination, a not unrealistic concern for someone who had allegedly come to power by violence). Reportedly, all food was tasted in his presence, and he made a practice of never sleeping twice in the same bed in his sumptuous palace. To guard against corruption, a board of censors was empowered to investigate cases of possible malfeasance and incompetence within the bureaucracy.

The ruler's authority beyond the confines of the capital may often have been limited, however. The empire was divided into provinces that were ruled by governors. At first, most of these governors were appointed by and reported to the ruler, but later the position became hereditary. The provinces themselves were divided into districts, each under a chief magistrate appointed by the governor. At the base of the government pyramid was the village, where the vast majority of the Indian people lived. The village was governed by a council of elders; membership in the council was normally hereditary and was shared by the wealthiest families in the village.

Caste and Class: Social Structures in Ancient India

When the Aryans arrived in India, they already possessed a strong class system based on a ruling warrior class. They apparently held the indigenous peoples in some contempt and assigned them to a lower position in society. The result was a set of social institutions and class divisions that have persisted with only minor changes down to the present day.

THE CASTE SYSTEM

At the base of the social system that emerged from the clash of cultures was the concept of the superiority of the invading peoples over their conquered subjects. In a sense, it became an issue of color, because the Aryan invaders, a primarily light-skinned people, were contemptuous of their subjects, who were dark. Light skin came to imply high status, whereas dark skin suggested the opposite.

The concept of color, however, was only the physical manifestation of a division that took place in Indian society on the basis of economic functions. Indian classes (called *varna*, literally, "color," and commonly known as "castes" in English) did not simply reflect an informal division of labor. Instead, they were a set of rigid social classifications that determined not only one's occupation but also one's status in society and one's hope for ultimate salvation (see "Escaping the Wheel of Life" later in this chapter). There were five major castes in Indian society in ancient times. At the top were two castes, collectively viewed as the aristocracy, which clearly represented the ruling elites in Aryan society prior to their arrival in India: the priests and the warriors.

The priestly caste, known as the *brahmins*, was usually considered to be at the top of the social scale. Descended from seers who had advised the ruler on religious matters in Aryan tribal society (*brahmin* meant "one possessed of *Brahman*," a term for the supreme god in the Hindu religion), they were eventually transformed into an official class after their religious role declined in importance. Megasthenes described this caste as follows:

From the time of their conception in the womb they are under the care and guardianship of learned men who go to the mother and . . . give her prudent hints and counsels, and the women who listen to them most willingly are thought to be the most fortunate in their offspring. After their birth the children are in the care of one person after another, and as they advance in years their masters are men of superior accomplishments. The philosophers reside in a grove in front of the city within a moderate-sized enclosure. They live in a simple style and lie on pallets of straw and [deer] skins. They abstain from animal food and sexual pleasures, and occupy their time in listening to serious discourse and in imparting knowledge to willing ears.[3]

The second caste was the *kshatriya*, the warriors. Although often listed below the *brahmins* in social status, many *kshatriyas* were probably descended from the ruling warrior class in Aryan society prior to the conquest of India and thus may have originally ranked socially above the *brahmins*, although they were ranked lower in religious terms. Like the *brahmins*, the *kshatriyas* were originally identified with a single occupation—fighting—but as the character of Aryan society changed, they often switched to other forms of employment.

The third-ranked caste in Indian society was the *vaisya* (literally, "commoner"). The *vaisyas* were usually viewed in economic terms as the merchant caste. Some historians have speculated that the *vaisyas* were originally guardians of the tribal herds but that after settling in India, many moved into commercial pursuits. Megasthenes noted that members of this caste "alone are permitted to hunt and keep cattle and to sell beasts of burden or to let them out on hire. In return for clearing the land of wild beasts and birds which infest sown fields, they receive an allowance of corn from the king. They lead a wandering life and dwell in tents."[4] Although this caste was ranked below the first two in social status, it shared with them the privilege of being considered "twice-born," a term referring to a ceremony at puberty whereby young males were initiated into adulthood and introduced into Indian society.

Below the three "twice-born" castes were the *sudras*, who represented the great bulk of the Indian population. The *sudras* were not considered fully Aryan, and the term probably originally referred to the conquered Dravidian population. Most *sudras* were peasants or artisans or worked at other forms of manual labor. They had only limited rights in society.

At the lowest level of Indian society, and in fact not even considered a legitimate part of the caste system itself, were the untouchables (also known as outcastes, or *pariahs*). The untouchables probably originated as a slave class consisting of prisoners of war, criminals, ethnic minorities, and other groups considered outside Indian society. Even after slavery was outlawed, the untouchables were given menial and degrading tasks that other Indians would not accept, such as collecting trash, handling dead bodies, or serving as butchers or tanners (handling dead meat). According to the estimate of one historian, they may have accounted for a little more than 5 percent of the total population of India in antiquity.

The life of the untouchables was extremely demeaning. They were not considered human, and their very presence was considered polluting to members of the other *varna*. No Indian would touch or eat food handled or prepared by an untouchable. Untouchables lived in special ghettos and were required to tap two sticks together to announce their presence when they traveled outside their quarters so that others could avoid them.

Technically, the caste divisions were absolute. Individuals supposedly were born, lived, and died in the same caste. In practice, some upward or downward mobility probably took place, and there was undoubtedly some flexibility in economic functions. But throughout most of Indian history, caste taboos remained strict. Members were generally not permitted to marry outside their caste (although in practice, men were occasionally allowed to marry below their caste but not above it).

The people of ancient India did not belong to a particular caste as individuals but as part of a larger kin group commonly referred to as the *jati*, a system of extended families that originated in ancient India and still exists in somewhat changed form today. Although the origins of the *jati* system are unknown (there are no indications of strict class distinctions in Harappan society), the *jati* eventually became identified with a specific caste living in a specific area and carrying out a specific function in society. Each caste was divided into thousands of separate *jatis*, each with its own separate economic function.

Caste was thus the basic social organization into which traditional Indian society was divided. Each *jati* was itself composed of hundreds or thousands of individual nuclear families and was governed by its own council of elders. Membership in this ruling council was usually hereditary and was based on the wealth or social status of particular families within the community.

In theory, each *jati* was assigned a particular form of economic activity. Obviously, though, not all families in a given caste could take part in the same vocation, and as time went on, members of a single *jati* commonly engaged in several different lines of work. Sometimes an entire *jati* would have to move its location in order to continue a particular form of activity. In other cases, a *jati* would adopt an entirely new occupation in order to remain in a certain area. Such changes in habitat or occupation introduced the possibility of movement up or down the social scale. In this way, an entire *jati* could sometimes engage in upward mobility, even though it was not possible for individuals, who were tied to their caste identity for life.

The caste system may sound highly constricting, but there were persuasive social and economic reasons why it survived for so many centuries. In the first place, it provided an identity for individuals in a highly hierarchical society. Although an individual might rank lower on the social scale than members of other castes, it was always possible to find others ranked even lower. Perhaps equally important, caste was a primitive form of welfare system. Each *jati* was obliged to provide for any of its members who were poor or destitute. Caste also provided an element of stability in a society that all too often was in a state of political anarchy.

DAILY LIFE IN ANCIENT INDIA

Beyond these rigid social stratifications was the Indian family. Not only was life centered around the family, but the family, not the individual, was the most basic unit in society. The ideal was an extended family, with three generations living under the same roof. It was essentially patriarchal, except along the Malabar coast, near the southwestern tip of the subcontinent, where a matriarchal form of social organization prevailed down to modern times. In the rest of India, the oldest male traditionally possessed legal authority over the entire family unit.

The family was linked together in a religious sense by a series of commemorative rites to ancestral members. This ritual originated in the Vedic era and consisted of family ceremonies to honor the departed and to link the living and the dead. The male family head was responsible for leading the ritual. At his death, his eldest son had the duty of conducting the funeral rites.

The importance of the father and the son in family ritual underlined the importance of males in Indian society. Male superiority was expressed in a variety of ways. Women could not serve as priests (although in practice, some were accepted as seers), nor were they normally permitted to study the Vedas. In general, males had a monopoly on education, since the primary goal of learning to read was to carry on family rituals. In high-class families, young men began Vedic studies with a *guru* (teacher). Some then went on to higher studies in one of the major cities. The goal of such an education might be either professional or religious.

In general, only males could inherit property, except in a few cases where there were no sons. According to law, a woman was always considered a minor. Divorce was prohibited, although it sometimes took place. According to the *Arthasastra*, a wife who had been deserted by her husband could seek a divorce. Polygamy was fairly rare and apparently occurred mainly among the higher classes, but husbands were permitted to take a second wife if the first was barren. Producing children was an important aspect of marriage, both because children provided security for their parents in old age and because they were a physical proof of male potency. Child marriage was common for young girls, whether because of the desire for children or because daughters represented an economic liability to their parents. But perhaps the most graphic symbol of women's subjection to men was the ritual of *sati* (often written *suttee*), which required the wife to throw herself on her dead husband's funeral pyre. The Greek visitor Megasthenes reported "that he had heard from some persons of wives burning themselves along with their deceased husbands and doing so gladly; and that those women who refused to burn themselves were held in disgrace."[5] All in all, it was undoubtedly a difficult existence. According to the *Law of Manu*, an early treatise on social organization and behavior in ancient India, probably written in the first or second century B.C.E., women were subordinated to men—first to their father, then to their husband, and finally to their sons:

> She should do nothing independently
>   even in her own house.
> In childhood subject to her father,
>   in youth to her husband,
> and when her husband is dead to her sons,
>   she should never enjoy independence. . . .
>
> She should always be cheerful,
>   and skillful in her domestic duties,
> with her household vessels well cleansed,
>   and her hand tight on the purse strings. . . .
>
> Though he be uncouth and prone to pleasure,
>   though he have no good points at all,
> the virtuous wife should ever
>   worship her lord as a god.[6]

At the root of female subordination to the male was the practical fact that as in most agricultural societies, men did most of the work in the fields. Females were viewed as having little utility outside the home and indeed were considered an economic burden, since parents were obliged to provide a dowry to acquire a husband for a daughter. Female children also appeared to offer little advantage in maintaining the family unit, since they joined the families of their husbands after the wedding ceremony.

Despite all of these indications of female subjection to the male, there are numerous signs that in some ways women often played an influential role in Indian society, and the Hindu code of behavior stressed that they should be treated with respect. Indians appeared to be fascinated by female sexuality, and tradition held that women often used their sexual powers to achieve domination over men. The author of the Mahabharata, a vast epic of early Indian society, complained that "the fire has never too many logs, the ocean never too many rivers, death never too many living souls, and fair-eyed woman never too many men." Despite the legal and social constraints, women often played an important role within the family unit, and many were admired and honored for their talents. It is probably significant that paintings and sculpture from ancient and medieval India frequently show women in a role equal to that of men.

Homosexuality was not unknown in India. It was condemned in the law books, however, and generally ignored by literature, which devoted its attention entirely to erotic heterosexuality. The *Kamasutra*, a textbook on sexual practices and techniques dating from the second century C.E. or slightly thereafter, mentions homosexuality briefly and with no apparent enthusiasm.

The Economy

The Aryan conquest did not drastically change the economic character of Indian society. Not only did most Aryans take up farming, but it is likely that agriculture expanded rapidly under Aryan rule with the invention of the iron plow and the spread of northern Indian culture into the Deccan Plateau. One consequence of this process was to shift the focus of Indian culture from the Indus valley farther eastward to the Ganges River valley, which even today is one of the most densely populated regions on earth. The flatter areas in the Deccan Plateau and in the coastal plains were also turned into cropland.

For most Indian farmers, life was harsh. Among the most fortunate were those who owned their own land, although they were required to pay taxes to the state. Many others were sharecroppers or landless laborers. They were subject to the vicissitudes of the market and often paid exorbitant rents to their landlord. Concentration of land in large holdings was limited by the tradition of dividing property among all the sons, but large estates worked by hired laborers or rented out to sharecroppers were not uncommon, particularly in areas where local *rajas* derived much of their wealth from their property.

Another problem for Indian farmers was the unpredictability of the climate. India is in the monsoon zone. The monsoon is a seasonal wind pattern in southern Asia that blows from the southwest during the summer months and from the northeast during the winter. The southwest monsoon is commonly marked by heavy rains. When the rains were late, thousands starved, particularly in the drier areas, which were especially dependent on rainfall. Strong governments attempted to deal with such problems by building state-operated granaries and maintaining the irrigation works; but strong governments were rare, and famine was probably all too common. The staple crops in the north were wheat, barley, and millet, with wet rice common in the fertile river valleys. In the south, grain and vegetables were supplemented by various tropical products, cotton, and spices such as pepper, ginger, cinnamon, and saffron.

By no means were all Indians farmers. As time passed, India became one of the most advanced trading and manufacturing civilizations in the ancient world. After the rise of the Mauryas, India's role in regional trade began to expand, and the subcontinent became a major transit point in a vast commercial network that extended from the rim of the Pacific to the Middle East and the Mediterranean Sea. This regional trade went both by sea and by camel caravan. Maritime trade across the Indian Ocean may have begun as early as the fifth century B.C.E. It extended eastward as far as Southeast Asia and China and southward as far as the straits between Africa and the island of Madagascar. Westward went spices, perfumes, jewels, textiles, precious stones and ivory, and wild animals. In return, India received gold, tin, lead, and wine.

India's expanding role as a manufacturing and commercial hub of the ancient world was undoubtedly a spur to the growth of the state. Under Chandragupta Maurya, the central government became actively involved in commercial and manufacturing activities. It owned mines and vast crown lands and undoubtedly earned massive profits from its role in regional commerce. Separate government departments were established for trade, agriculture, mining, and the manufacture of weapons, and the movement of private goods was vigorously taxed. Nevertheless, a significant private sector also flourished; it was dominated by great caste guilds, which monopolized key sectors of the economy. A money economy probably came into operation during the second century B.C.E., when copper and gold coins were introduced from the Middle East. This in turn led to the development of banking.

ESCAPING THE WHEEL OF LIFE: THE RELIGIOUS WORLD OF ANCIENT INDIA

Like Indian politics and society, Indian religion is a blend of Aryan and Dravidian culture. The intermingling of those two civilizations gave rise to an extraordinarily complex set of religious beliefs and practices, filled with diversity and contrast. Out of this cultural mix came two of the world's great religions, Buddhism and Hinduism, and several smaller ones, including Jainism and Sikhism.

Hinduism

Evidence about the earliest religious beliefs of the Aryan peoples comes primarily from sacred texts such as the Vedas, a set of four collections of hymns and religious ceremonies transmitted by memory through the centuries by Aryan priests. Many of these religious ideas were probably common to all of the Indo-European peoples before their separation into different groups at least four thousand years ago. Early Aryan beliefs were based on the common concept of a pantheon of gods and goddesses representing great forces of nature similar to the immortals of Greek mythology. The Aryan ancestor of the Greek father-god Zeus, for example, may have been the deity known in early Aryan tradition as Dyaus (see Chapter 4).

The parent god Dyaus was a somewhat distant figure, however, who was eventually overshadowed by other, more functional gods possessing more familiar human traits. For a while, the primary Aryan god was the great warrior god Indra. Indra summoned the Aryan tribal peoples to war and was represented in nature by thunder. Later, Indra declined in importance and was replaced by Varuna, lord of justice, who eventually evolved into the modern deity Vishnu. Other gods and goddesses represented various forces of nature or the needs of human beings, such as fire, fertility, and wealth.

The concept of sacrifice was a key element in Aryan religious belief in Vedic times. As in many other ancient cultures, the practice may have begun as human sacrifice, but later animals were used as substitutes, although human sacrifice was practiced in some isolated communities down to modern times. The priestly class, the *brahmins*, played a key role in these ceremonies.

Another element of Aryan religious belief in ancient times was the ideal of asceticism. By the sixth century B.C.E., self-sacrifice or even self-mutilation had begun to replace sacrifice as a means of placating or communicating with the gods. Apparently, the original motive for asceticism was to achieve magical powers, but later, in the Upanishads (a set of commentaries on the Vedas compiled in the sixth century B.C.E.), it was seen as a means of spiritual meditation that would enable the practitioner to reach beyond material reality to a world of truth and bliss beyond earthly joy and sorrow: "Those who practice penance and faith in the forest, the tranquil ones, the knowers of truth, living the life of wandering mendicancy—they depart, freed from passion, through the door of the sun, to where dwells, verily . . . the imperishable Soul."[7] It is possible that another motive was to permit those with strong religious convictions to communicate directly with metaphysical reality without having to rely on the priestly class at court.

Asceticism, of course, has been practiced in other religions, including Christianity and Islam, but it seems particularly identified with Hinduism, the religion that emerged from early Indian religious tradition. Eventually, asceticism evolved into the modern practice of body training that we know as *yoga* ("union"), which is accepted today as a meaningful element of Hindu religious practice.

REINCARNATION

Another new concept also probably began to appear around the time the Upanishads were written—the idea of reincarnation. This is the idea that the individual soul is reborn in a different form after death and progresses through several existences on the wheel of life until it reaches its final destination in a union with the Great World Soul, *Brahman*. Because life is harsh, this final release is the objective of all living souls.

A key element in this process is the idea of *karma*—that one's rebirth in a next life is determined by one's *karma* (actions) in this life. Hinduism places all living species on a vast scale of existence, including the four classes and the untouchables in human society. The current status of an individual soul, then, is not simply a cosmic accident but the inevitable result of actions that that soul has committed in a past existence.

At the top of the scale are the *brahmins*, who by definition are closest to ultimate release from the law of reincarnation. The *brahmins* are followed in descending order by the other castes in human society and the world of the beasts. Within the animal kingdom, an especially high position is reserved for the cow, which even today is revered by Hindus as a sacred beast. Some have speculated that the cow's sacred position may have descended from the concept of the sacred bull in Dravidian culture.

The concept of *karma* is governed by the *dharma,* a law regulating human behavior. The *dharma* imposes different requirements on different individuals depending on their status in society. Those high on the social scale, such as *brahmins* and *kshatriyas,* are held to a more strict form of behavior than are *sudras.* The *brahmin,* for example, is expected to abstain from eating meat, because that would entail the killing of another living being, thus interrupting its *karma.*

How the concept of reincarnation originated is not known, although it was apparently not unusual for early peoples to believe that the individual soul would be reborn in a different form in a later life. In any case, in India the concept may have had practical causes as well as consequences. In the first place, it tended to provide religious sanction for the rigid class divisions that had begun to emerge in Indian society after the Aryan conquest, and it provided moral and political justification for the privileges of those on the higher end of the scale.

At the same time, the concept of reincarnation provided certain compensations for those lower on the ladder of life. For example, it gave hope to the poor that if they behaved properly in this life, they might improve their condition in the next. It also provided a means for unassimilated groups such as ethnic minorities to find a place in Indian society while at the same time permitting them to maintain their distinctive way of life.

The ultimate goal of achieving "good" *karma,* as we have seen, was to escape the cycle of existence. To the sophisticated, the nature of that release was a spiritual union of the individual soul with the Great World Soul, *Brahman,* described in the Upanishads as a form of dreamless sleep, free from earthly desires. Such a concept, however, was undoubtedly too ethereal for the average Indian, who needed a more concrete form of heavenly salvation, a place of beauty and bliss after a life of disease and privation.

It was probably for this reason that the Hindu religion—in some ways so otherworldly and ascetic—came to be peopled with a multitude of very human gods and goddesses. It has been estimated that the Hindu pantheon contains more than 33,000 deities. Only a small number are primary ones, however, notably the so-called trinity of gods: Brahman the Creator, Vishnu the Preserver, and Siva (originally the Vedic god Rudra) the Destroyer. Although Brahman (sometimes in his concrete form called Brahma) is considered to be the highest god, Vishnu and Siva take precedence in the devotional exercises of many Hindus, who can be roughly divided into Vishnuites and Saivites. In addition to the trinity of gods, all of whom have wives with readily identifiable roles and personalities, there are

➤ **DANCING SIVA.** The Hindu deity Siva is often presented in the form of a bronze statue, performing a cosmic dance in which he simultaneously creates and destroys the universe. While his upper right hand creates the cosmos, his upper left hand reduces it in flames, and the lower two hands offer eternal blessing. Siva's dancing statues present to his followers the visual message of his power and compassion.

countless minor deities, each again with his or her own specific function, such as bringing good fortune, arranging a good marriage, or guaranteeing a son in childbirth.

The rich variety and earthy character of many Hindu deities are repugnant to many Christians and Muslims, to whom God is an all-seeing and transcendent deity. Many Hindus, however, regard the multitude of gods as simply different manifestations of one ultimate reality. The various deities also provide a useful means for ordinary Indians to personify their religious feelings. Even though some individuals among the early Aryans attempted to communicate with the gods through sacrifice or asceticism, most Indians undoubtedly sought to satisfy their own individual religious needs through devotion, which they expressed through ritual ceremonies and offerings at a Hindu temple. Such offerings were not only a way to seek salvation but also a means of satisfying all the aspirations of daily life.

Over the centuries, then, Hinduism changed radically from its origins in Aryan tribal society and became a religion of the vast majority of the Indian people. Concern with a transcendental union between the individual soul and the Great World Soul contrasted with practical desires for material wealth and happiness; ascetic self-denial contrasted with an earthy emphasis on the pleasures and values of sexual union between marriage partners. All of these became aspects of Hinduism, the religion of 70 percent of the Indian people.

Buddhism: The Middle Path

In the sixth century B.C.E., a new doctrine appeared in northern India that soon began to rival Hinduism's popularity throughout the subcontinent. This new doctrine was called Buddhism. The historical founder of Buddhism, Siddhartha Gautama, was a native of a small principality in the foothills of the Himalaya Mountains in what is today southern Nepal. He was born in the mid-sixth century B.C.E., the son of a ruling *kshatriya* family. According to tradition, the young Siddhartha was raised in affluent surroundings and trained, like many other members of his class, in the martial arts. On reaching maturity, he married and began to raise a family. However, at the age of twenty-nine, he suddenly discovered the pain of illness, the sorrow of death, and the degradation caused by old age in the lives of ordinary people and exclaimed: "Would that sickness, age, and death might be forever bound!" From that time on, he decided to dedicate his life to determining the cause and seeking the cure for human suffering.

To find the answers to these questions, Siddhartha abandoned his home and family and traveled widely. At first, he tried to follow the model of the ascetics, but he eventually decided that self-mortification did not lead to a greater understanding of life and abandoned the practice. Then one day, after a lengthy period of meditation under a tree, he finally achieved enlightenment as to the meaning of life and spent the remainder of his life preaching it. His conclusions, as embodied in his teachings, became the philosophy (or as some would have it, the religion) of Buddhism. According to legend, the Devil (the Indian term is *Mara*) attempted desperately to tempt him with political power and the company of beautiful girls. But Siddhartha Gautama resisted:

> *Pleasure is brief as a flash of lightning*
> *Or like an autumn shower, only for a moment. . . .*
> *Why should I then covet the pleasures you speak of?*
> *I see your bodies are full of all impurity:*
> *Birth and death, sickness and age are yours.*
> *I seek the highest prize, hard to attain by men—*
> *The true and constant wisdom of the wise.*[8]

How much the modern doctrine of Buddhism resembles the original teachings of Siddhartha Gautama is open to debate, since much time has elapsed since his death and

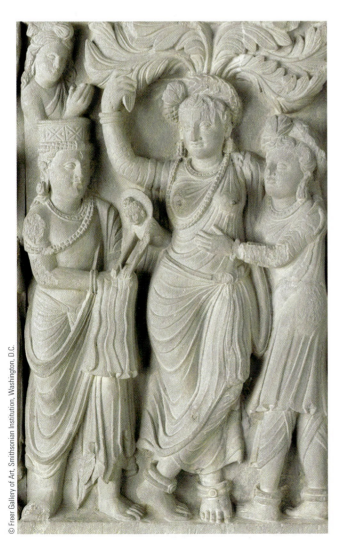

The Buddha and Jesus

As Buddhism evolved, transforming Gautama Buddha from mortal to god, Buddhist art changed as well. The representation of the Buddha in statuary and in relief panels began to illustrate the story of his life. Here the infant Siddhartha Gautama is seen emerging from the hip of his mother, Queen Maya, dressed in Greek-style draperies. Also shown is a fifth-century mosaic showing Jesus as the Good Shepherd. Notice that the heads of both the Buddha and Jesus are surrounded by a halo. The halo—or circle of light—is an ancient symbol of divinity. In ancient Hindu, Greek, and Roman art, the heads of gods were shown to emit a sunlike divine radiance. Early kings adopted crowns of gold and precious gems to symbolize their own divine authority.

HOW TO ACHIEVE ENLIGHTENMENT

One of the most famous passages in Buddhist literature is the sermon at Sarnath, which Siddhartha Gautama delivered to his followers in a deer park outside the holy city of Varanasi (Benares), in the Ganges River valley. Here he set forth the key ideas that would define Buddhist beliefs for centuries to come.

THE SERMON AT BENARES

Thus have I heard: at one time the Lord dwelt at Benares at Isipatana in the Deer Park. There the Lord addressed the five monks:—

"These two extremes, monks, are not to be practiced by one who has gone forth from the world. What are the two? That conjoined with the passions and luxury, low, vulgar, common, ignoble, and useless; and that conjoined with self-torture, painful, ignoble, and useless. Avoiding these two extremes the Tathagata has gained the enlightenment of the Middle Path, which produces insight and knowledge and tends to calm, to higher knowledge, enlightenment, Nirvana.

"And what, monks, is the Middle Path, of which the Tathagata has gained enlightenment, which produces insight and knowledge, and tends to calm, to higher knowledge, enlightenment, Nirvana? This is the noble Eightfold Way: namely, right view, right intention, right speech, right action, right livelihood, right effort, right mindfulness, right concentration. This, monks, is the Middle Path, of which the Tathagata has gained enlightenment, which produces insight and knowledge, and tends to calm, to higher knowledge, enlightenment, Nirvana.

1. Now this, monks, is the noble truth of pain: birth is painful, old age is painful, sickness is painful, death is painful, sorrow, lamentation, dejection, and despair are painful. Contact with unpleasant things is painful, not getting what one wishes is painful. In short the five groups of graspings are painful.

2. Now this, monks, is the noble truth of the cause of pain: the craving, which tends to rebirth, combined with pleasure and lust, finding pleasure here and there; namely, the craving for passion, the craving for existence, the craving for nonexistence.

3. Now this, monks, is the noble truth of the cessation of pain, the cessation without a remainder of craving, the abandonment, forsaking, release, nonattachment.

4. Now this, monks, is the noble truth of the way that leads to the cessation of pain: this is the noble Eightfold Way; namely, right view, right intention, right speech, right action, right livelihood, right effort, right mindfulness, right concentration.

"And when, monks, in these four noble truths my due knowledge and insight with its three sections and twelve divisions was well purified, then, monks, . . . I had attained the highest complete enlightenment. This I recognized. Knowledge arose in me, insight arose that the release of my mind is unshakable; this is my last existence; now there is no rebirth."

---

original texts relating his ideas are lacking. Nor is it certain that Siddhartha even intended to found a new religion or doctrine. In some respects, his ideas could be viewed as a reformist form of Hinduism, much as Martin Luther saw Protestantism as a reformation of Christianity. Siddhartha accepted much of the belief system of Hinduism, if not all of its practices. For example, he accepted the concept of reincarnation and the role of *karma* as a means of influencing the movement of individual souls up and down in the scale of life. He followed Hinduism in praising nonviolence and borrowed the idea of living a life of simplicity and chastity from the ascetics. Moreover, his vision of metaphysical reality—commonly known as Nirvana—is closer to the Hindu concept of *Brahman* than it is to the Christian concept of heavenly salvation. Nirvana, which involves an extinction of selfhood and a final reunion with the Great World Soul, is sometimes likened to a dreamless sleep or to a kind of "blowing out" (as of a candle). Buddhists occasionally remark that someone who asks for a description does not understand the concept.

At the same time, the new doctrine differed from existing Hindu practices in a number of key ways. In the first place, Siddhartha denied the existence of an individual soul. To him, the Hindu concept of *Atman*—the individual soul—meant that the soul was subject to rebirth and thus did not achieve a complete liberation from the cares of this world. In fact, Siddhartha denied the ultimate reality of the material world in its entirety and taught that it was an illusion to be transcended. Siddhartha's idea of achieving Nirvana was based on his conviction that the pain, poverty, and sorrow that afflict human beings are caused essentially by their attachment to the things of this world. Once worldly cares are abandoned, pain and sorrow can be overcome. With this knowledge comes *bodhi*, or wisdom (source of the term *Buddhism* and the familiar name for Gautama the Wise: Gautama Buddha).

Achieving this understanding is a key step on the road to Nirvana, which, as in Hinduism, is a form of release from the wheel of life. According to tradition, Siddhartha transmitted this message in a sermon to his disciples in a deer park at Sarnath (see the box above), not far from the modern city of Benares (also known as Varanasi). Like so many messages, it is deceptively simple and is enclosed in four noble truths: life is suffering; suffering is caused by desire; the way to end suffering is to end desire; and the way to end desire is to avoid the extremes of a life of vul-

The Voices of Silence

Most of what is known about the lives of women in ancient India comes from the Vedas or other texts written by men. Classical Sanskrit was the exclusive property of upper-caste males for use in religious and court functions. There are a few examples of women's writings that date from this period. In the first poem quoted here, a Buddhist nun living in the sixth century B.C.E. reflects on her sense of spiritual salvation and physical release from the drudgery of daily life. The other two poems were produced several hundred years later in southern India by anonymous female authors at a time when strict Hindu traditions had not yet been established in the area. Poetry and song were an essential part of daily life, as women sang while working in the fields, drawing water at the well, or reflecting on the hardships of their daily lives. The second poem quoted here breathes the sensuous joy of sex, while the third expresses the simultaneous grief and pride of a mother as she sends her only son off to war.

"A WOMAN WELL SET FREE! HOW FREE I AM"

A woman well set free! How free I am,
How wonderfully free, from kitchen drudgery.
Free from the harsh grip of hunger,
And from empty cooking pots,
Free too of that unscrupulous man,
The weaver of sunshades.
Calm now, and serene I am,
All lust and hatred purged.
To the shade of the spreading trees I go
And contemplate my happiness.

Translated by Uma Chakravarti and Kumkum Roy

"WHAT SHE SAID TO HER GIRLFRIEND"

What she said to her girlfriend:
On beaches washed by seas
older than the earth,
in the groves filled with bird-cries,
on the banks shaded by a punnai
clustered with flowers,
        when we made love
my eyes saw him
and my ears heard him;

my arms grow beautiful
in the coupling
and grow lean
as they come away.
        What shall I make of this?

Translated by A. K. Ramanujan

"HER PURPOSE IS FRIGHTENING, HER SPIRIT CRUEL"

Her purpose is frightening, her spirit cruel.
That she comes from an ancient house is fitting, surely.
In the battle the day before yesterday,
her father attacked an elephant and died there on the field.
In the battle yesterday,
her husband faced a row of troops and fell.
And today,
she hears the battle drum,
and, eager beyond reason, gives him a spear in his hand,
wraps a white garment around him,
smears his dry tuft with oil,
and, having nothing but her one son,
"Go!" she says, sending him to battle.

Translated by George L. Hart III

---

gar materialism and a life of self-torture and to follow the "Middle Path." This Middle Path, which is also known as the Eightfold Way, calls for right knowledge, right purpose, right speech, right conduct, right occupation, right effort, right awareness, and right meditation.

Buddhism also differed from Hinduism in its relative egalitarianism. Although Siddhartha accepted the idea of reincarnation (and hence the idea that human beings differ as a result of *karma* accumulated in a previous existence), he rejected the Hindu division of humanity into rigidly defined castes based on previous reincarnations and taught that all human beings could aspire to Nirvana as a result of their behavior in this life—a message that likely helped Buddhism win support among people at the lower end of the social scale.

In addition, Buddhism was much simpler than Hinduism. Siddhartha rejected the panoply of gods that had become identified with Hinduism and forbade his followers to worship his person or his image after his death. In fact, many Buddhists view Buddhism as a philosophy rather than a religion.

After Siddhartha Gautama's death in 480 B.C.E., dedicated disciples carried his message the length and breadth of India. Buddhist monasteries were established throughout the subcontinent, and temples and stupas (stone towers housing relics of the Buddha) sprang up throughout the countryside.

Women were permitted to join the monastic order but only in an inferior position. As Siddhartha had explained, women are "soon angered," "full of passion," and "stupid": "That is the reason . . . why women have no place in public assemblies . . . and do not earn their living by any profession." Still, the position of women tended to be better in Buddhist societies than it was elsewhere in ancient India (see the box above).

During the next centuries, Buddhism began to compete actively with Hindu beliefs, as well as with another new faith known as Jainism. Jainism was founded by Mahavira, a contemporary of Siddhartha Gautama. Resembling Buddhism in its rejection of the reality of the material world, Jainism was more extreme in practice. Whereas Siddhartha Gautama called for the "middle way" between passion and luxury and pain and self-torture, Mahavira preached a doctrine of extreme simplicity to his followers, who kept no possessions and relied on begging for a living. Some even rejected clothing and wandered through the world naked. Perhaps because of its insistence on a life of poverty, Jainism failed to attract enough adherents to become a major doctrine and never received official support. According to tradition, however, Chandragupta Maurya accepted Mahavira's doctrine after abdicating the throne and fasted to death in a Jain monastery.

THE REIGN OF ASOKA AND THE END OF THE MAURYAN EMPIRE

Buddhism received an important boost when Asoka, the grandson of Chandragupta Maurya, converted to Buddhism in the third century B.C.E. Asoka (269–232 B.C.E.) is widely considered the greatest ruler in the history of India. Reportedly, Asoka began his reign conquering, pillaging, and killing, but after his conversion to Buddhism, he began to regret his bloodthirsty past and attempted to rule benevolently.

Asoka directed that banyan trees and shelters be placed along the road to provide shade and rest for weary travelers. He sent Buddhist missionaries throughout India and ordered the erection of stone pillars with official edicts and Buddhist inscriptions to instruct people in the proper way (see Map 2.2). According to tradition, his son converted the island of Sri Lanka to Buddhism, and the peoples there accepted a tributary relationship with the Mauryan Empire.

After Asoka's death in 232 B.C.E., the Mauryan Empire began to decline. In 183 B.C.E., the last Mauryan ruler was overthrown by one of his military commanders, and India slipped back into disunity. A number of new kingdoms, some of them perhaps influenced by the memory of the Alexandrian conquests, arose along the fringes of the subcontinent in Bactria, known today as Afghanistan. In the first century C.E., Indo-European-speaking peoples fleeing from the nomadic Xiongnu warriors in Central Asia seized power in the area and proclaimed the new Kushan kingdom (see Chapter 9). For the next two centuries, the Kushanas extended their political sway over northern India as far as the central Ganges valley, while other kingdoms scuffled for predominance elsewhere on the subcontinent. India would not see unity again for another five hundred years.

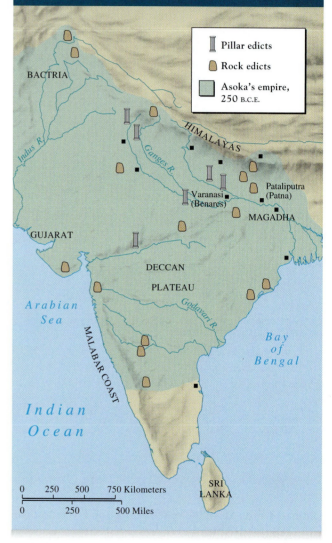

MAP 2.2 The Empire of Asoka. Asoka, the greatest of Indian monarchs, reigned over the Mauryan dynasty in the third century B.C.E. This map shows the extent of his empire, with the location of the pillar edicts that were erected along major trade routes. ➤ *What were the purposes of these pillars?*

Several reasons for India's failure to maintain a unified empire have been proposed. Some historians suggest that a decline in regional trade during the first millennium C.E. may have contributed to the growth of small land-based kingdoms, which drew their primary income from agriculture. The tenacity of the Aryan tradition with its emphasis on tribal rivalries may also have contributed. Although the Mauryan rulers tried to impose a more centralized organization, clan loyalties once again came to the fore after the collapse of the Mauryan dynasty. Furthermore, the behavior of the ruling class was characterized by what Indians call the "rule of the fishes," which glorified warfare as the natural activity of the king and the aris-

Chronology

ANCIENT INDIA

Harappan civilization	c. 2600–1900 B.C.E.
Arrival of the Aryans	c. 1500 B.C.E.
Life of Gautama Buddha	c. 560–480 B.C.E.
Invasion of India by Alexander the Great	326 B.C.E.
Mauryan dynasty founded	324 B.C.E.
Reign of Chandragupta Maurya	324–301 B.C.E.
Reign of Asoka	269–232 B.C.E.
Collapse of Mauryan dynasty	183 B.C.E.
Rise of Kushan kingdom	c. first century C.E.

tocracy. The *Arthasastra*, which set forth a model of a centralized Indian state, assumed that war was the "sport of kings."

☙ THE EXUBERANT WORLD OF INDIAN CULTURE

Few cultures in the world are as rich and varied as that of India. Most societies excel in some forms of artistic and literary achievement and not in others, but India has produced great works in almost all fields of cultural endeavor—art and sculpture, science, architecture, and literature.

Literature

The earliest known Indian literature consists of the four Vedas, which were passed down orally from generation to generation until they were finally written down after the Aryan conquest of India. The Rigveda dates from the second millennium B.C.E. and consists of over a thousand hymns that were used at religious ceremonies. The other three Vedas were written considerably later and contain instructions for performing ritual sacrifices and other ceremonies.

The language of the Vedas was Sanskrit, part of the Indo-European family of languages. After the Aryan conquest of India, Sanskrit gradually declined as a spoken language and was replaced in northern India by a simpler tongue known as Prakrit. Nevertheless, Sanskrit continued to be used as the language of the bureaucracy and literary expression for many centuries after that and, like Latin in medieval Europe, served as a common language of communication between various regions of India. In the south, a variety of Dravidian languages continued to be spoken.

After the development of a writing system sometime in the first millennium B.C.E., India's holy literature was probably inscribed on palm leaves stitched together into a book somewhat similar to the bamboo strips used during the same period in China. Also written for the first time were India's great historical epics, the Mahabharata and the Ramayana. Both of these epics may have originally been recited at religious ceremonies, but they are essentially historical writings that recount the martial exploits of great Aryan rulers and warriors.

The Mahabharata, consisting of more than ninety thousand stanzas, was probably written about 100 B.C.E. and describes in great detail a war between cousins for control of the kingdom about 1000 B.C.E. Interwoven in the narrative are many fantastic legends of the Hindu gods. Above all, the Mahabharata is a tale of moral confrontations. The most famous section of the book is the Bhagavadgita, a sermon by the legendary Indian figure Krishna on the eve of a major battle. In this sermon, Krishna sets forth one of the key ethical maxims of Indian society: in taking action, one must be indifferent to success or failure and consider only the moral rightness of the act itself.

The Ramayana, written at about the same time, is much shorter than the Mahabharata. It is an account of a semilegendary ruler named Rama who, as the result of a palace intrigue, is banished from the kingdom and forced to live as a hermit in the forest. Later, he fights the demon-king of Sri Lanka (Ceylon), who has kidnapped his beloved wife, Sita. Like the Mahabharata, the Ramayana is strongly imbued with religious and moral significance. Rama himself is portrayed as the ideal Aryan hero, a perfect ruler and an ideal son, while Sita projects the supreme duty of female chastity and wifely loyalty to her husband. The Ramayana is a story of the triumph of good over evil, duty over self-indulgence, and generosity over selfishness. It combines filial and erotic love, conflicts of human passion, character analysis, and poetic descriptions of nature (see the box on p. 42).

The Ramayana also has all the ingredients of an enthralling adventure: giants, wondrous flying chariots, invincible arrows and swords, and magic potions and mantras. One of the real heroes of the story is the monkey-king Hanuman, who flies from India to Sri Lanka to set the great battle in motion. It is no wonder that for millennia the Ramayana, including a hugely popular TV version produced in recent years, has remained a favorite among Indians of all age groups.

Architecture and Sculpture

After literature, the greatest achievements of early Indian civilization were in architecture and sculpture. Some of the earliest examples of Indian architecture stem from the time of Emperor Asoka, when Buddhism became the religion of the state. Until the time of the Mauryas, Aryan buildings had been constructed of wood. With the rise of

RAMA AND SITA

*O*ver the ages, the conclusion of the Ramayana has been the focus of considerable debate. After a long period of captivity at the hands of the demon Ravana, Sita is finally liberated by her husband, King Rama. Although the two enjoy a joyful reunion, the people of Rama's kingdom continue to voice suspicions that she has been defiled by her captor, and he is forced to banish her to a forest, where she gives birth to twin sons. The account reflects the tradition, expressed in the Arthasastra, that a king must place the needs of his subjects over his personal desires. Here we read of Rama's anguished decision as he consults with his brother, Lakshmana.

By accepting banishment, Sita bows to the authority of her husband and the established moral order. Subservient and long-suffering, she has been lauded as the ideal heroine and feminine role model, imitated by generations of Indian women. At the close of the Ramayana, Rama decides to take Sita back "before all [his] people." She continues to feel humiliated, however, and begs Mother Earth to open up and swallow her.

THE RAMAYANA

"A king must be blameless."

"Such words pierce my heart," said Lakshmana. "Fire himself proved her innocent. She is fired gold, poured into golden fire!"

Rama said, "Lakshmana, consider what is a king. Kings cannot afford blame. Ill fame is evil to kings; they above all men must be beyond reproach. . . . See into what a chasm of sorrow a king may fall. . . ."

Lakshmana said, "Gradually everything seems to change again, and even an Emperor must pay his way through life."

Rama faced his brother. "It must be! It's all the same, can't you see? Where there is growth there is decay; where there is prosperity there is ruin; and where there is birth there is death."

Lakshmana sighed hopelessly. "Well, what will you do?"

"Sita expects to go to the forests tomorrow. Let Sumantra the Charioteer drive you both there, and when you arrive by the river Ganga abandon her."

"She will die. Your child will die!"

"No," said Rama. "I command you! Not a word to anyone."

Lakshmana said, "Surely a king is remote and lonely, and very far from reason. We cannot speak to you. . . ."

Rama said, "Each person can be told what he will understand of the nature of the world, and no more than that—for the rest, take my word." . . .

Sita was forever beautiful. Wearing her ornaments she turned slowly around and looked at every person there. "Rama, let me prove my innocence, here before everyone."

"I give my permission," said Rama.

Then Sita stepped a little away from him and said, "Mother Earth, if I have been faithful to Rama take me home, hide me!"

Earth rolled and moved beneath our feet. With a great rumbling noise the ground broke apart near Sita and a deep chasm opened, lighted from below with bright lights like lightning flashes, from the castles of the Naga serpent kings. . . .

On that throne sat Mother Earth. Earth was not old, she was fair to look on, she was not sad but smiling. She wore flowers and a girdle of seas. Earth supports all life, but she feels no burden in all that. She is patient. She was patient then, under the Sun and Moon and through the rainfalls of countless years. She was patient with seasons and with kings and farmers; she endured all things and bore no line of care from it.

But this was the end of her long patience with Rama. Earth looked at her husband Janaka and smiled. Then she stretched out her arms and took her only child Sita on her lap. She folded her beautiful arms around her daughter and laid Sita's head softly against her shoulder as a mother would. Earth stroked her hair with her fair hands, and Sita closed her eyes like a little girl.

The throne sank back underground and they all were gone; the Nagas dove beneath the ground and the crevice closed gently over them, forever.

---

the empire, stone began to be used as artisans arrived in India seeking employment after the destruction of the Persian Empire by Alexander. Many of these stone carvers accepted the patronage of Emperor Asoka, who used them to spread Buddhist ideas throughout the subcontinent.

There were three main types of religious structure: the pillar, the stupa, and the rock chamber. During Asoka's reign, many stone columns were erected alongside roads to commemorate the events in the Buddha's life and mark pilgrim routes to holy places. Weighing up to 50 tons each and rising as high as 32 feet, these polished sandstone pillars were topped with a carved capital, usually depicting lions uttering the Buddha's message. Ten remain standing today.

A stupa was originally meant to house a relic of the Buddha, such as a lock of his hair or a branch of the famous Bodhi tree, and was constructed in the form of a burial mound (the pyramids in Egypt also derived from burial mounds). Eventually, the stupa became a place for devotion and the most familiar form of Buddhist architecture. It rose to considerable heights and was surmounted with a spire, possibly representing the stages of existence en route to Nirvana. According to legend, Asoka ordered the construction of 84,000 stupas throughout India to promote the Buddha's message. A few survive today.

The final form of early Indian architecture is the rock chamber carved out of a cliff on the side of a mountain.

© Borromeo/Art Resource, NY

ASOKA'S PILLAR. Stone pillars like this polished sandstone column, which is 32 feet high, were erected during the reign of Emperor Asoka in the third century B.C.E. Commemorating events in the life of the Buddha, announcing official edicts, or marking routes to the holy sites, they were placed on major trunk roads throughout the Indian subcontinent. The massive size of these pillars, some of which weighed up to 50 tons, underscores the engineering skills of the peoples of ancient India.

Asoka began the construction of these chambers to provide rooms to house monks or wandering ascetics and to serve as halls for religious ceremonies. The chambers were rectangular in form, with pillars, an altar, and a vault, reminiscent of Roman basilicas in the West. The three most famous chambers of this period are at Bhaja, Karli, and Ajanta; this last one contains twenty-nine rooms.

All three forms of architecture were embellished with decorations. Consisting of detailed reliefs and freestanding statues of deities, other human figures, and animals, these decorations are permeated with a sense of nature and the vitality of life. Many reflect an amalgamation of popular and sacred themes, of Buddhist, Vedic, and pre-Aryan religious motifs, such as male and female earth spirits. Until the second century C.E., Siddhartha Gautama was represented only through symbols, such as the wheel of life, the Bodhi tree, and the footprint, perhaps because artists felt that it was impossible to render a visual impression of the Buddha in the state of Nirvana. After the spread of Mahayana Buddhism in the second century, when the Buddha was portrayed as a god, his image began to appear in stone.

By this time, India had established its own unique religious art. The art is permeated by sensuousness and exuberance and is often overtly sexual. These scenes are

Courtesy William J. Duiker

A BUDDHIST CHAPEL. Carved out of solid rock cliffs during the Mauryan dynasty, these rock chambers served as small meditation halls for traveling Buddhist monks. Initially, they resembled freestanding shrines of wood and thatch from the Vedic period. Subsequently, chapels such as this fifth-century one at Ajanta evolved into elaborate structures reminiscent of Roman basilicas in the West. Witness the ornate columns, the ribbed vault, and the statue of the Buddha incorporated into the stupa.

meant to express otherworldly delights, not the pleasures of this world. The sensuous paradise that adorned the religious art of ancient India represented salvation and fulfillment for the ordinary Indian.

Science

Our knowledge of Indian science is limited by the paucity of written sources, but it is evident that ancient Indians had amassed an impressive amount of scientific knowledge in a number of areas. Especially notable was their work in astronomy, where they charted the movements of the heavenly bodies and recognized the spherical nature of the earth at an early date. Their ideas of physics were similar to those of the Greeks; matter was divided into the five elements of earth, air, fire, water, and ether. Many of their technological achievements are impressive, notably the quality of their textiles and the massive stone pillars erected during the reign of Asoka. The pillars weighed up to 50 tons each and were transported many miles to their final destination.

CONCLUSION

While the peoples of North Africa and the Middle East were actively building the first civilizations, a similar process was getting under way in the Indus River valley. Much has been learned about the nature of the Indus valley civilization in recent years, but without written records, there are inherent limits to our understanding. How did the Harappan people deal with the fundamental human problems mentioned at the close of Chapter 1? The answers remain tantalizingly elusive.

As often happened elsewhere, however, the collapse of Harappan civilization did not lead to the total disappearance of its culture. The new society that eventually emerged throughout the subcontinent after the coming of the Aryans was clearly an amalgam of two highly distinctive cultures, Aryan and Dravidian, each of which made a significant contribution to the politics, the social institutions, and the creative impulse of ancient Indian civilization.

With the rise of the Mauryan dynasty in the fourth century B.C.E., the distinctive features of a great civilization begin to be clearly visible. It was extensive in its scope, embracing the entire Indian subcontinent and eventually, in the form of Buddhism and Hinduism, spreading to China and Southeast Asia. But the underlying ethnic, linguistic, and cultural diversity of the Indian people posed a constant challenge to the unity of the state. After the collapse of the Mauryas, the subcontinent would not come under a single authority again for several hundred years.

In the meantime, another great experiment was taking place far to the northeast, across the Himalaya Mountains. Like many other civilizations of antiquity, the first Chinese state was concentrated on a major river system. And like them, too, its political and cultural achievements eventually spread far beyond their original habitat. In the next chapter, we turn to the civilization of ancient China.

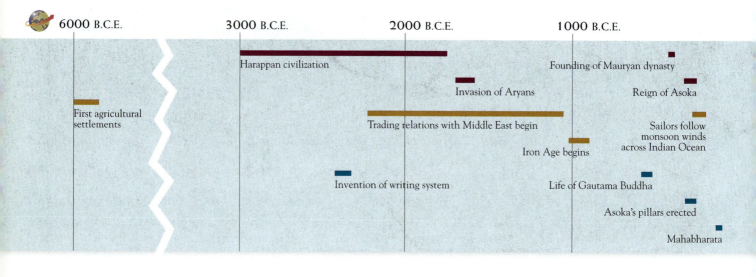

6000 B.C.E.   3000 B.C.E.   2000 B.C.E.   1000 B.C.E.

Harappan civilization

Founding of Mauryan dynasty

Invasion of Aryans

Reign of Asoka

First agricultural settlements

Trading relations with Middle East begin

Sailors follow monsoon winds across Indian Ocean

Iron Age begins

Invention of writing system

Life of Gautama Buddha

Asoka's pillars erected

Mahabharata

CHAPTER NOTES

1. Quoted in Richard Lannoy, *The Speaking Tree: A Study of Indian Culture and Society* (London, 1971), p. 318.
2. The quotation is from ibid., p. 319. Note also that the Law of Manu says that "punishment alone governs all created beings. . . . The whole world is kept in order by punishment, for a guiltless man is hard to find."
3. Strabo's Geography, book 15, quoted in Michael Edwardes, *A History of India: From the Earliest Times to the Present Day* (London, 1961), p. 55.
4. Ibid., p. 54.
5. Ibid., p. 57.
6. From the Law of Manu, quoted in A. L. Basham, *The Wonder That Was India* (London, 1961), pp. 180–181.
7. Mundaka Upanishad 1:2, quoted in William Theodore de Bary et al., eds., *Sources of Indian Tradition* (New York, 1966), pp. 28–29.
8. Quoted in Ananda K. Coomaraswamy, *Buddha and the Gospel of Buddhism* (New York, 1964), p. 34.

SUGGESTED READING

Several standard histories of India provide a good overview of the ancient period. One of the most readable and reliable is S. Wolpert, *New History of India,* 3d ed. (New York, 1989). V. A. Smith's edition of *The Oxford History of India,* 4th ed. (Oxford, 1981), although somewhat out of date, contains a wealth of information on various aspects of early Indian history. Also of note is H. H. Dodwell, ed., *The Cambridge History of India,* 6 vols. (Cambridge, 1922–1953).

By far the most informative and readable narrative on the history of India in premodern times is still A. L. Basham, *The Wonder That Was India* (London, 1961), which contains informative sections on prehistory, economy, language, art and literature, society, and everyday life. Also useful is A. L. Basham, ed., *A Cultural History of India* (Oxford, 1975). For a stimulating analysis of Indian culture and society in general, consult R. Lannoy, *The Speaking Tree: A Study of Indian Culture and Society* (London, 1971). R. Thapar, *Interpreting Early India* (Delhi, 1992), provides a recent view by an Indian historian.

Because of the relative paucity of archaeological exploration in South Asia, evidence for the Harappan period is not as voluminous as for areas such as Mesopotamia and the Nile valley. Some of the best work has been written by scholars who actually worked at the sites. For a relatively recent account, see J. M. Kenoyer, *Ancient Cities of the Indus Valley Civilization* (Karachi, 1998). A somewhat more extensive study is B. Allchin and R. Allchin, *The Birth of Indian Civilization, India and Pakistan Before 500 B.C.* (New York, 1968). For a detailed and well-illustrated analysis, see G. L. Possehl, ed., *The Harappan Civilization: A Contemporary Perspective* (Amherst, N.Y., 1983). Commercial relations between Harappa and its neighbors are treated in S. Ratnagar, *Encounters: The Westerly Trade of the Harappan Civilization* (Oxford, 1981). On the Mauryan period, see D. D. Kosambi, *The Culture and Civilization of Ancient India* (London, 1965), and R. Thapar, *Asoka and the Decline of the Mauryas* (Oxford, 1961).

There are a number of good books on the introduction of Buddhism into Indian society. Buddha's ideals are presented in A. K. Coomaraswamy, *Buddha and the Gospel of Buddhism* (London, 1916; rev. ed., New York, 1964), and E. Conze, *Buddhism: Its Essence and Development* (Oxford, 1951). Also see H. Nakamura and M. B. Dasgupta, *Indian Buddhism: A Survey with Bibliographical Notes* (New Delhi, 1987). H. Akira, *A History of Indian Buddhism: From Sakyamuni to Early Mahayana* (Honolulu, 1990), provides a detailed analysis of early activities by Siddhartha Gautama and his followers. The intimate relationship between Buddhism and commerce is discussed in Liu Hsin-ju, *Ancient India and Ancient China: Trades and Religious Exchanges* (Oxford, 1988).

Hinduism, its origins and development, is the subject of B. Walker, *Hindu World,* 2 vols. (London, 1969). For a more general treatment, see S. N. Dasgupta, *A History of Indian Philosophy,* 5 vols. (Cambridge, 1922–1955), and S. Radhakrishnan, *Indian Philosophy,* rev. ed., 2 vols. (London, 1958).

There are a number of excellent surveys of Indian art, including the comprehensive S. L. Huntington, *The Art of Ancient India: Buddhist, Hindu, Jain* (New York, 1985), and the concise *Indian Art* (London, 1976) by R. Craven. See also V. Dehejia's *Devi: The Great Goddess* (Washington, D.C., 1999) and *Indian Art* (London, 1997).

Few general surveys of Indian literature exist, perhaps because of the magnitude and diversity of India's literature. A good textbook for college students is E. C. Dimock, *The Literatures of India: An Introduction* (Chicago, 1974), which traces Indian literary achievement from the epics to the modern Hindi film.

Many editions of Sanskrit literature are available in English translation. Many are available in the multivolume *Harvard Oriental Series.* For a shorter annotated anthology of selections from the Indian classics, consult S. N. Hay, ed., *Sources of Indian Tradition,* 2 vols. (New York, 1988), or J. B. Alphonso-Karkala, *An Anthology of Indian Literature,* 2d rev. ed. (New Delhi, 1987), put out by the Indian Council for Cultural Relations.

The Mahabharata and Ramayana have been rewritten for 2,500 years. Fortunately, the vibrant versions, retold by William Buck and condensed to four hundred pages each, reproduce the spirit of the originals. See W. Buck, *Mahabharata* (Berkeley, Calif., 1973) and *Ramayana* (Berkeley, Calif., 1976). On the role played by women writers in ancient India, see S. Tharu and K. Lalita, eds., *Women Writing in India: 600 B.C. to the Present,* vol. 1 (New York, 1991).

INFOTRAC COLLEGE EDITION

Visit the source collections at infotrac.thomsonlearning.com and use the Search function with the following key terms.

Buddhism	Rigveda
Hinduism	Upanishad
India history	Vedas
Mahabharata	

WORLD HISTORY RESOURCES

Visit the *Essential World History* Companion Web Site for resources specific to this textbook:

http://history.wadsworth.com/duikeressentials02/

The CD in the back of this book and the World History Resource Center at http://history.wadsworth.com/world/ offer a variety of tools to help you succeed in this course, including access to quizzes; images; documents; interactive simulations, maps, and timelines; movie explorations; and a wealth of other sources.

Courtesy of William J. Duiker

CHINA IN ANTIQUITY

FOCUS QUESTIONS

- How did geography influence the civilization that arose in China?
- What were the major tenets of Confucianism, Legalism, and Daoism, and what role did each play in Chinese civilization?
- What were the key aspects of social and economic life in early China?
- What role did nomadic peoples play in early Chinese history?
- ➤ What concepts of kingship and political and governmental institutions characterized each of the major dynasties of early China—the Shang, the Zhou, the Qin, and the Han?

The Master said: "If the government seeks to rule by decree, and to maintain order by the use of punishment, the people will seek to evade punishment and have no sense of shame. But if government leads by virtue and governs through the rules of propriety, the people will feel shame and seek to correct their mistakes."

That statement is from the *Analects*, a collection of remarks by the Chinese philosopher Confucius that were gathered together by his disciples and published after his death in the fifth century B.C.E. Confucius lived at a time when Chinese society was in a state of increasing disarray. The political principles that had governed society since the founding of the Zhou dynasty six centuries earlier were widely ignored, and squabbling principalities scuffled for primacy as the power of the Zhou court steadily declined. The common people groaned under the weight of an oppressive manorial system that left them at the mercy of their feudal lords.

In the midst of this turmoil, Confucius traveled the length of the kingdom observing events and seeking employment as a political counselor. In the process, he attracted a number of disciples, to whom he expounded a set of ideas that in later years served as the guiding principles for the Chinese empire. Some of his ideas are strikingly modern in their thrust. Among them is the revolutionary proposition that government depends on the will of the people.

The civilization that produced Confucius had originated more than fifteen hundred years earlier as a collection of autonomous villages cultivating food crops along the two great river systems of East Asia, the Yellow and the Yangtze. This vibrant new civilization, which we know today as ancient China, expanded gradually over its neighboring areas. By the third century B.C.E., it had emerged as a great empire, as well as the dominant cultural and political force in the entire region. •

THE DAWN OF CHINESE CIVILIZATION

Human communities have existed in China for several hundred thousand years. Sometime around the eighth millennium B.C.E., early peoples living along riverbanks began to master the cultivation of crops.

Land and People

At first, these simple Neolithic communities were hardly more than villages, but as the inhabitants mastered the rudiments of agriculture, they gradually gave rise to more sophisticated and complex societies. In a pattern that we have already seen elsewhere, civilization gradually spread from these nuclear settlements in the valleys of the Yellow and Yangtze Rivers to other lowland areas of eastern and central China. The two great river valleys, then, can be considered the core regions in the development of Chinese civilization.

China, however, is more than a land of fertile fields. In fact, only 12 percent of the total land area is arable, compared with 23 percent in the United States. Much of the remainder consists of mountains and deserts that ring the country on its northern and western frontiers.

This often arid and forbidding landscape is a dominant feature of Chinese life and has played a significant role in Chinese history. The geographical barriers served to isolate the Chinese people from advanced agrarian societies in other parts of Asia. The frontier regions in the Gobi Desert, Central Asia, and the Tibetan plateau

were sparsely inhabited by peoples of Mongolian, Indo-European, or Turkish extraction. Most were pastoral societies, and like the other river valley civilizations, their contacts with the Chinese were often characterized by mutual distrust and conflict. Although less numerous than the Chinese, many of these peoples possessed impressive skills in war and were sometimes aggressive in seeking wealth or territory in the settled regions south of the Gobi Desert. Over the next two thousand years, the northern frontier became one of the great fault lines of conflict in Asia as Chinese armies attempted to protect precious farmlands from marauding peoples from beyond the frontier. When China was unified and blessed with capable rulers, it could usually keep the nomadic intruders at bay and even bring them under a loose form of Chinese administration. But in times of internal weakness, China was vulnerable to attack from the north, and on several occasions, nomadic peoples succeeded in overthrowing native Chinese rulers and setting up their own dynastic regimes.

The Shang Dynasty

Historians of China have traditionally dated the beginning of Chinese civilization to the founding of the Xia (Hsia) dynasty more than four thousand years ago. Legend maintains that the founder was a ruler named Yu, who is also credited with introducing irrigation and draining the floodwaters that periodically threatened to inundate the northern China plain. The Xia dynasty was replaced by a second dynasty, the Shang, around the sixteenth century B.C.E. (see Map 3.1). The late Shang capital at Anyang, just north of the Yellow River in north-central China, has been excavated by archaeologists. Among the finds were thousands of so-called oracle bones, ox and chicken bones or turtle shells that were used by Shang rulers for divination and to communicate with the gods. The inscriptions on these oracle bones are the earliest known form of Chinese writing and provide much of our information about the beginnings of civilization in China. They describe a culture gradually emerging from the Neolithic to the early Bronze Age.

POLITICAL ORGANIZATION

China under the Shang dynasty was a predominantly agricultural society ruled by an aristocratic class whose major occupation was war. One ancient chronicler complained that "the big affairs of state consist of sacrifice and soldiery."[1] Combat was carried on by means of two-horse chariots, whose speed and mobility assured local rulers of military superiority on the battlefield. The appearance of chariots in China in the mid-second millennium B.C.E. coincides roughly with similar developments elsewhere, leading some historians to suggest that the Shang ruling class may originally have invaded China from elsewhere

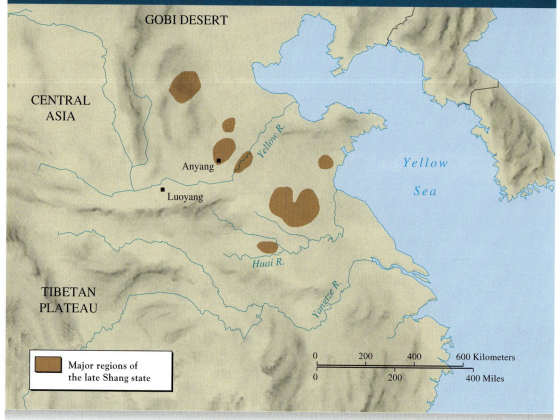

MAP 3.1 Shang China. This map shows the territory under the control of Shang rulers, who occupied parts of North China from the sixteenth to the eleventh centuries B.C.E. The capital of the Shang dynasty during its final phase was at Anyang.
➤ *What are the two major river systems on the map?*

GOBI DESERT

CENTRAL
ASIA

Anyang

Luoyang

Yellow R.

Yellow
Sea

Huai R.

Yangtze R.

TIBETAN
PLATEAU

Major regions of
the late Shang state

| 0 | 200 | 400 | 600 Kilometers |
| 0 | | 200 | 400 Miles |

in Asia. But items found in Shang burial mounds suggest that the Shang ruling elites were linear descendants of the indigenous Neolithic peoples in the area. If that was the case, the Shang may have acquired their knowledge of horse-drawn chariots through contact with chariot-making peoples in southern Russia and Kazakhstan.

The Shang king ruled with the assistance of a central bureaucracy in the capital city. His realm was divided into a number of territories governed by aristocratic chieftains, but the king appointed these chieftains and could apparently depose them at will. He was also responsible for the defense of the realm and controlled large armies that often fought on the fringes of the kingdom. The transcendent importance of the ruler was graphically displayed in the ritual sacrifices undertaken at his death, when hundreds of his retainers were buried with him in the royal tomb.

As the inscriptions on the oracle bones make clear, the Chinese ruling elite believed in the existence of supernatural forces and thought that they could communicate with those forces to obtain divine intervention on matters of this world. In fact, the purpose of the oracle bones was to communicate with the gods. This evidence also suggests that the king was already being viewed as an intermediary

between heaven and earth. In fact, an early Chinese character for king (王) consists of three horizontal lines connected by a single vertical line; the middle horizontal line represents the king's place between human society and the divine forces in nature.

SOCIAL STRUCTURES

In the Neolithic period, the farm village was apparently the basic social unit of China, at least in the core region of the Yellow River valley. Villages were organized by clans rather than by nuclear family units, and all residents probably took the common clan name of the entire village. In some cases, a village may have included more than one clan. The tribal origins of Chinese society may help explain the continued importance of the joint family in traditional China, as well as the relatively small number of family names in Chinese society. Even today there are only about four hundred commonly used family names in a society of more than one billion people.

By Shang times, the classes were becoming increasingly differentiated. It is likely that some poorer peasants did not own their farms but were obliged to work the land of

LIFE IN THE FIELDS

*T*he following passage is from The Book of Songs, a classic written during the early Zhou dynasty. This excerpt describes the calendar of peasant life on an estate in ancient China and indicates the various types of service that peasants provided for their lord.

THE BOOK OF SONGS

In the seventh month the Fire Star passes the meridian;
In the ninth month clothes are given out.
In the days of [our] first month, the wind blows cold;
In the days of [our] second, the air is cold.
Without coats, without garments of hair,
How could we get to the end of the year?
In the days of [our] third month we take our plows in hand;
In the days of [our] fourth we make our way to the fields.
Along with wives and children,
We eat in those south-lying acres.
The surveyor of the fields comes and is glad.

In the seventh month the Fire Star passes the meridian;
In the ninth month clothes are given out.
With the spring days the warmth begins,
And the oriole utters its song.
The young women take their deep baskets
And go along the small paths,
Looking for the tender [leaves of the] mulberry trees
As the spring days lengthen out,
They gather in crowds the white southern wood.
The girl's heart is wounded with sadness,
For she will soon be going with one of the young lords.

. . .

In the eighth month spinning is begun;
We make dark fabrics and yellow,
"With our red dye so bright,
We make robes for our young lords."

In the ninth month we prepare the stockyard,
And in the tenth we bring in the harvest.
The millets, the early and the late,
Together with paddy and hemp, beans and wheat.

. . .

Now we go up to work in the manor.
"In the day you gather the thatch-reeds;
In the evening twist them into rope;
Go quickly on to the roofs;
Soon you are to sow the grain."

In the days of [our] second month we cut the ice with
    tingling blows;
In the days of [our] third month [it is] stored in the
    icehouse.
In the days of [our] fourth month, very early,
A lamb with scallions is offered in sacrifice.
In the ninth month are shrewd frosts;
In the tenth month the stockyard is cleared.
With twin pitchers we hold the feast,
Killed for it is a young lamb.
Up we go into the lord's hall,
Raise the cup of buffalo horn;
"Long life for our lord; may he live forever and ever!"

---

the chieftain and other elite families in the village (see the box above). The aristocrats not only made war and served as officials, but they were also the primary landowners. In addition to the aristocratic elite and the peasants, there were a small number of merchants and artisans, as well as slaves, probably consisting primarily of criminals or prisoners taken in battle.

The Shang are perhaps best known for their mastery of the art of bronze casting (see "Metalwork and Sculpture" later in this chapter). It is also clear that the Shang had created a fairly sophisticated writing system that would evolve into the written language that is still used in China today.

 THE ZHOU DYNASTY

In the eleventh century B.C.E., the Shang dynasty was overthrown by an aggressive young state located somewhat to the west of Anyang, the Shang capital, and near the great bend of the Yellow River as it begins to flow directly eastward to the sea. The new dynasty, which called itself the Zhou (Chou), survived for about eight hundred years and was thus the longest-lived dynasty in the history of China. According to tradition, the last of the Shang rulers was a tyrant who oppressed the people (Chinese sources assert that he was a degenerate who built "ponds of wine" and ordered the composing of lustful music that "ruined the morale of the nation"),[2] leading the ruler of the principality of Zhou to revolt and establish a new dynasty.

Political Structures

The Zhou dynasty (1045–221 B.C.E.) adopted the political system of its predecessor, with some changes. The Shang practice of dividing the kingdom into a number of territories governed by officials appointed by the king was continued under the Zhou. At the apex of the government hierarchy was the Zhou king, who was served by a bureaucracy of growing size and complexity. It now included several ministries responsible for rites, education, law, and public works. Beyond the capital, near the modern

© Bradley D. Appleby

MUSIC IN THE ZHOU ERA. This set of bronze bells was discovered in a recent excavation of the tomb of a Zhou dynasty nobleman. Weighing over 2 tons and covering a range of five octaves, the sixty-five bells required five performers standing on either side. From early times in China, music was viewed not just as an aesthetic pleasure but also as a means of achieving political order and refining human character. Bells cast in bronze were first used as musical instruments in the Shang era. By the late Zhou, however, they had been replaced by strings and wind instruments, and the purpose of music shifted from ceremony to entertainment.

city of Xian, the Zhou kingdom was divided into a number of principalities, governed by members of the hereditary aristocracy, who were appointed by the king and were at least theoretically subordinated to his authority.

But the Zhou kings also introduced some innovations. According to the *Rites of Zhou,* one of the oldest surviving documents on statecraft, the Zhou dynasty ruled China because it possessed the "mandate of Heaven." According to this concept, Heaven (viewed as an impersonal law of nature rather than as an anthropomorphic deity) maintained order in the universe through the Zhou king, who thus ruled as a representative of Heaven but not as a divine being. The king, who was selected to rule because of his talent and virtue, was then responsible for governing the people with compassion and efficiency. It was his duty to propitiate the gods in order to protect the people from natural calamities or bad harvests. But if the king failed to rule effectively, he could, theoretically at least, be overthrown and replaced by a new ruler. As noted earlier, this idea was used to justify the Zhou conquest of the Shang. Eventually, the concept of the heavenly mandate would become a cardinal principle of Chinese statecraft. Each founder of

a new dynasty would routinely assert that he had earned the mandate of Heaven, and who could disprove it except by overthrowing the king? As a pragmatic Chinese proverb put it: "He who wins is the king; he who loses is the rebel."

By the sixth century B.C.E., the Zhou dynasty began to decline. As the power of the central government disintegrated, bitter internal rivalries arose among the various principalities, where the governing officials had succeeded in making their positions hereditary at the expense of the king. As the power of these officials grew, they began to regulate the local economy and seek reliable sources of revenue for their expanding armies.

Economy and Society

During the Zhou dynasty, the essential characteristics of Chinese economic and social institutions began to take shape. The Zhou continued the pattern of landownership that had existed under the Shang: the peasants worked on lands owned by their lord but also had land of their own that they cultivated for their own use. Each peasant family tilled an outer plot for its own use and then joined with other families to work the inner one for the hereditary lord (see the box on p. 49). As the following poem indicates, life for the average farmer was a difficult one. The "big rat" is probably a reference to the high taxes imposed on the peasants by the government or lord.

> *Big rat, big rat*
> *Do not eat my millet!*
> *Three years I have served you,*
> *But you will not care for me.*
> *I am going to leave you*
> *And go to that happy land;*
> *Happy land, happy land,*
> *Where I will find my place.*[3]

Trade and manufacturing were carried out by merchants and artisans, who lived in walled towns under the direct control of the local lord. Merchants did not operate independently but were considered the property of the local lord and on occasion could even be bought and sold like chattels. A class of slaves performed a variety of menial tasks and perhaps worked on local irrigation projects. Most of them were probably prisoners of war captured during conflicts with the neighboring principalities. Slaves probably did not constitute a large portion of the total population.

The period of the later Zhou, from the sixth to the third century B.C.E., was an era of significant economic growth and technological innovation, especially in agriculture. During that time, large-scale water control projects were undertaken to regulate the flow of rivers and distribute water evenly to the fields, as well as to construct canals to facilitate the transport of goods from one region to another.

Food production was also stimulated by a number of advances in farm technology. By the mid-sixth century B.C.E., the introduction of iron had led to the development of iron plowshares, which permitted deep plowing for the first time. Other innovations dating from the later Zhou were the use of natural fertilizer, the collar harness, and the technique of leaving land fallow to preserve or replenish nutrients in the soil. By the late Zhou dynasty, the cultivation of wet rice had become one of the prime sources of food in China. Although rice was difficult and time-consuming to produce, it replaced other grain crops in areas with a warm climate because of its good taste, relative ease of preparation, and high nutritious value.

The advances in agriculture, which enabled the population of China to rise as high as twenty million people during the late Zhou era, were also undoubtedly a major factor in the growth of commerce and manufacturing. During the late Zhou, economic wealth began to replace noble birth as the prime source of power and influence. Utensils made of iron became more common, and trade

© ChinaStock

◆-◆

Prized Possessions

Like the pharaohs in Egypt, Chinese rulers filled their tombs with prized possessions from daily life, some of which might prove useful in the next life. At left, we see the remains of a chariot and horses in a burial pit in Hebei province in China that dates from the early Zhou dynasty. At right, we see a small model boat from the tomb of Tutankhamen in the Valley of the Kings in Egypt.

Egyptian National Museum, Cairo, Egypt/Bridgeman Art Library

developed in a variety of useful commodities, including cloth, salt, and various manufactured goods.

One of the most important items of trade in ancient China was silk. Remains of silk material have been found on Shang bronzes, and a large number of fragments have been recovered in tombs dating from the mid-Zhou era. Silk cloth was used not only for clothing and quilts but also to wrap the bodies of the dead prior to burial. Fragments have been found throughout Central Asia and as far away as Athens, suggesting that the famous "Silk Road" stretching from central China westward to the Middle East and the Mediterranean Sea was in operation as early as the fifth century B.C.E. (see Map 3.4 on p. 60; see also Chapter 10).

With the development of trade and manufacturing, China began to move toward a money economy. The first form of money may have been seashells, but by the Zhou dynasty, pieces of iron shaped like a knife or round coins with a hole in the middle so they could be carried in strings of a thousand were being used. Most ordinary Chinese, however, simply used a system of barter. Taxes, rents, and even the salaries of government officials were normally paid in grain.

The Hundred Schools of Ancient Philosophy

In China, as in other great river valley societies, the birth of civilization was accompanied by the emergence of an organized effort to comprehend the nature of the cosmos and the role of human beings within it. Speculation over such questions began in the very early stages of civilization and culminated at the end of the Zhou era in the "hundred schools" of ancient philosophy, a wide-ranging debate over the nature of human beings, society, and the universe.

The Shang had begun to believe in the existence of one transcendent god who presided over all the forces of nature. As time went on, the Chinese concept of religion evolved from a vaguely anthropomorphic god to a somewhat more impersonal symbol of universal order known as Heaven (*Tian* or *T'ien*). There was also much speculation among Chinese intellectuals about the nature of the cosmic order. One of the earliest ideas was that the universe was divided into two primary forces of good and evil, light and dark, male and female, represented symbolically by the sun (*yang*) and the moon (*yin*). According to this theory, life was a dynamic process of interaction between the forces of *yang* and *yin*. Early Chinese could attempt only to understand the process and perhaps to have some minimal effect on its operation. They could not hope to reverse it.

The belief that there was some mysterious "law of nature" that could be interpreted by human beings led to various attempts to predict the future, such as the Shang oracle bones and other methods of divination.

Philosophers invented ways to interpret the will of nature, while shamans were employed at court to assist the emperor in his policy deliberations until at least the fifth century C.E. One of the most famous manuals used for this purpose was the *Yi Jing (I Ching)*, known in English as the *Book of Changes*.

CONFUCIANISM

Such efforts to divine the mysterious purposes of Heaven notwithstanding, Chinese thinking about metaphysical reality also contained a strain of pragmatism, which is readily apparent in the ideas of the great philosopher Confucius. Confucius (the name is the Latin form of his honorific title, Kung Fuci, or K'ung Fu-tzu, meaning Master Kung) was born in the state of Lu (in the modern province of Shandong) in 551 B.C.E. After reaching maturity, he apparently hoped to find employment as a political adviser in one of the principalities into which China was divided at that time, but he had little success in finding a patron. Nevertheless, he made an indelible mark on history as an independent political and social philosopher.

In conversations with his disciples, contained in the *Analects*, Confucius often adopted a detached and almost skeptical view of Heaven. "You are unable to serve man," he commented on one occasion, "how then can you hope to serve the spirits? While you do not know life, how can you know about death?" Confucius believed it was useless to speculate too much about metaphysical questions. Better by far to assume that there was a rational order to the universe and then concentrate one's attention on ordering the affairs of this world.[4]

Confucius' interest in philosophy, then, was essentially political and ethical. The universe was constructed in such a way that if human beings could act harmoniously in accordance with its purposes, their own affairs would prosper. Much of his concern was with human behavior. The key to proper behavior was to behave in accordance with the *Dao* (Way).

Two elements in the Confucian interpretation of the *Dao* are particularly worthy of mention. The first is the concept of duty. It was the responsibility of all individuals to subordinate their own interests and aspirations to the broader need of the family and the community. Confucius assumed that if each individual worked hard to fulfill his or her assigned destiny, the affairs of society as a whole would surely prosper as well. In this respect, it was important for the ruler to set a good example. If he followed his "kingly way," the beneficial effects would radiate throughout society (see the box on p. 53).

The second key element is the idea of humanity, sometimes translated as "human-heartedness." This concept involves a sense of compassion and empathy for others. It is similar in some ways to Christian concepts, but with a subtle twist. Whereas Christian teachings call on human beings to "behave toward others as you would have them

THE WAY OF THE GREAT LEARNING

F̲ew texts exist today that were written by Confucius himself. Most were written or edited by his disciples. The following text, titled The Great Learning, *was probably written two centuries after Confucius' death, but it illustrates his view that good government begins with the cultivation of individual morality and proper human relationships at the basic level. This conviction that to bring peace to the world, you must cultivate your own person continued to win general approval down to modern times. There are interesting similarities between such ideas and the views expressed in the Indian treatise* Arthasastra, *discussed in Chapter 2.*

THE GREAT LEARNING

The Way of the Great Learning consists in clearly exemplifying illustrious virtue, in loving the people, and in resting in the highest good.

Only when one knows where one is to rest can one have a fixed purpose. Only with a fixed purpose can one achieve calmness of mind. Only with calmness of mind can one attain serene repose. Only in serene repose can one carry on careful deliberation. Only through careful deliberation can one have achievement. Things have their roots and branches; affairs have their beginning and end. He who knows what comes first and what comes last comes himself near the Way.

The ancients who wished clearly to exemplify illustrious virtue throughout the world would first set up good government in their states. Wishing to govern well their states, they would first regulate their families. Wishing to regulate their families, they would first cultivate their persons. Wishing to cultivate their persons, they would first rectify their minds. Wishing to rectify their minds, they would first seek sincerity in their thoughts. Wishing for sincerity in their thoughts, they would first extend their knowledge. The extension of knowledge lay in the investigation of things. For only when things are investigated is knowledge extended; only when knowledge is extended are thoughts sincere; only when thoughts are sincere are minds rectified; only when minds are rectified are our persons cultivated; only when our persons are cultivated are our families regulated; only when families are regulated are states well governed; and only when states are well governed is there peace in the world.

From the emperor down to the common people, all, without exception, must consider cultivation of the individual character as the root. If the root is in disorder, it is impossible for the branches to be in order. To treat the important as unimportant and to treat the unimportant as important—this should never be. This is called knowing the root; this is called the perfection of knowledge.

behave toward you," the Confucian maxim is put in a different way: "Do not do unto others what you would not wish done to yourself." To many Chinese, this attitude symbolizes an element of tolerance in the Chinese character that has not always been practiced in other societies.[5]

In the generations after the death of Confucius, his message spread widely throughout China. Although he was an outspoken critic of his times and lamented the disappearance of what he regarded as the golden age of the early Zhou, Confucius was not just another disgruntled Chinese conservative mourning the passing of the good old days; rather, he was a revolutionary thinker, many of whose key ideas looked forward rather than backward. Perhaps his most striking political idea was that the government should be open to all men of superior quality, not limited to those of noble birth. As one of his disciples reports in the *Analects*: "The Master said, by nature, men are nearly alike; by practice, they get to be wide apart."[6]

The concept of rule by merit was, of course, not an unfamiliar idea in the China of his day; the *Rites of Zhou* had clearly stated that the king himself deserved to rule because of his talent and virtue, rather than as the result of noble birth. In practice, however, aristocratic privilege must often have opened the doors to political influence, and many of Confucius' contemporaries must have regarded his appeal for government by talent as both exciting and dangerous. Confucius did not explicitly question the right of the hereditary aristocracy to play a leading role in the political process, nor did his ideas have much effect in his lifetime. Still, they introduced a new concept that was later implemented in the form of a bureaucracy selected through a civil service examination (see "Confucianism and the State" later in this chapter).

Confucius' ideas had a strong impact on Chinese political thinkers of the late Zhou period, a time when the existing system was in disarray and open to serious question. But as with most great thinkers, Confucius' ideas were sufficiently ambiguous to be interpreted in very contradictory ways. Some, like the philosopher Mencius (370–290 B.C.E.), stressed the humanistic side of Confucian ideas, arguing that human beings were by nature good and hence could be taught their civic responsibilities by example. Mencius also stressed that the ruler had a duty to govern with compassion:

> Here is the way to win the empire: win the people and you win the empire. Here is the way to win the people: win their hearts and you win the people. Here is the way to win their hearts: give them and share with them what they like, and do not do to them what they do not like. The people turn to a human ruler as water flows downward or beasts take to wilderness.[7]

SEEKING THE ETERNAL DAO

The Dao De Jing (The Way of the Dao) is the great classic of philosophical Daoism (Taoism). Traditionally attributed to the legendary Chinese philosopher Lao Tzu (Old Master), it was probably written sometime during the era of Confucius. This opening passage illustrates two of the key ideas that characterize Daoist belief: it is impossible to define the nature of the universe, and "inaction" (not Confucian "action") is the key to ordering the affairs of human beings.

THE WAY OF THE DAO

The Tao that can be told of is not the eternal Tao;
The name that can be named is not the eternal name.
The Nameless is the origin of Heaven and Earth;
The Named is the mother of all things.

Therefore let there always be nonbeing, so we may see their
* subtlety.*
And let there always be being, so we may see their
* outcome.*
The two are the same,
But after they are produced, they have different names.
They both may be called deep and profound.

Deeper and more profound,
The door of all subtleties!
When the people of the world all know beauty as beauty,
There arises the recognition of ugliness.
When they all know the good as good,
There arises the recognition of evil.
Therefore:
Being and nonbeing produce each other;
Difficult and easy complete each other;
Long and short contrast each other;
High and low distinguish each other;
Sound and voice harmonize each other;
Front and behind accompany each other.

Therefore the sage manages affairs without action
And spreads doctrines without words.
All things arise, and he does not turn away from them.
He produces them but does not take possession of them.
He acts but does not rely on his own ability.
He accomplishes his task but does not claim credit for it.
It is precisely because he does not claim credit that his
* accomplishment remains with him.*

LEGALISM

Some thinkers, however, argued for a different approach. One school of thought that became quite popular during the "hundred schools" era in ancient China was the philosophy of Legalism. Taking issue with the view of Mencius that human nature was essentially good, the Legalists argued that human beings were by nature evil and would follow the correct path only if coerced by harsh laws and stiff punishments. These thinkers were referred to as the School of Law because they rejected the Confucian view that government by "superior men" could solve society's problems and argued instead for a system of impersonal laws.

The Legalists also disagreed with the Confucian belief that the universe has a moral core. They therefore believed that only firm action by the state could bring about social order. Fear of harsh punishment, more than the promise of material reward, could best motivate the common people to serve the interests of the ruler. Because human nature was essentially corrupt, officials could not be trusted to carry out their duties in a fair and evenhanded manner, and only a strong ruler could create an orderly society. All human actions should be subordinated to the effort to create a strong and prosperous state subject to his will.

DAOISM

One of the most popular alternatives to Confucianism was the philosophy of Daoism (frequently spelled Taoism). According to Chinese tradition, the Daoist school was founded by a contemporary of Confucius popularly known as Lao Tzu (Lao Zi), or the Old Master. Many modern scholars, however, are skeptical that Lao Tzu actually existed.

Obtaining a clear understanding of the original concepts of Daoism is difficult because its primary document, a short treatise known as the *Dao De Jing* (sometimes translated as *The Way of the Tao*), is an enigmatic book whose interpretation has baffled scholars for centuries. The opening line, for example, explains less what the *Dao* is than what it is not (see the box above).

Like Confucianism, Daoism does not anguish over the underlying meaning of the cosmos. Rather, it attempts to set forth proper forms of behavior for human beings here on earth. In most other respects, however, Daoism presents a view of life and its ultimate meaning that is almost diametrically opposed to that of Confucianism. Whereas Confucian doctrine asserts that it is the duty of human beings to work hard to improve life here on earth, Daoists contend that the true way to interpret the will of Heaven is not action but inaction (*wu wei*). The best way to act in harmony with the universal order is to act spontaneously and let nature take its course.

Such a message could be very appealing to those who were uncomfortable with the somewhat rigid flavor of the Confucian work ethic and preferred a more individualistic approach. Daoism achieved considerable popularity in the waning years of the Zhou dynasty. It was especially popular among intellectuals, who may have found it appealing as an escapist antidote in a world characterized by growing disorder.

POPULAR BELIEFS

Daoism also played a second role as a loose framework for popular spiritualistic and animistic beliefs among the common people. Popular Daoism was less a philosophy than a religion; it comprised a variety of rituals and forms of behavior that were regarded as a means of achieving heavenly salvation or even a state of immortality on earth. Daoist sorcerers practiced various types of mind- or body-training exercises in the hope of achieving power, sexual prowess, and long life.

Another aspect of popular religion was the belief that the spirits of deceased human beings lived in the atmosphere for a time before ascending to heaven or descending to hell. During that period, surviving family members had to care for the spirits through proper ritual, or they would become evil spirits and haunt the survivors. Foreign observers sometimes confused this practice as a form of ancestor worship.

Thus in ancient China, human beings were offered a variety of interpretations of the nature of the universe. Confucianism satisfied the need for a rational doctrine of nation building and social organization at a time when the existing political and social structure was beginning to disintegrate. Philosophical Daoism provided an alternative to Confucianism and a framework for a set of diverse animistic beliefs at the popular level. But neither could satisfy the deeper emotional needs that sometimes inspire the human spirit. Something else would be needed to fill the gap.

THE RISE OF THE CHINESE EMPIRE: THE QIN AND THE HAN

During the last two centuries of the Zhou dynasty (the fourth and third centuries B.C.E.), the authority of the king became increasingly nominal, and several of the small principalities into which the Zhou kingdom had been divided began to evolve into powerful states that presented a potential challenge to the Zhou ruler himself. At first, their mutual rivalries were in check, but by the late fifth century B.C.E., competition intensified into civil war, giving birth to the so-called Period of the Warring States. Powerful principalities vied with each other for preeminence and largely ignored the now purely titular authority of the Zhou court (see Map 3.2). New forms of warfare also emerged with the invention of iron weapons and the introduction of the foot soldier. Cavalry, too, made its first appearance, armed with the powerful crossbow.

Eventually, the relatively young state of Qin, located in the original homeland of the Zhou, became a key player in these conflicts. Benefiting from a strong defensive position in the mountains to the west of the great bend of the Yellow River, as well as from their control of the rich Sichuan plains, the Qin gradually subdued their main rivals through conquest or diplomatic maneuvering and created the first truly unified government in Chinese history.

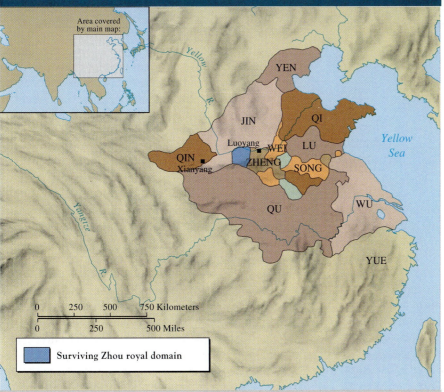

MAP 3.2 China During the Period of the Warring States. From the fifth to the third centuries B.C.E, China was locked in a period of civil strife known as the Period of the Warring States. This map shows the Zhou dynasty capital at Luoyang, along with the major states that were squabbling for precedence in the region. The state of Qin would eventually suppress its rivals and form the first unified Chinese empire, with its capital at Xianyang (near modern Xian). ➤ **Where is Qin located on the map?**

Area covered by main map:

YEN

JIN
QI

Luoyang WEI LU
QIN ZHENG
Xianyang SONG

QU WU

Yellow Sea

YUE

0   250   500   750 Kilometers
0   250   500 Miles

Surviving Zhou royal domain

MEMORANDUM ON THE BURNING OF BOOKS

*L*i Su, the author of the following passage, was a chief minister of the First Emperor of Qin. An exponent of Legalism, Li Su hoped to eliminate all rival theories on government. His recommendation to the emperor on the subject was recorded by the Han dynasty historian Sima Qian. The emperor approved the proposal and ordered all books contrary to the spirit of Legalist ideology to be destroyed on pain of death. Fortunately, some texts were preserved by being hidden or even memorized by their owners and were thus available to later generations. For centuries afterward, the First Emperor of Qin and his minister were singled out for criticism because of their intolerance and their effort to control the very minds of their subjects. Totalitarianism, it seems, is not exclusively a modern concept.

SIMA QIAN, *HISTORICAL RECORDS*

In earlier times the empire disintegrated and fell into disorder, and no one was capable of unifying it. Thereupon the various feudal lords rose to power. In their discourses they all praised the past in order to disparage the present and embellished empty words to confuse the truth. Everyone cherished his own favorite school of learning and criticized what had been instituted by the authorities. But at present Your Majesty possesses a unified empire, has regulated the distinctions of black and white, and has firmly established for yourself a position of sole supremacy. And yet these independent schools, joining with each other, criticize the codes of laws and instructions. Hearing of the promulgation of a decree, they criticize it, each from the standpoint of his own school. At home they disapprove of it in their hearts; going out they criticize it in the thoroughfare. They seek a reputation by discrediting their sovereign; they appear superior by expressing contrary views, and they lead the lowly multitude in the spreading of slander. If such license is not prohibited, the sovereign power will decline above and partisan factions will form below. It would be well to prohibit this.

Your servant suggests that all books in the imperial archives, save the memoirs of Ch'in, be burned. All persons in the empire, except members of the Academy of Learned Scholars, in possession of the *Book of Odes*, the *Book of History*, and discourses of the hundred philosophers should take them to the local governors and have them indiscriminately burned. Those who dare to talk to each other about the *Book of Odes* and the *Book of History* should be executed and their bodies exposed in the marketplace. Anyone referring to the past to criticize the present should, together with all members of his family, be put to death. Officials who fail to report cases that have come under their attention are equally guilty. After thirty days from the time of issuing the decree, those who have not destroyed their books are to be branded and sent to build the Great Wall. Books not to be destroyed will be those on medicine and pharmacy, divination by the tortoise and milfoil, and agriculture and arboriculture. People wishing to pursue learning should take the officials as their teachers.

The Qin Dynasty (221–206 B.C.E.)

One of the primary reasons for the triumph of the Qin was probably the character of the Qin ruler, known to history as Qin Shi Huangdi (Ch'in Shih Huang Ti), or the First Emperor of Qin. A man of forceful personality and immense ambition, Qin Shi Huangdi had ascended to the throne of Qin in 246 B.C.E. at the age of thirteen. Described by the Han dynasty historian Sima Qian as having "the chest of a bird of prey, the voice of a jackal, and the heart of a tiger," the new king of Qin found the Legalist views of his adviser Li Su (Li Ssu) only too appealing. In 221 B.C.E., Qin Shi Huangdi defeated the last of Qin's rivals and founded a new dynasty with himself as emperor.

The Qin dynasty transformed Chinese politics. Philosophical doctrines that had proliferated during the late Zhou period were prohibited, and Legalism was adopted as the official ideology. Those who opposed the policies of the new regime were punished and sometimes executed, while books presenting ideas contrary to the official orthodoxy were publicly put to the torch, perhaps the first example of book burning in history (see the box above).

Legalistic theory gave birth to a number of fundamental administrative and political developments, some of which would survive the Qin and serve as a model for future dynasties. In the first place, unlike the Zhou, the Qin was a highly centralized state. The central bureaucracy was divided into three primary ministries: a civil authority, a military authority, and a censorate, whose inspectors surveyed the efficiency of officials throughout the system. This would later become standard administrative procedure for future Chinese dynasties.

Below the central government were two levels of administration: provinces and counties. Unlike the Zhou system, officials at these levels did not inherit their positions but were appointed by the court and were subject to dismissal at the emperor's whim. The civil servants may have been chosen on the recommendation of other government officials. A penal code provided for harsh punishments for all wrongdoers. Officials were watched by the censors, who reported directly to the throne. Those guilty of malfeasance in office were executed.

Qin Shi Huangdi, who had a passion for centralization, unified the system of weights and measures, standardized

**The Qin Empire
221–206 B.C.E.**

the monetary system and the written forms of Chinese characters, and ordered the construction of a system of roads extending throughout the empire. He also attempted to eliminate the remaining powers of the landed aristocrats and divided their estates among the peasants, who were now taxed directly by the state. He thus eliminated potential rivals and secured tax revenues for the central government. Such a system may not have been advantageous to the peasants in all respects, however, since the central government could now collect taxes more effectively and mobilize the peasants for military service and for various public works projects.

The Qin dynasty was equally unsympathetic to the merchants, whom it viewed as parasites. Private commercial activities were severely restricted and heavily taxed, and many vital forms of commerce and manufacturing, including mining, wine making, and the distribution of salt, were placed under a government monopoly.

Qin Shi Huangdi was equally aggressive in foreign affairs. His armies continued the gradual advance to the south that had taken place during the final years of the Zhou dynasty, extending the border of China to the edge of the Red River in modern Vietnam. To supply the Qin armies operating in the area, a canal was dug that provided direct inland navigation from the Yangtze River in central China to what is now the modern city of Guangzhou (Canton) in the south.

BEYOND THE FRONTIER: THE NOMADIC PEOPLES AND THE GREAT WALL OF CHINA

The main area of concern for the Qin emperor, however, was in the north, where a nomadic people, known to the Chinese as the Xiongnu (Hsiung-nu) and possibly related to the Huns, who invaded Europe in the fourth century C.E. (see Chapter 5), had become increasingly active in the area of the Gobi Desert. The area north of the Yellow River had been sparsely inhabited since prehistoric times. The local population probably lived by hunting and fishing, practicing limited forms of agriculture, or herding animals such as cattle or sheep.

As the climate in the region became drier, people were forced to rely increasingly on animal husbandry as a means of livelihood. Their response was to master the art of riding on horseback and to adopt the nomadic life. Organized loosely into communities consisting of a number of kinship groups, they ranged far and wide in search of pasture for their herds of cattle, goats, or sheep.

But the new way of life presented its own challenges. Increased food production led to a growing population, which in times of drought outstripped the available resources. Rival groups then competed for the best pastures. After they mastered the art of fighting on horseback sometime during the middle of the first millennium B.C.E., territorial warfare became commonplace throughout the entire frontier region from the Pacific Ocean to Central Asia.

By the end of the Zhou dynasty in the third century B.C.E., the nomadic Xiongnu posed a serious threat to the security of China's northern frontier, and a number of Chinese principalities in the area began to build walls and fortifications to keep them out. But warriors on horseback possessed significant advantages over the infantry of the Chinese.

Qin Shi Huangdi's answer to the problem was to strengthen the walls to keep the marauders out. Today, of course, we know Qin Shi Huangdi's project as the Great Wall, which extends nearly 4,000 miles from the sandy wastes of Central Asia to the sea. It is constructed of massive granite blocks and is wide enough on top to provide a roadway for horse-drawn chariots. Although the wall that appears in most photographs today was built much later (see Chapter 16), some of the walls built by the Qin remain standing. Their construction was a massive project that required the efforts of thousands of laborers, many of whom met their deaths there and, according to legend, are now buried within the wall.

THE FALL OF THE QIN

The Legalist system put in place by the First Emperor of Qin was designed to achieve maximum efficiency as well as total security for the state. It did neither. Qin Shi Huangdi was apparently aware of the dangers of factions within the imperial family and established a class of eunuchs (males whose testicles have been removed) who served as personal attendants for himself and female members of the royal family. The eunuch system later became a standard feature of the Chinese imperial system. But as confidential advisers to the royal family, eunuchs were in a position of influence. The rivalry between the "inner" imperial court and the "outer" court of bureaucratic officials led to tensions that persisted until the end of the imperial system.

By ruthlessly gathering control over the empire into his own hands, Qin Shi Huangdi had hoped to establish a rule that, in the words of historian Sima Qian, "would be enjoyed by his sons for ten thousand generations." In fact, his centralizing zeal alienated many key groups. Landed aristocrats and Confucian intellectuals, as well as the common people, groaned under the censorship of thought and speech, harsh taxes, and forced labor projects. "He killed men," recounted the historian, "as though he thought he could never finish, he punished men as though he were afraid he would never get around to them all, and the whole world revolted against him."[8] Shortly after the emperor died in 210 B.C.E., the dynasty quickly descended into factional rivalry, and four years later it was overthrown.

The Glorious Han Dynasty (202 B.C.E.–221 C.E.)

The fall of the Qin was followed by a brief period of civil strife as aspiring successors competed for hegemony. Out of this strife emerged one of the greatest and most durable dynasties in Chinese history—the Han (see Map 3.3). The Han dynasty would later become so closely identified with the advance of Chinese civilization that even today the Chinese sometimes refer to themselves as "people of Han."

The founder of the Han dynasty was Liu Bang (Liu Pang), a commoner of peasant origin who would be known historically by his title of Han Gaozu (Han Kao Tsu, or Exalted Emperor of Han). Under his strong rule and that of his successors, the new dynasty quickly moved to consolidate its control over the empire and promote the welfare of its subjects. Efficient and benevolent, at least by the standards of the time, Gaozu maintained the centralized polit-

ical institutions of the Qin but abandoned their harsh Legalistic approach to law enforcement. Han rulers discovered in Confucian principles a useful foundation for the creation of a new state philosophy. Under the Han, Confucianism began to take on the character of an official ideology.

CONFUCIANISM AND THE STATE

The integration of Confucian doctrine with Legalist institutions, creating a system generally known as State Confucianism, did not take long to accomplish. For example, they borrowed the tripartite division of the central government into civilian and military authorities and a censorate. The government was headed by a "grand council" including representatives from all three segments of government. The Han also retained the system of local government, dividing the empire into provinces and districts.

Finally, the Han continued the Qin system of selecting government officials on the basis of merit rather than birth. Shortly after founding the new dynasty, Emperor Gaozu decreed that local officials would be asked to recommend promising candidates for public service. Thirty years later,

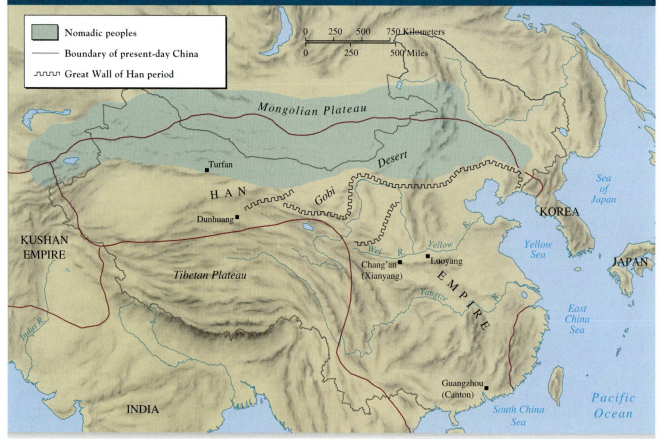

MAP 3.3 The Han Empire. This map shows the territory under control of the Han Empire at its greatest extent during the first century B.C.E. Note the expansion of Han rule to the west, as Chinese armies penetrated across the Silk Road into Central Asia. ➤ *Where is the Great Wall on the map?*

Nomadic peoples
Boundary of present-day China
Great Wall of Han period

Mongolian Plateau
Turfan
Gobi Desert
HAN
Dunhuang
KUSHAN EMPIRE
Tibetan Plateau
Indus R.
INDIA
Wei R.
Chang'an (Xianyang)
Yellow R.
Luoyang
EMPIRE
Yangtze
KOREA
Sea of Japan
Yellow Sea
JAPAN
East China Sea
Guangzhou (Canton)
South China Sea
Pacific Ocean

in 165 B.C.E., the first known civil service examination was administered to candidates for positions in the bureaucracy. Shortly after that, an academy was established to train candidates. The first candidates were almost all from aristocratic or other wealthy families, and the Han bureaucracy itself was still dominated by the traditional hereditary elite. Still, the principle of selecting officials on the basis of talent had been established and would eventually become standard practice.

Under the Han dynasty, the population increased rapidly—by some estimates rising from about twenty million to over sixty million at the height of the dynasty—creating a growing need for a large and efficient bureaucracy to maintain the state in proper working order. Unfortunately, the Han were unable to resolve all of the problems left over from the past. Factionalism at court remained a serious problem and undermined the efficiency of the central government.

SOCIETY AND ECONOMY IN THE HAN EMPIRE

Han rulers also retained some of the economic and social policies of their predecessors. In particular, they saw that a free peasantry paying taxes directly to the state would both limit the wealth and power of the great noble families and increase the state's revenues. The Han had difficulty preventing the recurrence of the economic inequities that had characterized the last years of the Zhou, however. The land taxes were relatively light, but the peasants also faced a number of other exactions, including military service and forced labor of up to one month annually. Although the use of iron tools brought new lands under the plow and food production increased steadily, the trebling of the population under the Han eventually reduced the average size of the individual farm plot to about one acre per capita, barely enough for survival. As time went on, many poor peasants were forced to sell their land and become tenant farmers, paying rents ranging up to half of the annual harvest. Thus land once again came to be concentrated in the hands of the powerful landed clans, which often owned thousands of acres worked by tenants.

Although such economic problems contributed to the eventual downfall of the dynasty, in general the Han era was one of unparalleled productivity and prosperity. The period was marked by a major expansion of trade, both domestic and foreign. This was not necessarily due to official encouragement. In fact, the Han were as suspicious of private merchants as their predecessors had been and levied stiff taxes on trade in an effort to limit commercial activities. Merchants were also subject to severe social constraints. They were disqualified from seeking office, restricted in their place of residence, and viewed in general as parasites providing little true value to Chinese society.

The state itself directed much trade and manufacturing; it manufactured weapons, for example, and operated shipyards, granaries, and mines. The government also moved cautiously into foreign trade, mostly with neighboring areas in Central and Southeast Asia, although trade relations were established with countries as far away as India and the Mediterranean (see Map 3.4). Some of this long-distance trade was carried by sea through southern ports like Guangzhou, but more was transported by overland caravans on the Silk Road (see Chapter 10) that led westward into Central Asia.

New technology contributed to the economic prosperity of the Han era. Significant progress was achieved in such areas as textile manufacturing, water mills, and iron casting; skill at ironworking led to the production of steel a few centuries later. Paper was invented under the Han, and the development of the rudder and fore-and-aft rigging permitted ships to sail into the wind for the first time. Thus equipped, Chinese merchant ships carrying heavy cargoes could sail throughout the islands of Southeast Asia and into the Indian Ocean.

Finally, the Han emperors continued the process of territorial expansion and consolidation that had begun under the Zhou and the Qin. Han rulers, notably Han Wudi (Han Wu Ti, or Martial Emperor of Han), successfully completed the assimilation into the empire of the regions south of the Yangtze River, including the Red River delta in what is today northern Vietnam. Han armies also marched westward as far as the Caspian Sea, pacifying nomadic tribal peoples and extending China's boundary far into Central Asia. The Han continued to have problems with the Xiongnu beyond the Great Wall to the north. Nomadic raids on Chinese territory continued intermittently to the end of the dynasty, once reaching almost to the gates of the capital city, now located at Chang'an (Ch'ang An, or Eternal Peace), on the site of modern Xian.

THE DECLINE AND FALL OF THE HAN

In 9 C.E., the reformist official Wang Mang, who was troubled by the plight of the peasants, seized power from the Han court and declared the foundation of a Xin (New) dynasty. The empire had been crumbling for decades. As frivolous or depraved rulers amused themselves with the pleasures of court life, the power and influence of the central government began to wane, and the great noble families filled the vacuum, amassing vast landed estates and transforming free farmers into tenants. Wang Mang tried to confiscate the great estates and abolish slavery. In so doing, however, he alienated powerful interests, who conspired to overthrow him. In 23 C.E., beset by administrative chaos and a collapse of the frontier defenses, Wang Mang was killed in a coup d'état.

For a time, strong leadership revived some of the glory of the early Han. The court did attempt to reduce land

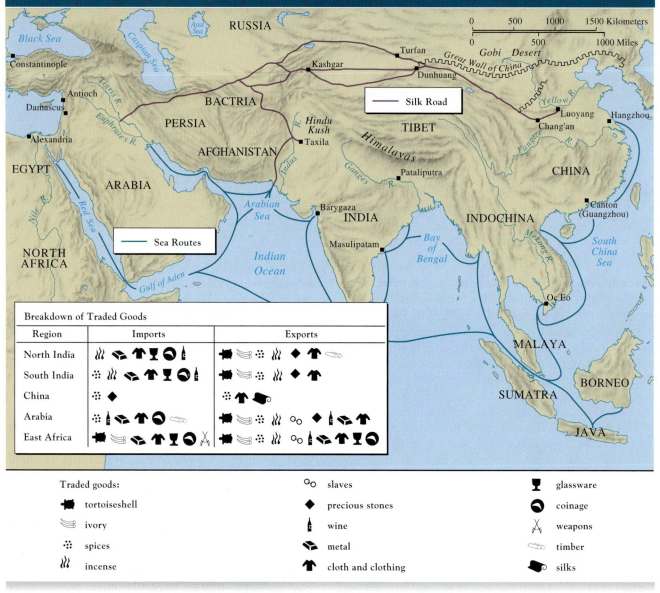

MAP 3.4 Trade Routes of the Ancient World. This map shows the various land and maritime routes that extended from China toward other civilizations that were located to the south and west of the Han empire. The various goods that were exchanged are identified at the bottom of the map. ➤ *What were the major goods exported by China?*

Breakdown of Traded Goods

Traded goods:
- tortoiseshell
- ivory
- spices
- incense
- slaves
- precious stones
- wine
- metal
- cloth and clothing
- glassware
- coinage
- weapons
- timber
- silks

taxes and carry out land resettlement programs. The growing popularity of nutritious crops like rice, wheat, and soybeans, along with the introduction of new crops such as alfalfa and grapes, helped boost food production. But the monopoly of land and power by the great landed families continued. Weak rulers were isolated within their imperial chambers and dominated by eunuchs and other powerful figures at court. Official corruption and the concentration of land in the hands of the wealthy led to widespread peasant unrest. The population of the empire, which had been estimated at about sixty million in China's first census in the year 2 C.E., had shrunk to

less than one-third that number two hundred years later. In the early third century C.E., the dynasty was finally brought to an end when power was seized by Cao Cao (Ts'ao Ts'ao), a general known to later generations as one of the main characters in the famous Chinese epic *The Romance of the Three Kingdoms*. But Cao Cao was unable to consolidate his power, and China entered a period of almost constant anarchy and internal division, compounded by invasions by northern tribal peoples. The next great dynasty did not arise until the beginning of the seventh century, four hundred years later.

Courtesy of William J. Duiker

OUTPOST OF EMPIRE. Located at the junction of two rivers passing through the sandy wastes of the Turfan Depression, in modern Xinjiang Province, the town of Jiaohe was one of the first outposts established by the Han dynasty as it expanded westward into Central Asia in the first century C.E. Previously inhabited by the Indo-European-speaking Tocharian peoples, eventually Jiaohe would become a prominent stopping point on the Silk Road before being overrun by the Mongols in the thirteenth century. The town was located on top of the plateau to the left. On the right side of the photograph are storage bins used today to dry grapes.

DAILY LIFE IN ANCIENT CHINA

Few social institutions have been as closely identified with China as the family. As in most agricultural civilizations, the family served as the basic economic and social unit in society. In traditional China, however, it took on an almost sacred quality as a microcosm of the entire social order.

In Neolithic times, the farm village, organized around the clan, was the basic social unit in China. By the Zhou dynasty, however, the smaller family unit took on increasing importance, in part because of the need for cooperation in agriculture. The cultivation of rice, which had become the primary crop along the Yangtze River and in the provinces to the south, is highly labor-intensive. The seedlings must be planted in several inches of water in a nursery bed and then transferred individually to the paddy beds, which must be irrigated constantly. During the harvest, the stalks must be cut and the kernels carefully separated from the stalks and husks. As a result, children—and the labor they supplied—were considered essential to the survival of the family, not only during their youthful years but also later, when sons were expected to provide for their parents. Loyalty to family members came to be considered even more important than loyalty to the broader community or the state.

At the crux of the concept of family was the idea of filial piety, which called on all members of the family to subordinate their needs and desires to the patriarchal head of the family. More broadly, it created a hierarchical system in which every family member had his or her place. All Chinese learned the "five relationships" that were the key to a proper social order. The son was subordinate to the father, the wife to her husband, the younger brother to the older brother, and all were subject to their king. The final relationship was the proper one between friend and friend. Only if all members of the family and the community as a whole behaved in a properly filial manner would society function effectively.

A stable family system based on obedient and hardworking members can serve as a bulwark for an efficient government, but putting loyalty to the family and the clan over loyalty to the state can also present a threat to a centralizing monarch. For that reason, the Qin dynasty attempted to assert the primacy of the state by weakening the role of the family.

But the efforts of the Qin to eradicate the family system ran against tradition and the dynamics of the Chinese economy, and under the Han, the family revived in importance. With official encouragement, the family became not only the primary economic unit; it was also the basic social unit for education, religious observances, and training in ethical principles.

We know much more about the lifestyle of the elites than that of the common people in ancient China. The first houses were probably constructed of wooden planks, but later Chinese mastered the art of building in tile and brick. By the first millennium B.C.E., most public buildings and the houses of the wealthy were probably constructed in this manner. Most Chinese, however, probably lived in simple houses of mud, wooden planks, or brick with thatch roofs.

Courtesy of William J. Duiker

✦ **FLOODED RICE FIELDS.** Rice, which was first cultivated in China as long as seven or eight thousand years ago, is a very labor-intensive crop that requires many workers to plant the seedlings and organize the distribution of water. Initially, the fields are flooded to facilitate the rooting of the rice seedlings and to add nutrients to the soil. Fish breeding in the flooded fields help keep mosquitoes and other insects in check. As the plants mature, the fields are drained, and the plants complete their four-month growing cycle in dry soil. Shown here is an example of terracing on a hillside to preserve water for the nourishment of young seedlings.

Chinese houses usually had little furniture; most people squatted or sat with their legs spread out on the packed mud floor. Chairs were apparently not introduced until the sixth or seventh century C.E. Clothing was simple, consisting of cotton trousers and shirts in the summer and wool or burlap in the winter.

The staple foods were millet in the north and rice in the south. Other common foods were wheat, barley, soybeans, mustard greens, and bamboo shoots. In early times, such foods were often consumed in the form of porridge, but by the Zhou dynasty, stir-frying in a wok was becoming common. When possible, the Chinese family would vary its diet of grain foods with vegetables, fruit (including pears, peaches, apricots, and plums), and fish or meat; but for most, such additions to the daily plate of rice, millet, or soybeans were a rare luxury.

Alcohol in the form of ale was drunk at least by the higher classes and by the early Zhou era had already begun to inspire official concern. According to the *Book of History*, "King Wen admonished . . . the young nobles . . . that they should not ordinarily use spirits; and throughout all the states he required that they should be drunk only on occasion of sacrifices, and that then virtue should preside so that there might be no drunkenness."[9]

Most Chinese lived in the countryside, but as time went on, cities began to play a larger role in society. The first towns were little more than forts for the local aristocracy; by the Zhou era, however, larger towns, usually located on the major trade routes, began to combine administrative and economic functions, serving as regional markets or manufacturing centers. Such cities were usually surrounded by a wall and a moat.

By the Han period, the major city in China was Chang'an, the imperial capital. The city covered a total area of nearly 40 square kilometers and was enclosed by a 12-foot earthen wall surrounded by a moat. Twelve gates provided entry into the city, and eight major avenues ran east-west or north-south; a center strip in each avenue was reserved for the emperor, whose palace and gardens occupied nearly half the southern and central part of the city.

The Humble Estate: Women in Ancient China

Female subservience was a key element in the social system of ancient China. As in many traditional societies, the male was considered of transcendent importance because of his role as food procurer or, in the case of farming communities, food producer. In ancient China, men worked in the fields and women raised children and served in the home. The Chinese written language graphically demonstrates how ancient Chinese society regarded the sexes. The character for man (**男**) combines the symbols for strength and a rice field, whereas the character for woman (**女**) represents a person in a posture of deference and respect. The character for peace (**安**) is a woman under a roof. A wife is symbolized by a woman with a broom.

Confucian thought accepted the dual roles of men and women in Chinese society. Men governed society. They carried on family ritual through the veneration of ancestors. They were the warriors, scholars, and ministers. Their dominant role was firmly enshrined in the legal system. Men were permitted to have more than one wife and to divorce a spouse who did not produce a male child. Women were denied the right to own property, and there was no dowry system in ancient China that would have provided the wife with a degree of financial security from her husband and his family.

Not surprisingly, women were taught to accept their secondary role in life. Ban Zhao, a prominent female historian of the Han dynasty whose own career was an exception to the rule, described that role as follows:

> To be humble, yielding, respectful and reverential; to put herself after others . . . these qualities are those exemplifying woman's low and humble estate. To retire late and rise early; not to shirk exertion from dawn to dark . . . this is called being diligent. To behave properly and decorously in serving her husband; to be serene and self-possessed, shunning jests and laughter . . . this is called being worthy of continuing the husband's lineage. If a woman possess the above-mentioned three qualities, then her reputation shall be excellent.[10]

Some women did become a force in politics, especially at court, where wives of the ruler or other female members of the royal family were often influential in palace intrigues. Such activities were frowned on, however, as the following passage from the *Book of Songs* attests:

> A clever man builds a city,
> A clever woman lays one low;
> With all her qualifications, that clever woman
> Is but an ill-omened bird.
> A woman with a long tongue
> Is a flight of steps leading to calamity;
> For disorder does not come from heaven,
> But is brought about by women.
> Among those who cannot be trained or taught
> Are women and eunuchs.[11]

CHINESE CULTURE

Modern knowledge about artistic achievements in ancient civilizations is limited because often little has survived the ravages of time. Fortunately, many ancient civilizations, such as Egypt and Mesopotamia, were located in relatively arid areas where many artifacts were preserved, even over thousands of years. In humid regions such as China, the cultural residue left by the civilizations of antiquity has been adversely affected by climate.

As a result, relatively little remains of the cultural achievements of the ancient Chinese aside from relics found in burial tombs. In recent years, a rich trove from the time of the Qin Empire has been unearthed near the tomb of Qin Shi Huangdi near Xian in central China and at burial sites elsewhere in the country. But little remains of the literature of ancient China and almost none of the painting, architecture, and music.

Metalwork and Sculpture

The pace of Chinese cultural development began to quicken during the Shang dynasty, when objects cast in bronze began to appear. A variety of bronze vessels were produced for use in preparing and serving food and drink in the ancestral rites.

The method of casting used was one reason for the extraordinary quality of Shang bronze work. Bronze workers in most ancient civilizations used the lost-wax method, where a model was first made in wax. After a clay mold had been formed around it, the model was heated so that the wax would disappear, and the empty space was filled with molten metal. In China, clay molds composed of several sections were tightly fitted together prior to the introduction of the liquid bronze. This technique, which had evolved from ceramic techniques used during the Neolithic period, enabled the artisans to apply the design directly to the mold and thus contributed to the clarity of line and rich surface decoration of the Shang bronzes.

Bronze casting became a large-scale business, and more than ten thousand vessels of an incredible variety of form and design survive today. The art of bronze working continued into the Zhou and the Han dynasties, but the quality and originality declined. The Shang bronzes remain the pinnacle of creative art in ancient China.

One reason for the decline of bronze casting in China was the rise in popularity of iron. Ironmaking developed in China around the ninth or eighth century B.C.E., much later than in the Middle East, where it had been mastered almost a millennium earlier. Once familiar with the process, however, the Chinese quickly moved to the forefront. Ironworkers in Europe and the Middle East, lacking the technology to achieve the high temperatures necessary to melt iron ore for casting, were forced to work with wrought iron, a cumbersome and expensive process. By the fourth century B.C.E., the Chinese had invented the technique of the blast furnace, powered by a person operating a bellows. They were therefore able to manufacture cast-iron ritual vessels and agricultural tools centuries before an equivalent technology appeared in the West.

A SHANG WINE VESSEL. Used initially as food containers in royal ceremonial rites during the Shang dynasty, Chinese bronzes were the product of an advanced technology unmatched by any contemporary civilization. This wine vessel displays a deep green patina as well as a monster motif, complete with large globular eyes, nostrils, and fangs, typical of many Shang bronzes. Known as the *taotie*, this fanciful beast is normally presented in silhouette as two dragons face-to-face so that each side forms half of the mask. Although the *taotie* presumably served as a guardian force against evil spirits, scholars are still not aware of its exact significance for early Chinese peoples.

© Robert Harding Picture Library

In 1974, in a remarkable discovery, farmers digging a well about 35 miles east of Xian unearthed a number of terra-cotta figures in an underground pit about one mile east of the burial mound of the First Emperor of Qin. Chinese archaeologists sent to work at the site discovered a vast terra-cotta army that they believed was a re-creation of Qin Shi Huangdi's imperial guard, which was to accompany the emperor on his journey to the next world.

The discovery of the terra-cotta army shows that the Chinese had come a long way from the human sacrifices that had taken place at the death of Shang sovereigns more than a thousand years earlier. But the project must have been ruinously expensive and is additional evidence of the burden the Qin ruler imposed on his subjects. One historian has estimated that one-third of the national income in Qin and Han times may have been spent on preparations for the ruler's afterlife.

Qin Shi Huangdi's ambitious effort to provide for his immortality became a pattern for his successors during the Han dynasty, although apparently on a somewhat more modest scale. In 1990, Chinese workers discovered a similar underground army for a Han emperor of the second century B.C.E. Like the imperial guard of the First Emperor of Qin, the underground soldiers were buried in parallel pits and possessed their own weapons and individual facial features. But they were smaller—only one-third the height of the average human adult—and were armed with wooden weapons and dressed in silk clothing, now decayed. A burial pit nearby indicates that as many as ten thousand workers, probably slaves or prisoners, died in the process of building the emperor's mausoleum, which took an estimated ten years to construct.

Language and Literature

Precisely when writing developed in China cannot be determined, but certainly by Shang times, as the oracle bones demonstrate, the Chinese had developed a simple but functional script. Like many other languages of antiquity, it was primarily ideographic and pictographic in form. Symbols, usually called "characters," were created to represent an idea or to form a picture of the object to be represented. For example, the Chinese characters for mountain (山), the sun (日), and the moon (月) were meant to represent the objects themselves. Other characters, such as "big" (大) (a man with his arms outstretched), represent an idea. The word "east" (東) symbolizes the sun coming up behind the trees.

Each character, of course, would be given a sound by the speaker when pronounced. In other cultures, this process led to the abandonment of the system of ideographs and the adoption of a written language based on phonetic symbols. The Chinese language, however, has never entirely abandoned its original ideographic format, although the phonetic element has developed into a significant part of the individual character. In that sense, the Chinese written language is virtually unique in the world today.

Even more important, if the written language had developed in the direction of a phonetic alphabet, it could no longer have served as the written system for all the peoples of an expanding civilization. Although the vast majority spoke a tongue derived from a parent Sinitic language (a system distinguished by its tonal nature, a characteristic that gives Chinese its lilting quality even today), the languages spoken in various regions of the country differed from each other in pronunciation and to a lesser degree in vocabulary and syntax; for the most part, they were (and are today) mutually unintelligible.

The Chinese answer to this problem was to give all the spoken languages the same writing system. Although any character might be pronounced differently in different regions of China, that character would be written the same way (after the standardization undertaken under the Qin) no matter where it was written. This system of written characters could be read by educated Chinese from one end of the country to the other. It became the language of the bureaucracy and the vehicle for the transmission of Chinese culture to all Chinese. The written language, however, was not identical with the spoken. Written Chinese evolved a totally separate vocabulary and grammatical structure from the spoken tongues. As a result, those who used it required special training.

The earliest extant form of Chinese literature dates from the Zhou dynasty. It was written on silk or strips of bamboo and consisted primarily of historical records such as the *Rites of Zhou*, philosophical treatises such as the *Analects* and *The Way of the Dao*, and poetry, as recorded in *The Book of Songs*. In later years, when Confucian principles had been elevated to a state ideology, the key works identified with the Confucian school were integrated into a set of so-called Confucian Classics. These works became required reading for generations of Chinese schoolchildren and introduced them to the forms of behavior that would be required of them as adults.

Under the Han dynasty, historical writing became the primary form of literary creativity. Historians such as Sima Qian and Ban Gu wrote works that became models for later dynastic histories. These historical works combined political and social history with biographies of key figures. Like so much literary work in China, their primary purpose was moral and political—to explain the underlying reasons for the rise and fall of individual human beings and dynasties.

CONCLUSION

By the time ancient China began to emerge as an organized state, the societies in Mesopotamia and the Nile valley had already reached an advanced level of civilization. Unfortunately, not enough is known about the early stages of these civilizations to allow us to determine why some developed earlier than others, but one likely reason for China's late arrival was that it was virtually isolated from other emerging centers of culture elsewhere in the world and thus was compelled to develop essentially on its own. Only at the end of the first millennium B.C.E. did the Han dynasty come into regular contact with other civilizations in South Asia, the Middle East, and the Mediterranean.

Once embarked on its own path toward the creation of a complex society, however, China achieved results that were in all respects the equal of its counterparts elsewhere. During the glory years of the Han dynasty, China extended the boundaries of its empire far into the sands of Central Asia and southward along the coast of the South China Sea into what is now Vietnam. The doctrine of State Confucianism provided an effective ideology for the state, and Chinese culture appeared unrivaled. In many respects, its scientific and technological achievements were unsurpassed.

One reason for China's striking success was undoubtedly that unlike its contemporary civilizations, it long was able to fend off the danger from nomadic peoples (along the northern frontier). By the end of the second century B.C.E., however, the Xiongnu were looming ominously, and tribal warriors began to nip at the borders of the empire. While the dynasty was strong, the problem was manageable, but when internal difficulties began to corrode the unity of the state, China became increasingly vulnerable to the threat from the north and entered its own time of troubles.

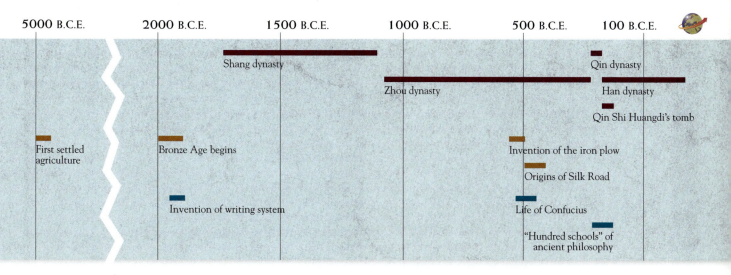

CHAPTER NOTES

1. *Book of Changes*, quoted in Chang Chi-yun, *Chinese History of Fifty Centuries*, vol. 1, *Ancient Times* (Taipei, 1962), p. 381
2. Quoted in E. N. Anderson, *The Food of China* (New Haven, Conn., 1988), p. 21.
3. From *The Book of Songs*, quoted in Sebastian de Grazia, ed., *Masters of Chinese Political Thought: From the Beginnings to the Han Dynasty* (New York, 1973), pp. 40–41.
4. James Legge, ed., *Confucian Analects* (Lun Yu)(Taipei, 1963), 11:11, 6:20.
5. Ibid., 15:23.
6. Ibid., 17:2.
7. *Book of Mencius* (Meng Zi), 4 A:9, quoted in William Theodore de Bary et al., eds., *Sources of Chinese Tradition* (New York, 1960), p. 107.
8. Burton Watson, *Records of the Grand Historian of China* (New York, 1961), vol. 2, pp. 32, 53.
9. Clae Waltham, *Shu Ching: Book of History* (Chicago, 1971), p. 154.
10. Lloyd E. Eastman, *Family, Fields, and Ancestors: Constancy and Change in China's Social and Economic History, 1550–1949* (New York, 1988), p. 19.
11. Quoted in Herbert A. Giles, *A History of Chinese Literature* (New York, 1923), p. 19.

SUGGESTED READING

Several general histories of China provide a useful overview of the period of antiquity. Perhaps the best known is the classic *East Asia: Tradition and Transformation* (Boston, 1973), by J. K. Fairbank, E. O. Reischauer, and A. M. Craig. For an authoritative overview of the ancient period, see M. Loewe and E. L. Shaughnessy, *The Cambridge History of Ancient China from the Origins of Civilization to 221 B.C.* (Cambridge, 1999). Political and social maps of China can be found in A. Herrmann, *A Historical Atlas of China* (Chicago, 1966).

The period of the Neolithic era and the Shang dynasty has received increasing attention in recent years. For an impressively documented and annotated overview, see Kwang-chih Chang, *Shang Civilization* (New Haven, Conn., 1980) and *Studies in Shang Archaeology* (New Haven, Conn., 1982). D. Keightley, *The Origins of Chinese Civilization* (Berkeley, Calif., 1983), presents a number of interesting articles on selected aspects of the period.

The Zhou and Qin dynasties have also received considerable attention. The former is exhaustively analyzed in Cho-yun Hsu and J. M. Linduff, *Western Zhou Civilization* (New Haven, Conn., 1988), and Li Xueqin, *Eastern Zhou and Qin Civilizations* (New Haven, Conn., 1985). The latter is a translation of an original work by a mainland Chinese scholar and is especially interesting for its treatment of the development of the silk industry and the money economy in ancient China. On bronze casting, see E. L. Shaughnessy, *Sources of Eastern Zhou History* (Berkeley, Calif., 1991). Also of value for its treatment of the formation of social classes is Cho-yun Hsu, *Ancient China in Transition* (Stanford, Calif., 1965).

There are a number of useful books on the Han dynasty. Zhong-shu Wang, *Han Civilization* (New Haven, Conn., 1982), presents evidence from the mainland on excavations from Han tombs and the old imperial capital of Chang'an. M. Loewe, *Everyday Life in Early Imperial China During the Han Period, 202 B.C.–220 A.D.* (London, 1968), contains useful material on religious beliefs and the development of social classes during the Han. Also see the lavishly illustrated *Han Civilization of China* (Oxford, 1982) by M. P. Serstevens. For a firsthand view, see B. Watson,

Records of the Grand Historian of China (New York, 1961), a translation of key passages from Sima Qian's history of the period.

The philosophy of ancient China has attracted considerable attention from Western scholars. Some standard works include A. Waley, *Three Ways of Thought in Ancient China* (New York, 1939); H. G. Creel, *Chinese Thought: From Confucius to Mao Tse-Tung* (Chicago, 1953); Feng Yu-lan, *A Short History of Chinese Philosophy* (New York, 1960); and F. Mote, *Intellectual Foundations of China*, 2d ed. (New York, 1989). On Confucius, see H. G. Creel, *Confucius: The Man and the Myth* (London, 1951), a sympathetic treatment that emphasizes the humanistic side of Confucian philosophy.

For works on general culture and science, consult the illustrated work by R. Temple, *The Genius of China: 3000 Years of Science, Discovery, and Invention* (New York, 1986), and J. Needham, *Science in Traditional China: A Comparative Perspective* (Boston, 1981). See also E. N. Anderson, *The Food of China* (New Haven, Conn., 1988).

The most comprehensive collection of original writings is W. T. de Bary and Irene Bloom, *Sources of Chinese Tradition*, 2d ed. (New York, 1999), which includes excerpts from most of the ancient texts. The complete translations of the Confucian Classics are in J. Legge, *The Chinese Classics*, 5 vols. (Hong Kong, 1960), with critical and exegetical notes. For an annotated version of Lao Tzu, see Wing-tsit Chan, *The Way of Lao Tzu* (Indianapolis, 1963).

For an introduction to classical Chinese literature, consult the three standard anthologies: Liu Wu-chi, *An Introduction to Chinese Literature* (New York, 1961); V. H. Mair, ed., *The Columbia Anthology of Traditional Chinese Literature* (New York, 1994); and S. Owen, ed., *An Anthology of Chinese Literature: Beginnings to 1911* (New York, 1996). For a comprehensive introduction to Chinese art, with good illustrations in color, consult M. Sullivan, *The Arts of China*, 4th ed. (Berkeley, Calif., 1999). Also see M. Tregear, *Chinese Art*, rev. ed. (London, 1997), and *Art Treasures in China* (New York, 1994). Also of interest is P. B. Ebrey, *The Cambridge Illustrated History of China* (Cambridge, 1999).

InfoTrac College Edition

Visit the source collections at infotrac.thomsonlearning.com and use the Search function with the following key terms.

China history

Confucius or Confucian

Han dynasty

Taoism or Daoism

World History Resources

Visit the *Essential World History* Companion Web Site for resources specific to this textbook:

http://history.wadsworth.com/duikeressentials02/

The CD in the back of this book and the World History Resource Center at http://history.wadsworth.com/world/ offer a variety of tools to help you succeed in this course, including access to quizzes; images; documents; interactive simulations, maps, and timelines; movie explorations; and a wealth of other sources.

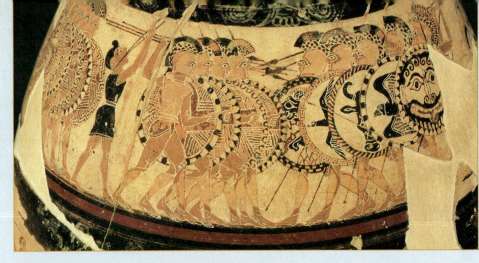

© Scala/Art Resource, NY

THE CIVILIZATION OF THE GREEKS

FOCUS QUESTIONS
- What was the *polis,* or city-state, and how did the city-states of Athens and Sparta differ?
- What effects did the Persian Wars and the Great Peloponnesian War have on Greek civilization?
- How was Alexander the Great able to amass his empire, and what was his legacy?
- How did the political, economic, and social institutions of the Hellenistic world differ from those of classical Greece?
- ➤ In what ways did the schools of philosophy and major religions of the Hellenistic period differ from those of the classical period, and what do those differences suggest about society in the two periods?

During the era of civil war in China known as the Period of the Warring States, a civil war also erupted on the northern shores of the Mediterranean Sea. In 431 B.C.E., two very different Greek city-states— Athens and Sparta—fought for domination of the Greek world. The people of Athens felt secure behind their walls and in the first winter of the war held a public funeral to honor those who had died in battle. On the day of the ceremony, the citizens of Athens joined in a procession, with the relatives of the dead wailing for their loved ones. As was the custom in Athens, one leading citizen was asked to address the crowd, and on this day it was Pericles who spoke to the people. He talked about the greatness of Athens and reminded the Athenians of the strength of their political system: "Our constitution," he said, "is called a democracy because power is in the hands not of a minority but of the whole people. When it is a question of settling private disputes, everyone is equal before the law. Just as our political life is free and open, so is our day-to-day life in our relations with each other. . . . Here each individual is interested not only in his own affairs but in the affairs of the state as well."

In this famous funeral oration, Pericles gave voice to the ideal of democracy and the importance of the individual, ideals that were quite different from those of ancient China, in which the individual was subordinated to a larger order based on obedience to an exalted emperor. The Greeks asked some basic questions about human life: What is the nature of the universe? What is the purpose of human existence? What is our relationship to divine forces? What constitutes a community? What constitutes a state? What is truth, and how do we realize it? Not only did the Greeks answer these questions, but they also derived a system of logical, analytical thought to examine them. Their answers and their system of rational thought laid the intellectual foundation of Western civilization's understanding of the human condition.

The remarkable story of ancient Greek civilization begins with the arrival of the Greeks around 1900 B.C.E. By the eighth century B.C.E., the characteristic institution of ancient Greek life, the *polis*, or city-state, had emerged. Greek civilization flourished and reached its height in the classical era of the fifth century B.C.E., but the inability of the Greek states to end their fratricidal warfare eventually left them vulnerable to the Macedonian king Philip II and helped bring an end to the era of independent Greek city-states.

Although the city-states were never the same after their defeat by the Macedonian monarch, it did not bring an end to the influence of the Greeks. Philip's son Alexander led the Macedonians and Greeks on a spectacular conquest of the Persian Empire and opened the door to the spread of Greek culture throughout the Middle East. ●

EARLY GREECE

Geography played an important role in Greek history. Compared to the landmasses of Mesopotamia and Egypt, Greece occupied a small area, a mountainous peninsula that encompassed only 45,000 square miles of territory, about the size of the state of Louisiana. The mountains and the sea were especially significant. Much of Greece consists of small plains and river valleys surrounded by mountain ranges 8,000 to 10,000 feet high. The mountains isolated Greeks from one another, causing Greek communities to follow their own separate paths and develop their own ways of life. Over a period of time, these communities became so fiercely attached to their independence that they were only too willing to fight one another to gain advantage. No doubt the small size of these independent Greek communities fostered participation in political affairs and unique cultural expressions, but the rivalry among them also led to the internecine warfare that ultimately devastated Greek society.

The sea also influenced Greek society. Greece had a long seacoast, dotted by bays and inlets that provided numerous harbors. The Greeks also inhabited a number of islands to the west, south, and particularly the east of the Greek mainland. It is no accident that the Greeks became seafarers who sailed out into the Aegean and Mediterranean Seas to make contact with the outside world and later to establish colonies that would spread Greek civilization throughout the Mediterranean.

Greek topography helped determine the major territories into which Greece was ultimately divided (see Map 4.1). South of the Gulf of Corinth was the Peloponnesus, virtually an island connected to the mainland by a narrow isthmus. Consisting mostly of hills, mountains, and small valleys, the Peloponnesus was home to the city-state of Sparta. Northeast of the Peloponnesus was the Attic peninsula (or Attica), the site of Athens, hemmed in by mountains to the north and west and surrounded by the sea to the south and east. Northwest of Attica was Boeotia in central Greece, with its chief city of Thebes. To the north of Boeotia was Thessaly, which contained the largest plains and became a great producer of grain and horses. To the north of Thessaly lay Macedonia, which was of minor importance in Greek history until 338 B.C.E., when the Macedonian king conquered the Greeks.

Minoan Crete

The earliest civilization in the Aegean region emerged on Crete, a large island southeast of the Greek mainland. By 2800 B.C.E., a Bronze Age civilization that used metals, especially bronze, in the construction of weapons had been established on Crete. This civilization was discovered by the English archaeologist Arthur Evans, who called it Minoan after Minos, the legendary king of Crete. Evans's excavations on Crete at the beginning of the twentieth

MACEDONIA

THRACE

Bosporus

EPIRUS

Propontis (Sea of Marmara)

Mt Olympus △

Hellespont

■ Troy

Corcyra

THESSALY

Aegean Sea

Lesbos

Mt Parnassus △
Delphi ■

Euboea

Chios

BOEOTIA

Ionian Sea

■ Thebes

ATTICA

IONIA

Gulf of Corinth

Corinth ■

Athens ■

Samos

■ Miletus

Olympia ■

Argos ■

Delos

Halicarnassus ■

PELOPONNESUS

Paros

MESSENIA

Sparta ■

Amorgos

LACONIA

Rhodes

Sea of Crete

Mediterranean Sea

Knossus ■

CRETE

```
0        100       200      300 Kilometers
0            100          200 Miles
```

century unearthed an enormous palace complex at Knossus, near modern Heracleion. The remains revealed a prosperous culture with Knossus as the apparent center of a far-ranging "sea empire" based on trade.

The Minoan civilization reached its height between 2000 and 1450 B.C.E. The palace at Knossus, the royal seat of the kings, was an elaborate structure that included numerous private living rooms for the royal family and workshops for making decorated vases, ivory figurines, and jewelry. Even bathrooms, with elaborate drains, like those found at Mohenjo-Daro in India, formed part of the complex. The rooms were decorated with brightly colored frescoes showing sporting events and nature scenes.

The centers of Minoan civilization on Crete suffered a sudden and catastrophic collapse around 1450 B.C.E. Some historians believe that a tidal wave triggered by a powerful volcanic eruption on the island of Thera was responsible for the devastation, but most historians maintain that the destruction was the result of invasion and pillage by mainland Greeks known as the Mycenaeans.

The Mycenaeans

The term *Mycenaean* is derived from Mycenae, a fortified site excavated by an amateur German archaeologist, Heinrich Schliemann, starting in 1870. Mycenae was one center in a civilization that flourished between 1600 and 1100 B.C.E. The Mycenaean Greeks were part of the Indo-European family of peoples (see Chapter 1) who spread from their original

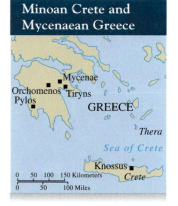

Minoan Crete and Mycenaean Greece

Mycenae

Orchomenos
Pylos

Tiryns

GREECE

Thera

Sea of Crete

Knossus
Crete

```
0    50   100   150 Kilometers
0        50        100 Miles
```

location into southern and western Europe, India, and Iran. One group entered the territory of Greece from the north around 1900 B.C.E. and eventually managed to gain control of the Greek mainland and develop a civilization.

Mycenaean civilization, which reached its high point between 1400 and 1200 B.C.E., consisted of a number of powerful monarchies that resided in fortified palace complexes. Like Mycenae, they were built on hills and surrounded by gigantic stone walls. These various centers of power probably formed a loose confederacy of independent states, with Mycenae being the strongest. The Mycenaeans were warriors who prided themselves on their heroic deeds in battle. Some scholars believe that the Mycenaeans spread outward and conquered Crete. The most famous of their supposed military adventures has come down to us in the epic poetry of Homer (see "Homer" later in this chapter). Did the Mycenaean Greeks, led by Agamemnon, king of Mycenae, sack the city of Troy on the northwestern coast of Asia Minor around 1250 B.C.E.? Ever since Schliemann began his excavations in 1870, scholars have debated this question. Many believe that Homer's account does have a basis in fact, even if the details have become shrouded in mystery.

By the late thirteenth century B.C.E., Mycenaean Greece was showing signs of serious trouble. Mycenae itself was torched around 1190 B.C.E., and other Mycenaean centers show similar patterns of destruction as new waves of Greek-speaking invaders moved into Greece from the north. By 1100, Mycenaean culture was coming to an end, and the Greek world was entering a new period of considerable insecurity.

THE GREEKS IN A DARK AGE (C. 1100–C. 750 B.C.E.)

After the collapse of Mycenaean civilization, Greece entered a difficult era of declining population and falling food production; not until 850 B.C.E. did farming—and Greece itself—revive. Because of both the difficult conditions and the fact that we have few records to help us reconstruct what happened in this period, historians refer to it as the Dark Age.

During the Dark Age, large numbers of Greeks left the mainland and migrated across the Aegean Sea to various islands and especially to the southwestern shore of Asia Minor, a strip of territory that came to be called Ionia. Two other major groups of Greeks settled in established parts of Greece. The Aeolians from northern and central Greece colonized the large island of Lesbos and the adjacent mainland. The Dorians established themselves in southwestern Greece, especially in the Peloponnesus, as well as on some south Aegean islands, including Crete.

As trade and economic activity began to recover, iron replaced bronze in the construction of weapons, making

them affordable for more people. At some point in the eighth century B.C.E., the Greeks adopted the Phoenician alphabet to give themselves a new system of writing. Near the very end of the Dark Age appeared the work of Homer, who has come to be viewed as one of the great poets of all time.

Homer

The first great epics of early Greece, the *Iliad* and the *Odyssey*, were based on stories that had been passed down from generation to generation. It is generally assumed that early in the eighth century B.C.E., Homer made use of these oral traditions to compose the *Iliad*, his epic poem of the Trojan War. The war was caused when Paris, a prince of Troy, kidnapped Helen, wife of the king of the Greek state of Sparta, outraging all the Greeks. Under the leadership of the Spartan king's brother, Agamemnon of Mycenae, the Greeks attacked Troy. After ten years of combat, the Greeks finally sacked the city. The *Iliad* is not so much the story of the war itself, however, as it is the tale of the Greek hero Achilles and how the "wrath of Achilles" led to disaster. The *Odyssey*, Homer's other masterpiece, is an epic romance that recounts the journeys of another Greek hero, Odysseus, after the fall of Troy and his eventual return to his wife, Penelope, after twenty years.

The Greeks regarded the *Iliad* and the *Odyssey* as authentic history as recorded by one poet, Homer. The epics gave the Greeks an idealized past, a legendary age of heroes, and the poems became standard texts for the education of generations of Greek males. As one Athenian stated, "My father was anxious to see me develop into a good man . . . and as a means to this end he compelled me to memorize all of Homer."[1] The values Homer inculcated were essentially the aristocratic values of courage and honor (see the box on p. 72). It was important to strive for the excellence befitting a hero, which the Greeks called *arete*. In the warrior-aristocratic world of Homer, *arete* is won in struggle or contest. Through his willingness to fight, the hero protects his family and friends, preserves his own honor and his family's, and earns his reputation. In the Homeric world, aristocratic women, too, were expected to pursue excellence. For example, Odysseus' wife, Penelope, remains faithful to her husband and displays great courage and intelligence in preserving their household during her husband's long absence.

To a later generation of Greeks, these heroic values formed the core of aristocratic virtue, a fact that explains the tremendous popularity of Homer as an educational tool. Homer gave the Greeks a universally accepted model of heroism, honor, and nobility. But in time, as city-states proliferated in Greece, new values of cooperation and community also transformed what the Greeks learned from Homer.

HOMER'S IDEAL OF EXCELLENCE

*T*he Iliad *and the* Odyssey, *which the Greeks believed were both written by Homer, were used as basic texts for the education of Greeks for hundreds of years during antiquity. This passage from the* Iliad, *describing the encounter between Hector, prince of Troy, and his wife, Andromache, illustrates the Greek ideal of gaining honor through combat. At the end of the passage, Homer also reveals what became the Greek attitude toward women: they are supposed to spin and weave and take care of their households and children.*

HOMER, *ILIAD*

Hector looked at his son and smiled, but said nothing. Andromache, bursting into tears, went up to him and put her hand in his. "Hector," she said, "you are possessed. This bravery of yours will be your end. You do not think of your little boy or your unhappy wife, whom you will make a widow soon. Some day the Achaeans [Greeks] are bound to kill you in a massed attack. And when I lose you I might as well be dead. . . . I have no father, no mother, now. . . . I had seven brothers too at home. In one day all of them went down to Hades' House. The great Achilles of the swift feet killed them all. . . .

"So you, Hector, are father and mother and brother to me, as well as my beloved husband. Have pity on me now; stay here on the tower; and do not make your boy an orphan and your wife a widow. . . ."

"All that, my dear," said the great Hector of the glittering helmet, "is surely my concern. But if I hid myself like a coward and refused to fight, I could never face the Trojans and the Trojan ladies in their trailing gowns. Besides, it would go against the grain, for I have trained myself always, like a good soldier, to take my place in the front line and win glory for my father and myself. . . ."

As he finished, glorious Hector held out his arms to take his boy. But the child shrank back with a cry to the bosom of his girdled nurse, alarmed by his father's appearance. He was frightened by the bronze of the helmet and the horsehair plume that he saw nodding grimly down at him. His father and his lady mother had to laugh. But noble Hector quickly took his helmet off and put the dazzling thing on the ground. Then he kissed his son, dandled him in his arms, and prayed to Zeus and the other gods: "Zeus, and you other gods, grant that this boy of mine may be, like me, preeminent in Troy; as strong and brave as I; a mighty king of Ilium. May people say, when he comes back from battle, 'Here is a better man than his father.' Let him bring home the bloodstained armor of the enemy he has killed, and make his mother happy."

Hector handed the boy to his wife, who took him to her fragrant breast. She was smiling through her tears, and when her husband saw this he was moved. He stroked her with his hand and said, "My dear, I beg you not to be too much distressed. No one is going to send me down to Hades before my proper time. But Fate is a thing that no man born of woman, coward or hero, can escape. Go home now, and attend to your own work, the loom and the spindle, and see that the maidservants get on with theirs. War is men's business; and this war is the business of every man in Ilium, myself above all."

THE GREEK CITY-STATES (C. 750–C. 500 B.C.E.)

During the Dark Age, Greek villages gradually expanded and evolved into independent city-states. By the eighth century B.C.E., the city-state, or what the Greeks called a *polis* (plural, *poleis*), had emerged as a unique and fundamental institution in Greek society.

The *Polis*

In the most basic sense, a *polis* could be defined as a small but autonomous political unit in which all major political, social, and religious activities were carried out at one central location. The *polis* consisted of a city, town, or village and its surrounding countryside. The city, town, or village was the focus, a central point where the citizens of the *polis* could assemble for political, social, and religious activities. In some *poleis*, this central meeting point was a hill, like the Acropolis at Athens, which could serve as a place of refuge during an attack and later in some sites came to be the religious center on which temples and public monuments were erected. Below the acropolis would be an *agora*, an open space or plaza that served both as a market and as a place where citizens could assemble.

Poleis could vary greatly in size, from a few square miles to a few hundred square miles. They also varied in population. Athens had a population of about 250,000 by the fifth century B.C.E. But most *poleis* were much smaller, consisting of only a few hundred to several thousand people.

Although our word *politics* is derived from the Greek term *polis*, the *polis* itself was much more than just a political institution. It was, above all, a community of citizens who shared a common identity and common goals. As a community, the *polis* consisted of citizens with political rights (adult males), citizens with no political rights (women and children), and noncitizens (slaves and resident aliens). All citizens of a *polis* possessed fundamental rights, but these rights were coupled with responsibilities. However, the loyalty that citizens had to their city-states

◆ **THE HOPLITE FORCES.**   The Greek hoplites were infantrymen equipped with large round shields and long thrusting spears. In battle, they advanced in tight phalanx formation and were dangerous opponents as long as this formation remained unbroken. This vase painting of the seventh century B.C.E. shows two groups of hoplite warriors engaged in battle. The piper on the left is leading another line of soldiers preparing to enter the fray.

also had a negative side. City-states distrusted one another, and the division of Greece into fiercely patriotic sovereign units heralded its ruin. "Greece" was not a united country but a geographical expression. The cultural unity of the Greeks did not mean much politically.

As the *polis* developed, so did a new military system. Greek fighting had previously been dominated by aristocratic cavalrymen, who reveled in individual duels with enemy soldiers. These aristocrats, who were large landowners, also dominated the political life of their city-states. By 700 B.C.E., however, hoplites had come to the fore. Hoplites were heavily armed infantrymen who wore bronze or leather helmets, breastplates, and greaves (shin guards). Each carried a round shield, a short sword, and a thrusting spear about 9 feet long. Hoplites advanced into battle as a unit, the tightly ordered phalanx, usually eight ranks deep. As long as the hoplites kept their order, were not outflanked, and did not break, they either secured victory or at the very least suffered no harm. If the phalanx broke its order, however, it was easily routed. Thus the safety of the phalanx depended on the solidarity and discipline of its members. As one poet of the seventh century B.C.E. noted, a good hoplite was a "short man . . . with a courageous heart, not to be uprooted from the spot where he plants his legs."[2]

The hoplite force had political as well as military repercussions. The aristocratic cavalry was now outdated. Since each hoplite provided his own armor, men of property, both aristocrats and small farmers, made up the new pha-

lanx. Those who could become hoplites and fight for the state could also challenge aristocratic control.

Colonization and the Rise of Tyrants

Between 750 and 550 B.C.E., large numbers of Greeks left their homeland to settle in distant lands. The growing gulf between rich and poor, overpopulation, and the development of trade were all factors that led to the establishment of colonies. Invariably, each colony saw itself as an independent *polis* whose links to the mother *polis* (*metropolis*) were not political but based on sharing common social, economic, and religious practices.

In the western Mediterranean, new Greek settlements were established along the coastline of southern Italy, southern France, eastern Spain, and northern Africa west of Egypt. To the north, the Greeks set up colonies in Thrace, where they sought good farmland to grow grains. Greeks also settled along the shores of the Black Sea and secured the approaches to it with cities on the Hellespont and Bosporus, most notably Byzantium, site of the later Constantinople (Istanbul). In establishing these settlements, the Greeks spread their culture throughout the Mediterranean basin.

Colonization also led to increased trade and industry. The Greeks on the mainland sent their pottery, wine, and olive oil to these areas; in return, they received grains and metals from the west and fish, timber, wheat, metals, and slaves from the Black Sea region. In many *poleis*, the expansion of trade and industry created a new group of rich men who desired political privileges commensurate with their wealth but found them impossible to gain because of the power of the ruling aristocrats.

The aspirations of the new industrial and commercial groups laid the groundwork for the rise of tyrants in the seventh and sixth centuries B.C.E. These men were not necessarily oppressive or wicked, as our word *tyrant* connotes. Greek tyrants were rulers who came to power in an unconstitutional way; a tyrant was not subject to the law. Many tyrants were actually aristocrats who opposed the control of the ruling aristocratic faction in their cities. Support for the tyrants, however, came from the new rich, who made their money in trade and industry, as well as from poor peasants, who were becoming increasingly indebted to landholding aristocrats. Both groups were opposed to the domination of political power by aristocratic oligarchies.

Once in power, the tyrants built new marketplaces, temples, and walls that not only glorified the city but also enhanced their own popularity. Tyrants also favored the interests of merchants and traders. Despite these achievements, however, tyranny was largely extinguished by the end of the sixth century B.C.E. Greeks believed in the rule of law, and tyranny made a mockery of that ideal.

Although tyranny did not last, it played a significant role in the evolution of Greek history by ending the rule of narrow aristocratic oligarchies. Once the tyrants were eliminated, the door was open to the participation of more people in governing the affairs of the community. Although this trend culminated in the development of democracy in some communities, in other states expanded oligarchies of one kind or another managed to remain in power. Greek states exhibited considerable variety in their governmental structures; this can perhaps best be seen by examining the two most famous and most powerful Greek city-states, Sparta and Athens.

Sparta

Located in the southwestern Peloponnesus, Sparta, like other Greek states, faced the need for more land. Instead of sending its people out to found new colonies, the Spartans conquered the neighboring Laconians and later, beginning around 730 B.C.E., undertook the conquest of neighboring Messenia despite its larger size and population. Messenia possessed a large, fertile plain ideal for growing grain. After its conquest in the seventh century B.C.E., many Messenians, like some of the Laconians earlier, were made helots (the name is derived from a Greek word for "capture") and forced to work for the Spartans. To ensure control over their conquered Laconian and Messenian helots, the Spartans made a conscious decision to establish a military state.

Sometime between 800 and 600 B.C.E., the Spartans instituted a series of reforms that are associated with the name of the lawgiver Lycurgus (see the box on p. 75). Although historians are not sure that Lycurgus ever existed, there is no doubt about the result of the reforms: the lives of Spartans were now rigidly organized and tightly controlled. Boys were taken from their mothers at the age of seven and put under control of the state. They lived in military-style barracks, where they were subjected to harsh discipline to make them tough and given an education that stressed military training and obedience to authority. At twenty, Spartan males were enrolled in the army for regular military service. Although allowed to marry, they continued to live in the barracks. All meals were eaten in public dining halls with fellow soldiers. Meals were simple; the famous Spartan black broth consisted of a piece of pork boiled in blood, salt, and vinegar, prompting a visitor who ate in a public mess to remark that he now understood why Spartans were not afraid to die. At thirty, Spartan males were allowed to vote in the assembly and live at home, but they remained in military service until the age of sixty.

While their husbands remained in military barracks, Spartan women lived at home. Because of this separation, Spartan women had greater freedom of movement and greater power in the household than was common elsewhere in Greece. Spartan women were expected to exercise and remain fit to bear and raise healthy children. Like the men, Spartan women engaged in athletic exercises in the nude. Many Spartan women upheld the strict Spartan values, expecting their husbands and sons to be brave in war. The story is told that as a Spartan mother was burying her son, an old woman came up to her and said, "You poor woman, what a misfortune." "No," replied the other, "because I bore him so that he might die for Sparta and that is what has happened, as I wished."[3]

The so-called Lycurgan reforms also reorganized the Spartan government, creating an oligarchy. Two kings were primarily responsible for military affairs and served as the leaders of the Spartan army on its campaigns. A group of five men, known as the ephors, were elected each year and were responsible for the education of youth and the conduct of all citizens. A council of elders, composed of the two kings and twenty-eight citizens over the age of sixty, decided on the issues that would be presented to an assembly. This assembly of all male citizens did not debate but only voted on the issues put before it by the council of elders.

To make their new military state secure, the Spartans deliberately turned their backs on the outside world. Foreigners, who might bring in new ideas, were discouraged from visiting Sparta. Nor were Spartans, except for military reasons, allowed to travel abroad where they might pick up new ideas that might be dangerous to the stability of the state. Likewise, Spartan citizens were discouraged from studying philosophy, literature, or the arts, any subject that might encourage new thoughts. The art of war was the Spartan ideal, and all other arts were frowned upon.

THE LYCURGAN REFORMS

*T*o maintain their control over the conquered Messenians, the Spartans instituted the reforms that created their military state. In this account of the lawgiver Lycurgus, who may or may not have been a real person, the Greek historian Plutarch discusses the effect of these reforms on the treatment and education of boys.

PLUTARCH, *LYCURGUS*

Lycurgus was of another mind; he would not have masters bought out of the market for his young Spartans, . . . nor was it lawful, indeed, for the father himself to breed up the children after his own fancy; but as soon as they were seven years old they were to be enrolled in certain companies and classes, where they all lived under the same order and discipline, doing their exercises and taking their play together. Of these, he who showed the most conduct and courage was made captain; they had their eyes always upon him, obeyed his orders, and underwent patiently whatsoever punishment he inflicted; so that the whole course of their education was one continued exercise of a ready and perfect obedience. The old men, too, were spectators of their performances, and often raised quarrels and disputes among them, to have a good opportunity of finding out their different characters, and of seeing which would be valiant, which a coward, when they should come to more dangerous encounters. Reading and writing they gave them, just enough to serve their turn; their chief care was to make them good subjects, and to teach them to endure pain and conquer in battle. To this end, as they grew in years, their discipline was proportionately increased; their heads were close-clipped, they were accustomed to go barefoot, and for the most part to play naked.

After they were twelve years old, they were no longer allowed to wear any undergarments; they had one coat to serve them a year; their bodies were hard and dry, with but little acquaintance of baths and unguents; these human indulgences they were allowed only on some few particular days in the year. They lodged together in little bands upon beds made of the rushes which grew by the banks of the river Eurotas, which they were to break off with their hands with a knife; if it were winter, they mingled some thistle down with their rushes, which it was thought had the property of giving warmth. By the time they were come to this age there was not any of the more hopeful boys who had not a lover to bear him company. The old men, too, had an eye upon them, coming often to the grounds to hear and see them contend either in wit or strength with one another, and this as seriously . . . as if they were their fathers, their tutors, or their magistrates; so that there scarcely was any time or place without someone present to put them in mind of their duty, and punish them if they had neglected it.

[Spartan boys were also encouraged to steal their food.] They stole, too, all other meat they could lay their hands on, looking out and watching all opportunities, when people were asleep or more careless than usual. If they were caught, they were not only punished with whipping, but hunger, too, being reduced to their ordinary allowance, which was but very slender, and so contrived on purpose, that they might set about to help themselves, and be forced to exercise their energy and address. This was the principal design of their hard fare.

Athens

By 700 B.C.E., Athens had established a unified *polis* on the peninsula of Attica. Although early Athens had been ruled by a monarchy, by the seventh century B.C.E. it had fallen under the control of its aristocrats. They possessed the best land and controlled political life by means of a council of nobles, assisted by a board of nine archons. Although there was an assembly of full citizens, it possessed few powers.

Near the end of the seventh century B.C.E., Athens faced political turmoil because of serious economic problems. Increasing numbers of Athenian farmers found themselves sold into slavery when they were unable to repay loans they had obtained from their aristocratic neighbors. Repeatedly, there were cries to cancel the debts and give land to the poor. Athens seemed on the verge of civil war.

The ruling Athenian aristocrats responded to this crisis in 594 B.C.E. by giving full power to Solon, a reform-minded aristocrat, to make changes. Solon canceled all land debts, outlawed new loans based on humans as collateral, and freed people who had fallen into slavery for debts. He refused, however, to carry out land redistribution. Thus Solon's reforms, though popular, did not truly solve Athens's problems. Aristocratic factions continued to vie for power, and poor peasants could not get land. Internal strife finally led to the very institution Solon had hoped to avoid—tyranny. Pisistratus, an aristocrat, seized power in 560 B.C.E. Pursuing a foreign policy that aided Athenian trade, Pisistratus remained popular with the mercantile and industrial classes. But the Athenians rebelled against his son and ended the tyranny in 510 B.C.E. When the aristocrats attempted to reestablish an aristocratic oligarchy, Cleisthenes, another aristocratic reformer, opposed their plan and, with the backing of the Athenian people, gained the upper hand in 508 B.C.E.

Cleisthenes set up a "council of five hundred" that supervised foreign affairs and the treasury and proposed laws that would be voted on by the assembly. The Athenian assembly, composed of all male citizens, was given final authority in the passing of laws after free and open debate. Since the assembly of citizens now had the central role in the Athenian political system, the reforms of Cleisthenes had created the foundations for Athenian democracy.

THE HIGH POINT OF GREEK CIVILIZATION: CLASSICAL GREECE

Classical Greece is the name given to the period of Greek history from around 500 B.C.E. to the conquest of Greece by the Macedonian king Philip II in 338 B.C.E. Many of the cultural contributions of the Greeks occurred during this period. The age began with a mighty confrontation between the Greek states and the mammoth Persian Empire.

The Challenge of Persia

As the Greeks spread throughout the Mediterranean, they came into contact with the Persian Empire to the east. The Ionian Greek cities in western Asia Minor had already fallen subject to the Persian Empire by the mid-sixth century B.C.E. An unsuccessful revolt by the Ionian cities in 499 B.C.E., assisted by the Athenians, led the Persian ruler Darius to seek revenge by attacking the mainland Greeks. In 490 B.C.E., the Persians landed an army on the plain of Marathon, only 26 miles from Athens. The Athenians and their allies were clearly outnumbered, but the Greek hoplites charged across the plain of Marathon and crushed the Persian forces.

Xerxes, the new Persian monarch after the death of Darius in 486 B.C.E., vowed revenge and planned to invade Greece. In preparation for the attack, some of the Greek states formed a defensive league under Spartan leadership, while the Athenians pursued a new military policy by undertaking the development of a navy. By the time of the Persian invasion in 480 B.C.E., the Athenians had produced a fleet of about two hundred vessels.

Xerxes led a massive invasion force into Greece: close to 150,000 troops, almost seven hundred naval ships, and hundreds of supply ships to keep the large army fed. The Greeks hoped to stop the Persians at the pass of Thermopylae, along the main road into central Greece. A Greek force numbering close to nine thousand men, under the leadership of a Spartan king and his contingent of three hundred Spartans, held off the Persian army for several days. The Spartan troops were especially brave. When told that Persian arrows would darken the sky in battle, one Spartan warrior supposedly responded: "That is good news. We will fight in the shade!" Unfortunately for the

Chronology

THE PERSIAN WARS

Rebellion of Greek cities in Asia Minor	499–494 B.C.E.
Battle of Marathon	490 B.C.E.
Xerxes' invasion of Greece	480–479 B.C.E.
Battles of Thermopylae and Salamis	480 B.C.E.
Battle of Plataea	479 B.C.E.

Greeks, a traitor told the Persians about a mountain path that would allow them to outflank the Greek force. The Spartans fought to the last man.

The Athenians, now threatened by the onslaught of the Persian forces, abandoned their city. While the Persians sacked and burned Athens, the Greek fleet remained offshore near the island of Salamis and challenged the Persian navy. Although the Greeks were outnumbered, they managed to outmaneuver the Persian fleet and utterly defeated it. A few months later, early in 479 B.C.E., the Greeks formed the largest Greek army seen up to that time and decisively defeated the Persian army at Plataea, northwest of Attica. The Greeks had won the war and were free to pursue their own destiny.

The Growth of an Athenian Empire in the Age of Pericles

After the defeat of the Persians, Athens took over the leadership of the Greek world against the Persians by forming a defensive alliance called the Delian League in the winter of 478–477 B.C.E. Its main headquarters was on the island of Delos, but its chief officials, including the treasurers and commanders of the fleet, were Athenian. Under the leadership of the Athenians, the Delian League pursued the attack against the Persian Empire. Virtually all of the Greek states in the Aegean were liberated from Persian control. In 454 B.C.E., the Athenians moved the treasury from Delos to Athens. By controlling the Delian League, Athens had created an empire.

At home, Athenians favored the new imperial policy, especially in the late 450s B.C.E., when an aristocrat named Pericles began to play an important political role. Under Pericles, Athens embarked on a policy of extending democracy at home and expanding its new empire abroad. This period of Athenian and Greek history, which historians have subsequently labeled the Age of Pericles, witnessed the height of Athenian power and the culmination of its brilliance as a civilization.

In the Age of Pericles, the Athenians became deeply attached to their democratic system. The sovereignty of the people was embodied in the assembly, which consisted of all male citizens over eighteen years of age. In the mid-fifth century, that was probably a group of about 43,000.

Meetings of the assembly were held every ten days on a hillside east of the Acropolis. Not all eligible citizens attended; the number present seldom reached six thousand. The assembly passed all laws, elected public officials, and made final decisions on war and foreign policy. Pericles also expanded the Athenians' involvement in their democracy by making lower-class citizens eligible for public offices formerly closed to them and introducing state pay for officerholders, including the widely held jury duty. Poor citizens could now afford to hold public office.

A large body of city magistrates, usually chosen by lot without regard to class, ran the government on a daily basis. Ten officials known as generals were responsible for military and civil affairs. Generals could be reelected, enabling individual leaders to play an important political role. Pericles, for example, was elected to the generalship fifteen times after 451 B.C.E.

Under Pericles, Athens became the leading center of Greek culture. The Persians had destroyed much of the city during the Persian Wars, but Pericles used the treasury money of the Delian League to launch a massive rebuilding program. New temples and statues soon proclaimed the greatness of Athens. Art, architecture, and philosophy flourished, and Pericles broadly boasted that Athens had become the "school of Greece." But the achievements of Athens alarmed the other Greek states, especially Sparta, and soon all Greece was confronted with a new war.

The Great Peloponnesian War and the Decline of the Greek States

During the forty years after the defeat of the Persians, the Greek world came to be divided into two major camps: Sparta and its supporters and the Athenian maritime empire. Sparta and its allies feared the growing Athenian empire. Then, too, Athens and Sparta had built two very different kinds of societies, and neither was able to tolerate the other's system. A series of disputes finally led to the outbreak of war in 431 B.C.E.

At the beginning of the war, both sides believed they had winning strategies. The Athenians planned to remain behind the protective walls of Athens; the overseas empire and the navy would keep them supplied. Pericles knew that the Spartans and their allies could beat the Athenians in open battles, which was the chief aim of the Spartan strategy. The Spartans and their allies attacked Athens, hoping that the Athenians would send out their army to fight beyond the walls. But Pericles was convinced that Athens was secure behind its walls and stayed put.

In the second year of the war, however, plague devastated the crowded city of Athens and wiped out possibly one-third of the population. Pericles himself died the following year (429 B.C.E.), a severe loss to Athens. Despite the decimation of the plague, the Athenians fought on in

a struggle that dragged on for another twenty-seven years. A crushing blow came in 405 B.C.E., when the Athenian fleet was destroyed at Aegospotami on the Hellespont. Athens was besieged and surrendered in 404 B.C.E., its walls torn down, its navy disbanded, and its empire destroyed. The war was finally over.

The Great Peloponnesian War weakened the major Greek states and led to new alliances among them. The next seventy years of Greek history are a sorry tale of efforts by Sparta, Athens, and Thebes, a new Greek power, to dominate Greek affairs. In continuing their petty wars, the Greeks remained oblivious to the growing power of Macedonia to their north and demonstrated convincingly that the genius of the Greeks did not lie in politics. Culture, however, was quite a different story.

The Culture of Classical Greece

The classical age was a period of remarkable intellectual and cultural growth throughout the Greek world, and Periclean Athens was the most important center of classical Greek culture.

THE WRITING OF HISTORY

History as we know it, as a systematic analysis of past events, was introduced to the Western world by the Greeks. Herodotus (c. 484–c. 425 B.C.E.) wrote *History of the Persian Wars*, a work commonly regarded as the first real history in Western civilization. The central theme of Herodotus' work is the conflict between the Greeks and the Persians, which he viewed as a struggle between Greek freedom and Persian despotism. Herodotus traveled extensively and questioned many people for his information. He was a master storyteller and sometimes included fanciful material, but he was also capable of exhibiting a critical attitude toward the materials he used.

Thucydides (c. 460–c. 400 B.C.E.) was by far the better historian, widely acknowledged as the greatest historian of the ancient world. Thucydides was an Athenian and a participant in the Peloponnesian War. A defeat in battle led the Athenian assembly to send him into exile, which gave him the opportunity to continue to write his *History of the Peloponnesian War*.

Unlike Herodotus, Thucydides was not concerned with underlying divine forces or gods as explanatory causal factors in history. He saw war and politics in purely rational terms, as the activities of human beings. He examined the causes of the Peloponnesian War in a clear and objective fashion, placing much emphasis on accuracy and the precision of his facts. Thucydides also provided remarkable insight into the human condition. He believed that political situations recur in similar fashion and that the study of history is of great value in understanding the present.

GREEK DRAMA

Like history, drama as we know it in Western culture was invented by the Greeks. Plays were presented in outdoor theaters as part of religious festivals. The form of Greek plays remained rather stable. Three male actors who wore masks acted all the parts, and a chorus, also male, played the role of groups of people or served as narrators. Action was very limited because the emphasis was on the story and its meaning.

The first Greek dramas were tragedies, plays based on the suffering of a hero and usually ending in disaster. Aeschylus (525–456 B.C.E.) is the first tragedian whose plays are known to us. As was customary in Greek tragedy, his plots are simple, and the entire drama focuses on a single tragic event and its meaning. Greek tragedies were sometimes presented in a trilogy (a set of three plays) built around a common theme. The only complete trilogy we possess, called the *Oresteia,* was composed by Aeschylus. The theme of this trilogy is derived from Homer. Agamemnon, the king of Mycenae, returns a hero from the defeat of Troy. His wife, Clytemnestra, avenges the sacrificial death of her daughter Iphigenia by murdering Agamemnon, who had been responsible for Iphigenia's death. In the second play of the trilogy, Agamemnon's son Orestes avenges his father by killing his mother. Orestes is then pursued by the avenging Furies, who torment him for killing his mother. Evil acts breed evil acts, and suffering is the human lot, suggests Aeschylus. In the end, however, reason triumphs over the forces of evil.

Another great Athenian playwright was Sophocles (c. 496–406 B.C.E.), whose most famous play was *Oedipus the King.* In this play, the oracle of Apollo foretells how a man (Oedipus) will kill his own father and marry his mother. Despite all attempts at prevention, the tragic events occur. Although it appears that Oedipus suffered the fate determined by the gods, Oedipus also accepts that he himself as a free man must bear responsibility for his actions: "It was Apollo, friends, Apollo, that brought this bitter bitterness, my sorrows, to completion. But the hand that struck me was none but my own."[4]

The third outstanding Athenian tragedian, Euripides (c. 485–406 B.C.E.), moved beyond his predecessors by creating more realistic characters. His plots became more complex, taking greater interest in real-life situations. Euripides was controversial; he questioned traditional moral and religious values. For example, he was critical of the traditional view that war was glorious. He portrayed war as brutal and barbaric and expressed deep compassion for the women and children who suffered from it.

Greek tragedies dealt with universal themes still relevant to our day. They probed such problems as the nature of good and evil, the rights of the individual, the nature of divine forces, and the essence of human beings. Over and over, the tragic lesson was repeated: humans were free and yet could operate only within limitations imposed by the gods. To strive to do the best may not always gain a person success in human terms but is nevertheless worthy of the endeavor. Greek pride in human accomplishment and independence is real. As the chorus chanted in Sophocles' *Antigone:* "Is there anything more wonderful on earth, our marvelous planet, than the miracle of man?"[5]

THE ARTS: THE CLASSICAL IDEAL

The artistic standards established by the Greeks of the classical period have largely dominated the arts of the Western world. Greek art was concerned with expressing eternally true ideals. Its subject matter was basically the human being, expressed harmoniously as an object of great beauty. The classical style, based on the ideals of reason, moderation, symmetry, balance, and harmony in all things, was meant to civilize the emotions.

In architecture, the most important form was the temple, dedicated to a god or goddess. At the center of Greek temples were walled rooms that housed the statues of deities and treasuries where gifts to the gods and goddesses were safeguarded. These central rooms were surrounded by a screen of columns that make Greek temples open structures rather than closed ones. The columns were originally made of wood but were changed to marble in the fifth century B.C.E.

Some of the finest examples of Greek classical architecture were built in fifth-century Athens. The most famous building, regarded as the greatest example of the classical Greek temple, was the Parthenon, built between 447 and 432 B.C.E. Consecrated to Athena, the patron goddess of Athens, the Parthenon was also dedicated to the glory of the city-state and its inhabitants. The structure typifies the principles of classical architecture: calmness, clarity, and the avoidance of superfluous detail.

Greek sculpture also developed a classical style. Statues of the male nude, the favorite subject of Greek sculptors, exhibited relaxed attitudes; their faces were self-assured, their bodies flexible and smoothly muscled. Although the figures possessed natural features that made them lifelike, Greek sculptors sought to achieve not realism but a standard of ideal beauty. Polyclitus, a fifth-century sculptor, wrote a treatise (now lost) on proportion that he illustrated in a work known as the *Doryphoros.* His theory maintained that the use of ideal proportions, based on mathematical ratios found in nature, could produce an ideal human form, beautiful in its perfected and refined features. This search for ideal beauty was the dominant feature of classical sculpture.

THE GREEK LOVE OF WISDOM

In classical Greece, Athens became the foremost intellectual and artistic center. Its reputation is perhaps strongest of all in philosophy, a Greek term that means

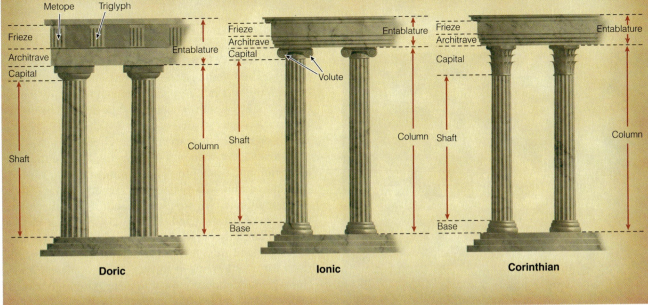

© Art Resource, NY

➤ **DORIC, IONIC, AND CORINTHIAN ORDERS.** The Greeks used different shapes and sizes in the columns of their temples. The Doric order, evolved first in the Dorian Peloponnesus, consisted of thick, fluted columns with simple capitals (the decorated tops of the columns). The Greeks considered the Doric order grave, dignified, and masculine. The Ionic style was first developed in western Asia Minor and consisted of slender columns with spiral-shaped capitals. The Greeks characterized the Ionic order as slender, elegant, and feminine in principle. Corinthian columns, with their more detailed capitals modeled after acanthus leaves, came later, near the end of the fifth century B.C.E.

"love of wisdom." Socrates, Plato, and Aristotle raised basic questions that have been debated for more than two thousand years; these are still largely the same philosophical questions we wrestle with today.

Socrates (469–399 B.C.E.) left no writings, but we know about him from his pupils. Socrates was a stonemason whose true love was philosophy. He taught a number of

➤ **THE PARTHENON.** The arts in classical Greece were designed to express the eternal ideals of reason, moderation, symmetry, balance, and harmony. In architecture, the most important form was the temple, and the classical example of this kind of architecture is the Parthenon, built between 447 and 432 B.C.E. Located on the Acropolis, the Parthenon was dedicated to Athena, the patron goddess of Athens, but it also served as a shining example of the power and wealth of the Athenian empire.

© Michael Holford, London

pupils, although not for pay, because he believed that the goal of education was solely to improve the individual. His approach, still known as the "Socratic method," uses a question-and-answer technique to lead pupils to see things for themselves using their own reason. Socrates believed that all knowledge was within each person; only critical examination was needed to call it forth. This was the real task of philosophy, since "the unexamined life is not worth living."

Socrates questioned authority, and this soon led him into trouble. Athens had had a tradition of free thought and inquiry, but defeat in the Peloponnesian War had created an environment intolerant of open debate and soul-searching. Socrates was accused and convicted of corrupting the youth of Athens by his teaching and sentenced to death.

One of Socrates' disciples was Plato (c. 429–347 B.C.E.), considered by many the greatest philosopher of Western civilization. Unlike his master Socrates, who wrote nothing, Plato wrote a great deal, often in the form of the dialogue. He was fascinated with the question of reality: How do we know what is real? According to Plato, a higher world of eternal, unchanging Ideas or Forms has always existed. To know these Forms is to know truth. These ideal Forms constitute reality and can be apprehended only by a trained mind, which, of course, is the goal of philosophy. The objects that we perceive with our senses are simply reflections of the ideal Forms. They are shadows; reality is in the Forms themselves.

Plato's ideas of government were set out in the dialogue titled *The Republic*. Based on his experience in Athens,

DORYPHOROS. This statue, known as the *Doryphoros*, or spear-carrier, is by the fifth-century B.C.E. sculptor Polyclitus, who believed it illustrated the ideal proportions of the human figure. Classical Greek sculpture moved away from the stiffness of earlier figures but retained the young male nude as its favorite subject matter. The statues became more lifelike, with relaxed poses and flexible, smoothly muscled bodies. The aim of sculpture, however, was not simply realism but rather the expression of ideal beauty.

group in Plato's ideal state were those who showed courage; they would be the warriors who protected society. All the rest made up the masses, essentially people driven not by wisdom or courage but by desire. They would be the producers of society—the artisans, tradespeople, and farmers. Contrary to common Greek custom, Plato also stressed that men and women should have the same education and equal access to all positions.

Plato established a school at Athens known as the Academy. One of his pupils, who studied there for twenty years, was Aristotle (384–322 B.C.E.). Aristotle did not accept Plato's theory of ideal Forms. Instead he believed that by examining individual objects, we can perceive their form and arrive at universal principles; but that these principles do not exist as a separate higher world of reality beyond material things but are a part of things themselves. Aristotle's interests, then, lay in analyzing and classifying things based on thorough research and investigation. His interests were wide-ranging, and he wrote treatises on an enormous number of subjects: ethics, logic, politics, poetry, astronomy, geology, biology, and physics.

Like Plato, Aristotle wished for an effective form of government that would rationally direct human affairs. Unlike Plato, he did not seek an ideal state but tried to find the best form of government by a rational examination of existing governments. For his *Politics*, Aristotle examined the constitutions of 158 states and identified three good forms of government: monarchy, aristocracy, and constitutional government. But based on his examination, he warned that monarchy can easily turn into tyranny, aristocracy into oligarchy, and constitutional government into radical democracy or anarchy. He favored constitutional government as the best form for most people.

Aristotle's philosophical and political ideas played an enormous role in the development of Western thought during the Middle Ages (see Chapter 12). So did his ideas on women. Aristotle maintained that women were biologically inferior to men: "A woman is, as it were, an infertile male. She is female in fact on account of a kind of inadequacy." Therefore, according to Aristotle, women must be subordinated to men, not only in the community but also in marriage: "The association between husband and wife is clearly an aristocracy. The man rules by virtue of merit, and in the sphere that is his by right; but he hands over to his wife such matters as are suitable for her."[7]

Greek Religion

Greek religion was intricately connected to every aspect of daily life; it was both social and practical. Public festivals, which originated from religious practices, served specific functions: boys were prepared to be warriors, girls to be mothers. Since religion was related to every aspect

Plato had come to distrust the workings of democracy. It was obvious to Plato that individuals could not attain an ethical life unless they lived in a just and rational state. Plato's search for the just state led him to construct an ideal state in which the population was divided into three basic groups. At the top was an upper class of philosopher-kings: "Unless . . . political power and philosophy meet together . . . there can be no rest from troubles . . . for states, nor yet, as I believe, for all mankind."[6] The second of life, citizens had to have a proper attitude toward the gods. Religion was a civic cult necessary for the well-being of the state. Temples dedicated to a god or goddess were the major buildings of Greek society.

The poetry of Homer gave an account of the gods that provided Greek religion with a definite structure. Over a period of time, most Greeks came to accept a common religion based on twelve chief gods and goddesses who were thought to live on Mount Olympus, the highest mountain in Greece. Among the twelve were Zeus, the chief god and father of many other gods; Athena, goddess of wisdom and crafts; Apollo, god of the sun and poetry; Aphrodite, goddess of love; and Poseidon, brother of Zeus and god of the seas and earthquakes. Although the twelve Olympian gods and goddesses were common to all Greeks, each *polis* usually singled out one of the twelve Olympians as the guardian deity of its community. Athena was the patron goddess of Athens, for example.

Greek religion did not have a body of doctrine, nor did it focus on morality. It gave little or no hope of life after death for most people. Because the Greeks wanted the gods to look favorably on their activities, ritual assumed enormous importance in Greek religion. Prayers were often combined with gifts to the gods based on the principle "I give so that you, the gods, will give in return." Ritual also meant sacrifices, whether of animals or agricultural products. Animal victims were burned on an altar in front of a temple or in front of a home.

Festivals also developed as a way to honor the gods and goddesses. Some of these (the Panhellenic celebrations) came to have international significance and were held at special locations, such as those dedicated to the worship of Zeus at Olympia or to Apollo at Delphi. Numerous events were held in honor of the gods at the great festivals, including athletic competitions to which all Greeks were invited. The first such games were held at the Olympic festival in 776 B.C.E. and then held every four years thereafter to honor Zeus. Initially, the Olympic contests consisted of foot races and wrestling, but later boxing, javelin throwing, and various other contests were added.

As another practical side of Greek religion, Greeks wanted to know the will of the gods. To do so, they made use of the oracle, a sacred shrine dedicated to a god or goddess who revealed the future. The most famous was the oracle of Apollo at Delphi, located on the side of Mount Parnassus, overlooking the Gulf of Corinth. At Delphi, a priestess, thought to be inspired by Apollo, listened to questions. Her responses were then interpreted by the priests and given in verse form to the person asking questions. Representatives of states and individuals traveled to Delphi to consult the oracle of Apollo. States might inquire whether they should undertake a military expedition. Responses were often enigmatic and at times even politically motivated. Croesus, the king of Lydia in Asia Minor who was known for his incredible wealth, sent messengers to the oracle at Delphi, asking "whether he shall go to war with the Persians." The oracle replied that if Croesus attacked the Persians, he would destroy a mighty empire. Overjoyed to hear these words, Croesus made war on the Persians but was crushed by his enemy. A mighty empire *was* destroyed—Croesus' own.

Daily Life in Classical Athens

The *polis* was, above all, a male community: only adult male citizens took part in public life. In Athens, this meant the exclusion of women, slaves, and foreign residents, or roughly 85 percent of the population of Attica. There were perhaps 150,000 citizens of Athens proper, of whom about 43,000 were adult males who exercised political power. Resident foreigners, who numbered about 35,000, received the protection of the laws but were also subject to some of the responsibilities of citizens, including military service and the funding of festivals. The remaining social group, the slaves, numbered around 100,000. Most slaves in Athens worked in the home as cooks and maids or worked in the fields. Some were owned by the state and worked on public construction projects.

The Athenian economy was largely based on agriculture and trade. Athenians grew grains, vegetables, and fruit for local consumption. Grapes and olives were cultivated for wine and olive oil, which were used locally and also exported. The Athenians raised sheep and goats for wool and dairy products. Because of the size of the population and the lack of abundant fertile land, Athens had to import 50 to 80 percent of its grain, a staple in the Athenian diet. Trade was thus very important to the Athenian economy.

The family was a central institution in ancient Athens. It was composed of husband, wife, and children, along with other dependent relatives and slaves who were part of the economic unit. The family's primary social function was to produce new citizens.

Women were citizens who could participate in most religious cults and festivals, but they were otherwise excluded from public life. They could not own property beyond personal items and always had a male guardian. An Athenian woman was expected to be a good wife. Her foremost obligation was to bear children, especially male children who would preserve the family line. Moreover, a wife was to take care of her family and her house, either doing the household work herself or supervising the slaves who did the actual work (see the box on p. 82).

Women were strictly controlled. Because they were married at the age of fourteen or fifteen, they were taught about their responsibilities early. Although many managed to learn to read and play musical instruments, they were not given any formal education. Unless attending funerals or festivals, women were expected to remain at home out of sight, and if they left the house, they were to be accompanied. A woman seen alone in public was assumed to be either poverty-stricken or not a citizen.

HOUSEHOLD MANAGEMENT
AND THE ROLE OF THE ATHENIAN WIFE

In the Athens of the fifth century B.C.E., a woman's place was in the home. She had two major responsibilities: the bearing and raising of children and the management of the household. In this dialogue on estate management, Xenophon relates the advice of an Attican gentleman on how to train a wife.

XENOPHON, OECONOMICUS

[Ischomachus addresses his new wife.] For it seems to me, dear, that the gods with great discernment have coupled together male and female, as they are called, chiefly in order that they may form a perfect partnership in mutual service. For, in the first place, that the various species of living creatures may not fail, they are joined in wedlock for the production of children. Secondly, offspring to support them in old age is provided by this union, to human beings, at any rate. Thirdly, human beings live not in the open air, like beasts, but obviously need shelter. Nevertheless, those who mean to win stores to fill the covered place, have need of someone to work at the open-air occupations; since plowing, sowing, planting, and grazing are all such open-air employments; and these supply the needful food. . . . For he made the man's body and mind more capable of enduring cold and heat, and journeys and campaigns; and therefore imposed on him the outdoor tasks. To the woman, since he has made her body less capable of such endurance, I take it that God has assigned the indoor tasks. And knowing that he had created in the woman and had imposed on her the nourishment of the infants, he meted out to her a larger portion of affection for newborn babes than to the man. . . . Now since we know, dear, what duties have been assigned to each of us by God, we must endeavor, each of us, to do the duties allotted to us as well as possible. . . .

Your duty will be to remain indoors and send out those servants whose work is outside, and superintend those who are to work indoors, and to receive the incomings, and distribute so much of them as must be spent, and watch over so much as is to be kept in store, and take care that the sum laid by for a year be not spent in a month. And when wool is brought to you, you must see that cloaks are made for those that want them. You must see too that the dry corn is in good condition for making food. One of the duties that fall to you, however, will perhaps seem rather thankless: you will have to see that any servant who is ill is cared for.

Male homosexuality was also a prominent feature of Athenian life. The Greek homosexual ideal was a relationship between a mature man and a young male. While the relationship was frequently physical, the Greeks also viewed it as educational. The older male (the "lover") won the love of his "beloved" through his value as a teacher and the devotion he demonstrated in training his charge. In a sense, this love relationship was seen as a way of initiating young males into the male world of political and military dominance. The Greeks did not feel that the coexistence of homosexual and heterosexual predilections created any special problems for individuals or their society.

THE RISE OF MACEDONIA AND THE CONQUESTS OF ALEXANDER

While the Greek city-states were caught up in fighting each other, a new and ultimately powerful kingdom to their north was emerging in its own right. To the Greeks, the Macedonians were little more than barbarians, a mostly rural folk organized into tribes rather than city-states. Not until the late fifth century B.C.E. did Macedonia emerge as a kingdom of any importance. But when Philip II (359–336 B.C.E.) came to the throne, he built an efficient army and turned Macedonia into the strongest power in the Greek world—one that was soon drawn into the conflicts among the Greeks.

The Athenians at last took notice of the new contender. Fear of Philip led them to ally with a number of other Greek states and confront the Macedonians at the Battle of Chaeronea, near Thebes, in 338 B.C.E. The Macedonian army crushed the Greeks, and Philip quickly gained control of all Greece, bringing an end to the freedom of the Greek city-states. He insisted that the Greek states form a league and then cooperate with him in a war against Persia. Before Philip could undertake his invasion of Asia, however, he was assassinated, leaving the task to his son Alexander.

Alexander the Great

Alexander was only twenty when he became king of Macedonia. He was in many ways prepared to rule by his father, who had taken Alexander along on military campaigns and had given him control of the cavalry at Chaeronea. After his father's assassination, Alexander moved quickly to assert his authority, securing the Macedonian frontiers and quashing a rebellion in Greece. He then turned to his father's dream, the invasion of the Persian Empire.

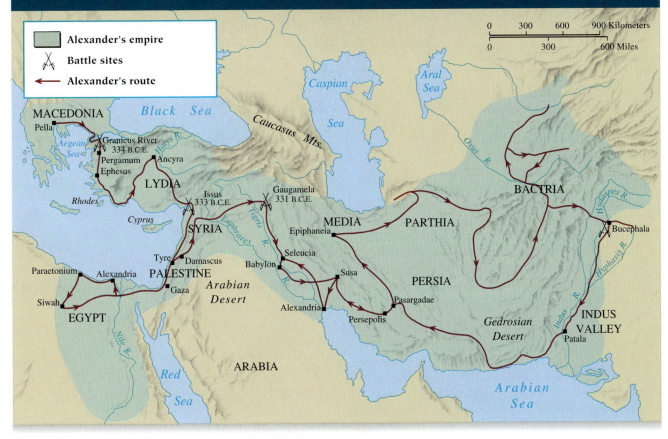

MAP 4.2   The Conquests of Alexander the Great.   In just twelve years, Alexander the Great conquered vast territories. Dominating lands from west of the Nile to east of the Indus, he brought the Persian Empire, Egypt, and much of the Middle East under his control and laid the foundations for the Hellenistic world. ➤ *Approximately how far did he and his troops travel during those twelve years?*

There is no doubt that Alexander was taking a chance in attacking Persia, which was still a strong state. In the spring of 334 B.C.E., Alexander entered Asia Minor with an army of some 37,000 men. About half were Macedonians, the rest Greeks and other allies. The cavalry, which would play an important role as a striking force, numbered about 5,000. By the following spring, the entire western half of Asia Minor was in Alexander's hands (see Map 4.2). Meanwhile, the Persian king, Darius III, mobilized his forces to stop Alexander's army, but the subsequent Battle of Issus resulted in yet another Macedonian success. Alexander then turned south, and by the winter of 332, Syria, Palestine, and Egypt were under his control.

In 331 B.C.E., Alexander turned east and fought a decisive battle with the Persians at Gaugamela, not far from Babylon. After his victory, Alexander entered Babylon and then proceeded to the Persian capitals at Susa and Persepolis, where he acquired the Persian treasuries and took possession of vast quantities of gold and silver. By 330, Alexander was again on the march, pursuing Darius. After Darius was killed by one of his own men, Alexander took

the title and office of the Great King of the Persians. Over the next three years, he moved east and northeast, as far as modern Pakistan. By summer 327 B.C.E., he had entered India, which at that time was divided into a number of warring states. In 326 B.C.E., Alexander and his armies arrived in the plains of northwestern India. At the Battle of the Hydaspes River, Alexander won a brutally fought battle (see the box on p. 84). When Alexander made clear his determination to march east to conquer more of India, his soldiers, weary of campaigning year after year, mutinied and refused to go further. Alexander returned to Babylon, where he planned more campaigns. But in June 323 B.C.E., weakened by wounds, fever, and probably excessive alcohol, he died at the age of thirty-two.

The Legacy of Alexander

Alexander is one of the most puzzling great figures in history. Historians relying on the same sources give vastly different pictures of him. Some portray him as an idealistic visionary and others as a ruthless Machiavellian. How did Alexander the Great view himself? We know that he

ALEXANDER MEETS AN INDIAN KING

In his campaigns in India, Alexander fought a number of difficult battles. At the Battle of the Hydaspes River, he faced a strong opponent in the Indian king Porus. After defeating Porus, Alexander treated him with respect, according to Arrian, Alexander's ancient biographer.

ARRIAN, *THE CAMPAIGNS OF ALEXANDER*

Throughout the action Porus had proved himself a man indeed, not only as a commander but as a soldier of the truest courage. When he saw his cavalry cut to pieces, most of his infantry dead, and his elephants killed or roaming riderless and bewildered about the field, his behaviour was very different from that of the Persian King Darius: unlike Darius, he did not lead the scramble to save his own skin, but so long as a single unit of his men held together, fought bravely on. It was only when he was himself wounded that he turned the elephant on which he rode and began to withdraw. . . . Alexander, anxious to save the life of this great soldier, sent . . . [to him] an Indian named Meroes, a man he had been told had long been Porus's friend. Porus listened to Meroes's message, stopped his elephant, and dismounted; he was much distressed by thirst, so when he had revived himself by drinking, he told Meroes to conduct him with all speed to Alexander.

Alexander, informed of his approach, rode out to meet him. . . .When they met, he reined in his horse, and looked at his adversary with admiration: he was a magnificent figure of a man, over seven feet high and of great personal beauty; his bearing had lost none of its pride; his air was of one brave man meeting another, of a king in the presence of a king, with whom he had fought honourably for his kingdom.

Alexander was the first to speak. "What," he said, "do you wish that I should do with you?" "Treat me as a king ought," Porus is said to have replied. "For my part," said Alexander, pleased by his answer, "your request shall be granted. But is there not something you would wish for yourself? Ask it." "Everything," said Porus, "is contained in this one request."

The dignity of these words gave Alexander even more pleasure, and he restored to Porus his sovereignty over his subjects, adding to his realm other territory of even greater extent. Thus he did indeed use a brave man as a king ought, and from that time forward found him in every way a loyal friend.

sought to imitate Achilles, the warrior-hero of Homer's *Iliad*. Alexander kept a copy of the *Iliad*—and a dagger—under his pillow. He also claimed to be descended from Heracles, the Greek hero who came to be worshiped as a god.

Regardless of his ideals, motives, or views about himself, one fact stands out: Alexander ushered in a new age, the Hellenistic era. The word *Hellenistic* is derived from a Greek word meaning "to imitate Greeks." It is an appropriate term to describe an age that saw the extension of the Greek language and ideas to the non-Greek world of the Middle East. Alexander's destruction of the Persian monarchy opened up opportunities for Greek engineers, intellectuals, merchants, administrators, and soldiers. Those who followed Alexander and his successors participated in a new political unity based on the principle of monarchy. His vision of empire no doubt inspired the Romans, who were the ultimate heirs of Alexander's political legacy.

But Alexander also left a cultural legacy. As a result of his conquests, Greek language, art, architecture, and literature spread throughout the Middle East. The urban centers of the Hellenistic age, many founded by Alexander and his successors, became springboards for the diffusion of Greek culture. While the Greeks spread their culture in the East, they were also inevitably influenced by Eastern ways. Thus Alexander's legacy was one of the earmarks of the Hellenistic era: the clash and fusion of different cultures.

THE HELLENISTIC KINGDOMS

The united empire that Alexander assembled through his conquests crumbled soon after his death. All too soon, the most important Macedonian generals were engaged in a struggle for power, and by 300 B.C.E., four Hellenistic kingdoms had emerged as the successors to Alexander (see Map 4.3): Macedonia under the Antigonid dynasty, Syria and the East under the Seleucids, the Attalid kingdom of Pergamum in western Asia Minor, and Egypt under the Ptolemies. All were eventually conquered by the Romans.

Alexander had planned to fuse Macedonians, Greeks, and easterners in his new empire by using Persians as officials and encouraging his soldiers to marry native women. The Hellenistic monarchs who succeeded him, however, relied only on Greeks and Macedonians to form the new ruling class. Even those easterners who did advance to important government posts had learned Greek, the language in which all government business was transacted. The Greek ruling class was determined to maintain its privileged position.

Alexander had founded numerous new cities and military settlements, and Hellenistic kings did likewise. The new population centers varied considerably in size and importance. Military settlements, intended to maintain order, might consist of only a few hundred men. The new independent cities attracted thousands of people. One of these new cities,

THE RISE OF MACEDONIA AND THE CONQUESTS OF ALEXANDER

Reign of Philip II	359–336 B.C.E.
Battle of Chaeronea; conquest of Greece	338 B.C.E.
Reign of Alexander the Great	336–323 B.C.E.
Alexander's invasion of Asia	334 B.C.E.
Battle of Gaugamela	331 B.C.E.
Fall of Persepolis	330 B.C.E.
Alexander's entry into India	327 B.C.E.
Death of Alexander	323 B.C.E.

Alexandria in Egypt, had become the largest city in the Mediterranean region by the first century B.C.E.

Hellenistic rulers encouraged a massive spread of Greek colonists to the Middle East. Greeks and Macedonians provided not only recruits for the army but also a pool of civilian administrators and workers who contributed to economic development. Even architects, engineers, dramatists, and actors were in demand in the new Greek cities. Many Greeks and Macedonians were quick to see the advantages of moving to the new urban centers and gladly sought their fortunes in the Middle East. The Greek cities of the Hellenistic era became the chief agents in the spread of Greek culture in the Middle East—as far east, in fact, as modern Afghanistan and India.

CULTURE IN THE HELLENISTIC WORLD

Although the Hellenistic kingdoms encompassed vast territories and many diverse peoples, the Greeks provided a sense of unity as a result of the diffusion of Greek culture throughout the Hellenistic world. The Hellenistic era was a period of considerable cultural accomplishment in many areas, especially science and philosophy. These achievements occurred throughout the Hellenistic world, although certain centers, especially the great city of Alexandria, stood out. Alexandria became home to poets, writers, philosophers, and scientists—scholars of all kinds. The library there became the largest in ancient times, with more than 500,000 scrolls.

MAP 4.3   The Hellenistic Kingdoms.   Alexander died unexpectedly at the age of thirty-two and did not designate a successor. Upon his death, his generals struggled for power, eventually creating four monarchies that spread Hellenistic culture and fostered trade and economic development. ➤ *Which kingdom encompassed most of the old Persian Empire?*

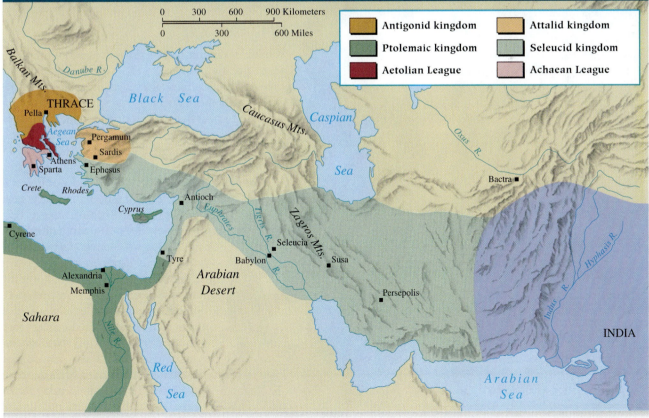

The founding of new cities and the rebuilding of old ones provided numerous opportunities for Greek architects and sculptors. The Hellenistic monarchs were particularly eager to spend their money to beautify and adorn the cities within their states. The buildings of the Greek homeland—gymnasiums, baths, theaters, and temples—lined the streets of these cities.

Both Hellenistic kings and rich citizens patronized sculptors. Hellenistic sculptors traveled throughout this world, attracted by the material rewards offered by wealthy patrons. These sculptors maintained the technical skill of the classical period, but they moved away from the idealism of fifth-century classicism to a more emotional and realistic art, which is evident in numerous statues of old women, drunks, and little children at play.

❖❖❖❖❖❖❖❖❖❖❖❖❖❖❖❖❖❖❖❖❖❖❖❖

Hellenistic Sculpture and a Greek-Style Buddha

Greek architects and sculptors were highly valued throughout the Hellenistic world. Shown at left is a terra-cotta statuette of a draped young woman, made as a tomb offering near Thebes, probably around 300 B.C.E. The incursion of Alexander into the western part of India resulted in some Greek cultural influence on India, and Hellenistic artistic styles affected some Indian artists. Especially noticeable, as shown at right in this stone sculpture of Buddha wearing a Greek-style toga, was the Buddhist Gandharan style, which in the first century B.C.E. combined Indian and Hellenistic artistic traditions.

The Art Archive/Kanellopoulos Museum Athens/Dagli Orti.

© Borromeo/Art Resource, NY

A Golden Age of Science

The Hellenistic era witnessed a more conscious separation of science from philosophy. In classical Greece, what we would call the physical and life sciences had been divisions of philosophical inquiry. Nevertheless, the Greeks, by the time of Aristotle, had already established an important principle of scientific investigation—empirical research or systematic observation as the basis for generalization. In the Hellenistic age, the sciences tended to be studied in their own right.

By far the most famous of the scientists of the Hellenistic period was Archimedes (287–212 B.C.E.). Archimedes was especially important for his work on the geometry of spheres and cylinders and for establishing the value of the mathematical constant pi. Archimedes was also a practical inventor. He may have devised the so-called Archimedean screw used to pump water out of mines and to lift irrigation water. During the Roman siege of his native city of Syracuse, he constructed a number of devices to thwart the attackers. Archimedes' accomplishments inspired a wealth of semilegendary stories. Supposedly, he discovered specific gravity by observing the water he displaced in his bath and became so excited by his realization that he jumped out of the water and ran home naked, shouting, "Eureka!" ("I have found it"). He is said to have emphasized the importance of levers by proclaiming to the king of Syracuse: "Give me a lever and a place to stand on, and I will move the earth." The king was so impressed that he encouraged Archimedes to lower his sights and build defensive weapons instead.

Philosophy

While Alexandria became the renowned cultural center of the Hellenistic world, Athens remained the prime center for philosophy. Even after Alexander the Great, the home of Socrates, Plato, and Aristotle continued to attract the most illustrious philosophers from the Greek world, who chose to establish their schools there. New schools of philosophical thought reinforced Athens's reputation as a philosophical center. Epicurus (341–270 B.C.E.), the founder of Epicureanism, established a school in Athens near the end of the fourth century B.C.E. Epicurus believed that human beings were free to follow self-interest as a basic motivating force. Happiness was the goal of life, and the means to achieve it was the pursuit of pleasure, the only true good. But the pursuit of pleasure was not meant in a physical, hedonistic sense (which is what our word *epicurean* has come to mean). Pleasure was not equated with satisfying one's desire in an active, gluttonous fashion but rather with freedom from emotional turmoil and worry—the freedom that came from a mind at rest. To achieve this kind of pleasure, one had to free oneself from public affairs and politics. But this was not a renunciation of all social life, for to Epicurus, a life could be complete only when it was based on friendship. Epicurus' own life in Athens was an embodiment of his teachings. He and his friends created their own private community where they could pursue their ideal of true happiness.

Another school of thought was Stoicism, which became the most popular philosophy of the Hellenistic world and later flourished in the Roman Empire as well. It was the product of a teacher named Zeno (335–263 B.C.E.), who came to Athens and began to teach in a public colonnade known as the Painted Portico (the *Stoa Poikile*—hence Stoicism). Like Epicureanism, Stoicism was concerned with how individuals find happiness. But Stoics took a radically different approach to the problem. To them, happiness, the supreme good, could be found only by living in harmony with the divine will, by which people gained inner peace. Life's problems could not disturb these people, and they could bear whatever life offered (hence our word *stoic*). Unlike Epicureans, Stoics did not believe in the need to separate oneself from the world and politics. Public service was regarded as noble, and the real Stoic was a good citizen and could even be a good government official. In fact, the Roman emperor Marcus Aurelius was a noted Stoic philosopher.

Both Epicureanism and Stoicism focused primarily on human happiness, and their popularity would suggest a fundamental change in the Greek lifestyle. In the classical Greek world, the happiness of individuals and the meaning of life were closely associated with the life of the *polis*. One found fulfillment in the community. In the Hellenistic kingdoms, the sense that one could find fulfillment through life in the *polis* had weakened. People sought new philosophies that offered personal happiness, and in the cosmopolitan world of the Hellenistic states, with their mixtures of peoples, a new openness to thoughts of universality could also emerge. For some people, Stoicism embodied this larger sense of community.

CONCLUSION

Unlike the great centralized empires of the Persians and the Chinese, ancient Greece consisted of a large number of small, independent city-states, most of which had only a few thousand inhabitants. Yet these ancient Greeks created a civilization that was the fountainhead of Western culture. Socrates, Plato, and Aristotle established the foundations of Western philosophy. Western literary forms are largely derived from Greek poetry and drama. Greek notions of harmony, proportion, and beauty have remained the touchstones for all subsequent Western art. A rational method of inquiry, so important to modern science, was conceived in ancient Greece. Many political terms are Greek in origin, and so are concepts of the rights and duties of citizenship, especially as they were conceived in Athens, the world's first great democracy. During their classical period, the Greeks raised and debated the fundamental questions about the purpose of human existence, the structure of human society, and the nature of the universe that have concerned thinkers ever since.

Yet despite all these achievements, there remains an element of tragedy about Greek civilization. Notwithstanding their brilliant accomplishments, the Greeks were unable to rise above the divisions and rivalries that caused them to fight each other and undermine their own civilization. Of course, their cultural contributions have outlived their political struggles. And the Hellenistic era, which emerged after the Greek city-states had lost their independence, made possible the spread of Greek ideas to larger areas.

During the Hellenistic period, Greek culture extended throughout the Middle East and made an impact wherever it was carried. Although the Hellenistic world achieved a degree of political stability, by the late third century B.C.E. signs of decline were beginning to multiply. Few Greeks realized the danger to the Hellenistic world of the growing power of Rome. But soon the Romans would inherit Alexander's empire and Greek culture, and we now turn to them to try to understand what made them such successful conquerors.

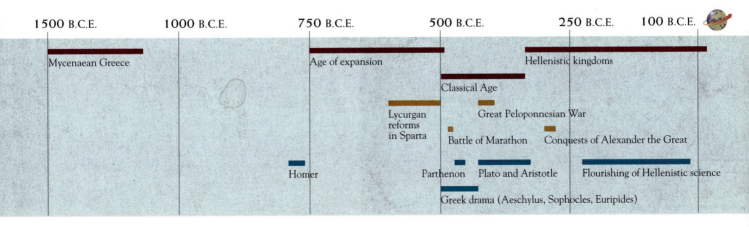

1500 B.C.E.   1000 B.C.E.   750 B.C.E.   500 B.C.E.   250 B.C.E.   100 B.C.E.

Mycenaean Greece

Age of expansion

Hellenistic kingdoms

Classical Age

Lycurgan reforms in Sparta

Great Peloponnesian War

Battle of Marathon

Conquests of Alexander the Great

Homer

Parthenon   Plato and Aristotle   Flourishing of Hellenistic science

Greek drama (Aeschylus, Sophocles, Euripides)

CHAPTER NOTES

1. Xenophon, *Symposium,* trans. O. J. Todd (Harmondsworth, England, 1946), 3:5.
2. Quoted in Thomas R. Martin, *Ancient Greece* (New Haven, Conn., 1996), p. 62.
3. The words from Plutarch are quoted in E. Fantham et al., *Women in the Classsical World* (New York, 1994), p. 64.
4. Sophocles, *Oedipus the King,* trans. David Grene (Chicago, 1959), pp. 68–69.
5. Sophocles, *Antigone,* trans. Don Taylor (London, 1986), p. 146.
6. Plato, *The Republic,* trans. F. M. Cornford (New York, 1945), pp. 178–179.
7. Quotations from Aristotle are in Sue Blundell, *Women in Ancient Greece* (London, 1995), pp. 106, 186.

SUGGESTED READING

A standard one-volume reference work for Greek history is J. B. Bury and R. Meiggs, *A History of Greece to the Death of Alexander the Great,* 4th ed. (New York, 1975). Other good general introductions to Greek history include T. R. Martin, *Ancient Greece* (New Haven, Conn., 1996); P. Cartledge, *The Cambridge Illustrated History of Ancient Greece* (Cambridge, 1998); and W. Donlan et. al., *Ancient Greece: A Political, Social, and Cultural History* (New York, 1998).

Early Greek history is examined in O. Murray, *Early Greece,* 2d ed. (Cambridge, Mass., 1993), and J. L. Fitton, *The Discovery of the Greek Bronze Age* (Cambridge, 1995).

A good general work on the Greek age of expansion is A. M. Snodgrass, *Archaic Greece* (London, 1980). On colonization, see J. Boardman, *The Greeks Overseas,* rev. ed. (Baltimore, 1980). On tyranny, see J. F. McFlew, *Tyranny and Political Culture in Ancient Greece* (Ithaca, N.Y., 1993). Sparta is examined in W. Forrest, *A History of Sparta, 950–121 B.C.,* 2d ed. (London, 1980), and P. Cartledge, *Spartan Reflections* (Berkeley, Calif., 2001). On early Athens, see the still valuable A. Jones, *Athenian Democracy* (London, 1957), and R. Osborne, *Demos* (Oxford, 1985). The Persian Wars are examined in P. Green, *The Greco-Persian Wars* (Berkeley, Calif., 1996).

A general history of classical Greece can be found in S. Hornblower, *The Greek World, 479–323 B.C.* (London, 1983). Important works on Athens include C. W. Fornara and L. J. Samons II, *Athens from Cleisthenes to Pericles* (Berkeley, Calif., 1991); D. Stockton, *The Classical Athenian Democracy* (Oxford, 1990); and D. Kagan, *Pericles of Athens and the Birth of Democracy* (New York, 1991). The best way to examine the Great Peloponnesian War is to read the work of Thucydides, *History of the Peloponnesian War,* trans. R. Warner (Harmondsworth, England, 1954).

A good brief study of Greek art is J. Boardman, *Greek Art* (London, 1985). On sculpture, see A. Stewart, *Greek Sculpture: An Exploration* (New Haven, Conn., 1990). A basic survey of architecture is H. W. Lawrence, *Greek Architecture* (Harmondsworth, England, 1983). On Greek drama, see the general work by J. De Romilly, *A Short History of Greek Literature* (Chicago, 1985). On Greek philosophy, a detailed study is available in W. K. C. Guthrie, *A History of Greek Philosophy,* 6 vols. (Cambridge, 1962–1981). On Greek religion, see J. N. Bremmer, *Greek Religion* (Oxford, 1994).

On the family and women in ancient Greece, see C. B. Patterson, *The Family in Greek History* (New York, 1998); E. Fantham et al., *Women in the Classical World* (New York, 1994); and S. Blundell, *Women in Ancient Greece* (Cambridge, Mass., 1995). On homosexuality, see E. Cantarella, *Bisexuality in the Ancient World* (New Haven, Conn., 1992).

The best general surveys of the Hellenistic era are F. W. Walbank, *The Hellenistic World* (London, 1981), and G. Shipley, *The Greek World After Alexander, 323–30 B.C.* (New York, 2000). For a good introduction to the early history of Macedonia, see E. N. Borza, *In the Shadow of Olympus: The Emergence of Macedon* (Princeton, N.J., 1990). There are considerable differences of opinion on Alexander the Great. The best biographies include R. L. Fox, *Alexander the Great* (London, 1973); J. R. Hamilton, *Alexander the Great* (London, 1973); and P. Green, *Alexander of Macedon* (Berkeley, Calif., 1991).

The best general survey of Hellenistic philosophy is A. A. Long, *Hellenistic Philosophy: Stoics, Epicureans, Skeptics,* 2d ed. (London, 1986). A superb work on Hellenistic science is G. E. R. Lloyd, *Greek Science After Aristotle* (London, 1973). On the entry of Rome into the Hellenistic world, see the basic work by E. S. Gruen, *The Hellenistic World and the Coming of Rome,* 2 vols. (Berkeley, Calif., 1984).

INFOTRAC COLLEGE EDITION

Visit the source collections at **infotrac.thomsonlearning.com** and use the Search function with the following key terms.

Alexander the Great	Peloponnesian War
Aristotle	Plato
Greece history	Socrates
Greek mythology	

WORLD HISTORY RESOURCES

Visit the *Essential World History* Companion Web Site for resources specific to this textbook:

http://history.wadsworth.com/duikeressentials02/

The CD in the back of this book and the World History Resource Center at **http://history.wadsworth.com/world/** offer a variety of tools to help you succeed in this course, including access to quizzes; images; documents; interactive simulations, maps, and timelines; movie explorations; and a wealth of other sources.

THE WORLD OF THE ROMANS

FOCUS QUESTIONS

- What policies and institutions help explain the Romans' success in conquering and then ruling their empire?
- What problems did Rome face during the last century of the Republic, and how were they ultimately resolved?
- What were the chief features of the Roman Empire at its height in the second century C.E., and what happened to bring it near collapse in the next century?
- What characteristics of Christianity enabled it to grow and ultimately to triumph?
- ➤ In what ways were the Roman Empire and the Chinese Han Empire similar, and in what ways were they different?

Although the Assyrians, Persians, and Indians under the Mauryan dynasty had created empires, they were neither as large nor as well controlled as the Han and Roman Empires that flourished at the beginning of the first millennium C.E. They were the largest political entities the world had yet seen (the Han Empire extended from Central Asia to the Pacific Ocean; the Roman Empire encompassed the lands around the Mediterranean, parts of the Middle East, and western and central Europe).

Roman history is the remarkable story of how a group of Latin-speaking people, who established a small community on a plain called Latium in central Italy, went on to conquer all of Italy and then the entire Mediterranean world. Why were the Romans able to do this? Scholars do not really know all the answers, but the Romans had their own explanation. Early Roman history is filled with legendary tales of the heroes who made Rome great. One of the best known is the story of Horatius at the bridge. Threatened by attack from the neighboring Etruscans, Roman farmers abandoned their fields and moved into the city, where they would be protected by the walls. One weak point in the Roman defenses, however, was a wooden bridge over the Tiber River. Horatius was on guard at the bridge when a sudden assault by the Etruscans caused many Roman troops to throw down their weapons and flee. Horatius urged them to make a stand at the bridge; when they hesitated, he told them to destroy the bridge behind him while he held the Etruscans back. Astonished at the sight of a single defender, the confused Etruscans threw their spears at Horatius, who caught them on his shield and barred the way. By the time the Etruscans were about to overwhelm the lone defender, the Roman soldiers had brought down the bridge. Horatius then dived fully armed into the water and swam safely to the other side through a hail of arrows. Rome had been saved by the courageous act of a Roman who knew his duty and was determined to carry it out. Courage, duty, determination—these qualities would serve the many Romans who believed that it was their divine mission to rule nations and peoples. As one writer proclaimed: "By heaven's will, my Rome shall be capital of the world." •

THE EMERGENCE OF ROME

Italy is a peninsula extending about 750 miles from north to south (see Map 5.1). It is not very wide, however, averaging about 120 miles across. The Apennines form a ridge down the middle of Italy that divides west from east. Nevertheless, Italy has some fairly large fertile plains that are ideal for farming. Most important are the Po River valley

MAP 5.1 Ancient Italy. Ancient Italy was home to several groups. Both the Etruscans in the north and the Greeks in the south had a major influence on the development of Rome. ➤ *Once Rome conquered the Etruscans, Sabines, Samnites, and other local groups, what aspects of the Italian peninsula helped make it defensible against outside enemies?*

in the north; the plain of Latium, on which Rome was located; and Campania to the south of Latium. To the east of the Italian peninsula is the Adriatic Sea and to the west the Tyrrhenian Sea, bounded by the large islands of Corsica and Sardinia. Sicily lies just west of the "toe" of the boot-shaped Italian peninsula.

Geography had an impact on Roman history. Although the Apennines bisected Italy, they were less rugged than the mountain ranges of Greece and did not divide the peninsula into many small isolated communities. Italy also possessed considerably more productive agricultural land than Greece, enabling it to support a large population. Rome's location was favorable from a geographical point of view. Located 18 miles inland on the Tiber River, Rome had access to the sea and yet was far enough inland to be safe from pirates. Built on seven hills, it was easily defended. Because the Tiber could be readily forded at Rome, the settlement became a natural crossing point for north-south traffic in western Italy. All in all, Rome had a good central location in Italy from which to expand.

Moreover, the Italian peninsula juts into the Mediterranean, making Italy an important crossroads between the western and eastern ends of the sea. Once Rome had unified Italy, involvement in Mediterranean affairs was natural. And after the Romans had conquered their Mediterranean empire, governing it was made easier by Italy's central location.

Early Rome

According to Roman legend, Rome was founded by twin brothers, Romulus and Remus, in 753 B.C.E., and archaeologists have found that by the eighth century B.C.E., a village of huts had been built on the tops of Rome's hills. The early Romans, basically a pastoral people, spoke Latin, which, like Greek, belongs to the Indo-European family of languages (see Table 1.2 in Chapter 1). The Roman historical tradition also maintained that early Rome (753–509 B.C.E.) had been under the control of seven kings and that two of the last three had been Etruscans, people who lived north of Rome in Etruria. Historians believe that the king list may have some historical accuracy. What is certain is that Rome did fall under the influence of the Etruscans for about a hundred years during the period of the kings and

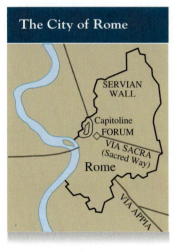

The City of Rome

SERVIAN WALL

Capitoline FORUM
VIA SACRA
(Sacred Way)

Rome

VIA APPIA

that by the beginning of the sixth century, under Etruscan influence, Rome began to emerge as a city. The Etruscans were responsible for an outstanding building program. They constructed the first roadbed of the chief street through Rome, the Sacred Way, before 575 B.C.E. and oversaw the development of temples, markets, shops, streets, and houses. By 509 B.C.E., supposedly when the monarchy was overthrown and a republican form of government was established, a new Rome had emerged, essentially a result of the fusion of Etruscan and native Roman elements.

THE ROMAN REPUBLIC

The transition from monarchy to a republican government was not easy. Rome felt threatened by enemies from every direction and, in the process of meeting these threats, embarked on a military course that led to the conquest of the entire Italian peninsula.

The Roman Conquest of Italy

At the beginning of the Republic, Rome was surrounded by enemies, including the Latin communities on the plain of Latium. If we are to believe Livy, one of the chief ancient sources for the history of the early Roman Repub-

lic, Rome was engaged in almost continuous warfare with these enemies for the next hundred years. In his account, Livy provided a detailed narrative of Roman efforts. Many of his stories were legendary in character; writing in the first century B.C.E., he used his stories to teach Romans the moral values and virtues that had made Rome great. These included tenacity, duty, courage, and especially discipline (see the box on p. 92).

By 340 B.C.E., Rome had crushed the Latin states in Latium. During the next fifty years, the Romans waged a fierce struggle with the Samnites, a hill people from the central Apennines, some of whom had settled in Campania, south of Rome. Rome was again victorious. The conquest of the Samnites gave Rome considerable control over a large part of Italy and also brought it into direct contact with the Greek communities. The Greeks had arrived on the Italian peninsula in large numbers during the age of Greek colonization (750–550 B.C.E.; see Chapter 4). Initially, the Greeks settled in southern Italy and then crept around the coast and up the peninsula. They also occupied the eastern two-thirds of Sicily. The Greeks had much influence on Rome. They cultivated olives and grapes, passed on their alphabet, and provided artistic and cultural models through their sculpture, architecture, and literature. Soon after their conquest of the Samnites, the Romans were involved in hostilities with some of these Greek cities and by 267 B.C.E. had completed their conquest of southern Italy. After crushing the remaining Etruscan states to the north in 264 B.C.E., Rome had conquered most of Italy.

To rule Italy, the Romans devised the Roman Confederation. Under this system, Rome allowed some peoples—especially the Latins—to have full Roman citizenship. Most of the remaining communities were made allies. They remained free to run their own local affairs but were required to provide soldiers for Rome. Moreover, the Romans made it clear that loyal allies could improve their status and even have hope of becoming Roman citizens. The Romans had found a way to give conquered peoples a stake in Rome's success.

In the course of their expansion throughout Italy, the Romans had pursued consistent policies that help explain their success. The Romans were superb diplomats who excelled in making the correct diplomatic decisions. In addition, the Romans were not only good soldiers but also persistent ones. The loss of an army or a fleet did not cause them to quit but spurred them on to build new armies and new fleets. Finally, the Romans had a practical sense of strategy. As they conquered, the Romans established colonies—fortified towns—at strategic locations throughout Italy. By building roads to these settlements and connecting them, the Romans created an impressive communications and military network that enabled them to rule effectively and efficiently. By insisting on military service from the allies in the Roman Confederation, Rome essentially mobilized the entire military manpower of all Italy for its wars.

CINCINNATUS SAVES ROME:
A ROMAN MORALITY TALE

There is perhaps no better account of how the virtues of duty and simplicity enabled good Roman citizens to prevail during the travails of the fifth century B.C.E. than Livy's account of Cincinnatus. He was chosen dictator, supposedly in 457 B.C.E., to defend Rome against the attacks of the Aequi. The position of dictator was a temporary expedient used only in emergencies; the consuls would resign, and a leader with unlimited power would be appointed for a limited period (usually six months). In this account, Cincinnatus did his duty, defeated the Aequi, and returned to his simple farm in just fifteen days.

LIVY, *THE EARLY HISTORY OF ROME*

The city was thrown into a state of turmoil, and the general alarm was as great as if Rome herself were surrounded. Nautius was sent for, but it was quickly decided that he was not the man to inspire full confidence; the situation evidently called for a dictator, and, with no dissentient voice, Lucius Quinctius Cincinnatus was named for the post.

Now I would solicit the particular attention of those numerous people who imagine that money is everything in this world, and that rank and ability are inseparable from wealth: let them observe that Cincinnatus, the one man in whom Rome reposed all her hope of survival, was at that moment working a little three-acre farm . . . west of the Tiber, just opposite the spot where the shipyards are today. A mission from the city found him at work on his land—digging a ditch, maybe, or plowing. Greetings were exchanged, and he was asked—with a prayer for divine blessing on himself and his country—to put on his toga and hear the Senate's instructions. This naturally surprised him, and, asking if all were well, he told his wife Racilia to run to their cottage and fetch his toga. The toga was brought, and wiping the grimy sweat from his hands and face he put it on; at once the envoys from the city saluted him, with congratulations, as Dictator, invited him to enter Rome, and informed him of the terrible danger of Municius' army. A state vessel was waiting for him on the river, and on the city bank he was welcomed by his three sons who had come to meet him, then by other kinsmen and friends, and finally by nearly the whole body of senators. Closely attended by all these people and preceded by his lictors he was then escorted to his residence through streets lined with great crowds of common folk who, be it said, were by no means so pleased to see the new Dictator, as they thought his power excessive and dreaded the way in which he was likely to use it.

[Cincinnatus proceeds to raise an army, march out, and defeat the Aequi.]

In Rome the Senate was convened by Quintus Fabius the City Prefect, and a decree was passed inviting Cincinnatus to enter in triumph with his troops. The chariot he rode in was preceded by the enemy commanders and the military standards, and followed by his army loaded with its spoils. . . . Cincinnatus finally resigned after holding office for fifteen days, having originally accepted it for a period of six months.

The Roman State

The chief executive officers of the Roman Republic were the consuls and praetors. Two consuls, chosen annually, administered the government and led the Roman army into battle. In 366 B.C.E., the office of praetor was created. The praetor was in charge of civil law (law as it applied to Roman citizens), but he could also lead armies and govern Rome when the consuls were away from the city. As the Romans' territory expanded, they added another praetor to judge cases in which one or both people were noncitizens. The Roman state also had a number of administrative officials who handled specialized duties, such as the administration of financial affairs and supervision of the public games of Rome.

The Roman senate came to hold an especially important position in the Roman Republic. The senate or council of elders was a select group of about three hundred men who served for life. The senate could only advise the magistrates, but this advice was not taken lightly and by the third century B.C.E. had virtually the force of law.

The Roman Republic had a number of popular assemblies. By far the most important was the centuriate assembly, essentially the Roman army functioning in its political role. Organized by classes based on wealth, it was structured in such a way that the wealthiest citizens always had a majority. This assembly elected the chief magistrates and passed laws. Another assembly, the council of the plebs, came into being as a result of the struggle of the orders.

THE STRUGGLE OF THE ORDERS: SOCIAL DIVISIONS IN THE ROMAN REPUBLIC

This struggle arose as a result of the division of early Rome into two groups, the patricians and the plebeians. The patricians were great landowners, who constituted an aristocratic governing class. Only they could be consuls, magistrates, and senators. Through their patronage of large numbers of dependent clients, they could control the centuriate assembly and many other facets of Roman life. The plebeians constituted the considerably larger group of nonpatrician large landowners, less wealthy landholders, artisans, merchants, and small farmers. Although they, too, were citizens, they did not have the same rights as the patricians. Both patricians and plebeians could vote, but only the patricians could be elected

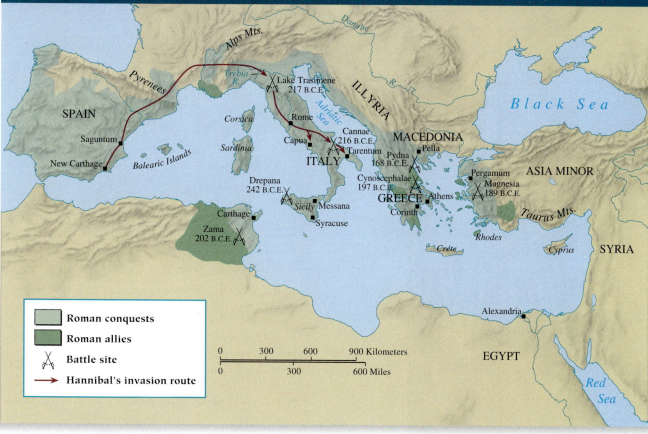

MAP 5.2 Roman Conquests in the Mediterranean, 264–133 B.C.E. Beginning with the Punic Wars, Rome expanded its holdings, first in the western Mediterranean at the expense of Carthage and later in Greece and western Asia Minor. ➤ *What aspects of Mediterranean geography, combined with the territorial holdings and aspirations of Rome and the Carthaginians, made the Punic Wars more likely?*

to governmental offices. Both had the right to make legal contracts and marriages, but intermarriage between patricians and plebeians was forbidden. At the beginning of the fifth century B.C.E., the plebeians began a struggle to seek both political and social equality with the patricians.

The struggle between the patricians and plebeians dragged on for hundreds of years, but it led to success for the plebeians. A popular assembly for plebeians only, called the council of the plebs, was created in 471 B.C.E., and new officials, known as tribunes of the plebs, were given the power to protect plebeians. A new law allowed marriages between patricians and plebeians, and in the fourth century B.C.E., plebeians were permitted to become consuls. Finally, in 287 B.C.E., the council of the plebs received the right to pass laws for all Romans.

The struggle between the patricians and plebeians, then, had a significant impact on the development of the Roman state. Theoretically, by 287 B.C.E., all Roman citizens were equal under the law, and all could strive for political office. But in reality, as a result of the right of intermarriage, a select number of patrician and plebeian families formed a new senatorial aristocracy that came to

dominate the political offices. The Roman Republic had not become a democracy.

The Roman Conquest of the Mediterranean (264–133 B.C.E.)

After their conquest of the Italian peninsula, the Romans found themselves face to face with a formidable Mediterranean power—Carthage. Founded around 800 B.C.E. on the coast of North Africa by Phoenicians, Carthage had flourished and assembled an enormous empire in the western Mediterranean. By the third century B.C.E., the Carthaginian Empire included the coast of northern Africa, southern Spain, Sardinia, Corsica, and western Sicily. With its monopoly of western Mediterranean trade, Carthage was the largest and richest state in the area. The presence of Carthaginians in Sicily, so close to the Italian coast, made the Romans apprehensive. In 264 B.C.E., the two powers began a lengthy struggle for control of the western Mediterranean (see Map 5.2).

In the First Punic War (the Latin word for Phoenician was *Punicus*), the Romans resolved to conquer Sicily.

British Museum, Photo © Michael Holford, London

⤜ **A ROMAN LEGIONARY.** The Roman legionaries, famed for their courage and tenacity, made possible Roman domination of the Mediterranean Sea. This tablet, dating from the first half of the third century B.C.E., shows a Roman legionary during the period of the Republic.

The Romans—a land power—realized that they could not win the war without a navy and promptly developed a substantial naval fleet. After a long struggle, a Roman fleet defeated the Carthaginian navy off Sicily, and the war quickly came to an end. In 241 B.C.E., Carthage gave up all rights to Sicily and had to pay an indemnity. Sicily became the first Roman province.

Carthage vowed revenge and extended its domains in Spain to compensate for the territory lost to Rome. When the Romans encouraged one of Carthage's Spanish allies to revolt against Carthage, Hannibal, the greatest of the Carthaginian generals, struck back, beginning the Second Punic War (218–201 B.C.E.).

This time, the Carthaginian strategy aimed at bringing the war home to the Romans and defeating them in their own backyard. Hannibal crossed the Alps with an army of thirty to forty thousand men and six thousand horses and elephants and inflicted a series of defeats on the Romans. At Cannae in 216 B.C.E., the Romans lost an army of almost forty thousand men. Rome seemed on the brink of disaster but refused to give up, raised yet another army, and began to reconquer some of the Italian cities that had gone over to Hannibal's side. They also sent troops to Spain, and by 206 B.C.E., Spain was freed of the Carthaginians.

The Romans then took the war directly to Carthage, forcing the Carthaginians to recall Hannibal from Italy. At the Battle of Zama in 202 B.C.E., the Romans crushed Hannibal's forces, and the war was over. By the peace treaty signed in 201 B.C.E., Carthage lost Spain, which became another Roman province. Rome had become the dominant power in the western Mediterranean.

Fifty years later, the Romans fought their third and final struggle with Carthage. For years, a number of Romans had called for the complete destruction of Carthage. The conservative politician Cato, for example, ended every speech he made to the senate with the words, "And I think Carthage must be destroyed." In 146 B.C.E., it was destroyed. For ten days, Roman soldiers burned and pulled down all of the city's buildings. The inhabitants—fifty thousand men, women, and children—were sold into slavery. The territory of Carthage became a Roman province called Africa.

During its struggle with Carthage, Rome also became involved in problems with the Hellenistic states in the eastern Mediterranean, and after the defeat of Carthage, Rome turned its attention there. In 148 B.C.E., Macedonia was made a Roman province, and two years later, Greece was placed under the control of the Roman governor of Macedonia. In 133 B.C.E., the king of Pergamum deeded his kingdom to Rome, giving Rome its first province in Asia. Rome was now master of the Mediterranean Sea.

THE DECLINE AND FALL OF THE ROMAN REPUBLIC (133–31 B.C.E.)

By the middle of the second century B.C.E., Roman domination of the Mediterranean Sea was complete. Yet the process of creating an empire had weakened the internal stability of Rome, leading to a series of crises that plagued the empire for the next hundred years.

Growing Unrest and a New Role for the Roman Army

By the second century B.C.E., the senate had become the effective governing body of the Roman state. It comprised three hundred men, drawn primarily from the landed aristocracy; they remained senators for life and held the chief magistracies of the Republic. The senate directed the wars of the third and second centuries and took control of both foreign and domestic policy, including financial affairs.

Of course, these aristocrats formed only a tiny minority of the Roman people. The backbone of the Roman state had traditionally been the small farmers. But over time, many small farmers had found themselves unable to compete with large, wealthy landowners and had lost their lands. By taking over state-owned land and by buying out small peasant owners, these landed aristocrats had amassed large estates (called *latifundia*) that used slave labor. Thus the rise of the *latifundia* contributed to a decline in the number of small citizen farmers. Since the latter group traditionally provided the foundation of the Roman army, the number of men available for military service declined. Moreover, many of these small farmers drifted to the cities, especially Rome, forming a large class of landless poor.

Some aristocrats tried to remedy this growing economic and social crisis. Two brothers, Tiberius and Gaius Gracchus, came to believe that the underlying cause of Rome's problems was the decline of the small farmer. To help the landless poor, they bypassed the senate by having the council of the plebs pass land-reform bills that called for the government to reclaim public land held by large landowners and to distribute it to landless Romans. Many senators, themselves large landowners whose estates included large areas of public land, were furious. A group of senators took the law into their own hands and murdered Tiberius in 133 B.C.E. Twelve years later, Gaius suf-

fered the same fate. The attempts of the Gracchus brothers to bring reforms had opened the door to further violence. Changes in the Roman army soon brought even worse problems.

In the closing years of the second century B.C.E., a Roman general named Marius began to recruit his armies in a new way. The Roman army had traditionally been a conscript army of small farmers who were landholders. Marius recruited volunteers from both the urban and rural poor who possessed no property. These volunteers swore an oath of loyalty to the general, not the senate, and thus inaugurated a professional-type army that might no longer be subject to the state. Moreover, to recruit these men, a general would promise them land, forcing generals to play politics in order to get laws passed that would provide the land for their veterans. Marius had created a new system of military recruitment that placed much power in the hands of the individual generals.

The Collapse of the Republic

The first century B.C.E. was characterized by two important features: the jostling for power of a number of powerful individuals and the civil wars generated by their conflicts. Three individuals came to hold enormous military and political power—Crassus, Pompey, and Julius Caesar. Crassus was known as the richest man in Rome and led a successful military command against a major slave rebellion. Pompey had returned from a successful military command in Spain in 71 B.C.E. and had been hailed as a military hero. Julius Caesar also had a military command in Spain. In 60 B.C.E., Caesar joined with Crassus and Pompey to form a coalition that historians call the First Triumvirate (*triumvirate* means "three-man rule").

The combined wealth and power of these three men was enormous, enabling them to dominate the political scene and achieve their basic aims: Pompey received a command in Spain, Crassus a command in Syria, and Caesar a special military command in Gaul (modern France). When Crassus was killed in battle in 53 B.C.E., it left two powerful men with armies in direct competition. During his time in Gaul, Caesar had conquered all of Gaul and gained fame, wealth, and military experience as well as an army of seasoned veterans who were loyal to him. When leading senators endorsed Pompey as the less harmful to their cause and voted for Caesar to lay down his command and return as a private citizen to Rome, Caesar refused. He chose to keep his army and moved into Italy illegally by crossing the Rubicon, the river that formed the southern boundary of his province. ("Crossing the Rubicon" is a phrase used today to mean being unable to turn back.) Caesar marched on Rome and defeated the forces of Pompey and his allies, leaving Caesar in complete control of the Roman government.

Caesar was officially made dictator in 47 B.C.E. and three years later was named dictator for life. Realizing the

THE ASSASSINATION OF JULIUS CAESAR

*W*hen it quickly became apparent that Julius Caesar had no intention of restoring the Republic as they conceived it, about sixty senators, many of them his friends or pardoned enemies, formed a conspiracy to assassinate the dictator. It was led by Gaius Cassius and Marcus Brutus, who naively imagined that this act would restore the traditional Republic. The conspirators set the Ides of March (March 15), 44 B.C.E., as the date for the assassination. Caesar was in the midst of preparations for a campaign in the eastern part of the empire. Although informed that there was a plot against his life, he chose to disregard the warning. This account of Caesar's death is taken from his biography by the Greek writer Plutarch.

PLUTARCH, *LIFE OF CAESAR*

Fate, however, is to all appearance more unavoidable than unexpected. For many strange prodigies and apparitions are said to have been observed shortly before this event. . . . One finds it also related by many that a soothsayer bade him [Caesar] prepare for some great danger on the Ides of March. When this day was come, Caesar, as he went to the senate, met this soothsayer, and said to him by way of raillery, "The Ides of March are come," who answered him calmly, "Yes, they are come, but they are not past. . . ."

All these things might happen by chance. But the place which was destined for the scene of this murder, in which the senate met that day, was the same in which Pompey's statue stood, and was one of the edifices which Pompey had raised and dedicated with his theater to the use of the public, plainly showing that there was something of a supernatural influence which guided the action and ordered it to that particular place. Cassius, just before the act, is said to have looked toward Pompey's statue, and silently implored his assistance. . . . When Caesar entered, the senate stood up to show their respect to him, and of Brutus' confederates, some came about his chair and stood behind it, others met him, pretending to add their petitions to those of Tillius Cimber, in behalf of his brother, who was in exile; and they followed him with their joint applications till he came to his seat.

When he was sat down, he refused to comply with their requests, and upon their urging him further began to reproach them severely for their importunities, when Tillius, laying hold of his robe with both his hands, pulled it down from his neck, which was the signal for the assault. Casca gave him the first cut in the neck, which was not mortal nor dangerous, as coming from one who at the beginning of such a bold action was probably very much disturbed; Caesar immediately turned about, and laid his hand upon the dagger and kept hold of it. And both of them at the same time cried out, he that received the blow, in Latin, "Vile Casca, what does this mean?" and he that gave it, in Greek to his brother, "Brother, help!" Upon this first onset, those who were not privy to the design were astonished, and their horror and amazement at what they saw were so great that they dared not fly nor assist Caesar, nor so much as speak a word. But those who came prepared for the business enclosed him on every side, with their naked daggers in their hands. Which way soever he turned he met with blows, and saw their swords leveled at his face and eyes, and was encompassed like a wild beast in the toils on every side. For it had been agreed they should each of them make a thrust at him, and flesh themselves with his blood: for which reason Brutus also gave him one stab in the groin. Some say that he fought and resisted all the rest, shifting his body to avoid the blows, and calling out for help, but that when he saw Brutus' sword drawn, he covered his face with his robe and submitted, letting himself fall, whether it were by chance or that he was pushed in that direction by his murderers, at the foot of the pedestal on which Pompey's statue stood, and which was thus wetted with his blood. So that Pompey himself seemed to have presided, as it were, over the revenge done upon his adversary, who lay here at his feet, and breathed out his soul through his multitude of wounds, for they say he received three-and-twenty. And the conspirators themselves were many of them wounded by each other, whilst they all leveled their blows at the same person.

---

need for reforms, he gave land to the poor and increased the senate to nine hundred members. By filling it with many of his supporters and increasing the number, he effectively weakened the power of the senate. He also reformed the calendar by introducing the Egyptian solar year of 365 days (with later changes in 1582, it became the basis of our own calendar). Caesar planned much more in the way of building projects and military adventures in the East, but in 44 B.C.E., a group of leading senators assassinated him (see the box above).

Within a few years after Caesar's death, two men had divided the Roman world between them—Octavian, Caesar's heir and grandnephew, taking the western portion and Antony, Caesar's ally and assistant, the eastern half. But the empire of the Romans, large as it was, was still too small for two masters, and Octavian and Antony eventually came into conflict. Antony allied himself closely with the Egyptian queen Cleopatra VII. At the Battle of Actium in Greece in 31 B.C.E., Octavian's forces smashed the army and navy of Antony and Cleopatra, who both fled to Egypt, where they committed suicide a year later. Octavian, at the age of thirty-two, stood supreme over the Roman world. The civil wars were ended. And so was the Republic.

THE DECLINE AND FALL OF THE REPUBLIC

Reforms of Tiberius Gracchus	133 B.C.E.
Reforms of Gaius Gracchus	123–121 B.C.E.
Marius: consecutive consulships	104–100 B.C.E.
First Triumvirate (Caesar, Pompey, Crassus)	60 B.C.E.
Caesar as dictator	47–44 B.C.E.
Octavian's defeat of Antony at Actium	31 B.C.E.

AUGUSTUS AND THE EARLY EMPIRE (31 B.C.E.–180 C.E.)

In 27 B.C.E., Octavian proclaimed the "restoration of the Republic." He understood that only traditional republican forms would satisfy the senatorial aristocracy. At the same time, Octavian was aware that the Republic could not be fully restored. Although he gave some power to the senate, Octavian in reality became the first Roman emperor. The senate awarded him the title of Augustus, "the revered one"—a fitting title in view of his power that had previously been reserved for gods. Augustus proved highly popular, but the chief source of his power was his continuing control of the army. The senate gave Augustus the title of *imperator* (our word *emperor*), or commander in chief.

Augustus maintained a standing army of twenty-eight legions or about 150,000 men (a legion was a military unit of about 5,000 troops). Only Roman citizens could be legionaries, while subject peoples could serve as auxiliary forces, which numbered around 130,000 under Augustus. Augustus was also responsible for setting up a praetorian guard of roughly 9,000 men who had the important task of guarding the emperor. Eventually, the praetorian guard would play a weighty role in making and deposing emperors.

While claiming to have restored the Republic, Augustus inaugurated a new system for governing the provinces. Under the Republic, the senate had appointed the governors of the provinces. Now certain provinces were given to the emperor, who assigned deputies known as legates to govern them. The senate continued to name the governors of the remaining provinces, but the authority of Augustus enabled him to overrule the senatorial governors and establish a uniform imperial policy.

Augustus also stabilized the frontiers of the Roman Empire. He conquered the central and maritime Alps and then expanded Roman control of the Balkan peninsula up to the Danube River. His attempt to conquer Germany failed when three Roman legions were massacred in 9 C.E. by a coalition of German tribes. His defeats in Germany taught Augustus that Rome's power was not unlimited and also devastated him; for months, he would beat his head on a door, shouting "Varus [the defeated Roman general in Germany], give me back my legions!"

Augustus died in 14 C.E. after dominating the Roman world for forty-five years. He had created a new order while placating the old by restoring traditional values, a fitting combination for a leader whose favorite maxim was "make haste slowly." By the time of his death, his new order was so well established that few agitated for an alternative. Indeed, as the Roman historian Tacitus pointed out, "Practically no one had ever seen truly Republican government. . . . Political equality was a thing of the past; all eyes watched for imperial commands."[1] The Republic was now only a memory and, given its last century of warfare, an unpleasant one at that. The new order was here to stay.

The Early Empire (14–180)

There was no serious opposition to Augustus' choice of his stepson Tiberius as his successor. By his actions, Augustus established the Julio-Claudian dynasty; the next four successors of Augustus were related to the family of Augustus or that of his wife, Livia.

Several major tendencies emerged during the reigns of the Julio-Claudians (14–68 C.E.). In general, more and more of the responsibilities that Augustus had given to the senate tended to be taken over by the emperors, who also instituted an imperial bureaucracy, staffed by talented freedmen, to run the government on a daily basis. As the Julio-Claudian successors of Augustus acted more openly as real rulers rather than "first citizens of the state," the opportunity for arbitrary and corrupt acts also increased. Nero (54–68), for example, freely eliminated people he wanted out of the way, including his own mother, whose murder he arranged. Without troops, the senators proved unable to oppose these excesses, but the Roman legions finally revolted. Abandoned by his guards, Nero chose to commit suicide by stabbing himself in the throat after uttering his final words, "What an artist the world is losing in me!"

THE FIVE GOOD EMPERORS (96–180)

At the beginning of the second century, five emperors created a period of peace and prosperity (known as the Pax Romana, the "Roman peace") that lasted almost one hundred years. These five "good emperors" treated the ruling classes with respect, cooperated with the senate, ended arbitrary executions, maintained peace in the empire, and supported generally beneficial domestic policies. Though absolute monarchs, they were known for their tolerance and diplomacy. By adopting capable men as their sons and successors, the first four of these emperors reduced the chances of succession problems.

Roman Empire at the end
of Augustus' reign, 14

Roman Empire at the end
of Trajan's reign, 117

Under the five good emperors, the powers of the emperor continued to expand at the expense of the senate. Increasingly, imperial officials appointed and directed by the emperor took over the running of the government. The good emperors also extended the scope of imperial administration to areas previously untouched by the imperial government. Trajan (98–117) implemented an alimentary program that provided state funds to assist poor parents in the raising and education of their children. The good emperors were widely praised for their extensive building programs. Trajan and Hadrian (117–138) were especially active in constructing public works—aqueducts, bridges, roads, and harbor facilities—throughout the empire.

FRONTIERS AND THE PROVINCES

Although Trajan extended Roman rule into Dacia (modern Romania), Mesopotamia, and the Sinai peninsula (see Map 5.3), his successors recognized that the empire was

overextended and pursued a policy of retrenchment. Hadrian withdrew Roman forces from much of Mesopotamia. Although he retained Dacia and Arabia, he went on the defensive in his frontier policy by reinforcing the fortifications along a line connecting the Rhine and Danube Rivers and building a defensive wall 80 miles long across northern Britain to keep the Scots out of Roman Britain. By the end of the second century, the Roman forces were established in permanent bases behind the frontiers.

At its height in the second century C.E., the Roman Empire was one of the greatest states the world had seen. It covered about 3.5 million square miles and had a population, like that of Han China, estimated at more than fifty million. While the emperors and the imperial administration provided a degree of unity, considerable leeway was given to local customs, and the privileges of Roman citizenship were extended to many people throughout the empire. In 212, the emperor Caracalla completed the process by giving Roman citizenship to every free inhabitant of the empire. Latin was the language of the western part of the empire, while Greek was used in the east. Roman culture spread to all parts of the empire and freely mixed with Greek culture, creating what has been called Greco-Roman civilization.

The administration and cultural life of the Roman Empire depended greatly on cities and towns. A provincial governor's staff was not large, so it was left to local city officials to act as Roman agents in carrying out many government functions, especially those related to taxes. Most towns and cities were not large by modern standards. The largest was Rome, but there were also some large cities in the east: Alexandria in Egypt numbered more than 300,000 inhabitants, and Ephesus in Asia Minor had 200,000. In the west, cities were usually small, with only a few thousand inhabitants. Cities were important in the spread of Roman culture, law, and the Latin language, and they resembled one another with their temples, markets, amphitheaters, and other public buildings.

ECONOMIC AND SOCIAL CONDITIONS

The Early Roman Empire was a period of considerable prosperity, with internal peace leading to unprecedented levels of trade. Merchants from all over the empire came to the chief Italian ports of Puteoli on the Bay of Naples and Ostia at the mouth of the Tiber. Trade, however, extended beyond the Roman boundaries and included even silk goods from China. The importation of large quantities of grain to feed the populace of Rome and an incredible quantity of luxury items for the wealthy upper classes in the west led to a steady drain of gold and silver coins from Italy to the eastern part of the empire.

Despite the profits from trade and commerce, agriculture remained the chief pursuit of most people and the underlying basis of Roman prosperity. Although the large *latifundia* still dominated agriculture, especially in southern and central Italy, small peasant farms continued to flourish, particularly in Etruria and the Po valley. Although large estates concentrating on sheep and cattle raising used slaves, the lands of some *latifundia* were also worked by free tenant farmers who paid rent in labor, produce, or sometimes cash.

The prosperity of the Roman world left an enormous gulf between rich and poor. The development of towns and cities, so important to the creation of any civilization, is based largely on the agricultural surpluses of the countryside. In ancient times, the margin of surplus produced by each farmer was relatively small. Therefore, the upper classes and urban populations had to be supported by the labor of a large number of agricultural producers, who never found it easy to produce much more than for themselves. In lean years, when there were no surpluses, the townspeople often took what they wanted, leaving little for the peasants.

One of the noticeable characteristics of Roman culture and society is the impact of the Greeks. Greek ambassadors, merchants, and artists traveled to Rome and spread Greek thought and practices. After their conquest of the Hellenistic kingdoms, Roman generals shipped Greek manuscripts and artworks back to Rome. Multitudes of educated Greek slaves labored in Roman households. Rich Romans hired Greek tutors and sent their sons to Athens to study. As the Roman poet Horace said, "Captive Greece took captive her rude conqueror." Greek thought captivated the less sophisticated Roman minds, and the Romans became willing transmitters of Greek culture.

Roman Literature

The Latin literature that first emerged in the third century B.C.E. was strongly influenced by Greek models. It was not until the last century of the Republic that the Romans began to produce a new poetry in which Latin poets were able to use various Greek forms to express their own feelings about people, social and political life, and love. The finest example of this can be seen in the work of Catullus (c. 87–54 B.C.E.), the finest lyric poet Rome produced and one of the greatest in world literature.

Catullus became a master at adapting and refining Greek forms of poetry to express his emotions. He wrote a variety of poems on, among other things, political figures, social customs, the use of language, the death of his brother, and the travails of love. Catullus became infatuated with Clodia, the promiscuous wife of a provincial governor, and addressed a number of poems to her (he called her Lesbia), describing his passionate love and hatred for her (Clodia had many other lovers besides Catullus):

> You used to say that you wished to know only Catullus,
> Lesbia, and wouldn't take even Jove before me!
> I didn't regard you just as my mistress then: I cherished you
> as a father does his sons or his daughters' husbands.
> Now that I know you, I burn for you even more fiercely,
> though I regard you as almost utterly worthless.
> How can that be, you ask? It's because such cruelty forces
> lust to assume the shrunken place of affection.[2]

The ability of Catullus to express in simple fashion his intense feelings and curiosity about himself and his world had a noticeable impact on later Latin poets.

The high point of Latin literature was reached in the age of Augustus, often called the golden age of Latin literature. The most distinguished poet of the Augustan age was Virgil (70–19 B.C.E.). The son of a small landholder in northern Italy, he welcomed the rule of Augustus and wrote his greatest work in the emperor's honor. Virgil's masterpiece was the *Aeneid,* an epic poem clearly intended to rival the work of Homer. The connection between Troy and Rome is made in the poem when Aeneas, a hero of Troy, survives the destruction of that city and eventually settles in Latium—establishing a link between Roman civilization and Greek history. Aeneas is portrayed as the ideal Roman—his virtues are duty, piety, and faithfulness. Virgil's overall purpose was to show that Aeneas had fulfilled his mission to establish the Romans in Italy and thereby start Rome on its divine mission to rule the world.

> Let others fashion from bronze more lifelike, breathing
>   images—
> For so they shall—and evoke living faces from marble;
> Others excel as orators, others track with their instruments
> The planets circling in heaven and predict when stars will
>   appear.
> But, Romans, never forget that government is your medium!
> Be this your art:—to practise men in the habit of peace,
> Generosity to the conquered, and firmness against
>   aggressors.[3]

As Virgil expressed it, ruling was Rome's gift.

Roman Art

The Romans were also dependent on the Greeks for artistic inspiration. The Romans developed a taste for Greek statues, which they placed not only in public buildings but also in their private houses. The Romans' own portrait sculpture was characterized by an intense realism that included even unpleasant physical details. Wall paintings and frescoes in the homes of the rich realistically depicted landscapes, portraits, and scenes from mythological stories.

The Romans excelled in architecture, a highly practical art. Although they continued to adapt Greek styles and made use of colonnades and rectangular structures, the Romans were also innovative. They made considerable use of curvilinear forms: the arch, vault, and dome. The Romans were also the first people in antiquity to use concrete on a massive scale. They constructed huge buildings—public baths, such as those of Caracalla, and amphitheaters capable of seating fifty thousand spectators. These large buildings were made possible by Roman engineering skills. These same skills were put to use in constructing roads, aqueducts, and bridges: a network of 50,000 miles of roads linked all parts of the empire, and in Rome, almost a dozen aqueducts kept the population of one million supplied with water.

Roman Law

One of Rome's chief gifts to the Mediterranean world of its day and to later generations was its system of law. Rome's first code of laws was the Twelve Tables of 450 B.C.E., but that was designed for a simple farming society and proved inadequate for later needs. So from the Twelve Tables the Romans developed a system of civil law that applied to all Roman citizens. As Rome expanded, problems arose between citizens and noncitizens and also among noncitizen residents of the empire. Although some of the rules of civil law could be used in these cases, special rules were often needed. Legislation to meet those needs gave rise to a body of law known as the law of nations, defined as the part of the law that applied to both Romans and foreigners. Under the influence of Stoicism, the Romans came to identify their law of nations with natural law, or universal law based on reason. This enabled them to establish standards of justice that applied to all people.

These standards of justice included principles that we would immediately recognize. A person was regarded as innocent until proved otherwise. People accused of wrongdoing were allowed to defend themselves before a judge. A judge, in turn, was expected to weigh evidence carefully before arriving at a decision. These principles lived on long after the fall of the Roman Empire.

The Roman Family

At the heart of the Roman social structure stood the family, headed by the *paterfamilias*—the dominant male. The household also included the wife, sons with their wives and children, unmarried daughters, and slaves. Like the Greeks, Roman males believed that females needed male guardians. The *paterfamilias* exercised that authority; upon his death, sons or nearest male relatives assumed the role of guardians.

Fathers arranged the marriages of daughters. In the Republic, women married "with legal control" passing from father to husband. By the mid-first century B.C.E., the dominant practice had changed to "without legal control," which meant that married daughters officially remained within the father's legal power. Since the fathers of most married women were dead, not being in the "legal control" of a husband entailed independent property rights that forceful women could translate into considerable power within the household and outside it.

Some parents in upper-class families provided education for their daughters by hiring private tutors or sending them to primary schools. However, at the age when boys were entering secondary schools, girls were pushed into marriage. The legal minimum age for marriage was twelve, although fourteen was a more common age in practice (for males, the legal minimum age was fourteen, and most men married later). Although some Roman doctors warned that early pregnancies could be dangerous for young girls, early marriages persisted because women died at a relatively young age. A good example is Tullia, Cicero's beloved daughter. She was married at sixteen, widowed at twenty-two, remarried one year later, divorced at twenty-eight, remarried at twenty-nine, and divorced at thirty-three. She died at thirty-four, which was not unusually young for women in Roman society.

⟫ **A ROMAN LADY.** Roman women, especially those of the upper class, developed comparatively more freedom than women in classical Athens despite the persistent male belief that women required guardianship. This mural decoration was found in the remains of a villa destroyed by the eruption of Mount Vesuvius.

By the second century C.E., significant changes were occurring in the Roman family. The *paterfamilias* no longer had absolute authority over his children; he could no longer sell his children into slavery or have them put to death. Moroever, the husband's absolute authority over his wife also disappeared, and by the late second century, women were no longer required to have guardians.

Upper-class Roman women in the Early Empire had considerable freedom and independence. They had acquired the right to own, inherit, and dispose of property. Unlike the Greeks, Roman wives were not segregated from males in the home but were appreciated as enjoyable company and were at the center of household social life. Upper-class women could attend races, the theater, and events in the amphitheater, although in the latter two places they were forced to sit in separate female sections. Women could not participate in politics, but the Early Empire saw a number of important women who influenced politics through their husbands, including Livia, the wife of Augustus; Agrippina, the mother of Nero; and Plotina, the wife of Trajan.

Slaves and Their Masters

Although slavery was a common institution throughout the ancient world, no people possessed more slaves or relied so much on slave labor as the Romans eventually did. Slaves were used in many ways in Roman society. The rich owned the most and the best. In the late Roman Republic, it became a badge of prestige to be attended by many slaves. Greek slaves were in much demand as tutors, musicians, doctors, and artists. Roman businessmen would employ them as shop assistants or craftspeople. Slaves were also used as farm laborers; in fact, huge gangs of slaves worked the large landed estates under pitiful conditions. Cato the Elder argued that it was cheaper to work them to death and then replace them than to treat them favorably. Many slaves of all nationalities were used as menial household workers, such as cooks, waiters, cleaners, and gardeners. Contractors used slave labor to build roads, aqueducts, and other public structures.

The treatment of Roman slaves varied. There are numerous instances of humane treatment by masters and situations where slaves even protected their owners from danger out of gratitude and esteem. Slaves were also subject to severe punishments, torture, abuse, and hard labor that drove some to run away, despite the stringent laws Romans had against aiding a runaway slave. Some slaves revolted against their owners and even murdered them, causing some Romans to live in unspoken fear of their slaves (see the box on p. 102).

Near the end of the second century B.C.E., large-scale slave revolts occurred in Sicily, where enormous gangs of slaves were subjected to horrible working conditions on large landed estates. Slaves were branded, beaten, fed little, worked in chains, and housed at night in underground prisons. It took three years (from 135 to 132 B.C.E.) to crush a revolt of seventy thousand slaves, and the great revolt on Sicily (104–101 B.C.E.) took a Roman army of seventeen thousand men to suppress. The most famous uprising on the Italian peninsula occurred in 73 B.C.E. Led by a gladiator named Spartacus, the revolt broke out in southern Italy and involved seventy thousand slaves. Spartacus managed to defeat several Roman armies before being trapped and killed in southern Italy in 71 B.C.E. Six thousand of his followers were crucified, the traditional form of execution for slaves.

Imperial Rome

At the center of the colossal Roman Empire was the ancient city of Rome. Truly a capital city, Rome had the largest population of any city in the empire, close to one million by the time of Augustus. Only Chang'an, the imperial capital of the Han Empire in China, had a comparable population during this time. For anyone with ambitions,

THE ROMAN FEAR OF SLAVES

The lowest stratum of the Roman population consisted of slaves. They were used extensively in households, at the court, as artisans in industrial enterprises, as business managers, and in numerous other ways. Although some historians have argued that slaves were treated more humanely during the Early Empire, these selections by the Roman historian Tacitus and the Roman statesman Pliny indicate that slaves still rebelled against their masters because of mistreatment. Many masters continued to live in fear of their slaves, as witnessed by the saying "As many enemies as you have slaves."

TACITUS, *THE ANNALS OF IMPERIAL ROME*

Soon afterwards the City Prefect, Lucius Pedanius Secundus, was murdered by one of his slaves [61 C.E.]. Either Pedanius had refused to free the murderer after agreeing to a price, or the slave, in a homosexual infatuation, found competition from his master intolerable. After the murder, ancient custom required that every slave residing under the same roof must be executed. But a crowd gathered, eager to save so many innocent lives; and rioting began. The senate-house was besieged. Inside, there was feeling against excessive severity, but the majority opposed any change. Among the latter was Gaius Cassius Longinus, who when his turn came spoke as follows. . . .

"An ex-consul has been deliberately murdered by a slave in his own home. None of his fellow-slaves prevented or betrayed the murderer, though the senatorial decree threatening the whole household with execution still stands. Exempt them from the penalty if you like. But then, if the City Prefect was not important enough to be immune; who will be? Who will have enough slaves to protect him if Pedanius' four hundred were too few? Who can

rely on his household's help if even fear for their own lives does not make them shield us?"

[The sentence of death was carried out.]

PLINY THE YOUNGER TO ACILIUS

This horrible affair demands more publicity than a letter—Larcius Macedo, a senator and ex-praetor, has fallen a victim to his own slaves. Admittedly he was a cruel and overbearing master, too ready to forget that his father had been a slave, or perhaps too keenly conscious of it. He was taking a bath in his house at Formiae when suddenly he found himself surrounded; one slave seized him by the throat while the others struck his face and hit him in the chest and stomach and—shocking to say—in his private parts. When they thought he was dead they threw him onto the hot pavement, to make sure he was not still alive. Whether unconscious or feigning to be so, he lay there motionless, thus making them believe that he was quite dead. Only then was he carried out, as if he had fainted with the heat, and received by his slaves who had remained faithful, while his concubines ran up, screaming frantically. Roused by their cries and revived by the cooler air he opened his eyes and made some movement to show that he was alive, it being now safe to do so. The guilty slaves fled, but most of them have been arrested and a search is being made for the others. Macedo was brought back to life with difficulty, but only for a few days; at least he died with the satisfaction of having revenged himself, for he lived to see the same punishment meted out as for murder. There you see the dangers, outrages, and insults to which we are exposed. No master can feel safe because he is kind and considerate; for it is their brutality, not their reasoning capacity, which leads slaves to murder masters.

Rome was the place to be. People from all over the empire resided there, with entire neighborhoods inhabited by members of specific groups, such as Greeks and Syrians.

Although it was the center of a great empire, Rome was also a great parasite. Beginning with Augustus, the emperors accepted responsibility for providing food for the urban populace, with about 200,000 people receiving free grain. Even with the free grain, conditions were grim for the poor.

In addition to food, entertainment was also provided on a grand scale for the inhabitants of Rome. The poet Juvenal said of the Roman masses: "But nowadays, with no vote to sell, their motto is 'Couldn't care less.' Time was when their plebiscite elected generals, heads of state, commanders of legions: but now they've pulled in their horns, there's only two things that concern them: Bread and Circuses."[4] Public spectacles were provided by the emperor as part of the great religious festivals celebrated by the state. Most famous were the gladiatorial shows, which took place in

amphitheaters. Perhaps the most famous was the amphitheater in Rome known as the Colosseum, designed to seat fifty thousand spectators. In most cities and towns, amphitheaters were the biggest buildings, rivaled only by the circuses (arenas) for races and the public baths.

Gladiatorial games were held from dawn to dusk. Contests to the death between trained fighters formed the central focus of these games, but the games included other forms of entertainment as well. Criminals of all ages and both sexes were sent into the arena without weapons to face certain death from wild animals who would tear them to pieces. Numerous types of animal contests were also held: wild beasts against each other, such as bears against buffaloes; staged hunts with men shooting safely from behind iron bars; and gladiators in the arena with bulls, tigers, and lions. It is recorded that five thousand beasts were killed in one day of games when Emperor Titus inaugurated the Colosseum in 80 C.E.

INTERIOR OF THE COLOSSEUM OF ROME. The Colosseum was a large amphitheater constructed under the emperor Vespasian and his son Titus. The amphitheaters in which the gladiatorial contests were held varied in size throughout the empire. The Roman emperors understood that gladiatorial shows and other forms of entertainment helped divert the poor and destitute from any political unrest.

CRISIS AND THE LATE EMPIRE

In the course of the third century, the Roman Empire came near to collapse. Military monarchy under the Severan rulers (193–235), which restored order after a series of civil wars, was followed by military anarchy. For the next forty-nine years, the Roman imperial throne was occupied by anyone who had the military strength to seize it—a total of twenty-two emperors, only two of whom did not meet a violent death. At the same time, the empire was beset by a series of invasions, no doubt exacerbated by the civil wars. In the east, the Sassanid Persians made inroads into Roman territory. Germanic tribes also poured into the Balkans, Gaul, and Spain. Not until the end of the third century were most of the boundaries restored.

Invasions, civil wars, and plague came close to causing an economic collapse of the Roman Empire in the third century. There was a noticeable decline in trade and small industry, and the labor shortage caused by plague affected both military recruiting and the economy. Farm production deteriorated significantly as fields were ravaged by invaders or, even more often, by the defending Roman armies. The monetary system began to collapse as a result of debased coinage and inflation. Armies were needed more than ever, but financial strains made it difficult to pay and enlist more soldiers. By the mid-third century, the state had to hire Germans to fight under Roman commanders.

The Reforms of Diocletian and Constantine

At the end of the third and beginning of the fourth centuries, the Roman Empire gained a new lease on life through the efforts of two strong emperors, Diocletian and Constantine. The Roman Empire was virtually transformed into a new state: the so-called Late Empire, which included a new governmental structure, a rigid economic and social system, and a new state religion—Christianity (see "Transformation of the Roman World" later in this chapter).

Both Diocletian (284–305) and Constantine (306–337) expanded imperial control by strengthening and enlarging the administrative bureaucracies of the Roman Empire. A hierarchy of officials exercised control at the various levels of government. The army was enlarged to half a million men, including German units. Mobile units were set up that could be quickly moved to support frontier troops when the borders were threatened.

Constantine's biggest project was the construction of a new capital city in the east, on the site of the Greek city of Byzantium on the shores of the Bosporus. Eventually renamed Constantinople (modern Istanbul), the city was developed for defensive reasons and had an excellent strategic location. Calling it his "New Rome," Constantine endowed the city with a forum, large palaces, and a vast amphitheater.

The political and military reforms of Diocletian and Constantine greatly enlarged two institutions—the army and the civil service—that drained most of the public funds. Though more revenues were needed to pay for the army and bureaucracy, the population was not growing, so the tax base could not be expanded. To ensure the tax base and keep the empire going despite the shortage of labor, the emperors issued edicts that forced people to remain in their designated vocations. Basic jobs, such as bakers and shippers, became hereditary. The fortunes of free tenant farmers also declined. Soon they found themselves bound to the land by large landowners who took advantage of depressed agricultural conditions to enlarge their landed estates.

In general, the economic and social policies of Diocletian and Constantine were based on an unprecedented degree of control and coercion. Although temporarily successful, such authoritarian policies in the long run stifled the very vitality the Late Empire needed to revive its sagging fortunes.

The End of the Western Roman Empire

The restored empire of Diocletian and Constantine limped along for more than a century. After Constantine, the empire continued to divide into western and eastern parts. The west came under increasing pressure from migrating Germanic peoples. Although the Romans had established a series of political frontiers in the western empire, Romans and Germans often came into contact across those boundaries. For some time, the Romans had hired Germanic tribes to fight other Germanic tribes that threatened Rome or enlisted groups of Germans to fight for Rome.

In the late fourth century, the Germanic tribes came under new pressure when the Huns, a fierce tribe of nomads from the steppes of Asia (who may have been related to the Xiongnu, the invaders of the Han Empire), moved into the Black Sea region. They devastated the Germanic Gothic confederation that dominated the region and forced some tribes out. One of the largest displaced groups, the Visigoths, crossed the Danube, crushed a Roman army in 378, and settled along the Danube, within the Roman Empire. But they were soon on the move again. Under their king, Alaric, they stormed into Italy and sacked Rome in 410. Then, at the urging of the emperor, they moved into Spain and southern Gaul as Roman allies.

The Roman experience with the Visigoths established a precedent. The emperors in the first half of the fifth century made alliances with whole groups of Germanic peoples, who settled peacefully in the western part of the empire. The Burgundians settled themselves in much of eastern Gaul, just south of another Germanic tribe called the Alemanni. Only the Vandals remained consistently hostile to the Romans. They sacked parts of Gaul, crossed the Pyrenees into Spain, and began to establish a Vandal kingdom there. Defeated by incoming Visigoths, the Vandals crossed the Strait of Gibraltar and conquered the province of Africa. In 455, the Vandals even attacked Rome and sacked it more ferociously than the Visigoths had in 410.

Increasingly, German military leaders dominated the imperial courts of the western empire. One such leader finally ended the charade of Roman imperial rule. In 476, Odoacer deposed the Roman emperor, Romulus Augustulus, and began to rule on his own. Meanwhile, another branch of the Goths, known as the Ostrogoths, under King Theodoric (493–526), marched into Italy, killed Odoacer, and established control of Italy in 493.

TRANSFORMATION OF THE ROMAN WORLD: THE DEVELOPMENT OF CHRISTIANITY

The rise of Christianity marked a fundamental break with the dominant values of the Greco-Roman world. To understand the rise of Christianity, we must first examine both the religious environment of the Roman world and the Jewish background from which Christianity emerged.

The Religious World of the Romans

Augustus had taken a number of steps to revive the Roman state religion, which had declined during the turmoil of the late Republic. The official state religion focused on the worship of a pantheon of Greco-Roman gods and goddesses, including Juno, the patron goddess of women; Minerva, the goddess of craftspeople; Mars, the god of war; and Jupiter Optimus Maximus ("best and greatest"), who became the patron deity of Rome and assumed a central place in the religious life of the city. The Romans believed that the observance of proper ritual by state priests brought them into a right relationship with the gods, thereby guaranteeing security, peace, and prosperity, and that their success in creating an empire confirmed the favor of the gods. As the first-century politician Cicero claimed, "We have overcome all the nations of the world because we have realized that the world is directed and governed by the gods."[5]

The polytheistic Romans were extremely tolerant of other religions. They allowed the worship of native gods and goddesses throughout their provinces and even adopted some of the local deities. In addition, beginning with Augustus, emperors were often officially made gods by the Roman senate, thus bolstering support for the emperors.

The desire for a more emotional spiritual experience led many people to the mystery religions of the Hellenistic east, which flooded into the western Roman world during the Early Empire. The mystery religions promised their followers entry into a higher world of reality and the promise of a future life superior to the present one. By participating in their ceremonies, an adherent could commune with spiritual beings and undergo purification that opened the door to life after death.

The Jewish Background

In Hellenistic times, the Jews had been granted considerable independence by their Seleucid rulers. By 6 C.E., however, Judaea (the lands of the old Jewish kingdom of Judah) had been made a Roman province and placed under the direction of a Roman procurator. But unrest continued, augmented by divisions among the Jews themselves. The Sadducees favored cooperation with the Romans. The Phar-

⟫ JESUS AND HIS APOSTLES. Pictured is a fourth-century C.E. fresco from a Roman catacomb depicting Jesus and his apostles (early disciples). Catacombs were underground cemeteries where early Christians buried their dead. Christian tradition holds that in times of imperial repression, Christians withdrew to the catacombs to pray and even hide.

isees, although they wanted Judaea to be free from Roman control, did not advocate violent means to achieve this goal. The Essenes were a Jewish sect that lived in a religious community near the Dead Sea. They, like most other Jews, awaited a messiah who would save Israel from oppression, usher in the kingdom of God, and establish paradise on earth. A fourth group, the Zealots, were militant extremists who advocated the violent overthrow of Roman rule. A Jewish revolt in 66 C.E. was crushed by the Romans four years later. The Jewish temple in Jerusalem was destroyed, and Roman power once more stood supreme in Judaea.

The Rise of Christianity

It was in the midst of the confusion and conflict in Judaea that Jesus of Nazareth (c. 6 B.C.E.–c. 29 C.E.) began his public preaching. Jesus—a Palestinian Jew—grew up in Galilee, an important center of the militant Zealots. Jesus' message was simple. He reassured his fellow Jews that he did not plan to undermine their traditional religion: "Do not think that I have come to abolish the Law or the Prophets; I have not come to abolish them but to fulfill them."[6] According to Jesus, what was important was not strict adherence to the letter of the law but the transformation of the inner person: "So in everything, do to others what you would have them do to you, for this sums up the Law and the Prophets."[7] God's command was simple—to love God and one another: "Love the Lord your God with all your heart and with all your soul and with all your mind and with all your strength. The second is this: Love your neighbor as yourself."[8] In the Sermon on the Mount (see the box on p. 106), Jesus presented the ethical concepts—humility, charity, and brotherly love—that would form the basis of the value system of medieval Western civilization.

To the Roman authorities of Palestine, Jesus was seen as a potential revolutionary who might transform Jewish expectations of a messianic kingdom into a revolt against Rome. Therefore, Jesus found himself denounced on many sides, and the procurator Pontius Pilate ordered his crucifixion. But that did not solve the problem. A few loyal followers of Jesus spread the story that Jesus had overcome death, had been resurrected, and had then ascended into heaven. The belief in Jesus' resurrection became an important tenet of Christian doctrine. Jesus was now hailed as "the anointed one" (*Christ* in Greek), the messiah who would return and usher in the kingdom of God on earth.

Christianity began, then, as a religious movement within Judaism and was viewed that way by Roman authorities for many decades. A prominent figure in early Christianity was Paul of Tarsus (c. 5–c. 67), who believed that the message of Jesus should be preached not only to Jews but to Gentiles (non-Jews) as well. Paul taught that Jesus was the Savior, the Son of God, who had come to earth to save all humans, who were all sinners as a result of Adam's sin of disobedience against God. By his death, Jesus had atoned for the sins of all humans and made possible their reconciliation with God and hence their salvation. By accepting Jesus as their Savior, they too could be saved.

At first, Christianity spread slowly. Although the teachings of early Christianity were mostly disseminated by the preaching of convinced Christians, written materials also appeared. Among them were a series of letters or epistles written by Paul outlining Christian beliefs for different Christian communities. Some of Jesus' disciples may also have preserved some of the sayings of the master in writing and would have passed on personal memories that became the basis of the written gospels—the "good news" concerning Jesus—which were written down between 50 and 150 and which attempted to give a record of Jesus' life and teachings and formed the core of the New Testament.

Although Jerusalem was the first center of Christianity, its destruction by the Romans in 70 C.E. dispersed the Christians and left individual Christian churches with considerable independence. By 100, Christian churches had been established in most of the major cities of the east and in some places in the western part of the empire. Many early Christians came from the ranks of Hellenized Jews and the Greek-speaking populations of the east. But in the second and third centuries, an increasing number of followers came from Latin-speaking peoples.

Initially, the Romans did not pay much attention to the Christians, whom they regarded at first as simply another Jewish sect. As time passed, however, the Roman attitude toward Christianity began to change. The Romans tolerated other religions as long as they did not threaten public order or public morals. Many Romans came to view Christians as harmful to the Roman state because they refused to worship the state gods and emperors. Because the Romans regarded such worship as important to the state, they saw the Christians' refusal as an act of treason, punishable by death. But to the Christians, who believed

CHRISTIAN IDEALS: THE SERMON ON THE MOUNT

Christianity was one of many religions competing for attention in the Roman Empire during the first and second centuries. The rise of Christianity marked a fundamental break with the value system of the upper-class elites who dominated the world of classical antiquity. As these excerpts from the Sermon on the Mount in the Gospel of Saint Matthew illustrate, Christians emphasized humility, charity, brotherly love, and a belief in the inner being and a spiritual kingdom superior to this material world. These values and principles were not those of classical Greco-Roman civilization as exemplified in the words and deeds of its leaders.

THE GOSPEL ACCORDING TO SAINT MATTHEW

Now when he saw the crowds, he went up on a mountainside and sat down. His disciples came to him, and he began to teach them, saying:

> Blessed are the poor in spirit: for theirs is the kingdom of heaven.
> Blessed are those who mourn: for they will be comforted.
> Blessed are the meek: for they will inherit the Earth.
> Blessed are those who hunger and thirst for righteousness: for they will be filled.
> Blessed are the merciful: for they will be shown mercy.
> Blessed are the pure in heart: for they will see God.
> Blessed are the peacemakers: for they will be called sons of God.
> Blessed are those who are persecuted because of righteousness: for theirs is the kingdom of heaven. . . .

You have heard that it was said, "Eye for eye, and tooth for tooth." But I tell you, Do not resist an evil person. If someone strikes you on the right cheek, turn to him the other also. . . .

You have heard that it was said, "Love your neighbor, and hate your enemy." But I tell you, Love your enemies and pray for those who persecute you. . . .

Do not store up for yourselves treasures on Earth, where moth and rust destroy, and where thieves break in and steal. But store up for yourselves treasures in heaven, where moth and rust do not destroy, and where thieves do not break in and steal. For where your treasure is, there your heart will be also. . . .

No one can serve two masters. Either he will hate the one and love the other, or he will be devoted to the one and despise the other. You cannot serve both God and Money.

Therefore I tell you, do not worry about your life, what you will eat or drink; or about your body, what you will wear. Is not life more important than food, and the body more important than clothes? Look at the birds of the air; they do not sow or reap or store away in barns, and yet your heavenly Father feeds them. Are you not much more valuable than they? . . . So do not worry, saying, What shall we eat? or What shall we drink? or What shall we wear? For the pagans run after all these things, and your heavenly Father knows that you need them. But seek first his kingdom and his righteousness, and all these things will be given to you as well.

---

there was only one God, the worship of state gods and the emperors meant committing idolatry and endangering their own salvation. Nevertheless, Roman persecution of Christians in the first and second centuries was only sporadic and local, never systematic. In the second century, Christians were largely ignored as harmless. By the end of the reigns of the five good emperors, Christians still represented a small minority, but one of considerable strength.

The Triumph of Christianity

The sporadic persecution of Christians by the Romans in the first and second centuries had done little to stop the growth of Christianity and had in fact served to strengthen Christianity as an institution in the second and third centuries by causing it to become more organized. Crucial to this change was the emerging role of the bishops, who began to assume more control over church communities. The Christian church was creating a well-defined hierarchical structure in which the bishops and clergy were salaried officers separate from the laity or regular church members.

Christianity grew slowly in the first century, took root in the second, and by the third had spread widely. Why was Christianity able to attract so many followers? First, the Christian message had much to offer the Roman world. The promise of salvation, made possible by Jesus' death and resurrection, made a resounding impact on a world full of suffering and injustice. Christianity seemed to imbue life with a meaning and purpose beyond the simple material things of everyday reality. Second, Christianity seemed familiar. It was regarded as simply another mystery religion, offering immortality as the result of the sacrificial death of a savior-god. At the same time, it offered more than the other mystery religions did. Jesus had been a human figure who was easy to relate to. Finally, Christianity fulfilled the human need to belong. Christians formed communities bound to one another, in which people could express their love by helping each other and offering assistance to the poor, sick, widows, and orphans. Christianity satisfied the need to belong in a way that the huge, impersonal, and remote Roman Empire could never do.

THE LATE EMPIRE—CHIEF RULERS AND EVENTS

Military monarchy (Severan dynasty)	193–235
Military anarchy	235–284
Diocletian	284–305
Constantine	306–337
Edict of Milan	313
Theodosius the Great	378–395
Sack of Rome by Visigoths	410
Sack of Rome by Vandals	455
Deposition of Romulus Augustulus	476

As the Christian church became more organized, some emperors in the third century responded with more systematic persecutions, but their schemes failed. The last great persecution was at the beginning of the fourth century, but by that time, Christianity had become too strong to be eradicated by force. After Constantine became the first Christian emperor, Christianity flourished. Although Constantine was not baptized until the end of his life, in 313 he issued the Edict of Milan officially tolerating Christianity. Under Theodosius the Great (378–395), it was made the official religion of the Roman Empire. In less than four centuries, Christianity had triumphed.

COMPARISON OF THE ROMAN AND HAN EMPIRES

At the beginning of the first millennium C.E., two great empires—the Roman Empire in the West and the Han Empire in the East—dominated large areas of the world. Although there was little contact between them, the Han Empire and the Roman Empire had some remarkable similarities. Both empires lasted for centuries, and both had remarkable success in establishing centralized control over their empires. They built elaborate systems of roads in order to rule efficiently and relied on provincial officials, and especially on towns and cities, for local administration. Architectural features found in the capital cities, Rome and Chang'an, were also transferred on a smaller scale to provincial towns and cities. In both empires, settled conditions led to a high level of agricultural production that sustained large populations, estimated at between fifty and sixty million in each empire. Although both empires expanded into areas that had different languages, ethnic groups, and ways of life, they managed to carry their legal and political institutions, their technical skills, and their languages throughout their empires.

The Roman and Han Empires had similar social and economic structures. The family stood at the heart of the social structure, with the male head of the family as all-powerful. Duty, courage, obedience, discipline—all were values inculcated by the family that helped make the empires strong. The wealth of both societies also depended on agriculture. Although a free peasantry was a backbone of strength and stability in each, the gradual conversion of free peasants into tenant farmers by wealthy landowners was common to both societies and ultimately served to undermine the power of their imperial governments.

Of course, there were also significant differences. Social mobility was less limited in Rome than in China. And merchants were more highly regarded and allowed more freedom in Rome than they were in China. The

Emperors, West and East

Two great empires with strong central governments dominated much of the ancient world. Shown here are two emperors from these empires. The Roman emperor Hadrian, who ruled from 117 to 138, was the third of the five good emperors. He had been adopted by the emperor Trajan to serve as his successor. Han Gaozu was the first emperor of the Han dynasty, which ruled China for four hundred years. He was responsible for bringing China back under central control by 202 B.C.E. but was killed in a frontier battle in 195 B.C.E.

© British Museum

© British Library

dynastic principle in China added a strong element of stability. With the mandate of Heaven, Chinese rulers had the authority to command by a mandate from divine forces that was easily passed on to other family members. Although Roman emperors were accorded divine status by the Roman senate after their death, accession to the Roman imperial throne depended less on solid dynastic principles and more on pure military force. As a result, over a period of centuries, Chinese imperial authority was far more stable.

Despite the differences, one major similarity remains—like the Han Empire, the Roman Empire was eventually faced with overwhelming problems. Both empires suffered from overexpansion, and both fortified their long borders with walls, forts, and military garrisons to guard against invasions of nomadic peoples. Both empires were eventually overcome by these peoples: the Han dynasty was weakened by the incursions of the Xiongnu, and the western Roman Empire eventually collapsed in the face of incursions by the Germanic peoples. Nevertheless, a significant difference between these two contemporary empires remained. Although the Han dynasty collapsed, the Chinese imperial tradition, as well as the class structure and set of values that sustained it, continued, and the Chinese Empire, under new dynasties, continued well into the twentieth century as a single political entity. The Roman Empire, on the other hand, collapsed and lived on only as an idea.

CONCLUSION

Between 509 and 264 B.C.E., the Latin-speaking community of Rome expanded and brought about the union of almost all of Italy under its control. Even more dramatically,

between 264 and 133 B.C.E., Rome expanded to the west and east and became master of the Mediterranean Sea and its surrounding territories, creating one of the largest empires in antiquity. Rome's republican institutions proved inadequate for the task of ruling an empire, however, and after a series of bloody civil wars, Octavian created a new order that would rule the empire in an orderly fashion. His successors established a Roman imperial state.

The Roman Empire experienced a lengthy period of peace and prosperity between 14 and 180. During this Pax Romana, trade flourished, and the provinces were governed efficiently. In the course of the third century, however, the Roman Empire came near to collapse due to invasions, civil wars, and economic decline. Although the emperors Diocletian and Constantine brought new life to the so-called Late Empire, their efforts shored up the empire only temporarily. Beginning in 395, the empire divided into western and eastern parts, and by 476, the Roman Empire in the west was being transformed.

Although the Roman Empire in the west ended and lived on only as an idea, Roman achievements were bequeathed to the future. The Romance languages of today (French, Italian, Spanish, Portuguese, and Romanian) are based on Latin. Western practices of impartial justice and trial by jury owe much to Roman law. As great builders, the Romans left monuments to their skills throughout Europe, some of which, such as aqueducts and roads, are still in use today. Aspects of Roman administrative practices survived in the Western world for centuries. The Romans also preserved the intellectual heritage of the Greco-Roman world of antiquity. Nevertheless, while many aspects of the Roman world would continue, the heirs of Rome created new civilizations—European, Islamic, and Byzantine—that would carry on yet another stage in the development of human society.

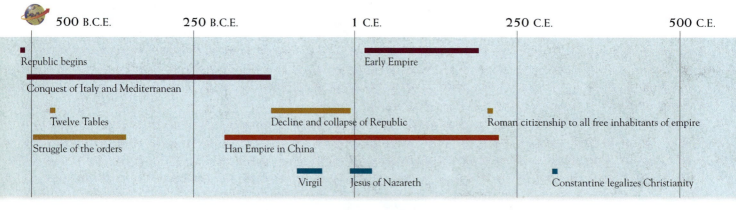

CHAPTER NOTES

1. Tacitus, *The Annals of Imperial Rome*, trans. Michael Grant (Harmondsworth, England, 1964), p. 31.
2. *The Poems of Catullus*, trans. Charles Martin (Baltimore, 1990), p. 109.
3. Virgil, *The Aeneid*, trans. C. Day Lewis (Garden City, N.Y., 1952), p. 154.
4. Juvenal, *The Sixteen Satires*, Satire 10.

5. Quoted in Chester Starr, *Past and Future in Ancient History* (Lanham, Md., 1987), pp. 38–39.

6. Matthew 5:17.

7. Matthew 7:12.

8. Mark 12:30–31.

SUGGESTED READING

For a general account of Roman history, see J. Boardman, J. Griffin, and O. Murray, eds., *The Oxford History of the Roman World* (Oxford, 1991). A standard one-volume reference on the Roman Republic is M. Cary and H. H. Scullard, *A History of Rome Down to the Reign of Constantine*, 3d ed. (New York, 1975). Good surveys of the Roman Republic include M. H. Crawford, *The Roman Republic*, 2d ed. (Cambridge, Mass., 1993); M. Le Glay, J.-L. Voisin, and Y. Le Bohec, *A History of Rome*, trans. A. Nevill (Oxford, 1996); and A. Kamm, *The Romans* (London, 1995). The history of early Rome is well covered in T. J. Cornell, *The Beginnings of Rome: Italy and Rome from the Bronze Age to the Punic Wars (c. 1000–264 B.C.)* (London, 1995).

Aspects of the Roman political structure can be studied in R. E. Mitchell, *Patricians and Plebeians: The Origin of the Roman State* (Ithaca, N.Y., 1990). Changes in Rome's economic life can be examined in A. H. M. Jones, *The Roman Economy* (Oxford, 1974). On the Roman social structure, see G. Alfoeldy, *The Social History of Rome* (London, 1985).

Accounts of Rome's expansion in the Mediterranean world are provided by J.-M. David, *The Roman Conquest of Italy*, trans. A. Nevill (Oxford, 1996), and R. M. Errington, *The Dawn of Empire: Rome's Rise to World Power* (Ithaca, N.Y., 1971).

An excellent account of basic problems in the history of the late Republic can be found in M. Beard and M. H. Crawford, *Rome in the Late Republic* (London, 1984). The classic work on the fall of the Republic is R. Syme, *The Roman Revolution* (Oxford, 1960). Also useful is D. Shotter, *The Fall of the Roman Republic* (London, 1994).

Good surveys of the Early Roman Empire include P. Garnsey and R. Saller, *The Roman Empire: Economy, Society and Culture* (London, 1987); C. Wells, *The Roman Empire*, 2d ed. (London, 1992); and J. Wacher, *The Roman Empire* (London, 1987). A fundamental work on Roman government and the role of the emperor is F. Millar, *The Emperor in the Roman World* (London, 1977).

The Roman army is examined in J. B. Campbell, *The Emperor and the Roman Army* (Oxford, 1984). On the provinces and Roman foreign policy, see E. N. Luttwak, *The Grand Strategy of the Roman Empire from the First Century A.D. to the Third* (Baltimore, 1976), and B. Isaac, *The Limits of Empire: The Roman Empire in the East* (Oxford, 1990).

A good survey of Roman literature can be found in R. M. Ogilvie, *Roman Literature and Society* (Harmondsworth, England, 1980). On Roman art and architecture, see R. Ling, *Roman Painting* (New York, 1991); D. E. Kleiner, *Roman Sculpture* (New Haven, Conn., 1992); and M. Wheeler, *Roman Art and Architecture* (London, 1964). A general study of daily life in Rome is F. Dupont, *Daily Life in Ancient Rome* (Oxford, 1994). Roman women are examined in S. Pomeroy, *Goddesses, Whores, Wives, and Slaves: Women in Classical Antiquity* (New York, 1976), and R. Baumann, *Women and Politics in Ancient Rome* (New York, 1995). On slavery, see K. R. Bradley, *Slavery and Rebellion in the Roman World* (Bloomington, Ind., 1989). On the gladiators, see T. Wiedemann, *Emperors and Gladiators* (New York, 1992).

On the Late Empire, see A. Cameron, *The Later Roman Empire* (Cambridge, Mass., 1993), and R. MacMullen, *Corruption and the Decline of Rome* (New Haven, Conn., 1988). On the fourth century, see T. D. Barnes, *The New Empire of Diocletian and Constantine* (Cambridge, Mass., 1982). Studies analyzing the aristocratic circles, the barbarian invasions, and the military problem include E. A. Thompson, *Romans and Barbarians* (Madison, Wis., 1982), and A. Ferrill, *The Fall of the Roman Empire: The Military Explanation* (London, 1986).

For a general introduction to early Christianity, see J. Court and K. Court, *The New Testament World* (Cambridge, 1990). Useful works on early Christianity include W. H. C. Frend, *The Rise of Christianity* (Philadelphia, 1984), and R. MacMullen, *Christianizing the Roman Empire* (New Haven, Conn., 1984). On Christian women, see D. M. Scholer, ed., *Women in Early Christianity* (New York, 1993), and R. Kraemer, *Her Share of the Blessings: Women's Religion Among the Pagans, Jews and Christians in the Graeco-Roman World* (Oxford, 1995).

INFOTRAC COLLEGE EDITION

Visit the source collections at infotrac.thomsonlearning.com and use the Search function with the following key terms.

Caesar	Roman history
Julius Caesar	Roman law
Roman empire	Roman republic

WORLD HISTORY RESOURCES

Visit the *Essential World History* Companion Web Site for resources specific to this textbook:

http://history.wadsworth.com/duikeressentials02/

The CD in the back of this book and the World History Resource Center at **http://history.wadsworth.com/world/** offer a variety of tools to help you succeed in this course, including access to quizzes; images; documents; interactive simulations, maps, and timelines; movie explorations; and a wealth of other sources.

THE FIRST CIVILIZATIONS AND THE RISE OF EMPIRES

*I*n Part I of this book, we have focused our attention on the emergence of the first civilizations during the ancient era. As we have seen, each civilization developed somewhat independently of the others, and we have therefore treated them as distinct entities, each with its own pattern of development. But clearly, these civilizations encountered a number of similar experiences, and contacts between the civilizations and with other nearby peoples sometimes played a significant role in their development. Let us now retrace our steps and evaluate the process in a comparative perspective. How and why did these first civilizations arise? What role did cross-cultural contacts play in their development? What was the nature of the relationship between these permanent settlements and nonagricultural peoples living elsewhere in the world? Finally, what brought about the demise of these early civilizations, and what legacy did they leave for their successors in the region?

An important stimulus behind the rise of all of these early civilizations was the development of settled agriculture, which unleashed a series of changes in the organization of human communities that culminated in the rise of large ancient empires. The exact time and place that crops were first cultivated successfully is uncertain. The first farmers, who may have lived as long as ten thousand years ago, undoubtedly used simple techniques and still relied primarily on other forms of food production, such as hunting, foraging, or pastoralism. The real breakthrough came when farmers began to cultivate crops along the floodplains of river systems. The advantage was that crops grown in such areas were not as dependent on rainfall and therefore produced a more reliable harvest. An additional benefit was that the sediment carried by the river waters deposited nutrients in the soil, thus enabling the farmer to cultivate a single plot of ground for many years without moving to a new location. Thus the first truly sedentary (that is, nonmigratory) societies were born.

The spread of this river valley agriculture in various parts of Asia and Africa was the decisive factor in the rise of the first civilizations. The increase in food production in these regions led to a significant growth in population, while efforts to control the flow of water to maximize the irrigation of cultivated areas and to protect the local inhabitants from hostile forces outside the community provoked the first steps toward cooperative activities on a large scale. The need to oversee the entire process brought about the emergence of an elite that was eventually transformed into a government.

As we have seen, the first clear steps in the rise of the first civilizations took place in the fourth and third millennia B.C.E. in Mesopotamia, northern Africa, India, and China. How the first governments took shape in these areas is not certain, but anthropologists studying the evolution of human communities in various parts of the world have discovered that one common stage in the process is the emergence of what are called "big men" within a single village or a collection of villages. By means of their military prowess, dominant personalities, or political acumen, these people gradually emerge as the leaders of that community.

The appearance of these sedentary societies had a major impact on the social organizations, religious beliefs, and way of life of the peoples living within their boundaries. With the increase in population and the development of centralized authority came the emergence of cities. Within these cities, new forms of livelihood appeared to satisfy the growing need for social services and consumer goods. Some people became artisans or merchants, while others became warriors, scholars, or priests. In some cases, the physical divisions within the first cities, with a royal palace surrounded by an imposing wall and separate from the remainder of the urban population, reflected the strict hierarchical character of the society as a whole.

Although the emergence of the first civilizations led to the appearance of major cities, the vast majority of the population undoubtedly consisted of peasants or slaves working on the lands of the wealthy. In general, rural peoples were less affected by the change than their urban counterparts. Most continued to live in simple mud-and-thatch huts and lacked the amenities that were increasingly available to the more affluent residents inside the city walls. Peasants in most societies still faced severe legal restrictions on their freedom of action and movement, and slavery was still commonly practiced in virtually all ancient societies.

Within these civilizations, the nature of social organization and relationships also began to change. As the concept of private property spread, people were less likely to live in large kinship groups, and the concept of the nuclear family became increasingly prevalent. Gender roles came to be differentiated, with men working in the fields or at various specialized occupations and women remaining in the home. Wives were less likely to be viewed as partners and more often as under the control of their husbands.

These new civilizations were also the scene of significant religious and cultural developments. All of them gave birth to new religions as a means of explaining the func-

RULERS AND GODS

All of the world's earliest civilizations believed that there was a close relationship between rulers and gods. In Egypt, pharaohs were considered gods whose role was to maintain the order and harmony of the universe in their own kingdom. In the words of an Egyptian hymn, "What is the king of Upper and Lower Egypt? He is a god by whose dealings one lives, the father and mother of all men, alone by himself, without an equal." In Mesopotamia, India, and China, rulers were thought to rule with divine assistance. Kings were often seen as rulers who derived their power from the gods and who were the agents or representatives of the gods. In ancient India, rulers claimed to be representatives of the gods because they were descended from Manu, the first man who had been made a king by Brahman, the chief god. Many Romans certainly believed that their success in creating an empire was a visible sign of divine favor. As the Roman statesman Cicero stated, "We have overcome all the nations of the world because we have realized that the world is directed and governed by the gods."

Their supposed connection to the gods also caused rulers to seek divine aid in the affairs of the world. This led to the art of divination, or an organized method to discover the intentions of the gods. In Mesopotamian and Roman society, one form of divination involved the examination of the livers of sacrificed animals; features seen in the livers were interpreted to foretell events to come. The Chinese used oracle bones to receive advice from supernatural forces that were beyond the power of human beings. Questions to the gods were scratched on turtle shells or animal bones, which were then exposed to fire. Shamans then interpreted the meaning of the resulting cracks on the surface of the shells or bones as messages from supernatural forces. The Greeks divined the will of the gods by use of the oracle, a sacred shrine dedicated to a god or goddess who revealed the future in response to a question.

Underlying all of these divinatory practices was a belief in a supernatural universe, that is, a world in which divine forces were in charge and in which humans were dependent for their own well-being on those divine forces. It was not until the Scientific Revolution of the modern world that many people began to believe in a natural world that was not governed by spiritual forces.

VISHNU. Brahma the Creator, Siva the Destroyer, and Vishnu the Preserver are the three chief Hindu gods of India. Vishnu is known as the Preserver because he mediates between Brahma and Siva and is thus responsible for maintaining the stability of the universe.

Fitzwilliam Museum, University of Cambridge

tioning of the forces of nature. The approval of gods was deemed crucial to a community's chances of success, and a professional class of priests emerged to govern relations with the divine world.

Writing was an important development in the evolution of these new civilizations. In China and Egypt, priests used writing to communicate with the gods. In Mesopotamia and the Indus River civilization, merchants relied on writing to maintain their accounts. Eventually, all of these civilizations used writing as a primary means of communication as well as of creative expression.

At first, these new civilizations had relatively little contact with peoples in the surrounding regions. But there is growing evidence that a pattern of regional trade had begun to develop in the Middle East, and probably in southern and eastern Asia as well, at a very early date. As the population increased, the volume of trade undoubtedly rose with it, and the new civilizations began to move outward to acquire new lands and access to needed resources. As they expanded, they began to encounter peoples along the periphery of their growing empires.

Not much evidence has survived to chronicle the nature of these first encounters, but it is likely that the results varied widely according to time and place. In some cases, the growing civilizations found it relatively easy to absorb isolated communities of agricultural or food-gathering peoples whom they encountered. Such was the case in southern China and in the southern part of the South Asian peninsula. But in other instances, notably among the nomadic or seminomadic peoples in central and northeastern Asia, the problem was more complicated and often resulted in bitter and extended conflict.

Contacts between these nomadic or seminomadic peoples and settled civilizations probably developed gradually over an extended period of time. Often the relationship, at least at the outset, was mutually beneficial, as each needed goods produced by the other. Nomadic peoples in Central Asia also served as an important conduit for goods and ideas between sedentary civilizations, transporting goods over long distances as early as 3000 B.C.E. Overland trade throughout southwestern Asia was already well established by the third millennium B.C.E. As we have seen, the Silk Road between China and the Mediterranean became an important avenue of long-distance commerce during the first millennium B.C.E.

Eventually, for reasons that are not always clear, the relationship between the settled peoples and the nomadic peoples became increasingly characterized by conflict. Where conflict occurred, the governments of the sedentary civilizations used a variety of techniques to resolve

THE USE OF METALS

Around 6000 B.C.E., people in western Asia discovered how to use metals. They soon realized the advantage in using metal rather than stone to make both tools and weapons. Metal could be shaped more exactly, allowing artisans to make more refined tools and weapons with sharp edges and more precise shapes. Copper, silver, and gold, which were commonly found in their elemental form, were the first metals to be used. These were relatively soft and could be easily pounded into different shapes. But an important step was taken when people discovered that a rock that contained metal could be heated to liquefy the metal (a process called smelting). The liquid metal could then be poured into molds of clay or stone to make precisely shaped tools and weapons.

Copper was the first metal to be used in making tools. The first known copper smelting furnace, dated to 3800 B.C.E., was found in the Sinai. At about the same time, however, artisans in Southeast Asia discovered that tin could be added to copper to make bronze. By 3000 B.C.E., artisans in West Asia were also making bronze. Bronze has a lower melting point, which makes it easier to cast, but it is also a harder metal than copper and corrodes less. By 1400 B.C.E., the Chinese were making bronze decorative objects as well as battle-axes and helmets. The widespread use of bronze has led historians to speak of the period from around 3000 to 1200 B.C.E. as the Bronze Age, although this is somewhat misleading, in that many peoples continued to use stone tools and weapons even after bronze became available.

But there were limitations to the use of bronze. Tin was not as available as copper, which made bronze tools and weapons expensive. After 1200 B.C.E., bronze was increasingly replaced by iron, which was probably first used around 1500 B.C.E. in western Asia, where the Hittites made new weapons from it. Between 1500 and 600 B.C.E., ironmaking spread across Europe, North Africa, and Asia. Bronze continued to be used, but mostly for jewelry and other domestic purposes. Iron was used to make tools and weapons with sharper edges. Because iron weapons were cheaper than bronze ones, larger numbers of warriors could be armed, and wars could be fought on a larger scale.

Iron was handled differently from bronze: it was heated until it could be beaten into a desired shape. Each hammering produced increased strength for the metal. This wrought iron, as it was called, was typical of iron manufacturing in the West until the Late Middle Ages. In China, however, the use of heat-resistant clay in the walls of their blast furnaces raised temperatures to 1,537 degrees Celsius, enabling artisans already in the fourth century B.C.E. to liquefy iron so that it too could be cast in a mold. Europeans would not develop such blast furnaces until the fifteenth century C.E.

BRONZE AXHEAD. This axhead was made around 2000 B.C.E. by pouring liquid metal into an ax-shaped mold of clay or stone. Artisans would then polish the surface of the ax to produce a sharp cutting edge.

© British Museum

	6000 B.C.E.	5000 B.C.E.	4000 B.C.E.	3000 B.C.E.	2000 B.C.E.
Middle East	Agriculture and Neolithic towns			Sumerian civilization	
India	First agricultural settlements			Harappan civilization	
China		First settled agriculture			
Egypt and the Mediterranean	Agriculture in the Nile Valley			Flowering of Egyptian civilization	

the problem, including negotiations, conquest, or alliance with other pastoral peoples to isolate their primary tormentors. We have seen all of these techniques at work in China, where the Qin and the Han tried a combination of the carrot and the stick to pacify the frontier and bring these unruly peoples under control. The Romans did not hesitate to ally with one Germanic tribe to ward off another.

As it turned out, few of these techniques had any lasting effect. The relationship along the frontier was inherently unstable and in the end was disastrous for the settled empires, all of whom were eventually destroyed or seriously weakened as the result of invasion from beyond the frontier. The first to experience such a fate was the Harappan civilization in the Indus River valley, which may have been brought down at least in part as a result of the intrusion by Indo-European Aryan peoples along the northern frontier. Several hundred years later, the peoples of Mesopotamia fell at the hands of the Assyrians, who were in turn conquered by the Indo-European-speaking Persians. The empire of the pharaohs was conquered by the Hyksos, and the Roman Empire was brought to its knees as the result of constant pressure from the Germanic tribes to the north. Although the empire of the Han was not overthrown by the Xiongnu, pressure along the northern frontier contributed to the weakening of the dynasty, and after its collapse in the early third century B.C.E., the entire northern part of the country was overrun by peoples from beyond the Great Wall.

At the same time, it is also increasingly evident that these early civilizations were brought to their knees not only by nomadic invasions but also by their own weaknesses, which made them increasingly vulnerable to attacks along the frontier. In the Roman Empire, bloated bureaucracies as well as excessive taxation to support them, an inability to achieve a workable political system, the decline of Roman military virtues and a reliance on noncitizen mercenaries, and population decline in part caused by plague all played a role in undermining Rome's ability to protect itself. In China, strains within Han society, more than depredations along the frontier, caused the collapse of the Han Empire.

Another possible factor in the decline and collapse of the first civilizations was the role of the environment. Much evidence suggests that ecological changes caused severe difficulties for peoples in the ancient world. Floods or drought may have brought an end to the Harappan civilization, and the infestation of salt water may have leached the nutrients from the soils of Mesopotamia. Imperial Rome may have suffered food shortages as a result of the desiccation of the wheat fields of northern Africa.

The fall of the ancient empires, of course, did not mark the end of civilization. Although the immediate consequences of the fall of Rome and the Han dynasty were a precipitous drop in world trade and a general decline of prosperity throughout the known world, new societies eventually rose on the ashes of the ancient empires. Although many were different in key respects from those they replaced, they still carried the legacy of their predecessors. In the meantime, the forces that had been unleashed in the civilizations of antiquity sent out strands of influence that were laying the basis for new societies elsewhere in the world: south of the Sahara in western and eastern Africa, where new societies were beginning to take shape; beyond the Alps in central Europe, where the Germanic peoples were in the process of forming a new society; in southeastern Asia, where the influence of India and China was beginning to help shape new societies among the trading and agricultural societies in the region; and across the Sea of Japan in the Japanese islands, where native rulers would import Chinese ideas to form a new civilization uniquely their own. In the meantime, new civilizations were on the verge of creation in the New World, across the oceans on the continents of North and South America.

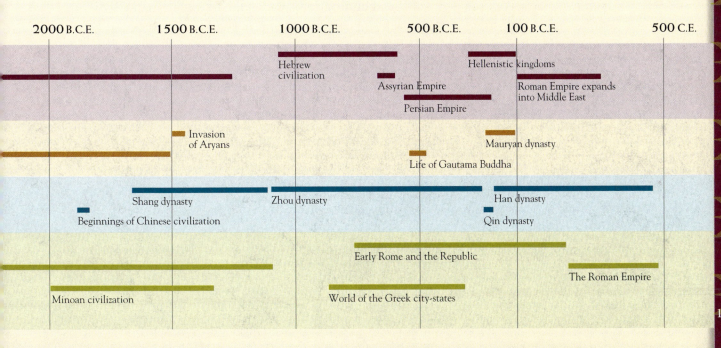

Part II

NEW PATTERNS OF CIVILIZATION

By the beginning of the first millennium C.E., the great states of the ancient world were in decline; some were even at the point of collapse. On the ruins of these ancient empires, new patterns of civilization began to take shape between 400 and 1400 C.E. In some cases, these new societies were built on the political and cultural foundations of their predecessors. The Tang dynasty in China and the Guptas in India both looked back to the ancient period to provide an ideological model for their own time. The Byzantine Empire carried on parts of the classical Greek tradition while also adopting the powerful creed of Christianity from the Roman Empire. In other cases, new states incorporated some elements of the former classical civilizations while embarking on markedly different directions, as in the new European civilization of the Middle Ages and the Arabic states in the Middle East.

In the meantime, complex societies were also beginning to appear in a number of other parts of the world—in Japan, in Southeast Asia, in sub-Saharan Africa, and in the Americas. Except for the Americas, which were developing in isolation, these civilizations were influenced to a greater or lesser degree by older or more powerful empires in the region, and all were increasingly linked by commercial and cultural contacts into the first "global civilization." At the same time, each was able to combine borrowed ideas with indigenous characteristics.

Like their classical predecessors, most of these new states obtained much of their wealth from agriculture. India, China, and medieval Europe were all predominantly agricultural societies. But what is most striking about the period is the growing importance of trade as a factor in national and global development.

Spring Festival on the River; Detail, The Metropolitan Museum of Art, Fletcher Fund, 1947, The A.W. Bahr Collection, (47.18.1)

It was during the first millennium C.E. that the great trade routes of the traditional world—the Silk Road from China to the Middle East and then on to the Mediterranean, the caravan trade route across the Sahara, and the commercial network that stretched across the Indian Ocean—all reached their maturity.

The expanding of regional and global trade also spread ideas. It was commerce that brought Buddhism to China and Southeast Asia and Islam to sub-Saharan Africa and the Indonesian archipelago. At first, the impact of these new ways of thinking was felt primarily in the cities, but eventually it began to spread to the countryside. Kings and princes became converts to the new faiths and provided funds and other forms of patronage in their support.

The spread of religious and cultural ideas sometimes led to conflict. The popularity of Buddhism led eventually to its suppression in China. Tensions between the Islamic and Christian worlds were particularly strong and culminated in the Crusades and the Christian reconquest of Spain and Portugal. But often the assimilation of new religions and cultural ideas took place peacefully, as with the spread of Islam into Africa. Christianity, aided by the zeal of its missionary monks, was an active agent in converting new peoples in central and eastern Europe and transforming their cultures.

© Courtesy of William J. Duiker

THE NEW WORLD

FOCUS QUESTIONS

- Who were the first Americans, and when and how did they arrive?
- What were the main characteristics of the civilizations of the Maya, the Aztecs, and the Inca?
- What role did religion play in the civilizations of the New World?
- What were the main characteristics of the stateless societies in the Americas, and how did they differ from the civilizations that arose in Central America and the Andes?
- ➤ In what ways were the civilizations of the New World similar to the early civilizations of the Old World, and in what ways were they different?

*I*n August 1519, five hundred Spanish soldiers of fortune left their anchorage near the modern city of Veracruz and began the long trek from the coast across the dusty plateau of Mexico to the capital of the Aztecs. At their head was Hernán Cortés, a Spanish conquistador who had just burned the ship on which he arrived to ensure that his followers would not launch a mutiny and sail back to Europe. In Tenochtitlán, the Aztec capital located at what is now Mexico City, Emperor Moctezuma received the news of the foreigners' presence and awaited their arrival with anticipation. According to Aztec legend, one of their ancestors, the godlike Quetzalcoatl, had left the area hundreds of years earlier, vowing to return one day to reclaim his heritage. Could this stranger with his band of men be Quetzalcoatl or his representative? When Cortés and his forces, now accompanied by a crowd of people they had encountered en route, reached the vicinity of Moctezuma's capital, the two men met face-to-face. With this encounter, the last barrier between the Old World and the previously unknown civilizations in the Western Hemisphere had been bridged, and a new era dawned.

The Aztecs were only the latest in a series of sophisticated societies that had sprung up at various locations in North and South America since human beings first crossed the Bering Strait several millennia earlier. Most of these early peoples, today often referred to as Amerindians, lived by hunting and fishing or by food gathering. But by the second millennium B.C.E., the first organized societies, based on agriculture, began to take root in Central and South America. One key area of development was on the plateau of central Mexico. Another was in the lowland regions along the Gulf of Mexico and extending into modern Guatemala. A third was in the central Andes Mountains, adjacent to the Pacific coast of South America. Others were just beginning to emerge in the river valleys and great plains of North America.

For the next two thousand years, these societies developed in isolation from their counterparts elsewhere in the world. This lack of contact with other human beings deprived them of access to technological and cultural developments taking place in Africa, Asia, and Europe. They did not know of the wheel, for example, and their written languages were rudimentary compared to equivalents in complex civilizations in other parts of the globe. But in other respects, their cultural achievements were the equal of those realized elsewhere. When the first European explorers arrived in the New World at the turn of the sixteenth century, they described much that they observed in glowing terms. •

THE FIRST AMERICANS

When the first human beings arrived in the New World has long been a matter of dispute. In the centuries following the voyages of Christopher Columbus, speculation centered on the possibility that the first settlers to reach the American continents had crossed the Atlantic Ocean. Were they the lost tribes of Israel? Were they Phoenician seafarers from Carthage? Were they refugees from the legendary lost continent of Atlantis? In all cases, the assumption was that they were relatively recent arrivals.

By the mid-nineteenth century, under the influence of the new Darwinian concept of evolution, a new theory developed. It proposed that the peopling of America had taken place much earlier as a result of the migration of small communities across the Bering Strait. Recent evidence, including numerous physical similarities between some early Americans and contemporary peoples living in northeastern Asia, has confirmed this hypothesis. The debate on when the migrations began continues, however. Archaeologist Louis Leakey, one of the pioneers in the search for the origins of humankind in Africa, suggested that the first hominids may have arrived in America as long as 100,000 years ago. Others estimate that the first Americans were members of *Homo sapiens sapiens* who crossed from Asia by foot between 10,000 and 15,000 years ago in pursuit of herds of bison and caribou that moved into the area in search of grazing land at the end of the last ice age. A recently discovered site at Cactus Hill, in central Virginia, shows signs of human habitation as early as 15,000 years ago. Genetic evidence now suggests the possibility of an earlier date, perhaps as early as 29,000 years ago. And other recent discoveries indicate that some early settlers may have originally come from Africa rather than from Asia. The question has not yet been definitively answered.

Nevertheless, it is now generally accepted that human beings were living in the New World at least 15,000 years ago. They gradually spread throughout the North American continent and had penetrated almost to the southern tip of South America by about 10,000 B.C.E. These first Americans were hunters and food gatherers who lived in small nomadic communities close to the source of their food supply. Although it is not known when agriculture was first practiced, beans and squash seeds have been found at sites that date back at least 8,000 years. The cultivation of maize (corn), and perhaps other crops as well, appears to have been under way in the lowland regions near the modern city of Veracruz and in the Yucatán peninsula farther to the east. There, in the region that archaeologists call Mesoamerica, one of the first civilizations in the New World began to appear.

EARLY CIVILIZATIONS IN CENTRAL AMERICA

The first signs of civilization in Mesoamerica appeared in the first millennium B.C.E., with the emergence of what is called Olmec culture in the hot and swampy lowlands along the coast of the Gulf of Mexico south of Veracruz (see Map 6.1). Olmec civilization was characterized by intensive agriculture along the muddy riverbanks in the area and by the carving of stone ornaments, tools, and monuments at sites such as San Lorenzo and La Venta. The site at La Venta includes a ceremonial precinct with

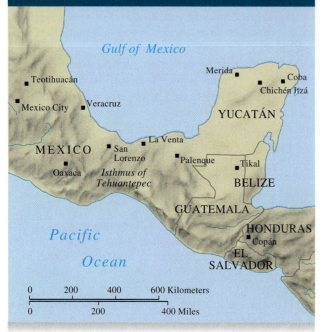

MAP **6.1** **The Heartland of Mesoamerica.** Mesoamerica was home to some of the first civilizations in the Western Hemisphere. This map shows the major urban settlements in the region. ➤ *What areas were most associated with Olmec, Mayan, and Aztec culture?*

all dominated by the massive Pyramid of the Sun, under which archaeologists have discovered the remains of sacrificial victims, probably put to death during the dedication of the structure. In the vicinity are the remains of a large market where goods from distant regions as well as agricultural produce grown by farmers in the vicinity were exchanged. The products traded included cacao, rubber, feathers, and various types of vegetables and meat. Pulque, a liquor extracted from the agave plant, was used in religious ceremonies. An obsidian mine nearby may explain the location of the city; obsidian is a volcanic glass that was prized in Mesoamerica for use in tools, mirrors, and the blades of sacrificial knives.

Most of the city consisted of one-story stucco apartment compounds; some were as large as 35,000 square feet, sufficient to house more than a hundred people. Each apartment was divided into several rooms, and the compounds were covered by flat roofs made of wooden beams, poles, and stucco. The compounds were separated by wide streets laid out on a rectangular grid and were entered through narrow alleys.

Living in the fertile Valley of Mexico, an upland plateau surrounded by magnificent snowcapped mountains, the inhabitants of Teotihuacán probably obtained the bulk of their wealth from agriculture. At that time, the valley floor was filled with swampy lakes containing the water runoff from the surrounding mountains. The combination of fertile soil and adequate water combined to make the valley one of the richest farming areas in Mesoamerica.

Sometime during the eighth century C.E., for unknown reasons, the wealth and power of the city began to decline. The next two centuries were a time of troubles throughout the region as principalities fought over limited farmland. The problem was later compounded when peoples from surrounding areas, attracted by the rich farmlands, migrated into the Valley of Mexico and began to compete for territory with small city-states already established there. As the local population expanded, farmers began to engage in more intensive agriculture. They drained the lakes to build *chinampas,* swampy islands crisscrossed by canals that provided water for their crops and easy transportation to local markets for their excess produce.

a 30-foot-high earthen pyramid, the largest of its date in all Mesoamerica. The Olmec peoples organized a widespread trading network, carried on religious rituals, and devised an as yet undeciphered system of hieroglyphs that is similar in some respects to later Mayan writing (see "Mayan Hieroglyphs" later in this chapter) and may be the ancestor of the first true writing systems in the New World.

Olmec society apparently consisted of several classes, including a class of skilled artisans who produced a series of massive stone heads, some of which are more than 10 feet high. The Olmec peoples supported themselves primarily by cultivating crops, such as corn and beans, but also engaged in fishing and hunting.

Eventually, Olmec civilization began to decline and apparently collapsed around the fourth century B.C.E. During its heyday, however, it extended from Mexico City to El Salvador and perhaps to the shores of the Pacific Ocean.

Teotihuacán: America's First Metropolis

The first major metropolis in Mesoamerica was the city of Teotihuacán, capital of an early kingdom about 30 miles northeast of Mexico City that arose around the third century B.C.E. and flourished for nearly a millennium until it collapsed under mysterious circumstances about 800 C.E. Along the main thoroughfare were temples and palaces,

The Mysterious Maya

Far to the east of the Valley of Mexico, in the Yucatán peninsula, another major civilization had taken form. This was the civilization of the Maya, which was older and just as sophisticated as the society at Teotihuacán.

Like the Aztecs and the inhabitants of Teotihuacán, the Maya trace their origins to the parent Olmec civilization in the lowlands along the Gulf of Mexico. It is not known when human beings first inhabited the Yucatán peninsula, but peoples contemporaneous with the Olmecs were already cultivating such crops as corn, yams, and manioc in the area during the first millennium B.C.E. As the pop-

© Will & Deni McIntyre/Photo Researchers, Inc.

The Pyramid

The monumental structure known as the pyramid was characteristic of two very different civilizations in antiquity. On the left are the three pyramids at Giza, across the Nile River from Cairo. At the rear is the Great Pyramid of Khufu, constructed around 2540 B.C.E. Centuries later, pyramids were also erected by the Maya, Aztecs, and Toltecs in Central America. Shown below is the Pyramid of the Sun at Teotihuacán, erected around 400 C.E. and certainly one of the most impressive pyramids in the Americas. It rises in four tiers to a height of over 200 feet.

© Richard A. Cooke III

ulation increased, an early civilization began to emerge along the Pacific coast directly to the south of the peninsula and in the highlands of modern Guatemala. Contacts were already established with the Olmecs to the west.

Since the area was a source for cacao trees and obsidian, the inhabitants soon developed relations with other early civilizations in the region. Cacao trees were the source of chocolate, which was used as a beverage by the upper classes, while cocoa beans, the fruit of the cacao tree, were used as currency in markets throughout the region.

As the population in the area increased, the inhabitants began to migrate into the central Yucatán peninsula to the north. The overcrowding forced farmers in the lowland areas to shift from slash-and-burn cultivation to swamp agriculture of the type practiced in the lake region of the Valley of Mexico. By the middle of the first millennium

C.E., the entire area was honeycombed with a patchwork of small city-states competing for land and resources. The most important city-states were probably Tikal and Copán, but it is doubtful that any one was sufficiently powerful to dominate the area. The largest urban centers such as Tikal may have had 100,000 inhabitants at their height.

The power of the rulers of the city-states was impressive. One of the monarchs at Copán—known to scholars as "18 Rabbit" from the hieroglyphs composing his name—ordered the construction of a grand palace requiring more than 30,000 person-days of labor. Around the ruler was a class of aristocrats whose wealth was probably based on the ownership of land farmed by their poorer relatives. Eventually, many of the aristocrats became priests or scribes at the royal court or adopted honored professions as sculptors or painters. As the society's wealth grew, so did the role of artisans and traders, who began to form a small middle class.

The majority of the population on the peninsula, however (estimated at roughly three million at the height of Mayan power), were farmers. They lived on their *chinampa* plots or on terraced hills in the highlands. Houses were built of adobe and thatch and probably resembled the houses of the majority of the population in the area today. There was a fairly clear-cut division of labor along gender lines. The men were responsible for fighting and hunting, the women for homemaking and the preparation of cornmeal, the staple food of much of the population.

Some noblewomen seem to have played important roles in both political and religious life. In the seventh century C.E., for example, Pacal became king of Palenque, one of the most powerful of the Mayan city-states, through the royal line of his mother and grandmother, thereby breaking the patrilineal descent twice. His mother ruled Palenque for three years and was the power behind the throne for her son's first twenty-five years of rule. Pacal legitimized his kingship by transforming his mother into a divine representation of the "first mother" goddess.

Mayan religion was polytheistic. Although the names were different, Mayan gods shared many of the characteristics of deities of nearby cultures. The supreme god was named Itzamna (Lizard House). Deities were ranked in order of importance, and some, like the jaguar god of night, were evil rather than good. Some scholars believe that many of the nature deities may have been viewed as manifestations of one supreme godhead (see the box on p. 121). As at Teotihuacán, human sacrifice (normally by decapitation) was practiced to propitiate the heavenly forces. Scenes from paintings and rock carvings depict a society preoccupied with war and the seizure of captives for sacrifice.

Physically, the Mayan cities were built around a ceremonial core dominated by a central pyramid surmounted by a shrine to the gods. Nearby were other temples, palaces, and a sacred ball court. Like many of their modern counterparts, Mayan cities suffered from urban sprawl, with separate suburbs for the poor and the middle class.

The ball court was a rectangular space surrounded by vertical walls with metal rings through which the contestants attempted to drive a hard rubber ball. Although the rules of the game are only imperfectly understood, it apparently had religious significance, and the vanquished players were sacrificed in ceremonies held after the close of the game. Most of the players were men, although there may have been some women's teams. Similar courts have been found at sites throughout Central and South America, with the earliest, located near Veracruz, dating back to around 1500 B.C.E.

➴ A MAYAN BLOODLETTING CEREMONY. The Mayan elite drew blood at various ritual ceremonies. Here we see Lady Xok, the wife of a king of Yaxchilian, passing a rope pierced with thorns along her tongue in a bloodletting ritual. Above her, the king holds a flaming torch. This vibrant scene from an eighth-century C.E. palace lintel demonstrates the excellence of Mayan stone sculpture as well as the sophisticated weaving techniques shown in the queen's elegant gown.

THE CREATION OF THE WORLD: A MAYAN VIEW

Popul Vuh, a sacred work of the ancient Maya, is an account of Mayan history and religious beliefs. No written version in the original Mayan script is extant, but shortly after the Spanish conquest, it was written down in Quiche (the spoken language of the Maya), using the Latin script, apparently from memory. This version was later translated into Spanish. The following excerpt from the opening lines of Popul Vuh recounts the Mayan myth of the creation.

POPUL VUH: THE SACRED BOOK OF THE MAYA

This is the account of how all was in suspense, all calm, in silence; all motionless, still, and the expanse of the sky was empty.

This is the first account, the first narrative. There was neither man, nor animal, birds, fishes, crabs, trees, stones, caves, ravines, grasses, nor forests; there was only the sky.

The surface of the earth had not appeared. There was only the calm sea and the great expanse of the sky.

There was nothing brought together, nothing which could make a noise, nor anything which might move, or tremble, or could make noise in the sky.

There was nothing standing; only the calm water, the placid sea, alone and tranquil. Nothing existed.

There was only immobility and silence in the darkness, in the night. Only the Creator, the Maker, Tepeu, Gucumatz, the Forefathers, were in the water surrounded with light. They were hidden under green and blue feathers, and were therefore called Gucumatz. By nature they were great sages and great thinkers. In this manner the sky existed and also the Heart of Heaven, which is the name of God and thus He is called.

Then came the word. Tepeu and Gucumatz came together in the darkness, in the night, and Tepeu and Gucumatz talked together. They talked then, discussing and deliberating; they agreed, they united their words and their thoughts.

Then while they meditated, it became clear to them that when dawn would break, man must appear. Then they planned the creation, and the growth of the trees and the thickets and the birth of life and the creation of man. Thus it was arranged in the darkness and in the night by the Heart of Heaven who is called Huracan.

The first is called Caculha Huracan. The second is Chipi-Caculha. The third is Raxa-Caculha. And these three are the Heart of Heaven.

So it was that they made perfect the work, when they did it after thinking and meditating upon it.

A BALL COURT. Throughout Mesoamerica, a dangerous game was played on ball courts such as this one. A large ball of solid rubber was propelled from the hip at such tremendous speed that players had to wear extensive padding. More than an athletic contest, the game had religious significance. The court is thought to have represented the cosmos and the ball the sun, and the losers were sacrificed to the gods in postgame ceremonies.

© Lee Boltin Picture Library

A SAMPLE OF MAYAN WRITING

*T*he Maya were the only Mesoamerican people to devise a complete written language. Like the Sumerian and Egyptian scripts, the Mayan system was composed of a mixture of ideographs and phonetic symbols, which were written in double columns to be read from left to right and top to bottom. The language was rudimentary in many ways. It had few adjectives or adverbs, and the numbering system used only three symbols: a shell for zero, a dot for one, and a bar for five.

During the classical era from 300 to 900 C.E., the Maya used the script to record dynastic statistics with deliberate precision, listing the date of the ruler's birth, his accession to power, and his marriage and death while highlighting victories in battle, the capture of prisoners, and ritual ceremonies. The symbols were carved on stone panels, stelae, and funerary urns or were painted with a brush on folding screen books made of bark paper; only four of these books from the late period remain extant today.

A sample of Mayan hieroglyphs is shown below.

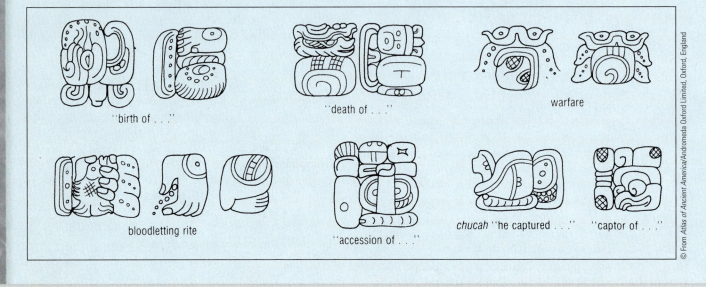

"birth of . . ."   "death of . . ."   warfare

bloodletting rite   "accession of . . ."   *chucah* "he captured . . ."   "captor of . . ."

MAYAN HIEROGLYPHS

In some ways, Mayan culture was more advanced than the later Aztec civilization in the Valley of Mexico. The Mayan writing system was much more sophisticated than the relatively primitive system used by the Aztecs (see the box above). Unfortunately, when the Spanish conquered the remains of Mayan civilization, they made no attempt to decipher the language with the assistance of natives familiar with the script. The Spanish bishop Diego de Landa, otherwise an astute and sympathetic observer of Mayan culture, remarked: "We found a large number of books in these characters and, as they contained nothing in which there were not to be seen superstition and lies of the devil, we burned them all, which they regretted to an amazing degree, and which caused them much affliction."[1]

The Mayan hieroglyphs remained undeciphered until scholars discovered that many passages contained symbols that recorded dates in the Mayan calendar. This calendar, which measures time back to a particular date in August 3114 B.C.E., required a sophisticated understanding of astronomical events and mathematics to compile. Starting with these known symbols as a foundation, modern scholars have gradually deciphered the script. Like the scripts of the Sumerians and ancient Egyptians, the Mayan hieroglyphs were both ideographic and phonetic and were becoming more phonetic as time passed.

One of the most important repositories of Mayan hieroglyphs is at Palenque, an archaeological site deep in the jungles in the neck of the Mexican peninsula, considerably to the west of the Yucatán. In a chamber located under the Temple of Inscriptions, archaeologists discovered a royal tomb and a massive limestone slab covered with hieroglyphs. By deciphering the message on the slab, archaeologists for the first time identified a historical figure in Mayan history. He was the ruler named Pacal, known from his glyph as "The Shield"; Pacal ordered the construction of the Temple of Inscriptions in the midseventh century, and it was his body that was buried in the tomb at the foot of the staircase leading down into the crypt.

As befits their intense interest in the passage of time, the Maya also had a sophisticated knowledge of astronomy and kept voluminous records of the movements of the heavenly bodies. There were practical reasons for their concern. The arrival of the planet Venus in the evening sky, for example, was a traditional time to prepare for war.

THE MYSTERY OF MAYAN DECLINE

Sometime in the eighth or ninth century, the classical Mayan civilization in the central Yucatán peninsula began to decline. At Copán, for example, it ended abruptly in 822 C.E., when work on various stone sculptures ordered by the ruler suddenly ceased. The end of Palenque, a rival state to the west, soon followed. What caused the decline? Recent evidence supports the theory that overcultivation of the land due to a growing population gradually reduced crop yields. Another theory is that a long drought, which lasted for almost two centuries in the ninth and tenth centuries C.E., may have played a major role. We do know that the period was characterized by an increase in internecine war among the states and the rise of powerful nobles.

Whatever the case, cities like Tikal and Palenque were abandoned to the jungles, though newer urban centers in the northern part of the peninsula, like Uxmal and Chichén Itzá, survived and continued to prosper. According to local history, this latter area was taken over by peoples known as the Toltecs, led by a man known as Kukulcan ("feathered serpent"), who migrated to the peninsula from Tula in central Mexico sometime in the tenth century. Some scholars believe this flight was associated with the legend of the departure of Quetzalcoatl, the feathered serpent who promised that he would someday return to reclaim his homeland.

The Toltecs apparently controlled the upper peninsula from their capital at Chichén Itzá for several centuries, and then they too declined. When the Spaniards arrived, the area was divided into a number of small principalities, and the cities such as Uxmal and Chichén Itzá had been abandoned.

The Aztecs

Among the groups moving into the Valley of Mexico after the fall of Teotihuacán were the Mexica (pronounced "Mesheeca"). No one knows their origins, although folk legend held that their original homeland was an island in a lake called Aztlán. From that legendary homeland comes the name *Aztec*, by which they are known to the modern world. Sometime during the early twelfth century, the Aztecs left their original habitat and, carrying an image of their patron deity, Huitzilopochtli, began a lengthy migration that climaxed with their arrival in the Valley of Mexico sometime late in the century.

Less sophisticated than many of their neighbors, the Aztecs were at first forced to seek alliances with stronger city-states. They were excellent warriors, however, and (like Sparta in ancient Greece and the state of Qin in Zhou dynasty China) had become the leading city-state in the lake region by the early fifteenth century. Establishing their capital at Tenochtitlán, on an island in the middle of Lake Texcoco, they set out to bring the entire region under their domination (see Map 6.2).

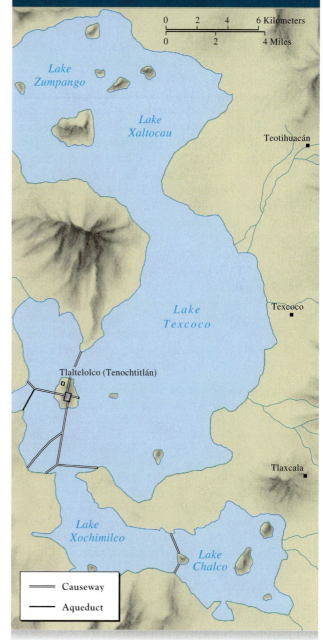

MAP 6.2 The Valley of Mexico Under Aztec Rule. The Aztecs were one of the most advanced peoples in pre-Columbian Central America. Their capital at Tlaltelolco was located at the site of modern-day Mexico City. Of the five lakes shown here, only Lake Texcoco remains today. ➤ *What was the importance of Teotihuacán?*

For the remainder of the fifteenth century, the Aztecs consolidated their control over much of what is modern Mexico, from the Atlantic to the Pacific Ocean and as far south as the Guatemalan border. The new kingdom was not a centralized state but a collection of semiautonomous territories. To provide a unifying focus for the kingdom, the Aztecs promoted their patron god, Huitzilopochtli, as the guiding deity of the entire population, which now numbered several million.

POLITICS AND SOCIETY

Like all great empires in ancient times, the Aztec state was authoritarian. Power was vested in the monarch, whose authority had both a divine and a secular character. The Aztec ruler claimed descent from the gods and served as an intermediary between the material and the metaphysical worlds. Unlike many of his counterparts in the Old World, however, the monarch did not obtain his position by a rigid law of succession. On the death of the ruler, his successor was selected from within the royal family by a small group of senior officials, who were also members of the family and were therefore eligible for the position. Once placed on the throne, the Aztec ruler was advised by a small council of lords, headed by a prime minister who served as the chief executive of the government, and a bureaucracy. Beyond the capital, the power of the central government was limited. Rulers of territories subject to the Aztecs were allowed considerable autonomy in return for paying tribute, in the form of goods or captives, to the central government. The most important government officials in the provinces were the tax collectors, who collected the tribute. They used the threat of military action against those who failed to carry out their tribute obligations and therefore, understandably, were not popular with the taxpayers. According to Bernal Díaz, a Spaniard who accompanied Hernán Cortés on his expedition to Tenochtitlán in 1519:

> All these towns complained about Montezuma [Moctezuma, the Aztec ruler at the time of the Cortés expedition] and his tax collectors, speaking in private so that the Mexican ambassadors should not hear them, however. They said these officials robbed them of all they possessed, and that if their wives and daughters were pretty they would violate them in front of their fathers and husbands and carry them away. They also said that the Mexicans [that is, the representatives from the capital] made the men work like slaves, compelling them to carry pine trunks and stone and firewood and maize overland and in canoes, and to perform other tasks, such as planting maize fields, and that they took away the people's lands as well for the service of their idols.[2]

Positions in the government bureaucracy were the exclusive privilege of the hereditary nobility, all of whom traced their lineage to the founding family of the Aztec clan. Male children in noble families were sent to temple schools, where they were exposed to a harsh regimen of manual labor, military training, and memorization of information about Aztec society and religion. On reaching adulthood, they would select a career in the military service, the government bureaucracy, or the priesthood.

The remainder of the population consisted of commoners, indentured workers, and slaves. Most indentured workers were landless laborers who contracted to work on the nobles' estates, while slaves served in the households of the wealthy. Slavery was not an inherited status, and the children of slaves were considered free citizens.

The vast majority of the population were commoners. All commoners were members of large kinship groups called *calpullis*. Each *calpulli*, often consisting of as many as a thousand members, was headed by an elected chief, who ran its day-to-day affairs and served as an intermediary with the central government. Each *calpulli* was responsible for providing taxes (usually in the form of goods) and conscript labor to the state.

Each *calpulli* maintained its own temples and schools and administered the land held by the community. Farmland within the *calpulli* was held in common and could not be sold, although it could be inherited within the family. In the cities, each *calpulli* occupied a separate neighborhood, where its members often performed a particular function, such as metalworking, stonecutting, weaving, carpentry, or commerce. Apparently, a large proportion of the population engaged in some form of trade, at least in the densely populated Valley of Mexico, where an estimated half of the people lived in an urban environment. Many farmers brought their goods to the markets via the canals and sold them directly to retailers.

Gender roles within the family were rigidly stratified. Male children were trained for war and were expected to serve in the army on reaching adulthood. Women were expected to work in the home, weave textiles, and raise children, although like their brothers, they were permitted to enter the priesthood (see the box on p. 125). As in most traditional societies, chastity and obedience were desirable female characteristics. Although women in Aztec society enjoyed more legal rights than women in some traditional Old World civilizations, they were still not equal to men. Women were permitted to own and inherit property and to enter into contracts. Marriage was usually monogamous, although noble families sometimes practiced polygyny (the state or practice of having more than one wife at a time). As in most societies at the time, parents usually selected their child's spouse, often for purposes of political or social advancement.

Classes in Aztec society were rigidly stratified. Commoners were not permitted to enter the nobility, although some occasionally rose to senior positions in the army or the priesthood as the result of exemplary service. As in medieval Europe, such occupations often provided a route of upward mobility for ambitious commoners. A woman of noble standing would sometimes marry a commoner because the children of such a union would inherit her higher status, and she could expect to be treated better by her husband's family, who would be proud of the marriage relationship.

AZTEC MIDWIFE RITUAL CHANTS

*M*ost Aztec women were burdened with time-consuming family chores, such as grinding corn into flour for tortillas and carrying heavy containers of water from local springs. Like their brothers, Aztec girls went to school, but rather than training for war, they learned spinning, weaving, and how to carry out family rituals. In the sixteenth century C.E., the Spanish priest Bernadino de Sahagun interviewed Aztec informants to compile a substantial account of traditional Aztec society. Here we read his narration of ritual chants used by midwives during childbirth. Compare the gender roles presented here with those of other ancient civilizations in preceding chapters.

BERNADINO DE SAHAGUN, THE FLORENTINE CODEX

My precious son, my youngest one . . . Heed, hearken: Thy home is not here, for thou art an eagle, thou art an ocelot. . . . Thou art the serpent, the bird of the lord of the near, of the nigh. Here is only the place of thy nest. Thou hast only been hatched here; thou hast only come, arrived. . . . Thou belongest out there. . . . Thou hast been sent into warfare. War is the desert, thy task. Thou shalt give drink, nourishment, food to the sun, the lord of the earth. . . . Perhaps thou wilt receive the gift, perhaps thou wilt merit death by the obsidian knife, the flowered death by the obsidian knife.

My beloved maiden . . . Thou wilt be in the heart of the home, thou wilt go nowhere, thou wilt nowhere become a wanderer, thou becomest the banked fire, the hearth stones. Here our Lord planteth thee, burieth thee. And thou wilt become fatigued, thou wilt become tired, thou art to provide water, to grind maize, to drudge; thou art to sweat by the ashes, by the hearth.

LAND OF THE FEATHERED SERPENT: AZTEC RELIGION AND CULTURE

The Aztecs, like their contemporaries throughout Mesoamerica, lived in an environment populated by a multitude of gods. Scholars have identified more than a hundred deities in the Aztec pantheon; some of them were nature spirits, like the rain god, Tlaloc, and some were patron deities, like the symbol of the Aztecs themselves, Huitzilopochtli. A supreme deity, called Ometeotl, represented the all-powerful and omnipresent forces of the heavens, but he was rather remote, and other gods, notably the feathered serpent Quetzalcoatl, had a more direct impact on the lives of the people. Representing the forces of creation, virtue, and learning and culture, Quetzalcoatl bears a distinct similarity to Siva in Hindu belief. According to Aztec tradition, this godlike being had left his homeland in the Valley of Mexico in the tenth century, promising to return in triumph (see "The Mystery of Mayan Decline" earlier in this chapter).

Aztec cosmology was based on a belief in the existence of two worlds, the material and the divine. The earth was the material world and took the form of a flat disk surrounded by water on all sides. The divine world, which

© Courtesy of William J. Duiker

QUETZALCOATL.
Quetzalcoatl was one of the favorite deities of the Central American peoples. His visage of a plumed serpent, as shown here, was prominent in the royal capital of Teotihuacán. According to legend, Quetzalcoatl, the leader of the Toltecs, was tricked into drunkenness and humiliated by a rival god. In disgrace, he left his homeland but promised to return. In 1519, the Aztec monarch Moctezuma welcomed Hernán Cortés, the leader of the Spanish expedition, believing that he was a representative of Quetzalcoatl.

consisted of both heaven and hell, was the abode of the gods. Human beings could aspire to a form of heavenly salvation but first had to pass through a transitional stage, somewhat like Christian purgatory, before reaching their final destination, where the soul was finally freed from the body. To prepare for the final day of judgment, as well as to help them engage in proper behavior through life, all citizens underwent religious training at temple schools during adolescence and took part in various rituals throughout their lives. The most devout were encouraged to study for the priesthood. Once accepted, they served at temples ranging from local branches at the *calpulli* level to the highest shrines in the ceremonial precinct at Tenochtitlán. In some respects, however, Aztec society may have been undergoing a process of secularization. By late Aztec times, athletic contests at the ball court had apparently lost some of their religious significance. Gambling was increasingly common, and wagering over the results of the matches was widespread. One province reportedly sent sixteen thousand rubber balls to the capital city of Tenochtitlán as its annual tribute to the royal court.

Aztec religion contained a distinct element of fatalism that was inherent in the creation myth, which described an unceasing struggle between the forces of good and evil throughout the universe. This struggle led to the creation and destruction of four worlds, or suns. The world was now living in the time of the fifth sun. But that world, too, was destined to end with the destruction of this earth and all that is within it:

> Even jade is shattered,
> Even gold is crushed,
> Even quetzal plumes are torn. . . .
> One does not live forever on this earth:
> We endure only for an instant![3]

In an effort to postpone the day of reckoning, the Aztecs practiced human sacrifice. The Aztecs believed that by appeasing the sun god, Huitzilopochtli, with sacrifices, they could delay the final destruction of their world. Victims were prepared for the ceremony through elaborate rituals and then brought to the holy shrine, where their hearts were ripped out of their chests and presented to the gods as a holy offering. It was an honor to be chosen for sacrifice, and captives were often used as sacrificial victims, since they represented valor, the trait the Aztecs prized most.

Like the art of the Olmecs, most Aztec architecture, art, and sculpture had religious significance. At the center of the capital city of Tenochtitlán was the sacred precinct, dominated by the massive pyramid dedicated to Huitzilopochtli and the rain god, Tlaloc. According to Bernal Díaz, at its base, the pyramid was equal to the plots of six large European town houses and tapered from there to the top, which was surmounted by a platform containing shrines to the gods and an altar for performing human sacrifices. The entire pyramid was covered with brightly colored paintings and sculptures.

Although little Aztec painting survives, it was evidently of high quality. Bernal Díaz compared the best work with that of Michelangelo. Artisans worked with stone and with soft metals such as gold and silver, which they cast using the lost-wax technique. They did not have the knowledge for making implements in bronze or iron, however. Stoneworking consisted primarily of representations of the gods and bas-reliefs depicting religious ceremonies. Among the most famous is the massive disk called the Stone of the Sun, carved for use at the central pyramid at Tenochtitlán.

The Aztecs had devised a form of writing based on hieroglyphs that represented an object or a concept. The symbols had no phonetic significance and did not constitute a writing system as such but could give the sense of a message and were probably used by civilian or religious officials as notes or memorandums for their orations. A trained class of scribes carefully painted the notes on paper made from the inner bark of fig trees. Unfortunately, many of these notes were destroyed by the Spaniards as part of their effort to eradicate all aspects of Aztec religion and culture.

THE DESTRUCTION OF AZTEC CIVILIZATION

For a century, the Aztec kingdom dominated much of central Mexico from the Atlantic to the Pacific coast, and its influence penetrated as far south as present-day Guatemala. Most local officials had accepted the sovereignty of the king in Tenochtitlán, but in Tlaxcallan to the east, the authorities were restive under Aztec rule.

In 1519, a Spanish expedition under the command of Hernán Cortés landed at Veracruz, on the Gulf of Mexico (see Chapter 14). Marching to Tenochtitlán at the head of a small contingent of troops, Cortés received a friendly welcome from the Aztec monarch Moctezuma Xocoyotzin (often called Montezuma), who initially believed his visitor was a representative of Quetzalcoatl, the godlike "feathered serpent." The king and his subjects were astounded to see men on horseback, for the horse had disappeared from the Americas at least ten thousand years earlier.

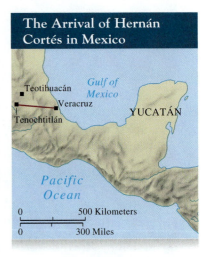

The Arrival of Hernán Cortés in Mexico

But tensions soon erupted between the Spaniards and the Aztecs, provoked in part by demands by Cortés that the Aztecs denounce their native beliefs and accept Christianity. When the Spanish took Moctezuma hostage and began to destroy Aztec religious shrines, the local population revolted and drove the invaders from the city. Receiving assistance from the state of Tlaxcallan, Cortés managed to fight his way back into the city. Meanwhile the Aztecs were beginning to suffer the first effects of the diseases brought by the Europeans, which would eventually wipe out the majority of the local population. In a battle that to many Aztecs must have seemed to symbolize the dying of the legendary fifth sun, the Aztecs were finally vanquished. Within months, their magnificent city and its temples, believed by the conquerors to be the work of Satan, had been destroyed.

THE FIRST CIVILIZATIONS IN SOUTH AMERICA

South America is a vast continent, characterized by extremes in climate and geography. The north is dominated by the mighty Amazon River, which flows through dense tropical jungles carrying a larger flow of water than any other river system in the world (see Map 6.3). Farther to the south, the jungles are replaced by prairies and steppes stretching westward to the Andes Mountains, which extend the entire length of the continent, from the Isthmus of Panama to the Strait of Magellan. Along the Pacific coast, on the western slopes of the mountains, are some of the driest desert regions in the world.

South America has been inhabited by human beings for more than twelve thousand years. Wall paintings discovered at the "cavern of the painted rock" in the Amazon region suggest that Stone Age peoples were living in the area at least eleven thousand years ago. Early peoples were hunters, fishermen, and food gatherers, but there are indications that irrigated farming was practiced in the northern fringe of the Andes Mountains as early as 2000 B.C.E. Other farming communities of similar age have been discovered in the Amazon River valley and on the western slopes of the Andes, where evidence of terraced agriculture dates back about four thousand years.

By the sixth millennium B.C.E., complex societies had emerged in the central Andes Mountains, in the region of modern Peru, Bolivia, and Ecuador. Archaeologists have discovered the remains of ceremonial precincts, complete with temples, ancestral tombs, and pyramids, similar to those of Mesoamerica. This early Andes civilization may have originated as early as about 2500 B.C.E. (archaeologists have recently discovered the remains of an ancient city in northwestern Peru, with several examples of public architecture and evidence of irrigated agriculture), but it reached its height during the first millennium B.C.E. with the emergence of the Chavin style, named for a site near the modern city of Chavin de Huantar, in the central mountains of modern Peru. The ceremonial precinct at

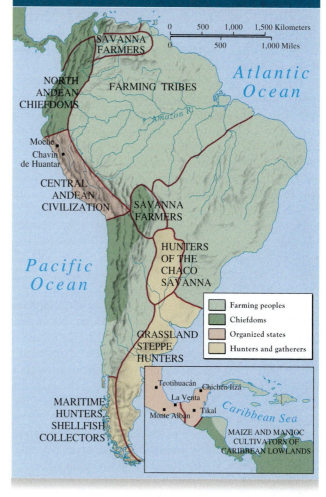

MAP 6.3 **Early Peoples and Cultures of Central and South America.** This map shows regions of early human settlements in Central and South America. Urban conglomerations appear in Mesoamerica (see inset) and along the western coast of South America. ➤ *Locate on the map the heartland of Incan civilization.*

the Chavin site contained an impressive stone temple complete with interior galleries, a stone-block ceiling, and a system of underground canals that probably channeled water into the temple complex for ritualistic purposes.

Moche

Early in the first millennium C.E., another advanced civilization, comprising a total area of over 2,500 square miles, appeared in northern Peru, in the valley of the Moche River, which flows from the foothills of the Andes into the Pacific Ocean. The capital city, large enough in territory to contain over ten thousand people, was dominated by two massive adobe pyramids rising as much as 100 feet high. The largest, known as the Pyramid of the Moon, covered a total of 15 acres and was adorned with painted murals depicting battles, ritual sacrifices, and various local deities.

Artifacts found at Moche, especially the metalwork and stone and ceramic figures, exhibit a high quality of artisanship. They were imitated at river valley sites throughout the surrounding area, which suggests that the authority of the Moche rulers may have extended as far as 400 miles along the coast. The artifacts also indicate that the people at Moche, like those in Central America, were preoccupied with warfare. The Moche were also fascinated by the heavens, and much of their art consisted of celestial symbols and astronomical constellations.

The Moche River valley is extremely arid, receiving less than an inch of rain annually. The peoples in the area compensated by building a sophisticated irrigation system to carry water from the river to the parched fields. At its zenith, Moche culture was spectacular. By the eighth century C.E., however, the civilization was in a state of collapse, the irrigation canals had been abandoned, and the remaining population suffered from severe malnutrition.

What had happened to bring Moche culture to this untimely end? Archaeologists speculate that environmental changes, perhaps brought on by changes in the water temperature known as El Niño, led to major flooding of coastal regions and the advance of sand dunes into the irrigated fields.

Three hundred years later, a new power, the kingdom of Chimor, with its capital at Chanchan, at the mouth of the Moche River, emerged in the area. Built almost entirely of adobe, Chanchan housed an estimated thirty thousand residents in an area of over 12 square miles that included a number of palace compounds surrounded by walls nearly 30 feet high. Like the Moche before them, the people of Chimor relied on irrigation to funnel the water from the river into their fields. An elaborate system of canals brought the water through hundreds of miles of hilly terrain to the fields near the coast. Nevertheless, by the fifteenth century, Chimor, too, had disappeared, a victim of floods and a series of earthquakes that destroyed the intricate irrigation system that had been the basis of its survival.

These early civilizations in the Andes were by no means isolated from other societies in the region. As early as 2000 B.C.E., local peoples had been venturing into the Pacific Ocean on wind-powered rafts constructed of balsa wood. By the late first millennium C.E., seafarers from the coast of Ecuador had established a vast trading network that extended southward to central Peru and as far north as western Mexico, over 2,000 miles away. Items transported included jewelry, beads, and metal goods.

The Inca

The Chimor kingdom was eventually succeeded in the late fifteenth century by an invading force from the mountains far to the south. In the late fourteenth century, the Incas were only a small community in the area of Cuzco, a city located at an altitude of 10,000 feet in the mountains of southern Peru. In the 1440s, however, under the leadership of their powerful ruler Pachakuti (sometimes called Pachacutec, or "he who transforms the world"), the Inca peoples launched a campaign of conquest that eventually brought the entire region under their authority. Under Pachakuti and his immediate successors, Topa Inca and Huayna Inca (the word *Inca* means "ruler"), the boundaries of the kingdom were extended as far as Ecuador, central Chile, and the edge of the Amazon basin.

THE FOUR QUARTERS: INCA POLITICS AND SOCIETY

Pachakuti created a highly centralized state (see Map 6.4). With a stunning concern for mathematical precision, he divided his empire, called Tahuantinsuyu, or "the world of the four quarters," into provinces and districts. Each

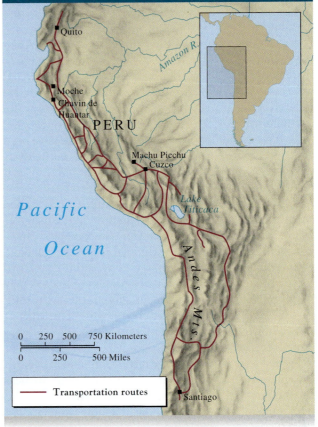

MAP 6.4   The Inca Empire About 1500 C.E. The Inca were the last civilization to flourish in South America prior to the arrival of the Spanish. The impressive system of roads constructed to facilitate communication shows the extent of Inca control throughout the Andes Mountains. ➤ *In what modern countries was the Inca state located?*

🌿 **MACHU PICCHU.** Situated in the Andes in modern Peru, Machu Picchu reflects the glory of Inca civilization. To farm such rugged terrain, the Incas constructed terraces and stone aqueducts. To span vast ravines, they built suspension bridges made of braided fiber and fastened them to stone abutments on the opposite banks. The most revered of the many temples and stone altars at Machu Picchu was the thronelike "hitching post of the sun," so called because of its close proximity to the sun god.

province contained about ten thousand residents (at least in theory) and was ruled by a governor related to the royal family. Excess inhabitants were transferred to other locations. The capital of Cuzco was divided into four quarters, or residential areas, and the social status and economic functions of the residents of each quarter were rigidly defined.

The state was built on forced labor. Often entire communities of workers were moved from one part of the country to another to open virgin lands or engage in massive construction projects. Under Pachakuti, the capital of Cuzco was transformed from a city of mud and thatch into an imposing metropolis of stone. The walls, built of close-fitting stones without the use of mortar, were a wonder to early European visitors. The most impressive structure in the city was a temple dedicated to the sun. According to a Spanish observer, "All four walls of the temple were covered from top to bottom with plates and slabs of gold."[4] Equally impressive are the ruins of the abandoned city of Machu Picchu, built on a lofty hilltop far above the Urubamba River.

Another major construction project was a system of 24,800 miles of highways and roads that extended from the border of modern Colombia to a point south of modern Santiago, Chile. Two major roadways extended in a north-south direction, one through the Andes Mountains and the other along the coast, with connecting routes between them. Rest houses and storage depots were placed along the roads. Suspension bridges made of braided fiber and fastened to stone abutments on opposite banks were built over ravines and waterways. Use of the highways was restricted to official and military purposes. Trained runners carried messages rapidly from one way station to another, enabling information to travel up to 140 miles in a single day.

In rural areas, the population lived mainly by farming. In the mountains, the most common form was terraced agriculture, watered by irrigation systems that carried precise amounts of water into the fields, which were planted with maize, potatoes, and other crops. The plots were tilled by collective labor regulated by the state. Like other aspects of Inca society, marriage was strictly regulated, and men and women were required to select a marriage partner from within the immediate tribal group. For women, there was one escape from a life of domestic servitude. Fortunate maidens were selected to serve as "chosen virgins" in temples throughout the country. Noblewomen were eligible to compete for service in the Temple of the Sun at Cuzco, while commoners might hope to serve in temples in the provincial capitals. Punishment for breaking the vow of chastity was harsh, and few evidently took the risk.

INCA CULTURE

Like many other civilizations in pre-Columbian Latin America, the Inca state was built on war. Soldiers for the 200,000-man Inca army, the largest and best armed in the region, were raised by universal male conscription. Military units were moved rapidly along the highway system and were housed in the rest houses located along the roadside. Since the Inca had no wheeled vehicles, supplies were

An Incan Aide-Mémoire

The Inca did not possess a written script. To record events and other aspects of their lives that they wished to remember, they used an ingenious system of knotted strings, called quipu. *This description of the process comes from the* Royal Commentaries of the Incas, *an account of Inca civilization and history written by Garcilaso de la Vega. Garcilaso, who was of mixed Inca and Spanish blood, was born shortly before the Spanish conquest of the Incan capital of Cuzco.*

GARCILASO DE LA VEGA, ROYAL COMMENTARIES OF THE INCAS

These men recorded on their knots all the tribute brought annually to the Inca, specifying everything by kind, species, and quality. They recorded the number of men who went to the wars, how many died in them, and how many were born and died every year, month by month. In short they may be said to have recorded on their knots everything that could be counted, even mentioning battles and fights, all the embassies that had come to visit the Inca, and all the speeches and arguments the king had uttered. But the purpose of the embassies or the contents of the speeches, or any other descriptive matter could not be recorded on the knots, consisting as it did of continuous spoken or written prose, which cannot be expressed by means of knots, since these can give only numbers and not words. To supply this want they used signs that indicated historical events or facts or the existence of any embassy, speech, or discussion in time of peace or war. Such speeches were preserved by the *quipu-camayus* by memory in a summarized form of a few words: they were committed to memory and taught by tradition to their successors and descendants from father to son. This was especially practiced in the villages or provinces where the event in question had occurred: there naturally such traditions were preserved better than elsewhere, because the natives would treasure them. Another method too was used for keeping alive in the memory of the people their deeds and the embassies they sent to the Inca and the replies he gave them. The *amautas* who were their philosophers and sages took the trouble to turn them into stories, no longer than fables, suitable for telling to children, young people, and the rustics of the countryside: they were thus passed from hand to hand and age to age, and preserved in the memories of all. Their stories were also recounted in the form of fables of an allegorical nature, some of which we have mentioned, while others will be referred to later. Similarly the *harauicus*, who were their poets, wrote short, compressed poems, embracing a history, or an embassy, or the king's reply. In short, everything that could not be recorded on the knots was included in these poems, which were sung at their triumphs and on the occasion of their greater festivals, and recited to the young Incas when they were armed knights. Thus they remembered their history.

---

carried on the backs of llamas. Once an area was placed under Incan authority, the local inhabitants were instructed in the Quechua language, which became the lingua franca of the state, and were introduced to the state religion. The Inca had no writing system but kept records using a system of knotted strings called *quipu* (see the box above).

As in the case of the Aztecs and the Maya, the lack of a fully developed writing system did not prevent the Inca from realizing a high level of cultural achievement. Most of what survives was recorded by the Spanish and consists of entertainment for the elites. The Inca had a highly developed tradition of court theater, including both tragic and comic works. There was also some poetry, composed in blank verse and often accompanied by music played on reed instruments.

THE CONQUEST OF THE INCA

The Inca Empire was still in existence when the first Spanish expeditions arrived in the central Andes. The leader of the Spanish invaders, Francisco Pizarro, was accompanied by only a few hundred companions, but like Cortés, he possessed steel weapons, gunpowder, and horses, none of which were familiar to his hosts. In the meantime, internal factionalism, combined with the onset of contagious diseases spread unknowingly by the Europeans, had weakened the ruling elite, and the empire fell rapidly to the Spanish forces in 1532. The last Inca ruler was tried by the Spaniards and executed. Pre-Columbian South America's greatest age was over.

✦ STATELESS SOCIETIES IN THE NEW WORLD

Beyond Central America and the high ridges of the Andes Mountains, on the Great Plains of North America, along the Amazon River in South America, and on the islands of the Caribbean Sea, other communities of Amerindians were also beginning to master the art of agriculture and to build organized societies.

Although human beings had occupied much of the continent of North America during the early phase of human settlement in the New World, the switch to farming as a means of survival did not occur until the third millennium B.C.E. at the earliest, and not until much later

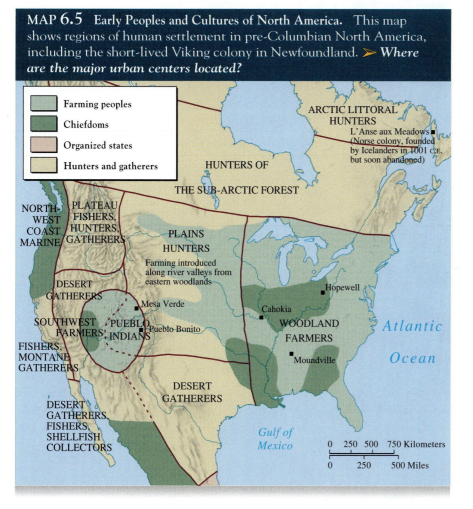

MAP 6.5 **Early Peoples and Cultures of North America.** This map shows regions of human settlement in pre-Columbian North America, including the short-lived Viking colony in Newfoundland. ➤ *Where are the major urban centers located?*

Legend:
- Farming peoples
- Chiefdoms
- Organized states
- Hunters and gatherers

ARCTIC LITTORAL HUNTERS
L'Anse aux Meadows (Norse colony, founded by Icelanders in 1001 C.E. but soon abandoned)

HUNTERS OF THE SUB-ARCTIC FOREST

NORTH WEST COAST MARINE

PLATEAU FISHERS, HUNTERS, GATHERERS

PLAINS HUNTERS
Farming introduced along river valleys from eastern woodlands

DESERT GATHERERS

Mesa Verde

SOUTHWEST FARMERS

PUEBLO INDIANS
Pueblo Bonito

FISHERS, MONTANE GATHERERS

Hopewell

Cahokia

WOODLAND FARMERS

Atlantic Ocean

Moundville

DESERT GATHERERS

DESERT GATHERERS, FISHERS, SHELLFISH COLLECTORS

Gulf of Mexico

0   250 500   750 Kilometers
0   250   500 Miles

in most areas of the continent. Until that time, most Amerindian communities lived by hunting, fishing, or foraging.

It was probably during the third millennium B.C.E. that peoples in selected parts of North America began to cultivate indigenous plants for food in a systematic way. As wild game and food became scarce, some communities began to place more emphasis on cultivating crops. This shift first occurred in the Mississippi River valley from Ohio, Indiana, and Illinois down to the Gulf of Mexico (see Map 6.5). Among the most commonly cultivated crops were maize, squash, beans, and various grasses.

As the population in the area increased, people began to congregate in villages, and sedentary communities began to develop in the alluvial lowlands, where the soil could be cultivated for many years at a time because of the nutrients deposited by the river water. Village councils were established to adjudicate disputes, and in a few cases, several villages banded together under the authority of a local chieftain. Urban centers began to appear, some of them inhabited by ten thousand people or more. At the same time, regional trade increased. The people of the Hopewell culture in Ohio ranged from the shores of Lake Superior to the Appalachian Mountains and the Gulf of

Mexico in search of metals, shells, obsidian, and manufactured items to support their economic needs and religious beliefs.

At the site of Cahokia, near the modern city of East Saint Louis, Illinois, archaeologists found a burial mound more than 98 feet high with a base larger than that of the Great Pyramid in Egypt. A hundred smaller mounds were also found in the vicinity. The town itself, which covered almost 300 acres and was surrounded by a wooden stockade, was apparently the administrative capital of much of the surrounding territory until its decline in the thirteenth century C.E. With a population of over twenty thousand, it was reportedly the largest city in North America until Philadelphia surpassed that number in the early nineteenth century. Cahokia carried on extensive trade with other communities throughout the region, and there are some signs of regular contacts with the civilizations in Mesoamerica, such as the presence of ball courts in the Central American style. But wars were not uncommon, leading the Iroquois, who inhabited much of the modern states of Pennsylvania and New York as well as parts of southern Canada, to create a tribal alliance called the League of Iroquois.

West of the Mississippi River basin, most Amerindian peoples lived by hunting or food gathering. During the first millennium C.E., knowledge of agriculture gradually spread up the rivers to the Great Plains, and farming was practiced as far west as southwestern Colorado, where the Anasazi peoples (Navajo for "alien ancient ones") established an extensive agricultural community in an area extending from northern New Mexico and Arizona to southwestern Colorado and parts of southern Utah. Although they apparently never discovered the wheel or used beasts of burden, the Anasazi created a system of roads that facilitated an extensive exchange of technology, products, and ideas throughout the region. By the ninth century, they had mastered the art of irrigation, which allowed them to expand their productive efforts to squash and beans, and had established an important urban center at Chaco Canyon, in southern New Mexico, where they built a walled city with dozens of three-story adobe houses with timbered roofs. Community religious functions were carried out in two large circular chambers called kivas. Clothing was made from hides or cotton cloth. At

© Courtesy of William J. Duiker

CLIFF PALACE AT MESA VERDE. Mesa Verde is one of the best-developed sites of the Anasazi peoples in southwestern North America. At one time, they were farmers who tilled the soil atop the mesas, but eventually they were forced to build their settlements in more protected locations. At Cliff Palace, shown here, adobe houses were hidden on the perpendicular face of the mesa. Access was achieved only by a perilous descent via indented finger- and toeholds on the rock face.

its height, Pueblo Bonito contained several hundred compounds housing several thousand residents. Another urban community was eventually established along a cliff face at Mesa Verde, in southwestern Colorado.

Sometime during the late twelfth and thirteenth centuries, however, these settlements were suddenly abandoned, and the inhabitants migrated southward. Their descendants, the Zuni and the Hopi, now occupy pueblos in central Arizona and New Mexico. For years, archaeologists surmised that a severe drought was the cause of the migration, but in recent years, new evidence has raised doubts that decreasing rainfall, by itself, was a sufficient explanation. An increase in internecine warfare, perhaps brought about by climatic changes, may also have played a role in the decision to relocate. Some archaeologists point to evidence that cannibalism was practiced at Pueblo Bonito and suggest that migrants from the south may have arrived in the area, provoking bitter rivalries within Anasazi society. In any event, with increasing aridity and the importation of the horse by the Spanish in the sixteenth century, hunting revived, and mounted nomads like

the Apache and the Navajo came to dominate much of the Southwest.

East of the Andes Mountains in South America, other Amerindian societies were beginning to make the transition to agriculture. Perhaps the most prominent were the Arawak, a people living along the Orinoco River in modern Venezuela. Having begun to cultivate manioc (a tuber used today in the manufacture of tapioca) along the banks of the river, they gradually migrated down to the coast and then proceeded to move eastward along the northern coast of the continent. Some occupied the islands of the Caribbean Sea. In their new island habitat, they lived by a mixture of fishing, hunting, and cultivating maize, beans, manioc, and squash, as well as other crops such as peanuts, peppers, and pineapples. As the population increased, a pattern of political organization above the village level appeared, along with recognizable social classes headed by a chieftain whose authority included control over the economy. The Arawak practiced human sacrifice, and some urban centers contained ball courts, suggesting the possibility of contacts with Mesoamerica.

In most such societies, where clear-cut class stratifications had not as yet taken place, men and women were considered of equal status. Men were responsible for hunting, warfare, and dealing with outsiders, while women were accountable for the crops, the distribution of food, maintaining the household, and bearing and raising the children. Their roles were complementary and were often viewed as a divine division of labor. In such cases, women in the stateless societies of North America held positions of greater respect than their counterparts in the river valley civilizations of the Old World.

 ## CONCLUSION

The first human beings did not arrive in the New World until quite late in the prehistorical period. For the next several millennia, their descendants were forced to respond to the challenges of the environment in total isolation from other parts of the world. Nevertheless, around 5000 B.C.E., farming settlements began to appear in river valleys and upland areas in both Central and South America. Not long afterward—as measured in historical time—organized communities located along the coast of the Gulf of Mexico and the western slopes of the central Andes Mountains embarked on the long march toward civilization. Along the same path, although perhaps somewhat less advanced in technological terms, were the emerging societies of North America, which were beginning to expand their commercial and cultural links with civilizations farther to the south and had already laid the foundations for future urbanization. Although the total number of people living in the New World is a matter of debate, some scholars estimate a figure between ten and twenty million.

What is perhaps most striking about the developments in the New World is how closely the process paralleled that in the Old. Although the civilizations in Central and South America were less advanced in terms of technology (the lack of iron and the wheel, for example, and the absence of a sophisticated writing system), in many other respects, the states in Central America and the Andes were the equal of those that we will discuss in later chapters. One need only point to the awed comments of early Spanish visitors, who said that the cities of the Aztecs were the equal of Seville and the other great metropolitan centers of Spain.

What was most repugnant to those early European visitors were the religious beliefs and practices of the civilizations that they encountered. They were repelled by the worship of strange idols and even more by the human sacrifices on a massive scale. Before rushing to judgment, however, we should remember that similar practices had been carried out in many societies of the Old World, including the ancient civilizations of Egypt, India, and China. The Spaniards were perhaps most surprised to discover that civilizations that in other respects had achieved such a high degree of culture also practiced human sacrifice.

In recent years, some scholars have speculated that the peoples in the Americas were more peaceful than their counterparts in the Old World. The bulk of the evidence, however, suggests that the Amerindian peoples were every bit as addicted to warfare as those of the ancient empires of Africa and Asia. In the end, military prowess was of little help when the peoples of the Americas encountered the first visitors from overseas. The Europeans' advanced military technology and their mastery of horseback riding gave them a major advantage over the local population. Just as sedentary peoples in ancient Europe were often overwhelmed by nomads migrating westward from the steppes of Central Asia, so the armies of the Aztecs and Incas were no match for the Spanish conquistadors, whose mobility on horseback had been increased through recent European contacts with Arab warriors in North Africa and the Middle East. Yet it should be noted that in the New World as in the Old, many of the first civilizations formed by the human species appear to have been brought to an end as much by environmental changes as by war. In the next chapter, we shall return to the Old World, where new civilizations were in the process of replacing the ancient empires.

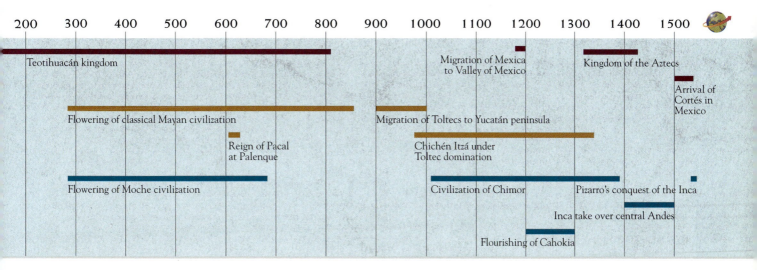

CHAPTER NOTES

1. Quoted in Sylvanus G. Morley and George W. Brainerd, *The Ancient Maya* (Stanford, Calif., 1983), p. 513.
2. Bernal Díaz, *The Conquest of New Spain* (Harmondsworth, England, 1975), p. 210.
3. Michael D. Coe, Dean Snow, and Elizabeth P. Benson, *Atlas of Ancient America* (New York, 1988), p. 149.
4. Garcilaso de la Vega (El Inca), *Royal Commentaries of the Incas and General History of Peru*, pt. 1, trans. Harold V. Livermore (Austin, Tex., 1966), p. 180.

SUGGESTED READING

For a profusely illustrated and informative overview of the early civilizations of the Americas, see M. D. Coe, D. Snow, and E. P. Benson, *Atlas of Ancient America* (New York, 1988). The first arrival of human beings in the New World is discussed in B. Fagan, *The Great Journey: The Peopling of Ancient America* (London, 1987).

For an early classical work on Mayan civilization, see S. G. Morley and G. W. Brainerd, *The Ancient Maya* (Stanford, Calif., 1983). N. Hammond, *Ancient Maya Civilization* (New Brunswick, N.J., 1982), provides a general survey for the nonspecialist. See also M. D. Coe, *The Maya* (London, 1993), and J. Sabloff, *The New Archeology and the Ancient Maya* (New York, 1990).

For an overview of Aztec civilization in Mexico, see B. Fagan, *The Aztecs* (New York, 1984). S. D. Gillespie, *The Aztec Kings: The Construction of Rulership in Mexican History* (Tucson, Ariz., 1989), is an imaginative effort to uncover the symbolic meaning in Aztec traditions. For a provocative study of religious traditions in a comparative context, see B. Fagan, *From Black Land to Fifth Sun* (Reading, Mass., 1998). On the Olmecs, see E. P. Benson, *The Olmec and Their Neighbors* (Washington, D.C., 1981), and M. D. Coe and R. A. Diehl, *In the Land of the Olmec* (Austin, Tex., 1980).

Much of our information about the lives of the peoples of ancient Central America comes from Spanish writers who visited or lived in the area during the sixteenth and seventeenth centuries. For the original Spanish conquest of Mexico, see H. Cortés, *Letters from Mexico* (New Haven, Conn., 1986), and B. Díaz, *The Conquest of New Spain* (Harmondsworth, England, 1975). See also D. Duran, *The Aztecs: The History of the Indies of New Spain* (New York, 1964).

On the Inca and their predecessors, see R. W. Keatinge, ed., *Peruvian Prehistory: An Overview of Pre-Inca and Inca Society* (Cambridge, 1988); G. Bankes, *Peru Before Pizarro* (Oxford, 1977); and E. P. Lanning, *Peru Before the Incas* (Englewood Cliffs, N.J., 1967). The arrival of the Spanish is chronicled in C. Howard, *Pizarro and the Conquest of Peru* (New York, 1967). For an extended account of Inca civilization, see G. de la Vega (El Inca), *Royal Commentaries of the Incas and General History of Peru* (Austin, Tex., 1966).

On the art and culture of the ancient Americas, see M. E. Miller, *Maya Art and Architecture* (London, 1999); E. Pasztory, *Pre-Columbian Art* (Cambridge, 1998); and L. Schele and M. E. Miller, *The Blood of Kings: Ritual and Dynasty in Maya Art* (New York, 1992). Writing systems are discussed in D. H. Kelley, *Deciphering the Maya Script* (Austin, Tex., 1976), and J. E. S. Thompson, *Maya Hieroglyphic Writing: An Introduction* (Norman, Okla., 1971).

On social issues, see L. Schele and D. Freidel, *A Forest of Kings: The Untold Story of the Ancient Maya* (New York, 1990); R. van Zantwijk, *The Aztec Arrangement: The Social History of Pre-Spanish Mexico* (Norman, Okla., 1985); and N. Shoemaker, *Negotiators of Change: Historical Perspectives on Native American Women* (New York, 1995).

INFOTRAC COLLEGE EDITION

Visit the source collections at **infotrac.thomsonlearning.com** and use the Search function with the following key terms.

Aztec	Latin American history	Maya or Mayan
Inca or Incan	Machu Picchu	

WORLD HISTORY RESOURCES

Visit the *Essential World History* Companion Web Site for resources specific to this textbook:

http://history.wadsworth.com/duikeressentials02/

The CD in the back of this book and the World History Resource Center at **http://history.wadsworth.com/world/** offer a variety of tools to help you succeed in this course, including access to quizzes; images; documents; interactive simulations, maps, and timelines; movie explorations; and a wealth of other sources.

Courtesy of William J. Duiker

ISLAM AND BYZANTIUM

FOCUS QUESTIONS

- What are the main tenets of Islam, and how does the religion compare with Judaism and Christianity?
- Why did the Arabs undergo such a rapid expansion in the seventh and eighth centuries, and why were they so successful in amassing an empire?
- What were the basic political structures of the Arab Empire under the Umayyads and the Abbasids, and how did the Seljuk Turks, the Crusades, and the Mongols affect Islamic civilization?
- What were the main features of Islamic society and culture?
- ➤ What were the main characteristics of Byzantine and Islamic civilizations, and why and in what ways did they come into conflict?

The collapse of Roman power in the Mediterranean led to the emergence of three new civilizations. In the west, Roman elements combined with German influences and Christianity to form a new Christian European civilization (see Chapter 12). The eastern part of the old Roman Empire, increasingly Greek in culture, continued to flourish as the Christian Byzantine Empire. Although the European civilization of the west and the Byzantine civilization of the east came to share a common bond in Christianity, it proved incapable of keeping them in harmony politically as the two civilizations continued to move apart. The rise of an Islamic Empire, Rome's third heir, resulted in the loss of the southern and eastern Mediterranean worlds of the old Roman Empire to a religious power that was neither Roman nor Christian and brought a conflict between the Islamic and Byzantine worlds in the eastern Mediterranean that lasted for centuries.

In the year 570, in the Arabian city of Mecca, there was born a child named Muhammad whose life changed the course of world history. The son of a merchant, Muhammad grew to maturity in a time of transition. Old empires that had once ruled the entire Middle East were only a distant memory. The region was now divided into many separate states, and the people adhered to many different faiths.

Within a few decades of Muhammad's death, the Middle East was united once again. The initial triumph was primarily political and military. Arab armies marched westward across North Africa and eastward into Mesopotamia and Persia, imposing their authority and creating a new empire that stretched from the Iberian peninsula to the Indus valley. But Arab rule also brought with it a new religion and a new culture—Islam.

Islamic beliefs and culture exerted a powerful influence in all areas occupied by Arab armies. Initially, Arab beliefs and customs, as reflected through the prism of Muhammad's teachings, transformed the societies and cultures of the peoples living in the new empire. But eventually, the distinctive political and cultural forces that had long characterized the region began to reassert themselves. Factional struggles led to the decline and then the destruction of the Arab Empire. Invading forces from Central Asia established their control over the great mercantile cities of the region, while Christian crusaders attacked the empire from the west. New states formed in Spain, North Africa, and Persia and began to put their own stamp on the cultures of the region. Like the empires that had preceded it, the Arab Empire, with its capital at Baghdad, became a thing of the past. Still, the Arab conquest left a powerful legacy that survived the decline of Arab political power. •

THE RISE OF ISLAM

The Arabs were a Semitic-speaking people of southwestern Asia with a long history. The Greek historian Herodotus had applied the name *Arab* to the entire peninsula, calling it Arabia. In 106 B.C.E., the Romans extended their authority to the Arabian peninsula, transforming it into a province of their growing empire.

During Roman times, the region was inhabited primarily by the Bedouin Arabs, nomadic peoples who came originally from the northern part of the peninsula. Bedouin society was organized on a tribal basis. The ruling member of the tribe was called the *sheikh* and was selected from one of the leading families by a council of elders called the *majlis*. The *sheikh* ruled the tribe with the consent of the council. Each tribe was autonomous but felt a general sense of allegiance to the larger unity of all the clans in the region. In early times, the Bedouins had supported themselves primarily by sheepherding or by raiding passing caravans, but after the domestication of the camel during the first millennium B.C.E., the Bedouins began to participate in the caravan trade themselves and became major carriers of goods between the Persian Gulf and the Mediterranean Sea.

The Arabs of pre-Islamic times were polytheistic, with a supreme god known as Allah presiding over a community of spirits. It was a communal faith, involving all members of the tribe, and had no priesthood. The supreme deity was symbolized by a sacred stone. Each tribe possessed its own stone, but all worshiped a massive black meteorite, which was located in a central shrine called the Ka'aba in the commercial city of Mecca.

In the fifth and sixth centuries C.E., the economic importance of the Arabian peninsula began to increase. As a result of the political disorder in Mesopotamia—a consequence of the constant wars between the Byzantine and Persian Empires—and in Egypt, the trade routes that ran directly across the peninsula or down the Red Sea became increasingly risky, and a third route, which passed from the Mediterranean through Mecca to Yemen and then by ship across the Indian Ocean, became more popular (see Map 7.1). The communities in that part of the peninsula benefited from the change. As a consequence, relations between the Bedouins of the desert and the increasingly wealthy merchants of the towns began to become strained.

The Role of Muhammad

Into this intense world stepped Muhammad (also known as Mohammed), a man whose spiritual visions unified the Arab world with a speed no one would have suspected possible. Born in Mecca to a merchant family and orphaned at the age of six, Muhammad (570–632) grew up to become a caravan manager and eventually married a rich widow, Khadija, who was also his employer. For several years, he lived in Mecca as a merchant but was apparently troubled by the growing gap between the Bedouin values of honesty and generosity (he himself was a member of the local Hashemite clan of the Quraishi tribe) and the acquisitive behavior of the affluent commercial elites in the city. Deeply concerned, he began to visit the nearby hills to meditate in isolation.

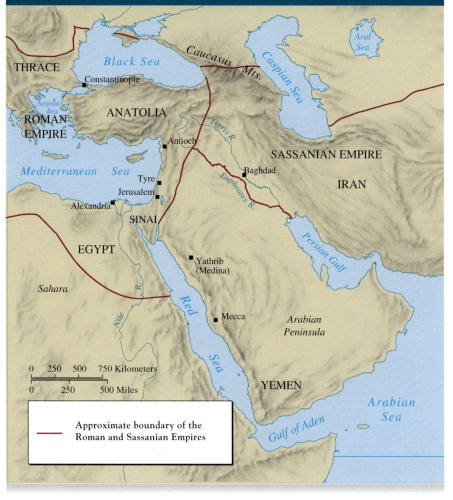

MAP 7.1 **The Middle East in the Time of Muhammad.** When Islam began to spread throughout the Middle East in the early seventh century, the dominant states in the region were the Roman Empire in the eastern Mediterranean and the Sassanian Empire in Persia. ➤ *What were the major territorial divisions existing at the time and the key sites connected to the rise of Islam?*

THRACE
Black Sea
Constantinople
Caucasus Mts.
Caspian Sea
Aral Sea
Aegean Sea
ROMAN EMPIRE
ANATOLIA
Antioch
Tigris R.
Baghdad
SASSANIAN EMPIRE
Euphrates R.
IRAN
Mediterranean Sea
Tyre
Jerusalem
Alexandria
SINAI
EGYPT
Sahara
Nile R.
Yathrib (Medina)
Red Sea
Mecca
Arabian Peninsula
Persian Gulf
0   250   500   750 Kilometers
0   250   500 Miles
YEMEN
Gulf of Aden
Arabian Sea

Approximate boundary of the Roman and Sassanian Empires

the Book," believers in a faith based on scripture.

After returning home, Muhammad set out to comply with Gabriel's command by preaching to the residents of Mecca about his revelations. At first, many were convinced that he was a madman or a charlatan. Others were undoubtedly concerned that his vigorous attacks on traditional beliefs and the corrupt society around him could severely shake the social and political order. After three years of proselytizing, he had only thirty followers.

Discouraged by the systematic persecution of his followers, which was undertaken with a brutality reminiscent of the cruelties suffered by early Christians, as well as the failure of the Meccans to accept his message, in 622 Muhammad and some of his closest supporters (mostly from his own Hashemite clan) left the city and retreated north to the rival city of Yathrib, later renamed Medina, or "city of the Prophet." That flight, known in history as the Hegira (*Hijrah*), marks the first date on the official calendar of Islam. At Medina, Muhammad failed in his original purpose—to convert the Jewish community in Medina to his beliefs. But he was successful in winning support from many residents of the city as well as from Bedouins in the surrounding countryside. From this mixture, he formed the first Muslim community (the *umma*). Returning to his birthplace at the head of a considerable military force, Muhammad conquered Mecca and converted the townspeople to the new faith. In 630, he made a symbolic visit to the Ka'aba, where he declared it a sacred shrine of Islam and ordered the destruction of the idols of the traditional faith. Two years later, Muhammad died, just as Islam was beginning to spread throughout the peninsula.

The Teachings of Muhammad

Like Christianity and Judaism, Islam is monotheistic. Allah is the all-powerful being who created the universe and everything in it. Islam is also concerned with salvation and offers the hope of an afterlife. Those who hope to achieve it must subject themselves to the will of Allah.

On one of these occasions, he experienced visions and heard a voice that he was convinced was inspired by Allah. According to tradition, the message was conveyed by the angel Gabriel, who commanded Muhammad to preach the revelations that he would be given.

Muhammad was acquainted with Jewish and Christian beliefs and came to believe that while Allah had already revealed himself in part through Moses and Jesus—and thus through the Hebraic and Christian traditions—the final revelations were now being given to him. Out of his revelations, which were eventually dictated to scribes, came the Koran or Qur'an, the holy scriptures of Islam (*Islam* means "submission," implying submission to the will of Allah). The Koran contained the guidelines by which followers of Allah, known as Muslims (practitioners of Islam), were to live. Like the Christians and the Jews, Muslims (also known as Moslems) were a "people of

THE KORAN AND THE SPREAD OF THE MUSLIM FAITH

The Koran is the sacred book of Islam, holding a place comparable to that of the Bible in Christianity. In this selection from Chapter 47, it is apparent that Islam encourages the spreading of the faith. A garden of paradise quite unlike the arid desert homeland of the Arab warriors awaited all believers who died for Allah. In many Islamic countries today, militants are encouraged to battle with their enemies by the promise of entry into paradise as described here.

THE KORAN: CHAPTER 47, "MUHAMMAD, REVEALED AT MEDINA"

Allah will bring to nothing the deeds of those who disbelieve and debar others from His path. As for the faithful who do good works and believe in what is revealed to Muhammad—which is the truth from their Lord—He will forgive them their sins and ennoble their state.

This, because the unbelievers follow falsehood, while the faithful follow the truth from their Lord. Thus Allah coins their sayings for mankind.

When you meet the unbelievers in the battlefield strike off their heads and, when you have laid them low, bind your captives firmly. Then grant them their freedom or take ransom from them, until War shall lay down her armour.

Thus shall you do. Had Allah willed, He could Himself have punished them; but He has ordained it thus that He might test you, the one by the other.

As for those who are slain in the cause of Allah, He will not allow their works to perish. He will vouchsafe them guidance and ennoble their state; He will admit them to the Paradise He has made known to them.

Believers, if you help Allah, Allah will help you and make you strong. But the unbelievers shall be consigned to perdition. He will bring their deeds to nothing. Because they have opposed His revelations, He will frustrate their works.

Have they never journeyed through the land and seen what was the end of those who have gone before them? Allah destroyed them utterly. A similar fate awaits the unbelievers, because Allah is the protector of the faithful; because the unbelievers have no protector.

Allah will admit those who embrace the true faith and do good works to gardens watered by running streams. The unbelievers take their fill of pleasure and eat as the beasts eat: but Hell shall be their home. . . .

This is the Paradise which the righteous have been promised. There shall flow in it rivers of unpolluted water, and rivers of milk forever fresh; rivers of delectable wine and rivers of clearest honey. They shall eat therein of every fruit and receive forgiveness from their Lord. Is this like the lot of those who shall abide in Hell forever and drink scalding water which will tear their bowels? . . .

Know that there is no god but Allah. Implore Him to forgive your sins and to forgive the true believers, men and women. Allah knows your busy haunts and resting places.

Unlike Christianity, Islam makes no claim to the divinity of its founder. Muhammad, like Jesus, Moses, and other figures of the Old Testament, was a prophet, but he was also a man like other men. Because human beings rejected his earlier messengers, Allah sent his final revelation through Muhammad.

At the heart of Islam is the Koran (meaning "recitation"), with its basic message that there is no God but Allah and Muhammad is his Prophet (see the box above). Consisting of 114 *suras* (chapters) that were drawn together into an integrated whole by a committee established after Muhammad's death, the Koran is not only the sacred book of Islam but also an ethical guidebook and a code of law and political theory combined.

Islam was a direct and simple faith, emphasizing the need to obey the will of Allah. This meant following a basic ethical code that consisted of what are popularly termed the Five Pillars of Islam: belief in Allah and Muhammad as his Prophet; standard prayer five times a day and public prayer on Friday at midday to worship Allah; observation of the holy month of Ramadan, including fasting from dawn to sunset; making a pilgrimage, if possible, to Mecca at least once in one's lifetime; and giving alms (called the *zakat*) to the poor and unfortunate. The faithful who observed the law were guaranteed a place in an eternal paradise with the sensuous delights so obviously lacking in the midst of the Arabian desert.

Islam was not just a set of religious beliefs but a way of life as well. After the death of Muhammad, Muslim scholars, known as the *ulama*, drew up a law code, called the *Shari'a*, to provide believers with a set of prescriptions to regulate their daily lives. Much of the *Shari'a* was drawn from the Koran or from the *Hadith*, a collection of the sayings of the Prophet that was used to supplement the revelations contained in the holy scriptures.

Believers were subject to strict behavioral requirements. In addition to the Five Pillars, Muslims were forbidden to gamble, to eat pork, to drink alcoholic beverages, and to engage in dishonest behavior. Sexual mores were also strict. Contacts between unmarried men and women were discouraged, and ideally marriages were to be arranged by the parents. In accordance with Bedouin custom, polygyny was permitted, but Muhammad attempted to limit the practice by restricting males to four wives.

Courtesy of William J. Duiker

THE QUIET SPIRIT OF A MOSQUE. For Muslims, the mosque is a revered oasis for worship, reflection, and the reading of the Koran. The practicing Muslim is required to pray to Allah five times a day. While women normally pray at home, men are expected to visit a mosque. If a mosque is not available, they may pray wherever they are at the time of the muezzin's (a muezzin is a Muslim crier) call. At that time, each Muslim stops whatever he is doing and kneels down, facing Mecca, on his portable prayer rug. Above all, the mosque is a place for quiet devotion, a refuge from the bustle of daily life. The artwork in a mosque should reflect motifs from the Koran. In this illustration, two of the faithful pray in a mosque under iron lamps on plush layers of carpets decorated with Koranic symbols.

THE ARAB EMPIRE AND ITS SUCCESSORS

The death of Muhammad presented his followers with a dilemma. Although Muhammad had not claimed divine qualities, Muslims saw no separation between political and religious authority. Submission to the will of Allah meant submission to his Prophet, Muhammad. According to the Koran, "Whoso obeyeth the messenger obeyeth Allah."[1] Muhammad's charismatic authority and political skills had been at the heart of his success. But he never named a successor, and although he had several daughters, he left no sons. In a male-oriented society, who would lead the community of the faithful?

Shortly after Muhammad's death, a number of his closest followers selected Abu Bakr, a wealthy merchant from Medina who was Muhammad's father-in-law and one of his first supporters, as caliph (*khalifa*, literally "successor"). The caliph was the temporal leader of the Islamic community and was also considered, in general terms, to be a religious leader, or *imam*. Under Abu Bakr's prudent leadership, the movement succeeded in suppressing factional tendencies among some of the Bedouin tribes in the peninsula and began to direct its attention to wider fields. Muhammad had used the Arabic tribal custom of the *razzia* or raid in the struggle against his enemies. Now his successors turned to the same custom to expand the authority of the movement. The Koran called this activity "striving in the way of the Lord," or *jihad*. Although sometimes translated as "holy war," the term is ambiguous and has been subject to varying interpretations.

Creation of an Empire

Once the Arabs had become unified under Muhammad's successor, they began to conduct a *jihad* on a larger scale, directing outward against neighboring peoples the energy they had formerly directed against each other. The Byzantine and Persian Empires were the first to feel the strength of the newly united Arabs, now aroused to a peak of zeal by their common faith. At Yarmuk in 636, the Muslims defeated the Byzantine army. Four years later, they took possession of the Byzantine province of Syria. To the east, the Arabs defeated a Persian force in 637 and then went on to conquer the entire empire of the Sassanids by 650. In the meantime, Egypt and other areas of North Africa were also brought under Arab authority (see Chapter 8).

What accounts for this rapid expansion of the Arabs after the rise of Islam in the early seventh century? Historians have proposed various explanations, ranging from a prolonged drought on the Arabian peninsula to the desire of Islam's leaders to channel the energies of their new converts. Another hypothesis is that the expansion was deliberately planned by the ruling elites in Mecca to extend their trade routes and bring surplus-producing regions under their control. Whatever the case, Islam's ability to unify the Bedouin peoples certainly played a role. Although the Arab triumph was made substantially easier by the ongoing conflict between the Byzantine and Persian Empires, which had weakened both powers, the strength of the Bedouin armies should not be overlooked. Led by a series of brilliant generals, the Arabs put together a large, highly motivated army, whose valor was enhanced

ISLAM AND BYZANTIUM • CHAPTER 7   **139**

by the belief that Muslim warriors who died in battle were guaranteed a place in paradise.

Once the armies had prevailed, Arab administration of the conquered areas was generally tolerant. Sometimes, due to a shortage of trained Arab administrators, government was left to local officials. Conversion to Islam was voluntary in accordance with the maxim in the Koran that "there shall be no compulsion in religion."[2] Those who chose not to convert were required only to submit to Muslim rule and pay a head tax in return for exemption from military service, which was required of all Muslim males. Under such conditions, the local populations often welcomed Arab rule as preferable to Byzantine rule or that of the Sassanid dynasty in Persia. Furthermore, the simple and direct character of the new religion, as well as its egalitarian qualities (all people were viewed as equal in the eyes of Allah), were undoubtedly attractive to peoples throughout the region.

Succession Problems and the Rise of the Umayyads

The main challenge to the growing empire came from within. Some of Muhammad's followers had not agreed with the selection of Abu Bakr as the first caliph and promoted the candidacy of Muhammad Ali, Muhammad's cousin and son-in-law, as an alternative. Ali's claim was ignored by other leaders, however, and after Abu Bakr's death, the office was passed to Umar, another of Muhammad's followers. In 656, Umar's successor, Uthman, was assassinated, and Ali was finally selected for the position. But Ali's rivals were convinced that he had been implicated in the death of his predecessor, and a factional struggle broke out within the Muslim leadership. In 661, Ali himself was assassinated, and Mu'awiya, the governor of Syria and one of Ali's chief rivals, replaced him in office. Mu'awiya thereupon made the caliphate hereditary in his own family, called the Umayyads, who were a branch of the Quraishi tribe. The new caliphate, with its capital at Damascus, remained in power for nearly a century.

The factional struggle within Islam did not bring an end to Arab expansion. At the beginning of the eighth century, new attacks were launched at both the western and the eastern ends of the Mediterranean world (see Map 7.2). Arab armies advanced across North Africa and conquered the Berbers, a primarily pastoral people living along the Mediterranean coast and in the mountains in the interior. Then, around 710, Arab forces, supplemented by Berber allies under their commander, Tariq, crossed the

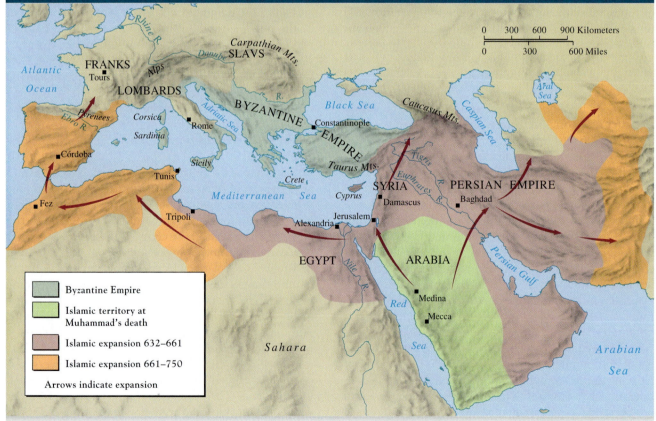

MAP 7.2 The Expansion of Islam. This map shows the expansion of the Islamic faith from its origins in the Arabian peninsula. Muhammad's followers carried the religion as far west as Spain and southern France and eastward to India and Southeast Asia. ➤ *In which of these areas is the Muslim faith still the dominant religion?*

Strait of Gibraltar and occupied southern Spain. The Visigothic kingdom, already weakened by internecine warfare, quickly collapsed, and by 725, most of the Iberian peninsula had become a Muslim state with its center in Andalusia. Seven years later, an Arab force, making a foray into southern France, was defeated by the army of Charles Martel between Tours and Poitiers. Some historians think that internal exhaustion would have forced the invaders to retreat even without their defeat at the hands of the Franks. In any event, the Battle of Tours (or Poitiers) would be the high-water mark of Arab expansion in Europe.

In the meantime, in 717, another Muslim force had launched an attack on Constantinople with the hope of destroying the Byzantine Empire. But the Byzantines' use of "Greek fire," a petroleum-based compound containing quicklime and sulfur, destroyed the Muslim fleet, thus saving the empire and indirectly Christian Europe, since the fall of Constantinople would have opened the door to an Arab invasion of eastern Europe. The Byzantine Empire and Islam now established an uneasy frontier in southern Asia Minor.

Arab power also extended to the east, consolidating Islamic rule in Mesopotamia and Persia and northward into Central Asia. But factional disputes continued to plague the empire. Many Muslims of non-Arab extraction resented the favoritism shown by local administrators to Arabs. In some cases, resentment led to revolt, as in Iraq, where Ali's second son, Hussein, disputed the legitimacy of the Umayyads and incited his supporters—to be known in the future as Shi'ites (from the Arabic phrase shi'at Ali, "partisans of Ali")—to rise up against Umayyad rule in 680. Hussein's forces were defeated, but a schism between Shi'ite and Sunni (usually translated as "orthodox") Muslims had been created that continues to this day.

Umayyad rule, always (in historian Arthur Goldschmidt's words) "more political than pious," created resentment, not only in Mesopotamia but also in North Africa, where Berber resistance continued, especially in the mountainous areas south of the coastal plains. The Umayyads contributed to their own demise by their decadent behavior. One caliph allegedly swam in a pool of wine and then imbibed enough of the contents to lower the wine level significantly. Finally, in 750, a revolt led by Abu al-Abbas, a descendant of Muhammad's uncle, led to the overthrow of the Umayyads and the establishment of the Abbasid dynasty (750–1258) in what is now Iraq.

The Abbasids

The Abbasid caliphs brought political, economic, and cultural change to the world of Islam. While stressing religious orthodoxy, they tried to break down the distinctions between Arab and non-Arab Muslims. All Muslims were now allowed to hold both civil and military offices. This change helped open Islamic culture to the influences of the occupied civilizations. Many Arabs now began to intermarry with the peoples they had conquered. In 762, the Abbasids built a new capital city at Baghdad, on the Tigris River far to the east of the Umayyad capital at Damascus. The new capital was strategically positioned to take advantage of river traffic to the Persian Gulf and also lay astride the caravan route from the Mediterranean to Central Asia. The move eastward allowed Persian influence to come to the fore, encouraging a new cultural orientation. Under the Abbasids, judges, merchants, and government officials, rather than warriors, were viewed as the ideal citizens.

The new Abbasid caliphate experienced a period of splendid rule well into the ninth century. Best known of the caliphs of the time was Harun al-Rashid (786–809), or Harun "the Upright," whose reign is often described as the golden age of the Abbasid caliphate. His son al-Ma'mun (813–833) was a patron of learning who founded an astronomical observatory and established a foundation for undertaking translations of classical Greek works. This was also a period of growing economic prosperity. The Arabs had conquered many of the richest provinces of the Roman Empire and now controlled the routes to the east (see Map 7.3). Baghdad became the center of an enormous commercial market that extended into Europe, Central Asia, and Africa, greatly adding to the wealth of the Islamic world and promoting an exchange of culture, ideas, and technology from one end of the known world to the other. Paper was introduced from China and eventually passed on to North Africa and Europe. Crops from India and Southeast Asia, such as rice, sugar, sorghum, and cotton, moved toward the west, while glass, wine, and indigo dye were introduced into China.

Under the Abbasids, the caliphs became more regal. More kings than spiritual leaders, described by such august phrases as the "caliph of God," they ruled by autocratic means, hardly distinguishable from the kings and emperors in neighboring civilizations. A thirteenth-century Chinese author, who compiled a world geography based on accounts by Chinese travelers, left the following description of one of the later caliphs:

> The king wears a turban of silk brocade and foreign cotton stuff (buckram). On each new moon and full moon he puts on an eight-sided flat-topped headdress of pure gold, set with the most precious jewels in the world. His robe is of silk brocade and is bound around him with a jade girdle. On his feet he wears golden shoes. . . . The king's throne is set with pearls and precious stones, and the steps of the throne are covered with pure gold.[3]

As the caliph took on more of the trappings of a hereditary autocrat, the bureaucracy assisting him in administering the expanding empire grew more complex as well. The caliph was advised by a council (called a diwan) headed by a prime minister, known as a vizier (wazir). The caliph did not attend meetings of the diwan in the normal

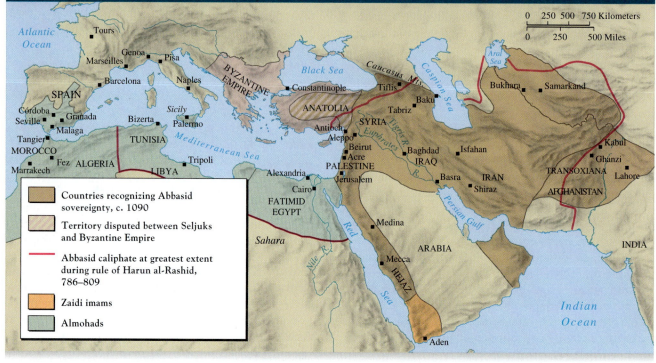

MAP 7.3 The Abbasid Caliphate at the Height of Its Power. The Abbasids arose in the eighth century as the defenders of the Muslim faith and established their capital at Baghdad. With its prowess as a trading state, the caliphate was the most powerful and extensive state in the region for several centuries. ➤ **What were the major urban centers under the influence of Islam, as shown on this map?**

Legend:
- Countries recognizing Abbasid sovereignty, c. 1090
- Territory disputed between Seljuks and Byzantine Empire
- Abbasid caliphate at greatest extent during rule of Harun al-Rashid, 786–809
- Zaidi imams
- Almohads

manner but sat behind a screen and then communicated his divine will to the *vizier*. Some historians have ascribed the change in the caliphate to Persian influence, which permeated the empire after the capital was moved to Baghdad. Persian influence was indeed strong (the mother of the caliph al-Ma'mun, for example, was a Persian), but more likely, the increase in pomp and circumstance was a natural consequence of the growing power and prosperity of the empire.

However, an element of instability lurked beneath the surface. Disputes over the succession to the caliphate were common. At Harun's death, the rivalry between his two sons, Amin and al-Ma'mun, led to civil war and the destruction of Baghdad. As described by the tenth-century Muslim historian al-Mas'udi, "Mansions were destroyed, most remarkable monuments obliterated; prices soared. . . . Brother turned his sword against brother, son against father, as some fought for Amin, others for Ma'mun. Houses and palaces fueled the flames; property was put to the sack."[4]

Vast wealth also contributed to financial corruption. By awarding important positions to court favorites, the Abbasid caliphs began to undermine the foundations of their own power and eventually became mere figureheads. Under Harun al-Rashid, members of his Hashemite clan received large pensions from the state treasury, and his wife, Zubaida, reportedly spent vast sums while shopping

on a pilgrimage to Mecca. One powerful family, the Barmakids, amassed vast wealth and power until Harun al-Rashid eliminated the entire clan in a fit of jealousy.

The life of luxury enjoyed by the caliph and other political and economic elites in Baghdad seemingly undermined the stern fiber of Arab society as well as the strict moral code of Islam. Strictures against sexual promiscuity were widely ignored, and caliphs were rumored to maintain thousands of concubines in their harems. Divorce was common, homosexuality was widely practiced, and alcohol was consumed in public despite Islamic law's prohibition against imbibing spirits.

The process of disintegration was accelerated by changes that were taking place within the armed forces and the bureaucracy of the empire. Given the shortage of qualified Arabs for key positions in the army and the administration, the caliphate began to recruit officials from among the non-Arab peoples in the empire, such as Persians and Turks from Central Asia. These people gradually became a dominant force in the army and administration. Eventually, provincial rulers began to break away from central control and establish their own independent dynasties. Spain had already established its own caliphate when a prince of the Umayyad dynasty had escaped execution and fled there in 750. Morocco became independent, and in 973, a new Shi'ite dynasty under the Fatimids was established in Egypt with its capital at Cairo. With increasing disarray in the empire, the Islamic world was held together only by the common commitment to the Koran and the use of Arabic as the prevailing means of communication.

The Seljuk Turks

In the eleventh century, the Abbasid caliphate faced an even more serious threat in the form of the Seljuk Turks. The Seljuk Turks were a nomadic people from Central Asia who had converted to Islam and flourished as military mercenaries for the Abbasid caliphate, where they were known for their ability as mounted archers. Moving gradually into Iran and Armenia as the Abbasids weakened, the Seljuk Turks grew in number until by the eleventh century, they were able to occupy the eastern provinces of the Abbasid empire. In 1055, a Turkish leader captured Baghdad and assumed command of the empire with the title of sultan (the term means "holder of power"). While the Abbasid caliph remained the chief representative of Sunni religious authority, the real military and political power of the state was in the hands of the Seljuk Turks. The latter did not establish their headquarters in Baghdad, which now entered a period of decline.

By the last quarter of the eleventh century, the Seljuks were exerting military pressure on Egypt and the Byzantine Empire. In 1071, when the Byzantines foolishly challenged the Turks, their army was routed at Manzikert, near Lake Van in eastern Turkey, and the victors took over most of the Anatolian peninsula (see Map 7.4). In dire straits, the Byzantine Empire turned to the west for help, setting in motion the papal pleas that led to the Crusades.

In Europe, and undoubtedly within the Muslim world itself, the arrival of the Turks was regarded as a disaster. The Turks were viewed as barbarians who destroyed civilizations and oppressed populations. In fact, in many respects, Turkish rule in the Middle East was probably beneficial. Converted to Islam, the Turkish rulers temporarily brought an end to the fraternal squabbles between Sunni and Shi'ite Muslims, while supporting the Sunnites. They put their energies into revitalizing Islamic law and institutions and provided much-needed political stability to the empire, which helped restore its former prosperity.

The Crusades

Just before the end of the eleventh century, the Byzantine emperor Alexius I desperately called for assistance from other Christian states in Europe to protect his empire against the invading Seljuk Turks. As part of his appeal, he said that the Muslims were desecrating Christian shrines in the Holy Land and also molesting Christian pilgrims en route to the shrines. In actuality, the Muslims had never threatened the shrines or cut off Christian access to them. But tension between Christendom and Islam was on the rise, and the Byzantine emperor's appeal received a ready response

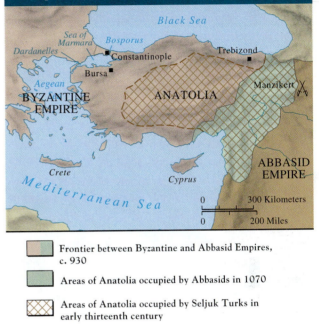

MAP **7.4** **The Turkish Occupation of Anatolia.** This map shows the expansion of Turkic-speaking peoples into the Anatolian peninsula in the tenth and eleventh centuries. The Ottoman Turks established their capital at Bursa in 1335 and eventually at Constantinople in 1453. ➤ *What was at the time the major obstacle to Ottoman expansion into Europe?*

☐ Frontier between Byzantine and Abbasid Empires, c. 930

☐ Areas of Anatolia occupied by Abbasids in 1070

☒ Areas of Anatolia occupied by Seljuk Turks in early thirteenth century

in Europe. Beginning in 1096 and continuing into the thirteenth century, a series of Christian raids on Islamic territories known as the Crusades brought the Holy Land and adjacent areas on the Mediterranean coast from Antioch to the Sinai peninsula under Christian rule (see Chapter 12).

At first, Muslim rulers in the area were taken aback by the invading crusaders, whose armored cavalry presented a new challenge to local warriors, and their response was ineffectual. The Seljuk Turks by that time were preoccupied with events taking place farther to the east and took no action themselves. But in 1169, Sunni Muslims under the leadership of Saladin (Salah al-Din), vizier to the last Fatimid caliph, brought an end to the Fatimid dynasty. Proclaiming himself sultan, Saladin succeeded in establishing his control over both Egypt and Syria, thereby confronting the Christian states in the area with united Muslim power on two fronts. In 1187, Saladin's army invaded the kingdom of Jerusalem and destroyed the Christian forces concentrated there. Further operations reduced Christian occupation in the area to a handful of fortresses along the northern coast. Unlike the Christians, however, Saladin did not permit a massacre of the civilian population and even tolerated the continuation of Christian religious services in conquered territories.

The Medieval Castle

The earliest castles that appeared in the ninth century in Europe were built of wood, but by the eleventh century, they were beginning to be constructed of the more common fieldstone held together by mortar. By the end of the eleventh century, an even greater sophistication in building castles occurred as a result of the Crusades. So impressed were the crusaders by the innovative defensive features they saw in Muslim fortified palaces that they began to incorporate similar ideas into their castles. In Syria in 1131, the crusaders, making use of the building skills of their Muslim enemies, began construction of the imposing citadel known as the Krak des Chevaliers (Castle of the Knights), seen above (at top). This new model of a massive fortress of solid masonry spread to western Europe, as is evident in the castle shown above (at bottom), built in the late twelfth century at Dover, England, for King Henry II.

The Christians returned for another try a few years after the fall of Jerusalem, but the campaign succeeded only in securing some of the coastal cities. Although the Christians would retain a toehold on the coast for much of the thirteenth century (Acre, their last stronghold, fell to the Muslims in 1291), they were no longer a significant force in Middle Eastern affairs. In retrospect,

the Crusades had only minimal importance in the history of the Middle East and may even have served to unite the forces of Islam against the foreign invaders, thus creating a residue of distrust toward Christians that continues to resonate through the Islamic world today (see the box on p. 145). Far more important in their impact were the Mongols, a pastoral people who swept out of the Gobi Desert in the early thirteenth century to seize control over much of the known world (see Chapter 10). Beginning with the advances of Genghis Khan in northern China, Mongol armies later spread across Central Asia, and in 1258, under the leadership of Hulegu, brother of the more famous Khubilai Khan, they seized Persia and Mesopotamia, bringing an end to the caliphate at Baghdad.

The Mongols

Unlike the Seljuk Turks, the Mongols were not Muslims, and they found it difficult to adapt to the settled conditions that they found in the major cities in the Middle East. Their treatment of the local population in conquered territories was brutal (according to one historian, after

THE CRUSADES IN MUSLIM EYES

*U*samah, an early-twelfth-century Muslim warrior and gentleman, had close associations with the crusaders. When he was ninety years old, he wrote his memoirs including many entertaining observations on the crusaders, or "Franks" as he called them. Here Usamah is astounded at the Franks' rudeness to Muslims and at their assumption of cultural superiority.

USAMAH, BOOK OF REFLECTIONS

1. Everyone who is a fresh emigrant from the Frankish lands is ruder in character than those who have become acclimatized and have held long association with the Moslems. Here is an illustration of their rude character.

Whenever I visited Jerusalem I always entered the Aqsa Mosque, beside which stood a small mosque which the Franks had converted into a church. When I used to enter the Aqsa Mosque, which was occupied by the Templars [an order of crusading knights], who were my friends, the Templars would evacuate the little adjoining mosque so that I might pray in it. One day I entered this mosque, repeated the first formula, "Allah is great," and stood up in the act of praying, upon which one of the Franks rushed on me, got hold of me, and turned my face eastward, saying, "This is the way thou shouldst pray!" A group of Templars hastened to him, seized him, and repelled him from me. I resumed my prayer. The same man, while the others were otherwise busy, rushed once more on me and turned my face eastward, saying, "This is the way thou shouldst pray!" The

Templars again came in to him and expelled him. They apologized to me, saying, "This is a stranger who has only recently arrived from the land of the Franks, and he has never before seen anyone praying except eastward." Thereupon I said to myself, "I have had enough prayer." So I went out, and have ever been surprised at the conduct of this devil of a man, at the change in the color of his face, his trembling, and his sentiment at the sight of one praying toward the qiblah.

2. In the army of King Fulk, son of Fulk, was a Frankish reverend knight who had just arrived from their land in order to make the holy pilgrimage and then return home. He was of my intimate fellowship and kept such constant company with me that he began to call me "my brother." Between us were mutual bonds of amity and friendship. When he resolved to return by sea to his homeland, he said to me:

"My brother, I am leaving for my country and I want thee to send with me thy son (my son, who was then fourteen years old, was at that time in my company) to our country, where he can see the knights and learn wisdom and chivalry. When he returns, he will be like a wise man."

Thus there fell upon my ears words which would never come out of the head of a sensible man; for even if my son were to be taken captive, his captivity could not bring him a worse misfortune than carrying him into the lands of the Franks.

conquering a city, they wiped out not only entire families but also their household pets) and destructive to the economy. Cities were razed to the ground, and dams and other irrigation works were destroyed, reducing prosperous agricultural societies to the point of mass starvation. The Mongols advanced as far as the Red Sea, but their attempt to seize Egypt failed, in part because of the effective resistance posed by the Mamluks (a Turkish military class originally composed of slaves; sometimes written as Mamelukes), who had recently overthrown the administration set up by Saladin and seized power for themselves.

Eventually, the Mongol rulers in the Middle East began to take on the characteristics of the peoples that they had conquered. Mongol elites converted to Islam, Persian influence became predominant at court, and the cities began to be rebuilt. By the fourteenth century, the Mongol Empire began to split into separate kingdoms and then to disintegrate. In the meantime, however, the old Islamic empire originally established by the Arabs in the seventh and eighth centuries had come to an end. The new center of Islamic civilization was in Cairo, now about to

promote a renaissance in Muslim culture under the sponsorship of the Mamluks.

To the north, another new force began to appear on the horizon with the rise of the Ottoman Turks on the Anatolian peninsula. In 1453, Sultan Mehmet II seized Constantinople and brought an end to the decrepit Byzantine Empire. Then the Ottomans began to turn their attention to the rest of the Middle East (see Chapter 15).

ISLAMIC CIVILIZATION

To be a Muslim is not simply to worship Allah but also to live according to his law as revealed in the Koran, which is viewed as fundamental and immutable doctrine, not to be revised by human beings.

As Allah has decreed, so must humans behave. Therefore, Islamic doctrine must be consulted to determine questions of politics, economic behavior, civil and criminal law, and social ethics. In Islamic society, there is no rigid demarcation between church and state, between the sacred and the secular.

The Wealth of Araby: Trade and Cities in the Middle East

As we have noted, this era was probably, overall, one of the most prosperous periods in the history of the Middle East. Trade flourished, not only in the Islamic world but also with China (now in a period of efflorescence during the era of the Tang and the Song dynasties—see Chapter 10), with the Byzantine Empire, and with the trading societies in Southeast Asia (see Chapter 9). Trade goods were carried both by ship and by the "fleets of the desert," the camel caravans that traversed the arid land from Morocco in the far west to the countries beyond the Caspian Sea. From the Sahara came gold and slaves; from China, silk and porcelain; from East Africa, gold, ivory, and rhinoceros horn; and from the lands of South Asia, sandalwood, cotton, wheat, sugar, and spices. Within the empire, Egypt contributed grain; Iraq, linens, dates, and precious stones; Spain, leather goods, olives, and wine; and western India, various textile goods. The exchange of goods was facilitated by the development of banking and the use of currency and letters of credit.

Under these conditions, urban areas flourished. While the Abbasids were in power, Baghdad was probably the greatest city in the empire. After the rise of the Fatimids in Egypt, the focus of trade shifted to Cairo, described by the traveler Leo Africanus as "one of the greatest and most famous cities in all the whole world, filled with stately and admirable palaces and colleges, and most sumptuous temples."[5] Other great commercial cities included Basra at the head of the Persian Gulf, Aden at the southern tip of the Arabian peninsula, Damascus in modern Syria, and Marrakech in Morocco. In the cities, the inhabitants were generally segregated by religion, with Muslims, Jews, and Christians living in separate neighborhoods. But all were equally subject to the most common threats to urban life—fire, flood, and disease.

The most impressive urban buildings were usually the palace for the caliph or the local governor and the great mosque. Houses were often constructed of stone or brick around a timber frame. The larger houses were often built around an interior courtyard, where the residents could retreat from the dust, noise, and heat of the city streets. Sometimes domestic animals such as goats or sheep would be stabled there. The houses of the wealthy were often multistoried, with balconies and windows covered with latticework to provide privacy for those inside. The poor in both urban and rural areas lived in simpler houses composed of clay or unfired bricks.

Eating habits varied in accordance with economic standing and religious preference. Muslims did not eat pork, but those who could afford it often served other meats, such as mutton, lamb, poultry, or fish. Fruit, spices, and various sweets were delicacies. The poor were generally forced to survive on boiled millet or peas with an occasional lump of meat or fat. Bread—white or whole meal—could be found on tables throughout the region except in the deserts, where boiled grain was the staple food.

Islamic Society

In some ways, Arab society was probably one of the most egalitarian of its time. Both the principles of Islam, which held that all were equal in the eyes of Allah, and the importance of trade to the prosperity of the state probably contributed to this egalitarianism. Although there was a fairly well defined upper class, consisting of the ruling families, senior officials, tribal elites, and the wealthiest merchants, there was no hereditary nobility as in many contemporary societies, and the merchants enjoyed a degree of respect that they did not receive in Europe, China, or India.

Though the Arab Empire was more urbanized than most other societies at the time, the bulk of the population continued to live in the countryside and supported itself by farming or herding animals. During the early stages, most of the farmland was owned by independent peasants, but later some concentration of land in the hands of wealthy owners began to take place. In river valleys like the Tigris and Euphrates and the Nile, the majority of the farmers probably continued to be independent peasants.

Not all benefited from the high degree of social mobility in the Islamic world, however. Slavery was widespread. Since a Muslim could not be enslaved, the supply came from sub-Saharan Africa or from non-Islamic populations elsewhere in Asia. Most slaves were employed in the army (which was sometimes a road to power, as in the case of the Mamluks) or as domestic servants, who were sometimes permitted to purchase their freedom. The slaves who worked the large estates experienced the worst living conditions and rose in revolt on several occasions.

The Islamic principle of human equality also fell short in the treatment of women. Although the Koran instructed men to treat women with respect, and women did have the right to own and inherit property, in general the male was dominant in Muslim society. Polygyny was permitted, and the right of divorce was in practice restricted to the husband, although some schools of legal thought permitted women to stipulate that their husband could have only one wife or to seek a separation in certain specific circumstances. Adultery and homosexuality were stringently forbidden (although such prohibitions were frequently ignored in practice), and Islamic custom required that women be cloistered in their homes (thus the tradition of the harem) and prohibited from social contacts with males outside their own family. The custom of requiring women to cover virtually all parts of their body when appearing in public was common in urban areas and continues to be practiced in many Islamic societies today. It should be noted, however, that these customs owed more

"DRAW THEIR VEILS OVER THEIR BOSOMS"

*P*rior to the Islamic era, many upper-class women greeted men on the street, entertained their husband's friends at home, went on pilgrimages to Mecca, and even accompanied their husbands to battle. Such women were neither veiled nor secluded. Muhammad, however, specified that his own wives, who (according to the Koran) were "not like any other women," should be modestly attired and should be addressed by men from behind a curtain. Over the centuries, Muslim theologians, fearful that female sexuality could threaten the established order, interpreted Muhammad's "modest attire" and his reference to curtains to mean segregated seclusion and body concealment for all Muslim women. In fact, one strict scholar in fourteenth-century Cairo went so far as to prescribe that ideally a woman should be allowed to leave her home only three times in her life: when entering her husband's home after marriage, after the death of parents, and after her own death.

In traditional Islamic societies, veiling and seclusion were more prevalent among urban women than among their rural counterparts. The latter, who worked in the fields and rarely saw people outside their extended family, were less restricted. In this excerpt from the Koran, women are instructed to "guard their modesty" and "draw veils over their bosoms." Nowhere in the Koran, however, does it stipulate that women should be sequestered or covered from head to toe.

THE KORAN: CHAPTER 24

And say to the believing women
That they should lower
Their gaze and guard
Their modesty: that they
Should not display their
Beauty and ornaments except
What [must ordinarily] appear
Thereof: that they should
Draw their veils over
Their bosoms and not display
Their beauty except
To their husbands, their fathers,
Their husbands' fathers, their sons,
Their husbands' sons,
Their brothers or their brothers' sons,
Or their sisters' sons,
Or their women, or the slaves
Whom their right hands
Possess, or male servants
Free of physical needs,
Or small children who
Have no sense of the shame
Of sex; and that they
Should not strike their feet
In order to draw attention
To their hidden ornaments.

to traditional Arab practice than to Koranic law (see the box above).

As Islam spread, it assimilated many of the cultural attributes of the peoples it conquered. Consequently, upper-class women in the Arabian peninsula were forced to abandon their freedoms and accept the conditions of a newly imposed patriarchal system. Like women in neighboring regions in the Middle East, they would henceforth don the veil and live in seclusion and submissiveness.

The Culture of Islam

The Arabs were truly heirs to many elements of the remaining Greco-Roman culture of the Roman Empire, and they assimilated Byzantine and Persian culture just as readily. In the eighth and ninth centuries, numerous Greek, Syrian, and Persian scientific and philosophical works were translated into Arabic. As the chief language in the southern Mediterranean and the Middle East, Arabic became an international language.

The spread of Islam led to the emergence of a new culture throughout the Arab Empire. This was true in all

fields of endeavor, from literature to art and architecture. But pre-Islamic traditions were not extinguished and frequently combined with Muslim motifs, resulting in creative works of great imagination and originality.

PHILOSOPHY AND SCIENCE

During the centuries following the rise of the Arab Empire, it was the Islamic world that was most responsible for preserving and spreading the scientific and philosophical achievements of ancient civilizations. At a time when ancient Greek philosophy was largely unknown in Europe, key works by Aristotle, Plato, and other Greek philosophers were translated into Arabic and stored in a "house of wisdom" in Baghdad, where they were read and studied by Muslim scholars. Through the writings of the Spanish Muslim philosopher Ibn Rushd (known in the West as Averroës), many of these works eventually became known in Europe and influenced Christian thought. Texts on mathematics and linguistics were brought from India. The process was undoubtedly stimulated by the introduction of paper manufacturing from China in the eighth century.

By the end of the century, the first paper factories had been established in Baghdad, and booksellers and libraries soon followed. The first paper mill in Europe appeared in the Pyrenees region of Spain in the twelfth century.

Although Islamic scholars are justly praised for preserving much of classical knowledge for the West, they also made considerable advances of their own. Nowhere is this more evident than in mathematics and the natural sciences. Islamic scholars adopted and passed on the numerical system of India, including the use of the zero, and a ninth-century Iranian mathematician created the mathematical discipline of algebra (*al-jebr*). In astronomy, Muslims set up an observatory at Baghdad to study the positions of the stars. They were aware that the earth was round and in the ninth century produced a world map based on the tradition of the Greco-Roman astronomer Ptolemy.

Muslim scholars also made many new discoveries in optics and chemistry and, with the assistance of texts on anatomy by the ancient Greek physician Galen (c. 180–200 C.E.), developed medicine as a distinctive field of scientific inquiry. Especially well known was Ibn Sina (980–1037). Known as Avicenna in the West, he compiled a medical encyclopedia that, among other things, emphasized the contagious nature of certain diseases and showed how they could be spread by contaminated water supplies. After its translation into Latin, Avicenna's work became a basic medical textbook for medieval European university students.

ISLAMIC LITERATURE

Islam brought major changes to the literature of the Middle East. Muslims regarded the Koran as their greatest literary work, but pre-Islamic traditions continued to influence writers throughout the region.

In the West, the most famous works of Middle Eastern literature are undoubtedly the *Rubaiyat* of Omar Khayyam and *Tales from 1001 Nights* (also called *The Arabian Nights*). Paradoxically, these two works are not as popular with Middle Eastern readers. Little is known of the life or the poetry of the twelfth-century poet Omar Khayyam. He did not write down his poems but composed them orally over wine with friends at a neighborhood tavern. They were recorded later by friends or scribes. Many poems attributed to him were actually written long after his death. Among them is the well-known couplet translated into English in the nineteenth century: "Here with a loaf of bread beneath the bough, a flask of wine, a book of verse, and thou."

Omar Khayyam's poetry is simple and down to earth. Key themes are the impermanence of life, the impossibility of knowing God, and disbelief in an afterlife. Ironically, recent translations of his work appeal to modern attitudes of skepticism and minimalist simplicity that may make him even more popular in the West:

In youth I studied for a little while;
Later I boasted of my mastery.
Yet this was all the lesson that I learned:
We come from dust, and with the wind are gone.

Of all the travelers on this endless road
No one returns to tell us where it leads,
There's little in this world but greed and need;
Leave nothing here, for you will not return. . . .

Since no one can be certain of tomorrow,
It's better not to fill the heart with care.
Drink wine by moonlight, darling, for the moon
Will shine long after this, and find us not.[6]

Like Omar Khayyam's verse, *The Arabian Nights* was loosely translated into European languages and adapted to Western tastes. A composite of folktales, fables, and romances of Indian and indigenous origin, the stories interweave the natural with the supernatural. The earliest stories were told orally and were later transcribed, with many later additions, in Arabic and Persian versions. The famous story of Aladdin and the Magic Lamp, for example, was an eighteenth-century addition. Nevertheless, *The Arabian Nights* has entertained readers for centuries, allowing them to enter a land of wish fulfillment through extraordinary plots, sensuality, comic and tragic situations, and a cast of unforgettable characters.

Some Arabic and Persian literature reflected the deep spiritual and ethical concerns of the Koran. Many writers, however, carried Islamic thought in novel directions. The thirteenth-century poet Rumi, for example, embraced Sufism, a form of religious belief that called for a mystical relationship between Allah and human beings (the term *Sufism* stems from the Arabic word for "wool," referring to the rough wool garments that its adherents wore). Converted to Sufism by a wandering dervish (dervishes, from the word for "poor" in Persian, sought to achieve a mystical union with Allah through dancing and chanting in an ecstatic trance), Rumi abandoned orthodox Islam to embrace God directly through ecstatic love. Realizing that love transcends intellect, he sought to reach God through a trance attained by the whirling dance of the dervish, set to mesmerizing music. As he twirled, the poet extemporized some of the most passionate lyrical verse ever conceived.

The Islamic world also made a major contribution to historical writing, another discipline that was stimulated by the introduction of paper manufacturing. The first great Islamic historian was al-Mas'udi. Born in Baghdad in 896, he wrote about both the Muslim and the non-Muslim world, traveling widely in the process. His *Meadows of Gold* is the source of much of our knowledge about the golden age of the Abbasid caliphate. Translations of his work reveal a wide-ranging mind and a keen intellect, combined with a human touch that practitioners of the art in our century might find reason to emulate. Equaling al-Mas'udi in talent and reputation was the fourteenth-century historian Ibn Khaldun. Combining scholarship with government service, Ibn Khaldun was one of the first historians to attempt a philosophy of history.

ISLAMIC ART AND ARCHITECTURE

The art of Islam is a blend of Arab, Turkish, and Persian traditions. The ultimate expression of Islamic art is to be found in the magnificent Muslim mosques, which were built to proclaim the spiritual and political legitimacy of the new religion to the world. The largest mosque ever built, the Great Mosque of Samarra (848–852), covered 10 acres and contained 464 pillars in aisles surrounding the court. Remains of the massive 30-foot-high outer wall still stand, but the most famous section of the Samarra mosque was its 90-foot-tall minaret, the tower accompanying a mosque from which the muezzin (crier) calls the faithful to prayer five times a day.

No discussion of mosques would be complete without mentioning the famous ninth-century mosque at Córdoba in southern Spain, which is still in remarkable condition. Its 514 columns supporting double horseshoe arches transform this architectural wonder into a unique forest of trees pointing upward, contributing to a light and airy effect. The unparalleled sumptuousness and elegance make the Córdoba mosque one of the wonders of world art, let alone Islamic art.

Since the Muslim religion combines spiritual and political power in one, palaces also reflected the glory of Islam. Beginning in the eighth century with the spectacular castles of Syria, the rulers constructed large brick domiciles reminiscent of Roman design, with protective walls, gates, and baths. With a central courtyard surrounded by two-story arcades and massive gate-towers, they resembled fortresses as much as palaces. Characteristic of such "desert palaces" was the gallery over the entrance gate, with holes through which boiling oil could be poured down on the heads of attacking forces. Unfortunately, none of these structures has survived.

The ultimate remaining Islamic palace is the fourteenth-century Alhambra in Spain. The extensive succession of courtyards, rooms, gardens, and fountains created a fairy-tale castle perched high above the city of Granada. Every inch of surface is decorated in intricate floral and semiabstract patterns; much of the decoration is done in carved plasterwork so fine that it resembles lace.

One of the most significant contributions of Islamic art is the knotted woolen rug. Originating in the pre-Muslim era, rugs were initially used to insulate stone palaces against the cold as well as to warm shepherds' tents. Eventually they were applied to religious purposes, since every practicing Muslim is required to pray five times a day on clean ground. Small rugs served as prayer mats for individual use, while larger and more elaborate ones were given by rulers as rewards for political favors.

In villages throughout the Middle East, the art of rug weaving has been passed down from mother to daughter over the centuries. Small girls as young as four years old took part in the process by helping to spin and prepare the wool shorn from the family sheep. By the age of six, girls would begin their first

>> THE MOSQUE AT CÓRDOBA. Perhaps the most impressive of all Islamic religious structures is the Mosque of Córdoba, in southern Spain, which was built between the eighth and tenth centuries. Shown here is the interior of the mosque, with some of the columns that give the entire structure an effect of mass as well as lightness.

© Scala/Art Resource, NY

Courtesy of William J. Duiker

⟫ **THE ALHAMBRA IN GRANADA.** Islamic civilization reached its zenith with the fourteenth-century fairy-tale castle of Alhambra in southern Spain. Perched on a hill high above the city of Granada and framed by snowcapped mountains, the Alhambra is widely considered the most perfect expression of Islamic art. Renowned for its lacelike plaster decorations and imaginative use of reflecting pools and fountains, the Alhambra stands as an exquisite gem of Islam.

rug, and before adolescence, their slender fingers would be producing fine carpets. Eventually, rugs began to be manufactured in workshops by professional artisans, who reproduced the designs from detailed painted diagrams.

Most decorations on the rugs, as well as on all forms of Islamic art, consisted of Arabic script and natural plant and figurative motifs. Repeated continuously in naturalistic or semiabstract geometrical patterns called arabesques, these decorations completely covered the surface and left no area undecorated. This dense decor was also evident in

brick, mosaic, and stucco ornamentation and culminated in the magnificent tile work of later centuries.

No representation of the prophet Muhammad ever adorned a mosque, in painting or in any other art form. Although no passage of the Koran forbids representational painting, the *Hadith,* an early collection of the Prophet's sayings, warned against any attempt to imitate God through artistic creation or idolatry. From the time of the Dome of the Rock, no figurative representations appear in Islamic religious art.

THE BYZANTINE EMPIRE

In the fourth century, a noticeable separation between the western and eastern parts of the Roman Empire began to develop. In the course of the fifth century, while the Germans moved into the western part of the empire and established various kingdoms, the Roman Empire in the east, centered on Constantinople, continued to exist and even prosper.

The Reign of Justinian (527–565)

In the sixth century, the empire in the east came under the control of one of its most remarkable rulers, the emperor Justinian. As the nephew and heir of the previous emperor, Justinian had been well trained in imperial administration. He was determined to reestablish the Roman Empire in the entire Mediterranean world.

Justinian's army under Belisarius, probably the best general of the late Roman world, presented a formidable force. Belisarius sailed to North Africa and quickly destroyed the Vandals in two major battles. From North

Courtesy of William J. Duiker

⟫ **THE KORAN AS SCULPTURED DESIGN.** Muslim sculptors and artists, reflecting the official view that any visual representation of the prophet Muhammad was blasphemous, turned to geometric patterns, as well as to flowers and animals, as a means of fulfilling their creative urge. The predominant motif, however, was the reproduction of Koranic verses in the Arabic script. Calligraphy, which was almost as important in the Middle East as it was in traditional China, used the Arabic script to decorate all of the Islamic arts, from painting to pottery, tile and iron work, and wall decorations such as this carved plaster panel in a courtyard of the Alhambra palace in Spain. Since a recitation from the Koran was an important component of the daily devotional activities for all practicing Muslims, elaborate scriptural panels such as this one perfectly blended the spiritual and the artistic realms.

THE EMPEROR JUSTINIAN AND HIS COURT. As the seat of Byzantine power in Italy, the town of Ravenna became adorned with examples of Byzantine art. The church of San Vitale at Ravenna contains some of the finest examples of sixth-century Byzantine mosaics, in which small pieces of colored glass were attached to the wall to form these figures and their surroundings. The emperor is seen as both head of state (he wears a jeweled crown and a purple robe) and head of the church (he carries a gold bowl symbolizing the body of Jesus).

Africa, he led his forces onto the Italian peninsula after occupying Sicily in 535. But it was not until 552 that the Ostrogoths were finally defeated. Justinian appeared to have achieved his goals. He had restored the imperial Mediterranean world; his empire included Italy, part of Spain, North Africa, Asia Minor, Palestine, and Syria (see Map 7.5). But the conquest of the western empire proved fleeting. Only three years after Justinian's death, the Lombards entered Italy. Although the eastern empire maintained the fiction of Italy as a province, its forces were limited to southern and central Italy, Sicily, and coastal areas, such as the territory around Ravenna.

THE CODIFICATION OF ROMAN LAW

Though his conquests proved short-lived, Justinian made a lasting contribution through his codification of Roman law. The eastern empire was heir to a vast quantity of materials connected to the development of Roman law. Justinian had been thoroughly trained in imperial government and was well acquainted with Roman law. He wished to codify and simplify this mass of materials.

To accomplish his goal, Justinian authorized the jurist Trebonian to make a systematic compilation of imperial edicts. The result was the Code of Law, the first part of the *Corpus Iuris Civilis* (Body of Civil Law), completed in 529. Four years later, two other parts of the *Corpus* appeared: the *Digest*, a compendium of writings of Roman jurists, and the *Institutes*, a brief summary of the chief principles of Roman law that could be used as a textbook on Roman law. The fourth part of the *Corpus* was the *Novels*, a compilation of the most important new edicts issued during Justinian's reign.

Justinian's codification of Roman law became the basis of imperial law in the Byzantine Empire until its end in 1453. More important, however, since it was written in Latin (it was in fact the last product of eastern Roman culture to be written in Latin, which was soon replaced by Greek), it was also eventually used in the West and became the basis of the legal system of all of continental Europe.

LIFE IN CONSTANTINOPLE: THE EMPEROR'S BUILDING PROGRAM

After riots destroyed much of Constantinople during a revolt against the emperor's rule in 532, Justinian rebuilt the city and gave it the appearance it would keep for almost a thousand years. With a population estimated in the hundreds of thousands, Constantinople was the largest city in Europe during the Middle Ages. It viewed itself as the center of an empire and a special Christian city.

Until the twelfth century, Constantinople was Europe's greatest commercial center. The city was the chief entrepôt for the exchange of products between West and East. Highly desired in Europe were the products of the East: silk from China, spices from Southeast Asia and India, jewelry and ivory from India (the latter used by artisans for church items), wheat and furs from southern Russia, and flax and honey from the Balkans. Many of these eastern goods were then shipped to the Mediterranean area and northern Europe.

Moreover, imported raw materials were used in Constantinople for local industries. During Justinian's reign, two Christian monks smuggled silkworms from China to begin a silk industry. The state had a monopoly on the production of silk cloth, and the workshops themselves were housed in

MAP 7.5 The Byzantine Empire in the Time of Justinian. The Byzantine emperor Justinian briefly restored much of the Mediterranean portion of the old Roman Empire. His general Belisarius quickly conquered the Vandals in North Africa but wrested Italy from the Ostrogoths only after a long and devastating struggle.

➤ *Examine Map 5.3 in Chapter 5. What former Roman territories lay outside Justinian's control?*

Empire before Justinian

Territory gained by Justinian

Constantinople's royal palace complex. European demand for silk cloth made it the city's most lucrative product.

Much of Constantinople's appearance in the Early Middle Ages was due to Justinian's program of rebuilding in the sixth century. The city was dominated by an immense palace complex, a huge arena known as the Hippodrome, and hundreds of churches. Justinian added many new buildings. His public works projects included roads, bridges, walls, public baths, law courts, and colossal underground reservoirs to hold the city's water supply. Churches were his special passion, and in Constantinople alone he built or rebuilt thirty-four of them. His greatest achievement was the famous Hagia Sophia, the Church of the Holy Wisdom.

Completed in 537, Hagia Sophia was designed by a Greek architect who did not use the simple, flat-roofed basilica of Western architecture. The center of Hagia Sophia consisted of four huge piers crowned by an enormous dome, which seemed to be floating in space. This effect was emphasized by Procopius, the court historian,

who, at Justinian's request, wrote a treatise on the emperor's building projects: "From the lightness of the building, it does not appear to rest upon a solid foundation, but to cover the place beneath as though it were suspended from heaven by the fabled golden chain."[7] In part, this impression was created by putting forty-two windows around the base of the dome, which allowed an incredible play of light within the cathedral. Light served to remind the worshipers of God. As darkness is illumined by invisible light, so too it was believed the world is illumined by invisible spirit.

The royal palace complex, Hagia Sophia, and the Hippodrome were the three greatest buildings in Constantinople. This last was a huge amphitheater, constructed of brick covered by marble, holding between forty and sixty thousand spectators. Although gladiator fights were held there, the main events were the chariot races; twenty-four would usually be presented in one day. The citizens of Constantinople were passionate fans of chariot racing. Successful charioteers were acclaimed as heroes and honored with public statues. Crowds in the Hippodrome also took on political significance. Being a member of the two chief factions of charioteers—the Blues or the Greens—was the only real outlet for political expression. Even emperors had to be aware of their demands and attitudes: the loss of a race in the Hippodrome frequently resulted in bloody riots, and rioting could threaten the emperor's power.

From Eastern Roman to Byzantine Empire

Justinian's accomplishments had been spectacular, but when he died, he left the eastern Roman Empire with serious problems: too much distant territory to protect, an empty treasury, a smaller population after a plague, and renewed threats to the frontiers. In the first half of the seventh century, during the reign of Heraclius (610–641), the empire faced attacks from the Persians to the east and the Slavs to the north.

The empire was left exhausted by these struggles. In the midst of them, it had developed a new system of defense by creating a new administrative unit, the *theme*, which combined civilian and military offices in the hands of the same person. Thus the civil governor was also the military leader of the area. Although this innovation helped the empire survive, it also fostered increased militarization. By the mid-seventh century, it had become apparent that a restored Mediterranean empire was simply beyond the resources of the eastern empire, which now increasingly turned its back on the Latin west. A renewed series of external threats in the second half of the seventh century strengthened this development.

The most serious challenge to the eastern empire was presented by the rise of Islam, which, as noted earlier in the chapter, created a powerful new force that swept through the east. The defeat of the eastern Roman army at Yarmuk in 636 meant the loss of the provinces of Syria and Palestine. The Arabs also moved into the old Persian Empire and conquered it. The failed Arab attempt to besiege Constantinople in 717 left Arabs and eastern Roman forces facing each other along a frontier in southern Asia Minor.

Problems also arose along the northern frontier, especially in the Balkans, where an Asiatic people known as the Bulgars had arrived earlier in the sixth century. In 679, the Bulgars defeated the eastern Roman forces and took possession of the lower Danube valley, setting up a strong Bulgarian kingdom.

By the beginning of the eighth century, the eastern Roman Empire was greatly diminished in size, consisting only of the eastern Balkans and Asia Minor. It was now an eastern Mediterranean state. These external challenges had important internal repercussions as well. By the eighth century, the eastern Roman Empire had been transformed into what historians call the Byzantine Empire (sometimes referred to as Byzantium), a civilization with its own unique character that would last until 1453. (Constantinople was built on the site of an older city named Byzantium—hence the term *Byzantine*.)

THE BYZANTINE EMPIRE IN THE EIGHTH CENTURY

The Byzantine Empire was a Greek state. Latin fell into disuse as Greek became not only the common language of the Byzantine Empire but its official language as well.

The Byzantine Empire was also a Christian state, built on a faith in Jesus that was shared in a profound way by almost all its citizens. An enormous amount of artistic talent was poured into church construction, church ceremonies, and church decoration. Spiritual principles deeply permeated Byzantine art. The importance of religion to the Byzantines explains why theological disputes took on an exaggerated form. The most famous of these disputes, the so-called iconoclastic controversy, threatened the stability of the empire in the first half of the eighth century.

Beginning in the sixth century, the use of religious images, especially in the form of icons or pictures of sacred figures, became so widespread that charges of idolatry (the worship of images) began to be heard. The use of images or icons had been justified by the argument that icons were not worshiped but were simply used to help illiterate people understand their religion. This argument failed to stop the iconoclasts, as the opponents of icons were called. Beginning in 730, the Byzantine emperor Leo III (717–741) outlawed the use of icons. Strong resistance ensued, especially from monks. Leo III also used the iconoclastic controversy to add to the prestige of the patriarch of Constantinople, the highest church official in the east and second in dignity only to the bishop of Rome. The Roman popes were opposed to the iconoclastic edicts, and their opposition created considerable dissension between the popes and the Byzantine emperors. Late in the eighth century, the Byzantine rulers reversed their stand on the use of images, but not before considerable damage had been done to the unity of the Christian church. Although the final separation between Roman Catholicism and Greek Orthodoxy (as the Christian religion in the Byzantine Empire was called) did not occur until 1054, the iconoclastic controversy was important in moving both sides in that direction.

The emperor occupied a crucial position in the Byzantine state. Portrayed as chosen by God, the Byzantine emperor was crowned in sacred ceremonies, and his subjects were expected to prostrate themselves in his presence. His power was considered absolute and was limited in practice only by deposition or assassination. Because the emperor appointed the patriarch, he also exercised control over both church and state. The Byzantines believed that God had commanded their state to preserve the true faith—Orthodox Christianity. Emperor, clergy, and civic officials were all bound together in service to this ideal. It can be said that spiritual values truly held the Byzantine state together.

By 750, it was apparent that two of Rome's heirs, the Germanic kingdoms and the Byzantine Empire, were moving in different directions. Nevertheless, Byzantine influence on the medieval Western world was significant. The images of a Roman imperial state that continued to haunt the West had a living reality in the Byzantine state. The legal system of the West came to owe much to Justinian's codification of Roman law. In addition, the Byzantine Empire served in part as a buffer state, protecting the West for a long time from incursions from the east.

The Zenith of Byzantine Civilization

In the seventh and eighth centuries, the Byzantine Empire had lost much of its territory to Slavs, Bulgars, and Muslims. By 750, the empire consisted only of Asia Minor, some lands in the Balkans, and the southern coast of Italy. Although Byzantium was beset with internal dissension and invasions in the ninth century, it was able to deal with them and not only endured but even expanded, reaching its high point in the tenth century, which some historians have called the golden age of Byzantine civilization.

During the reign of Michael III (842–867), the Byzantine Empire began to experience a revival. Iconoclasm was finally abolished in 843, and reforms were made in education, church life, the military, and the peasant economy. There was a noticeable intellectual renewal. But the Byzantine Empire under Michael was still plagued by persistent problems. The Bulgars mounted new attacks, and the Arabs continued to harass the empire. Moreover, a new church problem with political repercussions erupted over differences between the pope as leader of the western Christian church and the patriarch of Constantinople as leader of the eastern (or Orthodox) Christian church. Patriarch Photius condemned the pope as a heretic for accepting a revised form of the Nicene Creed stating that the Holy Spirit proceeded from the Father and the Son instead of "the Holy Spirit, who proceeds from the Father." A council of eastern bishops followed Photius' wishes and excommunicated the pope, creating the so-called Photian schism. Although the differences were later papered over, this controversy served to further the division between the eastern and western Christian churches.

The Byzantine Empire, c. 750

THE MACEDONIAN DYNASTY

The problems that arose during Michael's reign were effectively dealt with by a new dynasty of Byzantine emperors known as the Macedonians (867–1056), who managed to hold off the external enemies, go over to the offensive, and reestablish domestic order. Supported by the church, the emperors thought of the Byzantine Empire as a continuation of the Christian Roman Empire of late antiquity. Although for diplomatic reasons they occasionally recognized the imperial title of western emperors, such as Charlemagne and Otto I, they still regarded them as little more than barbarian parvenus.

The Macedonian emperors could boast of a remarkable number of achievements in the late ninth and tenth centuries. They worked to strengthen the position of the free farmers, who felt threatened by the attempts of landed aristocrats to expand their estates at the farmers' expense. The emperors were well aware that the free farmers made up the rank and file of the Byzantine cavalry and provided the military strength of the empire. The Macedonian emperors also fostered a burst of economic prosperity by expanding trade relations with western Europe, especially by selling silks and metalwork. Thanks to this prosperity, the city of Constantinople flourished. Foreign visitors continued to be astounded by its size, wealth, and physical surroundings. To western Europeans, it was the stuff of legends and fables (see the box on p. 155).

In this period of prosperity, Byzantine cultural influence expanded due to the active missionary efforts of eastern Byzantine Christians. Eastern Orthodox Christianity was spread to eastern European peoples, such as the Bulgars and Serbs. Perhaps the greatest missionary success occurred when the prince of Kiev in Russia converted to Christianity in 987.

Under the Macedonian rulers, Byzantium enjoyed a strong civil service, talented emperors, and military advances. The Byzantine civil service was staffed by well-educated, competent aristocrats from Constantinople who oversaw the collection of taxes, domestic administration, and foreign policy. At the same time, the Macedonian dynasty produced some truly outstanding emperors skilled in administration and law, including Leo VI (886–912) and Basil II (976–1025). In the tenth century, competent emperors combined with a number of talented generals to mobilize the empire's military resources and take the offensive. The Bulgars were defeated, and both the eastern and western parts of Bulgaria were annexed to the empire. The Byzantines went on to add the islands of Crete and Cyprus to the empire and defeat the Muslim

A Western View of the Byzantine Empire

*B*ishop Liudprand of Cremona undertook diplomatic missions to Constantinople on behalf of two western kings, Berengar of Italy and Otto I of Germany. This selection is taken from his description of his mission to the Byzantine emperor Constantine VII in 949 as an envoy for Berengar, king of Italy from 950 until his overthrow by Otto I of Germany in 964. Liudprand had mixed feelings about Byzantium: admiration, yet also envy and hostility because of its superior wealth.

LIUDPRAND OF CREMONA, ANTAPODOSIS

Next to the imperial residence at Constantinople there is a palace of remarkable size and beauty which the Greeks call Magnavra . . . the name being equivalent to "Fresh breeze." In order to receive some Spanish envoys, who had recently arrived, as well as myself . . . , Constantine gave orders that this palace should be got ready. . . .

Before the emperor's seat stood a tree, made of bronze gilded over, whose branches were filled with birds, also made of gilded bronze, which uttered different cries, each according to its varying species. The throne itself was so marvelously fashioned that at one moment it seemed a low structure, and at another it rose high into the air. It was of immense size and was guarded by lions, made either of bronze or of wood covered over with gold, who beat the ground with their tails and gave a dreadful roar with open mouth and quivering tongue. Leaning upon the shoulders of two eunuchs I was brought into the emperor's presence. At my approach the lions began to roar and the birds to cry out, each according to its kind; but I was neither terrified nor surprised, for I had previously made enquiry about all these things from people who were well acquainted with them. So after I had three times made obeisance to the emperor with my face upon the ground, I lifted my head, and behold! The man whom just before I had seen sitting on a moderately elevated seat had now changed his raiment and was sitting on the level of the ceiling. How it was done I could not imagine, unless perhaps he was lifted up by some such sort of device as we use for raising the timbers of a wine press. On that occasion he did not address me personally, . . . but by the intermediary of a secretary he enquired about Berengar's doings and asked after his health. I made a fitting reply and then, at a nod from the interpreter, left his presence and retired to my lodging.

It would give me some pleasure also to record here what I did then for Berengar. . . . The Spanish envoys . . . had brought handsome gifts from their masters to the emperor Constantine. I for my part had brought nothing from Berengar except a letter and that was full of lies. I was very greatly disturbed and shamed at this and began to consider anxiously what I had better do. In my doubt and perplexity it finally occurred to me that I might offer the gifts, which on my account I had brought for the emperor, as coming from Berengar, and trick out my humble present with fine words. I therefore presented him with nine excellent cuirasses, seven excellent shields with gilded bosses, two silver gilt cauldrons, some swords, spears, and spits, and what was more precious to the emperor than anything, four carzimasia; that being the Greek name for young eunuchs who have had both their testicles and their penis removed. This operation is performed by traders at Verdun, who take the boys into Spain and make a huge profit.

---

forces in Syria, expanding the empire to the upper Euphrates. By the end of the reign of Basil II in 1025, the Byzantine Empire was the largest it had been since the beginning of the seventh century.

New Challenges to the Byzantine Empire

The Macedonian dynasty of the tenth and eleventh centuries had restored much of the power of the Byzantine Empire; its incompetent successors, however, reversed most of the gains. After the Macedonian dynasty was extinguished in 1056, the empire was beset by internal struggles for power between ambitious military leaders and aristocratic families who attempted to buy the support of the great landowners of Anatolia by allowing them greater control over their peasants. This policy was self-destructive, however, because the peasant-warrior was the traditional backbone of the Byzantine state.

The growing division between the Catholic church of the West and the Eastern Orthodox church of the Byzantine Empire also weakened the Byzantine state. The Eastern Orthodox church was unwilling to accept the pope's claim that he was the sole head of the church. This dispute reached a climax in 1054 when Pope Leo IX and Patriarch Michael

The Byzantine Empire, 1025

Chronology

THE BYZANTINE EMPIRE

Justinian codifies Roman law	529–533
Reconquest of Italy by the Byzantines	535–552
Completion of Hagia Sophia	537
Attacks on the empire in reign of Heraclius	610–641
Arab defeat of Byzantines at Yarmuk	636
Defeat by the Bulgars; losses in the Balkans	679
Leo III and iconoclasm	717–741
Revival under Michael III	842–867
Macedonian dynasty	867–1056
Leo VI	886–912
Basil II	976–1025
Schism between Eastern Orthodox church and Catholic church	1054
Turkish defeat of Byzantines at Manzikert	1071
Revival under Alexius I Comnenus	1081–1118
Latin Empire of Constantinople	1204–1261
Revival of Byzantine Empire	1261
Fall of the empire	1453

Cerularius, head of the Byzantine church, formally excommunicated each other, initiating a schism between the two great branches of Christianity that has not been completely healed to this day.

The Byzantine Empire faced external threats to its security as well. The greatest challenge came from the Seljuk Turks who had moved into Asia Minor—the heartland of the empire and its main source of food and manpower. After the Byzantine forces were disastrously defeated at Manzikert by a Turkish army in 1071, the Turks advanced into Anatolia, where many peasants, already disgusted by their exploitation at the hands of Byzantine landowners, readily accepted Turkish control (see Map 7.4 on p. 143).

A new dynasty, however, soon breathed new life into the Byzantine Empire. The Comneni, under Alexius I Comnenus (1081–1118), were victorious on the Greek Adriatic coast against the Normans, defeated the Pechenegs in the Balkans, and stopped the Turks in Anatolia. Lacking the resources to undertake additional campaigns against the Turks, Emperor Alexius I turned to the West for military assistance. The positive response to the emperor's request led to the Crusades. The Byzantine Empire lived to regret it.

Impact of the Crusades

Ultimately, the Crusades had an enormous impact on the Byzantine Empire. In the First Crusade, the mostly French bands of crusading knights ignored their oath of allegiance and promises to Byzantine Emperor Alexis and organized their own crusader states in Palestine (see Chapter 12). Even more disastrous was the Fourth Crusade. On its way to Palestine, the crusading army became involved in a dispute over the succession to the Byzantine throne. The Venetian leaders of the Fourth Crusade saw an opportunity to neutralize their greatest commercial competitor, the Byzantine Empire. Diverted to Constantinople, the crusaders sacked the great capital city in 1204 and set up the Latin Empire of Constantinople. Some parts of the Byzantine Empire managed to survive under Byzantine princes. In 1259, Michael Paleologus, a Greek military leader, took control of the kingdom of Nicaea in western Asia Minor and led a Byzantine army in recapturing Constantinople two years later.

The Byzantine Empire had been saved, but it was no longer a great Mediterranean power. The restored empire now consisted of the city of Constantinople and its surrounding territory along with some lands in Asia Minor. Though reduced in size, the empire limped along for another two centuries until its weakened condition finally enabled the Ottoman Turks to conquer it in 1453.

CONCLUSION

After the collapse of Roman power in the west, the eastern Roman Empire, centered on Constantinople, continued in the eastern Mediterranean and eventually emerged as the unique Christian civilization known as the Byzantine Empire, which flourished for hundreds of years. One of the greatest challenges to the Byzantine Empire, however, came from a new force—Islam—that blossomed in the Arabian peninsula and spread rapidly throughout the Middle East. In the eyes of some Europeans during the Middle Ages, the Arab Empire was a malevolent force that posed a serious threat to the security of Christianity. Their fears were not entirely misplaced, for within half a century after the death of Islam's founder, Muhammad, Arab armies overran Christian states in North Africa and the Iberian peninsula, and Turkish Muslims moved eastward onto the fringes of the Indian subcontinent.

But although the teachings of Muhammad brought war and conquest to much of the known world, they also brought hope and a sense of political and economic stability to peoples throughout the region. Thus for many people in the medieval Mediterranean world, the arrival of Islam was a welcome event. Islam brought a code of law and a written language to societies that had previously not possessed them. Finally, by creating a revitalized trade network stretching from West Africa to East Asia, it established a vehicle for the exchange of technology and ideas that brought untold wealth to thousands and a better life to millions.

Like other empires in the region, the Arab Empire did not last. It fell victim to a combination of internal and external pressures, and by the end of the thirteenth century, it was no more than a memory. But it left a powerful legacy in Islam, which remains one of the great religions of the world. In succeeding centuries, Islam began to penetrate into new areas beyond the edge of the Sahara and across the Indian Ocean into the islands of the Indonesian archipelago.

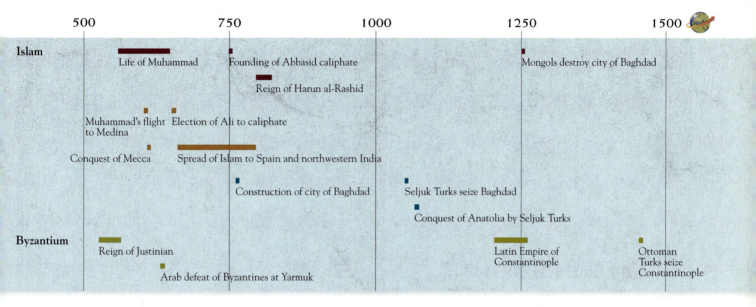

Islam

500 — Life of Muhammad

750 — Founding of Abbasid caliphate / Reign of Harun al-Rashid

Muhammad's flight to Medina / Election of Ali to caliphate

Conquest of Mecca / Spread of Islam to Spain and northwestern India

Construction of city of Baghdad

1250 — Mongols destroy city of Baghdad

Seljuk Turks seize Baghdad / Conquest of Anatolia by Seljuk Turks

Byzantium

Reign of Justinian

Arab defeat of Byzantines at Yarmuk

Latin Empire of Constantinople

1500 — Ottoman Turks seize Constantinople

CHAPTER NOTES

1. Mohammed Marmaduke Pickthall, trans., *The Meaning of the Glorious Koran* (New York, 1953), p. 89.
2. Quoted in Thomas W. Lippman, *Understanding Islam: An Introduction to the Moslem World* (New York, 1982), p. 118.
3. Friedrich Hirth and W. W. Rockhill, trans., *Chau Ju-kua: His Work on the Chinese and Arab Trade in the Twelfth and Thirteenth Centuries, Entitled Chu-fan-chi* (New York, 1966), p. 115.
4. al-Mas'udi, *The Meadows of Gold: The Abbasids*, ed. Paul Lunde and Caroline Stone (London, 1989), p. 151.
5. Leo Africanus, *The History and Description of Africa and of the Notable Things Therein Contained* (New York, n.d.), pp. 820–821.
6. Ehsan Yarshater, ed., *Persian Literature* (Albany, N.Y., 1988), pp. 154–159.
7. Procopius, *Buildings of Justinian* (London, 1897), p. 9.

SUGGESTED READING

Standard works on the Arab Empire and the rise of Islam include B. Lewis, *The Arabs in History* (New York, 1961), and T. Lippman, *Understanding Islam: An Introduction to the Moslem World* (New York, 1982). More recent is G. E. Perry, *The Middle East: Fourteen Islamic Centuries*, 2d ed. (Englewood Cliffs, N.J., 1992). Worthwhile studies include B. Lewis, *The Middle East: A Brief History of the Last 2,000 Years* (New York, 1986); K. Armstrong, *Islam: A Short History* (New York, 2000); and J. L. Esposito, ed., *The Oxford History of Islam* (New York, 1999). For anthropological background, see D. Bates and A. Rassam, *Peoples and Cultures of the Middle East* (Englewood Cliffs, N.J., 1983).

On Islam, see F. Denny, *An Introduction to Islam* (New York, 1985), and J. L. Esposito, *Islam: The Straight Path* (New York, 1988). Among the various translations of the Koran, two of the best for the introductory student are N. J. Dawood, trans., *The Koran* (Harmondsworth, England, 1990), and M. M. Pickthall, trans., *The Meaning of the Glorious Koran* (New York, 1953). See also R. W. Bulliet, *Conversion to Islam in the Medieval Period: An Essay in Quantitative History* (Cambridge, 1979), and K. Armstrong, *Muhammad: A Biography of the Prophet* (San Francisco, 1993).

Specialized works on various historical periods are numerous. For a view of the Crusades from an Arab perspective, see A. Maalouf,

The Crusades Through Arab Eyes (London, 1984), and C. Hillenbrand, The Crusades: Islamic Perspectives (New York, 2001). On the Mamluks, see R. Irwin, The Middle East in the Middle Ages: The Early Mamluk Sultanate, 1250–1382 (Carbondale, Ill., 1986). In God of Battles: Christianity and Islam (Princeton, N.J., 1998), P. Partner compares the expansionist tendencies of the two great religions.

On the economy, see E. Ashtor, A Social and Economic History of the Near East in the Middle Ages (Berkeley, Calif., 1976); K. N. Chaudhuri, Asia Before Europe: Economy and Civilization of the Indian Ocean from the Rise of Islam to 1750 (Cambridge, 1990); and C. Issawi, The Middle East Economy: Decline and Recovery (Princeton, N.J., 1995). On the crucial role of the camel in Middle Eastern society, see the interesting study by R. W. Bulliet, The Camel and the Wheel (Cambridge, 1975).

On women, see F. Hussain, ed., Muslim Women (New York, 1984); G. Nashat and J. E. Tucker, Women in the Middle East and North Africa (Bloomington, Ind., 1998); S. S. Hughes and B. Hughes, Women in World History, vol. 1 (London, 1995); and L. Ahmed, Women and Gender in Islam (New Haven, Conn., 1992).

For the best introduction to Islamic literature, consult J. Kritzeck, ed., Anthology of Islamic Literature (New York, 1964), with its concise commentaries and introduction. An excellent introduction to Persian literature can be found in E. Yarshater, ed., Persian Literature (Albany, N.Y., 1988). For the student, H. Haddawy, trans., The Arabian Nights (New York, 1990) is the best version. It presents 271 "nights" in a clear and colorful style.

For the best introduction to Islamic art, consult the concise yet comprehensive work by D. T. Rice, Islamic Art, rev. ed. (London, 1975). Also see J. Bloom and S. Blair, Islamic Arts (London, 1997). For carpets, a beautifully illustrated source is E. Sakhai, The Story of Carpets (London, 1991).

A brief but good introduction to Byzantine history can be found in J. Haldon, Byzantium: A History (Charleston, S.C., 2000). The best single political history is G. Ostrogorsky, A History of the Byzantine State, 2d ed. (New Brunswick, N.J., 1968). For a comprehensive survey of the Byzantine Empire, see W. Treadgold, A History of the Byzantine State and Society (Stanford, Calif., 1997). On Justinian, see J. Moorhead, Justinian (London, 1995). The role of the Christian church is discussed in J. Hussey, The Orthodox Church in the Byzantine Empire (Oxford, 1986). The zenith of Byzantine civilization is examined in R. Jenkins, Byzantium: The Imperial Centuries, 610–1071 (New York, 1969).

INFOTRAC COLLEGE EDITION

Visit the source collections at **infotrac.thomsonlearning.com** and use the Search function with the following key terms.

Byzantium	Islam
Caliph or Caliphate	Koran
Crusades	Sufi or Sufism or Rumi

WORLD HISTORY RESOURCES

Visit the *Essential World History* Companion Web Site for resources specific to this textbook:

http://history.wadsworth.com/duikeressentials02/

 The CD in the back of this book and the World History Resource Center at **http://history.wadsworth.com/world/** offer a variety of tools to help you succeed in this course, including access to quizzes; images; documents; interactive simulations, maps, and timelines; movie explorations; and a wealth of other sources.

EARLY CIVILIZATIONS IN AFRICA

CHAPTER OUTLINE

- THE LAND
- THE EMERGENCE OF CIVILIZATION
- THE COMING OF ISLAM
- STATES AND STATELESS SOCIETIES IN SOUTHERN AFRICA
- AFRICAN SOCIETY
- AFRICAN CULTURE
- CONCLUSION

FOCUS QUESTIONS

- What effects did the coming of Islam and the Arabs have on African religion, society, political structures, trade, and culture?
- What were the main characteristics of the West African states of Ghana and Mali?
- What roles did lineage groups, women, and slavery play in African society?
- What are some of the characteristics of African sculpture and carvings, music, and architecture, and what purpose did these forms of creative expression serve in African society?
- ➤ What were the main developments in African history before the coming of Islam, and what contacts did early African civilizations and societies have with civilizations outside Africa?

*I*n 1871, the German explorer Karl Mauch began to search southern Africa's central plateau for the colossal stone ruins of a legendary lost civilization. In late August, he found what he had been looking for. According to his diary: "Presently I stood before it and beheld a wall of a height of about 20 feet of granite bricks. Very close by there was a place where a kind of footpath led over rubble into the interior. Following this path I stumbled over masses of rubble and parts of walls and dense thickets. I stopped in front of a towerlike structure. Altogether it rose to a height of about 30 feet." Mauch was convinced that "a civilized nation must once have lived here." Like many other nineteenth-century Europeans, however, Mauch was equally convinced that the Africans who had lived there could never have built such splendid structures as the ones he had found at Great Zimbabwe. To Mauch and other archaeologists, Great Zimbabwe must have been the work of "a northern race closely akin to the Phoenician and Egyptian." It was not until the twentieth century that Europeans could overcome their prejudices and finally admit that Africans south of Egypt had also developed advanced civilizations with spectacular achievements.

The continent of Africa has played a central role in the long evolution of humankind. It was in Africa that the first hominids appeared more than three million years ago. It was probably in Africa that the immediate ancestors of modern human beings—*Homo sapiens*—emerged for the first time. Both the cultivation of crops and the domestication of animals may have occurred first in Africa. Certainly, one of the first states appeared in Africa, in the Nile valley in the northeastern corner of the continent, in the form of the kingdom of the pharaohs. Recent evidence suggests that Egyptian civilization was significantly influenced by cultural developments taking place to the south, in Nubia, in modern Sudan.

After the decline of the Egyptian empire during the first millennium B.C.E., the focus of social change began to shift from the lower Nile valley to other areas of the continent: to West Africa, where a series of major trading states began to take part in the caravan trade with the Mediterranean through the vast wastes of the Sahara; to the region of the upper Nile River, where the states of Kush and Axum dominated trade for several centuries; and to the eastern coast from the Horn of Africa to the straits between the continent and the island of Madagascar, where African peoples began to play an active role in the commercial traffic of the Indian Ocean. In the meantime, a gradual movement of agricultural peoples brought Iron Age farming to the central portion of the continent, leading eventually to the creation of several states in the Congo River basin and the plateau region south of the Zambezi River. When European seafarers began to round the Cape of Good Hope at the end of

the fifteenth century C.E., Western historians would herald their voyages as the beginning of the Age of Discovery. That label was a misnomer, however, for the peoples of Africa had played a significant role in the changing human experience since ancient times. •

THE LAND

After Asia, Africa is the largest of the continents (see Map 8.1). It stretches nearly 5,000 miles from the Cape of Good Hope in the south to the Mediterranean in the north and extends a similar distance from Cape Verde on the west coast to the Horn of Africa on the Indian Ocean. Africa is as diverse as it is vast. The northern coast, washed by the Mediterranean Sea, is mountainous for much of its length. South of the mountains lies the greatest desert on earth, the Sahara, which stretches from the Atlantic to the Indian Ocean. To the east is the Nile River, heart of the ancient Egyptian civilization. Beyond that lies the Red Sea, separating Africa from Asia.

The Sahara acts as a great divide separating the northern coast from the rest of the continent. Africa south of the Sahara is divided into a number of major regions. In the west is the so-called hump of Africa, which juts like a massive shoulder into the Atlantic Ocean. Here the Sahara gradually gives way to grasslands in the interior and then to tropical jungles along the coast. This region, dominated by the Niger River, is rich in natural resources and was the home of many ancient civilizations.

Far to the east, bordering the Indian Ocean, is a very different terrain of snowcapped mountains, upland plateaus, and lakes. Much of this region is grassland populated by wild beasts, which have given it the modern designation of Safari Country. Here, in the East African Rift valley in the lake district of modern Kenya, early hominids began their long trek toward civilization several million years ago.

Farther to the south lies the Congo basin, with its jungles watered by the mighty Congo River. The jungles of equatorial Africa then fade gradually into the hills, plateaus, and deserts of the south. This rich land contains some of the most valuable mineral resources known today.

THE EMERGENCE OF CIVILIZATION

It is not certain when agriculture was first practiced on the continent of Africa. Until recently, historians assumed that crops were first cultivated in the lower Nile valley (the northern part near the Mediterranean) about seven or eight thousand years ago, when wheat and barley were

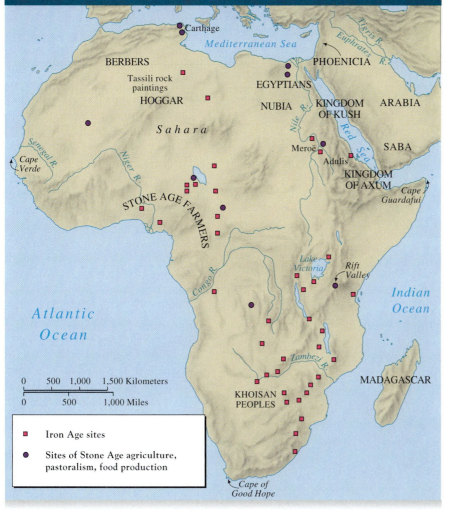

MAP 8.1 Ancient Africa. Modern human beings, known as *Homo sapiens*, first evolved on the continent of Africa. Some key sites of early human settlement are shown on this map. ➤ *Which are the main river systems on the continent of Africa?*

Map labels: Carthage, Mediterranean Sea, BERBERS, Tassili rock paintings, HOGGAR, Sahara, Cape Verde, Senegal R., Niger R., STONE AGE FARMERS, Congo R., Atlantic Ocean, Lake Victoria, Zambezi R., KHOISAN PEOPLES, Cape of Good Hope, PHOENICIA, EGYPTIANS, NUBIA, KINGDOM OF KUSH, ARABIA, Nile, Red Sea, SABA, Meroë, Adulis, KINGDOM OF AXUM, Cape Guardafui, Tigris R., Euphrates R., Rift Valley, Indian Ocean, MADAGASCAR

Scale: 0 500 1,000 1,500 Kilometers / 0 500 1,000 Miles

Legend:
- ■ Iron Age sites
- ● Sites of Stone Age agriculture, pastoralism, food production

than in Egypt. A drawing on an incense burner dated to 3100 B.C.E. or earlier depicts a seated ruler with the falcon motif later adopted by the pharaohs of Egypt. Some scholars suggest that the Nubian concept of kingship may have spread to the north, past the cataracts along the Nile, where it eventually gave birth to the better-known civilization of Egypt.

Whatever the truth of such conjectures, it is clear that contacts between the upper and lower Nile had been established by the late third millennium B.C.E., when Egyptian merchants traveled to Nubia to obtain ivory, ebony, frankincense, and leopard skins. A few centuries later, Nubia had become an Egyptian tributary. At the end of the second millennium B.C.E., Nubia profited from the disintegration of the Egyptian New Kingdom to become the independent state of Kush. Egyptian influence continued, however, as Kushite culture borrowed extensively from Egypt, including religious beliefs, the practice of interring kings in pyramids, and hieroglyphs.

Although its economy was probably founded primarily on agriculture and animal husbandry, Kush developed into a major trading state that endured for hundreds of years. Its commercial activities were stimulated by the discovery of iron ore in a floodplain near the river at Meroë. Strategically located at the point where a land route across the desert to the north intersected the Nile River, Meroë eventually became the capital of the state. In addition to iron products, Kush supplied goods from Central and East Africa, notably ivory, gold, ebony, and slaves, to the Roman Empire, Arabia, and India. At first, goods were transported by donkey caravans to the point where the river north was navigable. By the last centuries of the first millennium B.C.E., however, the donkeys were being replaced by camels, newly introduced from the Arabian peninsula.

Little is known about Kushite society, but it seems likely that it was predominantly urban. Initially foreign trade was probably a monopoly of the state, but the extensive luxury goods in the numerous private tombs in the vicinity indicate that at one time, material prosperity was relatively widespread. This suggests that commercial activities were being conducted by a substantial merchant class.

introduced, possibly from the Middle East. Eventually, as explained in Chapter 1, this area gave rise to the civilization of ancient Egypt.

Kush

Recent evidence suggests that this hypothesis may need some revision. South of Egypt, near the junction of the White and the Blue Nile, is an area known historically as Nubia. Some archaeologists suggest that agriculture may have appeared first in Nubia rather than in the lower Nile valley. Stone Age farmers from Nubia may have begun to cultivate local crops such as sorghum and millet along the banks of the upper Nile (the southern part near the river's source) as early as the eleventh millennium B.C.E.

Recent archaeological finds also imply that the first true African kingdom may have been located in Nubia rather

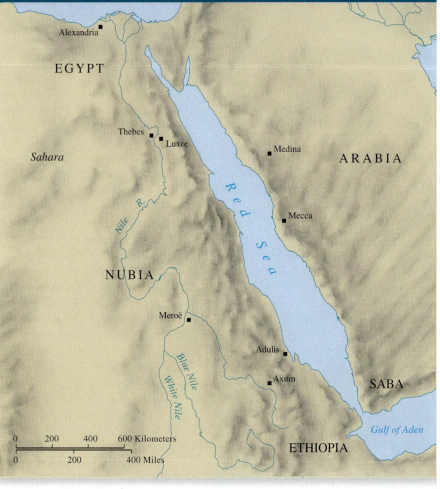

MAP 8.2 **Ancient Ethiopia and Nubia.** The first civilizations to appear on the African continent emerged in the Nile River valley. Early in the first century C.E., the state of Axum emerged in what is modern-day Ethiopia. ➤ *Where are the major urban settlements in the region, as shown on this map?*

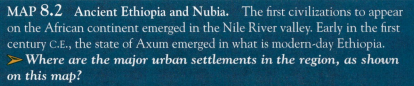

vived for centuries as an independent state. Like Saba, Axum owed much of its prosperity to its location on the commercial trade route between India and the Mediterranean, and Greek ships from the Ptolemaic kingdom in Egypt stopped regularly at the port of Adulis on the Red Sea. Axum exported ivory, frankincense, myrrh, and slaves, while its primary imports were textiles, metal goods, wine, and olive oil. For a time, Axum competed for control of the ivory trade with the neighboring state of Kush, and hunters from Axum armed with imported iron weapons scoured the entire region for elephants. Probably as a result of this competition, in the fourth century C.E., the Axumite ruler, claiming he had been provoked, launched an invasion of Kush and conquered it.

Perhaps the most distinctive feature of Axumite civilization was its religion. Originally, the rulers of Axum (who claimed descent from King Solomon through the visit of the queen of Sheba to Israel in biblical times) followed the religion of their predecessors in Saba. But in the fourth century C.E., Axumite rulers adopted Christianity from the Egyptians. This commitment to the Egyptian form of Christianity (often called Coptic, from the local language of the day) was retained even after the collapse of Axum and the expansion of Islam through the area in later centuries. Later, Axum (now renamed Ethiopia) would be identified by Europeans as the "hermit kingdom" and the home of Prester John, a legendary Christian king of East Africa.

Axum, Son of Saba

In the first millennium C.E., Kush declined and was eventually conquered by Axum, a new power located in the highlands of modern Ethiopia (see Map 8.2). Axum had been founded during the first millennium B.C.E. as a colony of the kingdom of Saba (popularly known as Sheba) across the Red Sea on the southern tip of the Arabian peninsula. During antiquity, Saba was a major trading state, serving as a transit point for goods carried from South Asia into the lands surrounding the Mediterranean. Biblical sources credited the "queen of Sheba" with vast wealth and resources. In fact, much of that wealth had originated much farther to the east and passed through Saba en route to the countries adjacent to the Mediterranean.

When Saba declined, perhaps because of the desiccation of the Arabian Desert, Axum broke away and sur-

The Sahara and Its Environs

Kush and Axum were part of the ancient trading network originally established by the Egyptians and were affected in various ways by the cross-cultural contacts that took place throughout that region. Elsewhere in Africa, somewhat different patterns prevailed; they varied from area to area depending on the geography and climate.

At one time, when the world's climate was much colder than it is today, Central Africa may have been one of the few areas that was habitable for the first hominids. Later, from 8000 to 4000 B.C.E., a warm, humid climate prevailed in the Sahara, creating lakes and ponds, as well as vast grasslands (known as savannas) replete with game. Rock paintings found in what are today some of the most uninhabitable parts of the region are a clear indication that the environment was much different several thousand years ago.

By 7000 B.C.E., the peoples of the Sahara were herding animals—first sheep and goats and later cattle. During the sixth and fifth millennia B.C.E., the climate became more arid, however, and the desertification of the Sahara began. From the rock paintings, which for the most part date from the fourth and third millennia B.C.E., we know that by that time, the herds were being supplemented by fishing and limited cultivation of crops such as millet, sorghum, and a drought-resistant form of dry rice. After 3000 B.C.E., as the desiccation of the Sahara proceeded and the lakes dried up, farming began to spread into the savannas on the southern fringes of the desert and eventually into the tropical forest areas to the south, where crops were no longer limited to drought-resistant cereals but could include tropical fruits and tubers.

Historians do not know when goods first began to be exchanged across the Sahara in a north-south direction, but during the first millennium B.C.E., the commercial center of Carthage on the Mediterranean had become a focal point of the trans-Saharan trade. The Berbers, a pastoral people of North Africa, served as intermediaries, carrying food products and manufactured goods from Carthage across the desert and exchanging them for salt, gold and copper, skins, various agricultural products, and perhaps slaves.

This trade initiated a process of cultural exchange that would exert a significant impact on the peoples of tropical Africa. Among other things, it may have spread the knowledge of ironworking south of the desert. Although historians once believed that ironworking knowledge reached sub-Saharan Africa from Meroë in the upper Nile valley in the first centuries C.E., recent finds suggest that the peoples along the Niger River were smelting iron five or six hundred years earlier. Some scholars believe that the technique developed independently there, but others believe that it was introduced by the Berbers, who had learned it from the Carthaginians.

Whatever the case, the Nok culture in northern Nigeria eventually became one of the most active ironworking societies in Africa. Excavations have unearthed numerous terra-cotta and iron figures, as well as stone and iron farm implements, dating back as far as 500 B.C.E. The remains of smelting furnaces confirm that the iron was produced locally.

Early in the first millennium C.E., the introduction of the camel provided a major stimulus to the trans-Saharan trade. With its ability to store considerable amounts of food and water, the camel was far better equipped to handle the arduous conditions of the desert than the ox, which had been used

✦✦✦✦✦✦✦✦✦✦✦✦✦✦✦✦✦✦✦✦✦✦✦✦✦✦✦✦✦✦✦✦✦✦✦✦

The Stele

A stele is a stone slab or pillar, usually decorated or inscribed, and placed upright. Stelae were often used to commemorate the accomplishments of a ruler or significant figure. Shown at the left is the tallest of the Axum stelae still standing, in present-day Ethiopia. The stone stelae in Axum in the fourth century B.C.E. marked the location of royal tombs with inscriptions commemorating the glories of the kings. An earlier famous stele, seen in the center, is that of Hammurabi (who ruled from 1792 to 1750 B.C.E.; see Chapter 1), which depicts Hammurabi standing in front of a seated god. Below the scene is an inscription of the Code of Hammurabi. A similar kind of stone pillar, shown at the right, was erected in India during the reign of Asoka in the third century B.C.E. (see Chapter 2) to commemorate events in the life of the Buddha. Archaeologists have also found stelae in ancient China, Greece, and Mexico.

© Werner Forman/Art Resource, NY

© Réunion des Musées Nationaux/Art Resource, NY

© Borromeo/Art Resource

previously. The camel caravans of the Berbers became known as the "fleets of the desert."

East Africa

South of Axum, along the shores of the Indian Ocean and in the inland plateau that stretches from the mountains of Ethiopia through the lake district of Central Africa, lived a mixture of peoples, some living by hunting and food gathering and others following pastoral pursuits.

Beginning in the first millennium B.C.E., new peoples began to migrate into East Africa from the west. Farming peoples speaking dialects of the Bantu family of languages began to move from the region of the Niger River into East Africa and the Congo River basin. They were probably responsible for introducing the widespread cultivation of crops and knowledge of ironworking to much of East Africa, although there are signs of some limited iron smelting in the area before their arrival.

The Bantu settled in rural communities based on subsistence farming. The primary crops were millet and sorghum, along with yams, melons, and beans. The land was often tilled with both iron and stone tools, and the former were usually manufactured in a local smelter. Some people kept domestic animals such as cattle, sheep, goats, or chickens or supplemented their diets by hunting and food gathering. Because the population was minimal and an ample supply of cultivable land was available, most settlements were relatively small; each village formed a self-sufficient political and economic entity.

As early as the era of the New Kingdom in the second millennium B.C.E., Egyptian ships had plied the waters off the East African coast in search of gold, ivory, palm oil, and perhaps slaves. By the first century C.E., the region was an established part of a trading network that included the Mediterranean and the Red Sea. In that century, a Greek seafarer from Alexandria wrote an account of his travels down the coast from Cape Guardafui at the tip of the Horn of Africa to the Strait of Madagascar thousands of miles to the south. Called the *Periplus*, this work provides generally accurate descriptions of the peoples and settlements along the African coast and the trade goods they supplied.

According to the *Periplus*, the port of Rhapta (possibly modern Dar es Salaam) was a commercial metropolis, exporting ivory, rhinoceros horn, and tortoiseshell and importing glass, wine, grain, and metal goods such as weapons and tools. The identity of the peoples taking part in this trade is not clear, but it seems likely that the area was already inhabited by a mixture of local peoples and immigrants from the Arabian peninsula. Out of this mixture would eventually emerge an African-Arabian "Swahili" culture (see "East Africa: The Land of Zanj" later in this chapter) that continues to exist in coastal areas today. Beyond Rhapta was "unexplored ocean." Some contemporary observers believed that the Indian and Atlantic Oceans were connected. Others were convinced that the Indian Ocean was an enclosed sea and that the continent of Africa could not be circumnavigated.

Trade across the Indian Ocean and down the coast of East Africa, facilitated by the monsoon winds, would gradually become one of the most lucrative sources of commercial profit in the ancient and medieval worlds. Although the origins of the trade remain shrouded in mystery, traders eventually came by sea from as far away as the mainland of Southeast Asia. Early in the first millennium C.E., Malay peoples bringing cinnamon to the Middle East began to cross the Indian Ocean directly and landed on the southeastern coast of Africa. Eventually, a Malay settlement was established on the island of Madagascar, where the population is still of mixed Malay-African origin. Historians suspect that Malay immigrants were responsible for introducing such Southeast Asian foods as the banana and the yam to Africa. With its high yield and ability to grow in uncultivated rain forest, the banana often became the preferred crop of the Bantu peoples.

Southern Africa

South of the East African plateau and the Congo basin is a vast land of hills, grasslands, and arid desert stretching almost to the Cape of Good Hope at the tip of the continent. As Bantu-speaking farmers spread southward during the final centuries of the first millennium B.C.E., they began to encounter Stone Age peoples in the area who still lived primarily by hunting and foraging. These peoples, many of whom apparently belonged to the Khoisan family of languages (Khoisan languages are distinguished by their numerous "clicking" sounds), were lighter in skin color and generally shorter than the Bantu speakers who were arriving from the north.

Available evidence suggests that early relations between these two peoples were relatively harmonious. Intermarriage between members of the two groups was apparently not unusual, and many of the Khoisan-speaking peoples were gradually absorbed into what became a dominantly Bantu-speaking pastoral and agricultural society that spread throughout much of southern Africa during the first millennium C.E.

THE COMING OF ISLAM

As we saw in Chapter 7, the rise of Islam during the first half of the seventh century C.E. had ramifications far beyond the Arabian peninsula. Arab armies swept across North Africa, incorporating it into the Arab Empire and isolating the Christian state of Axum to the south. Although East Africa and West Africa south of the Sahara were not conquered by the Arab forces, Islam eventually penetrated these areas as well.

African Religious Beliefs Before Islam

When Islam arrived, most African societies already had well-developed systems of religious beliefs. Like other aspects of African life, early African religious beliefs varied from place to place, but certain characteristics appear to have been shared by most African societies. One of these common features was a belief in a single creator god. The supreme god of the Bantu, for example, was a pantheistic force from whom all things came. Sometimes the creator god was accompanied by a whole pantheon of lesser deities. The Ashanti people of Ghana in West Africa believed in a supreme being called Nyame, whose sons were lesser gods. Each son served a different purpose: one was the rainmaker, another the compassionate, and a third was responsible for the sunshine. This heavenly hierarchy paralleled earthly arrangements: worship of Nyame was the exclusive preserve of the king through his priests; lesser officials and the common people worshiped Nyame's sons, who might intercede with their father on behalf of ordinary Africans.

Many African religions also shared a belief in a form of afterlife during which the soul floated in the atmosphere through eternity. Belief in an afterlife was closely connected to the importance of ancestors and the lineage, or clan, in African society. Each lineage group could trace itself back to a founding ancestor or group of ancestors. These ancestral souls would not be extinguished as long as the lineage group continued to perform rituals in their name. The rituals could also benefit the lineage group on earth, for the ancestral souls, being closer to the gods, had the power to influence, for good or evil, the lives of their descendants.

Such beliefs were challenged but not always replaced by the arrival of Islam. In some ways, the tenets of Islam were in con-

➤➤ A POWER OBJECT. One of the important aspects of many traditional African religions is the close communion between the worlds of the living and the dead. The artifact shown here (known as a *nkisi*) is a sacred object used by the people of Kongo to harness the power of the spirits to solve problems encountered in their daily lives. Nails were driven into the object (normally a male statue or a two-headed dog) to arouse its inner spirits, who would be activated to identify the source of the problem and resolve it. Over the stomach of this artifact is a container for medicines to assist in the healing ritual.

Dallas Museum of Art, Foundation for the Arts Collection, gift of the McDermott Foundation

flict with traditional African beliefs and customs. Although the concept of a single transcendent deity presented no problems in many African societies, Islam's rejection of spirit worship and a priestly class ran counter to the beliefs of many Africans and was often ignored in practice. Similarly, as various Muslim travelers observed, Islam's insistence on the separation of the sexes contrasted with the relatively informal relationships that prevailed in many African societies and was probably slow to take root. In the long run, imported ideas were synthesized with native beliefs to create a unique brand of Africanized Islam.

The Arabs in North Africa

In 641, Arab forces advanced into Egypt, seized the delta of the Nile River, and brought two centuries of Byzantine rule to an end. To guard against attacks from the Byzantine fleet, the Arabs eventually built a new capital at Cairo, inland from the previous Byzantine capital of Alexandria, and began to consolidate their control over the entire region.

The Arab conquerors were probably welcomed by many, if not the majority, of the local inhabitants. Although Egypt had been a thriving commercial center under the Byzantines, the average Egyptian had not shared in this prosperity. Tax rates were generally high, and Christians were subjected to periodic persecution by the Byzantines, who viewed the local Coptic faith and other sects in the area as heresies. Although the new rulers continued to obtain much of their revenue from taxing the local farming population, tax rates were generally lower than they had been under the corrupt Byzantine government, and conversion to Islam brought exemption from taxation. During the next generations, many Egyptians converted to the Muslim faith, but Islam did not move into the upper Nile valley until several hundred years later. As Islam spread southward, it was adopted by many lowland peoples, but it had less success in the mountains of Ethiopia, where Coptic Christianity continued to win adherents (see the next section).

In the meantime, Arab rule was gradually being extended westward along the Mediterranean coast. When the Romans conquered Carthage in 146

B.C.E., they had called their new province Africa, thus introducing a name that would eventually be applied to the entire continent. After the fall of the Roman Empire, much of the area had reverted to the control of local Berber chieftains, but the Byzantines captured Carthage in the mid-sixth century C.E. In 690, the city was seized by the Arabs, who then began to extend their control over the entire area, which they called Al Maghrib ("the west").

At first, the local Berber peoples resisted their new conquerors. The Berbers were tough fighters, and for several generations, Arab rule was limited to the towns and lowland coastal areas. But Arab persistence eventually paid off, and by the early eighth century, the entire North African coast as far west as the Strait of Gibraltar was under Arab rule. The Arabs were now poised to cross the strait and expand into southern Europe and to push south beyond the fringes of the Sahara.

The Kingdom of Ethiopia: A Christian Island in a Muslim Sea

By the end of the sixth century C.E., the kingdom of Axum, long a dominant force in the trade network through the Red Sea, was in a state of decline. Both over-exploitation of farmland and a shift in trade routes away from the Red Sea to the Arabian peninsula and Persian Gulf contributed to this decline. By the beginning of the ninth century, the capital had been moved farther into the mountainous interior, and Axum was gradually transformed from a maritime power into an isolated agricultural society.

The rise of Islam on the Arabian peninsula hastened this process, as the Arab world increasingly began to serve as the focus of the regional trade passing through the area. By the eighth century, a number of Muslim trading states had been established on the African coast of the Red Sea, a development that contributed to the transformation of Axum into a landlocked society with primarily agricultural interests. At first, relations between Christian Axum and its Muslim neighbors were relatively peaceful, as the larger and more powerful Axumite kingdom attempted with some success to compel the coastal Islamic states to accept a tributary relationship. Axum's role in the local commercial network temporarily revived, and the area became a prime source for ivory, resins like frankincense and myrrh, and slaves. Slaves came primarily from the south, where Axum had been attempting to subjugate restive tribal peoples living in the Amharic plateau beyond its southern border.

Beginning in the twelfth century, however, relations between Axum and its neighbors deteriorated as the Muslim states along the coast began to move inland to gain control over the growing trade in slaves and ivory. Axum responded with force and at first had some success in reasserting its hegemony over the area. But in the early

Origins of agriculture in Africa	c. 7000 B.C.E.
Desiccation of the Sahara	Begins c. 5000 B.C.E.
Kingship appears in the Nile valley	c. 3100 B.C.E.
Kingdom of Kush in Nubia	c. 500 B.C.E.
Iron Age begins	c. sixth century B.C.E.
Beginnings of trans-Saharan trade	c. first millennium B.C.E.
Rise of Axum	First century C.E.
Conquest of Kush by Axum	Fourth century C.E.
Arrival of Bantus in East Africa	Early centuries C.E.
Arrival of Malays on Madagascar	Second century C.E.
Origins of Ghana	Fifth century C.E.
Arab takeover of lower Nile valley	641 C.E.
Development of Swahili culture	c. first millennium C.E.
Spread of Islam across North Africa	Seventh century C.E.
Spread of Islam in Horn of Africa	Ninth century C.E.
Decline of Ghana	Twelfth century C.E.
Establishment of Zagwe dynasty in Ethiopia	c. 1150
Rise of Mali	c. 1250
Kingdom of Zimbabwe	c. 1300–c. 1450
Portuguese ships explore West African coast	Mid-fifteenth century

fourteenth century, the Muslim state of Adal, located at the juncture of the Indian Ocean and the Red Sea, launched a new attack on the Christian kingdom.

Axum also underwent significant internal change during this period. The Zagwe dynasty, which seized control of the country in the mid-twelfth century, centralized the government and extended the Christian faith throughout the kingdom, now known as Ethiopia. Military commanders or civilian officials who had personal or kinship ties with the royal court established vast landed estates to maintain security and facilitate the collection of taxes from the local population. In the meantime, Christian missionaries established monasteries and churches to propagate the faith in outlying areas. Close relations were reestablished with leaders of the Coptic church in Egypt and with Christian officials in the Holy Land. This process was continued by the Solomonids, who succeeded the Zagwe dynasty in 1270. But by the early fifteenth century, the state had become more deeply involved in an expanding conflict with Muslim Adal to the east, a conflict that lasted for over a century and gradually took on the characteristics of a holy war.

East Africa: The Land of Zanj

The rise of Islam also had a lasting impact on the coast of East Africa, which the Greeks had called Azania and the Arabs called Zanj. During the seventh and eighth centuries, peoples from the Arabian peninsula and the Persian Gulf began to settle at ports along the coast and on the small islands offshore. Then, according to legend, in the middle of the tenth century, a Persian from Shiraz, a city in southern Iran, sailed to the area with his six sons. As his small fleet stopped along the coast, each son disembarked on one of the coastal islands and founded a small community; these settlements eventually grew into important commercial centers such as Mombasa, Pemba, Zanzibar (literally, "the coast of Zanj"), and Kilwa.

Although the legend underestimates the degree to which the area had already become a major participant in local commerce as well as the role of the local inhabitants in the process, it does reflect the importance of Arab and Persian immigrants in the formation of a string of trading ports stretching from Mogadishu (today the capital of Somalia) in the north to Kilwa (south of present-day Dar es Salaam) in the south. Kilwa became especially important as it was near the southern limit for a ship hop-ing to complete the round-trip journey in a single season. Goods such as ivory, gold, and rhinoceros horn were exported across the Indian Ocean to countries as far away as China, while imports included iron goods, glassware, Indian textiles, and Chinese porcelain. Merchants in these cities often amassed considerable profit, as evidenced by their lavish stone palaces, some of which still stand in the modern cities of Mombasa and Zanzibar. Though now in ruins, Kilwa was one of the most magnificent cities of its day. The fourteenth-century Arab traveler Ibn Battuta described it as "amongst the most beautiful of cities and most elegantly built. All of it is of wood, and the ceilings of its houses are of *al-dis* [reeds]."[1]

Most of the coastal states were self-governing, although sometimes several towns were grouped together under a single dominant authority. Government revenue came primarily from taxes imposed on commerce. Some trade went on between these coastal city-states and the peoples of the interior, who provided gold and iron, ivory, and various agricultural goods and animal products in return for textiles, manufactured articles, and weapons. Relations apparently varied, and the coastal merchants sometimes resorted to force to obtain goods from the inland peoples. A Portuguese visitor recounted that "the men [of Mombasa] are oft-times at war and but seldom at peace with those of the mainland, and they carry on trade with them, bringing thence great store of honey, wax, and ivory."[2]

By the twelfth and thirteenth centuries, a mixed African-Arabian culture, eventually known as Swahili (from the Arabic *sahel* meaning "coast"; thus, "peoples of the coast"), began to emerge throughout the coastal area. Intermarriage between the immigrants and the local population was common, although a distinct Arab community,

Courtesy of William J. Duiker

> **A LOST CITY IN AFRICA.** Gedi was founded in the early fourteenth century and abandoned three hundred years later. Its romantic ruins suggest the grandeur of the Swahili civilization that once flourished along the eastern coast of Africa. Located 60 miles north of Mombasa, in present-day Kenya, Gedi once contained several thousand residents but was eventually abandoned after it was attacked by nomadic peoples from the north. Today the ruins of the town, surrounded by a 9-foot wall, seem dwarfed by towering baobab trees populated only by chattering monkeys. Shown here is the entrance to the palace, which probably served as the residence of the chief official in the town. Neighboring houses, constructed of coral stone, contain sumptuous rooms, with separate women's quarters and enclosed lavatories with urinal channels and double-sink washing benches.

The States of West Africa

During the eighth century, merchants from the Maghrib began to carry Muslim beliefs to the savanna areas south of the Sahara. At first, conversion took place on an individual basis rather than through official encouragement. The first rulers to convert to Islam were the royal family of Gao at the end of the tenth century. Five hundred years later, most of the population in the grasslands south of the Sahara had accepted Islam.

The expansion of Islam into West Africa had a major impact on the political system. By introducing Arabic as the first written language in the region and Muslim law codes and administrative practices from the Middle East, Islam provided local rulers with the tools to increase their authority and the efficiency of their governments. Moreover, as Islam gradually spread throughout the region, a common religion united previously diverse peoples into a more coherent community.

When Islam arrived in the grasslands south of the Sahara, the region was beginning to undergo significant political and social change. A number of major trading states were in the making, and they eventually transformed the Sahara into one of the leading avenues of world trade, crisscrossed by caravan routes leading to destinations as far away as the Atlantic Ocean, the Mediterranean, and the Red Sea (see Map 8.3).

GHANA

The first of these great commercial states was Ghana, which emerged in the fifth century C.E. in the upper Niger valley, a grassland region between the Sahara and the tropical forests along the West African coast (the modern state of Ghana, which takes its name from the trading society under discussion here, is located in the forest region to the south). The majority of the people in the area were Iron Age farmers living in villages under the authority of a local chieftain. Gradually, these local communities were united to form the kingdom of Ghana.

Although the people of the region had traditionally lived from agriculture, a primary reason for Ghana's growing importance was gold. The heartland of the state was located near one of the richest gold-producing areas in all of Africa. Ghanaian merchants transported the gold to Morocco, whence it was distributed throughout the known world. This trade began in ancient times, as the Greek historian Herodotus relates:

The Carthaginians also tell us that they trade with a race of men who live in a part of Libya beyond the Pillars of Heracles [the Strait of Gibraltar]. On reaching this country, they unload their goods, arrange them tidily along the beach, and then, returning to their boats, raise a smoke. Seeing the smoke, the natives come down to the beach, place on the

Courtesy of William J. Duiker

ground a certain quantity of gold in exchange for the goods,
and go off again to a distance. The Carthaginians then come
ashore and take a look at the gold; and if they think it represents a fair price for their wares, they collect it and go away;
if, on the other hand, it seems too little, they go back aboard
and wait, and the natives come and add to the gold until they
are satisfied. There is perfect honesty on both sides; the
Carthaginians never touch the gold until it equals in value
what they have offered for sale, and the natives never touch
the goods until the gold has been taken away.[3]

Later, Ghana became known to Arab-speaking peoples in
North Africa as "the land of gold." Actually, the name was
misleading, for the gold did not come from Ghana, but
from a neighboring people, who sold it to merchants from
Ghana.

Eventually other exports from Ghana found their
way to the bazaars of the Mediterranean coast and
beyond—ivory, ostrich feathers, hides, leather goods, and
ultimately slaves. The origins of the slave trade in the area
probably go back to the first millennium B.C.E., when
Berber tribesmen seized African villagers in the regions
south of the Sahara and sold them for profit to buyers
in Europe and the Middle East. In return, Ghana imported
metal goods (especially weapons), textiles, horses, and
salt.

Much of the trade across the desert was still conducted
by the nomadic Berbers, but Ghanaian merchants played
an active role as intermediaries, trading tropical products such as bananas, kola nuts, and palm oil from the forest states of Guinea along the Atlantic coast to the south.
By the eighth and ninth centuries, much of this trade was
conducted by Muslim merchants, who purchased the
goods from local traders (using iron and copper cash or
cowrie shells from Southeast Asia as the primary means of
exchange) and then sold them to Berbers, who carried
them across the desert. The merchants who carried on this
trade often became quite wealthy and lived in splendor in
cities like Saleh, the capital of Ghana. So did the king,
of course, who taxed the merchants as well as the farmers and the producers.

Like other West African kings, the king of Ghana
ruled by divine right and was assisted by a hereditary
aristocracy composed of the leading members of the
prominent clans, who also served as district chiefs responsible for maintaining law and order and collecting
taxes. The king was responsible for maintaining the
security of his kingdom, serving as an intermediary with
local deities, and functioning as the chief law officer
to adjudicate disputes. The kings of Ghana did not
convert to Islam themselves, although they welcomed
Muslim merchants and apparently did not discourage
their subjects from adopting the new faith (see the box on
p. 170).

MALI

The state of Ghana flourished for several hundred years,
but by the twelfth century, weakened by ruinous wars with
Berber tribesmen, it had begun to decline; it collapsed at
the end of the century. In its place rose a number of new
trading societies, including large territorial states like Mali
and Songhai in the west, Kanem-Bornu in the east, and

Description of a Ghanaian Capital

After its first appearance in West Africa in the decades following the death of Muhammad, Islam competed with native African religions for followers. Eventually several local rulers converted to the Muslim faith. This passage by the Arab geographer al-Bakri shows how both religions flourished side by side in the state of Ghana during the eleventh century.

AL-BAKRI'S DESCRIPTION OF GHANA

The king's residence comprises a palace and conical huts, the whole surrounded by a fence like a wall. Around the royal town are huts and groves of thorn trees where live the magicians who control their religious rites. These groves, where they keep their idols and bury their kings, are protected by guards who permit no one to enter or find out what goes on in them.

None of those who belong to the imperial religion may wear tailored garments except the king himself and the heir-presumptive, his sister's son. The rest of the people wear wrappers of cotton, silk or brocade according to their means. Most of the men shave their beards and the women their heads. The king adorns himself with female ornaments around the neck and arms. On his head he wears gold-embroidered caps covered with turbans of finest cotton. He gives audience to the people for the redressing of grievances in a hut around which are placed 10 horses covered in golden cloth. Behind him stand 10 slaves carrying shields and swords mounted with gold. On his right are the sons of vassal kings, their heads plaited with gold and wearing costly garments. On the ground around him are seated his ministers, whilst the governor of the city sits before him. On guard at the door are dogs of fine pedigree, wearing collars adorned with gold and silver. The royal audience is announced by the beating of a drum, called daba, made out of a long piece of hollowed-out wood. When the people have gathered, his coreligionists draw near upon their knees sprinkling dust upon their heads as a sign of respect, whilst the Muslims clap hands as their form of greeting.

---

small commercial city-states like the Hausa states, located in what is today northern Nigeria (see Map 8.4).

The greatest of the states that emerged after the destruction of Ghana was Mali. Extending from the Atlantic coast inland as far as the trading cities of Timbuktu and Gao on the Niger River, Mali built its wealth and power on the gold trade. But the heartland of Mali was situated south of the Sahara in the savanna region, where sufficient moisture enabled farmers to grow such crops as sorghum, millet, and rice. The farmers lived in villages ruled by a local chieftain (called a *mansa*), who served as both religious and administrative leader and was responsible for forwarding tax revenues from the village to higher levels of government.

The primary wealth of the country was accumulated in the cities. Here lived the merchants, who were primarily of local origin, although many were now practicing Muslims. Commercial activities were taxed but were apparently so lucrative that both the merchants and the kings prospered. One of the most powerful kings of Mali was Mansa Musa (1312–1337), whose primary contribution to his people was probably not economic prosperity but the Muslim faith. Mansa Musa strongly encouraged the building of mosques and the study of the Koran in his kingdom and imported scholars and books to introduce his subjects to the message of Allah. One visitor from Europe, writing in the late fifteenth century, reported that in Timbuktu "are a great store of doctors, judges, priests, and other learned men, that are bountifully maintained at the king's cost and charges. And hither are brought divers manuscripts of written books out of Barbary [North

Africa] which are sold for more money than any other merchandise."[4]

STATES AND STATELESS SOCIETIES IN SOUTHERN AFRICA

In the southern half of the African continent, from the great basin of the Congo River to the Cape of Good Hope, states formed somewhat more slowly than in the north. Until the eleventh century C.E., most of the peoples in this region lived in what are sometimes called "stateless societies," characterized by autonomous villages organized by clans and ruled by a local chieftain or clan head. Beginning in the eleventh century, in some parts of southern Africa, these independent villages gradually began to consolidate. Out of these groupings came the first states.

One area where this process occurred was the Congo River valley, where the combination of fertile land and nearby deposits of copper and iron enabled the inhabitants to enjoy an agricultural surplus and engage in regional commerce. Two new states in particular underwent this transition. Sometime during the fourteenth century, the kingdom of Luba was founded in the center of the continent, in a rich agricultural and fishing area near the shores of Lake Kisale. Luba had a relatively centralized government, in which the king appointed provincial governors, who were responsible for collecting tribute from the village chiefs. At about the same time, the kingdom of Kongo

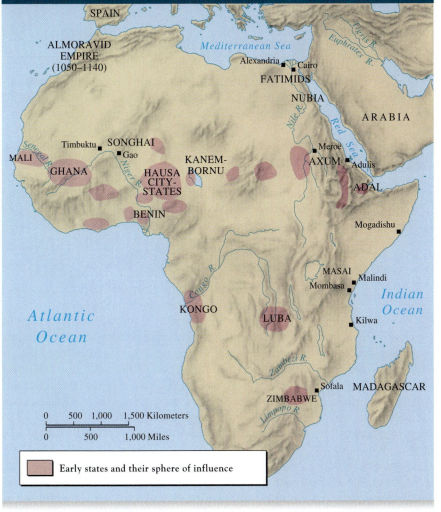

MAP 8.4 The Emergence of States in Africa. By the end of the first millennium C.E., organized states had begun to appear in various parts of Africa. ➤ *What were some of the key states at the time, as shown on the map?*

Map labels: SPAIN · ALMORAVID EMPIRE (1050–1140) · Mediterranean Sea · Alexandria · Cairo · FATIMIDS · NUBIA · ARABIA · Tigris R. · Euphrates R. · Nile R. · Red Sea · Meroë · AXUM · Adulis · ADAL · Mogadishu · Timbuktu · SONGHAI · Gao · Senegal R. · Niger R. · MALI · GHANA · HAUSA CITY-STATES · KANEM-BORNU · BENIN · Congo R. · KONGO · LUBA · MASAI · Malindi · Mombasa · Indian Ocean · Kilwa · Atlantic Ocean · Zambezi R. · Sofala · MADAGASCAR · ZIMBABWE · Limpopo R.

0 500 1,000 1,500 Kilometers
0 500 1,000 Miles

■ Early states and their sphere of influence

ber of dehorned cows. . . . They live together in small villages, in houses made of reed mats, which do not keep out the rain."[5]

Zimbabwe

Farther to the east, the situation was somewhat different. In the grassland regions immediately to the south of the Zambezi River, a mixed economy involving farming, cattle herding, and commercial pursuits had begun to develop during the early centuries of the first millennium C.E. Characteristically villages in this area were constructed inside walled enclosures to protect the animals at night. The most famous of these communities was Zimbabwe, located on the plateau of the same name between the Zambezi and Limpopo Rivers. From the twelfth century to the middle of the fifteenth, Zimbabwe was the most powerful and most prosperous state in the region and played a major role in the gold trade with the Swahili trading communities on the eastern coast.

The ruins of Zimbabwe's capital, known as Great Zimbabwe (the term *Zimbabwe* means "sacred house" in the Bantu language), provide a vivid illustration of the kingdom's power and influence. Strategically situated between substantial gold reserves to the west

was formed just south of the mouth of the Congo River on the Atlantic coast.

These new states were primarily agricultural, although both had a thriving manufacturing sector and took an active part in the growing exchange of goods throughout the region. As time passed, both began to expand southward to absorb the mixed farming and pastoral peoples in the area of modern Angola. In the drier grassland area to the south, other small communities continued to support themselves by herding, hunting, or food gathering. We know little about these peoples, however, since they possessed no writing system and had few visitors. A Portuguese sailor who encountered them in the late sixteenth century reported, "These people are herdsmen and cultivators. . . . Their main crop is millet, which they grind between two stones or in wooden mortars to make flour. . . . Their wealth consists mainly in their huge num-

and a small river leading to the coast, Great Zimbabwe was well placed to benefit from the expansion of trade between the coast and the interior. The town sits on a hill overlooking the river and is surrounded by stone walls, which enclosed an area large enough to hold over ten thousand residents. The houses of the wealthy were built of cement on stone foundations, while those of the common people were of dried mud with thatched roofs. In the valley below is the royal palace, surrounded by a stone wall 30 feet high. Artifacts found at the site include household implements and ornaments made of gold and copper, as well as jewelry and even porcelain imported from China.

Most of the royal wealth probably came from two sources: the ownership of cattle and the king's ability to levy heavy taxes on the gold that passed through the kingdom en route to the coast. By the middle of the fifteenth century, however, the city was apparently abandoned,

⟾ **GREAT ZIMBABWE.** Situated on an important trade route and a center for cattle and agriculture, Great Zimbabwe was originally settled by pastoral peoples during the first millennium B.C.E. Later it became the capital of a prosperous state. Its 30-foot walls were the first in Africa to be constructed without the use of mortar. The walled palace shown here indicates why Great Zimbabwe is generally regarded as the most impressive archaeological site in southern Africa.

possibly because of environmental damage caused by overgrazing. With the decline of Zimbabwe, the focus of economic power began to shift northward to the valley of the Zambezi River.

South of the Limpopo River, pastoralism and hunting continued to be the primary means of livelihood. As we saw earlier, some of these peoples had been absorbed by the Iron Age farming communities that spread southward from Central Africa during the first millennium C.E. Others remained independent in isolated villages or small kingdoms, although they often carried on active trade with the growing states to their north.

One such people were the San, called Bushmen by later Europeans. A hunting and foraging people who spoke a Khoisan language, the San lived in small family communities of twenty to twenty-five members throughout southern Africa from Namibia in the west to the Drakensberg Mountains near the southeastern coast. Scholars have learned about the early life of the San by interviewing their modern descendants and by studying rock paintings found in caves throughout the area. These multicolored paintings, which predate the coming of the Europeans, were drawn with a brush made of small feathers fastened to a reed. They depict various aspects of the San's lifestyle, including their hunting techniques and religious rituals.

When the Europeans arrived in the area, they regarded the San as troublesome pests who raided their cattle. One nineteenth-century European missionary dismissed the San contemptuously, saying, "He has no religion, no laws, no government, no recognized authority, no patrimony,

no fixed abode."[6] Over time, as the Europeans constantly encroached on their hunting grounds, the San found it virtually impossible to maintain their way of life. Only a few survive today, most of them in the Kalahari Desert in Botswana.

◆ AFRICAN SOCIETY

Drawing generalizations about social organization, cultural development, and daily life in traditional Africa is difficult because of the diversity of the continent and the absence of written languages in much of the area. Historians must therefore rely on accounts of the occasional visitor, such as al-Mas'udi and the famous fourteenth-century chronicler Ibn Battuta. Such travelers, however, tended to come into contact mostly with the wealthy and the powerful, leaving us to speculate about what life was like for ordinary Africans during this early period.

Urban Life

African towns often began as fortified walled villages and gradually evolved into larger communities serving several purposes. Here, of course, were the center of government and the teeming markets filled with goods from distant regions. Here also were artisans skilled in metal- or woodworking, pottery making, and other crafts. Unlike the rural areas, where a village was usually composed of a single lineage group or clan, the towns drew their residents from several clans, although individual clans usually lived in their own compounds and were governed by their own clan heads.

In the states of West Africa, the focal point of the major towns was the royal precinct. The relationship between the ruler and the merchant class differed from the situation in most Asian societies, where the royal family and the aristocracy were largely isolated from the remainder of the population. In Africa, the chasm between the king and the common people was not so great. Often the ruler would hold an audience to allow people to voice their complaints or to welcome visitors from foreign countries.

This is not to say that the king was not elevated above all others in status. In wealthier states, the walls of the audience chamber would be covered with sheets of beaten silver and gold, and the king would be surrounded by hundreds of armed soldiers and some of his trusted advisers. Nevertheless the symbiotic relationship between the ruler and merchant class served to reduce the gap between the king and his subjects. The relationship was mutually beneficial, since the merchants received honors and favors from the palace while the king's coffers were filled with taxes paid by the merchants. Certainly it was to the benefit of the king to maintain law and order in his domain so that the merchants could ply their trade. As Ibn Battuta observed, among the good qualities of the peoples of West

Africa was the prevalence of peace in the region. "The traveler is not afraid in it," he remarked, "nor is he who lives there in fear of the thief or of the robber by violence."[7]

Village Life

The vast majority of Africans lived in small rural villages. Their identities were established by their membership in a nuclear family and a lineage group. At the basic level was the nuclear family composed of parents and preadult children; sometimes it included an elderly grandparent and other family dependents as well. They lived in small round huts constructed of packed mud and topped with a conical thatch roof. In most African societies, these nuclear family units would in turn be combined into larger kinship communities known as households or lineage groups.

The lineage group was similar in many respects to the clan in China or the caste system in India in that it was normally based on kinship ties, although sometimes outsiders such as friends or other dependents may have been admitted to membership. Throughout the precolonial era, lineages served, in the words of one historian, as the "basic building blocks" of African society. The authority of the leading members of the lineage group was substantial. As in China, the elders had considerable power over the economic functions of the other people in the group, which provided mutual support for all members.

A village would usually be composed of a single lineage group, although some communities may have consisted of several unrelated families. At the head of the village was the familiar "big man," who was often assisted by a council of representatives of the various households in the community. Often the "big man" was believed to possess supernatural powers, and as the village grew in size and power, he might eventually be transformed into a local chieftain or monarch.

The Role of Women

Although generalizations are risky, we can say that women were usually subordinate to men in Africa, as in most early societies. In some cases, they were valued for the work they could do or for their role in increasing the size of the lineage group. Polygyny was not uncommon, particularly in Muslim societies. Women often worked in the fields while the men of the village tended the cattle or went on hunting expeditions. In some communities, the women specialized in commercial activities. In one area in southern Africa, young girls were sent into the mines to extract gold because of their smaller physiques.

But there were some key differences between the role of women in Africa and elsewhere. In many African societies, lineage was matrilinear rather than patrilinear. In the words of Ibn Battuta, "A man does not pass on inheritance except to the sons of his sister to the exclusion of his own sons."[8] He said he had never encountered this custom before except among the unbelievers of the Malabar coast in India. Women were often permitted to inherit property, and the husband was often expected to move into his wife's house.

Relations between the sexes were also sometimes more relaxed than in China or India, with none of the taboos characteristic of those societies. Again, in the words of Ibn Battuta, himself a Muslim:

> With regard to their women, they are not modest in the presence of men, they do not veil themselves in spite of their perseverance in the prayers. . . . The women there have friends and companions amongst men outside the prohibited degrees of marriage [i.e., other than brothers, fathers, etc.]. Likewise for the men, there are companions from amongst women outside the prohibited degrees. One of them would enter his house to find his wife with her companion and would not disapprove of that conduct.

When Ibn Battuta asked an African acquaintance about these customs, the latter responded: "Women's companionship with men in our country is honorable and takes place in a good way: there is no suspicion about it. They are not like the women in your country." Ibn Battuta noted his astonishment at such a "thoughtless" answer and did not accept further invitations to visit his friend's house.[9]

Such informal attitudes toward the relationship between the sexes were not found everywhere in Africa and were probably curtailed as many Africans converted to Islam (see the box on p. 174). But it is a testimony to the tenacity of traditional customs that the relatively puritanical views about the role of women in society brought by Muslims from the Middle East made little impression even among Muslim families in West Africa.

Slavery

African slavery is often associated with the period after 1500. Indeed, the slave trade did reach enormous proportions in the seventeenth and eighteenth centuries, when European slave ships transported millions of unfortunate victims abroad to Europe or the Americas (see Chapter 14).

Slavery did not originate with the coming of the Europeans, however. It had been practiced in Africa since ancient times and probably originated with prisoners of war who were forced into perpetual servitude. Slavery was common in ancient Egypt and became especially prevalent during the New Kingdom, when slaving expeditions brought back thousands of captives from the upper Nile to be used in labor gangs, for tribute, and even as human sacrifices.

Slavery persisted during the early period of state building, in the first and early second millennia C.E. Berber tribes may have regularly raided agricultural communities south of the Sahara for captives who were transported northward and eventually sold throughout the Mediterranean. Some were enrolled as soldiers, while others, often women, were used as domestic servants in the homes of

WOMEN AND ISLAM IN
NORTH AFRICA

In Muslim societies in North Africa, as elsewhere, women were required to cover their bodies to avoid giving temptations to men, but Islam's puritanical insistence on the separation of the sexes contrasted with the relatively informal relationships that prevailed in many African societies. In this excerpt from The History and Description of Africa, *Leo Africanus describes the customs along the Mediterranean coast of Africa. A resident of Spain of Muslim parentage who was captured by Christian corsairs in 1518 and later served under Pope Leo X, Leo Africanus undertook many visits to Africa.*

LEO AFRICANUS, *THE HISTORY AND DESCRIPTION OF AFRICA*

Their women (according to the guise of that country) go very gorgeously attired: they wear linen gowns dyed black, with exceeding wide sleeves, over which sometimes they cast a mantle of the same color or of blue, the corners of which mantle are very [attractively] fastened about their shoulders with a fine silver clasp. Likewise they have rings hanging at their ears, which for the most part are made of silver; they wear many rings also upon their fingers. Moreover they usually wear about their thighs and ankles certain scarfs and rings, after the fashion of the Africans. They cover their faces with certain masks having only two holes for the eyes to peep out at. If any man chance to meet with them, they presently hide their faces, passing by him with silence, except it be some of their allies or kinsfolks; for unto them they always [uncover] their faces, neither is there any use of the said mask so long as they be in presence. These Arabians when they travel any journey (as they oftentimes do) they set their women upon certain saddles made handsomely of wicker for the same purpose, and fastened to their camel backs, neither be they anything too wide, but fit only for a woman to sit in. When they go to the wars each man carries his wife with him, to the end that she may cheer up her good man, and give him encouragement. Their damsels which are unmarried do usually paint their faces, breasts, arms, hands, and fingers with a kind of counterfeit color: which is accounted a most decent custom among them.

---

the well-to-do. The use of captives for forced labor or for sale was apparently also common in African societies farther to the south and along the eastern coast.

Life was difficult for the average slave. The least fortunate were probably those who worked on plantations owned by the royal family or other wealthy landowners. Those pressed into service as soldiers were sometimes more fortunate, since in Muslim societies in the Middle East, they might at some point win their freedom. Many slaves were employed in the royal household or as domestic servants in private homes. In general, these slaves probably had the most tolerable existence. Although they were not ordinarily permitted to purchase their freedom, their living conditions were often decent and sometimes practically indistinguishable from those of the free individuals in the household. In some societies in North Africa, slaves reportedly made up as much as 75 percent of the entire population. Elsewhere the percentage was much lower, in some cases less than 10 percent.

AFRICAN CULTURE

In early Africa, as in much of the rest of the world at the time, creative expression, whether in the form of painting, literature, or music, was above all a means of serving religion. Though to the uninitiated a wooden mask or the bronze and iron statuary of southern Nigeria is simply a work of art, to the artist it was often a means of expressing religious convictions. Some African historians reject the use of the term *art* to describe such artifacts because they were produced for religious rather than aesthetic purposes.

Painting and Sculpture

The earliest extant art forms in Africa are rock paintings. The most famous examples are in the Tassili Mountains in the central Sahara, where the earliest paintings may date back as far as 5000 B.C.E., though the majority are a millennium or so younger. Some of the later paintings depict the two-horse chariots used to transport goods prior to the introduction of the camel. Rock paintings are also found elsewhere in the continent, including the Nile valley and in eastern and southern Africa. Those of the San peoples of southern Africa are especially interesting for their illustrations of ritual ceremonies in which village shamans induce rain, propitiate the spirits, or cure illnesses.

More familiar perhaps are African wood carvings and sculpture. Wood-carvers throughout the continent produced remarkable masks (actually headpieces) and statuary. The carvings often represent gods, spirits, or ancestral figures and were believed to embody the spiritual powers of the subject in symbolic form. Terra-cotta and metal figurines served a similar purpose.

In the thirteenth and fourteenth centuries C.E., metalworkers at Ife in what is now southern Nigeria produced handsome bronze and iron statues using the lost-wax method, in which melted wax is replaced in a mold by molten metal. The Ife sculptures may in turn have influenced artists in Benin, in West Africa, who produced equally impressive works in bronze during the same period. The Benin sculptures include bronze heads, relief plaques depicting life at court, ornaments, and figures of various animals.

Westerners once regarded African wood carvings and metal sculpture as a form of "primitive art," but the label is not appropriate. The metal sculpture of Benin, for example, is highly sophisticated, and some of the best works are considered masterpieces. Such artistic works were often created by artisans in the employ of the royal court.

Music

Like sculpture and wood carving, African music and dance often served a religious function. With their characteristic heavy rhythmic beat, dances were a means of communicating with the spirits, and the frenzied movements that are often identified with African dance were intended to represent the spirits acting through humans.

African music during the traditional period varied to some degree from one society to another. A wide variety of instruments were used, including drums and other percussion instruments, xylophones, bells, horns and flutes, and stringed instruments like the fiddle, harp, and zither. Still, the music throughout the continent had sufficient common characteristics to justify a few generalizations. In the first place, a strong rhythmic pattern was an important feature of most African music, although the desired effect was achieved through a wide variety of means, including gourds, pots, bells, sticks beaten together, and hand clapping as well as drums.

Another important feature of African music was the integration of voice and instrument into a total musical experience. Musical instruments and the human voice were often woven together to tell a story, and instruments, such as the famous "talking drum," were often used to represent the voice. Choral music and individual voices were frequently used in a pattern of repetition and variation, sometimes known as "call and response." Through this technique, the audience participated in the music by uttering a single phrase over and over as a choral response to the changing call sung by the soloist. Sometimes instrumental music achieved a similar result.

Much music was produced in the context of social rituals, such as weddings and funerals, religious ceremonies, and official inaugurations. It could also serve an educational purpose by passing on to the young people information about the history and social traditions of the community. In the absence of written languages in sub-Saharan Africa (except for the Arabic script, used in Muslim societies in East and West Africa), music served as the primary means of transmitting folk legends and religious traditions from generation to generation. Storytelling, which was usually undertaken by a priestly class or a specialized class of storytellers, served a similar function.

Architecture

No aspect of African artistic creativity is more varied than architecture. From the pyramids along the Nile to the ruins of Great Zimbabwe south of the Zambezi River, from the Moorish palaces at Zanzibar to the turreted mud mosques of West Africa, African architecture shows a striking diversity of approach and technique that is unmatched in other areas of creative endeavor.

The earliest surviving architectural form found in Africa is the pyramid. The Kushite kingdom at Meroë apparently adopted the pyramidal form from Egypt during the last centuries of the first millennium B.C.E. Although used for the same purpose as their earlier counterparts at Giza, the pyramids at Meroë were distinctive in style; they were much smaller and were topped with a flat platform rather than rising to a point. Remains of temples with massive carved pillars at Meroë also reflect Egyptian influence.

Farther to the south, the kingdom of Axum was developing its own architectural traditions. Most distinctive were the carved stone pillars, known as stelae (see the photo on p. 163), that were used to mark the tombs of dead kings. Some stood as high as 100 feet. The advent of Christianity eventually had an impact on Axumite architecture. During the Zagwe dynasty in the twelfth and thirteenth centuries C.E., churches carved out of solid rock were constructed throughout the country. Stylistically they combined indigenous techniques inherited from the pre-Christian period with elements borrowed from Christian churches in the Holy Land.

In West Africa, buildings constructed in stone were apparently a rarity until the emergence of states during the first millennium C.E. At that time, the royal palace, as well as other buildings of civic importance, were often built of stone or cement, while the houses of the majority of the population continued to be constructed of dried mud. On his visit to the state of Guinea on the West African coast, the sixteenth-century traveler Leo Africanus noted that the houses of the ruler and other elites were built of chalk with roofs of straw. Even then, however, well into the state-building period, mosques were often built of mud.

Along the east coast, the architecture of the elite tended to reflect Middle Eastern styles. In the coastal towns and islands from Mogadishu to Kilwa, the houses of the wealthy were built of stone and reflected Moorish influence. As elsewhere, the common people lived in huts of mud, thatch, or palm leaves (see the box on p. 176). Mosques were built of stone.

The most famous stone buildings in sub-Saharan Africa are those at Great Zimbabwe. Constructed of carefully cut stones that were set in place without mortar, the great wall and the public buildings at Great Zimbabwe are an impressive monument to the architectural creativity of the peoples of the region.

A CHINESE VIEW OF AFRICA

This passage from Chau Ju-kua's thirteenth-century treatise on geography describes various aspects of life along the eastern coast of Africa in what is now Somalia, including the urban architecture. The author was an inspector of foreign trade in the city of Quanzhou (sometimes called Zayton) on the southern coast of China. His account was compiled from reports of seafarers. Note the varied uses that the local people make of a whale carcass.

CHAU JU-KUA ON EAST AFRICA

The inhabitants of the Chung-li country [the Somali coast] go bareheaded and barefooted; they wrap themselves in cotton stuffs, but they dare not wear jackets, for the wearing of jackets and turbans is a privilege reserved to the ministers and the king's courtiers. The king lives in a brick house covered with glazed tiles, but the people live in huts made of palm leaves and covered with grass-thatched roofs. Their daily food consists of baked flour cakes, sheep's and camel's milk. There are great numbers of cattle, sheep, and camels. . . .

There are many sorcerers among them who are able to change themselves into birds, beasts, or aquatic animals, and by these means keep the ignorant people in a state of terror. If some of them in trading with some foreign ship have a quarrel, the sorcerers pronounce a charm over the ship so that it can neither go forward nor backward, and they only release the ship when it has settled the dispute. The government has formally forbidden this practice.

When one of the inhabitants dies, and they are about to bury him in his coffin, his kinsfolk from near and far come to condole. Each person, flourishing a sword in his hand, goes in and asks the mourners the cause of the person's death. If he was killed by the hand of man, each one says, we will revenge him on the murderer with these swords. Should the mourners reply that he was not killed by any one, but that he came to his end by the will of Heaven, they throw away their swords and break into violent wailing.

Every year there are driven on the coast a great many dead fish measuring two hundred feet in length and twenty feet through the body. The people do not eat the flesh of these fish, but they cut out their brains, marrow, and eyes, from which they get oil. They mix this oil with lime to caulk their boats, and use it also in lamps. The poor people use the ribs of these fish to make rafters, the backbones for door leaves, and they cut off vertebrae to make mortars with.

THE MOSQUE AT JENNE, MALI. With the opening of the gold fields south of Mali, in present-day Ghana, Jenne became an important trading center for gold. Shown here is its distinctive fourteenth-century mosque made of unbaked clay without reinforcements. The projecting timbers offer easy access for repairing the mud exterior, as was regularly required.

A WEST AFRICAN ORAL TRADITION

*I*n this passage from the West African Epic of Son-Jara, Son-Jara's sister, Sugulun Kulunkan, offers to seduce his enemy Sumamuru in order to obtain the Manden secret, or magic spell, needed to control the kingdom of Mali. Sumamuru divulges his all-powerful secret and is rebuked by his mother; both son and mother then disown one another with the trenchant symbols of the slashed breast and cut cloth. After each line of the verse, the bard's assistant would shout the endorsement "true," perhaps the distant origin of today's African American practice of approving each line of religious oratory with "Amen." The subversion of a powerful man by the enticements of a seductive woman is reminiscent of the biblical story of Samson and Delilah.

THE EPIC OF SON-JARA

Son-Jara's flesh-and-blood sister, Sugulun Kulunkan,
She said, "O Magan Son-Jara,
"One person cannot fight this war.
"Let me go seek Sumamuru.
"Were I then to reach him,
"To you I will deliver him,
"So that the folk of the Manden be yours,
"And all the Mandenland you shield."
Sugulun Kulunkan arose,
And went up to the gates of Sumamuru's fortress:
. . .
"Come open the gates, Susu Mountain Sumamuru!
"Come make me your bed companion!"
Sumamuru came to the gates:
"What manner of person are you?"
"It is I Sugulun Kulunkan!"
"Well, now, Sugulun Kulunkan,
"If you have come to trap me,

"To turn me over to some person,
"Know that none can ever vanquish me.
"I have found the Manden secret,
"And made the Manden sacrifice,
"And in five score millet stalks placed it,
"And buried them here in the earth.
"'Tis I who found the Manden secret,
"And made the Manden sacrifice,
"And in a red piebald bull did place it,
"And buried it here in the earth.
"Know that none can vanquish me.
"'Tis I who found the Manden secret
"And made a sacrifice to it,
"And in a pure white cock did place it.
"Were you to kill it,
"And uproot some barren groundnut plants,
"And strip them of their leaves,
"And spread them round the fortress,
"And uproot more barren peanut plants,
"And fling them into the fortress,
"Only then can I be vanquished."
His mother sprang forward at that:
"Heh! Susu Mountain Sumamuru!
"Never tell all to a woman,
"To a one-night woman!
"The woman is not safe, Sumamuru."
Sumamuru sprang towards his mother,
And came and seized his mother,
And slashed off her breast with a knife, magasi!
She went and got the old menstrual cloth.
"Ah! Sumamuru!" she swore.
"If your birth was ever a fact,
"I have cut your old menstrual cloth!"

Literature

Literature in the sense of written works did not exist in sub-Saharan Africa during the early traditional period, except in regions where Islam had brought the Arabic script from the Middle East. But African societies compensated for the absence of a written language with a rich tradition of oral lore. The bard, or professional storyteller, was an ancient African institution by which history was transmitted orally from generation to generation. In many West African societies, bards were highly esteemed and served as counselors to kings as well as protectors of local tradition. Bards were revered for their oratory and singing skills, phenomenal memory, and astute interpretation of history. As one African scholar wrote, the death of a bard was equivalent to the burning of a library.

Bards served several necessary functions in society. They were chroniclers of history, preservers of social customs and proper conduct, and entertainers who possessed a monopoly over the playing of several musical instruments, which accompanied their narratives. Because of their unique position above normal society, bards often played the role of mediator between hostile families or clans in a community. They were also credited with possessing occult powers and could read divinations and give blessings and curses. Traditionally bards also served as advisers to the king, sometimes inciting him to action (such as going to battle) through the passion of their poetry. When captured by the enemy, bards were often treated with respect and released or compelled to serve the victor with their art.

One of the most famous West African epics is *The Epic of Son-Jara* (also known as *Sunjata* or *Sundiata*). Passed down orally by bards for more than seven hundred years, it relates the heroic exploits of Son-Jara, the founder and ruler (1230–1255) of Mali's empire. Although Mansa Musa is famous throughout the world because of his flamboyant pilgrimage to Mecca in the fourteenth century, Son-Jara is more celebrated in West Africa because of the dynamic and unbroken oral traditions of the West African peoples (see the box above).

In addition to the bards, women too were appreciated for their storytelling talents, as well as for their role as purveyors of the moral values and religious beliefs of African societies. In societies that lacked a written tradition, women represented the glue that held the community together. Through the recitation of fables, proverbs, poems, and songs, mothers conditioned the communal bonding and moral fiber of succeeding generations in a way that was rarely encountered in the patriarchal societies of Europe, eastern and southern Asia, and the Middle East. Such activities were not only vital aspects of education in traditional Africa, but they also offered a welcome respite from the drudgery of everyday life and a spark to develop the imagination and artistic awareness of the young. Renowned for its many proverbs, Africa also offers the following: "A good story is like a garden carried in the pocket."

 CONCLUSION

Thanks to the dedicated work of a generation of archaeologists, anthropologists, and historians, we now have a much better understanding of the evolution of human societies in Africa than we did a few decades ago. Intensive efforts by archaeologists have demonstrated beyond reasonable doubt that the first hominids lived there. Recent evidence suggests that farming may have been practiced in Africa more than twelve thousand years ago, and the concept of kingship may have originated not in Sumer or in Egypt but in the upper Nile valley as long ago as the fourth millennium B.C.E.

Less is known about more recent African history, partly because of the paucity of written records. Still, historians have established that the first civilizations had begun to take shape in sub-Saharan Africa by the first millennium C.E., while the continent as a whole was an active participant in emerging regional and global trade with the Mediterranean world and across the Indian Ocean.

Thus the peoples of Africa were not as isolated from the main currents of human history as was once assumed. Although the state-building process in sub-Saharan Africa was still in its early stages compared with the ancient civilizations of India, China, and Mesopotamia, in many respects these new states were as impressive and sophisticated as their counterparts elsewhere in the world.

In the fifteenth century, a new factor was added to the equation. Urged on by the tireless efforts of Prince Henry the Navigator, Portuguese fleets began to probe southward along the coast of West Africa. At first, their sponsors were in search of gold and slaves, but at the end of the century, Vasco da Gama's voyage around the Cape of Good Hope signaled Portugal's determination to dominate the commerce of the Indian Ocean in the future. The new situation posed a challenge to the peoples of Africa, whose nascent states and technology would be severely tested by the rapacious demands of the Europeans (see Chapter 14).

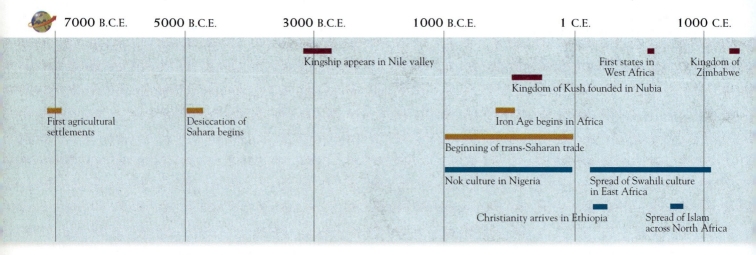

| 7000 B.C.E. | 5000 B.C.E. | 3000 B.C.E. | 1000 B.C.E. | 1 C.E. | 1000 C.E. |

Kingship appears in Nile valley

First states in West Africa

Kingdom of Zimbabwe

Kingdom of Kush founded in Nubia

First agricultural settlements

Desiccation of Sahara begins

Iron Age begins in Africa

Beginning of trans-Saharan trade

Nok culture in Nigeria

Spread of Swahili culture in East Africa

Christianity arrives in Ethiopia

Spread of Islam across North Africa

CHAPTER NOTES

1. Said Hamdun and Noel King, eds., *Ibn Battuta in Africa* (London, 1975), p. 19.
2. *The Book of Duarte Barbosa* (Nedeln, Liechtenstein, 1967), p. 28.
3. Herodotus, *The Histories*, trans. Aubrey de Sélincourt (Baltimore, 1964), p. 307.
4. Quoted in Margaret Shinnie, *Ancient African Kingdoms* (London, 1965), p. 60.

5. C. R. Boxer, ed., *The Tragic History of the Sea, 1589–1622* (Cambridge, 1959), pp. 121–122.
6. Quoted in Brian Fagan, *New Treasures of the Past: Fresh Finds That Deepen Our Understanding of the Archaeology of Man* (Leicester, England, 1987), p. 154.

7. Hamdun and King, *Ibn Battuta in Africa*, p. 47.
8. Ibid., p. 28.
9. Ibid., pp. 28–30.

SUGGESTED READING

In few areas of world history is scholarship advancing as rapidly as in African history. New information is constantly forcing archaeologists and historians to revise their assumptions about the early history of the continent. Standard texts therefore quickly become out-of-date as their conclusions are supplanted by new evidence.

Still, there are several worthwhile general surveys that provide a useful overview of the early period of African history. The dean of African historians, and certainly one of the most readable, is B. Davidson. For a sympathetic portrayal of the African people, see his *African History* (New York, 1968) and *Lost Cities in Africa*, rev. ed. (Boston, 1970). Other respected accounts are R. Oliver and J. D. Fage, *A Short History of Africa* (Middlesex, England, 1986); J. M. Harris, *Africans and Their History* (New York, 1972); and V. B. Khapoya, *The African Experience: An Introduction* (Englewood Cliffs, N.J., 1994). A more detailed interpretation, by four respected historians, is P. Curtin et al., *African History* (Boston, 1978). For a readable treatment incorporating more-recent evidence, see K. Shillington, *History of Africa* (New York, 1989). R. O. Collins, ed., *Problems in African History: The Precolonial Centuries* (New York, 1993), provides a useful collection of scholarly articles on key issues in precolonial Africa.

Specialized studies are beginning to appear with frequency on many areas of the continent. For a popular account of archaeological finds, see B. Fagan, *New Treasures of the Past: Fresh Finds That Deepen Our Understanding of the Archaeology of Man* (Leicester, England, 1987). For a more detailed treatment of the early period, see the early volumes in *The Cambridge History of Africa* (Cambridge, 1976–1986). See also R. Oliver and B. Fagan, *Africa in the Iron Age* (Cambridge, 1975). C. Ehret, *An African Classical Age: Eastern and Southern Africa in World History, 1000 B.C. to 400 A.D.* (Charlottesville, Va., 1998), applies historical linguistics to make up for the lack of documentary evidence in the precolonial era. J. D. Clarke and S. A. Brandt, eds., *From Hunters to Farmers* (Berkeley, Calif., 1984), takes an economic approach. Also see D. A. Welsby, *The Kingdom of Kush: The Napataean Meroitic Empire* (London, 1996), and J. Middleton, *Swahili: An African Mercantile Civilization* (New Haven, Conn., 1992). For a fascinating account of trans-Saharan trade, see E. W. Bovill, *The Golden Trade of the Moors: West African Kingdoms in the Fourteenth Century*, 2d ed. (Princeton, N.J., 1995). On the cultural background, see R. Olaniyan, ed., *African History and Culture* (Lagos, Nigeria, 1982), and J. Vansina, *Paths in the Rainforest: Toward a History of Political Tradition in Equatorial Africa* (Madison, Wis., 1990). Although there exist many editions of *The Epic of Son-Jara*, based on recitations of different bards, the most conclusive edition is by F.-D. Sisòkò, translated and thoroughly annotated by J. W. Johnson (Bloomington, Ind., 1992).

On East Africa, see D. Nurse and T. Spear, *The Swahili: Reconstituting the History and Language of an African Society, 800–1500* (Philadelphia, 1985). The maritime story is recounted with documents in G. S. P. Freeman-Grenville, *The East African Coast: Select Documents from the First to the Earlier Nineteenth Century* (Oxford, 1962). For the larger picture, see K. N. Chaudhuri, *Trade and Civilization in the Indian Ocean: An Economic History from the Rise of Islam to 1750* (Cambridge, 1985). On the early history of Ethiopia, see the classic work by S. H. Sellassie, *Ancient and Medieval Ethiopian History* (1972), and J. D. Fage and R. Oliver, eds., *The Cambridge History of Africa*, vol. 4 (Cambridge, 1977–1985).

For useful general surveys of southern Africa, see N. Parsons, *A New History of Southern Africa* (New York, 1983), and K. Shillington, *A History of Southern Africa* (Essex, England, 1987), a profusely illustrated account. For an excellent introduction to African art, see M. B. Visond et al., *A History of Art in Africa* (New York, 2001); R. Hackett, *Art and Religion in Africa* (London, 1996); and S. Adams et al., *Calls and Response: Journeys in African Art* (New Haven, Conn., 2000).

INFOTRAC COLLEGE EDITION

Visit the source collections at infotrac.thomsonlearning.com and use the Search function with the following key terms.

Africa	Bantu
Africa history	Slave trade

WORLD HISTORY RESOURCES

Visit the *Essential World History* Companion Web Site for resources specific to this textbook:

http://history.wadsworth.com/duikeressentials02/

The CD in the back of this book and the World History Resource Center at **http://history.wadsworth.com/world/** offer a variety of tools to help you succeed in this course, including access to quizzes; images; documents; interactive simulations, maps, and timelines; movie explorations; and a wealth of other sources.

Courtesy of William J. Duiker

Chapter 9

THE EXPANSION OF CIVILIZATION IN SOUTHERN ASIA

CHAPTER OUTLINE
- INDIA FROM THE MAURYAS TO THE MUGHALS
- THE GOLDEN REGION: EARLY SOUTHEAST ASIA
- CONCLUSION

FOCUS QUESTIONS
- How did Buddhism change in the centuries after Siddhartha Gautama's death, and why did it ultimately decline in popularity in India?
- What impact did Muslim rule have on Indian society?
- What are some of the most important cultural achievements of Indian civilization in the era between the Mauryas and the Mughals?
- What were the main characteristics of Southeast Asian social and economic life, culture, and religion before 1500 C.E.?
- ➤ How did Indian civilization influence the civilizations that arose in Southeast Asia?

As the traveler wandered through the length and breadth of the land, he carefully recorded his impressions of the people, from the king down to his most insignificant subject. Their dress, he remarked, was quite different from that of his own country. People wore loose-fitting clothing gathered at the armpits. Most garments were white and were fashioned of cotton, wool, or silk. The robes of the women fell to the ground and completely covered their shoulders. In some areas, the common people wore garments made of leaves or bark or even went naked.

The visitor was especially impressed with the people's personal cleanliness. All wash themselves before eating, he said, and when they complete their meal, they clean their teeth with a willow stick and wash their hands and mouths. After relieving themselves, they wash their bodies and use perfume of sandalwood or turmeric.

The visitor was Xuan Zang (Hsuan Tsang), a Buddhist monk from China who traveled to India in the seventh century C.E. to search for holy scriptures to take back to his own country for translation into Chinese. Because little of the literature of the Indian people from that period survives, Xuan Zang's observations are a valuable resource for our knowledge of the daily lives of the people and show us that the *dhoti* and the *sari*, common forms of Indian dress today, have a long history on the subcontinent. •

INDIA FROM THE MAURYAS TO THE MUGHALS

The India that Xuan Zang visited was no longer the unified land it had been under the Mauryan dynasty. The overthrow of the Mauryas in the early second century B.C.E. had been followed by several hundred years of disunity, when the subcontinent was divided into a number of separate kingdoms and principalities. The dominant force in the north was the Kushan state, established by Indo-European-speaking peoples who had been driven out of what is now China's Xinjiang province by the Xiongnu (see Chapter 3). The Kushans penetrated into the mountains north of the Indus River, where they eventually formed a kingdom with its capital at Bactria, not far from modern Kabul. Over the next two centuries, the Kushans expanded their supremacy along the Indus River and into the central Ganges valley. Then the dynasty began to weaken, and it collapsed sometime in the third century C.E. After the disintegration of the Kushan state, northern India remained divided until the rise of the Gupta dynasty in the early fourth century. The Guptas revived the ancient tradition of the Mauryas for nearly two hundred years until they too were overthrown in about 500 C.E.

Meanwhile, to the south, a number of kingdoms arose among the Dravidian peoples of the Deccan Plateau, which had been only partly under Mauryan rule. The most famous of these kingdoms was Cola (sometimes spelled Chola) on the southeastern coast. Cola developed into a major trading power and sent merchant fleets eastward across the Bay of Bengal, where they introduced Indian culture as well as Indian goods to the peoples of Southeast Asia. In the fourth century C.E., Cola was overthrown by the Pallavas, who ruled from their capital at Kanchipuram (known today as Kanchi), just southwest of modern Madras, for the next four hundred years.

The Kushan Kingdom: Sitting Astride the Silk Road

The Kushan kingdom, with its power base beyond the Khyber Pass in modern Afghanistan, became the dominant political force in northern India in the centuries immediately after the fall of the Mauryas. Sitting astride the main trade routes across the northern half of the subcontinent, the Kushans thrived on the commerce that passed through the area. The bulk of that trade was between the Roman Empire and China and was transported along the route known as the Silk Road, one segment of which passed through the mountains northwest of India (see Chapter 10). From there, goods were shipped to Rome through the Persian Gulf or the Red Sea.

Trade between India and Europe had begun even before the rise of the Roman Empire, but it expanded rapidly in the first century C.E., when sailors mastered the pattern of the monsoon winds in the Indian Ocean (from the southwest in the summer and the northeast in the winter). Commerce between the Mediterranean and the Indian Ocean, as described in the *Periplus*, a first-century C.E. account by a Greek participant, was extensive and often profitable, and it resulted in the establishment of several small Roman settlements along the Indian coast. Rome imported ivory, indigo, textiles, precious stones, and pepper from India and silk from China. The Romans sometimes paid cash for these goods but also exported silver, wine, perfume, slaves, and glass and cloth from Egypt. Overall, Rome appears to have imported much more than it sold to the Far East, leading Emperor Tiberius to grumble that "the ladies and their baubles are transferring our money to foreigners."

The emergence of the Kushan kingdom as a major commercial power was due not only to its role as an intermediary in the Rome-China trade but also to the rising popularity of Buddhism. During the second century C.E. (the precise dates of his reign are unknown), Kanishka, the greatest of the Kushan monarchs, began to patronize Buddhism. Under Kanishka and his successors, an intimate and mutually beneficial relationship was established between Buddhist monasteries and the local merchant community in thriving urban centers like Taxila and Varanasi. Merchants were eager to build stupas and donate money to monasteries in return for social prestige and the implied promise of a better life in this world or the hereafter.

For their part, the wealthy monasteries ceased to be simple communities where monks could find a refuge from the material cares of the world; instead they became major consumers of luxury goods provided by their affluent patrons. Monasteries and their inhabitants became increasingly involved in the economic life of society, and Buddhist architecture began to be richly decorated with precious stones and glass purchased from local merchants or imported from abroad. The process was highly reminiscent of the changes that occurred in the church in medieval Europe.

It was from the Kushan kingdom that Buddhism began its long journey across the wastes of Central Asia to China and other societies in eastern Asia. As trade between the two regions increased, merchants and missionaries flowed

THE GOOD LIFE IN MEDIEVAL INDIA

Much of what we know about life in medieval India comes from the accounts of Chinese missionaries who visited the subcontinent in search of documents recording the teachings of the Buddha. Here the Buddhist monk Fa Xian, who spent several years there in the fifth century C.E., *reports on conditions in the kingdom of Mathura (Mo-tu-lo), a vassal state in western India that was part of the Gupta Empire. Although he could not have been pleased that the Gupta monarchs had adopted the Hindu faith, he found that the people were contented and prosperous except for the outcastes, whom he called Chandalas.*

FA XIAN, *THE TRAVELS OF FA XIAN*

Going southeast from this somewhat less than 80 *joyanas*, we passed very many temples one after another, with some myriad of priests in them. Having passed these places, we arrived at a certain country. This country is called Mo-tu-lo. Once more we followed the Pu-na river. On the sides of the river, both right and left, are twenty *sangharamas*, with perhaps 3,000 priests. The law of Buddha is progressing and flourishing. Beyond the deserts are the countries of western India. The kings of these countries are all firm believers in the law of Buddha. They remove their caps of state when they make offerings to the priests. The members of the royal household and the chief ministers personally direct the food giving; when the distribution of food is over, they spread a carpet on the ground opposite the chief seat (the president's seat) and sit down before it. They dare not sit on couches in the presence of the priests. The rules relating to the almsgiving of kings have been handed down from the time of Buddha till now. Southward from this is the so-called middle country (Madhyadesa). The climate of this country is warm and equable, without frost or snow. The people are very well off, without poll tax or official restrictions. Only those who till the royal lands return a portion of profit of the land. If they desire to go, they go; if they like to stop, they stop. The kings govern without corporal punishment; criminals are fined, according to circumstances, lightly or heavily. Even in cases of repeated rebellion they only cut off the right hand. The king's personal attendants, who guard him on the right and left, have fixed salaries. Throughout the country the people kill no living thing nor drink wine, nor do they eat garlic or onions, with the exception of Chandalas only. The Chandalas are named "evil men" and dwell apart from others; if they enter a town or market, they sound a piece of wood in order to separate themselves; then men, knowing who they are, avoid coming in contact with them. In this country they do not keep swine nor fowls, and do not deal in cattle; they have no shambles [slaughterhouses] or wine shops in their marketplaces. In selling they use cowrie shells. The Chandalas only hunt and sell flesh.

---

from Bactria over the trade routes snaking through the mountains toward the northeast. At various stopping points on the trail, pilgrims erected statues and decorated mountain caves with magnificent frescoes depicting the life of the Buddha and his message to his followers. One of the most prominent of these centers was at Bamiyan, not far from modern-day Kabul, where believers carved two mammoth statues of the Buddha out of a sheer sandstone cliff. According to the Chinese pilgrim Fa Xian (see the box above), when he visited the area in 400 C.E., over a thousand monks were attending a religious ceremony at the site.

The Gupta Dynasty

The Kushan kingdom came to an end under uncertain conditions sometime in the third century C.E. In 320, a new state was established in the central Ganges valley by a local raja named Chandragupta (no relation to Chandragupta Maurya, the founder of the Mauryan dynasty). Chandragupta located his capital at Pataliputra, the site of the now decaying palace of the Mauryas. Under his successor Samudragupta, the territory under Gupta rule was extended into surrounding areas, and eventually the new kingdom became the dominant political force throughout northern India. It also established a loose suzerainty over the Dravidian state of Pallava to the south, thus becoming the greatest state in the subcontinent since the decline of the Mauryan Empire. Under a succession of powerful, efficient, and highly cultured monarchs, notably Samudragupta and Chandragupta II, India enjoyed a new "classical age" of civilization (see Map 9.1).

The Gupta era was a time of prosperity and thriving commerce with China, Southeast Asia, and the Mediterranean. Great cities, notable for their temples and Buddhist monasteries as well as for their economic prosperity, rose along the main trade routes throughout the subcontinent. The religious trade also prospered, as pilgrims from across India and as far away as China came to visit the major religious centers.

As in the Mauryan Empire, much of the trade in the Gupta Empire was managed or regulated by the government. The Guptas owned mines and vast crown lands and earned massive profits from their commercial dealings. But there was also a large private sector, dominated by great caste guilds that monopolized key sectors of the economy. A money economy had probably been in operation since the second century B.C.E., when copper and gold coins had been introduced from the Middle East. This in turn led to the development of banking. Nevertheless, there are indications that the circulation of coins was limited. The Chinese missionary Xuan Zang, who visited India early in the seventh century, remarked that most commercial transactions were conducted by barter.[1]

But the good fortunes of the Guptas proved to be relatively short-lived. Beginning in the late fifth century C.E., incursions by nomadic warriors from the northwest gradually reduced the power of the empire. Soon northern India was once more divided into myriad small kingdoms engaged in seemingly constant conflict.

Buddhism at Bay

The Chinese pilgrims who traveled to India during the Gupta era found a Buddhism that had changed in a number of ways in the centuries since the time of Siddhartha Gautama. They also found a doctrine that was beginning to decline in popularity in the face of a resurgent Hinduism.

The transformation in Buddhism had come about in part because the earliest written sources were transcribed two centuries after Siddhartha's death and in part because his message was reinterpreted as it became part of the everyday life of the people. Abstract concepts of a Nirvana that cannot be described began to be replaced, at least in the popular mind, with more concrete visions of heavenly salvation, and Siddhartha was increasingly regarded as a divinity rather than as a sage. The Buddha's teachings that all four classes were equal gave way to the familiar Hindu conviction that some people, by reason of previous reincarnations, were closer to Nirvana than others.

These developments led to a split in the movement. Purists emphasized what they insisted were the original teachings of the Buddha (describing themselves as the school of Theravada, or "the teachings of the elders"). Followers of Theravada considered Buddhism a way of life, not a salvationist creed. Theravada stressed the importance of strict adherence to personal behavior and the quest for understanding as a means of release from the wheel of life.

In the meantime, another interpretation of Buddhist doctrine was emerging in the northwest. Here Buddhist believers, perhaps hoping to compete with other salvationist faiths circulating in the region, began to promote the view that Nirvana could be achieved through devotion and not just through painstaking attention to one's behavior. According to advocates of this school, eventually to be known as Mahayana ("greater vehicle"), Theravada teachings were too demanding or too strict for ordinary people to follow and therefore favored the wealthy, who were more apt to have the time and resources to spend weeks or months away from their everyday occupations. Mahayana Buddhists referred to their rivals as Hinayana, or "lesser vehicle," because in Theravada fewer would reach enlightenment. Mahayana thus attempted to provide hope for the masses in their efforts to reach

The Buddhas at Bamiyan and Dunhuang

By their sheer size, the towering Buddhas cut out of a mountain cliff at Bamiyan (in present-day Afghanistan) expressed the builder's perception of the Buddha as encompassing the entire universe. The statues were painted and gilded, as in ancient Greece. The drapery on the 175-foot statue shown on the left reflects the fusion of cultural influences from several regions along the Silk Road, combining Chinese, Indian, Persian, and Greco-Roman styles. Tragically, in 2001, Muslim extremists destroyed the two largest Buddhist statues at the site, decrying them as "idols of the gods of the infidels." At the right is an eighth-century wall banner of the Buddha from the Buddhist caves at Dunhuang, a Chinese town on the Silk Road at the edge of the Gobi Desert. Like the statues at Bamiyan, this portrayal of the Buddha was meant to attract monks and merchants along the Silk Road and to spread the wisdom and compassion of the Buddha. Although this banner was painted by a Chinese artist in a Chinese manner, it also shows Indian influences.

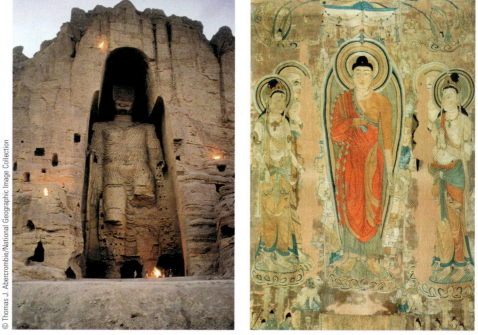

© Thomas J. Abercrombie/National Geographic Image Collection

© The Art Archive/British Museum

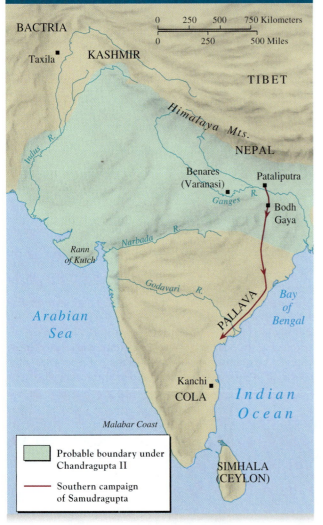

MAP 9.1 The Gupta Empire. This map shows the extent of the Gupta Empire, the only major state to arise in the Indian subcontinent during the first millennium C.E. The arrow indicates the military campaign into southern India led by King Samudragupta.

➤ *How did the Gupta Empire differ in territorial extent from its great predecessor, the Mauryan Empire?*

BACTRIA

KASHMIR

Taxila

TIBET

0   250   500   750 Kilometers
0   250   500 Miles

Himalaya Mts.

Indus R.

NEPAL

Benares
(Varanasi)

Pataliputra

Ganges R.

Bodh
Gaya

Narbada R.

*Rann
of Kutch*

Godavari R.

PALLAVA

*Arabian
Sea*

*Bay
of
Bengal*

Kanchi
COLA

*Indian
Ocean*

Malabar Coast

Probable boundary under
Chandragupta II

Southern campaign
of Samudragupta

SIMHALA
(CEYLON)

hisattva applied only to Siddhartha Gautama himself, denounced such ideas as "the teaching of demons." But to their proponents, such ideas extended the hope of salvation to the masses. Mahayana Buddhists revered the saintly individuals who, according to tradition, had become bodhisattvas at death and erected temples in their honor where the local population could pray and render offerings.

A final distinguishing characteristic of Mahayana Buddhism was its reinterpretation of Buddhism as a religion rather than as a philosophy. Although Mahayana had philosophical aspects, its adherents increasingly regarded the Buddha as a divine figure, and an elaborate Buddhist cosmology developed. Nirvana was not a form of extinction but a true heaven.

Under Kushan rule, Mahayana achieved considerable popularity in northern India and for a while even made inroads in such Theravada strongholds as the island of Sri Lanka. But in the end, neither Mahayana nor Theravada was able to retain its popularity in Indian society. By the seventh century C.E., Theravada had declined rapidly on the subcontinent, although it retained its foothold in Sri Lanka and across the Bay of Bengal in Southeast Asia, where it remained an influential force to modern times. Mahayana prospered in the northwest for centuries, but eventually it was supplanted by a revived Hinduism and later by a new arrival, Islam. But Mahayana too would find better fortunes abroad, as it was carried over the Silk Road or by sea to China and then to Korea and Japan (see Chapters 10 and 11). In all three countries, Buddhism has coexisted with Confucian doctrine and indigenous beliefs to the present.

Why was Buddhism unable to retain its popularity in its native India, although it became a major force elsewhere in Asia? Some have speculated that in denying the existence of the soul, Buddhism ran counter to traditional Hindu belief. Perhaps, too, one of Buddhism's strengths was also a weakness. In rejecting the class divisions that defined the Indian way of life, Buddhism appealed to those very groups who lacked an accepted place in Hindu society, such as the untouchables. But at the same time, it represented a threat to those with a higher status. Moreover, by emphasizing the responsibility of each person to seek an individual path to Nirvana, Buddhism undermined the strong social bonds of the Indian caste system.

Perhaps a final factor in the decline of Buddhism was the revival of Hinduism. In its early development, Hinduism had been highly elitist. Not only was observance of court ritual a monopoly of the *brahmin* class, but the major route to individual salvation, asceticism, was hardly realistic for the average Indian. However, in the centuries after the fall of the Mauryas, a growing emphasis on devotion (*bhakti*) as a means of religious observance brought the possibility of improving one's *karma* by means of ritual acts within the reach of Indians of all classes. It seems

Nirvana, but to the followers of Theravada, it did so at the expense of an insistence on proper behavior.

To advocates of the Mahayana school, salvation could also come from the intercession of a bodhisattva ("he who possesses the essence of Buddhahood"). According to Mahayana beliefs, some individuals who had achieved bodhi and were thus eligible to enter the state of Nirvana after death chose instead, because of their great compassion, to remain on earth in spirit form to help all human beings achieve release from the life cycle. Followers of Theravada, who believed the concept of bod-

Courtesy of William J. Duiker

❧ **MAMALLAPURAM SHORE TEMPLE.** Mamallapuram ("the city of the great warrior") was so named by one of the powerful kings of the Pallavan kingdom on the eastern coast of South India. From this port, ships embarked on naval expeditions to Sri Lanka and far-off destinations in Southeast Asia. Although the site was originally identified with the Hindu deity Vishnu, in the eighth century C.E. a Pallavan monarch built this shore temple in honor of Vishnu's rival deity, Siva. It stands as a visual confirmation of the revival of the Hindu faith in southern India at the time. As with many other stone monuments from antiquity, such as the Sphinx in Egypt, centuries of wind and rain have eroded the ornate carvings that originally covered the large granite blocks.

likely that Hindu devotionalism rose precisely to combat the inroads of Buddhism and reduce the latter's appeal among the Indian population. The Chinese Buddhist missionary Fa Xian, who visited India in the mid-Gupta era, reported that mutual hostility between the Buddhists and the *brahmins* was quite strong:

> Leaving the southern gate of the capital city, on the east side of the road is a place where Buddha once dwelt. Whilst here he bit [a piece from] the willow stick and fixed it in the earth; immediately it grew up seven feet high, neither more nor less. The unbelievers and Brahmans, filled with jealousy, cut it down and scattered the leaves far and wide, but yet it always sprang up again in the same place as before.[2]

For a while, Buddhism was probably able to stave off the Hindu challenge by its own salvationist creed of Mahayana, which also emphasized the role of devotion, but the days of Buddhism as a dominant faith in the subcontinent were numbered.

Islam on the March

While India was still suffering from the disarray left by the collapse of the Gupta Empire, a new and dynamic force in the form of Islam was arising in the Arabian peninsula

to the west. As we have seen, during the seventh and eighth centuries, Arab armies carried the new faith westward to the Iberian peninsula and eastward across the arid wastelands of Persia and into the rugged mountains of the Hindu Kush. Islam first reached India through the Arabs in the eighth century, but a second onslaught in the tenth and eleventh centuries by Turkic-speaking converts had a more lasting effect.

Although Arab merchants had been active along the Indian coasts for centuries, Arab armies did not reach India until the early eighth century. When Indian pirates attacked Arab shipping near the delta of the Indus River, the Muslim ruler in Iraq demanded an apology from the ruler of Sind, a Hindu state in the Indus valley. When the latter refused, Muslim forces conquered lower Sind in 711 and then moved northward into the Punjab, bringing Arab rule into the frontier regions of the subcontinent for the first time.

For the next three centuries, Islam made no further advances into India. But a second phase began at the end of the tenth century with the rise of the state of Ghazni, located in the area of the old Kushan kingdom in present-day Afghanistan. The new kingdom was founded in 962 when Turkic-speaking slaves seized power from the Samanids, a Persian dynasty. When the founder of the new state died in 997, his son, Mahmud of Ghazni (997–1030), succeeded him. Brilliant and ambitious, Mahmud used his patrimony as a base of operations for sporadic forays against neighboring Hindu kingdoms to the southeast. Before his death in 1030, he was able to extend his rule throughout the upper Indus valley and as far south as the Indian Ocean (see Map 9.2). In wealth and cultural brilliance, his court at Ghazni rivaled that of the Abbasid dynasty in neighboring Baghdad. But his achievements had a dark side. Describing Mahmud's conquests in northwestern India, the contemporary historian al-Biruni wrote:

> Mahmud utterly ruined the prosperity of the country, and performed wonderful exploits by which the Hindus became like atoms scattered in all directions, and like a tale of old in the mouth of the people. Their scattered remains cherish, of course, the most inveterate aversion towards all Muslims. This is the reason, too, why Hindu sciences have retired far away from those parts of the country conquered by us, and have fled to places which our hand cannot yet reach, to Kashmir, Benares, and other places.[3]

Resistance against the advances of Mahmud and his successors into northern India was led by the Rajputs, aristocratic Hindu clans who were probably descended from tribal groups that had penetrated into northwestern

India from Central Asia in earlier centuries. The Rajputs possessed a strong military tradition and fought bravely, but their military tactics, based on infantry supported by elephants, were no match for the fearsome cavalry of the invaders, whose ability to strike with lightning speed contrasted sharply with the slow-footed forces of their adversaries. Although the power of Ghazni declined after Mahmud's death, a successor state in the area resumed the advance in the late twelfth century, and by 1200, Muslim power, in the form of a new Delhi sultanate, had been extended over the entire plain of northern India.

South of the Ganges River valley, Muslim influence spread more slowly and in fact had little immediate impact. Muslim armies launched occasional forays into the Deccan Plateau, but at first, they had little success, even though the area was divided among a number of warring kingdoms, including the Colas along the eastern coast and the Pandyas far to the south.

One reason the Delhi sultanate failed to take advantage of the disarray of its rivals was the threat posed by the Mongols on the northwestern frontier (see Chapter 10). Mongol armies unleashed by the great tribal warrior Genghis Khan occupied Baghdad and destroyed the Abbasid caliphate in the 1250s, while other forces occupied the Punjab around Lahore, from which they threatened Delhi on several occasions. For the

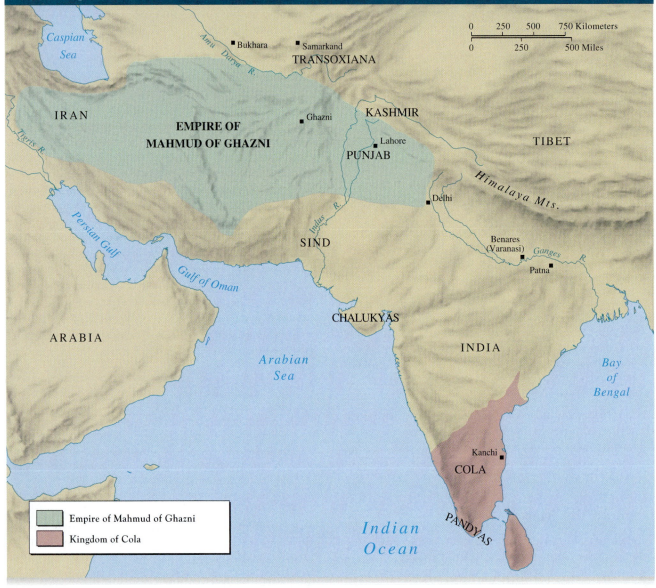

MAP 9.2 India at the Death of Mahmud of Ghazni. Beginning in the tenth century, Turkic-speaking peoples invaded northwestern India and introduced Islam to the peoples in the area. Most famous was the empire of Mahmud of Ghazni. ➤ *Which of the great trading states of southern India are located on the map?*

MEDIEVAL INDIA

Kushan kingdom	c. 150 B.C.E.–c. 200 C.E.
Gupta dynasty	320–600s
Chandragupta I	320–c. 330
Samudragupta	c. 330–375
Chandragupta II	375–415
Arrival of Fa Xian in India	c. 406
First Buddhist temples at Ellora	Seventh century
Travels of Xuan Zang in India	630–643
Conquest of Sind by Arab armies	c. 711
Mahmud of Ghazni	997–1030
Mongol invasion of northern India	1221
Delhi sultanate at peak	1220
Invasion of Tamerlane	1398

next half-century, the attention of the sultanate was focused on the Mongols. That threat finally declined in the early fourteenth century with the gradual breakup of the Mongol Empire, and a new Islamic state emerged in the form of a new Tughluq dynasty (1320–1413), which extended its power into the Deccan Plateau. In praise of his sovereign, the Tughluq monarch Ala-ud-din, the poet Amir Khusrau exclaimed:

Happy be Hindustan, with its splendor of religion,
Where Islamic law enjoys perfect honor and dignity;
In learning Delhi now rivals Bukhara;
Islam has been made manifest by the rulers.
From Ghazni to the very shore of the ocean
You see Islam in its glory.[4]

Such happiness was not destined to endure, however. During the latter half of the fourteenth century, the Tughluq dynasty gradually fell into decline. In 1398, a new military force crossed the Indus River from the northwest, raided the capital of Delhi, and then withdrew. According to some contemporary historians, as many as 100,000 Hindu prisoners were massacred before the gates of the city. Such was India's first encounter with Tamerlane.

Tamerlane (b. 1330s), also known as Timur-i-lang (Timur the Lame), was the ruler of a Mongol khanate based in Samarkand to the north of the Pamir Mountains. His kingdom had been founded on the ruins of the Mongol Empire, which had begun to disintegrate as a result of succession struggles in the thirteenth century. Tamerlane, the son of a local aristocrat, seized power in

Samarkand in 1369 and immediately launched a program of conquest. During the 1380s, he brought the entire region east of the Caspian Sea under his authority and then conquered Baghdad and occupied Mesopotamia (see Map 9.3). After his brief foray into northern India, he turned to the west and raided the Anatolian peninsula. Defeating the army of the Ottoman Turks, he advanced almost as far as the Bosporus before withdrawing. "The last of the great nomadic conquerors," as one recent historian described him, died in 1405 in the midst of a final military campaign.

The passing of Tamerlane removed a major menace from the diverse states of the Indian subcontinent. But the respite from external challenge was not a long one. By the end of the fifteenth century, two new challenges had appeared from beyond the horizon: the Mughals, a newly emerging nomadic power beyond the Khyber Pass in the north, and the Portuguese traders, who arrived by sea from the eastern coast of Africa in search of gold and spices. Both, in different ways, would exert a major impact on the later course of Indian civilization.

ISLAM AND INDIAN SOCIETY

Like their counterparts in other areas that came under Islamic rule, many Muslim rulers in India were quite tolerant of other faiths and used peaceful means, if any, to encourage nonbelievers to convert to Islam. Even the more enlightened, however, could be fierce when their religious zeal was aroused. One ruler, on being informed that a Hindu fair had been held near Delhi, ordered the promoters of the event put to death. Hindu temples were razed, and mosques were erected in their place. Eventually, however, most Muslim rulers realized that not all Hindus could be converted and recognized the necessity of accepting what to them was an alien and repugnant religion. While Hindu religious practices were generally tolerated, non-Muslims were compelled to pay a tax to the state. Some Hindus likely converted to Islam to avoid paying the tax, but they were then expected to make the traditional charitable contribution required of Muslims in all Islamic societies.

Over time, millions of Hindus did turn to the Muslim faith. Some were individuals or groups in the employ of the Muslim ruling class, such as government officials, artisans, or merchants catering to the needs of the court. But many others were probably peasants from the *sudra* class or even untouchables who found in the egalitarian message of Islam a way of removing the stigma of low-class status in the Hindu social hierarchy.

Seldom have two major religions been so strikingly different. Whereas Hinduism tolerated a belief in the existence of several deities (although admittedly they were all considered by some to be manifestations of one supreme god), Islam was uncompromisingly monotheistic. Whereas Hinduism was hierarchical, Islam was egalitarian. Whereas

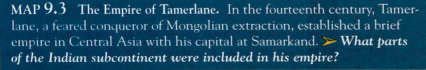

MAP 9.3 The Empire of Tamerlane. In the fourteenth century, Tamerlane, a feared conqueror of Mongolian extraction, established a brief empire in Central Asia with his capital at Samarkand. ➤ *What parts of the Indian subcontinent were included in his empire?*

Hinduism featured a priestly class to serve as an intermediary with the ultimate force of the universe, Islam permitted no one to come between believers and their god. Such differences contributed to the mutual hostility that developed between the adherents of the two faiths in the Indian subcontinent, but more mundane issues, such as the Muslim habit of eating beef and the idolatry and sexual frankness in Hindu art, were probably a greater source of antagonism at the popular level (see the box on p. 189).

In other cases, the two peoples borrowed from each other. Some Muslim rulers found the Indian idea of divine kingship appealing. In their turn, Hindu rajas learned by bitter experience the superiority of cavalry mounted on horses instead of elephants, the primary assault weapon in early India. Some upper-class Hindu males were attracted to the Muslim tradition of *purdah* and began to keep their women in seclusion (termed locally "behind the curtain") from everyday society. Hindu sources claimed that one reason for adopting the custom was to protect Hindu women from the roving eyes of foreigners. But it is likely that many Indian families adopted the practice for reasons of prestige or because they were convinced that *purdah* was a practical means of protecting female virtue.

All in all, Muslim rule probably did not have a significant impact on the lives of most Indian women. *Purdah* was practiced more commonly among high castes than among the lower castes. Though it was probably of little consolation, sexual relations in poor and low-caste families were relatively egalitarian, as men and women worked together on press gangs or in the fields. Muslim customs apparently had little effect on the Hindu tradition of *sati*. In fact, in many respects, Muslim women had more rights than their Hindu counterparts. They had more property rights than Hindu women and were legally permitted to divorce under certain conditions and to remarry after the death of their husband. The primary role for Indian women in general, however, was to produce children. Sons were preferred over daughters, not only because they alone could conduct ancestral rights but also because a daughter was a financial liability. A daughter required that her father provide a costly dowry when she married, yet after the wedding, she would transfer her labor assets to her husband's family. Still, women shared with men a position in the Indian religious pantheon. The Hindu female deity, known as Devi, was celebrated by both men and women as the source of cosmic power, bestower of wishes, and symbol of fertility.

Overall the Muslims continued to view themselves as foreign conquerors and generally maintained a strict separation between the Muslim ruling class and the mass of the Hindu population. Although a few Hindus rose to important positions in the local bureaucracy, most high posts in the central government and the provinces were reserved for Muslims. Only with the founding of the Mughal dynasty was a serious effort undertaken to reconcile the differences.

One result of this effort was the religion of the Sikhs ("disciples"). Founded by the guru Nanak in the early sixteenth century in the Punjab, Sikhism attempted to integrate the best of the two faiths in a single religion. Sikhism originated in the devotionalist movement in Hinduism, which taught that God was the single true reality. All else is illusion. But Nanak rejected the Hindu tradition of asceticism and mortification of the flesh and, like Muhammad, taught his disciples to participate in the world. Sikhism achieved considerable popularity in northwest-

THE ISLAMIC CONQUEST OF INDIA

One consequence of the Muslim conquest of northern India was the imposition of many Islamic customs on Hindu society. In this excerpt, the fourteenth-century Muslim historian Zia-ud-din Barani describes the attempt of one Muslim ruler, Ala-ud-din, to forbid the use of alcohol and gambling, two practices expressly forbidden in Muslim society. Ala-ud-din had seized power in Delhi from a rival in 1294.

A MUSLIM RULER SUPPRESSES HINDU PRACTICES

He forbade wine, beer, and intoxicating drugs to be used or sold; dicing, too, was prohibited. Vintners and beer sellers were turned out of the city, and the heavy taxes which had been levied from them were abolished. All the china and glass vessels of the Sultan's banqueting room were broken and thrown outside the gate of Badaun, where they formed a mound. Jars and casks of wine were emptied out there till they made mire as if it were the season of the rains. The Sultan himself entirely gave up wine parties. Self-respecting people at once followed his example; but the ne'er-do-wells went on making wine and spir-

its and hid the leather bottles in loads of hay or firewood and by various such tricks smuggled it into the city. Inspectors and gatekeepers and spies diligently sought to seize the contraband and the smugglers; and when seized the wine was given to the elephants, and the importers and sellers and drinkers [were] flogged and given short terms of imprisonment. So many were they, however, that holes had to be dug for their incarceration outside the great thoroughfare of the Badaun gate, and many of the wine bibbers died from the rigor of their confinement and others were taken out half-dead and were long in recovering their health. The terror of these holes deterred many from drinking. Those who could not give it up had to journey ten or twelve leagues to get a drink, for at half that distance, four or five leagues from Delhi, wine could not be publicly sold or drunk. The prevention of drinking proving very difficult, the Sultan enacted that people might distill and drink privately in their own homes, if drinking parties were not held and the liquor not sold. After the prohibition of drinking, conspiracies diminished.

---

ern India, where Islam and Hinduism confronted each other directly, and eventually evolved into a militant faith that fiercely protected its adherents against its two larger rivals. In the end, Sikhism did not reconcile Hinduism and Islam but provided an alternative to them.

One complication for both Muslims and Hindus as they tried to come to terms with the existence of a mixed society was the problem of caste. Could non-Hindus form castes, and if so, how were these castes related to the Hindu castes? Where did the Turkic-speaking elites who made up the ruling class in many of the Islamic states fit into the equation?

The problem was resolved in a pragmatic manner that probably followed an earlier tradition of assimilating non-Hindu tribal groups into the system. Members of the Turkic ruling groups formed social groups that were roughly equivalent to the Hindu *brahmin* or *kshatriya* caste. Ordinary Indians who converted to Islam also formed Muslim castes, although at a lower level on the social scale. Many who did so were probably artisans who converted en masse to obtain the privileges that conversion could bring.

In most of India, then, Muslim rule did not substantially disrupt the caste system. One perceptive European visitor in the early sixteenth century reported that in Malabar, along the southwestern coast, there were separate castes for fishing, pottery making, weaving, carpentry and metalworking, salt mining, sorcery, and labor on the plantations. There were separate castes for doing the laundry, one for the elite and the other for the common people (see the box on p. 190).

Economy and Daily Life

India's landed and commercial elites lived in the cities, often in conditions of considerable opulence. The rulers, of course, possessed the most wealth. One maharaja of a relatively small state in southern India, for example, had over 100,000 soldiers in his pay along with nine hundred elephants and twenty thousand horses. Another maintained a thousand high-caste women to serve as sweepers of his palace. Each carried a broom and a brass basin containing a mixture of cow dung and water and followed him from one house to another, plastering the path where he was to tread. Most urban dwellers, of course, did not live in such style. Xuan Zang, the Chinese Buddhist missionary who visited India in the early seventh century, left us a description of ordinary homes in urban areas:

> Their houses are surrounded by low walls, and form the suburbs. The earth being soft and muddy, the walls of the towns are mostly built of brick or tiles. The towers on the walls are constructed of wood or bamboo; the houses have balconies and belvederes, which are made of wood, with a coating of lime or mortar, and covered with tiles. The different buildings have the same form as those in China; rushes, or dry branches, or tiles, or boards are used for covering them. The walls are covered with lime and mud, mixed with cow's dung for purity. At different seasons they scatter flowers about. Such are some of their different customs.[5]

The majority of India's population (estimated at slightly more than 100 million in the first millennium C.E.),

UNTOUCHABLES IN SOUTH INDIA

Some of the best descriptions of Indian society in the late medieval era came from European merchants and missionaries. The following passage was written by the Portuguese traveler Duarte Barbosa and describes an untouchable caste on the southwestern coast of India in the early sixteenth century. The Nayres mentioned in this excerpt were a higher caste in the region.

DUARTE BARBOSA, FROM THE LAND OF MALABAR

And there is yet another caste of Heathen lower than these whom they call Poleas, who among all the rest are held to be accursed and excommunicate; they dwell in the fields and open campaigns [plots] in secret lurking places, whither folk of good caste never go save by mischance, and live in huts very strait and mean. They are tillers of rice with buffaloes and oxen. They never speak to the Nayres save from afar off, shouting so that they may hear them, and when they go along the roads they utter loud cries, that they may be let past, and whosoever hears them leaves the road, and stands in the wood till they have passed by; and if anyone, whether man or woman, touches them his kinsfolk slay him forthwith, and in vengeance therefore they slay Poleas until they weary without suffering any punishment. In certain months of the year they do their utmost to touch some Nayre woman by night as secretly as they can, and this only for the sake of doing evil. They go by in order to get into the houses of the Nayres to touch women, and during these months the women guard themselves carefully, and if they touch any woman, even though none have seen it, and there may be no witnesses, yet she declares it at once, crying out, and she will stay no longer in her house that her caste may not be destroyed; in general she flees to the house of some other low caste folk, and hides herself, that her kinsfolk may not slay her; and that thence she may help herself and be sold to foreigners, which is ofttimes done. And the manner of touching is this, even though no words are exchanged, they throw something at her, a stone or a stick, and if it touches her she is touched and ruined. These people are also great sorcerers and thieves; they are a very evil race.

---

however, lived on the land. Most were peasants who tilled small plots with a wooden plow pulled by oxen and paid a percentage of the harvest to their landlord. The landlord in turn forwarded part of the payment to the local ruler. In effect, the landlord functioned as a tax collector for the king, who retained ultimate ownership of all farmland in his domain. At best, most peasants lived at the subsistence level. At worst, they were forced into debt and fell victim to moneylenders who charged exorbitant rates of interest.

In the north and in the upland regions of the Deccan Plateau, the primary grain crops were wheat and barley. In the Ganges valley and the southern coastal plains, the main crop was rice. Vegetables were grown everywhere, and southern India produced many spices, fruits, sugarcane, and cotton. The cotton plant apparently originated in the Indus River valley and spread from there. Although some cotton was cultivated in Spain and North Africa by the eighth and ninth centuries, India remained the primary producer of cotton goods. Spices such as cinnamon, pepper, ginger, sandalwood, cardamom, and cumin were also major export products.

Agriculture, of course, was not the only source of wealth in India. Since ancient times, the subcontinent had served as a major entrepôt for trade between the Middle East and the Pacific basin, as well as the source of other goods shipped throughout the known world. Although civil strife and piracy, heavy taxation of the business community by local rulers to finance their fratricidal wars, and increased customs duties between principalities may have contributed to a decline in internal trade, the level of foreign trade remained high, particularly in the Dravidian kingdoms in the south and along the northwestern coast, which were located along the traditional trade routes to the Middle East and the Mediterranean Sea. Much of this foreign trade was carried on by wealthy Hindu castes with close ties to the royal courts. But there were other participants as well, including such non-Hindu minorities as the Muslims, the Parsis, and the Jain community. The Parsis, expatriates from Persia who practiced the Zoroastrian religion, dominated banking and the textile industry in the cities bordering the Rann of Kutch. Later they would become a dominant economic force in the modern city of Mumbai (Bombay). The Jains became prominent in trade and manufacturing even though their faith emphasized simplicity and the rejection of materialism.

According to early European travelers, merchants often lived quite well. One Portuguese observer described the "Moorish" population in Bengal as follows:

They have girdles of cloth, and over them silk scarves; they carry in their girdles daggers garnished with silver and gold, according to the rank of the person who carries them; on their fingers many rings set with rich jewels, and cotton turbans on their heads. They are luxurious, eat well and spend freely, and have many other extravagances as well. They bathe often in great tanks which they have in their houses. Everyone has three or four wives or as many as he can maintain. They keep them carefully shut up, and treat them very well, giving them great store of gold, silver and apparel of fine silk.[6]

Outside these relatively small, specialized trading communities, most manufacturing and commerce were in the hands of petty traders and artisans, who were generally limited to local markets. This failure to build on the promise of antiquity has led some historians to ask why India failed to produce an expansion of commerce and growth of cities similar to the developments that began in Europe during the High Middle Ages or even in China during the Song dynasty (see Chapter 10). Some have pointed to the traditionally low status of artisans and merchants in Indian society, symbolized by the comment in the *Arthasastra* that merchants were "thieves that are not called by the name of thief."[7] Yet commercial activities were frowned on in many areas in Europe throughout the Middle Ages, a fact that did not prevent the emergence of capitalist societies in much of the West.

Another factor may have been the monopoly on foreign trade held by the government in many areas of India. More important, perhaps, was the impact of the caste system, which reduced the ability of entrepreneurs to expand their activities and have dealings with other members of the commercial and manufacturing community. Successful artisans, for example, normally could not set up as merchants to market their products, nor could merchants compete for buyers outside their normal area of operations. The complex interlocking relationships among the various castes in a given region were a powerful factor inhibiting the development of a thriving commercial sector in medieval India.

The Wonder of Indian Culture

The era between the Mauryas and the Mughals in India was a period of cultural evolution as Indian writers and artists built on the literary and artistic achievements of their predecessors. This is not to say, however, that Indian culture rested on its ancient laurels. To the contrary, it was an era of tremendous innovation in all fields of creative endeavor.

ART AND ARCHITECTURE

At the end of antiquity, the primary forms of religious architecture were the Buddhist cave temples and monasteries. The next millennium witnessed the evolution of religious architecture from underground cavity to monumental structure.

The twenty-eight caves of Ajanta in the Deccan Plateau are one of India's greatest artistic achievements. They are as impressive for their sculpture and painting as for their architecture. Except for a few examples from the second century B.C.E., most of the caves were carved out of solid rock over an incredibly short period of eighteen years, from 460 to 478 C.E. In contrast to the early unadorned temple halls, these temples were exuberantly decorated with ornate pillars, friezes, beamed ceilings, and statues of the Buddha and bodhisattvas. Several caves served as monasteries, which by then had been transformed from simple holes in the wall to large complexes with living apartments, halls, and shrines to the Buddha.

All of the inner surfaces of the caves, including the ceilings, sculptures, walls, door frames, and pillars, were painted in vivid colors. Perhaps best known are the wall paintings, which illustrate the various lives and incarnations of the Buddha. Similar rock paintings focusing on secular subjects can be found at Sigiriya, a fifth-century royal palace on the island of Sri Lanka.

Among the most impressive rock carvings in southern India are the cave temples at Mamallapuram (also known

➤ ROCK PAINTINGS AT SIGIRIYA, SRI LANKA. Starting in the third century B.C.E., engineers on the island of Sri Lanka developed a sophisticated irrigation system consisting of dams, reservoirs, water tanks, and canals. One of the most impressive examples was built by the fifth-century C.E. kingdom of Sigiriya, in the center of the island. The royal palace, perched for protective purposes on the summit of a 650-foot-high rock mesa, contains extensive water gardens, fountains, and swimming pools to provide royal entertainment. Portraits of serving girls from the king's harem, such as the one shown here, were painted high up along the cliff wall. Many such paintings were destroyed by Buddhist monks when they reclaimed the area after the king's sudden death. Fortunately, a few have survived to captivate viewers over the centuries.

Courtesy of William J. Duiker

as Mahabalipuram), south of the modern city of Madras. The sculpture, called *Descent of the Ganges River*, depicts the role played by Siva in intercepting the heavenly waters of the Ganges and allowing them to fall gently on the earth. Mamallapuram also boasts an eighth-century shore temple (see illustration on p. 185), which is one of the earliest surviving freestanding structures in the subcontinent.

From the eighth century until the time of the Mughals, Indian architects built a multitude of magnificent Hindu temples, now constructed exclusively above ground. Each temple consisted of a central shrine surmounted by a sizable tower, a hall for worshipers, a vestibule, and a porch, all set in a rectangular courtyard that might also contain other minor shrines. Temples became progressively more ornate until the eleventh century, when the sculpture began to dominate the structure itself. The towers became higher and the temple complexes more intricate, some becoming virtual walled compounds set one within the other and resembling a town in themselves.

The greatest example of medieval Hindu temple art is probably Khajuraho. Of the original eighty temples, dating from the tenth century, twenty remain standing today. All of the towers are buttressed at various levels on the sides, giving the whole a sense of unity and creating a vertical movement similar to Mount Kailasa in the Himalayas, sacred to Hindus. Everywhere the viewer is entertained by voluptuous temple dancers bringing life to the massive structures. One is removing a thorn from her foot, another is applying eye makeup, and yet another is wringing out her hair.

LITERATURE

During this period, Indian authors produced a prodigious number of written works, both religious and secular. Indian religious poetry was written in Sanskrit and also in the languages of southern India. As Hinduism was transformed from a contemplative to a more devotional religion, its poetry became more ardent and erotic and prompted a sense of divine ecstasy. Much of the religious verse extolled the lives and heroic acts of Siva, Vishnu, Rama, and Krishna by repeating the same themes over and over, which is also a characteristic of Indian art. In the eighth century, a tradition of poet-saints inspired by intense mystical devotion to a deity emerged in southern India. Many were women who sought to escape the drudgery of domestic toil through an imagined sexual union with the god-lover. Such was the case for the twelfth-century mystic whose poem here expresses her sensuous joy in the physical-mystical union with her god:

> It was like a stream
> running into the dry bed
> of a lake,
> like rain pouring on plants
> parched to sticks.
> It was like this world's pleasure

> and the way to the other,
> both walking towards me.
> Seeing the feet of the master,
> O lord white as jasmine
> I was made worthwhile.[8]

The great secular literature of traditional India was also written in Sanskrit in the form of poetry, drama, and prose. Some of the best medieval Indian poetry is found in single-stanza poems, which create an entire emotional scene in just four lines. Witness this poem by the poet Amaru:

> We'll see what comes of it, I thought,
>   and I hardened my heart against her.
> What, won't the villain speak to me? she
>   thought, flying into a rage.
> And there we stood, sedulously refusing to look one
>   another in the face,
> Until at last I managed an unconvincing laugh,
>   and her tears robbed me of my resolution.[9]

One of India's most famous authors was Kalidasa, who lived during the Gupta dynasty. Although little is known of him, including his dates, he probably wrote for the court of Chandragupta II (375–415 C.E.). Even today, Kalidasa's hundred-verse poem, *The Cloud Messenger*, remains one of the most popular Sanskrit poems.

In addition to being a poet, Kalidasa was also a great dramatist. He wrote three plays, all dramatic romances that blend the erotic with the heroic and the comic. *Shakuntala*, perhaps the best-known play in all Indian literature, tells the story of a king who, while out hunting, falls in love with the maiden Shakuntala. He asks her to marry him and offers her a ring of betrothal but is suddenly recalled to his kingdom on urgent business. Shakuntala, who is pregnant, goes to him, but the king has been cursed by a hermit and no longer recognizes her. With the help of the gods, the king eventually does recall their love and is reunited with Shakuntala and their son.

Like poetry, prose developed in India from the Vedic period. The use of prose was well established by the sixth and seventh centuries C.E. This is truly astonishing considering that the novel did not appear until the tenth century in Japan and until the seventeenth century in Europe.

One of the greatest masters of Sanskrit prose was Dandin, who lived during the seventh century. In *The Ten Princes*, he created a fantastic and exciting world that fuses history and fiction. His keen powers of observation, details of low life, and humor give his writing considerable vitality.

MUSIC

Another area of Indian creativity that developed during this era was music. Ancient Indian music had come from the chanting of the Vedic hymns and thus inevitably had a strong metaphysical and spiritual flavor. The actual physical vibrations of music (*nada*) were considered to be related to the spiritual world. An off-key or sloppy rendition of a sacred text could upset the harmony and balance of the entire universe.

In form, Indian classical music is based on a scale, called a *raga*. There are dozens, if not hundreds, of separate scales, which are grouped into separate categories depending on the time of day during which they are to be performed. The performers use a stringed instrument called a *sitar* and various types of wind instruments and drums. The performers select a basic *raga* and then are free to improvise the melodic structure and rhythm. A good performer never performs a particular *raga* the same way twice. As with jazz music in the West, the audience is concerned not so much with faithful reproduction as with the performer's creativity.

THE GOLDEN REGION: EARLY SOUTHEAST ASIA

Between China and India lies the region that today is called Southeast Asia. It has two major components: a mainland region extending southward from the Chinese border down to the tip of the Malay peninsula and an extensive archipelago, most of which is part of present-day Indonesia and the Philippines. Travel between the islands and regions to the west, north, and east was not difficult, so Southeast Asia has historically served as a vast land bridge for the movement of peoples between China, the Indian subcontinent, and the more than 25,000 islands of the South Pacific.

Mainland Southeast Asia consists of several north-south mountain ranges, separated by river valleys that run in a southerly or southeasterly direction. During the first millennium C.E., two groups of migrants—the Thai from southwestern China and the Burmans from the Tibetan highlands—came down these valleys in search of new homelands, as earlier peoples had done before them. Once in Southeast Asia, most of these migrants settled in the fertile deltas of the rivers—the Irrawaddy and the Salween in Burma, the Chao Phraya in Thailand, and the Red River and the Mekong in Vietnam—or in lowland areas in the islands to the south.

Although the river valleys facilitated north-south travel on the Southeast Asian mainland, movement between east and west was relatively difficult. The mountains are densely forested and often infested with malaria-carrying mosquitoes. Consequently the lowland peoples in the river valleys were often isolated from each other and had only limited contacts with the upland peoples in the mountains. These geographical barriers may help explain why Southeast Asia is one of the few regions in Asia that was never unified under a single government.

Given Southeast Asia's location between China and India, it is not surprising that both civilizations influenced

developments in the region. In 111 B.C.E., Vietnam was conquered by the Han dynasty and remained under Chinese control for more than a millennium (see Chapter 11). The Indian states never exerted much political control over Southeast Asia, but their influence was pervasive nevertheless. By the first centuries C.E., Indian merchants were sailing to Southeast Asia; they were soon followed by Buddhist and Hindu missionaries. Indian influence can be seen in many aspects of Southeast Asian culture, from political institutions to religion, architecture, language, and literature.

Paddy Fields and Spices: The States of Southeast Asia

The traditional states of Southeast Asia can generally be divided between agricultural societies and trading societies. The distinction between farming and trade was a product of the environment. The agricultural societies—notably, Vietnam, Angkor in what is now Cambodia, and the Burman state of Pagan—were situated in rich river deltas that were conducive to the development of a wet rice economy (see Map 9.4). Although all produced some goods for regional markets, none was tempted to turn to commerce as the prime source of national income. In fact, none was situated astride the main trade routes that crisscrossed the region.

The kingdom of Angkor, which took shape in the ninth century, was the most powerful state to emerge in mainland Southeast Asia before the sixteenth century. The remains of its capital city, Angkor Thom, give a sense of the magnificence of Angkor civilization. The city formed a square 2 miles on each side. Its massive stone walls were several feet thick and were surrounded by a moat. Four main gates led into the city, which at its height had a substantial population. By the fourteenth century, however, Angkor had begun to decline, and in 1432, Angkor Thom was destroyed by the Thai, who had migrated into the region from southwestern China in the thirteenth century and established their capital at Ayuthaya, in lower Thailand, in 1351.

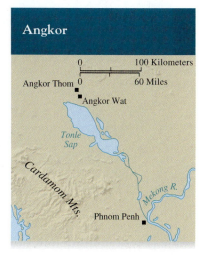

The islands of the Indonesian archipelago gave rise to two of the region's most notable trading societies—Srivijaya and Majapahit. Both were based in large part on spices. As the wealth of the Arab Empire in the Middle East and then of western Europe increased, so did the

MAP 9.4 Southeast Asia in the Thirteenth Century. This map indicates the major states that arose in Southeast Asia in the early second millennium C.E. Some, like Angkor and Dai Viet, were predominantly agricultural. Others, like Srivijaya and Champa, were commercial.
➤ *Which of these empires were soon to disappear?*

the Dravidian kingdoms of southern India and a commercial rival of Srivijaya, inflicted a devastating defeat on the island kingdom. Although Srivijaya survived, it was unable to regain its former dominance, in part because the main trade route had shifted to the east, through the Strait of Sunda and directly out into the Indian Ocean. In the late thirteenth century, this shift in trade patterns led to the founding of a new kingdom of Majapahit on the island of Java. In the mid-fourteenth century, Majapahit succeeded in uniting most of the archipelago and perhaps even part of the Southeast Asian mainland under its rule (see the box on p. 195).

Indian influence was evident in all of these societies to various degrees. Based on models from the Dravidian kingdoms of southern India, Southeast Asian kings were believed to possess special godlike qualities that set them apart from ordinary people. In some societies such as Angkor, the most prominent royal advisers constituted a *brahmin* class on the Indian model. In Pagan and Angkor, some division of the population into separate classes based on occupation and ethnic background seems to have occurred, although these divisions do not seem to have developed the rigidity of Indian castes.

India also supplied Southeast Asians with a writing system. The societies of the region had no written scripts for their spoken languages before the arrival of the Indian merchants and missionaries. Indian phonetic symbols were borrowed and used to record the spoken language. Initially Southeast Asian literature was written in the Indian Sanskrit but eventually came to be written in the local languages. Southeast Asian authors borrowed popular Indian themes, such as stories from the Buddhist scriptures and tales from the Ramayana.

A popular form of entertainment among the common people, the *wayang kulit,* or shadow play, may have come originally from India or possibly China, but it became a distinctive art form in Java and other islands of the Indonesian archipelago. In a shadow play, flat leather puppets were manipulated behind an illuminated screen while

demand for the products of East Asia. Merchant fleets from India and the Arabian peninsula sailed to the Indonesian islands to buy cloves, pepper, nutmeg, cinnamon, precious woods, and other exotic products coveted by the wealthy. In the eighth century, Srivijaya, located along the eastern coast of Sumatra, became a powerful commercial state that dominated the trade route passing through the Strait of Malacca, at that time the most convenient route from East Asia into the Indian Ocean. The rulers of Srivijaya had helped bring the route to prominence by controlling the pirates who had previously plagued shipping in the strait. Another inducement was Srivijaya's capital at Palembang, a deepwater port where sailors could wait out the change in the monsoon season before making their return voyage. In 1025, however, Cola, one of

THE LEGENDARY GRANDEUR
OF MAJAPAHIT

The Nagarkertagama, written by the court poet Prapanca in 1365, was the national epic of the kingdom of Majapahit. This passage describes the relationship between the kingdom and neighboring countries in the region.

PRAPANCA, NAGARKERTAGAMA

Such is the excellence of His Majesty the Prince who reigns at Majapahit as absolute monarch. His is praised like the moon in autumn, since he fills all the world with joy. The evil-doers are like the red lotus, the good—who love him wholeheartedly—are like the white lotus. His retinue, treasures, chariots, elephants, horses, etc., are [immeasurable] like the sea.

The land of Java is becoming more and more famous for its blessed state throughout the world. "Only Jambudwipa [India] and Java," so people say, "are mentioned for their superiority, good countries as they are, because of the multitude of men experienced in the doctrine . . . ; whatever 'work' turns up, they are very able to handle it."

First comes the Illustrious Brahmaraja, the excellent brahmin, an irreproachable, great poet and expert of the religious traditions; he has complete knowledge of the speculative as well as all the other philosophies, . . . the system of dialectical [logic], etc. And [then] the holy Shamana, very pious, virtuous, experienced in the Vedas and the six pure activities. And also the Illustrious Vishnu, powerful in Samaveda incantations, with which he aims to increase the country's prosperity.

For this reason all kinds of people have continually come from other countries, in multitudes. There are Jambudwipa, Kamboja [Cambodia], China, Yawana [Annam], Champa, Kannataka [in South China], etc., Goda [Gaur] and Siam—these are the places whence they come from. They come by ship with numerous merchants; monks and brahmins are the principal ones who as they come are regaled and are well pleased during their stay.

And in each month of Phalguna [February–March] His Majesty the Prince is honored and celebrated in his residence. Then the high state officials come from all over Java, the heads of districts, and the judicial officials . . . ; also the [people from] other islands, Bali, etc., all come with tributes so numerous that they are uninterrupted, to honor him. Traders and merchants fill the market in dense crowds with all their wares in great variety.

---

the narrator recited tales from the Indian classics. The plays were often accompanied by gamelan, a type of music performed by an orchestra composed primarily of percussion instruments such as gongs and drums that apparently originated in Java.

Daily Life

Because of the diversity of ethnic backgrounds, religions, and cultures, making generalizations about daily life in Southeast Asia during the early historical period is difficult. Nevertheless, it appears that Southeast Asian societies did not always apply the social distinctions that were sometimes imported from India.

Still, traditional societies in Southeast Asia had some clearly hierarchical characteristics. At the top of the social ladder were the hereditary aristocrats, who monopolized both political power and economic wealth and enjoyed a borrowed aura of charisma by virtue of their proximity to the ruler. Most aristocrats lived in the major cities, which were the main source of power, wealth, and foreign influence. Beyond the major cities lived the mass of the population, composed of farmers, fishers, artisans, and merchants. In most Southeast Asian societies, the vast majority were probably rice farmers, living at a bare level of subsistence and paying heavy rents or taxes to a landlord or a local ruler.

The average Southeast Asian peasant was not actively engaged in commerce except as a consumer of various necessities. But accounts by foreign visitors indicate that in the Malay world, some were involved in growing or mining products for export, such as tropical food products, precious woods, tin, and precious gems. Most of the regional trade was carried on by local merchants, who purchased products from local growers and then transported them to the major port cities. During the early state-building era, roads were few and relatively primitive, so most of the trade was transported by small boats down rivers to the major ports along the coast. There the goods were loaded onto larger ships for delivery outside the region. Growers of export goods in areas near the coast were thus indirectly involved in the regional trade network but received few economic benefits from the relationship.

As we might expect from an area of such ethnic and cultural diversity, social structures differed significantly from country to country. In the Indianized states on the mainland, the tradition of a hereditary tribal aristocracy was probably accentuated by the Hindu practice of dividing the population into separate classes, called *varna* in imitation of the Indian model. In Angkor and Pagan, for example, the divisions were based on occupation or ethnic background. Some people were considered free subjects of the king, although there may have been legal restrictions against changing occupations. Others, however, may have been indentured to an employer. Each community was under a chieftain, who in turn was subordinated to a higher official responsible for passing on the tax revenues of each group to the central government.

In the kingdoms in the Malay peninsula and the Indonesian archipelago, social relations were generally less formal. Most of the people in the region, whether farmers, fishers, or artisans, lived in small *kampongs* (Malay for "villages") in wooden houses built on stilts to avoid flooding during the monsoon season. Some of the farmers were probably sharecroppers who paid a part of their harvest to a landlord, who was often a member of the aristocracy. But in other areas, the tradition of free farming was strong.

The women of Southeast Asia during this era have been described as the most fortunate in the world. Although most women worked side by side with men in the fields, as in Africa they often played an active role in trading activities. Not only did this lead to a higher literacy rate among women than among their male counterparts, but it also allowed them more financial independence than their counterparts in China and India, a fact that was noticed by the Chinese traveler Zhou Daguan at the end of the thirteenth century: "In Cambodia it is the women who take charge of trade. For this reason a Chinese arriving in the country loses no time in getting himself a mate, for he will find her commercial instincts a great asset."[10]

Although, as elsewhere, warfare was normally part of the male domain, women sometimes played a role as bodyguards as well. According to Zhou Daguan, women were used to protect the royal family in Angkor, as well as in kingdoms located on the islands of Java and Sumatra. While there is no evidence that such female units ever engaged in battle, they did give rise to wondrous tales of amazon warriors in the writings of foreign travelers such as the fourteenth-century Muslim adventurer Ibn Battuta.

One reason for the enhanced status of women in traditional Southeast Asia is that the nuclear family was more common than the joint family system prevalent in China and the Indian subcontinent. Throughout the region, wealth in marriage was passed from the male to the female, in contrast to the dowry system applied in China and India. In most societies, virginity was usually not a valued commodity in brokering a marriage, and divorce proceedings could be initiated by either party. Still, most marriages were monogamous, and marital fidelity was taken seriously.

The relative availability of cultivable land in the region may help explain the absence of joint families. Joint families under patriarchal leadership tend to be found in areas where land is scarce and individual families must work together to conserve resources and maximize income. With the exception of a few crowded river valleys, few areas in Southeast Asia had a high population density per acre of cultivable land. Throughout most of the area, water was plentiful, and the land was relatively fertile. In parts of Indonesia, it was possible to survive by living off the produce of wild fruit trees—bananas, coconuts, mangoes, and a variety of other tropical fruits.

World of the Spirits: Religious Belief

Indian religions also had a profound effect on Southeast Asia. Traditional religious beliefs in the region took the familiar form of spirit worship and animism that we have seen in other cultures. Southeast Asians believed that spirits dwelled in the mountains, rivers, streams, and other sacred places in their environment. Mountains were probably particularly sacred, since they were considered to be the abode of ancestral spirits, the place to which the souls of all the departed would retire after death.

When Hindu and Buddhist ideas began to penetrate the area early in the first millennium C.E., they exerted a strong appeal among local elites. Not only did the new doctrines offer a more convincing explanation of the nature of the cosmos, but they also provided local rulers with a means of enhancing their prestige and power and conferred an aura of legitimacy on their relations with their subjects. In Angkor, the king's duties included performing sacred rituals on the mountain in the capital city; in time, the ritual became a state cult uniting Hindu gods with local nature deities and ancestral spirits in a complex pantheon.

This state cult, financed by the royal court, eventually led to the construction of temples throughout the country. Many of these temples housed thousands of priests and retainers and amassed great wealth, including vast estates farmed by local peasants. It has been estimated that there were as many as 300,000 priests in Angkor at the height of its power. This vast wealth, which was often exempt from taxes, may be one explanation for the gradual decline of Angkor in the thirteenth and fourteenth centuries.

Initially the spread of Hindu and Buddhist doctrines took place mostly among the elite. Although the common people participated in the state cult and helped construct the temples, they did not give up their traditional beliefs in local deities and ancestral spirits. A major transformation began in the eleventh century, however, when Theravada Buddhism began to penetrate the kingdom of Pagan in mainland Southeast Asia from the island of Sri Lanka. From Pagan, it spread rapidly to other areas in Southeast Asia and eventually became the religion of the masses throughout the mainland west of the Annamite Mountains.

Theravada's appeal to the peoples of Southeast Asia is reminiscent of the original attraction of Buddhist thought centuries earlier on the Indian subcontinent. By teaching that individuals could seek Nirvana through their own actions rather than through the intercession of the ruler or a priest, Theravada was more accessible to the masses than the state cults promoted by the rulers. During the next centuries, Theravada gradually undermined the influence of state-supported religions and became the dominant faith in several mainland societies, including Burma, Thailand, Laos, and Cambodia.

Theravada did not penetrate far into the Malay peninsula or the Indonesian island chain, perhaps because it entered Southeast Asia through Burma farther to the north. But the Malay world found its own popular alternative to state religions when Islam began to enter the area in the thirteenth and fourteenth centuries. Because Islam's expansion into Southeast Asia took place for the most part after 1500, its emergence as a major force in the region will be discussed in a later chapter.

Not surprisingly, Indian influence extended to the Buddhist and Hindu temples of Southeast Asia. Temple archi-tecture reflecting Gupta or southern Indian styles began to appear in Southeast Asia during the first centuries C.E. Most famous is the Buddhist temple at Borobudur, in central Java. Begun in the late eighth century at the behest of a king of Sailendra (an agricultural kingdom based in

The Island of Java

THE TEMPLE OF BOROBUDUR. The colossal pyramid temple at Borobudur, on the island of Java, is one of the greatest Buddhist monuments. Constructed in the eighth century, it depicts the path to spiritual enlightenment in stone. The reliefs along the lowest walls depict the world of desire, while the higher levels represent the world of the spirit, culminating at the summit with the empty and closed stupa, signifying the state of Nirvana. Shortly after it was built, Borobudur was abandoned, as a new ruler switched his allegiance to Hinduism and ordered the erection of the Hindu temple of Prambanan nearby. Shown in the insert is a depiction of an eighth-century sailing vessel of the type that plied the waters of southern Asia at the time. The carvings on the face of the temple are virtually the only visual record of the nature of society in eighth-century Java.

eastern Java), Borobudur is a massive stupa with nine terraces. Sculpted on the sides of each terrace are bas-reliefs depicting the nine stages in the life of Siddhartha Gautama, from childhood to his final release from the chain of human existence. Surmounted by hollow bell-like towers containing representations of the Buddha and capped by a single stupa, the structure dominates the landscape for miles around.

Second only to Borobudur in technical excellence and even more massive in size are the ruins of the old capital city of Angkor Thom. The temple of Angkor Wat is the most famous and arguably the most beautiful of all the existing structures at Angkor Thom. Built on the model of the legendary Mount Meru (the home of the gods in Hindu tradition), it combines Indian architectural techniques with native inspiration in a structure of impressive delicacy and grace. In existence for more than six hundred

years, Angkor Wat serves as a bridge between the Hindu and Buddhist architectural styles.

CONCLUSION

During the more than fifteen hundred years from the fall of the Mauryas to the rise of the Mughals, Indian civilization faced a number of severe challenges. One challenge was primarily external and took the form of a continuous threat from beyond the mountains in the northwest. A second was generated by internal causes and stemmed from the tradition of factionalism and internal rivalry that had marked relations within the aristocracy since the Aryan invasion in the second millennium B.C.E. (see Chapter 2). Despite the abortive efforts of the Guptas, that tradition continued almost without interrup-

❧ **ANGKOR WAT.** The Khmer rulers of Angkor constructed a number of remarkable temples and palaces. Devised as either Hindu or Buddhist shrines, the temples also reflected the power and sanctity of the king. This twelfth-century temple known as Angkor Wat is renowned both for its spectacular architecture and for the thousands of fine bas-reliefs relating Hindu legends and Khmer history. Most memorable are the heavenly dancing maidens and the royal processions with elephants and soldiers.

Courtesy of William J. Duiker

tion down to the founding of the Mughal Empire in the sixteenth century.

The third challenge was primarily cultural and appeared in the religious divisions between Hindus and Buddhists, and later between Hindus and Muslims, that took place throughout much of this period. It is a measure of the strength and resilience of Hindu tradition that it was able to surmount the challenge of Buddhism and by the late first millennium C.E. reassert its dominant position in Indian society. But that triumph was short-lived. Like so many other areas in the region of southern Asia, by 1000 C.E., it was beset by a new challenge presented by nomadic forces from Central Asia. One result of the foreign conquest of northern India was the introduction of Islam into the region.

During the same period that Indian civilization faced these challenges at home, it was having a profound impact on the emerging states of Southeast Asia. Situated at the crossroads between two oceans and two great civilizations, Southeast Asia has long served as a bridge linking peoples and cultures, and it is not surprising that as complex societies began to develop in the area, they were strongly influenced by the older civilizations of neighboring China and India. At the same time, the Southeast Asian peoples put their own unique stamp on the ideas that they adopted and eventually rejected those that were inappropriate to local conditions.

The result was a region characterized by an almost unparalleled cultural richness and diversity, reflecting influences from as far away as the Middle East, yet preserving indigenous elements that were deeply rooted in the local culture. Unfortunately that very diversity posed potential problems for the peoples of Southeast Asia as they faced a new challenge from beyond the horizon. We shall deal with that challenge when we return to the region in a later chapter. In the meantime, we must turn our attention to the other major civilization that spread its shadow over the societies of southern Asia— China.

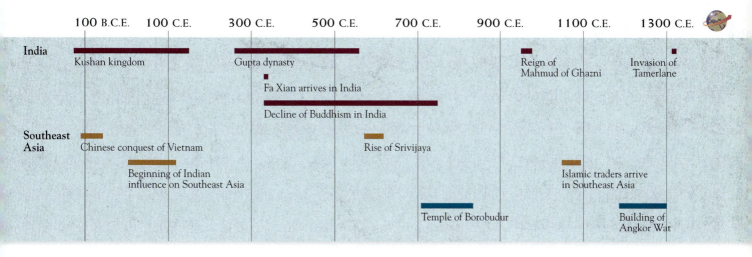

	100 B.C.E.	100 C.E.	300 C.E.	500 C.E.	700 C.E.	900 C.E.	1100 C.E.	1300 C.E.

India
Kushan kingdom
Gupta dynasty
Fa Xian arrives in India
Decline of Buddhism in India
Reign of Mahmud of Ghazni
Invasion of Tamerlane

Southeast Asia
Chinese conquest of Vietnam
Beginning of Indian influence on Southeast Asia
Rise of Srivijaya
Islamic traders arrive in Southeast Asia
Temple of Borobudur
Building of Angkor Wat

CHAPTER NOTES

1. Hiuen Tsiang, *Si-Yu-Ki: Buddhist Records of the Western World*, trans. Samuel Beal (London, n.d.), pp. 89–90.
2. "Fo-Kwo-Ki" (Travels of Fa Xian), in ibid., ch. 20, p. xliii.
3. E. C. Sachau, *Alberoni's India* (London, 1914), vol. 1, p. 22, quoted in S. M. Ikram, *Muslim Civilization in India* (New York, 1964), pp. 31–32.
4. Quoted in Ikram, *Muslim Civilization in India*, p. 68.
5. Hiuen Tsiang, *Si-Yu-Ki*, pp. 73–74.
6. Duarte Barbosa, *The Book of Duarte Barbosa* (Nedeln, Liechtenstein, 1967), pp. 147–148.
7. Quoted in Richard Lannoy, *The Speaking Tree: A Study of Indian Culture and Society* (London, 1971), p. 232.
8. Quoted in S. Tharu and K. Lalita, *Women Writing in India*, vol. 1 (New York, 1991), p. 77.
9. Quoted in A. L. Basham, *The Wonder That Was India* (London, 1954), p. 426.
10. Quoted in S. S. Hughes and B. Hughes, *Women in World History*, vol. 1 (Armonk, N.Y., 1995), p. 217.

SUGGESTED READING

The period from the decline of the Mauryas to the rise of the Mughals in India is not especially rich in terms of materials in English. Still, a number of the standard texts on Indian history contain useful sections on the period. Particularly good are A. L. Basham, *The Wonder That Was India* (London, 1954), and S. Wolpert, *New History of India* (New York, 1989).

A number of studies of Indian society and culture deal with this period. See, for example, R. Lannoy, *The Speaking Tree: A Study of Indian Culture and Society* (London, 1971), for a sophisticated interpretation of Indian culture during the medieval period. On Buddhism, see H. Nakamura, *Indian Buddhism: A Survey with Bibliographical Notes* (Delhi, 1987), and H. Akira, *A History of Indian Buddhism from Sakyamuni to Early Mahayana* (Honolulu, 1990). For an interesting treatment of the Buddhist influence on commercial activities that is reminiscent of the role of Christianity in Europe, see L. Xinru, *Ancient India and Ancient China: Trade and Religious Changes*, A.D. 1–600 (Delhi, 1988).

For a discussion of women's issues, see S. S. Hughes and B. Hughes, *Women in World History*, vol. 1 (Armonk, N.Y., 1995); S. Tharu and K. Lalita, *Women Writing in India*, vol. 1 (New York, 1991); and V. Dehejia, *Devi: The Great Goddess* (Washington, D.C., 1999).

The most comprehensive treatment of the Indian economy and, in particular, the regional trade throughout the Indian Ocean is K. N. Chaudhuri, *Trade and Civilization in the Indian Ocean: An Economic History from the Rise of Islam to 1750* (Cambridge, 1985), a groundbreaking comparative study. See also his more recent and massive *Asia Before Europe: Economy and Civilization of the Indian Ocean from the Rise of Islam to 1750* (Cambridge, 1990), which owes a considerable debt to F. Braudel's classical work on the Mediterranean Sea.

For an overview of events in Central Asia during this period, see D. Christian, *Inner Eurasia from Prehistory to the Mongol Empire* (Oxford, 1998), and C. E. Bosworth, *The Later Ghaznavids: Splendor and Decay* (New York, 1977). On the career of Tamerlane, see B. F. Manz, *The Rise and Rule of Tamerlane* (Cambridge, 1989).

For Indian art during the medieval period, see S. Huntington, *The Art of Ancient India: Buddhist, Hindu, and Jain* (New York, 1985), and V. Dehejia, *Indian Art* (London, 1997).

For an introduction to Indian literature, see E. C. Dimock, *The Literature of India: An Introduction* (Chicago, 1974), and A. K. Warder, *Indian Kavya Literature*, 5 vols. (Delhi, 1972–1988).

The early history of Southeast Asia is not as well documented as that of China or India. Except for Vietnam, where histories written in Chinese appeared shortly after the Chinese conquest, written materials on societies in the region are relatively sparse. Historians were therefore compelled to rely on stone inscriptions and the accounts of travelers and historians from other countries. As a result, the history of precolonial Southeast Asia was presented, as it were, from the outside looking in. A few classic studies, however, presented a useful overview and retain their value. For example, see R. Burling, *Hill Farms and Padi Fields: Life in Mainland Southeast Asia* (Englewood Cliffs, N.J., 1965); P. Wheatley, *The Golden Khersonese: Studies in the Historical Geography of the Malay Peninsula Before A.D. 1500* (Kuala Lumpur, 1961); and G. Coedes, *The Making of Southeast Asia* (Berkeley, Calif., 1966). More recently, some scholars have tended to emphasize the role of indigenous forces in the evolution of the region. See, for example, two works by O. W. Wolters, *Early Indonesian Commerce: A Study of the Origins of Srivijaya* (Ithaca, N.Y., 1967) and *The Fall of Srivijaya in Malay History* (Ithaca, N.Y., 1970). For an overview of modern scholarship on the region, see N. Tarling, ed., *The Cambridge History of Southeast Asia*, vol. 1 (Cambridge, 1999).

Impressive advances are now being made in the field of prehistory. See P. Bellwood, *Prehistory of the Indo-Malaysian Archipelago* (Honolulu, 1997), and C. Higham, *The Archaeology of Mainland Southeast Asia* (Cambridge, 1989). Also see C. Higham, *The Bronze Age of Southeast Asia* (Cambridge, 1996).

The role of commerce has been highlighted as a key aspect in the development of the region. For two fascinating accounts, see K. R. Hall, *Maritime Trade and State Development in Early Southeast Asia* (Honolulu, 1985), and A. Reid, *Southeast Asia in the Era of Commerce, 1450–1680: The Lands Below the Winds* (New Haven, Conn., 1989). The latter is also quite useful on the role of women.

INFOTRAC COLLEGE EDITION

Visit the source collections at infotrac.thomsonlearning.com and use the Search function with the following key terms.

Buddhism
Hinduism
India history
Tamerlane

WORLD HISTORY RESOURCES

Visit the *Essential World History* Companion Web Site for resources specific to this textbook:

http://history.wadsworth.com/duikeressentials02/

The CD in the back of this book and the World History Resource Center at **http://history.wadsworth.com/world/** offer a variety of tools to help you succeed in this course, including access to quizzes; images; documents; interactive simulations, maps, and timelines; movie explorations; and a wealth of other sources.

© Burstein Collection/CORBIS

FOCUS QUESTIONS

- How did Chinese historians traditionally view Chinese history, and has this view of China's past been challenged in any way?
- Why were the Mongols able to amass an empire, and what were the main characteristics of their rule in China?
- What roles did Buddhism, Daoism, and Neo-Confucianism play in Chinese intellectual life in the period between the Sui dynasty and the Ming?
- What were the main achievements in Chinese literature and art in the period between the Tang dynasty and the Ming, and what technological innovations and intellectual developments contributed to these achievements?
- ➤ What major changes in political structures and social and economic life occurred during the Sui, Tang, and Song dynasties?

FROM THE TANG TO THE MONGOLS: THE FLOWERING OF TRADITIONAL CHINA

On his first visit to the city, the traveler was mightily impressed. Its streets were so straight and wide that he could see through the city from one end to the other. Along the wide boulevards were beautiful palaces and inns in great profusion. The city was laid out in squares 'like a chessboard,' and within each square were spacious courts and gardens. Truly, said the visitor, this must be one of the largest and wealthiest cities on earth—a city so splendid that 'it is impossible to give a description that should do it justice.'[1]

The visitor was Marco Polo, and the city was Khanbaliq (later known as Beijing), capital of the Yuan dynasty (1279–1368) and one of the great commercial centers of the Chinese Empire. Marco Polo was an Italian merchant who had traveled to China in the late thirteenth century and then served as an official at the court of Khubilai

Khan. His diary, published after his return to Italy almost twenty years later, astonished readers with tales of this magnificent but unknown civilization far to the east.

When Marco Polo arrived, China was ruled by the Mongols, a nomadic people from Central Asia who had recently assumed control of the Chinese Empire. The Yuan dynasty, as the Mongol rulers were called, was only one of a succession of dynasties to rule China after the collapse of the Han in the third century C.E. The end of the Han had led to a period of internal division that lasted nearly four hundred years and was aggravated by the threat posed by nomadic peoples from the north. This time of troubles ended in the early seventh century, when a dynamic new dynasty, the Tang, came to power.

To this point, Chinese history appeared to be following a pattern similar to that of India, where the passing of the Mauryan dynasty in the second century B.C.E. unleashed a period of internal division that lasted for several hundred years. But China did not recapitulate the Indian experience. The Tang dynasty led China to some of its finest achievements and was succeeded by the Song, who ruled most of China for nearly three hundred years. The Song were in turn overthrown by the Mongols in the late thirteenth century, who then gave way to a powerful new native dynasty, the Ming, in 1368. Dynasty followed dynasty, with periods of extraordinary cultural achievement alternating with periods of internal disorder, but in general, Chinese society continued to build on the political and cultural foundations of the Zhou and the Han.

Chinese historians, viewing this vast process as it evolved over time, began to hypothesize that Chinese history was cyclical, driven by the dynamic interplay of the forces of good and evil, *yang* and *yin,* growth and decay. Beyond the forces of conflict and change lay the essential continuity of Chinese history, based on the timeless principles established by Confucius and other thinkers during the Zhou dynasty in antiquity. If India often appeared to be a politically and culturally diverse entity, only sporadically knit together by ambitious rulers, China, in the eyes of its historians, was a coherent civilization struggling to relive the glories of its ancient golden age while contending against the divisive forces operating throughout the cosmos. •

CHINA AFTER THE HAN

After the collapse of the Han dynasty at the beginning of the third century C.E., China fell into an extended period of division and civil war. Taking advantage of the absence of organized government in China, nomadic forces from the Gobi Desert penetrated south of the Great Wall and established their own rule over northern China. In the Yangtze valley and farther to the south, native Chinese rule was maintained, but constant civil war and instability led later historians to refer to the period as the "era of the six dynasties."

The collapse of the Han Empire had a marked effect on the Chinese psyche. The Confucian principles that emphasized hard work, the subordination of the individual to community interests, and belief in the essentially rational order of the universe came under severe challenge, and many Chinese intellectuals began to reject the stuffy moralism and complacency of State Confucianism and sought emotional satisfaction in hedonistic pursuits or philosophical Daoism.

Eccentric behavior and a preference for philosophical Daoism became a common response to a corrupt age. A group of writers known as the "seven sages of the bamboo forest" exemplified the period. Among the best known was the poet Liu Ling, whose odd behavior is described in this oft-quoted passage:

> Liu Ling was an inveterate drinker and indulged himself to the full. Sometimes he stripped off his clothes and sat in his room stark naked. Some men saw him and rebuked him. Liu Ling said, "Heaven and earth are my dwelling, and my house is my trousers. Why are you all coming into my trousers?"[2]

But neither popular beliefs in the supernatural nor philosophical Daoism could satisfy deeper emotional needs or provide solace in time of sorrow or the hope of a better life in the hereafter. Instead Buddhism filled that gap.

Buddhism was brought to China in the first or second century C.E., probably by missionaries and merchants traveling over the Silk Road. The concept of rebirth was probably unfamiliar to most Chinese, and the intellectual hairsplitting that often accompanied discussion of

Courtesy of William J. Duiker

THE BIG GOOSE PAGODA. When the Buddhist pilgrim Xuan Zang returned to China from India in the mid-seventh century C.E., he settled in the capital of Chang'an, where, under orders from the Tang emperor, he began to translate Buddhist texts in his possession from Sanskrit into Chinese. The Big Goose Pagoda, shown here, was erected shortly afterward to house them. Originally known as the Pagoda of the Classics, the structure consists of seven stories and is over 240 feet tall.

Buddha's message in India was somewhat too esoteric for Chinese tastes. Still, in the difficult years surrounding the decline of the Han dynasty, Buddhist ideas, especially those of the Mahayana school, began to find adherents among intellectuals and ordinary people alike. As Buddhism increased in popularity, it was frequently attacked by supporters of Confucianism and Daoism for its foreign origins. But such sniping did not halt the progress of Buddhism, and eventually the new faith was assimilated into Chinese culture, assisted by the efforts of such tireless advocates as the missionaries Fa Xian and Xuan Zang and the support of ruling elites in both northern and southern China (see "The Rise and Decline of Buddhism and Daoism" later in this chapter).

CHINA REUNIFIED: THE SUI, THE TANG, AND THE SONG

After nearly four centuries of internal division, China was unified once again in 581 when Yang Jian (Yang Chien), a member of a respected aristocratic family in northern China, founded a new dynasty, known as the Sui (581–618 C.E.). Yang Jian (who is also known by his reign title of Sui Wendi, or Sui Wen Ti) established his capital at the historic metropolis of Chang'an and began to extend his authority throughout the heartland of China.

Like his predecessors, the new emperor sought to create a unifying ideology for the state to enhance its efficiency. But whereas Liu Bang, the founder of the Han dynasty, had adopted Confucianism as the official doctrine to hold the empire together, Yang Jian turned to Daoism and Buddhism. He founded monasteries for both doctrines in the capital and appointed Buddhist monks to key positions as political advisers.

Yang Jian was a builder as well as a conqueror, ordering the construction of a new canal from the capital to the confluence of the Wei and Yellow Rivers nearly 100 miles to the east. His son, Emperor Sui Yangdi (Sui Yang Ti), continued the process, and the 1,400-mile-long Grand Canal, linking the two great rivers of China, the Yellow and the Yangtze, was completed during his reign. The new canal facilitated the shipment of grain and other commodities from the rice-rich southern provinces to the densely populated north. Sui Yangdi also used the canal as an imperial highway for inspecting his empire and dispatching troops to troubled provinces.

Despite such efforts to project the majesty of the imperial personage, the Sui dynasty came to an end immediately after Sui Yangdi's death. The Sui emperor was a tyrannical ruler, and his expensive military campaigns aroused widespread unrest. After his return from a failed campaign against Korea in 618, the emperor was murdered in his palace. One of his generals, Li Yuan, took advantage of the instability that ensued and declared the foundation of a new dynasty, known as the Tang (T'ang). Building on the successes of its predecessor, the Tang lasted for three hundred years, until 907.

Li Yuan ruled for a brief period and then was elbowed aside by his son, Li Shimin (Li Shih-min), who assumed the reign title Tang Taizong (T'ang T'ai-tsung). Under his vigorous leadership, the Tang launched a program of internal renewal and external expansion that would make it one of the greatest dynasties in the long history of China (see Map 10.1). Under the Tang, the northwest was pacified and given the name of Xinjiang, or "new region." A long conflict with Tibet led for the first time to the extension of Chinese control over the vast and desolate plateau north of the Himalaya Mountains. The southern provinces

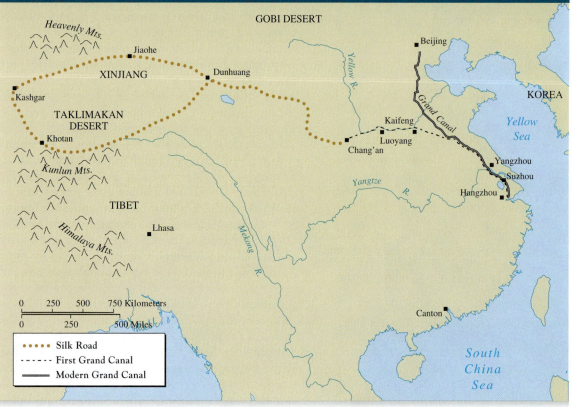

MAP 10.1 China Under the Tang. The era of the Tang dynasty was one of the greatest periods in the long history of China. Tang influence spread from the heartland of China into neighboring regions, including Central and Southeast Asia. ➤ *Where are the Grand Canal and the Silk Road, as located on the map?*

below the Yangtze were fully assimilated into the Chinese Empire, and the imperial court established commercial and diplomatic relations with the states of Southeast Asia. With reason, China now claimed to be the foremost power in East Asia, and the emperor demanded fealty and tribute from all his fellow rulers beyond the frontier. Korea accepted tribute status and attempted to adopt the Chinese model, and the Japanese dispatched official missions to China to learn more about its customs and institutions (see Chapter 11).

Finally the Tang dynasty witnessed a flowering of Chinese culture. Many modern observers feel that the era represents the apogee of Chinese creativity in poetry and sculpture. One reason for this explosion of culture was the influence of Buddhism, which affected art, literature, and philosophy, as well as religion and politics. Monasteries sprang up throughout China, and (as under the Sui) Buddhist monks served as advisers at the Tang imperial court. The city of Chang'an, now restored to the glory it had known as the

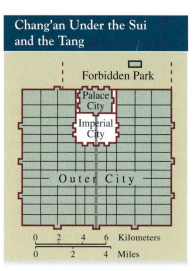

Chang'an Under the Sui and the Tang

capital of the Han dynasty, once again became the seat of the empire. It was possibly the greatest city in the world of its time, with an estimated population of nearly two million. The city was filled with temples and palaces, and its markets teemed with goods from all over the known world.

But the Tang, like the Han, sowed the seeds of their own destruction. Tang rulers could not prevent the rise of internal forces that would ultimately weaken the dynasty and bring it to an end. Two ubiquitous problems were court intrigues and official corruption. In 755, rebellious forces briefly seized control of the capital of Chang'an. Although the revolt was eventually suppressed, the Tang never fully recovered from the catastrophe. The loss of power by the central government led to increased influence by great landed families inside China and chronic instability along the northern and western frontiers, where local military commanders ruled virtually without central government interference. It was an eerie repetition of the final decades of the Han.

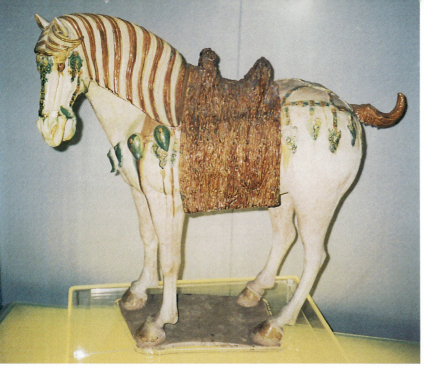

➤ A TANG HORSE. During the Tang dynasty, trade between China, India, and the Middle East along the famous Silk Road increased rapidly and introduced new Central Asian motifs to Chinese culture. Ceramic representations of the sturdy Central Asian horse and the two-humped Bactrian camel were often produced as decorative objects in the homes of the wealthy or as tomb figures. Preserved for us today, these ceramic studies of horses and camels, as well as of officials, court ladies, and servants, painted in brilliant gold, green, and blue lead glazes, are impressive examples of Tang cultural achievement.

The end finally came in the early tenth century, when border troubles with northern nomadic peoples called the Khitan increased, leading to the final collapse of the dynasty in 907. The Tang had followed the classic strategy of "using a barbarian to oppose a barbarian" by allying with a trading people called the Uighurs (a Turkic-speaking people who had taken over many of the caravan routes along the Silk Road) against their old rivals. But yet another nomadic people called the Kirghiz defeated the Uighurs and then turned on the Tang government in its moment of weakness and overthrew it.

China slipped once again into chaos. This time, the period of foreign invasion and division was much shorter. In 960, a new dynasty, known as the Song (960–1279), rose to power. From the start, however, the Song (Sung) rulers encountered more problems than their predecessors. Although the founding emperor, Song Taizu (Sung T'ai-tsu), was able to co-opt many of the powerful military commanders whose rivalry had brought the Tang dynasty to an end, he was unable to reconquer the northwestern part of the country from the nomadic Khitan peoples. The emperor therefore established his capital farther to the east, at Kaifeng, where the Grand Canal intersected the Yellow River. Later, when pressures from the nomads in the north increased, the court was forced to move the capital even farther south, to Hangzhou (Hangchow), on the coast just south of the Yangtze River delta; the emperors who ruled from Hangzhou are known as the southern Song. The Song also lost control over Tibet. Despite its

political and military weaknesses, the dynasty nevertheless ruled during a period of economic expansion, prosperity, and cultural achievement and is therefore considered among the more successful Chinese dynasties. The population of the empire had risen to an estimated forty million people, slightly more than that of the continent of Europe.

Yet the Song dynasty was never able to surmount the external challenge from the north, and that failure eventually brought about the end of the dynasty. During its final decades, the Song rulers were forced to pay tribute to the Jurchen peoples from Manchuria. In the early thirteenth century, the Song, ignoring precedent and the fate of the Tang, formed an alliance with the Mongols, a new and obscure nomadic people from the Gobi Desert. As under the Tang, the decision proved to be a disaster. Within a few years, the Mongols had become a much more serious threat to China than the Jurchen. After defeating the Jurchen, the Mongols turned their attention to the Song, advancing on Song territory from both the north and the west. By this time, the Song Empire had been weakened by internal factionalism and a loss of tax revenues. After a series of river battles and sieges marked by the use of catapults and gunpowder, the Song were defeated, and the conquerors announced the creation of a new Yuan (Mongol) dynasty. Ironically the Mongols had first learned about gunpowder from the Chinese.

Political Structures: The Triumph of Confucianism

During the nearly seven hundred years from the Sui to the end of the Song, a mature political system based on principles originally established during the Qin and Han dynasties gradually emerged in China. After the Tang dynasty's brief flirtation with Buddhism, State Confucianism became the ideological cement that held the system together. The development of this system took several centuries, and it did not reach its height until the period of the Song dynasty.

EQUAL OPPORTUNITY IN CHINA: THE CIVIL SERVICE EXAMINATION

At the apex of the government hierarchy was the Grand Council, assisted by a secretariat and a chancellery; it included representatives from all three authorities—civil, military, and censorate. Under the Grand Council was the Department of State Affairs, composed of ministries responsible for justice, military affairs, personnel, public works, revenue, and rites (ritual). This department was in effect the equivalent of a modern cabinet.

The Tang dynasty adopted the practice of selecting bureaucrats through civil service examinations. One way of strengthening the power of the central administration was to make the civil service examination system the primary route to an official career. To reduce the power of the noble families, relatives of individuals serving in the imperial court, as well as eunuchs, were prohibited from taking the examinations. But if the Song rulers' objective was to make the bureaucracy more subservient to the court, they may have been disappointed. The rising professionalism of the bureaucracy, which numbered about ten thousand in the imperial capital, with an equal number at the local level, provided it with an esprit de corps and an influence that sometimes enabled it to resist the whims of individual emperors.

Under the Song, the examination system attained the form that it would retain in later centuries. In general, three levels of examinations were administered. The first was a qualifying examination given annually at the provincial capital. Candidates who succeeded in this first stage were considered qualified but normally were not given positions in the bureaucracy except at the local level. Many stopped at this level and accepted positions as village teachers to train other candidates. Candidates who wished to go on could take a second examination given at the capital every three years. Successful candidates could apply for an official position. Some went on to take the final examination, which was given in the imperial palace once every three years. Those who passed were eligible for high positions in the central bureaucracy or for appointments as district magistrates.

By Song times, examinations were based entirely on the Confucian classics. Candidates were expected to memorize passages and to be able to define the moral lessons they contained. The system guaranteed that successful candidates—and therefore officials—would have received a full dose of Confucian political and social ethics. Many students complained about the rigors of memorization and the irrelevance of the process. Others brought crib notes into the examination hall (one enterprising candidate concealed an entire Confucian text in the lining of his cloak).

The Song authorities ignored such criticisms, but they did open the system to more people by allowing all males except criminals or members of certain restricted occupations to take the examinations. To provide potential candidates with schooling, training academies were set up at the provincial and district level. Without such academies, only individuals fortunate enough to receive training in the classics in family-run schools would have had the expertise to pass the examinations. In time, the majority of candidates came from the landed gentry, nonaristocratic landowners who controlled much of the wealth in the countryside. Because the gentry prized education and became the primary upholders of the Confucian tradition, they were often called the scholar-gentry.

But certain aspects of the system still prevented it from truly providing equal opportunity to all. In the first place, only males were eligible. Then again, the Song did not attempt to establish a system of universal elementary education. In practice, only those who had been given a basic education in the classics at home were able to enter the state-run academies and compete for a position in the bureaucracy. The poor had little chance.

Nor could the system guarantee an honest, efficient bureaucracy. Official arrogance, bureaucratic infighting, corruption, and legalistic interpretations of government regulations were as prevalent in medieval China as in bureaucracies the world over. Nepotism was a particular problem, since many Chinese, following Confucius, held that filial duty transcended loyalty to the community.

Despite such weaknesses, the civil service examination system was an impressive achievement for its day and probably provided a more efficient government and more opportunity for upward mobility than were found in any other civilization of its time. Most Western governments, for example, only began to recruit officials on the basis of merit in the nineteenth century. Furthermore, by regulating the content of the examinations, the system helped provide China with a cultural uniformity lacking in empires elsewhere in Asia.

LOCAL GOVERNMENT

The Song dynasty maintained the local government institutions that it had inherited from its predecessors. At the base of the government pyramid was the district (or county), governed by a magistrate. The magistrate, assisted by his staff of three or four officials and several other menial employees, was responsible for maintaining law and order and collecting taxes within his jurisdiction. A district could exceed 100,000 people. Below the district was the basic unit of Chinese government, the village. Because villages were so numerous in China, the central government did not appoint an official at that level and allowed the villages to administer themselves. Village government was normally in the hands of a council of elders, usually assisted by a chief. The council, usually made up of the heads of influential families in the village, maintained the local irrigation and transportation network, adjudicated local disputes, organized and maintained a militia, and assisted in collecting taxes (usually paid in grain) and delivering them to the district magistrate.

Economy and Society

During the long period between the Sui and the Song, the Chinese economy, like the government, grew considerably in size and complexity. China was still an agricultural society, but major changes were taking place within the economy and the social structure. The urban sector of the economy was becoming increasingly important, new social classes were beginning to appear, and the economic focus of the empire was beginning to shift from the Yellow River valley in the north to the Yangtze River valley in the center—a process that was encouraged both by the expansion of cultivation in the Yangtze delta and by the control exerted over the north by nomadic peoples during the Song.

The economic revival began shortly after the rise of the Tang. During the long period of internal division, land had become concentrated in the hands of aristocratic families, with most peasants reduced to serfdom or slavery. The early Tang tried to reduce the power of the landed nobility and maximize tax revenues by adopting the ancient "equal field" system, in which land was allocated to farmers for life in return for an annual tax payment and three weeks of conscript labor.

At first, the new system was vigorously enforced and led to increased rural prosperity and government revenue. But eventually, the rich and the politically influential learned to manipulate the system for their own benefit and accumulated huge tracts of land. The growing population, caused by a rise in food production and the extended period of social stability, also put steady pressure on the system. Finally the government abandoned the effort to equalize landholdings and returned the land to private hands while attempting to prevent inequalities through the tax system. The failure to resolve the land problem contributed to the fall of the Tang dynasty in the early tenth century.

The Song tried to resolve the land problem by returning to the successful programs of the early Tang and reducing the power of the wealthy landed aristocrats. During the late eleventh century, the reformist official Wang Anshi (Wang An-shih) attempted to limit the size of landholdings through progressive land taxes and provided cheap credit to poor farmers to help them avoid bankruptcy. His reforms met with some success, but other developments probably contributed more to the general agricultural prosperity under the Song. These included the opening of new lands in the Yangtze River valley, improvements in irrigation techniques such as the chain pump (a circular chain of square pallets on a treadmill that enabled farmers to lift considerable amounts of water or mud to a higher level), and the introduction of a new strain of quick-growing rice from Southeast Asia, which permitted farmers in warmer regions to plant and harvest two crops each year.

Major changes also took place in the Chinese urban economy, which witnessed a significant increase in trade and manufacturing. Despite the restrictive policies of the state, the urban sector grew steadily larger and more complex, helped by several new technological developments. During the Tang, the Chinese mastered the art of manufacturing steel by mixing cast iron and wrought iron. The blast furnace was heated to a high temperature by burning coal, which had been used as a fuel in China from about the fourth century C.E. The resulting product was used in the manufacture of swords, sickles, and even suits of armor. By the eleventh century, more than 35,000 tons of steel were being produced annually. The introduction of cotton offered new opportunities in textile manufacturing. Gunpowder was invented by the Chinese during the Tang dynasty and used primarily for explosives and a primitive form of flamethrower; it reached the West via the Arabs in the twelfth century.

OCEAN TRADE AND THE SILK ROAD

The nature of trade was also changing. In the past, most long-distance trade had been undertaken by state monopoly. By the time of the Song, private commerce was being actively encouraged, and many merchants engaged in shipping as well as in wholesale and retail trade. Guilds began to appear, along with a new money economy. Paper currency began to be used in the eighth and ninth centuries. Credit (at first called "flying money") also made its first appearance during the Tang. With the increased circulation of paper money, banking began to develop as merchants found that strings of copper coins were too cumbersome for their increasingly complex operations. Equally useful, if more prosaic, was the invention of the abacus, an early form of calculator that simplified the calculations needed for commercial transactions.

Long-distance trade, both overland and by sea, expanded under the Tang and the Song. Trade with countries and peoples to the west had been carried on for centuries (see Chapter 3), but it had declined dramatically between the fourth and sixth centuries C.E. as a result of the collapse of the Han and Roman Empires. It began to revive with the rise of the Tang and the simultaneous unification of much of the Middle East under the Arabs. During the Tang era, the Silk Road revived and then reached its zenith. Much of the trade was carried by the Turkic-speaking Uighurs. During the Tang, Uighur caravans of two-humped Bactrian camels (a hardy variety native to Iran and regions to the northeast) carried goods back and forth between China and the countries of South Asia and the Middle East.

In actuality, the Silk Road was composed of a number of separate routes. The first to be used, probably because of the jade found in the mountains south of Khotan, ran along the southern rim of the Taklimakan Desert via Kashgar and thence through the Pamir Mountains into Bactria. Eventually, however, this area began to dry up, and traders were forced to seek other routes. From a climatic standpoint, the best route for the Silk Road was to the north of the Tian Shan (Heavenly Mountains), where moisture-laden northwesterly winds created pastures where animals could graze. But the area was frequently infested by bandits who preyed on unwary travelers. Most caravans therefore followed the southern route, which passed along the northern fringes of the Taklimakan Desert to Kashgar and down into northwestern India. Travelers avoided the direct route through the desert (in the Uighur language, the name means "go in and you won't come out") and trudged from oasis to oasis along the southern slopes of the Tian Shan. The oases were created by the water runoff from winter snows in the mountains, which then dried up in the searing heat of the desert.

The Silk Road was so hazardous that shipping goods by sea became increasingly popular. China had long been engaged in sea trade with other countries in the region, but most of the commerce was originally in the hands of Korean, Japanese, or Southeast Asian merchants. Chinese maritime trade, however, was stimulated by the invention of the compass and technical improvements in shipbuilding such as the sternpost rudder and the lug sail (which enabled ships to sail close to the wind). If Marco Polo's observations can be believed, by the thirteenth century, Chinese junks (a type of seagoing ship popular in Asian waters that employed square sails and a flat bottom) had multiple sails and weighed up to 2,000 tons, much more than contemporary ships in the West. The Chinese governor of Canton in the early twelfth century remarked:

> According to the government regulations concerning sea-going ships, the larger ones can carry several hundred men, and the smaller ones may have more than a hundred men on board. . . . The ship's pilots are acquainted with the configuration of the coasts; at night they steer by the stars, and in the daytime by the Sun. In dark weather they look at the south-pointing needle. They also use a line a hundred feet long with a hook at the end, which they let down to take samples of mud from the seabottom; by its appearance and smell they can determine their whereabouts.[3]

A wide variety of goods passed through Chinese ports. The Chinese exported tea, silk, and porcelain to the countries beyond the South China Sea, receiving exotic woods, precious stones, and various tropical goods in exchange. Seaports on the southern China coast exported sweet oranges, lemons, and peaches in return for grapes, walnuts, and pomegranates. Along the Silk Road to China came raw hides, furs, and horses. Chinese aristocrats, their appetite for material consumption stimulated by the affluence of Chinese society during much of the Tang and Song periods, were fascinated by the exotic goods and the flora and fauna of the desert and the tropical lands of the South Seas. The city of Chang'an became the eastern terminus of the Silk Road and perhaps the wealthiest city in the world during the Tang era. The major port of exit in southern China was Canton, where an estimated 100,000 merchants lived.

Some of this trade was a product of the tribute system, which the Chinese rulers used as an element of their foreign policy. The Chinese viewed the outside world as they viewed their own society—in a hierarchical manner. Rulers of smaller countries along the periphery were viewed as "younger brothers" of the Chinese emperor and owed fealty to him. Foreign rulers who accepted the relationship were required to pay tribute and to promise not to harbor enemies of the Chinese Empire. In return, they obtained legitimacy and access to the vast Chinese market.

DAILY LIFE IN TRADITIONAL CHINA

These political and economic changes affected Chinese society during the Tang and Song eras. For one thing, it became much more complex. Whereas previously China had been almost exclusively rural, with a small urban class of merchants, artisans, and workers almost entirely dependent on the state, the cities had now grown into an important, if statistically still insignificant, part of the population. Urban life, too, had changed. Cities were no longer primarily administrative centers dominated by officials and their families but now included a much broader mix of officials, merchants, artisans, touts, and entertainers. Unlike the situation in Europe, however, Chinese cities did not possess special privileges that protected their residents from the rapacity of the central government.

In the countryside, equally significant changes were taking place, as the relatively rigid demarcation between the landed aristocracy and the mass of the rural population gave way to a more complex mixture of landed gentry, free farmers, sharecroppers, and landless laborers. There was also a class of "base people," consisting of actors, butchers, and prostitutes, who possessed only limited legal rights and were not permitted to take the civil service examination.

Perhaps the most significant development was the rise of the landed gentry as the most influential force in Chinese society. The gentry class controlled much of the wealth in the rural areas and produced the majority of the candidates for the bureaucracy. By virtue of their possession of land and specialized knowledge of the Confucian classics, the gentry had replaced the aristocracy as the political and economic elite of Chinese society. Unlike the aristocracy, however, the gentry did not form an exclusive class separated by the accident of birth from the remainder of the population. Upward and downward mobility between the scholar-gentry class and the remainder of the population was not uncommon and may have been a key factor in the stability and longevity of the system. A position in the bureaucracy opened the doors to wealth and prestige for the individual and his family but was no guarantee of success, and the fortunes of individual families might experience a rapid rise and fall. The soaring ambitions and arrogance of China's landed gentry are vividly described in the following wish list set in poetry by a young bridegroom of the Tang dynasty:

> Chinese slaves to take charge of treasury and barn,
> Foreign slaves to take care of my cattle and sheep.
> Strong-legged slaves to run by saddle and stirrup when I ride,
> Powerful slaves to till the fields with might and main,
> Handsome slaves to play the harp and hand the wine;
> Slim-waisted slaves to sing me songs, and dance;
> Dwarfs to hold the candle by my dining-couch.[4]

For affluent Chinese in this era, life offered many more pleasures than had been available to their ancestors. There

Public Entertainment in China and Japan

Besides being an artistic masterpiece, the Chinese scroll shown at the top, known as *Spring Festival on the River*, is one of the most remarkable social documents of early twelfth-century China. Nearly 33 feet long, it records with encyclopedic detail various aspects of Chinese society, from the imperial court down to the lowliest peasants, as they prepare for the spring festival. The screen painting on the bottom, probably from the fifteenth century, depicts a form of Japanese public entertainment (see Chapter 11). On the left, the well-behaved upper-class spectators observe the graceful dancers on stage in a dignified manner, while the ordinary people down at the front display themselves as a rowdy crowd.

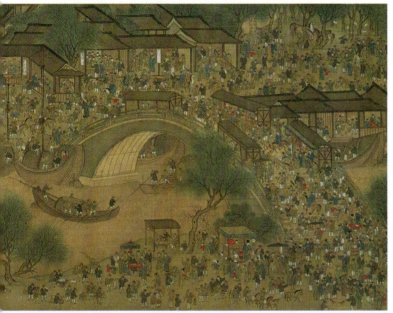

Spring Festival on the River; Detail, The Metropolitan Museum of Art, Fletcher Fund, 1947, The A.W. Bahr Collection, (47.18.1)

© Werner Forman/Art Resource, NY

were new forms of entertainment, such as playing cards and chess (brought from India, although an early form had been invented in China during the Zhou dynasty); new forms of transportation, such as the paddle-wheel boat and horseback riding (made possible by the introduction of the stirrup); better means of communication (block printing was first invented in the eighth century C.E.); and new tastes for the palate introduced from lands beyond the frontier. Tea had been introduced from the Burmese frontier by monks as early as the Han dynasty, and brandy and other concentrated spirits produced by the distillation of alcohol made their appearance in the seventh century.

The vast majority of the Chinese people still lived off the land in villages ranging in size from a few dozen residents to several thousand. The life of the farmers was bounded by their village. Although many communities were connected to the outside world by roads or rivers, the average Chinese rarely left the confines of their native village except for an occasional visit to a nearby market town.

An even more basic unit than the village in the lives of most Chinese, of course, was the family. The ideal was the joint family with at least three generations under one roof. Because of the heavy labor requirements of rice farming, the tradition of the joint family was especially prevalent in the south. When a son married, he was expected to bring his new wife back to live in his parents' home (see the box on p. 210).

Chinese village architecture reflected these traditions. Most family dwellings were simple, consisting of one or at most two rooms. They were usually constructed of dried mud, stone, or brick, depending on available materials and the prosperity of the family. Roofs were of thatch or tile, and the floors were usually of packed dirt. Large houses were often built in a square around an inner courtyard, thus guaranteeing privacy from the outside world.

Within the family unit, the eldest male theoretically ruled as an autocrat. He was responsible for presiding over ancestral rites at an altar, usually in the main room of the house. He had traditional legal rights over his wife, and if she did not provide him with a male heir, he was permitted to take a second wife. She, however, had no recourse to divorce. As the old saying went, "Marry a chicken, follow the chicken; marry a dog, follow the dog." Wealthy Chinese might keep concubines, who lived in a separate room in the house and sometimes competed with the legal wife for precedence.

In accordance with Confucian tradition, children were expected, above all, to obey their parents, who not only determined their children's careers but also selected their marriage partners. Filial piety was viewed as an absolute moral good, above virtually all other moral obligations.

THE SAINTLY MISS WU

The idea that a wife should sacrifice her wants to the needs of her husband and family was deeply embedded in traditional Chinese society. Widows in particular had few rights, and their remarriage was strongly condemned. In this account from a story by Hung Mai, a twelfth-century writer, the widowed Miss Wu wins the respect of the entire community by faithfully serving her mother-in-law.

HUNG MAI, A SONG FAMILY SAGA

Miss Wu served her mother-in-law very filially. Her mother-in-law had an eye ailment and felt sorry for her daughter-in-law's solitary and poverty-stricken situation, so suggested that they call in a son-in-law for her and thereby get an adoptive heir. Miss Wu announced in tears, "A woman does not serve two husbands. I will support you. Don't talk this way." Her mother-in-law, seeing that she was determined, did not press her. Miss Wu did spinning, washing, sewing, cooking, and cleaning for her neighbors, earning perhaps a hundred cash a day, all of which she gave to her mother-in-law to cover the cost of firewood and food. If she was given any meat, she would wrap it up to take home. . . .

Once when her mother-in-law was cooking rice, a neighbor called to her, and to avoid overcooking the rice she dumped it into a pan. Owing to her bad eyes, however, she mistakenly put it in the dirty chamber pot. When Miss Wu returned and saw it, she did not say a word. She went to a neighbor to borrow some cooked rice for her mother-in-law and took the dirty rice and washed it to eat herself.

One day in the daytime neighbors saw [Miss Wu] ascending into the sky amid colored clouds. Startled, they told her mother-in-law, who said, "Don't be foolish. She just came back from pounding rice for someone, and is lying down on the bed. Go and look." They went to the room and peeked in and saw her sound asleep. Amazed, they left.

When Miss Wu woke up, her mother-in-law told her what happened, and she said, "I just dreamed of two young boys in blue clothes holding documents and riding on the clouds. They grabbed my clothes and said the Emperor of Heaven had summoned me. They took me to the gate of heaven and I was brought in to see the emperor, who was seated beside a balustrade. He said, 'Although you are just a lowly ignorant village woman, you are able to serve your old mother-in-law sincerely and work hard. You really deserve respect.' He gave me a cup of aromatic wine and a string of cash, saying, 'I will supply you. From now on you will not need to work for others.' I bowed to thank him and came back, accompanied by the two boys. Then I woke up."

There was in fact a thousand cash on the bed, and the room was filled with a fragrance. They then realized that the neighbors' vision had been a spirit journey. From this point on even more people asked her to work for them, and she never refused. But the money that had been given to her she kept for her mother-in-law's use. Whatever they used promptly reappeared, so the thousand cash was never exhausted. The mother-in-law also regained her sight in both eyes.

Female children were considered less desirable than males because they could not undertake heavy work in the fields or carry on the family traditions. Poor families often sold their daughters to wealthy villagers to serve as concubines, and female infanticide to ensure there would be food for the remainder of the family was not uncommon in times of famine. Concubines had few legal rights; female domestic servants, even fewer.

During the Song era, two new practices emerged that changed the equation for women seeking to obtain a successful marriage contract. First, a new form of dowry appeared. Whereas previously the prospective husband offered the bride's family a bride price, now the reverse became the norm, with the bride's parents paying the groom's family a dowry. With the prosperity that characterized Chinese society during much of the Song era, affluent parents sought to buy a satisfactory husband for their daughter, preferably one with a higher social standing and good prospects for an official career.

A second source of marital bait during the Song period was the promise of a bride with tiny bound feet. The process of foot binding, carried out on girls aged five to thirteen, was excruciatingly painful, since it bent and compressed the foot to half its normal size by imprisoning it in restrictive bandages. But the procedure was often performed by ambitious mothers intent on assuring their daughters of the best possible prospects for marriage. Bound feet represented submissiveness and self-discipline, two required attributes for the ideal Confucian wife.

Throughout northern China, foot binding became a common practice for women of all social classes. It was less common in southern China, where the cultivation of wet rice could not be carried out with bandaged feet; there it tended to be limited to the scholar-gentry class. Still, most Chinese women with bound feet contributed to the labor force to supplement the family income. Although foot binding was eventually prohibited, the practice lasted into the twentieth century, particularly in rural villages.

As in most traditional societies, there were exceptions to the low status of women in Chinese society. Women had substantial property rights and retained control over their dowries even after divorce or the death of the husband. Wives were frequently an influential force within the home, often handling the accounts and taking primary responsibility for raising the children. Some were active in politics. The outstanding example was Wu Zhao (c. 625–c. 706), popularly known as Empress Wu. Selected by Emperor Tang Taizong as a concubine, after his death she rose to a position of supreme power at court. At first, she was content to rule through her sons, but in 690, she declared herself empress of China. For her presumption, she has been vilified by later Chinese historians, but she was actually a quite capable ruler. She was responsible for giving meaning to the civil service examination system and was the first to select graduates of the examinations for the highest positions in government. During her last years, she reportedly fell under the influence of courtiers and was deposed in 705, when she was probably around eighty.

EXPLOSION IN CENTRAL ASIA: THE MONGOL EMPIRE

The Mongols, who succeeded the Song as the rulers of China in 1279, rose to power in Asia with stunning rapidity. When Genghis Khan (also known as Chinggis Khan), the founder of Mongol greatness, was born, the Mongols were a relatively obscure pastoral people in the region of modern Outer Mongolia. Like most of the nomadic peoples in the region, they were organized loosely into clans and tribes and even lacked a common name for themselves. Rivalry among the various tribes over pasture, livestock, and booty was intense and increased at the end of the twelfth century as a result of a growing population and the consequent overgrazing of pastures.

Born in 1162, Genghis Khan (his original name was Temuchin, or Temujin) was the son of one of the more impoverished nobles of his tribe. While he was still a child, his father was murdered by a rival, and the youngster was temporarily forced to seek refuge in the wilderness. Nevertheless, through his prowess and the power of his personality, he gradually unified the Mongol tribes. In 1206, he was elected Genghis Khan ("universal ruler") at a massive tribal meeting. From that time on, he devoted himself to military pursuits. Mongol nomads were now forced to pay taxes and were subject to military conscription. "Man's highest joy," Genghis Khan reportedly remarked, "is in victory: to conquer one's enemies, to pursue them,

to deprive them of their possessions, to make their beloved weep, to ride on their horses, and to embrace their wives and daughters."[5]

The army that Genghis Khan unleashed on the world was not exceptionally large—less than 130,000 men in 1227, at a time when the total Mongol population numbered between one and two million. But their mastery of military tactics set the Mongols apart from their rivals. Their tireless flying columns of mounted warriors surrounded their enemies and harassed them like cattle, luring them into pursuit, then ambushing them with flank attacks. John Plano Carpini, a contemporary Franciscan friar, described their tactics:

> As soon as they discover the enemy they charge and each one unleashes three or four arrows. If they see that they can't break him, they retreat in order to entice the enemy to pursue, thus luring him into an ambush prepared in advance. . . . Their military stratagems are numerous. At the moment of an enemy cavalry attack, they place prisoners and foreign auxiliaries in the forefront of their own position, while positioning the bulk of their own troops on the right and left wings to envelop the adversary, thus giving the enemy the impression that they are more numerous than in reality. If the adversary defends himself well, they open their ranks to let him pass through in flight, after which they launch in pursuit and kill as many as possible.[6]

In the years after the election of Temuchin as universal ruler, the Mongols, now in possession of a new type of compound bow, which added both power and distance, defeated tribal groups to their west and then turned their attention to the seminomadic non-Chinese kingdoms in northern China. There they discovered that their adversaries were armed with a weapon called a fire-lance, an early form of flamethrower. Gunpowder had been invented in China during the late Tang period, and by the early thirteenth century, a type of fire-lance had been developed that could spew out a combination of flame and projectiles that could travel 30 or 40 yards and inflict considerable damage on the enemy. By the end of the thirteenth century, the fire-lance had evolved into the much more effective handgun and cannon. These inventions came too late to save China from the Mongols, however, and were transmitted to Europe by the early fourteenth century by foreigners employed by the Mongol rulers of China.

While some Mongol armies were engaged in the conquest of northern China, others traveled farther afield and advanced as far as central Europe (see the box on p. 212). Only the death of the Great Khan may have prevented

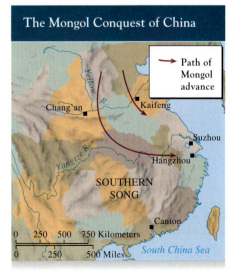

The Mongol Conquest of China

Path of Mongol advance

Chang'an
Kaifeng
Suzhou
Hangzhou
SOUTHERN SONG
Canton

0   250   500   750 Kilometers
0   250   500 Miles

South China Sea

A LETTER TO THE POPE

In 1243, Pope Innocent IV dispatched the Franciscan friar John Plano Carpini to the Mongol headquarters at Karakorum to appeal to the Great Khan to cease his attacks on Christians. After a considerable wait, Carpini was given the following reply, which could not have pleased the pope. The letter was discovered in the Vatican archives.

A LETTER FROM KUYUK KHAN TO POPE INNOCENT IV

By the power of the Eternal Heaven, We are the all-embracing Khan of all the Great Nations. It is our command:

This is a decree, sent to the great Pope that he may know and pay heed.

After holding counsel with the monarchs under your suzerainty, you have sent us an offer of subordination, which we have accepted from the hands of your envoy.

If you should act up to your word, then you, the great Pope, should come in person with the monarchs to pay us homage and we should thereupon instruct you concerning the commands of the Yasak.

Furthermore, you have said it would be well for us to become Christians. You write to me in person about this matter, and have addressed to me a request. This, your request, we cannot understand.

Furthermore, you have written me these words: "You have attacked all the territories of the Magyars and other Christians, at which I am astonished. Tell me, what was

their crime?" These, your words, we likewise cannot understand. Jenghiz Khan and Ogatai Khakan revealed the commands of Heaven. But those whom you name would not believe the commands of Heaven. Those of whom you speak showed themselves highly presumptuous and slew our envoys. Therefore, in accordance with the commands of the Eternal Heaven the inhabitants of the aforesaid countries have been slain and annihilated. If not by the command of Heaven, how can anyone slay or conquer out of his own strength?

And when you say: "I am a Christian. I pray to God. I arraign and despise others," how do you know who is pleasing to God and to whom He allots His grace? How can you know it, that you speak such words?

Thanks to the power of the Eternal Heaven, all lands have been given to us from sunrise to sunset. How could anyone act other than in accordance with the commands of Heaven? Now your own upright heart must tell you: "We will become subject to you, and will place our powers at your disposal." You in person, at the head of the monarchs, all of you, without exception, must come to tender us service and pay us homage, then only will we recognize your submission. But if you do not obey the commands of Heaven, and run counter to our orders, we shall know that you are our foe.

That is what we have to tell you. If you fail to act in accordance therewith, how can we foresee what will happen to you? Heaven alone knows.

---

an all-out Mongol attack on western Europe. In 1231, the Mongols attacked Persia and then defeated the Abbasids at Baghdad in 1258 (see Chapter 7). Mongol forces attacked the Song from the west in the 1260s and finally defeated the remnants of the Song navy in 1279.

By then, the Mongol Empire was quite different from what it had been under its founder. Prior to the conquests of Genghis Khan, the Mongols had been purely nomadic. They lived in round tents covered with felt (called yurts) that were easily transported. For food, the Mongols depended on milk and meat from their herds and game from hunting.

To administer the new empire, Genghis Khan set up a capital city at Karakorum, in present-day Outer Mongolia, but prohibited his fellow Mongols from practicing sedentary occupations or living in cities. But under his successors, Mongol aristocrats began to enter administrative positions, and commoners took up sedentary occupations as farmers or merchants. As one khan remarked, quoting his Chinese adviser, "Although you inherited the Chinese Empire on horseback, you cannot rule it from that position."[7]

The territorial nature of the empire also changed. Following tribal custom, at the death of the ruling khan, the

territory was distributed among his heirs. Genghis Khan's empire was thus divided into several separate khanates, each under the autonomous rule of one of his sons by his principal wife (see Map 10.2). One of his sons was awarded the khanate of Chaghadai in Central Asia with its capital at Samarkand; another ruled Persia from the conquered city of Baghdad; a third took charge of the khanate of Kipchak (commonly known as the Golden Horde). But it was one of his grandsons, named Khubilai Khan (who ruled from 1260 to 1294), who completed the conquest of the Song and established a new Chinese dynasty, called the Yuan. Khubilai moved the capital of China northward to Khanbaliq ("city of the khan"), which was located on a major trunk route from the Great Wall to the plains of northern China. Later the city would be known by the Chinese name Beijing, or Peking ("northern capital").

Mongol Rule in China

At first, China's new rulers exhibited impressive vitality. Mongol rulers adapted to the Chinese political system and made use of local talents in the bureaucracy, although the

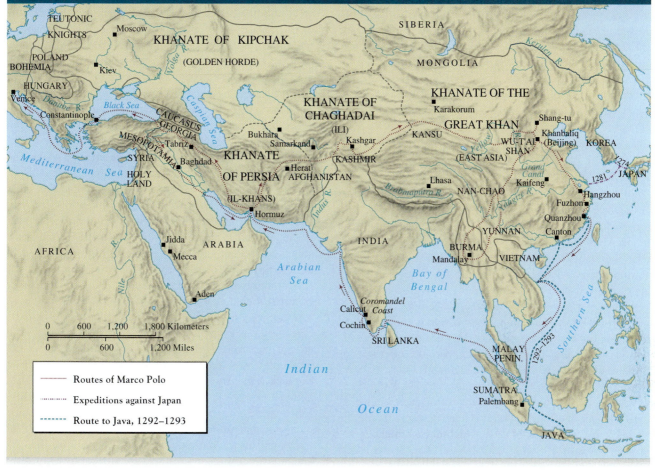

MAP 10.2 Asia Under the Mongols. This map shows the expansion of Mongol power throughout Eurasia in the thirteenth century. After the death of Genghis Khan, the empire was divided into four separate khanates. ➤ *In what modern-day countries were the four khanates located?*

Routes of Marco Polo

Expeditions against Japan

Route to Java, 1292–1293

highest positions were usually reserved for Mongols. The tripartite division of the administration into civilian, military, and censorate was retained, as were the six ministries. Eventually even the civil service system was revived, as was the state cult of Confucius, although Khubilai Khan himself was a Buddhist. Some leading Mongols followed their ruler in converting to Buddhism, but most commoners retained their traditional religion. In general, the Mongols remained apart as a separate class with their own laws.

The Mongols' greatest achievement may have been the prosperity they fostered. They continued the relatively tolerant economic policies of the southern Song, and by bringing the entire Eurasian landmass under a single rule, they encouraged long-distance trade, particularly along the Silk

Khanbaliq (Beijing) Under the Mongols

MONGOL CITY

Imperial City

NATIVE CITY

Built 1267–1271

Road, now dominated by Muslim merchants from Central Asia. To promote trade, the Grand Canal was extended from the Yellow River to the capital. Adjacent to the canal, a paved highway was constructed that extended all the way from the Song capital of Hangzhou to its Mongol counterpart at Khanbaliq. According to the Italian merchant Marco Polo, who resided there during the reign of Khubilai Khan (see the box on p. 214), the new capital was a magnificent city 24 miles in diameter where "so many pleasures may be found that one fancies himself to be in Paradise." The urban area was surrounded by thick walls of earth penetrated by twelve massive gates.

But the Yuan eventually fell victim to the same fate that had afflicted other powerful dynasties in China. Excessive spending on foreign

KHANBALIQ, CAPITAL OF KHUBILAI KHAN

When the Italian merchant and adventurer Marco Polo returned from China to Europe in the late thirteenth century, he wrote a lengthy description of his experiences, later to be popularized in book form as The Travels of Marco Polo. Here he describes the Chinese capital city of Khanbaliq, which he called Cambaluc and would later be known as Peking or Beijing, as it existed during the height of the Mongol dynasty. Although the magnificent gates and palaces that he saw no longer exist today, the layout of modern Beijing is much as it is presented here, with wide streets built at right angles and ending at massive gates that once offered an entryway through the wall that surrounded the imperial city.

THE TRAVELS OF MARCO POLO

Now there was on that spot in old times a great and noble city called Cambaluc, which is as much as to say in our tongue "The city of the emperor." But the great Khan was informed by his astrologers that this city would prove rebellious, and raise great disorders against his imperial authority. So he caused the present city to be built close beside the old one, with only a river between them. And he caused the people of the old city to be removed to the new town that he had founded; and this is called Taidu. However, he allowed a portion of the people which he did not suspect to remain in the old city, because the new one could not hold the whole of them, big as it is.

As regards the size of this new city you must know that it has a compass of twenty-four miles, for each side of it hath a length of six miles, and it is four square. And it is all walled round with walls of earth which have a thickness of full ten paces at bottom, and a height of more than ten paces; but they are not so thick at top, for they diminish in thickness as they rise, so that at top they are only about three paces thick. And they are provided throughout with loop-holed battlements, which are all whitewashed.

There are twelve gates, and over each gate there is a great and handsome palace, so that there are on each side of the square three gates and five palaces; for I ought to mention there is at each angle also a great and handsome palace. In those palaces are vast halls in which are kept the arms of the city garrison.

The streets are so straight and wide that you can see right along them from end to end and from one gate to the other. And up and down the city there are beautiful palaces, and many great and fine hostelries, and fine houses in great numbers. All the plots of ground on which the houses of the city are built are four square, and laid out with straight lines; all the plots being occupied by great and spacious palaces, with courts and gardens of proportionate size. All these plots were assigned to different heads of families. Each square plot is encompassed by handsome streets for traffic; and thus the whole city is arranged in squares just like a chessboard, and disposed in a manner so perfect and masterly that it is impossible to give a description that should do it justice.

Moreover, in the middle of the city there is a great clock—that is to say, a bell—which is struck at night. And after it has struck three times no one must go out in the city, unless it be for the needs of a woman in labor, or of the sick. And those who go about on such errands are bound to carry lanterns with them. Moreover, the established guard at each gate of the city is one thousand armed men; not that you are to imagine this guard is kept up for fear of any attack, but only as a guard of honor for the sovereign, who resides there, and to prevent thieves from doing mischief in the town.

---

campaigns, inadequate tax revenues, factionalism and corruption at court and in the bureaucracy, and growing internal instability all contributed to the dynasty's demise. Khubilai Khan's successors lacked his administrative genius, and by the middle of the fourteenth century, the Yuan dynasty in China, like the Mongol khanates elsewhere in Central Asia, had fallen into a rapid decline.

The immediate instrument of Mongol defeat was Zhu Yuanzhang (Chu Yuan-chang), the son of a poor peasant in the lower Yangtze valley. After losing most of his family in the famine of the 1340s, Zhu became an itinerant monk and then the leader of a band of bandits. In the 1360s, unrest spread throughout the country, and after defeating a number of rivals, Zhu Yuanzhang put an end to the disintegrating Yuan regime and declared the foundation of a new Ming ("bright") dynasty (which lasted from 1369 to 1644).

IN SEARCH OF THE WAY

By the time of the Sui dynasty, Buddhism and Daoism had emerged as major rivals of Confucianism as the ruling ideology of the state. But during the last half of the Tang dynasty, Confucianism revived and once again became dominant at court, a position it would retain to the end of the dynastic period in the early twentieth century. Buddhist and Daoist beliefs, however, remained popular at the local level.

The Rise and Decline of Buddhism and Daoism

As noted earlier, Buddhism arrived in China with merchants from India and found its first adherents among the merchant community and intellectuals intrigued by

the new ideas. During the chaotic centuries following the collapse of the Han dynasty, Buddhism and Daoism appealed to those who were searching for more emotional and spiritual satisfaction than Confucianism could provide. Both faiths reached beyond the common people and found support among the ruling classes as well.

As Buddhism attracted more followers, it began to take on Chinese characteristics and divided into a number of separate sects. Some, like the *Chan* (*Zen* in Japanese) sect, called for mind training and a strict regimen as a means of seeking enlightenment. Others, like the Pure Land sect, stressed the role of devotion, an approach that was more appealing to ordinary Chinese, who lacked the time and inclination for strict monastic discipline. Still others were mystical sects, like Tantrism, which emphasized the importance of magical symbols and ritual in seeking a preferred way to enlightenment. Some Buddhist groups, like their Daoist counterparts, had political objectives. The White Lotus sect, founded in 1133, often adopted the form of a rebel movement, seeking political reform or the overthrow of a dynasty and forecasting a new era when a "savior Buddha" would come to earth to herald the advent of a new age. Most believers, however, assimilated Buddhism into their daily lives, where it joined Confucian ideology and spirit worship as an element in the highly eclectic and tolerant Chinese worldview.

The burgeoning popularity of Buddhism continued into the early years of the Tang dynasty. Early Tang rulers lent their support to the Buddhist monasteries that had been established throughout the country. But ultimately, Buddhism and Daoism lost favor at court and were increasingly subjected to official persecution. Envious Daoists and Confucianists made a point of criticizing the foreign origins of Buddhist doctrines, which one prominent Confucian scholar characterized as nothing but "silly relics." But another reason for this change of heart may have been financial. The great Buddhist monasteries had accumulated thousands of acres of land and serfs that were exempt from paying taxes to the state. Such wealth contributed to the corruption of the monks and other Buddhist officials and in turn aroused popular resentment and official disapproval. As the state attempted to eliminate the great landholdings of the aristocracy, the large monasteries also attracted its attention. During the later Tang, countless temples and monasteries were destroyed, and over 100,000 monks were compelled to leave the monasteries and return to secular life.

Yet there were probably deeper political and ideological reasons for the growing antagonism between Buddhism and the state. By preaching the illusory nature of the material world, Buddhism was denying the very essence of Confucian teachings—the necessity for filial piety and hard work. By encouraging young Chinese to abandon their rice fields and seek refuge and wisdom in the monasteries, Buddhism was undermining the foundation stones of Chinese society—the family unit and the work ethic. In the last analysis, Buddhism was incompatible with the activist element in Chinese society, an orientation that was most effectively expressed by State Confucianism. In the competition with Confucianism for support by the state, Buddhism, like Daoism, was almost certain to lose.

Neo-Confucianism: The Investigation of Things

Into the vacuum left by the decline of Buddhism and Daoism stepped a revived Confucianism. Challenged by Buddhist and Daoist ideas about the nature of the universe, Confucian thinkers began to flesh out the spare metaphysical structure of classical Confucian doctrine with a set of sophisticated theories about the nature of the cosmos and humans' place in it.

The fundamental purpose of neo-Confucianism, as the new doctrine was called, was to unite the metaphysical speculations of Buddhism and Daoism with the pragmatic Confucian approach to society. In response to Buddhism and Daoism, neo-Confucianism maintained that the world is real, not illusory, and that fulfillment comes from participation, not withdrawal.

The primary contributor to this intellectual effort was the philosopher Zhu Xi (Chu Hsi). Raised during the southern Song era, Zhu Xi accepted the division of the world into a material world and a transcendent world (called by neo-Confucianists the Supreme Ultimate, or *Tai Ji*). The latter was roughly equivalent to the *Dao*, or Way, in classical Confucian philosophy. To Zhu Xi, this Supreme Ultimate was a set of abstract principles governed by the law of *yin* and *yang* and the five elements.

Courtesy of William J. Duiker

LONGMEN CAVES BUDDHIST SCULPTURE. The Silk Road, which stretched through Central Asia from the Middle East to China, was an avenue for ideas as well as trade. Over the centuries, Christian, Buddhist, and Muslim teachings came to China across the sandy wastes of the Taklimakan Basin. In the seventh century, the Tang emperor Gaozong commissioned this massive temple carving as part of the large complex of cave art devoted to Buddha at Longmen in central China. Bold and grandiose in their construction, these statues reflect the glory that was the Tang dynasty.

Human beings served as a link between the two halves of this bifurcated universe. Although human beings live in the material world, each individual has an identity that is linked with the Supreme Ultimate, and the goal of individual action is to transcend the material world in a Buddhist sense to achieve an essential identity with the Supreme Ultimate. According to Zhu Xi and his followers, the means of transcending the material world is self-cultivation, which is achieved by the "investigation of things." During the remainder of the Song dynasty and into the early years of the Ming, Zhu Xi's ideas became the central core of Confucian ideology and a favorite source of questions for the civil service examinations.

Neo-Confucianism remained the state doctrine until the end of the dynastic system in the twentieth century. Some historians have asked whether the doctrine can help to explain why China failed to experience scientific and industrial revolutions of the sort that occurred in the West. In particular, it has been suggested that neo-Confucianism tended to encourage an emphasis on the elucidation of moral principles rather than the expansion of scientific knowledge. Though the Chinese excelled in practical technology, inventing gunpowder, the compass (first used by seafarers during the Song dynasty), printing and paper, and cast iron, among other things, they had less interest in scientific theory. Their relative backwardness in mathematics is a good example. Chinese scholars had no knowledge of the principles of geometry and lagged behind other advanced civilizations in astronomy, physics, and optics. Until the Mongol era, they had no knowledge of Arabic numerals and lacked the concept of zero. Even after that time, they continued to use a cumbersome numbering system based on Chinese characters.

Furthermore, intellectual affairs in China continued to be dominated by the scholar-gentry, the chief upholders of neo-Confucianism, who not only had little interest in the natural sciences or economic change but also viewed them as a threat to their own dominant status in Chinese society. The commercial middle class, who lacked social status and an independent position in society, had little say in intellectual matters. In contrast, in the West, an urban middle class emerged that was a source not only of wealth but also of social prestige, political power, and intellectual ideas. The impetus for the intellectual revolution in the West came from the members of the commercial bourgeoisie, who were interested in the conquest of nature and the development of technology. In China, however, the scholar-gentry continued to focus on the sources of human behavior and a correct understanding of the relationship between humankind and the universe. The result was an intellectual environment that valued continuity over change and tradition over innovation.

THE APOGEE OF CHINESE CULTURE

The period between the Tang and the Ming dynasties was in many ways the great age of achievement in Chinese literature and art. Enriched by Buddhist and Daoist images and themes, Chinese poetry and painting reached the pinnacle of their creativity. Porcelain emerged as the highest form of Chinese ceramics, and sculpture flourished under the influence of styles imported from India and Central Asia.

TWO TANG POETS

Li Bo was one of the great poets of the Tang dynasty. The first selection is probably the best-known poem in China and has been memorized by schoolchildren for centuries. The second poem, titled "Drinking Alone in Moonlight," reflects the poet's carefree attitude toward life.

Du Fu, Li Bo's prime competitor as the greatest poet of the Tang dynasty, was often the more reflective of the two. In the final piece here, the poet has returned to his home in the capital after a rebellion against the dynasty has left the city in ruins.

LI BO, "QUIET NIGHT THOUGHTS"

Beside my bed the bright moonbeams bound
Almost as if there were frost on the ground.
Raising up, I gaze at the Mountain moon;
Lying back, I think of my old hometown.

LI BO, "DRINKING ALONE IN MOONLIGHT"

Among the flowers, with a jug of wine,
I drink all alone—no one to share.
Raising my cup, I welcome the moon.
And my shadow joins us, making a threesome.

Alas! the moon won't take part in the drinking,
And my shadow just does whatever I do.
But I'm friends for a while with the moon and my shadow,
And we caper in revels well suited to spring.
As I sing the moon seems to sway back and forth;
As I dance my shadow goes flopping about.
As long as I'm sober we'll enjoy one another,
And when I get drunk, we'll go our own ways:
Forever committed to carefree play,
We'll all meet again in the Milky Way!

DU FU, "SPRING PROSPECT"

The capital is taken. The hills and streams are left,
And with spring in the city the grass and trees grown dense.
Mourning the times, the flowers trickle their tears;
Saddened with parting, the birds make my heart flutter.
The army beacons have flamed for three months;
A letter from home would be worth ten thousand in gold.
My white hairs I have anxiously scratched ever shorter;
But such disarray! Even hairpins will do no good!

Literature

The development of Chinese literature was stimulated by two technological innovations: the invention of paper during the Han dynasty and the invention of woodblock printing during the Tang. At first, paper was used for clothing, wrapping material, toilet tissue, and even armor, but by the first century B.C.E., it was being used for writing as well.

In the seventh century C.E., the Chinese developed the technique of carving an entire page of text into a wooden block, inking it, and then pressing it onto a sheet of paper. Ordinarily a text was printed on a long sheet of paper like a scroll. Then the paper was folded and stitched together to form a book. The earliest printed book known today is a Buddhist text published in 868 C.E.; it is more than 16 feet long. Although the Chinese eventually developed movable type as well, block printing continued to be used until relatively modern times because of the large number of Chinese characters needed to produce a lengthy text. Even with printing, books remained too expensive for most Chinese, but they did help popularize all forms of literary writing among the educated elite.

During the post-Han era, historical writing and essays continued to be favorite forms of literary activity. Each dynasty produced an official dynastic history of its predecessor to elucidate sober maxims about the qualities of good and evil in human nature, and local gazetteers added to the general knowledge about the various regions.

But it was in poetry, above all, that Chinese of the Tang to the Ming dynasties most effectively expressed their literary talents. Chinese poems celebrated the beauty of nature, the changes of the seasons, the joys of friendship and drink, and sadness at the brevity of life, old age, and parting. Love poems existed but were neither as intense as Western verse nor as sensual as Indian poetry.

The nature of the Chinese language imposed certain characteristics on Chinese poetry, the first being compactness. The most popular forms were four-line and eight-line poems, with five or seven words in each line. Because Chinese grammar does not rely on case or gender and makes no distinction between verb tenses, five-character Chinese poems were not only brief but often cryptic and ambiguous.

Two Tang poets, Li Bo (Li Po, sometimes known as Li Bai or Li Taibo) and Du Fu (Tu Fu), symbolized the genius of the era as well as the two most popular styles. Li Bo was a free spirit. His writing often centered on nature and shifted easily between moods of revelry and melancholy. One of his best-known poems is "Drinking Alone in Moonlight" (see the box above).

Whereas Li Bo was a carefree Daoist, Du Fu was a sober Confucian. His poems often dealt with historical issues or ethical themes, befitting a scholar-official living during the chaotic times of the late Tang era. Many of his works reflect a concern with social injustice and the plight of the unfortunate rarely to be found in the writings of his contemporaries (see the box on p. 217). Neither the poetry nor the prose of the great writers of the Tang and Song dynasties was written for or ever reached the majority of the Chinese population.

By the Song dynasty, China had sixty million people, one million in Hangzhou alone. With the growth of cities came an increased demand for popular entertainment. Although the Tang dynasty had imposed a curfew on urban residents, the Song did not. The city gates and bridges were closed at dark, but food stalls and entertainment continued through the night. At fairgrounds throughout the year, one could find comedians, musicians, boxers, fencers, wrestlers, acrobats, puppets and marionettes, shadow plays, and especially storytellers.

During the Yuan dynasty, new forms of literary creativity, including popular theater and the novel, began to appear. One of the most famous novels was *Tale of the Marshes*, an often violent tale of bandit heroes who at the end of the northern Song banded together to oppose government taxes and official oppression. They rob from those in power to share with the poor. *Tale of the Marshes* is the first prose fiction that describes the daily ordeal of ordinary Chinese people in their own language. Unlike the picaresque novel in the West, *Tale of the Marshes* does not limit itself to the exploits of one hero, offering instead 108 different story lines. This multitude of plots is a natural outgrowth of the tradition of the professional storyteller, who attempts to keep the audience's attention by recounting as many adventures as the market will bear.

Art

Although painting flourished in China under the Han and reached a level of artistic excellence under the Tang, little remains from those periods. The painting of the Song and the Yuan, however, is considered the apogee of painting in traditional China.

Like literature, Chinese painting found part of its inspiration in Buddhist and Daoist sources. Some of the best surviving examples of the Tang period are the Buddhist wall paintings in the caves at Dunhuang, in Central Asia (see p. 183 in Chapter 9). Like the few surviving Tang scroll paintings, these wall paintings display a love of color and refinement that are reminiscent of styles in India and Iran.

Daoism ultimately had a greater influence than Buddhism on Chinese painting. From early times, Chinese artists removed themselves to the mountains to write and paint and find the *Dao*, or Way, in nature. In the fifth century, one Chinese painter, who was too old to travel, began to paint mountain scenes from memory and announced that depicting nature could function as a substitute for contemplating nature itself. Painting, he said, could be the means of realizing the *Dao*. This explains in part the emphasis on nature in traditional Chinese painting. The word *landscape* in Chinese means "mountain-water," and the Daoist search for balance between earth and water, hard and soft, *yang* and *yin*, is at play in the tradition of Chinese painting.

To represent the totality of nature, Chinese artists attempted to reveal the quintessential forms of the land-

LADIES PREPARING SILK. Although the Tang dynasty was a very prolific period in the development of Chinese painting, very few examples survive to the present day. Fortunately, copying the works of previous masters was a common tradition in China. Here we see a twelfth-century copy of a Tang painting showing ladies preparing newly woven silk. Two women are stretching a bolt of silk while a third irons the cloth with a pan containing burning coals. Silk was a highly prized luxury item in elite circles throughout the imperial period in China.

to portray human beings as insignificant in the midst of nature. In contrast to the focus on the human body and personality in Western art, Chinese art presented people as tiny figures fishing in a small boat, meditating on a cliff, or wandering up a hillside trail, coexisting with but not dominating nature.

The Chinese displayed their paintings on long scrolls of silk or paper that were attached to a wooden cylindrical bar at the bottom. Varying in length from 3 to 20 feet, the paintings were unfolded slowly so that the eye could enjoy each segment, one after the other, beginning at the bottom with water or a village and moving upward into the hills to the mountain peaks and the sky.

By the tenth century, Chinese painters began to eliminate color from their paintings, preferring the challenge of capturing the distilled essence of the landscape in washes of black ink on white silk. Borrowing from calligraphy, now a sophisticated and revered art, they emphasized the brush stroke and created black-and-white landscapes characterized by a gravity of mood and dominated by overpowering mountains.

Second only to painting in creativity was the field of ceramics, notably, the manufacture of porcelain. Made of fine clay baked at unusually high temperatures in a kiln, porcelain was first produced during the period after the fall of the Han and became popular during the Tang era. During the Song, porcelain came into its own. The translucent character of Chinese porcelain represented the final product of a technique that did not reach Europe until the eighteenth century.

National Palace Museum, Taipei, Taiwan, Republic of China

❧ A MOUNTAIN SCENE. As a means of reproducing the totality of nature, Chinese artists often attempted to visualize physical reality. In this famous eleventh-century painting by Fan K'uan, the mountain seems to take on an existence all its own, independent of the interpretation of the artist. Daoist influence is evident here in that human beings play an insignificant role in the grand scheme of nature. Two tiny figures driving mules, a bridge, and a half-hidden temple are eclipsed by the mountain.

scape. Rather than depicting the actual realistic shape of a specific mountain, they tried to portray the idea of "mountain." Empty spaces were left in the paintings because in the Daoist vision, one cannot know the whole truth. Daoist influence was also evident in the tendency

CONCLUSION

Traditionally Chinese historians believed that Chinese history tended to be cyclical. The pattern of history was marked by the rise and fall of great dynasties, interspersed with periods of internal division and foreign invasion. Underlying the waxing and waning of dynasties was the essential continuity of Chinese civilization.

This view of the dynamic forces of Chinese history was long accepted as valid by historians in China and in the West and led many to assert that Chinese history was unique and could not be placed in a European or universal framework. Whereas Western history was linear, leading steadily away from the past, China's always returned to its moorings and was rooted in the values and institutions of antiquity.

In recent years, however, this traditional view of a changeless China has come under increasing challenge from historians who see patterns of change that made the China of 1400 a very different place from the country that had existed at the rise of the Tang dynasty in 600. To these scholars, China had passed through its own version of the "middle ages" and was on the verge of beginning a linear evolution into a posttraditional society.

As we have seen, China at the beginning of the Ming had advanced in many ways since the end of the great Han dynasty over a thousand years earlier. The industrial and commercial sector had grown considerably in size, complexity, and technological capacity, while in the countryside, the concentration of political and economic power in the hands of the aristocracy had been replaced by a more stable and equitable mixture of landed gentry, freehold farmers, and sharecroppers. In addition, Chinese society had achieved a level of stability and social tranquillity that was the envy of observers from other lands near and far. The civil service provided an avenue of upward mobility that was unavailable elsewhere in the world, and the state tolerated a diversity of beliefs that responded to the emotional needs and preferences of the Chinese people. In many respects, China's achievements were unsurpassed throughout the world and marked a major advance beyond the world of antiquity.

Yet there were also some key similarities between the China of the Ming and the China of late antiquity. Ming China was still a predominantly agrarian society, with wealth based primarily on the ownership of land. Commercial activities flourished but remained under a high level of government regulation and by no means represented a major proportion of the national income. China also remained a relatively centralized empire based on an official ideology that stressed the virtue of hard work, social conformity, and hierarchy.

Thus the significant change that China experienced during its medieval era can probably be best described as change within continuity, an evolutionary working out of trends that had first become visible during the Han dynasty or even earlier. The result was a civilization that was the envy of its neighbors and of the world. It also influenced other states in the region, including Japan, Korea, and Vietnam. It is to these societies along the Chinese rimlands that we now turn.

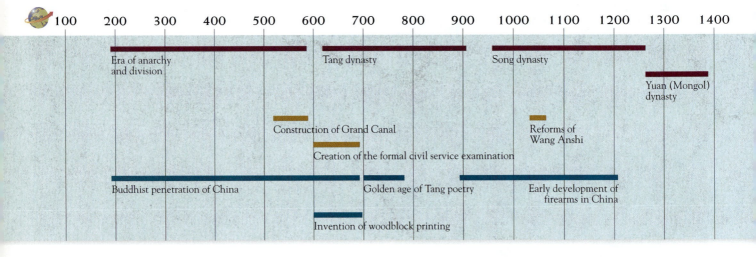

CHAPTER NOTES

1. *The Travels of Marco Polo* (New York, n.d.), p. 119.
2. Quoted in Arthur F. Wright, *Buddhism in Chinese History* (Stanford, Calif., 1959), p. 30.
3. Chu-yu, *P'ing-chow Table Talks*, quoted in Robert Temple, *The Genius of China: 3,000 Years of Science, Discovery, and Invention* (New York, 1986), p. 150.
4. Quoted in Edward H. Schafer, *The Golden Peaches of Samarkand: A Study of T'ang Exotics* (Berkeley, Calif., 1963), p. 43.
5. Quoted in John K. Fairbank, Edwin O. Reischauer, and Albert M. Craig, *East Asia: Tradition and Transformation* (Boston, 1973), p. 164.
6. Quoted in Rene Grousset, *L'Empire des Steppes* (Paris, 1939), p. 285.
7. A. M. Khazanov, *Nomads and the Outside World* (Cambridge, 1983), p. 241.

SUGGESTED READING

For an authoritative overview of the early imperial era in China, see M. Elvin, *The Pattern of the Chinese Past* (Stanford, Calif., 1973). A global perspective is presented in S. A. M. Adshead, *China in World History* (New York, 1988).

A vast body of material is available on almost all periods of early Chinese history. For the post-Han period, see A. E. Dien, ed., *State and Society in Early Medieval China* (Stanford, Calif., 1990), and D. Twitchett and M. Loewe, *Cambridge History of China*, vol. 3, *Medieval China* (Cambridge, 1986).

For a readable treatment of the brief but tempestuous Sui dynasty, see A. F. Wright, *The Sui Dynasty* (New York, 1978). For an interpretation of the Song dynasty, see J. T. C. Liu, *China Turning Inward: Intellectual Changes in the Early Twelfth Century* (Cambridge, Mass., 1988). Song problems with the northern frontier are chronicled in Tao Jing-shen, *Two Sons of Heaven: Studies in Sung-Liao Relations* (Tucson, Ariz., 1988).

There are a number of good studies on the Mongol period in Chinese history. See, for example, W. A. Langlois, *China Under Mongol Rule* (Princeton, N.J., 1981), and J. W. Dardess, *Conquerors and Confucians: Aspects of Political Change in Late Yuan China* (New York, 1973). M. Rossabi, *Khubilai Khan: His Life and Times* (Berkeley, Calif., 1988), is a biography of the dynasty's greatest emperor, while M. Rossabi, ed., *China Among Equals: The Middle Kingdom and Its Neighbors* (Berkeley, Calif., 1983), deals with foreign affairs. For a provocative interpretation of Chinese relations with nomadic peoples, see T. J. Barfield, *The Perilous Frontier: Nomadic Empires and China* (Cambridge, 1989). An analytic account of the dynamics of nomadic society is A. M. Khazanov, *Nomads and the Outside World* (Cambridge, 1983).

The emergence of urban culture during this era is analyzed in C. K. Heng, *Cities of Aristocrats and Bureaucrats: The Development of Medieval Chinese Cityscapes* (Honolulu, 1999).

For an introduction to women's issues during this period, consult P. B. Ebrey, *The Inner Quarters: Marriage and the Lives of Chinese Women in the Sung Period* (Berkeley, Calif., 1993); *Chu Hsi's Family Rituals* (Princeton, N.J., 1991); and "Women, Marriage, and the Family in Chinese History," in P. S. Ropp, *Heritage of China: Contemporary Perspectives on Chinese Civilization* (Berkeley, Calif., 1990). For an overview of Chinese foot binding, see C. F. Blake, "Foot-Binding in Neo-Confucian China and the Appropriation of Female Labor," *Signs* 19 (Spring, 1994).

On Central Asia, two popular accounts are J. Myrdal, *The Silk Road* (New York, 1979), and N. Marty, *The Silk Road* (Methuen, Mass., 1987). A more interpretive approach is found in S. A. M. Adshead, *Central Asia in World History* (New York, 1993). See also E. T. Grotenhuis, ed., *Along the Silk Road* (Washington, D.C., 2002).

The period from the fall of the Han to the early Ming was an important period in Chinese intellectual history. For developments in Confucianism, see Carsun Chang, *The Development of Neo-Confucian Thought*, 2 vols. (New Haven, Conn., 1963). For a more scholarly study, see W. T. de Bary, *Self and Society in Ming Thought* (New York, 1970). A classic survey of the role of Buddhism in Chinese society is A. F. Wright, *Buddhism in Chinese History* (Stanford, Calif., 1959).

The classic work on Chinese literature is Liu Wu-chi, *An Introduction to Chinese Literature* (Bloomington, Ind., 1966). Also consult the more recent and scholarly S. Owen, *An Anthology of Chinese Literature: Beginnings to 1911* (New York, 1996), and V. Mair, *The Columbia Anthology of Traditional Chinese Literature* (New York, 1994). For poetry, see Liu Wu-chi and I. Yucheng Lo, *Sunflower Splendor: Three Thousand Years of Chinese Poetry* (Bloomington, Ind., 1975), and S. Owen, *The Great Age of Chinese Poetry: The High T'ang* (New Haven, Conn., 1981), the latter presenting poems in both Chinese and English.

For a comprehensive introduction to Chinese art, see the classic M. Sullivan, *The Arts of China*, 4th ed. (Berkeley, Calif., 1999); M. Tregear, *Chinese Art*, rev. ed. (London, 1997); and C. Clunas, *Art in China* (Oxford, 1997). The standard introduction to Chinese painting can be found in J. Cahill, *Chinese Painting* (New York, 1985), and Yang Xin et al., *Three Thousand Years of Chinese Painting* (New Haven, Conn., 1997).

INFOTRAC COLLEGE EDITION

Visit the source collections at infotrac.thomsonlearning.com and use the Search function with the following key terms.

China and Buddhism
China history
Mongol
Tang dynasty or Song dynasty
Taoism or Daoism

WORLD HISTORY RESOURCES

Visit the *Essential World History* Companion Web Site for resources specific to this textbook:

http://history.wadsworth.com/duikeressentials02/

The CD in the back of this book and the World History Resource Center at http://history.wadsworth.com/world/ offer a variety of tools to help you succeed in this course, including access to quizzes; images; documents; interactive simulations, maps, and timelines; movie explorations; and a wealth of other sources.

© Kyoto National Museum, Kyoto, Japan with permission
from the Kozan-ji Temple, Kyoto

THE EAST ASIAN RIMLANDS: EARLY JAPAN, KOREA, AND VIETNAM

FOCUS QUESTIONS

- What centralizing and decentralizing forces were at work in Japan before 1500, and how did they influence the political and governmental structures that arose?
- What were the main characteristics of economic and social life in early Japan?
- What were the most important cultural achievements of early Japan, and how do they illustrate the Japanese ability to blend indigenous and imported elements?
- What were the main developments in Korean and Vietnamese history before 1500?
- ➤ How did Chinese civilization influence the civilizations that arose in Japan, Korea, and Vietnam?

These people, the exasperated official complained, are like birds and beasts. "They wear their hair tied up and go barefoot, while for clothing they simply cut a hole in a piece of cloth for their head or they fasten their garments on the left side [in barbarian style]." Their women are untrustworthy "and promiscuously wander about." In some areas, he said, "men and women go naked without shame" and are little better than bugs.[1]

The speaker was Xue Tong, a Chinese administrator stationed in northern Vietnam at the end of the Han dynasty. His comments vividly reflected the frustration of Chinese bureaucrats faced with what they regarded as the uncivilized behavior of the untutored peoples living along the frontiers of the Chinese Empire. To Xue Tong and other upright Confucian officials like him, it was hopeless to try to civilize such people.

Such comments should not surprise us. During ancient times, China was the most technologically advanced society in East Asia. To the north and west were nomadic pastoral peoples whose military exploits were often impressive but whose political and cultural attainments were still limited, at least by comparison with the great river valley civilizations of the day. In inland areas south of the Yangtze River were scattered clumps of rice farmers and hill peoples, most of whom had not yet entered the era of state building and certainly had little knowledge of the niceties of Confucian ethics.

But Xue Tong and officials like him were being a little too hasty in their judgments. Along the fringes of Chinese civilization were a number of other agricultural societies that were beginning to follow a pattern of development similar to that of China, although somewhat later in time. One of these was in the islands of Japan, where an organized agricultural society was beginning to take shape just about the time Xue Tong was complaining about the barbarian peoples in the south. These developments may have been hastened by events on the Korean peninsula, where an advanced Neolithic society had begun to develop a few centuries earlier. Even in the Red River valley, where Xue Tong viewed the local inhabitants with such disdain, a relatively advanced civilization had been in existence for several hundred years before the area was conquered by the Han dynasty in the second century B.C.E.

All of these early agricultural societies were eventually influenced to some degree by their great neighbor, China. Vietnam remained under Chinese rule for a thousand years. Korea retained its separate existence but was long a tributary state of China and in many ways followed the cultural example of its larger patron. Only Japan retained both its political independence and its cultural uniqueness. Yet even the Japanese were strongly influenced by the glittering culture of their powerful neighbor, and today many Japanese institutions and customs still bear the imprint of several centuries of borrowing from the "Middle Kingdom" (as China was called). In this chapter, we will take a closer look at these emerging societies along the Chinese rimlands and consider how their cultural achievements reflected or contrasted with those of the Chinese Empire. •

JAPAN: LAND OF THE RISING SUN

The geographical environment helps explain some of the historical differences between Chinese and Japanese society. Whereas China is a continental civilization, Japan is an island country. It consists of four main islands (see Map 11.1): Hokkaido in the north, the main island of Honshu in the center, and the two smaller islands of Kyushu and Shikoku in the southwest. Its total land area is about 146,000 square miles, about the size of the state of Montana. Japan's main islands are at approximately the same latitude as the eastern seaboard of the United States.

Like the eastern United States, Japan is blessed with a temperate climate. It is slightly warmer on the east coast, which is washed by the Pacific current that sweeps up from the south, and has a number of natural harbors that provide protection from the winds and high waves of the Pacific Ocean. As a consequence, in recent times, the majority of the Japanese people have tended to live along the east coast, especially in the flat plains surrounding the cities of Tokyo, Osaka, and Kyoto. In these favorable environmental conditions, Japanese farmers have been able to harvest two crops of rice annually since early times.

By no means, however, is Japan an agricultural paradise. Like China, much of the country is mountainous, with only about 20 percent of the total land area suitable for cultivation. These mountains are of volcanic origin, since the Japanese islands are located at the juncture of the Asian and Pacific tectonic plates. This location is both an advantage and a disadvantage. Volcanic soils are extremely fertile, which helps explain the exceptionally high productivity of Japanese farmers. At the same time, the area

MAP 11.1 Early Japan. This map shows key cities in Japan during the early development of the Japanese state. ➤ *What was the original heartland of Japanese civilization on the main island of Honshu?*

is prone to earthquakes, such as the famous earthquake of 1923, which destroyed almost the entire city of Tokyo.

The fact that Japan is an island country has had a significant impact on Japanese history. As we have seen, the continental character of Chinese civilization, with its constant threat of invasion from the north, had a number of consequences for Chinese history. One effect was to make the Chinese more sensitive to the preservation of their culture from destruction at the hands of non-Chinese invaders. Proud of their own considerable cultural achievements and their dominant position throughout the region, the Chinese have traditionally been reluctant to dilute the purity of their culture with foreign innovations. Culture more than race is a determinant of the Chinese sense of identity.

By contrast, the island character of Japan probably had the effect of strengthening the Japanese sense of ethnic and cultural distinctiveness. Although the Japanese view of themselves as the most ethnically homogeneous people in East Asia may not be entirely accurate (the modern Japanese probably represent a mix of peoples, much like their neighbors on the continent), their sense of racial and cultural homogeneity has enabled them to import ideas from abroad without worrying that the borrowings will destroy the uniqueness of their own culture.

A Gift from the Gods: Prehistoric Japan

According to an ancient legend recorded in historical chronicles written in the eighth century C.E., the islands of Japan were formed as a result of the marriage of the god Izanagi and the goddess Izanami. After giving birth to Japan, Izanami gave birth to a sun goddess whose name was Amaterasu. A descendant of Amaterasu later descended to earth and became the founder of the Japanese nation. This Japanese creation myth is reminiscent of similar beliefs in other ancient societies, which often saw themselves as the product of a union of deities. What is interesting about the Japanese version is that it has survived into modern times as an explanation for the uniqueness of the Japanese people and the divinity of the Japanese emperor, who is still believed by some Japanese to be a direct descendant of the sun goddess Amaterasu.

Modern scholars have a more prosaic explanation for the origins of Japanese civilization. According to archaeological evidence, the Japanese islands have been occupied by human beings for at least 100,000 years. The earliest known Neolithic inhabitants, known as the Jomon people from the cord pattern of their pottery, lived in the islands as much as 10,000 years ago. They lived by hunting, fishing, and food gathering and probably had not mastered the techniques of agriculture.

Agriculture probably first appeared in Japan sometime during the first millennium B.C.E., although some archaeologists believe that the Jomon people had already learned how to cultivate some food crops considerably earlier than that. About 400 B.C.E., rice cultivation was introduced, probably by immigrants from the mainland by way of the Korean peninsula. Until recently, historians believed that these immigrants drove out the existing inhabitants of the area and gave rise to the emerging Yayoi culture (named for the site near Tokyo where pottery from the period was found). It is now thought, however, that Yayoi culture was a product of a mixture between the Jomon people and the new arrivals, enriched by imports such as wet-rice agriculture, which had been brought by the immigrants from the mainland. In any event, it seems clear that the Yayoi peoples were the ancestors of the vast majority of present-day Japanese.

At first, the Yayoi lived primarily on the southern island of Kyushu, but eventually they moved northward onto the main island of Honshu, conquering, assimilating, or driving out the previous inhabitants of the area, some of whose descendants, known as the Ainu, still live in the northern islands. Finally, in the first centuries C.E., the Yayoi settled in the Yamato plain in the vicinity of the modern cities of Osaka and Kyoto. Japanese legend recounts the story of a "divine warrior" (in Japanese, *Jimmu*) who led his people eastward from the island of Kyushu to establish a kingdom in the Yamato plain.

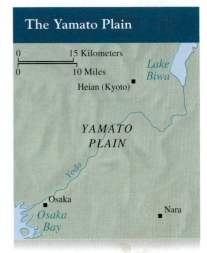

In central Honshu, the Yayoi set up a tribal society based on a number of clans, called *uji*. Each *uji* was ruled by a hereditary chieftain, who provided protection to the local population in return for a proportion of the annual harvest. The population itself was divided between a small aristocratic class and the majority of the population, composed of rice farmers, artisans, and other household servants of the aristocrats. Yayoi society was highly decentralized, although eventually the chieftain of the dominant clan in the Yamato region, who claimed to be descended from the sun goddess Amaterasu, achieved a kind of titular primacy. There is no evidence, however, of a central ruler equivalent in power to the Chinese rulers of the Shang and the Zhou eras.

The Rise of the Japanese State

Although the Japanese had been aware of China for centuries, they paid relatively little attention to their more advanced neighbor until the early seventh century, when the rise of the centralized and expansionistic Tang dynasty presented a challenge. The Tang began to meddle in the

THE SEVENTEEN-ARTICLE CONSTITUTION

The following excerpt from the Nihon Shoki (The Chronicles of Japan) is a passage from the seventeen-article constitution promulgated in 604 C.E. Although the opening section reflects Chinese influence in its emphasis on social harmony, there is also a strong focus on obedience and hierarchy. The constitution was put into practice during the reign of the famous Prince Shotoku.

THE CHRONICLES OF JAPAN

Summer, 4th month, 3rd day [12th year of Empress Suiko, 604 C.E.]. The Crown Prince personally drafted and promulgated a constitution consisting of seventeen articles, which are as follows:

I. Harmony is to be cherished, and opposition for opposition's sake must be avoided as a matter of principle. Men are often influenced by partisan feelings, except a few sagacious ones. Hence there are some who disobey their lords and fathers, or who dispute with their neighboring villages. If those above are harmonious and those below are cordial, their discussion will be guided by a spirit of conciliation, and reason shall naturally prevail. There will be nothing that cannot be accomplished.

II. With all our heart, revere the three treasures. The three treasures, consisting of Buddha, the Doctrine, and the Monastic Order, are the final refuge of the four generated beings, and are the supreme objects of worship in all countries. Can any man in any age ever fail to respect these teachings? Few men are utterly devoid of goodness, and men can be taught to follow the teachings. Unless they take refuge in the three treasures, there is no way of rectifying their misdeeds.

III. When an imperial command is given, obey it with reverence. The sovereign is likened to heaven, and his subjects are likened to earth. With heaven providing the cover and earth supporting it, the four seasons proceed in orderly fashion, giving sustenance to all that which is in nature. If earth attempts to overtake the functions of heaven, it destroys everything. . . . If there is no reverence shown to the imperial command, ruin will automatically result. . . .

VII. Every man must be given his clearly delineated responsibility. If a wise man is entrusted with office, the sound of praise arises. If a wicked man holds office, disturbances become frequent. . . . In all things, great or small, find the right man, and the country will be well governed. . . . In this manner, the state will be lasting and its sacerdotal functions will be free from danger.

---

affairs of the Korean peninsula, conquering the southwestern coast and arousing anxiety in Japan. Yamato rulers attempted to deal with the potential threat posed by the Chinese in two ways. First, they sought alliances with the remaining Korean states. Second, they attempted to centralize their authority so that they could mount a more effective resistance in the event of a Chinese invasion. The key figure in this effort was Shotoku Taishi (572–622), a leading aristocrat in one of the dominant clans in the Yamato region. Prince Shotoku sent missions to the Tang capital, Chang'an, to learn about the political institutions already in use in the relatively centralized Tang kingdom (see Map 11.2).

EMULATING THE CHINESE MODEL

Shotoku Taishi then launched a series of reforms to create a new system based roughly on the Chinese model. In the so-called seventeen-article constitution, he called for the creation of a centralized government under a supreme ruler and a merit system for selecting and ranking public officials (see the box above). His objective was to limit the powers of the hereditary nobility and enhance the prestige and authority of the Yamato ruler, who claimed divine status and was now emerging as the symbol of the unique character of the Japanese nation. In reality, there is evidence that places the origins of the Yamato clan on the Korean peninsula.

After Shotoku Taishi's death in 622, his successors continued to introduce reforms based on the Chinese model to make the government more efficient. In a series of so-called Taika ("great change") reforms that began in the mid-seventh century, the Grand Council of State was established, presiding over a cabinet of eight ministries. To the traditional six ministries of Tang China were added ministers representing the central secretariat and the imperial household. The territory of Japan was divided into administrative districts on the Chinese pattern. The rural village, composed ideally of fifty households, was the basic unit of government. The village chief was responsible for "the maintenance of the household registers, the assigning of the sowing of crops and the cultivation of mulberry trees, the prevention of offenses, and the requisitioning of taxes and forced labor." A law code was introduced, and a new tax system was established; now all farmland technically belonged to the state, so taxes were paid directly to the central government rather than through the local nobility, as had previously been the case.

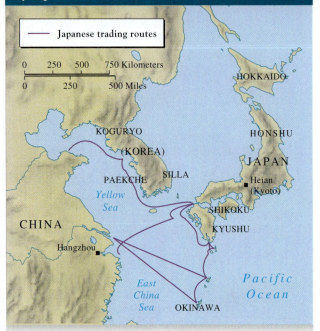

MAP 11.2 Japan's Relations with China and Korea. This map shows the Japanese islands at the time of the Yamato state. Maritime routes taken by Japanese traders and missionaries to China are indicated. ➤ **What are the four major islands of Japan?**

As a result of their new acquaintance with China, the Japanese also developed a strong interest in Buddhism. Some of the first Japanese to travel to China during this period were Buddhist pilgrims hoping to learn more about the exciting new doctrine and bring back scriptures. Buddhism became quite popular among the aristocrats, who endowed wealthy monasteries that became active in Japanese politics. At first, the new faith did not penetrate to the masses, but eventually, popular sects such as the Pure Land sect, an import from China, won many adherents among the common people.

THE NARA AND HEIAN PERIODS

Initial efforts to build a new state modeled roughly after the Tang state were successful. After Shotoku Taishi's death in 622, political influence fell into the hands of the powerful Fujiwara clan, which managed to marry into the ruling family and continue the reforms Shotoku had begun. In 710, a new capital, laid out on a grid similar to the great Tang city of Chang'an, was established at Nara, on the eastern edge of the Yamato plain. The Yamato ruler began to use the title "son of Heaven" in the Chinese fashion. In deference to the allegedly divine character of the ruling family, the mandate remained in perpetuity in the imperial house rather than being

bestowed on an individual who was selected by Heaven because of his talent and virtue, as was the case in China.

Had these reforms succeeded, Japan might have followed the Chinese pattern and developed a centralized bureaucratic government. But as time passed, the central government proved unable to curb the power of the aristocracy. Unlike in Tang China, the civil service examinations in Japan were not open to all but were restricted to individuals of noble birth. Leading officials were awarded large tracts of land, and they and other powerful families were able to keep the taxes from the lands for themselves. Increasingly starved for revenue, the central government steadily lost power and influence.

In 794, the emperor moved the capital to his family's original power base at nearby Heian, on the site of present-day Kyoto. The new capital was laid out in the now familiar Chang'an checkerboard pattern, but on a larger scale than at Nara. Now increasingly self-confident, the rulers ceased to emulate the Tang and sent no more missions to Chang'an. At Heian, the emperor—as the head of the royal line descended from the sun goddess was now officially styled—continued to rule in name, but actual power was in the hands of the Fujiwara clan, which had managed through intermarriage to link its fortunes closely with the imperial family. A senior member of the clan began to serve as regent (in practice, the chief executive of the government) for the emperor.

What was occurring was a return to the decentralization that had existed prior to Shotoku Taishi. The central government's attempts to impose taxes directly on the rice lands failed, and rural areas came under the control of powerful families whose wealth was based on the ownership of tax-exempt farmland (called *shoen*). To avoid paying taxes, peasants would often surrender their lands to a local aristocrat, who would then allow the peasants to cultivate the lands in return for the payment of rent. To obtain protection from government officials, these local aristocrats might in turn grant title of their lands to a more powerful aristocrat with influence at court. In return, these individuals would receive inheritable rights to a portion of the income from the estate.

With the decline of central power at Heian, local aristocrats tended to take justice into their own hands and increasingly used military force to protect their interests. A new class of military retainers called the samurai emerged whose purpose was to protect the security and property of their patron. They frequently drew their leaders from disappointed aristocratic office seekers, who thus began to occupy a prestigious position in local society, where they often served an administrative as well as a military function. The samurai lived a life of simplicity and self-sacrifice and were expected to maintain an intense and unquestioning loyalty to their lord. Bonds of loyalty were also quite strong among members of the samurai class, and homosexuality was common. Like the knights of medieval Europe, the samurai fought on horseback (although a samurai carried a sword and a bow and arrows rather than lance and shield) and were supposed to live by a strict warrior code, known in Japan as *Bushido*, or "way of the warrior" (see the box on p. 228). As time went on, they became a major force and almost a surrogate government in much of the Japanese countryside.

THE KAMAKURA SHOGUNATE AND AFTER

By the end of the twelfth century, as rivalries among noble families led to almost constant civil war, once again centralizing forces asserted themselves. This time the instrument was a powerful noble from a warrior clan named Minamoto Yoritomo (1142–1199), who defeated several rivals and set up his power base on the Kamakura peninsula, south of the modern city of Tokyo. To strengthen the state, he created a more centralized government (the *bakufu*, or "tent government") under a powerful military leader, known as the shogun (general). The shogun attempted to increase the powers of the central government while reducing rival aristocratic clans to vassal status. This "shogunate system," in which the emperor was the titular authority while the shogun exercised actual power, served as the political system in Japan until the second half of the nineteenth century.

The system worked effectively, and it was fortunate that it did, because during the next century, Japan faced the most serious challenge it had yet confronted. The Mongols, who had destroyed the Song dynasty in China, were now attempting to assert their hegemony throughout all of Asia (see Chapter 10). In 1266, Emperor Khubilai Khan demanded tribute from Japan. When the Japanese refused, he invaded with an army of over 30,000 troops. Bad weather and difficult conditions forced a retreat, but the Mongols tried again in 1281. An army nearly 150,000 strong landed on the northern coast of Kyushu. The Japanese were able to contain them for two months until virtually the entire Mongol fleet was destroyed by a massive typhoon—a "divine wind" (*kamikaze*). Japan would not face a foreign invader again until American forces landed on the Japanese islands in the summer of 1945.

The resistance to the Mongols had put a heavy strain on the system, however, and in 1333, the Kamakura shogunate was overthrown by a coalition of powerful clans. A new shogun, supplied by the Ashikaga family, arose in Kyoto and attempted to continue the shogunate system. But the Ashikaga were unable to restore the centralized power of their predecessors. With the central government reduced to a shell, the power of the local landed aristocracy increased to an unprecedented degree. Heads of great noble families, now called daimyo ("great names"), controlled vast landed estates that owed no taxes to the government or to the court in Kyoto. As clan rivalries continued, the daimyo relied increasingly on the samurai for protection, and political power came into the hands of a loose coalition of noble families.

➤ **SAMURAI.** During the Kamakura period, painters began to depict the adventures of the new warrior class. Here is an imposing mounted samurai warrior, the Japanese equivalent of the medieval knight in fief-holding Europe. Like his European counterpart, the samurai was supposed to live by a strict moral code and was expected to maintain an unquestioning loyalty to his liege lord. Above all, a samurai's life was one of simplicity and self-sacrifice.

JAPAN'S WARRIOR CLASS

The samurai was the Japanese equivalent of the medieval European knight. Like the knight, he was expected to adhere to a strict moral code. Although this passage comes from a document dating only to the seventeenth century, it shows the importance of hierarchy and duty in a society influenced by the doctrine of Confucius. Note the similarity with Krishna's discourse on the duties of an Indian warrior in Chapter 2.

THE WAY OF THE SAMURAI

The master once said: . . . Generation after generation men have taken their livelihood from tilling the soil, or devised and manufactured tools, or produced profit from mutual trade, so that peoples' needs were satisfied. Thus the occupations of farmer, artisan, and merchant necessarily grew up as complementary to one another. However, the samurai eats food without growing it, uses utensils without manufacturing them, and profits without buying or selling. . . . The samurai is one who does not cultivate, does not manufacture, and does not engage in trade, but it cannot be that he has no function at all as a samurai. . . .

If one deeply fixes his attention on what I have said and examines closely one's own function, it will become clear what the business of the samurai is. The business of the samurai consists in reflecting on his own station in life, in discharging loyal service to his master if he has one, in deepening his fidelity in associations with friends, and, with due consideration of his own position, in devoting himself to duty above all. . . . The samurai dispenses with the business of the farmer, artisan, and merchant and confines himself to practicing this Way; should there be someone in the three classes of the common people who transgresses against these moral principles, the samurai summarily punishes him and thus upholds proper moral principles in the land. . . . Outwardly he stands in physical readiness for any call to service, and inwardly he strives to fulfill the Way of the lord and subject, friend and friend, father and son, older and younger brother, and husband and wife. Within his heart he keeps to the ways of peace, but without he keeps his weapons ready for use. The three classes of the common people make him their teacher and respect him. By following his teachings, they are enabled to understand what is fundamental and what is secondary.

Herein lies the Way of the samurai, the means by which he earns his clothing, food, and shelter; and by which his heart is put at ease, and he is enabled to pay back at length his obligation to his lord and the kindness of his parents. Were there no such duty, it would be as though one were to steal the kindness of one's parents, greedily devour the income of one's master, and make one's whole life a career of robbery and brigandage. This would be very grievous.

By the end of the fifteenth century, Japan was again close to anarchy. A disastrous civil conflict known as the Onin War (1467–1477) led to the virtual destruction of the capital city of Kyoto and the disintegration of the shogunate. With the disappearance of any central authority, powerful aristocrats in rural areas now seized total control over large territories and ruled as independent great lords. Territorial rivalries and claims of precedence led to almost constant warfare in this period of "warring states," as it is called (in obvious parallel with a similar era during the Zhou dynasty in China). The trend back toward central authority did not begin until the last quarter of the sixteenth century.

Economic and Social Structures

From the time the Yayoi culture was first established on the Japanese islands, Japan was a predominantly agrarian society. Although Japan lacked the spacious valleys and deltas of the river valley societies, its inhabitants were able to take advantage of their limited amount of tillable land and plentiful rainfall to create a society based on the cultivation of wet rice.

As in China, commerce was slow to develop in Japan. During ancient times, each *uji* had a local artisan class, composed of weavers, carpenters, and ironworkers, but trade was essentially local and was regulated by the local clan leaders. With the rise of the Yamato state, a money economy gradually began to develop, although most trade was still conducted through barter until the twelfth century, when metal coins introduced from China became more popular.

Trade and manufacturing began to develop more rapidly during the Kamakura period, with the appearance of trimonthly markets in the larger towns and the emergence of such industries as paper, iron casting, and porcelain. Foreign trade, mainly with Korea and China, began during the eleventh century. Japan exported raw materials, paintings, swords, and other manufactured items in return for silk, porcelain, books, and copper cash. Some Japanese traders were so aggressive in pressing their interests that authorities in China and Korea attempted to limit the number of Japanese commercial missions that could visit each year. Such restrictions were often ignored, however, and encouraged some Japanese traders to turn to piracy.

Significantly, manufacturing and commerce developed rapidly during the more decentralized period of the Ashikaga shogunate and the era of the warring states, perhaps because of the rapid growth in the wealth and autonomy of local daimyo families. Market towns, now operating on a full money economy, began to appear, and local manufacturers formed guilds to protect their mutual interests.

Sometimes local peasants would sell products made in their homes, such as clothing made of silk or hemp, household items, or food products, at the markets. In general, however, trade and manufacturing remained under the control of the local daimyo, who would often provide tax breaks to local guilds in return for other benefits. Although Japan remained a primarily agricultural society, it was on the verge of a major advance in manufacturing.

DAILY LIFE

One of the first descriptions of the life of the Japanese people comes from a Chinese dynastic history from the third century C.E. It describes lords and peasants living in an agricultural society that was based on the cultivation of wet rice. Laws had been enacted to punish offenders, local trade was conducted in markets, and government granaries stored the grain that was paid as taxes.

Life for the common people probably changed very little over the next several hundred years. Most were peasants who worked on land owned by their lord or, in some cases, by the state or by Buddhist monasteries. By no means, however, were all peasants equal either economically or socially. Although in ancient times, all land was owned by the state and peasants working the land were taxed at an equal rate depending on the nature of the crop, after the Yamato era variations began to develop. At the top were local officials who were often well-to-do peasants. They were responsible for organizing collective labor services and collecting tax grain from the peasants and in turn were exempt from such obligations themselves.

The mass of the peasants were under the authority of these local officials. In theory, peasants were free to dispose of their harvest as they saw fit after paying their tax quota, but in practical terms, their freedom was limited. Those who were unable to pay the tax sank to the level of

genin, or landless laborers, who could be bought and sold by their proprietors like slaves along with the land on which they worked. Some fled to escape such a fate and attempted to survive by clearing plots of land in the mountains or by becoming bandits.

In addition to the genin, the bottom of the social scale was occupied by the eta, a class of hereditary slaves who were responsible for what were considered degrading occupations, such as curing leather and burying the dead. The origins of the eta are not entirely clear, but they probably were descendants of prisoners of war, criminals, or mountain dwellers who were not related to the dominant Yamato peoples. As we shall see, the eta are still a distinctive part of Japanese society, and although their full legal rights are guaranteed under the current constitution, discrimination against them is not uncommon.

Daily life for ordinary people in early Japan resembled that of their counterparts throughout much of Asia. The vast majority lived in small villages, several of which normally made up a single shoen. Housing was simple. Most lived in small two-room houses of timber, mud, or thatch, with dirt floors covered by straw or woven mats (the origin, perhaps, of the well-known tatami, or woven-mat floor, of more modern times). Their diet consisted of rice (if some was left after the payment of the grain tax), wild grasses, millet, roots, and some fish and birds. Life must have been difficult at best; as one eighth-century poet lamented:

> Here I lie on straw
> Spread on bare earth,
> With my parents at my pillow,
> My wife and children at my feet,
> All huddled in grief and tears.
> No fire sends up smoke
> At the cooking place,
> And in the cauldron
> A spider spins its web.[2]

Evidence about the relations between men and women in early Japan presents a mixed picture. The Chinese dynastic history reports that "in their meetings and daily living, there is no distinction between . . . men and women." It notes that a woman "adept in the ways of shamanism" had briefly ruled Japan in the third century C.E. But it also remarks that polygyny was common, with nobles normally having four or five wives and commoners two or three.[3] An eighth-century law code guaranteed the inheritance rights of women, and wives abandoned by their husbands were permitted to obtain a divorce and remarry. A husband could divorce his wife if she did not produce a male child, committed adultery, disobeyed her parents-in-law, talked too much, engaged in theft, was jealous, or had a serious illness.[4]

When Buddhism was introduced, women were initially relegated to a subordinate position in the new faith. Although they were permitted to take up monastic life—

many widows entered a monastery at the death of their husbands—they were not permitted to visit Buddhist holy places, nor were they even (in the accepted wisdom) equal with men in the afterlife. One Buddhist commentary from the late thirteenth century said that a woman could not attain enlightenment because "her sin is grievous, and so she is not allowed to enter the lofty palace of the great Brahma, nor to look upon the clouds which hover over his ministers and people."[5] Other Buddhist scholars were more egalitarian: "Learning the Law of Buddha and achieving release from illusion have nothing to do with whether one happens to be a man or a woman."[6] Such views ultimately prevailed, and women were eventually allowed to participate fully in Buddhist activities in medieval Japan.

Although women did not possess the full legal and social rights of their male counterparts, they played an active role at various levels of Japanese society. Aristocratic women were prominent at court, and some, such as the author Lady Murasaki, became renowned for their artistic or literary talents. Though few commoners could aspire to such prominence, women often appear in the scroll paintings of the period along with men, doing the spring planting, threshing and hulling the rice, and acting as carriers, peddlers, salespersons, and entertainers.

In Search of the Pure Land: Religion in Early Japan

In Japan, as elsewhere, religious belief began with the worship of nature spirits. Early Japanese worshiped spirits, called *kami*, who resided in trees, rivers and streams, and mountains. They also believed in ancestral spirits present in the atmosphere. In Japan, these beliefs eventually evolved into a kind of state religion called Shinto (the "Sacred Way" or the "Way of the Gods"), which is still practiced today. Shinto still serves as an ideological and emotional

force that knits the Japanese into a single people and nation.

Shinto does not have a complex metaphysical superstructure or an elaborate moral code. It does require certain ritual acts, usually undertaken at a shrine, and a process of purification, which may have originated in prim-

Urban Life in Medieval Japan and Europe

Like Europe in the Middle Ages, medieval Japan was largely an agricultural society, but during their medieval periods, both began to develop trade and manufacturing in growing urban areas. Intraregional trade was transported by horse-drawn carts or by boats on rivers or along the coast. Portrayed at the top is a detail from a thirteenth-century scroll depicting the bustle and general confusion of the city of Edo (now Tokyo). On the bottom is a similar scene from a fourteenth-century painting by Ambrogio Lorenzetti. He portrays a street scene in Siena, Italy. In the street are donkeys loaded with goods, a goatherd driving his flock through the town, and two women from the country bringing their goods into the town. In the background, a shoemaker is at work in his shop, a teacher is instructing his students, a man is selling spices, and a tailor is cutting a piece of cloth.

Courtesy of the Tokyo National Museum

© Scala/Art Resource, NY

itive concerns about death, childbirth, illness, and menstruation. This traditional concern about physical purity may help explain the strong Japanese concern for personal cleanliness and the practice of denying women entrance to the holy places.

Another feature of Shinto is its stress on the beauty of nature and the importance of nature itself in Japanese life. Shinto shrines are usually located in places of exceptional beauty and are often dedicated to a nearby physical feature. As time passed, such primitive beliefs contributed to the characteristic Japanese love of nature. In this sense, early Shinto beliefs have been incorporated into the lives of all Japanese.

In time, Shinto evolved into a state doctrine that was linked with belief in the divinity of the emperor and the sacredness of the Japanese nation. A national shrine was established at Ise, north of the early capital of Nara, where the emperor annually paid tribute to the sun goddess. But although Shinto had evolved well beyond its primitive origins, like its counterparts elsewhere it could not satisfy all the religious and emotional needs of the Japanese people. For those needs, the Japanese turned to Buddhism.

As we have seen, Buddhism was introduced into Japan from China during the sixth century C.E. and had begun to spread beyond the court to the general population by the eighth century. As in China, most Japanese saw no contradiction between worshiping both the Buddha and their local nature gods, many of whom were considered to be later manifestations of the Buddha. Most of the Buddhist sects that had achieved popularity in China were established in Japan, and many of them attracted powerful patrons at court. Great monasteries were established that competed in wealth and influence with the noble families that had traditionally ruled the country.

Perhaps the two most influential Buddhist sects were the Pure Land (Jodo) sect and Zen (in Chinese, Chan or Ch'an). The Pure Land sect, which taught that devotion alone could lead to enlightenment and release, was very popular among the common people, for whom monastic life was one of the few routes to upward mobility. Among the aristocracy, the most influential school was Zen, which exerted a significant impact on Japanese life and culture during the era of the warring states. In its emphasis on austerity, self-discipline, and communion with nature, Zen complemented many traditional beliefs in Japanese society and became an important component of the samurai warrior's code.

In Zen teachings, there were various ways to achieve enlightenment (*satori* in Japanese). Some stressed that it could be achieved suddenly. One monk, for example, reportedly achieved *satori* by listening to the sound of a bamboo striking against roof tiles; another, by carefully watching the opening of peach blossoms in the spring. But other practitioners, sometimes called adepts, said that enlightenment could come only through studying the scriptures and arduous self-discipline (known as *zazen*, or "seated Zen"). Seated Zen involved a lengthy process of meditation that cleansed the mind of extraneous thoughts so that it could concentrate on the essential.

Sources of Traditional Japanese Culture

Nowhere is the Japanese genius for blending indigenous and imported elements into an effective whole better demonstrated than in culture. In such widely diverse fields as art, architecture, sculpture, and literature, the Japanese from early times showed an impressive capacity to borrow selectively from abroad without destroying essential native elements.

Growing contact with China during the period of the rise of the Yamato state stimulated Japanese artists. Missions sent to China and Korea during the seventh and eighth centuries returned with examples of Tang literature, sculpture, and painting, all of which influenced the Japanese.

LITERATURE

Borrowing from Chinese models was somewhat complicated, however, since the early Japanese had no writing system for recording their own spoken language and initially adopted the Chinese written language for writing. But resourceful Japanese soon began to adapt the Chinese written characters so that they could be used for recording the Japanese language. In some cases, Chinese characters were given Japanese pronunciations. But Chinese characters ordinarily could not be used to record Japanese words, which normally contain more than one syllable. Sometimes the Japanese simply used Chinese characters as phonetic symbols that were combined to form Japanese words. Later they simplified the characters into phonetic symbols that were used alongside Chinese characters. This hybrid system continues to be used today.

At first, most educated Japanese preferred to write in Chinese, and a court literature—consisting of essays, poetry, and official histories—appeared in the classical Chinese language. But spoken Japanese never totally disappeared among the educated classes and eventually became the instrument of a unique literature. With the lessening of Chinese cultural influence in the tenth century, Japanese verse resurfaced. Between the tenth and fifteenth centuries, twenty imperial anthologies of poetry were compiled. Initially they were written primarily by courtiers, but with the fall of the Heian court and the rise of the warrior and merchant classes, all literate segments of society began to produce poetry.

Japanese poetry is unique. It expresses its themes in a simple form, a characteristic stemming from traditional Japanese aesthetics, Zen religion, and the language itself. The aim of the Japanese poet was to create a mood, perhaps the melancholic effect of gently falling cherry blossoms or leaves. With a few specific references, the poet suggested a whole world, just as Zen Buddhism sought

A SAMPLE OF LINKED VERSE

*O*ne of the distinctive features of medieval Japanese literature was the technique of "linked verse." In a manner similar to haiku poetry today, such poems, known as renga, were written by groups of individuals who would join together to compose the poem, verse by verse. The following example, by three famous poets named Sogi, Shohaku, and Socho, is one of the most famous of the period.

THE THREE POETS AT MINASE

Snow clinging to slope,   Sogi
   On mist-enshrouded mountains
   At eveningtime.
In the distance flows   Shohaku
   Through plum-scented villages.

Willows cluster   Socho
   In the river breeze
   As spring appears.
The sound of a boat being poled   Sogi
   In the clearness at dawn
Still the moon lingers   Shohaku
   As fog o'er-spreads
   The night.
A frost-covered meadow;   Socho
   Autumn has drawn to a close.
Against the wishes   Sogi
   Of droning insects
   The grasses wither.

---

enlightenment from a sudden perception. Poets often alluded to earlier poems by repeating their images with small changes, a technique that was viewed not as plagiarism but as an elaboration on the meaning of the earlier poem.

By the fourteenth century, the technique of the "linked verse" had become the most popular form of Japanese poetry. Known as *haiku*, it is composed of seventeen syllables divided into lines of five, seven, and five syllables. The poems usually focused on images from nature and called attention to the mutability of life. Often the poetry was written by several individuals alternately composing verses and linking them together into long sequences of hundreds and even thousands of lines (see the box above).

Poetry served a unique function at the Heian court, where it was the initial means of communication between lovers. By custom, aristocratic women were isolated from all contact with men outside their immediate family and spent their days hidden behind screens. Some amused themselves by writing poetry. When courtship began, poetic exchanges were the only means a woman had to attract her prospective lover, who would be enticed solely by her poetic art.

During the Heian period, male courtiers wrote in Chinese, believing that Chinese civilization was superior and worthy of emulation. Like the Chinese, they viewed prose fiction as "vulgar gossip." Nevertheless, from the ninth century to the twelfth, Japanese women were prolific writers of prose fiction in Japanese. Excluded from school, they learned to read and write at home and wrote diaries and stories to pass the time. Some of the most talented women were invited to court as authors in residence.

In the increasingly pessimistic world of the warring states of the Kamakura period (1185–1333), Japanese novels typically focused on a solitary figure who is aloof from the refinements of the court and faces battle and possibly death. Another genre, that of the heroic war tale, came out of the new warrior class. These works described the military exploits of warriors, coupled with an overwhelming sense of sadness and loneliness.

The famous classical Japanese drama known as *No* also originated during this period. *No* developed out of a variety of entertainment forms, such as dancing and juggling, that were part of the native tradition or had been imported from China and other regions of Asia. The plots were normally based on stories from Japanese history or legend. Eventually *No* evolved into a highly stylized drama in which the performers wore masks and danced to the accompaniment of instrumental music. Like much of Japanese culture, *No* was restrained, graceful, and refined.

ART AND ARCHITECTURE

In art and architecture, as in literature, the Japanese pursued their interest in beauty, simplicity, and nature. To some degree, Japanese artists and architects were influenced by Chinese forms. As they became familiar with Chinese architecture, Japanese rulers and aristocrats tried to emulate the splendor of Tang civilization and began constructing their palaces and temples in Chinese style.

During the Heian period (794–1185), the search for beauty was reflected in various art forms, such as narrative hand scrolls, screens, sliding door panels, fans, and lacquer decoration. As in the case of literature, nature themes dominated, such as seashore scenes, a spring rain, moon and mist, or flowering wisteria and cherry blossoms. All were intended to evoke an emotional response on the part of the viewer. Japanese painting suggested the frail beauty of nature by presenting it on a smaller scale. The majestic mountain in a Chinese painting became a more intimate Japanese landscape with rolling hills and a rice field. Faces were rarely shown, and human drama was indicated by a woman lying prostrate or hiding her face in her sleeve. Tension was shown by two people talking at a great distance or with their backs to one another.

❧ **A SEATED BUDDHA.** Buddhist statuary originated in India and China and evolved as a popular art form in Japan from the seventh century on. Characteristic of these statues are the *mudras*, or hand and body positions by which the Buddha communicated with his followers. Here his connected fingers indicate meditation. Whereas earlier Japanese sculptors worked in bronze, the depletion of metal reserves eventually necessitated the use of wood. This remarkable eleventh-century gilded wood carving, over 10 feet in height, is composed of fifty-three pieces of cypress and exudes a feeling of stability and calm, expressing the Buddha's deep spirituality. He is seated on a bed of lotus leaves, a Buddhist symbol for purity arising out of the mire.

During the Kamakura period (1185–1333), the hand scroll with its physical realism and action-packed paintings of the new warrior class achieved great popularity. Reflecting these chaotic times, the art of portraiture flourished, and a scroll would include a full gallery of warriors and holy men in starkly realistic detail, including such unflattering features as stubble, worry lines on a forehead, and crooked teeth. Japanese sculptors also produced naturalistic wooden statues of generals, nobles, and saints. By far the most distinctive, however, were the fierce heavenly "guardian kings," who still intimidate the viewer today.

Zen Buddhism, an import from China in the thirteenth century, also influenced Japanese aesthetics. With its emphasis on immediate enlightenment without recourse to intellectual analysis and elaborate ritual, Zen reinforced the Japanese predilection for simplicity and self-discipline. During this era, Zen philosophy found expression in the Japanese garden, the tea ceremony, the art of flower arranging, pottery and ceramics, and miniature plant display (the famous *bonsai*, literally "pot scenery").

Landscapes served as an important means of expression in both Japanese art and architecture. Japanese gardens were initially modeled on Chinese examples. Early court texts during the Heian period emphasized the importance of including a stream or pond when creating a garden. The landscape surrounding the fourteenth-century Golden Pavilion in Kyoto displays a harmony of garden, water, and architecture that makes it one of the treasures of the world. Because of the shortage of water in the city, later gardens concentrated on rock composition, using white pebbles to represent water.

Like the Japanese garden, the tea ceremony represents the fusion of Zen and aesthetics. Developed in the fifteenth century, it was practiced in a simple room devoid of external ornament except for a *tatami* floor, sliding doors, and an alcove with a writing desk and asymmetrical shelves. The participants could therefore focus completely on the activity of pouring and drinking tea. "Tea and Zen have the same flavor," goes the Japanese saying. Considered the ultimate symbol of spiritual deliverance, the tea ceremony had great aesthetic value and moral significance in traditional times just as it does today.

Japan and the Chinese Model

Few societies in Asia have historically been as isolated as Japan. Cut off from the mainland by 120 miles of frequently turbulent ocean, the Japanese had only minimal contact with the outside world during most of their early development.

Whether this isolation was ultimately beneficial to Japanese society cannot be determined. On one hand, the lack of knowledge of developments taking place elsewhere probably delayed the process of change in Japan. On the other hand, the Japanese were spared the destructive invasions that afflicted other ancient civilizations. Certainly, once the Japanese became acquainted with Chinese culture at the height of the Tang era, they were quick to take advantage of the opportunity. In the space of a few decades, the young state adopted many aspects of Chinese society and culture and thereby introduced major changes into Japanese life.

Nevertheless, Japanese political institutions failed to follow all aspects of the Chinese pattern. Despite Prince Shotoku's effort to make effective use of the imperial traditions of Tang China, the decentralizing forces inside Japanese society remained dominant throughout the period under discussion in this chapter. Adoption of the

Courtesy of William J. Duiker

© Charles Gupton

➤ RYOANJI TEMPLE GARDEN IN KYOTO.   As the result of
a water shortage in the fifteenth century, Japanese landscape
designers began to make increasing use of rocks and pebbles to
represent water. In the Ryoanji Temple in the hills west of Kyoto,
seventeen rocks surrounded by wavy raked pebbles are arranged
in five groups to suggest mountains emerging from the sea. Here
we experience the quintessential Japanese aesthetic expression of
allusion, simplicity, restraint, and tranquillity.

➤ THE GOLDEN PAVILION IN KYOTO.   The landscape surrounding the Golden Pavilion displays a harmony of garden, water,
and architecture that makes it one of the treasures of the world.
Constructed in the fourteenth century as a retreat for the shoguns
to withdraw from their administrative chores, the pavilion is
named for the gold foil that covered its exterior. Completely
destroyed by an arsonist in 1950 as a protest against the commer-
cialism of modern Buddhism, it was rebuilt and reopened in 1987.
The use of water as a backdrop is especially noteworthy in Chinese
and Japanese landscapes, as well as in the Middle East.

eases (such as smallpox and measles) imported inadvertently from China led to a marked decline in the population of the islands, reducing the food output and
preventing the population from coalescing in more com-
pact urban centers.

In any event, Japan was not the only society in Asia
to assimilate ideas from abroad while at the same time preserving customs and institutions inherited from the past.
Across the Sea of Japan to the west and several thousand
miles to the south, other Asian peoples were embarked on
a similar journey. We now turn to their experience.

period under discussion in this chapter. Adoption of the
Confucian civil service examination did not lead to a
breakdown of Japanese social divisions; instead the examination was administered in a manner that preserved and
strengthened them. Although Buddhist and Daoist doctrines made a significant contribution to Japanese religious
practices, Shinto beliefs continued to play a major role
in shaping the Japanese worldview.

Why Japan did not follow the Chinese road to centralized authority has been the subject of some debate
among historians. Some argue that the answer lies in dif-
fering cultural traditions, while others suggest that Chinese institutions and values were introduced too rapidly
to be assimilated effectively by Japanese society. One factor may have been the absence of a foreign threat (except
for the Mongols) in Japan. A recent view holds that dis-

KOREA: BRIDGE TO THE EAST

No society in East Asia was more strongly influenced by
the Chinese model than Korea. Slightly larger than the
state of Minnesota, the Korean peninsula was probably first
settled by Altaic-speaking fishing and hunting peoples
from neighboring Manchuria during the Neolithic Age.
Because the area is relatively mountainous (only about
one-fifth of the peninsula is adaptable to cultivation),
farming was apparently not practiced until about 2000
B.C.E. The other aspect of Korea's geography that has profoundly affected its history is its proximity to both China
and Japan.

Korea's Three Kingdoms

In 109 B.C.E., the northern part of the peninsula came under direct Chinese rule. During the next several generations, the area was ruled by the Han dynasty, which divided the territory into provinces and introduced Chinese institutions. With the decline of the Han in the third century C.E., power gradually shifted to local tribal leaders, who drove out the Chinese administrators but continued to absorb Chinese cultural influence. Eventually three separate kingdoms emerged on the peninsula: Koguryo in the north, Paekche in the southwest, and Silla in the southeast. The Japanese, who had recently established their own state on the Yamato plain, maintained a small colony on the southern coast.

The Three Kingdoms

From the fourth to the seventh centuries, the three kingdoms were bitter rivals for influence and territory on the peninsula. At the same time, all began to absorb Chinese political and cultural institutions. Chinese influence was most notable in Koguryo, where Buddhism was introduced in the late fourth century C.E. and the first Confucian academy on the peninsula was established in the capital at Pyongyang. All three kingdoms also appear to have accepted a tributary relationship with one or another of the squabbling states that emerged in China after the fall of the Han. The kingdom of Silla, less exposed than its two rivals to Chinese influence, was at first the weakest of the three, but eventually its greater internal cohesion—perhaps a consequence of the tenacity of its tribal traditions—enabled it to become the dominant power on the peninsula. Then the rulers of Silla forced the Chinese to withdraw from all but the area adjacent to the Yalu River. To pacify the haughty Chinese, Silla accepted tributary status under the Tang dynasty. The remaining Japanese colonies in the south were eliminated.

With the country unified for the first time, the rulers of Silla attempted to use Chinese political institutions and ideology to forge a centralized state. Buddhism, now rising in popularity, became the state religion, and Korean monks followed the paths of their Japanese counterparts on journeys to the Middle Kingdom. Chinese architecture and art became dominant in the capital at Kyongju and other urban centers, and the written Chinese language became the official means of communication at court. But powerful aristocratic families, long dominant in the southeastern part of the peninsula, were still influential at court. They were able to prevent the adoption of the Tang civil service examination system and resisted the distribution of manorial lands to the poor. The failure to adopt the Chinese model was fatal. Squabbling among noble families steadily increased, and after the assassination of the king of Silla in 780, the country sank into civil war.

Unification

In the early tenth century, a new dynasty called Koryo (the root of the modern word for Korea) arose in the north. The new kingdom adopted Chinese political institutions in an effort to strengthen its power and unify its territory. The civil service examination system was introduced in 958, but as in Japan, the bureaucracy continued to be dominated by influential aristocratic families.

The Koryo dynasty remained in power for four hundred years, protected from invasion by the absence of a strong dynasty in neighboring China. Under the Koryo, industry and commerce slowly began to develop, but as in China, agriculture was the prime source of wealth. In theory, all land was the property of the king, but in actuality, noble families controlled their holdings. The lands were worked by peasants who were subject to burdens similar to those of European serfs. At the bottom of society was a class of "base people" (chonmin), composed of slaves, artisans, and other specialized workers.

From a cultural point of view, the Koryo era was one of high achievement. Buddhist monasteries, run by sects introduced from China, including Pure Land and Zen (Chan), controlled vast territories, while their monks served as royal advisers at court. At first, Buddhist themes dominated in Korean art and sculpture, and the entire Tripitaka (the "three baskets" of the Buddhist canon) was printed using wooden blocks. Eventually, however, with the appearance of landscape painting and porcelain, Confucian themes began to predominate.

Under the Mongols

Like its predecessor in Silla, the kingdom of Koryo was unable to overcome the power of the nobility and the absence of a reliable tax base. In the thirteenth century, the Mongols seized the northern part of the country and assimilated it into the Yuan Empire. The weakened kingdom of Koryo became a tributary of the Great Khan in Khanbaliq (see Chapter 10).

The era of Mongol rule was one of profound suffering for the Korean people, especially the thousands of peasants and artisans who were compelled to perform forced labor to help build the ships in preparation for Khubilai Khan's invasion of Japan. On the positive side, the Mongols introduced many new ideas and technology from China and farther afield. The Koryo dynasty had managed

↬ **PULGUKSA BELL TOWER**   Among the greatest architectural achievements on the Korean penin-sula is the Pulguksa (Monastery of the Land of Buddha), built near Kyongju, the ancient capital of Silla, in the eighth century C.E. Shown here is the bell tower, located in the midst of beautiful parklands on the monastery grounds. Young Korean couples often come to this monastery after their weddings to be photographed in the stunning surroundings.

to survive, but only by accepting Mongol authority, and when the power of the Mongols declined, the kingdom declined with it. With the rise to power of the Ming in China, Koryo collapsed, and power was seized by the military commander Yi Song-gye, who declared the founding of the new Yi dynasty in 1392. Once again, the Korean people were in charge of their own destiny.

VIETNAM: THE SMALLER DRAGON

While the Korean people were attempting to establish their own identity in the shadow of the powerful Chinese Empire, the peoples of Vietnam, on China's southern frontier, were trying to do the same. The Vietnamese began to practice irrigated agriculture in the flooded regions of the Red River delta at an early date and entered the Bronze Age sometime during the second millennium

B.C.E. By about 200 B.C.E., a young state had begun to form in the area but immediately encountered the expanding power of the Qin Empire (see Chapter 3). The Vietnamese were not easy to subdue, however, and the collapse of the Qin dynasty temporarily enabled them to preserve their independence. Nevertheless, a century later, they were absorbed into the Han Empire.

At first, the Han were satisfied to rule the delta as an autonomous region under the administration of the local landed aristocracy. But Chinese taxes were oppressive, and in 39 C.E., a revolt led by the Trung Sisters (widows of local nobles who had been executed by the Chinese) briefly brought Han rule to an end. The Chinese soon suppressed the rebellion, however, and began to rule the area directly through officials dispatched from China. In time, however, these foreign officials began to intermarry with the local nobility and form a Sino-Vietnamese ruling class who, though trained in Chinese culture, began to identify with the cause of Vietnamese autonomy.

A PLEA TO THE EMPEROR

Like many other societies in premodern East and South-east Asia, the kingdom of Vietnam regularly paid tribute to the imperial court in China. The arrangement was often beneficial to both sides, as the tributary states received a form of international recognition from the relationship, as well as trade privileges in the massive Chinese market. China, for its part, assured itself that neighboring areas would not harbor dissident elements hostile to its own security.

In this document, contained in a historical chronicle written by Le Tac in the fourteenth century, a claimant to the Vietnamese throne seeks recognition from the Song emperor while offering trib-ute to the Son of Heaven in China. Note the way in which the claimant, Le Hoan, founder of the early Le dynasty (980–1009), demeans the character of the Vietnamese people in comparison with the sophisticated ways of imperial China.

LE HOAN, *ESSAY ON ANNAM*

My ancestors have received favors from the Imperial Court. Living in a faraway country at a corner of the sea [Annam], they have been granted the seals of investiture for that barbarian area and have always paid to the Impe-rial ministers the tribute and respect they owed. But recently our House has been little favored by Heaven; however, the death of our ancestors has not prevented us from promptly delivering the tribute. . . .

But now the leadership of the country is in dispute and investiture has not yet been conferred by China. My father, Pou-ling, and my eldest brother, Lienn, formerly enjoyed the favors of the [Chinese] Empire, which endowed them with the titles and functions of office. They zealously and humbly protected their country, neither daring to appear lazy or neg-ligent. . . . [But then] the good fortune of our House began to crumble. The mandarins [officials], the army, the people, the court elders, and members of my family, all . . . entreated me to lead the army. . . . My people, who are wild mountain-dwellers, have unpleasant and violent customs; they are a people who live in caves and have disorderly and impetuous habits. I feared that trouble would arise if I did not yield to their wishes. From prudence I therefore assumed power tem-porarily. . . . I hope that His Majesty will place my country among His other tributary states by granting me the investi-ture. He will instill peace in the heart of His little servant by allowing me to govern the patrimony my parents left me. Then shall I administer my barbarian and remote people. . . . I shall send tributes of precious stones and ivory, and before the Golden Gate I shall express my loyalty.

For nearly a thousand years, the Vietnamese were exposed to the art, architecture, literature, philosophy, and written language of China as the Chinese attempted to integrate the area culturally as well as politically and administratively into their empire. To all intents and purposes, the Red River delta, then known to the Chinese as the "pacified South" (Annam), became a part of China.

The Rise of Great Viet

Despite the Chinese efforts to assimilate Vietnam, the Vietnamese sense of ethnic and cultural identity proved inextinguishable, and in the tenth century, the Vietnam-ese took advantage of the collapse of the Tang dynasty in China to overthrow Chinese rule.

The new Vietnamese state, which called itself Dai Viet (Great Viet), became a dynamic new force on the South-east Asian mainland. As the population of the Red River delta expanded, Dai Viet soon came into conflict with Champa, its neighbor to the south. Located along the cen-tral coast of modern Vietnam, Champa was a trading soci-ety based on Indian cultural traditions. Over the next several centuries, the two states fought on numerous occa-sions. By the end of the fifteenth century, Dai Viet had conquered Champa. The Vietnamese then resumed their march southward, establishing agricultural settlements in the newly conquered territory. By the seventeenth cen-tury, the Vietnamese had reached the Gulf of Siam.

The Vietnamese faced an even more serious challenge from the north. The Song dynasty in China, beset with its own problems on the northern frontier, even-tually accepted the Dai Viet ruler's offer of tribute status (see the box above), but later dynas-ties attempted to reinte-grate the Red River delta into the Chinese Empire. The first effort was made in the late thirteenth century by the Mongols, who attempted on two occasions to conquer the Vietnamese. After a series of bloody bat-tles, during which the Vietnamese displayed an impressive capacity for guerrilla warfare, the invaders were driven out. A little over a century later, the Ming dynasty tried again, and for twenty years Vietnam was once more under Chi-nese rule. In 1428, the Vietnamese evicted the Chinese again, but the experience had contributed to the strong sense of Vietnamese identity.

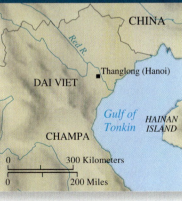

The Kingdom of Dai Viet, 1100

Chronology

EARLY KOREA AND VIETNAM

Chinese conquest of Korea and Vietnam	First century B.C.E.
Trung Sisters' Revolt	39 C.E.
Foundation of Champa	192
Era of Three Kingdoms in Korea	Fourth–seventh centuries
Restoration of Vietnamese independence	939
Mongol invasion of Korea and Vietnam	1257–1285
Foundation of Yi dynasty in Korea	1392
Vietnamese conquest of Champa	1471

THE CHINESE LEGACY

Despite their stubborn resistance to Chinese rule, after the restoration of independence in the tenth century, Vietnamese rulers quickly discovered the convenience of the Confucian model in administering a river valley society and therefore attempted to follow Chinese practice in forming their own state. The ruler styled himself an emperor like his counterpart to the north (although he prudently termed himself a king in his direct dealings with the Chinese court), adopted Chinese court rituals, claimed the Mandate of Heaven, and arrogated to himself the same authority and privileges in his dealings with his subjects. But unlike a Chinese emperor, who had no particular symbolic role as defender of the Chinese people or Chinese culture, a Vietnamese monarch was viewed, above all, as the symbol and defender of Vietnamese independence.

Like their Chinese counterparts, Vietnamese rulers fought to preserve their authority from the challenges of powerful aristocratic families and turned to the Chinese bureaucratic model, including civil service examinations, as a means of doing so. Under the pressure of strong monarchs, the concept of merit eventually took hold, and the power of the landed aristocracy was weakened if not entirely broken. The Vietnamese adopted much of the Chinese administrative structure, including the six ministries, the censorate, and the various levels of provincial and local administration.

Another aspect of the Chinese legacy was the spread of Buddhist, Daoist, and Confucian ideas, which supplemented the Viets' traditional belief in nature spirits. Buddhist precepts became popular among the local population,

who integrated the new faith into their existing belief system by founding Buddhist temples dedicated to the local village deity in the hope of guaranteeing an abundant harvest. Upper-class Vietnamese educated in the Confucian classics tended to follow the more agnostic Confucian doctrine, but some joined Buddhist monasteries. Daoism also flourished at all levels of society and, as in China, provided a structure for animistic beliefs and practices that still predominated at the village level.

During the early period of independence, Vietnamese culture also borrowed liberally from its larger neighbor. Educated Vietnamese tried their hand at Chinese poetry, wrote dynastic histories in the Chinese style, and followed Chinese models in sculpture, architecture, and porcelain. Many of the notable buildings of the medieval period, such as the Temple of Literature and the famous One-Pillar Pagoda in Hanoi, are classic examples of Chinese architecture.

But there were signs that Vietnamese creativity would eventually transcend the bounds of Chinese cultural norms. Although most classical writing was undertaken in literary Chinese, the only form of literary expression deemed suitable by Confucian conservatives, an adaptation of Chinese written characters, called *chu nom* ("southern characters"), was devised to provide a written system for spoken Vietnamese. In use by the early ninth century, it eventually began to be used for the composition of essays and poetry in the Vietnamese language. Such pioneering efforts would lead in later centuries to the emergence of a vigorous national literature totally independent of Chinese forms.

Society and Family Life

Vietnamese social institutions and customs were also strongly influenced by those of China. As in China, the introduction of a Confucian system and the adoption of civil service examinations undermined the role of the old landed aristocrats and led eventually to their replacement by the scholar-gentry class. Also as in China, the examinations were open to most males, regardless of family background, which opened the door to a degree of social mobility unknown in most of the states elsewhere in the region. Candidates for the bureaucracy read many of the same Confucian classics and absorbed the same ethical principles as their counterparts in China. At the same time, they were also exposed to the classic works of Vietnamese history, which strengthened their sense that Vietnam was a distinct culture similar to, but separate from, that of China.

The vast majority of the Vietnamese people, however, were peasants. Most were small landholders or sharecroppers who rented their plots from wealthier farmers, but large estates were rare due to the systematic efforts of the central government to prevent the rise of a powerful local landed elite.

Family life in Vietnam was similar in many respects to that in China. The Confucian concept of family took hold during the period of Chinese rule, along with the related concepts of filial piety and gender inequality. Perhaps the most striking difference between family traditions in China and Vietnam was that Vietnamese women possessed more rights both in practice and by law. Since ancient times, wives had been permitted to own property and initiate divorce proceedings. One consequence of Chinese rule was a growing emphasis on male dominance, but the tradition of women's rights was never totally extinguished and was legally recognized in a law code promulgated in 1460.

Moreover, Vietnam had a strong historical tradition associating heroic women with the defense of the homeland. The Trung Sisters were the first but by no means the only example. In the following passage, a Vietnamese historian of the eighteenth century recounts their story:

> The imperial court was far away; local officials were greedy and oppressive. At that time the country of one hundred sons was the country of the women of Lord To. The ladies [the Trung Sisters] used the female arts against their irreconcilable foe; skirts and hairpins sang of patriotic righteousness, uttered a solemn oath at the inner door of the ladies' quarters, expelled the governor, and seized the capital. . . . Were they not grand heroines? . . . Our two ladies brought forward an army of all the people, and, establishing a royal court that settled affairs in the territories of the sixty-five strongholds, shook their skirts over the Hundred Yueh [the Vietnamese people].[7]

CONCLUSION

There are some tantalizing similarities among the three countries we have examined in this chapter. All borrowed liberally from the Chinese model. At the same time, all adapted Chinese institutions and values to the conditions prevailing in their own societies. Though all expressed admiration and respect for China's achievement, all sought to keep Chinese power at a distance.

As an island nation, Japan was the most successful of the three in protecting its political sovereignty and its cultural identity. Both Korea and Vietnam were compelled on various occasions to defend their independence by force of arms. That experience may have shaped their strong sense of national distinctiveness, which we shall discuss further in a later chapter.

The appeal of Chinese institutions can undoubtedly be explained by the fact that Japan, Korea, and Vietnam were all agrarian societies, much like their larger neighbor. But it is undoubtedly significant that the aspect of Chinese political culture that was least amenable to adoption abroad was the civil service examination system. The Confucian concept of meritocracy ran directly counter to the strong aristocratic tradition that flourished in all three societies during their early stage of development. Even when the system was adopted, it was put to quite different uses. Only in Vietnam did the concept of merit eventually triumph over that of birth, as strong rulers of Dai Viet attempted to initiate the Chinese model as a means of creating a centralized system of government.

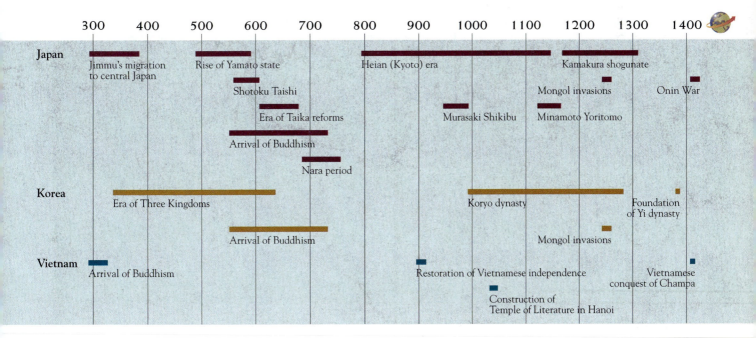

CHAPTER NOTES

1. Keith W. Taylor, *The Birth of Vietnam* (Berkeley, Calif., 1983), p. 75.
2. Quoted in David John Lu, *Sources of Japanese History*, vol. 1 (New York, 1974), p. 7.
3. From "The History of Wei," quoted in ibid., p. 10.
4. From "The Law of Households," quoted in ibid., p. 32.
5. From "On the Salvation of Women," quoted in ibid., p. 127.
6. Quoted in Barbara Ruch, "The Other Side of Culture in Medieval Japan," in Kozo Yamamura, ed., *The Cambridge History of Japan*, vol. 3, *Medieval Japan* (Cambridge, 1990), p. 506.
7. Quoted in Taylor, *The Birth of Vietnam*, pp. 336–337.

SUGGESTED READING

Some of the standard treatments of the rise of Japanese civilization appear in textbooks dealing with the early history of East Asia. Two of the best are J. K. Fairbank, E. O. Reischauer, and A. M. Craig, *East Asia: Tradition and Transformation* (Boston, 1973), and C. Schirokauer, *A Brief History of Chinese and Japanese Civilizations* (San Diego, Calif., 1989). A number of historical works deal specifically with early Japan. G. Sansom, *A History of Japan to 1334* (Stanford, Calif., 1958), is now somewhat out of date but is still informative and very well written. For more-recent scholarship on the early period, see the first three volumes of *The Cambridge History of Japan*, ed. J. W. Hall et al. (Cambridge, 1988).

The best available collections of documents on the early history of Japan are D. J. Lu, ed., *Sources of Japanese History*, vol. 1 (New York, 1974), and Theodore de Bary et al., eds., *Sources of Japanese Tradition*, vol. 1 (New York, 2002).

For specialized books on the early historical period, see R. J. Pearson, ed., *Windows on the Japanese Past: Studies in Archaeology and Prehistory* (Ann Arbor, Mich., 1986). J. W. Hall, *Government and Local Power in Japan, 500–1700* (Princeton, N.J., 1966), provides a detailed analysis of the development of Japanese political institutions. The relationship between disease and state building is analyzed in W. W. Farris, *Population, Disease, and Land in Early Japan, 645–900* (Cambridge, 1985). The Kamakura period is covered in J. P. Mass, ed., *Court and Bakufu in Japan: Essays in Kamakura History* (New Haven, Conn., 1982). See also H. P. Varley, *The Onin War* (New York, 1977). For Japanese Buddhism, see W. T. de Bary, ed., *The Buddhist Tradition in India, China, and Japan* (New York, 1972).

A concise and provocative introduction to women's issues during this period in Japan, as well as in other parts of the world, can be found in S. S. Hughes and B. Hughes, *Women in World History* (Armonk, N.Y., 1995). For a tenth-century account of daily life for women at the Japanese court, see I. Morris, trans. and ed., *The Pillow Book of Sei Shonagon* (New York, 1991). For the changes that took place from matrilocal and matrilineal marriages to a patriarchal society, consult H. Tonomura, "Black Hair and Red Trousers: Gendering the Flesh in Medieval Japan," in *American Historical Review* 99 (1994).

The best introduction to Japanese literature for college students is still the concise and insightful D. Keene, *Japanese Literature: An Introduction for Western Readers* (London, 1953). The most comprehensive anthology is D. Keene, *Anthology of Japanese Literature* (New York, 1955), while the best history of Japanese literature, also by D. Keene, is *Seeds in the Heart: Japanese Literature from Earlier Times to the Late Sixteenth Century* (New York, 1993).

For the most comprehensive introduction to Japanese art, consult P. Mason, *History of Japanese Art* (New York, 1993). Also see the concise J. Stanley-Baker, *Japanese Art* (London, 1984). For a stimulating text with magnificent illustrations, see D. Elisseeff and V. Elisseeff, *Art of Japan* (New York, 1985). See also J. E. Kidder Jr., *The Art of Japan* (London, 1985), for an insightful text accompanied by beautiful photographs.

For an informative and readable history of Korea, see Lee Ki-baik, *A New History of Korea* (Cambridge, 1984). P. H. Lee, ed., *Sourcebook of Korean Civilization*, vol. 1 (New York, 1993), is a rich collection of documents dating from the period prior to the sixteenth century.

Vietnam often receives little attention in general studies of Southeast Asia because it was part of the Chinese Empire for much of the traditional period. For a detailed investigation of the origins of Vietnamese civilization, see K. W. Taylor, *The Birth of Vietnam* (Berkeley, Calif., 1983). T. Hodgkin, *Vietnam: The Revolutionary Path* (New York, 1981), provides an overall survey of Vietnamese history to modern times. See also J. Buttinger, *The Smaller Dragon: A Political History of Vietnam* (New York, 1966).

InfoTrac
College Edition

Visit the source collections at infotrac.thomsonlearning.com and use the Search function with the following key terms.

Asia history
Japan history
Korea history
Shinto
Zen Buddhism

World History
Resources

Visit the *Essential World History* Companion Web Site for resources specific to this textbook:

http://history.wadsworth.com/duikeressentials02/

The CD in the back of this book and the World History Resource Center at http://history.wadsworth.com/world/ offer a variety of tools to help you succeed in this course, including access to quizzes; images; documents; interactive simulations, maps, and timelines; movie explorations; and a wealth of other sources.

The Art Archive, London, from the collections of the British Library

THE MAKING OF EUROPE IN THE MIDDLE AGES

FOCUS QUESTIONS
- What contributions did the Romans, the Christian church, and the Germanic peoples make to the new civilization that emerged in Europe after the collapse of the western Roman Empire?
- What roles did aristocrats, peasants, and townspeople play in medieval European civilization, and how did their lifestyles differ?
- What were the main aspects of the political, economic, and spiritual revivals that took place in Europe during the High Middle Ages?
- What were the major intellectual and cultural achievements of European civilization in the High Middle Ages?
- ➤ What problems did Europeans face during the fourteenth century, and what impact did those problems have on European economic, social, and religious life?

*I*n 800, Charlemagne, the king of the Franks, journeyed to Rome to help Pope Leo III, head of the Catholic church, who was barely clinging to power in the face of rebellious Romans. On Christmas Day, Charlemagne and his family, attended by Romans and Franks, crowded into Saint Peter's Basilica to hear Mass. Quite unexpectedly, according to a Frankish writer, "as the king rose from praying before the tomb of the blessed apostle Peter, Pope Leo placed a golden crown on his head." The people in the church shouted, "Long life and victory to Charles Augustus, crowned by God the great and peace-loving Emperor of the Romans." Seemingly, the Roman

Empire in the west had been reborn, and Charles had become the first Roman emperor since 476. But this "Roman emperor" was actually a German king, and he had been crowned by the head of the western Christian church. In truth, the coronation of Charlemagne was a sign not of the rebirth of the Roman Empire but of the emergence of a new European civilization that came into being in western Europe after the collapse of the western Roman Empire.

This new civilization—European civilization—was formed by the coming together of three major elements: the legacy of the Romans, the Christian church, and the Germanic peoples who moved in and settled the western empire. European civilization developed during a period that historians call the Middle Ages, or the medieval period, which lasted from about 500 to about 1400. To historians who first used the title, the Middle Ages was a middle period between the ancient world and the modern world. •

TRANSFORMATION OF THE ROMAN WORLD

Already by the third century C.E., Germanic peoples had begun to move into the lands of the Roman Empire. By 500, the western Roman Empire had been replaced politically by a series of states ruled by German kings.

The New Germanic Kingdoms

The fusion of Romans and Germans took different forms in the various Germanic kingdoms. Both the kingdom of the Ostrogoths in Italy and the kingdom of the Visigoths in Spain (see Map 12.1) maintained the Roman structure for the larger native populations, while a Germanic warrior caste came to dominate. Over a period of time, Germans and natives began to fuse. In Britain, however, when the Roman armies abandoned Britain at the beginning of the fifth century, the Angles and Saxons, Germanic tribes from Denmark and northern Germany, moved in and settled there.

Only one of the German states on the European continent proved long-lasting—the kingdom of the Franks. The establishment of a Frankish kingdom was the work of Clovis (c. 482–511), who became a Catholic Christian around 500. By 510, Clovis had established a powerful new Frankish kingdom stretching from the Pyrenees in the west to German lands in the east (modern France and western Germany). After Clovis's death, however, as was the Frankish custom, his sons divided his newly created kingdom, and during the sixth and seventh centuries, the once-united Frankish kingdom came to be divided into three major areas: Neustria, Austrasia, and Burgundy.

THE SOCIETY OF THE GERMANIC PEOPLES

As Germans and Romans intermarried and began to create a new society, some of the social customs of the Germanic peoples came to play an important role. The crucial social bond among the Germanic peoples was the family, especially the extended family of husbands, wives, children, brothers, sisters, cousins, and grandparents. Males were dominant and made all the important decisions. A woman obeyed her father until she married and then fell under the legal domination of her husband. For most women, life consisted of domestic labor: providing food and clothing for the household, caring for the children, and assisting with farming chores.

The German conception of family affected the way Germanic law treated the problem of crime and punishment. In the Roman system, as in our own, a crime such as murder was considered an offense against society or the state and was handled by a court that heard evidence and arrived at a decision. Germanic law was personal. An injury by one person against another could lead to a blood feud in which the family of the injured party took revenge on the family of the wrongdoer. Feuds could lead to savage acts of revenge, such as hacking off hands or feet or gouging out eyes. Because this system could easily get out of control, an alternative system arose that made use of a fine called *wergeld*, which was the amount paid by a wrongdoer to the family of the person injured or killed. *Wergeld*, which means "money for a man," was the value of a person in monetary terms. That value varied considerably according to social status. An offense against a nobleman, for example, cost considerably more than one against a slave.

The Role of the Christian Church

By the end of the fourth century, Christianity had become the predominant religion of the Roman Empire. As the official Roman state disintegrated, the Christian church played an increasingly important role in the growth of the new European civilization.

THE ORGANIZATION OF THE CHURCH

By the fourth century, the Christian church had developed a system of government. The Christian community in each city was headed by a bishop, whose area of jurisdiction was known as a bishopric, or diocese; the bishoprics

Political Divisions of Britain

- Angles
- Saxons
- Jutes
- Britons

bishops of Rome were considered Peter's successors and came to be known as popes (from the Latin word *papa*, meaning "father"). By the sixth century, popes had been successful in extending papal authority over the Christian church in the west and converting the pagan peoples of Germanic Europe. Their primary instrument of conversion was the monastic movement.

THE MONKS AND THEIR MISSIONS

A monk (in Latin, *monachus*, meaning "someone who lives alone") was a man who sought to live a life divorced from the world, cut off from ordinary human society, in order to pursue an ideal of total dedication to God. As the monastic ideal spread, a new form of monasticism based on living together in a community soon became the dominant form. Saint Benedict (c. 480–c. 543), who founded a monastic house for which he wrote a set of rules, established the basic form of monastic life in the western Christian church.

Benedict's rule divided each day into a series of activities, with primary emphasis on prayer and manual labor. Physical work of some kind was required of all monks for several hours a day because idleness was "the enemy of the soul." At the very heart of community practice was prayer, the proper "work of God." Although this included private meditation and reading, all monks gathered together seven times during the day for common prayer and chanting of psalms. The Benedictine life was a communal one. Monks ate, worked, slept, and worshiped together.

Each Benedictine monastery was strictly ruled by an abbot, or "father" of the monastery, who had complete authority over his fellow monks. Unquestioning obedience to the will of the abbot was expected of every monk. Each Benedictine monastery held lands that enabled it to be a self-sustaining community, isolated from and independent

of each Roman province were joined together under the direction of an archbishop. The bishops of four great cities—Rome, Jerusalem, Alexandria, and Antioch—held positions of special power in church affairs. Soon, however, one of them—the bishop of Rome—claimed that he was the sole leader of the western Christian church, which came to be known as the Roman Catholic church. According to church tradition, Jesus had given the keys to the kingdom of heaven to Peter, who was considered the chief apostle and the first bishop of Rome. Subsequent

The Granger Collection

⟫ **THE CORONATION OF CHARLEMAGNE.** After rebellion in 799 forced Pope Leo III to seek refuge at Charlemagne's court, Charlemagne went to Rome to settle the affair. There, on Christmas Day 800, he was crowned emperor of the Romans by the pope. This manuscript illustration shows Leo III placing a crown on Charlemagne's head.

of the world surrounding it. Within the monastery, however, monks were to fulfill their vow of poverty: "Let all things be common to all, as it is written, lest anyone should say that anything is his own."[1] Only men could be monks, but women, called nuns, also began to withdraw from the world to dedicate themselves to God.

Monasticism played an indispensable role in early medieval civilization. Monks became the new heroes of Christian civilization, and their dedication to God became the highest ideal of Christian life. They were the social workers of their communities: monks provided schools for the young, hospitality for travelers, and hospitals for the sick.

Monks also copied Latin works and passed on the legacy of the ancient world to the new European civilization. Monasteries became centers of learning wherever they were located, and monks worked to spread Christianity to all of Europe.

Women played an important role in the monastic missionary movement and the conversion of the Germanic kingdoms. Some served as abbesses (an abbess was the head of a monastery or a convent for nuns); many abbesses came from aristocratic families, especially in Anglo-Saxon England. In the kingdom of Northumbria, for example, Saint Hilda founded the monastery of Whitby in 657. As abbess, she was responsible for making learning an important part of the life of the monastery.

Charlemagne and the Carolingians

During the seventh and eighth centuries, as the kings of the Frankish kingdom gradually lost their power, the mayors of the palace—the chief officers of the king's household—assumed more control of the kingdom. One of these mayors, Pepin, finally took the logical step of assuming the kingship of the Frankish state for himself and his family. Upon his death in 768, his son came to the throne of the Frankish kingdom.

This new king was the dynamic and powerful ruler known to history as Charles the Great (768–814), or Charlemagne (from the Latin *Carolus Magnus*). He was determined and decisive, intelligent and inquisitive, a strong statesman, and a pious Christian. Himself unable to read or write, he was a wise patron of learning. In a series of military campaigns, he greatly expanded the territory he had inherited and created what came to be known as the Carolingian Empire. At its height, Charlemagne's empire covered much of western and central Europe; not until the time of Napoleon in the nineteenth century would an empire of its size be seen again in Europe.

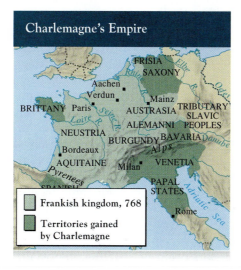

Charlemagne's Empire

FRISIA
SAXONY
Aachen
Verdun
Mainz
BRITTANY Paris AUSTRASIA TRIBUTARY SLAVIC PEOPLES
ALEMANNI
NEUSTRIA BURGUNDY BAVARIA
Bordeaux Alps
AQUITAINE Milan VENETIA
Pyrenees PAPAL STATES
SPANISH
Rome

☐ Frankish kingdom, 768
☐ Territories gained by Charlemagne

As Charlemagne's power grew, so did his prestige as the most powerful Christian ruler; one monk even wrote that he ruled the "kingdom of Europe." In 800, Charlemagne acquired a new title: emperor of the Romans. Charlemagne's coronation as Roman emperor demonstrated the strength, even after three hundred years, of the concept of an enduring Roman Empire. More important, it symbolized the fusion of the Roman, Christian, and Germanic elements that formed the base of European civilization. A Germanic king had been crowned emperor of the Romans by the spiritual leader of western Christendom. A new civilization had emerged.

THE WORLD OF LORDS AND VASSALS

The Carolingian Empire began to disintegrate soon after Charlemagne's death in 814, and less than thirty years later, in 843, it was divided among his grandsons into three major sections. At the same time, powerful nobles gained even more power in their own local territories while the Carolingian rulers fought each other. Invasions in different parts of the old Carolingian world added to the process of disintegration.

Invasions of the Ninth and Tenth Centuries

In the ninth and tenth centuries, western Europe was beset by a wave of invasions. Muslims attacked the southern coasts of Europe and sent raiding parties into southern France. The Magyars, a people from western Asia, moved into central Europe at the end of the ninth century and settled on the plains of Hungary, from where they made forays into western Europe. Finally crushed at the Battle of Lechfeld in Germany in 955, the Magyars converted to Christianity and settled down to create the kingdom of Hungary.

The most far-reaching attacks of the time came from the Northmen or Norsemen of Scandinavia, also known to us as the Vikings. The Vikings were warriors whose love of adventure and search for booty and new avenues of trade may have led them to invade other areas of Europe. Viking ships were the best of the period. Long and narrow with beautifully carved arched prows, the Viking dragon ships carried about fifty men. Their shallow draft enabled them to sail up European rivers and attack places at some distance inland. In the ninth century, Vikings sacked villages and towns, destroyed churches, and easily defeated small local armies.

By the mid-ninth century, the Northmen had begun to build winter settlements in different areas of Europe. By 850, groups of Norsemen from Norway had settled in Ireland, and Danes occupied northeastern England by 878. Beginning in 911, the ruler of the western Frankish lands gave one band of Vikings land at the mouth of the Seine River, forming a section of France that came to be known as Normandy. This policy of settling the Vikings and converting them to Christianity was a deliberate one; by their conversion to Christianity, the Vikings were soon made a part of European civilization.

The Development of Fief-Holding

The disintegration of central authority in the Carolingian world and the invasions by Muslims, Magyars, and Vikings led to the emergence of a new type of relationship between free individuals. When governments ceased to be able to defend their subjects, it became important to find some powerful lord who could offer protection in return for service. The contract sworn between a lord and his subordinate (known as a vassal) is the basis of a form of social organization that later generations of historians viewed as an organized system of government, which they called feudalism. But feudalism was never a system, and many historians today prefer to avoid using the term.

With the breakdown of royal governments, powerful nobles took control of large areas of land. They needed men to fight for them, so the practice arose of giving grants of land to vassals who in return would fight for their lord. The Frankish army had originally consisted of foot soldiers, dressed in coats of mail and armed with swords. But in the eighth century, a military change began to occur when larger horses and the stirrup were introduced. Earlier, horsemen had been throwers of spears. Now they came to be armored in coats of mail (the larger horse could carry the weight) and wielded long lances that enabled them to act as battering rams (the stirrup kept them on their horses). For almost five hundred years, warfare in Europe would be dominated by these mounted warriors, or knights, as they came to be called.

Of course, it was expensive to have a horse, armor, and weapons. It also took time and much practice to learn to wield these instruments skillfully from horseback. Consequently lords who wanted men to fight for them had to grant each vassal a piece of land that provided for the support of the vassal and his family. In return for the land, the vassal provided his lord with his fighting skills. Each needed the other. In the society of the Early Middle Ages (from 500 to 1000), where there was little trade and wealth was based primarily on land, land became the most important gift a lord could give to a vassal in return for his military service.

By the ninth century, the grant of land made to a vassal had become known as a fief. A fief was a piece of land held from the lord by a vassal in return for military service, but vassals who held such grants of land came to exercise rights of jurisdiction or political and legal authority within these fiefs. As the Carolingian world disintegrated politically under the impact of internal dissension and invasions, an increasing number of powerful lords arose who were now responsible for keeping order.

Fief-holding came to be characterized by a set of practices, known as the feudal contract, that determined the relationship between a lord and his vassal. The major obligation of a vassal to his lord was to perform military service, usually about forty days a year. A vassal was also required to appear at his lord's court when summoned to give advice to the lord. He might also be asked to sit in judgment in a legal case, since the important vassals of a lord were peers and only they could judge each other. Finally, vassals were also responsible for aids, or financial payments to the lord, on a number of occasions, among them the knighting of the lord's eldest son, the marriage of his eldest daughter, and the ransom of the lord's person if he were captured.

Under the feudal contract, a lord also had responsibilities toward his vassals. His major obligation was to protect his vassal, either by defending him militarily or by taking his side in a court of law. The lord was also responsible for the maintenance of the vassal, usually by granting him a fief.

The Nobility of the Middle Ages

In the High Middle Ages (the period between 1000 and 1300), European society, like that of Japan during the same period, was dominated by men whose chief concern was warfare. Like the Japanese samurai, many nobles loved war. As one nobleman wrote:

> And well I like to hear the call of "Help" and see the
>   wounded fall,
> Loudly for mercy praying,
> And see the dead, both great and small,
> Pierced by sharp spearheads one and all.[2]

The men of war were the lords and vassals of medieval society.

The lords were the kings, dukes, counts, barons, and viscounts (and even bishops and archbishops) who had extensive landholdings and wielded considerable political influence. They formed an aristocracy or nobility of people who held real political, economic, and social power. Both the great lords and ordinary knights were warriors, and the institution of knighthood united them. But there were also social divisions among them based on extremes of wealth and landholdings.

Although aristocratic women could legally hold property, most women remained under the control of men—their fathers until they married and their husbands after that. Nevertheless, these women had many opportunities for playing important roles. Because the lord was often away at war or at court, the lady of the castle had to manage the estate. Households could include large numbers of officials and servants, so this was no small responsibility. Maintaining the financial accounts alone took considerable financial knowledge. The lady of the castle was also responsible on a regular basis for overseeing the food supply and maintaining all the other supplies needed for the smooth operation of the household.

Although women were expected to be subservient to their husbands, there were many strong women who advised and sometimes even dominated their husbands. Perhaps most famous was Eleanor of Aquitaine (c. 1122–1204). Married to King Louis VII of France, Eleanor accompanied her husband on a Crusade, but her alleged affair with her uncle during the Crusade led Louis to have their marriage annulled. Eleanor then married Henry, duke of Normandy, who became King Henry II of England (1154–1189). She took an active role in politics, even assisting her sons in rebelling against Henry in 1173 and 1174.

EVOLUTION OF THE EUROPEAN KINGDOMS

The domination of society by the nobility reached its apex in the High Middle Ages. At the same time, kings began extending their power, and out of this growth in the monarchies would eventually come the European states that dominated much of later European history.

England in the High Middle Ages

On October 14, 1066, an army of heavily armed knights under William of Normandy landed on the coast of England and soundly defeated King Harold and his Anglo-Saxon foot soldiers. William was crowned king of England at Christmastime in London and then began the process of combining Anglo-Saxon and Norman institutions to create a new England. Many of the Norman knights were given parcels of land that they held as fiefs from the new English king. William made all nobles swear an oath of loyalty to him as sole ruler of England and insisted that all people owed loyalty to the king. All in all, William of Normandy established a strong, centralized monarchy.

In the twelfth century, the power of the English monarchy was greatly enlarged during the reign of Henry II (1154–1189). The new king was particularly successful in strengthening the power of the royal courts. Henry expanded the number of criminal cases to be tried in the king's court and also devised means for taking property cases from local courts to the royal courts. Henry's goals were clear: expanding the power of the royal courts expanded the king's power and, of course, brought revenues into his coffers. Moreover, since the royal courts were now found throughout England, a body of common law (law that was common to the whole kingdom) began to replace the different law codes that often varied from place to place.

Many English nobles came to resent the ongoing growth of the king's power and rose in rebellion during the reign of King John (1199–1216). At Runnymeade in 1215, John was forced to seal the Magna Carta (the Great Charter) guaranteeing feudal liberties. Feudal custom had always recognized that the relationship between king and vassals was based on mutual rights and obligations. The Magna Carta gave written recognition to that fact and was used in later years to support the idea that a monarch's power was limited.

During the reign of Edward I (1272–1307), an institution of great importance in the development of representative government—the English Parliament—also emerged. Originally the word *parliament* was applied to meetings of the king's Great Council, in which the greater barons and chief prelates of the church met with the king's judges and principal advisers to deal with judicial affairs. But in his need for money, Edward I in 1295 invited two knights from every county and two residents from each town to meet with the Great Council to consent to new taxes. This was the first Parliament.

The English Parliament, then, came to be composed of two knights from every county and two burgesses from every borough as well as the barons and ecclesiastical lords. Eventually barons and church lords formed the House of Lords; knights and burgesses, the House of Commons. The Parliaments of Edward I approved taxes, discussed politics, passed laws, and handled judicial business. The law of the realm was beginning to be determined not by the king alone but by the king in consultation with representatives of various groups that constituted the community.

Growth of the French Kingdom

In 843, the Carolingian Empire had been divided into three major sections. The western Frankish lands formed the core of the eventual kingdom of France. In 987, after the death of the last Carolingian king, the western Frank-

ish nobles chose Hugh Capet as the new king, thus establishing the Capetian dynasty of French kings. Although they carried the title of kings, the Capetians had little real power. They controlled as the royal domain only the lands around Paris known as the Île-de-France. As kings of France, the Capetians were formally the overlords of the great lords of France, such as the dukes of Normandy, Brittany, Burgundy, and Aquitaine. In reality, however, many of the dukes were considerably more powerful than the Capetian kings.

The reign of King Philip II Augustus (1180–1223) was an important turning point in the growth of the French monarchy. Philip II waged war against the Plantagenet rulers of England, who also ruled the French territories of Normandy, Maine, Anjou, and Aquitaine, and was successful in gaining control of most of these territories, thus enlarging the power of the French monarchy (see Map 12.2). To administer justice and collect royal revenues in his new territories, Philip appointed new royal officials,

MAP 12.2 **Europe in the High Middle Ages.** Although the nobility dominated much of European society in the High Middle Ages, kings began the process of extending their power in more effective ways, creating the monarchies that would form the European states. ➤ *Which were the strongest monarchical states by 1300? Why?*

thus inaugurating a French royal bureaucracy in the thirteenth century.

Capetian rulers after Philip II continued to add lands to the royal domain. Philip IV the Fair (1285–1314) was especially effective in strengthening the French monarchy. He reinforced the royal bureaucracy and also brought a French parliament into being by asking representatives of the three estates, or classes—the clergy (first estate), the nobles (second estate), and the townspeople (third estate)—to meet with him. They did so in 1302, inaugurating the Estates-General, the first French parliament, although it had little real power. By the end of the thirteenth century, France was the largest, wealthiest, and best-governed monarchical state in Europe.

The Lands of the Holy Roman Empire

In the tenth century, the powerful dukes of the Saxons became kings of the eastern Frankish kingdom (or Germany, as it came to be called). The best known of the Saxon kings of Germany was Otto I (936–973), who intervened in Italian politics and for his efforts was crowned by the pope in 962 as emperor of the Romans, reviving a title that had not been used since the time of Charlemagne. Otto's creation of a new "Roman Empire" in the hands of the eastern Franks (or Germans) added a tremendous burden to the king of Germany, who now took on the onerous task of ruling Italy as well.

In the eleventh century, German kings created a strong monarchy and a powerful empire by leading armies into Italy. The German kings also tried to bolster their power by using their position as emperors to exploit the resources of Italy. But this tended to backfire; many a German king lost armies in Italy in pursuit of a dream of empire, and no German dynasty demonstrates this better than the Hohenstaufens.

The two most famous members of the Hohenstaufen dynasty, Frederick I (1152–1190) and Frederick II (1212–1250), tried to create a new kind of empire. Frederick I planned to get his chief revenues from Italy as the center of a "holy empire," as he called it (hence the name Holy Roman Empire). But his attempt to conquer northern Italy ran into severe opposition from the pope and the cities of northern Italy. An alliance of these north Italian cities, with the support of the pope, defeated the forces of Emperor Frederick I in 1176.

The main goal of Frederick II was the establishment of a strong centralized state in Italy dominated by the kingdom he had inherited in Sicily. Frederick's major task was to gain control of northern Italy. In attempting to conquer Italy, however, he became involved in a deadly struggle with the popes, who feared that a single ruler of northern and southern Italy meant the end of papal power in central Italy. The north Italian cities were also unwilling to give up their freedom. Frederick waged a bitter struggle in northern Italy, winning many battles but ultimately losing the war.

The struggle between popes and emperors had dire consequences for the Holy Roman Empire. By spending their time fighting in Italy, the German emperors left Germany in the hands of powerful German lords who ignored the emperor and created their own independent kingdoms. This ensured that the German monarchy would remain weak and incapable of maintaining a centralized monarchical state; thus the German Holy Roman Emperor had no real power over either Germany or Italy. Unlike France and England, neither Germany nor Italy created a unified national monarchy in the Middle Ages. Both Germany and Italy consisted of many small, independent states, a situation that changed little until the nineteenth century.

The Slavic Peoples of Central and Eastern Europe

East of the Carolingian Empire lay a spacious plain through which a number of Asiatic nomads, including the Huns, Bulgars, Avars, and Magyars, had pushed their way westward. Eastern Europe was ravaged by these successive waves of invaders who found it relatively easy to create large empires that were in turn overthrown by the next invaders. Over a period of time, the invaders themselves were largely assimilated with the native Slavic peoples of the area.

The Slavic peoples were originally a single people in central Europe, but they gradually divided into three major groups: the western, southern, and eastern Slavs (see Map 12.3). The western Slavs eventually formed the Polish and Bohemian kingdoms. German Christian missionaries converted both the Czechs in Bohemia and the Slavs in Poland by the tenth century. The non-Slavic kingdom of Hungary, which emerged after the Magyars settled down after their defeat in 955, was also converted to Christianity by German missionaries. The Poles, Czechs, and Hungarians all accepted Catholic or western Christianity and became closely tied to the Roman Catholic church and its Latin culture.

The southern and eastern Slavic populations took a different path: the Slavic peoples of Moravia were converted to the Orthodox Christianity of the Byzantine Empire by two Byzantine missionary brothers, Cyril and Methodius, who began their activities in 863. They created the Slavonic (Cyrillic) alphabet, translated the Bible into Slavonic, and developed Slavonic church services. While the southern Slavic peoples accepted Christianity, a split eventually developed between the Croats, who accepted the Roman Catholic church, and the Serbs, who remained loyal to Orthodox Christianity.

Although the Bulgars were originally an Asiatic people who conquered much of the Balkan peninsula, they were eventually absorbed by the larger native south Slavic population. Together they formed a largely Slavic Bulgarian kingdom that embraced the church services earlier developed by Cyril and Methodius.

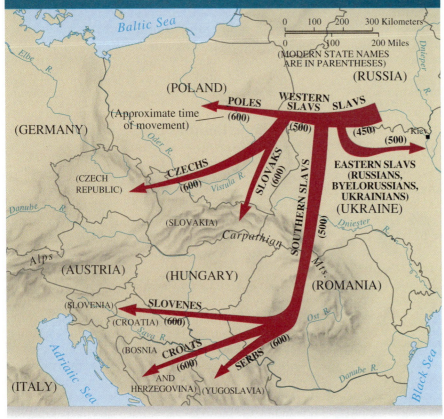

MAP 12.3 The Migrations of the Slavs. Originally from east-central Europe, the Slavic people broke into three groups. The western Slavs converted to Catholic Christianity, while the eastern Slavs and southern Slavs, under the influence of the Byzantine Empire, embraced the Eastern Orthodox faith. ➤ *What connections do these Slavic migrations have with what we today characterize as eastern Europe?*

The eastern Slavic peoples, from whom the modern Russians, Byelorussians, and Ukrainians are descended, had settled in the territory of present-day Ukraine and European Russia. There, beginning in the late eighth century, they began to encounter Swedish Vikings who moved down the extensive network of rivers into the lands of the eastern Slavs in search of booty and new trade routes (see the box on p. 251). These Vikings built trading settlements and eventually came to dominate the native peoples, who called them "the Rus," from which the name *Russia* is derived.

THE DEVELOPMENT OF RUSSIA

A Viking leader named Oleg (c. 873–913) settled in Kiev at the beginning of the tenth century and created the Rus state known as the principality of Kiev. His successors extended their control over the eastern Slavs and expanded the territory of Kiev until it included the territory between the Baltic and Black Seas and the Danube and Volga Rivers. By marrying Slavic wives, the Viking ruling class was gradually assimilated into the Slavic population.

The growth of the principality of Kiev attracted religious missionaries, especially from the Byzantine Empire. One Rus ruler, Vladimir (c. 980–1015), married the Byzantine emperor's sister and officially accepted Christianity for himself and his people in 987. From the end of the tenth century, Byzantine Christianity became the model for Russian religious life.

The Kievan Rus state prospered and reached its high point in the first half of the eleventh century. But civil wars and new invasions by Asiatic nomads caused the principality of Kiev to collapse, and the sack of Kiev by north Russian princes in 1169 brought an end to the first Russian state. That first Russian state had remained closely tied to the Byzantine Empire, not to the new Europe. In the thirteenth century, the Mongols conquered Russia and cut it off even more from Europe.

The Mongols had exploded on the scene in the thirteenth century, moving east into China and west into the Middle East and central Europe. Although they conquered Russia, they were not numerous enough to settle the vast Russian lands. They occupied only part of Russia but required Russian princes to pay tribute to them. One Russian prince soon emerged as more powerful than the others. Alexander Nevsky, prince of Novgorod, defeated a German invading army in northwestern Russia in 1242. His cooperation with the Mongols won him their favor. The khan, leader of the western part of the Mongol Empire, rewarded Alexander Nevsky with the title of grand-prince, enabling his descendants to become the princes of Moscow and eventually leaders of all Russia.

THE WORLD OF PEASANTS AND TOWNSPEOPLE

In the Early Middle Ages, Europe had a relatively small population, but in the High Middle Ages, the number of people nearly doubled, from 38 to 74 million. What

A MUSLIM'S DESCRIPTION
OF THE RUS

Despite the difficulties that travel presented, early medieval civilization did witness some contact among the various cultures. This might occur through trade, diplomacy, or the conquest and migration of peoples. This document is a description of the Swedish Rus, who eventually merged with the native Slavic peoples to form the principality of Kiev, commonly regarded as the first Russian state. It was written by Ibn Fadlan, a Muslim diplomat sent from Baghdad in 921 to a settlement on the Volga River. His comments on the filthiness of the Rus reflect the Muslim preoccupation with cleanliness.

IBN FADLAN, DESCRIPTION OF THE RUS

I saw the Rus folk when they arrived on their trading mission and settled at the river Atul (Volga). Never had I seen people of more perfect physique. They are tall as date palms, and reddish in color. They wear neither coat nor kaftan, but each man carried a cape which covers one half of his body, leaving one hand free. No one is ever parted from his axe, sword, and knife. Their swords are Frankish in design, broad, flat, and fluted. Each man has a number of trees, figures, and the like from the fingernails to the neck. Each woman carried on her bosom a container made of iron, silver, copper, or gold—its size and substance depending on her man's wealth.

They [the Rus] are the filthiest of God's creatures. They do not wash after discharging their natural functions, neither do they wash their hands after meals. They are as lousy as donkeys. They arrive from their distant lands and lay their ships alongside the banks of the Atul, which is a great river, and there they build big houses on its shores. Ten or twenty of them may live together in one house, and each of them has a couch of his own where he sits and diverts himself with the pretty slave girls whom he had brought along for sale. He will make love with one of them while a comrade looks on; sometimes they indulge in a communal orgy, and, if a customer should turn up to buy a girl, the Rus man will not let her go till he has finished with her.

They wash their hands and faces every day in incredibly filthy water. Every morning the girl brings her master a large bowl of water in which he washes his hands and face and hair, then blows his nose into it and spits into it. When he has finished the girl takes the bowl to his neighbor—who repeats the performance. Thus the bowl goes the rounds of the entire household. . . .

If one of the Rus folk falls sick they put him in a tent by himself and leave bread and water for him. They do not visit him, however, or speak to him, especially if he is a serf. Should he recover he rejoins the others; if he dies they burn him. But if he happens to be a serf they leave him for the dogs and vultures to devour. If they catch a robber they hang him to a tree until he is torn to shreds by wind and weather.

---

accounted for this dramatic increase? For one thing, conditions in Europe were more settled and more peaceful after the invasions of the Early Middle Ages had ended. For another, agricultural production surged after 1000.

The New Agriculture

During the High Middle Ages, Europeans began to farm in new ways. An improvement in climate resulted in better growing conditions, but an important factor in increasing food production was the expansion of cultivated or arable land, accomplished by clearing forested areas. Peasants of the eleventh and twelfth centuries cut down trees and drained swamps until by the thirteenth century, Europeans had more acreage available for farming than at any time before or since.

Technological changes also furthered the development of farming. The Middle Ages saw an explosion of labor-saving devices, many of which were made from iron, which was mined in different areas of Europe. Iron was used to make scythes, axes, and hoes for use on farms as well as saws, hammers, and nails for building purposes. Iron was crucial in making the *carruca*, a heavy, wheeled plow with an iron plowshare pulled by teams of horses, which could turn over the heavy clay soil north of the Alps.

Besides using horsepower, the High Middle Ages harnessed the power of water and wind to do jobs formerly done by humans or animals. Located along streams, mills powered by water were used to grind grains and produce flour. Where rivers were lacking or not easily dammed, Europeans developed windmills to harness the power of the wind.

The shift from a two-field to a three-field system also contributed to the increase in food production. In the Early Middle Ages, peasants planted one field while another of equal size was allowed to lie fallow to regain its fertility. Now estates were divided into three parts. One field was planted in the fall with winter grains, such as rye and wheat, while spring grains, such as oats or barley, and vegetables, such as peas or beans, were planted in the second field. The third was allowed to lie fallow. By rotating their use, only one-third rather than one-half of the land lay fallow at any time. The rotation of crops also kept the soil from being exhausted so quickly, and more crops could now be grown.

Chronology

THE EUROPEAN KINGDOMS

England

Norman conquest	1066
William the Conqueror	1066–1087
Henry II	1154–1189
John	1199–1216
Magna Carta	1215
Edward I	1272–1307
First Parliament	1295

France

Philip II Augustus	1180–1223
Philip IV	1285–1314
First Estates-General	1302

Germany and the Empire

Otto I	936–973
Frederick I Barbarossa	1152–1190
Northern Italian cities defeat Frederick	1176
Frederick II	1212–1250

The Eastern World

Mongol conquest of Russia	1230s
Alexander Nevsky, prince of Novgorod	c. 1220–1263

The Manorial System

The landholding class of nobles and knights contained a military elite whose ability to function as warriors depended on having the leisure time to pursue the arts of war. Landed estates, located on the fiefs given to a vassal by his lord and worked by a dependent peasant class, provided the economic sustenance that made this way of life possible. A manor or villa was simply an agricultural estate operated by a lord and worked by peasants. Although a large class of free peasants continued to exist, increasing numbers of free peasants became serfs—persons bound to the land and required to provide labor services, pay rents, and be subject to the lord's jurisdiction. By the ninth century, probably 60 percent of the population of western Europe had become serfs.

Labor services consisted of working the lord's demesne, the land retained by the lord, which might consist of one-third to one-half of the cultivated lands scattered throughout the manor. The rest would be used by the peasants for themselves. Building barns and digging ditches were also part of the labor services. Serfs usually worked about three days a week for their lord and paid rents by giving the lord a share of every product they raised.

Serfs were legally bound to the lord's lands and could not leave without his permission. Although free to marry,

serfs could not marry anyone outside their manor without the lord's approval. Moreover, lords sometimes exercised public rights or political authority on their lands, which gave them the right to try peasants in their own courts.

Daily Life of the Peasantry

The lifestyle of the peasants was quite simple. Their cottages consisted of wood frames surrounded by sticks with the space between them filled with rubble and then plastered over with clay. Roofs were simply thatched. The houses of poorer peasants consisted of a single room, but others had at least two rooms—a main room for cooking, eating, and other activities and another room for sleeping.

Peasant women occupied both an important and difficult position in manorial society. They were expected to carry and bear their children and at the same time fulfill their obligation to labor in the fields. Their ability to manage the household might determine whether a peasant family would starve or survive in difficult times.

Though simple, a peasant's daily diet was adequate when food was available. The staple of the peasant diet, and the medieval diet in general, was bread. Women made the dough for the bread at home, then brought their loaves to be baked in community ovens, which were owned by the lord of the manor. Peasant bread was highly nutritious, containing not only wheat and rye but also barley, millet, and oats, giving it a dark appearance and a very heavy, hard texture. Bread was supplemented by numerous vegetables from the household gardens, cheese from cow's or goat's milk, nuts and berries from woodlands, and fruits, such as apples, pears, and cherries. Chickens provided eggs and sometimes meat.

The Revival of Trade

Medieval Europe was overwhelmingly an agrarian society, with most people living in small villages. In the eleventh and twelfth centuries, however, new elements were introduced that began to transform the economic foundation of European civilization: a revival of trade, the emergence of specialized craftspeople and artisans, and the growth and development of towns.

The revival of trade was a gradual process. During the chaotic conditions of the Early Middle Ages, large-scale trade had declined in western Europe except for Byzantine contacts with Italy and the Jewish traders who moved back and forth between the Muslim and Christian worlds. By the end of the tenth century, however, people were emerging in Europe with both the skills and the products for commercial activity. Cities in Italy took the lead in this revival of trade. Venice, for example, emerged as a town by the end of the eighth century, developed a mercantile fleet, and by the end of the tenth century had become the chief western trading center for Byzantine and Islamic commerce. In the High Middle Ages, Italian merchants became even more daring in their trade activities. They established trading posts in Cairo, Damascus, and a number of Black Sea ports, where they acquired goods brought by Muslim merchants from India, China, and Southeast Asia. A few Italian merchants even journeyed to India and China in search of trade (see the box on p. 254).

While the northern Italian cities were busy trading in the Mediterranean, the towns of Flanders were doing likewise in northern Europe. Flanders, the area along the coast of present-day Belgium and northern France, was known for its high-quality woolen cloth. The location of Flanders made it an ideal center for the traders of northern Europe. Merchants from England, Scandinavia, France, and Germany converged there to trade their goods for woolen cloth. Flanders prospered in the eleventh and twelfth centuries. By the twelfth century, a regular exchange of goods had developed between Flanders and Italy, the two major centers of northern and southern European trade.

As trade increased, both gold and silver came to be in demand at fairs and trading markets of all kinds. Slowly a money economy began to emerge. New trading companies and banking firms were set up to manage the exchange and sale of goods. All of these new practices were part of the rise of commercial capitalism, an economic system in which people invested in trade and goods in order to make profits.

The Growth of Cities

The revival of trade led to a revival of cities. Towns had greatly declined in the Early Middle Ages, especially in Europe north of the Alps. Old Roman cities continued

The New Agriculture in the Medieval World

New agricultural methods and techniques in the Middle Ages enabled peasants in both Europe and China to increase food production. This general improvement in diet was a factor in supporting noticeably larger populations in both areas. At the bottom, a thirteenth-century illustration shows a group of English peasants harvesting grain. Overseeing their work is a bailiff, or manager, who supervised the work of the peasants. At the right, a twelfth-century painting shows Chinese peasants transplanting month-old seedlings from the nursery bed to their permanent field. Rice became the staple food in China.

AN ITALIAN BANKER DISCUSSES TRADING BETWEEN EUROPE AND CHINA

Working on behalf of a banking guild in Florence, Francesco Balducci Pegolotti journeyed to England and Cyprus. As a result of his contacts with many Italian merchants, he acquired considerable information about long-distance trade between Europe and China. In this account, written in 1340, he provides advice for Italian merchants.

FRANCESCO BALDUCCI PEGOLOTTI, AN ACCOUNT OF TRADERS BETWEEN EUROPE AND CHINA

In the first place, you must let your beard grow long and not shave. And at Tana [modern Rostov] you should furnish yourself with a guide. And you must not try to save money in the matter of guides by taking a bad one instead of a good one. For the additional wages of the good one will not cost you so much as you will save by having him. And besides the guide it will be well to take at least two good menservants who are acquainted with the Turkish tongue. . . .

The road you travel from Tana to China is perfectly safe, whether by day or night, according to what the mer-chants say who have used it. Only if the merchant, in going or coming, should die upon the road, everything belonging to him will become the possession of the lord in the country in which he dies. . . . And in like manner if he dies in China. . . .

China is a province which contains a multitude of cities and towns. Among others there is one in particular, that is to say the capital city, to which many merchants are attracted, and in which there is a vast amount of trade; and this city is called Khanbaliq [modern Beijing]. And the said city has a circuit of one hundred miles, and is all full of people and houses and of dwellers in the said city. . . .

Whatever silver the merchants may carry with them as far as China, the emperor of China will take from them and put into his treasury. And to merchants who thus bring silver they give that paper money of theirs in exchange . . . and with this money you can readily buy silk and all other merchandise that you have a desire to buy. And all the people of the country are bound to receive it. And yet you shall not pay a higher price for your goods because your money is of paper.

---

to exist but had dwindled in size and population. With the revival of trade, merchants began to settle in these old cities, followed by craftspeople or artisans, people who on manors or elsewhere had developed skills and now saw an opportunity to ply their trade and make goods that could be sold by the merchants. In the course of the eleventh and twelfth centuries, the old Roman cities came alive with new populations and growth.

Beginning in the late tenth century, many new cities or towns were also founded, particularly in northern Europe. Usually a group of merchants established a settlement near some fortified stronghold, such as a castle or monastery. (This explains why so many place names in Europe end in *borough*, *burgh*, *burg*, or *bourg*, which means "fortress" or "walled enclosure.") Castles were particularly favored because they were generally located along trade routes; the lords of the castle also offered protection. If the settlement prospered and expanded, new walls were built to protect it.

Although lords wanted to treat towns and townspeople as they would their vassals and serfs, cities had totally different needs and a different perspective. Townspeople needed mobility to trade. Consequently these merchants and artisans (who came to be called *burghers* or *bourgeois*, from the same root as *borough* and *burg*) needed their own unique laws to meet their requirements and were willing to pay for them. In many instances, lords and kings saw that they could also make money and were willing to sell to the townspeople the liberties they were beginning to demand, including the right to bequeath goods and sell property, freedom from any military obligation to the lord, and written urban laws that guaranteed their freedom. Some towns also obtained the right to govern themselves by choosing their own officials and administering their own courts of law.

As time went on, medieval cities developed their own governments for running the affairs of the community. Only males who were born in the city or had lived there for a particular length of time were defined as citizens. In many cities, these citizens elected members of a city coun-cil who served as judges and city officials and passed laws.

Medieval cities remained relatively small in compari-son to either ancient or modern cities. A large trading city would number about 5,000 inhabitants. By 1200, London was the largest city in England with 30,000 people. Oth-erwise, north of the Alps, only a few great urban centers of commerce, such as Bruges and Ghent, had a population close to 40,000. Italian cities tended to be larger, with Venice, Florence, Genoa, Milan, and Naples numbering almost 100,000. Even the largest European city, however, seemed small alongside the Byzantine capital of Constan-tinople or the Arab cities of Damascus, Baghdad, and Cairo.

DAILY LIFE IN THE MEDIEVAL CITY

Medieval towns were surrounded by stone walls that were expensive to build, so the space within was precious. Con-sequently most medieval cities featured narrow, winding streets with houses crowded against each other and second and third stories extending out over the streets. Because dwellings were built mostly of wood before the fourteenth century and candles and wood fires were used for light and heat, fire was a constant threat. Medieval cities burned rapidly once a fire started.

Most of the people who lived in cities were merchants involved in trade and artisans engaged in manufacturing a wide range of goods, such as cloth, metalwork, shoes, and leather goods. Generally merchants and artisans had their own sections within a city. The merchant area included warehouses, inns, and taverns. Artisan sections were usually divided along craft lines. From the twelfth century on, craftspeople began to organize themselves into guilds, and by the thirteenth century, there were individual guilds for virtually every craft. Each craft had its own street where its activity was pursued.

The physical environment of medieval cities was not pleasant. They were often dirty and rife with smells from animal and human waste deposited in backyard privies or on the streets. Cities were unable to stop water pollution, especially from the tanning and animal-slaughtering industries, which dumped their waste products into the river.

Because of the pollution, cities did not use the rivers for drinking water but relied instead on wells. Private and public baths also existed in medieval towns. Paris, for example, had thirty-two public baths for men and women. City laws did not allow lepers and people with "bad reputations" to use them. This did not, however, prevent public baths from being known for permissiveness due to public nudity. One contemporary commented on what occurred in public bathhouses: "Shameful things. Men make a point of staying all night in the public baths and women at the break of day come in and through 'ignorance' find themselves in the men's rooms."[3]

In medieval cities, women, in addition to supervising the household, purchasing food, preparing meals, raising the children, and managing the family finances, were also often expected to help their husbands in their trades. Some women also developed their own trades to earn extra money. When some master craftspeople died, their widows even carried on their trades. Some women in medieval towns were thus able to lead lives of considerable independence.

CHRISTIANITY AND MEDIEVAL CIVILIZATION

Christianity was an integral part of the fabric of European society and the consciousness of Europe. Papal directives affected the actions of kings and princes alike, and Christian teachings and practices touched the lives of all Europeans.

The Papal Monarchy

Since the fifth century, the popes of the Catholic church had reigned supreme over the affairs of the church. They had also come to exercise control over the territories in central Italy that came to be known as the Papal States, which kept the popes involved in political matters, often at the expense of their spiritual obligations. At the same time, the church became increasingly entangled in the evolving feudal relationships. High officials of the church, such as bishops and abbots, came to hold their offices as fiefs from nobles. As vassals, they were obliged to carry out the usual duties, including military service. Of course, lords assumed the right to choose their vassals and thus came to appoint bishops and abbots.

REFORM OF THE PAPACY

By the eleventh century, church leaders realized the need to free the church from the interference of lords in the appointment of church officials. Lay investiture was the practice by which secular rulers both chose nominees to church offices and invested them with the symbols of their office. Pope Gregory VII (1073–1085) decided to fight this practice. Gregory claimed that he—the pope—was God's "vicar on earth" and that the pope's authority extended over all of Christendom, including its rulers. In 1075, he issued a decree forbidding high-ranking clerics from receiving their investiture from lay leaders.

Gregory VII soon found himself in conflict with the king of Germany over his actions. King Henry IV (1056–1106) of Germany was also a determined man who had appointed high-ranking clerics, especially bishops, as his vassals in order to use them as administrators. Henry had no intention of obeying a decree that challenged the very heart of his administration.

The struggle between Henry IV and Gregory VII, which is known as the Investiture Controversy, was one of the great conflicts between church and state in the High Middle Ages. It dragged on until a new German king and a new pope reached a compromise in 1122 called the Concordat of Worms. Under this agreement, a bishop in Germany was first elected by church officials. After election, the nominee paid homage to the king as his lord, who then invested him with the symbols of temporal office. A representative of the pope, however, then invested the new bishop with the symbols of his spiritual office.

THE CHURCH SUPREME

The popes of the twelfth century did not abandon the reform ideals of Pope Gregory VII, but they were more inclined to consolidate their power and build a strong administrative system. During the papacy of Pope Innocent III (1198–1216), the Catholic church reached the height of its power. At the beginning of his pontificate, in a letter to a priest, the pope made a clear statement of his views on papal supremacy:

> As God, the creator of the universe, set two great lights in the firmament of heaven, the greater light to rule the day, and the lesser light to rule the night, so He set two great dignities in the firmament of the universal church, . . . the greater to rule the day, that is, souls, and the lesser to rule the night, that is, bodies. These dignities are the papal authority and the royal power. And just as the moon gets her light from the sun, and is inferior to the sun . . . so the royal power gets the splendor of its dignity from the papal authority.[4]

Innocent III's actions were those of a man who believed that he, the pope, was the supreme judge of European affairs. To achieve his political ends, he did not hesitate to use the spiritual weapons at his command, especially the interdict, which forbade priests to dispense the sacraments of the church in the hope that the people, deprived of the comforts of religion, would exert pressure against their ruler.

New Religious Orders and New Spiritual Ideals

Between 1050 and 1150, a wave of religious enthusiasm seized Europe, leading to a spectacular growth in the number of monasteries and the emergence of new monastic orders. Most important was the Cistercian order, founded in 1098 by a group of monks dissatisfied with the lack of a strict discipline at their own Benedictine monastery. The Cistercians were strict. They ate a simple diet and possessed only a single robe apiece. More time for prayer and manual labor was provided by shortening the number of hours spent at religious services. The Cistercians played a major role in developing a new, activist spiritual model for twelfth-century Europe. A Benedictine monk often spent hours in prayer to honor God. The Cistercian ideal had a different emphasis: "Arise, soldier of Christ, arise! Get up off the ground and return to the battle from which you have fled! Fight more boldly after your flight, and triumph in glory!"[5] These were the words of Saint Bernard of Clairvaux (1090–1153), who more than any

other person embodied the new spiritual ideal of Cistercian monasticism.

Women were also actively involved in the spiritual movements of the age. The number of women joining religious houses grew dramatically in the High Middle Ages. Most nuns were from the ranks of the landed aristocracy. Convents were convenient for families unable or unwilling to find husbands for their daughters and for aristocratic women who did not wish to marry. Female intellectuals found them a haven for their activities. Most of the learned women of the Middle Ages were nuns.

In the thirteenth century, two new religious orders emerged that had a profound impact on the lives of ordinary people. Like their founder, Saint Francis of Assisi (1182–1226), the Franciscans lived among the people, preaching repentance and aiding the poor. Their calls for a return to the simplicity and poverty of the early church, reinforced by their own example, were especially effective and made them very popular.

Dominicans arose out of the desire of a Spanish priest, Dominic de Guzmán (1170–1221), to defend church teachings from heresy—beliefs contrary to official church doctrine. Dominic was an intellectual who came to believe that a new religious order of men who lived lives of poverty but were learned and capable of preaching effectively would best be able to attack heresy. The Dominicans became especially well known for their roles as the inquisitors of the papal Inquisition.

The Holy Office, as the papal Inquisition was formally called, was a court that had been established by the church to find and try heretics. Anyone accused of heresy who

A GROUP OF NUNS. Although still viewed by the medieval church as inferior to men, women were as susceptible to the spiritual fervor of the twelfth century as men, and female monasticism grew accordingly. This miniature shows a group of Flemish nuns listening to the preaching of an abbot, Gilles li Muisis. The nun wearing a white robe at the far left is a novice.

refused to confess was still considered guilty and was turned over to the state for execution. To the Christians of the thirteenth century, who believed that there was only one path to salvation, heresy was a crime against God and against humanity. In their minds, force should be used to save souls from damnation.

THE CULTURE OF THE HIGH MIDDLE AGES

The High Middle Ages was a time of extraordinary intellectual and artistic vitality. It witnessed the birth of universities and a building spree that left Europe bedecked with churches and cathedrals.

The Rise of Universities

The university as we know it—with faculty, students, and degrees—is a product of the High Middle Ages. The word *university* is derived from the Latin word *universitas*, meaning a corporation or guild, and referred to either a corporation of teachers or a corporation of students. Medieval universities were educational guilds or corporations that produced educated and trained individuals.

The first European university appeared in Bologna, Italy, where a great teacher named Irnerius (1088–1125), who taught Roman law, attracted students from all over Europe. Most of them were laymen, usually older individuals who were administrators for kings and princes and were eager to learn more about law to apply it in their own jobs. To protect themselves, students at Bologna formed a guild or *universitas*, which was recognized by Emperor Frederick Barbarossa and given a charter in 1158. Kings, popes, and princes soon competed to found new universities, and by the end of the Middle Ages, there were eighty universities in Europe, most of them in England, France, Italy, and Germany.

University students (all men—women did not attend universities in the Middle Ages) began their studies with the traditional liberal arts curriculum, which consisted of grammar, rhetoric, logic, arithmetic, geometry, music, and astronomy. Teaching was done by the lecture method. The word *lecture* is derived from the Latin verb for "read." Before the development of the printing press in the fifteenth century, books were expensive and few students could afford them, so teachers read from a basic text (such as a collection of laws if the subject was law) and then added their explanations. No exams were given after a series of lectures, but when a student applied for a degree, he was given a comprehensive oral examination by a committee of teachers. The exam was taken after a four- or six-year period of study. The first degree a student could earn was a bachelor of arts; later he might receive a master of arts.

After completing the liberal arts curriculum, a student could go on to study law, medicine, or theology. The study of law, medicine, or theology could take a decade or more. A student who passed his final oral examinations was granted a doctor's degree, which officially enabled him to teach his subject. Students who received degrees from medieval universities could pursue other careers besides teaching that proved to be much more lucrative. A law degree was necessary for those who wished to serve as advisers to kings and princes. The growing administrative bureaucracies of popes and kings also demanded a supply of clerks with a university education who could keep records and draw up official documents. Universities provided the teachers, administrators, lawyers, and doctors for medieval society.

The Development of Scholasticism

The importance of Christianity in medieval society made it certain that theology would play a central role in the European intellectual world. Theology, the formal study of religion, was "queen of the sciences" in the new universities.

Beginning in the eleventh century, the effort to apply reason or logical analysis to the church's basic theological doctrines had a significant impact on the study of theology. The word *scholasticism* is used to refer to the philosophical and theological system of the medieval schools. Scholasticism tried to reconcile faith and reason, to demonstrate that what was accepted on faith was in harmony with what could be learned by reason.

The overriding task of scholasticism was to harmonize Christian teachings with the work of the Greek philosopher Aristotle. In the twelfth century, due largely to the work of Muslim and Jewish scholars, western Europe was introduced to a large number of Greek scientific and philosophical works, including the works of Aristotle. However, Aristotle's works threw many theologians into consternation. Aristotle was so highly regarded that he was called "the philosopher"; yet he had arrived at his conclusions by rational thought, not by faith, and some of his doctrines contradicted the teachings of the church. The most famous attempt to reconcile Aristotle and the doctrines of Christianity was that of Saint Thomas Aquinas.

Thomas Aquinas (1225–1274) is best known for his *Summa Theologica* (*A Summa of Theology*—a summa was a compendium of knowledge that attempted to bring together all the received learning of the preceding centuries on a given subject). Aquinas's masterpiece was organized according to the dialectical method of the scholastics. Aquinas first posed a question, cited sources that offered opposing opinions on the question, and then resolved the matter by arriving at his own conclusions. In this fashion, Aquinas raised and discussed some six hundred articles.

Aquinas's reputation derives from his masterful attempt to reconcile faith and reason. He took it for granted that there were truths derived by reason and truths derived by faith. He was certain, however, that the two truths could not be in conflict. The natural mind, unaided by faith, could arrive at truths concerning the physical universe. Without the help of God's grace, however, reason alone could not grasp spiritual truths, such as the Trinity (the manifestation of God in three separate yet identical persons—Father, Son, and Holy Spirit) or the Incarnation (Jesus' simultaneous identity as God and human).

The Gothic Cathedral

Begun in the twelfth century and brought to perfection in the thirteenth, the Gothic cathedral remains one of the greatest artistic triumphs of the High Middle Ages. Soaring skyward, as if to reach heaven, it was a fitting symbol for medieval people's preoccupation with God.

Two fundamental innovations of the twelfth century made Gothic cathedrals possible. The combination of ribbed vaults and pointed arches replaced the barrel vault of earlier churches and enabled builders to make Gothic churches higher. The use of pointed arches and ribbed vaults created an impression of upward movement, a sense of weightless upward thrust that implied the energy of God. Another technical innovation, the flying buttress, basically a heavy arched pier of stone built onto the outside of the walls, made it possible to distribute the weight of the church's vaulted ceilings outward and down and thus eliminate the heavy walls used in earlier churches to hold the weight of the massive barrel vaults. Thus Gothic cathedrals could be built with thin walls containing magnificent stained-glass windows, which created a play of light inside that varied with the sun at different times of the day. The extensive use of colored light in Gothic cathedrals was not accidental but reflected the belief that natural light was a symbol of the divine light of God.

The first fully Gothic church was the abbey of Saint-Denis near Paris, inspired by its famous Abbot Suger (1122–1151) and built between 1140 and 1150. Although the Gothic style was a product of northern France, by the mid-thirteenth century, French Gothic architecture had spread to virtually all of Europe. French Gothic architecture was seen most brilliantly in cathedrals in Paris (Notre-Dame), Reims, Amiens, and Chartres.

A Gothic cathedral was the work of the entire community. All classes contributed to its construction. Master masons, who were both architects and engineers, designed them, and stonemasons and other craftspeople were paid a daily wage and provided the skilled labor to build them. A Gothic cathedral symbolized the chief preoccupation of a medieval Christian community, its dedication to a spiritual ideal. The largest buildings of an era reflect the values of its society. The Gothic cathedral, with its towers soaring toward heaven, gave witness to an age when a spiritual impulse underlay most aspects of life.

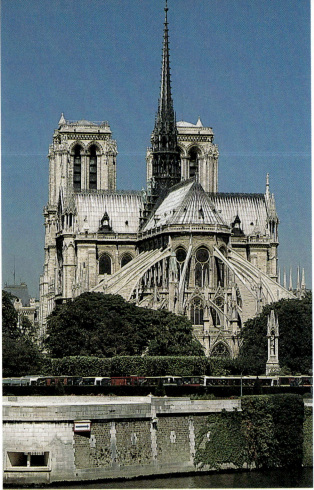

© Sylvain Grandadam/Photo Researchers, Inc.

THE GOTHIC CATHEDRAL. The Gothic cathedral was one of the great artistic triumphs of the High Middle Ages. Seen here is the cathedral of Notre-Dame in Paris. Begun in 1163, it was not completed until the beginning of the fourteenth century.

THE EXPANSION OF MEDIEVAL EUROPE: THE CRUSADES

As it developed, European civilization remained largely confined to one geographical area. Some Europeans, especially merchants, had contacts with parts of Asia and Africa, and Viking explorers even reached the eastern fringes of North America in the tenth and eleventh centuries. But at the end of the eleventh century, Europeans began their first concerted attempt to expand beyond the frontiers of Europe by conquering the land of Palestine.

The First Crusades

The Crusades were based on the idea of a holy war against the infidels or unbelievers. The wrath of Christians was directed against the Muslims, and at the end of the eleventh century, Christian Europe found itself with a glorious opportunity to attack them. The immediate impetus

THE SIEGE OF JERUSALEM: CHRISTIAN AND MUSLIM PERSPECTIVES

During the First Crusade, Christian knights laid siege to Jerusalem in June 1099. The first excerpt is taken from an account by Fulcher of Chartres, who accompanied the crusaders to the Holy Land. The second selection is by a Muslim writer, Ibn al-Athir, whose account of the First Crusade can be found in his history of the Muslim world.

FULCHER OF CHARTRES, *CHRONICLE OF THE FIRST CRUSADE*

Then the Franks entered the city magnificently at the noonday hour on Friday, the day of the week when Christ redeemed the whole world on the cross. With trumpets sounding and with everything in an uproar, exclaiming: "Help, God!" they vigorously pushed into the city, and straightaway raised the banner on the top of the wall. All the heathen, completely terrified, changed their boldness to swift flight through the narrow streets of the quarters. The more quickly they fled, the more quickly they were put to flight.

Count Raymond and his men, who were bravely assailing the city in another section, did not perceive this until they saw the Saracens [Muslims] jumping from the top of the wall. Seeing this, they joyfully ran to the city as quickly as they could, and helped the others pursue and kill the wicked enemy.

Then some, both Arabs and Ethiopians, fled into the Tower of David; others shut themselves in the Temple of the Lord and of Solomon, where in the halls a very great attack was made on them. Nowhere was there a place where the Saracens could escape swordsmen.

On the top of Solomon's Temple, to which they had climbed in fleeing, many were shot to death with arrows and cast down headlong from the roof. Within this Temple, about ten thousand were beheaded. If you had been there, your feet would have been stained up to the ankles with the blood of the slain. What more shall I tell? Not one of them was allowed to live. They did not spare the women and children.

ACCOUNT OF IBN AL-ATHIR

In fact Jerusalem was taken from the north on the morning of Friday 22 Sha'ban 492/15 July 1099. The population was put to the sword by the Franks, who pillaged the area for a week. A band of Muslims barricaded themselves into the Oratory of David and fought on for several days. They were granted their lives in return for surrendering. The Franks honored their word, and the group left by night for Ascalon. In the Masjid al-Aqsa the Franks slaughtered more than 70,000 people, among them a large number of Imams and Muslim scholars, devout and ascetic men who had left their homelands to live lives of pious seclusion in the Holy Place. The Franks stripped the Dome of the Rock of more than forty silver candelabra, each of them weighing 3,600 drams, and a great silver lamp weighing forty-four Syrian pounds, as well as a hundred and fifty smaller candelabra and more than twenty gold ones, and a great deal more booty. Refugees from Syria reached Baghdad in Ramadan, among them the qadi Abu sa'd al-Harawi. They told the Caliph's ministers a story that wrung their hearts and brought tears to their eyes. On Friday they went to the Cathedral Mosque and begged for help, weeping so that their hearers wept with them as they described the sufferings of the Muslims in the Holy City: the men killed, the women and children taken prisoner, the homes pillaged. Because of the terrible hardships they had suffered, they were allowed to break the fast.

---

for the Crusades came when the Byzantine emperor, Alexius I, asked Pope Urban II for help against the Seljuk Turks, who were Muslims. The pope saw a golden opportunity to provide papal leadership for a great cause: to rally the warriors of Europe for the liberation of Jerusalem and the Holy Land (Palestine) from the infidel. At the Council of Clermont in southern France near the end of 1095, Urban II challenged Christians to take up their weapons and join in a holy war to recover the Holy Land.

Three organized crusading bands of noble warriors, most of them French, made their way eastward. After the capture of Antioch in 1098, much of the crusading host proceeded down the Palestinian coast, evading the well-defended coastal cities, and reached Jerusalem in June 1099. After a five-week siege, the Holy City was taken amid a horrible massacre of the inhabitants—men, women, and children (see the box above).

After further conquest of Palestinian lands, the crusaders ignored the wishes of the Byzantine emperor and organized four Latin crusader states. Because the crusader kingdoms were surrounded by Muslims hostile to them, they grew increasingly dependent on the Italian commercial cities for supplies from Europe. Some Italian cities, such as Genoa, Pisa, and above all, Venice, grew rich and powerful in the process.

But it was not easy for the crusader kingdoms to maintain themselves. Already by the 1120s, the Muslims had begun to strike back. The fall of one of the Latin kingdoms in 1144 led to renewed calls for another Crusade, especially from the monastic firebrand Saint Bernard of Clairvaux. He exclaimed: "Now, on account of our sins, the enemies of the cross have begun to show their faces. . . . What are you doing, you servants of the cross? Will you throw to the dogs that which is most holy? Will you cast

Chronology

THE CRUSADES

Urban's call for a Crusade at Clermont	1095
First Crusade	1096–1099
Second Crusade	1147–1149
Saladin's conquest of Jerusalem	1187
Third Crusade	1189–1192
Fourth Crusade—sack of Constantinople	1204
Latin Empire of Constantinople	1204–1261

pearls before swine?"[6] Bernard even managed to enlist two powerful rulers, but their Second Crusade proved to be a total failure.

The Third Crusade was a reaction to the fall of the Holy City of Jerusalem in 1187 to the Muslim forces under Saladin. Now all of Christendom was ablaze with calls for a new Crusade. Three major monarchs agreed to lead their forces in person: Emperor Frederick Barbarossa of Germany (1152–1190), Richard I the Lionhearted of England (1189–1199), and Philip II Augustus, king of France (1180–1223). Some of the crusaders finally arrived in the East by 1189 only to encounter problems. Frederick Barbarossa drowned while swimming in a local river, and his army quickly disintegrated. The English and French arrived by sea and met with success against the coastal cities, where they had the support of their fleets, but when they moved inland, they failed miserably. Eventually, after Philip went home, Richard the Lionhearted negotiated a settlement whereby Saladin agreed to allow Christian pilgrims free access to Jerusalem.

The Later Crusades

After the death of Saladin in 1193, Pope Innocent III initiated the Fourth Crusade. On its way to the East, the crusading army became involved in a dispute over the succession to the Byzantine throne. The Venetian leaders of the Fourth Crusade saw an opportunity to neutralize their greatest commercial competitor, the Byzantine Empire. Diverted to Constantinople, the crusaders sacked the great capital city of Byzantium in 1204 and set up the new Latin Empire of Constantinople. Not until 1261 did a Byzantine army recapture Constantinople. In the meantime, additional Crusades were undertaken to reconquer the Holy Land. All of them were largely disasters, and by the end of the thirteenth century, the European military effort to capture Palestine was recognized as a complete failure.

THE LATE MIDDLE AGES: A TIME OF TROUBLES IN EUROPE

At the beginning of the fourteenth century, changes in weather patterns in Europe ushered in what has been called a "little ice age." Shortened growing seasons and disastrous weather conditions, including heavy storms and constant rain, led to widespread famine and hunger. Soon an even greater catastrophe struck.

The Black Death

The Black Death (plague) of the mid-fourteenth century was the most devastating natural disaster in European history, ravaging Europe's population and causing economic, social, political, and cultural upheaval. People were horrified by an evil force they could not understand and by the subsequent breakdown of all normal human relations.

Bubonic plague was the most common and most important form of plague in the diffusion of the Black Death and was spread by black rats infested with fleas who were host to the deadly bacterium *Yersinia pestis*. This great plague originated in Asia. After disappearing from Europe and the Middle East in the Middle Ages, bubonic plague continued to haunt areas of southwestern China. Rats accompanying Mongol troops spread the plague into central and northwestern China and into Central Asia in the mid-thirteenth century. From there, trading caravans brought the plague to Caffa, on the Black Sea, in 1346.

The plague reached Europe in October 1347 when Genoese merchants brought it from Caffa to the island of Sicily off the coast of Italy. It quickly spread to southern Italy and southern France by the end of 1347. Diffusion of the Black Death followed commercial trade routes. In 1348, it spread through Spain, France, and the Low Countries and into Germany. By the end of that year, it had moved to England, ravaging it in 1349. By the end of 1349, the plague had reached northern Europe and Scandinavia. Eastern Europe and Russia were affected by 1351.

Mortality figures for the Black Death were incredibly high. Especially hard hit were Italy's crowded cities, where 50 to 60 percent of the people died. One citizen of Florence wrote, "A great many breathed their last in the public streets, day and night; a large number perished in their homes, and it was only by the stench of their decaying bodies that they proclaimed their deaths to their neighbors. Everywhere the city was teeming with corpses."[7] In England and Germany, entire villages simply disappeared. It has been estimated that out of a total European population of 75 million, as many as 38 million people may have died of the plague between 1347 and 1351.

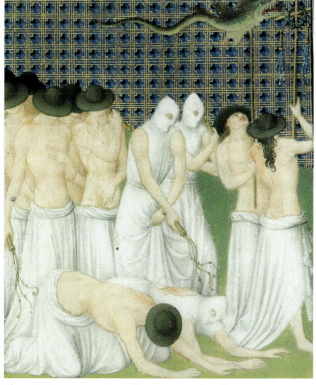

Metropolitan Museum of Art, New York, The Cloisters Collection, 1954 (54.1.1) Photograph © 1987 The Metropolitan Museum of Art

THE FLAGELLANTS. Reactions to the plague were extreme at times. Believing that asceticism could atone for humanity's sins and win God's forgiveness, flagellants wandered from town to town flogging themselves and each other with whips, as in this illustration.

The attempt of contemporaries to explain the Black Death and mitigate its harshness led to extreme sorts of behavior. To many, either the plague had been sent by God as a punishment for humans' sins, or it had been caused by the devil. Some, known as the flagellants, resorted to extreme measures to gain God's forgiveness. Groups of flagellants, both men and women, wandered from town to town, flogging each other with whips to beg the forgiveness of a God who, they felt, had sent the plague to punish humans for their sinful ways. One contemporary chronicler described their activies:

> The penitents went about, coming first out of Germany. They were men who did public penance and scourged themselves with whips of hard knotted leather with little iron spikes. Some made themselves bleed very badly between the shoulder blades and some foolish women had cloths ready to catch the blood and smear it on their eyes, saying it was miraculous blood. While they were doing penance, they sang very mournful songs about the nativity and the passion of Our Lord. The object of this penance was to put a stop to the mortality, for in that time . . . at least a third of all the people in the world died.[8]

The flagellants created mass hysteria wherever they went, and authorities worked overtime to crush the movement.

An outbreak of virulent anti-Semitism also accompanied the Black Death. Jews were accused of causing the plague by poisoning town wells. The worst pogroms against this minority were carried out in Germany, where more than sixty major Jewish communities had been exterminated by 1351 (see the box on p. 262). Many Jews fled eastward to Russia and especially to Poland, where the king offered them protection. Eastern Europe became home to large Jewish communities.

Economic Dislocation and Social Upheaval

The death of so many people in the fourteenth century also had severe economic consequences. Trade declined, and some industries suffered greatly. A shortage of workers caused a dramatic rise in the price of labor, while the decline in the number of people lowered the demand for food, resulting in falling prices. Landlords were now paying more for labor at the same time that their rental income was declining. Concurrently the decline in the number of peasants after the Black Death made it easier for some to convert their labor services to rent, thus freeing them from serfdom. But there were limits to how much the peasants could advance. They faced the same economic hurdles as the lords, who also attempted to impose wage restrictions and reinstate old forms of labor service. Peasant complaints became widespread and soon gave rise to rural revolts.

The English Peasants' Revolt of 1381 was the most prominent of all. After the Black Death, the English peasants had enjoyed improved conditions with greater freedom and higher wages or lower rents. Aristocratic landlords had fought back with legislation to depress wages and an effort to reimpose old feudal dues. The most immediate cause of the revolt, however, was the monarchy's attempt to raise revenues by imposing a poll tax, a flat charge on each adult member of the population. Peasants in eastern England refused to pay the tax and expelled the collectors forcibly from their villages. Rebellion spread as peasants burned down the manor houses of artistocrats, lawyers, and government officials. Soon, however, the young king, Richard II (1377–1399), with the assistance of aristocrats, arrested hundreds of the rebels and ended the revolt.

Although the peasant revolts sometimes resulted in short-term gains for the participants, the uprisings were easily crushed and their gains quickly lost. Accustomed to ruling, the established classes easily combined and stifled dissent.

Political Instability

Famine, plague, economic turmoil, and social upheaval were not the only problems of the fourteenth century. War and political instability must also be added to the list. Of

A Medieval Holocaust: The Cremation
of the Strasbourg Jews

In their attempt to explain the widespread horrors of the Black Death, medieval Christian communities looked for scapegoats. As at the time of the Crusades, the Jews were accused of poisoning wells and hence spreading the plague. This selection by a contemporary chronicler, written in 1349, gives an account of how Christians in the town of Strasbourg in the Holy Roman Empire dealt with their Jewish community. It is apparent that financial gain was also an important factor in killing the Jews.

JACOB VON KÖNIGSHOFEN, "THE CREMATION OF THE STRASBOURG JEWS"

In the year 1349 there occurred the greatest epidemic that ever happened. Death went from one end of the earth to the other. . . . And from what this epidemic came, all wise teachers and physicians could only say that it was God's will. . . . This epidemic also came to Strasbourg in the summer of the above-mentioned year, and it is estimated that about sixteen thousand people died.

In the matter of this plague the Jews throughout the world were reviled and accused in all lands of having caused it through the poison which they are said to have put into the water and the wells—that is what they were accused of—and for this reason the Jews were burnt all the way from the Mediterranean into Germany. . . .

[The account then goes on to discuss the situation of the Jews in the city of Strasbourg.]

On Saturday . . . they burnt the Jews on a wooden platform in their cemetery. There were about two thousand people of them. Those who wanted to baptize themselves were spared. [Some say that about a thousand accepted baptism.] Many small children were taken out of the fire and baptized against the will of their fathers and mothers. And everything that was owed to the Jews was canceled, and the Jews had to surrender all pledges and notes that they had taken for debts. The council, however, took the cash that the Jews possessed and divided it among the workingmen proportionately. The money was indeed the thing that killed the Jews. If they had been poor and if the feudal lords had not been in debt to them, they would not have been burnt. . . .

Thus were the Jews burnt at Strasbourg, and in the same year in all the cities of the Rhine, whether Free Cities or Imperial Cities or cities belonging to the lords. In some towns they burnt the Jews after a trial; in others, without a trial. In some cities the Jews themselves set fire to their houses and cremated themselves.

It was decided in Strasbourg that no Jew should enter the city for a hundred years, but before twenty years had passed, the council and magistrates agreed that they ought to admit the Jews again into the city for twenty years. And so the Jews came back again to Strasbourg in the year 1368 after the birth of our Lord.

---

all the struggles that ensued in the fourteenth century, the Hundred Years' War was the most violent.

THE HUNDRED YEARS' WAR

In the thirteenth century, the English king, Henry III, still held one small possession in France known as the duchy of Gascony. As duke of Gascony, the English king pledged loyalty as a vassal to the French king, but when King Philip VI of France (1328–1350) seized Gascony in 1337, the duke of Gascony—King Edward III of England (1327–1377)—declared war on Philip. The attack on Gascony was a convenient excuse; Edward III had already laid claim to the throne of France after the senior branch of the Capetian dynasty had become extinct in 1328.

The Hundred Years' War began in a burst of knightly enthusiasm. The French army of 1337 still relied largely on heavily armed noble cavalrymen, who looked with contempt on foot soldiers and crossbowmen, whom they regarded as social inferiors. The English, too, used heavily armed cavalry, but they relied even more on large numbers of paid foot soldiers. Armed with pikes, many of these soldiers had also adopted the longbow, invented by the Welsh. The longbow had greater striking power, longer range, and more rapid speed of fire than the crossbow.

The first major battle of the Hundred Years' War occurred in 1346 at Crécy, just south of Flanders. The larger French army followed no battle plan but simply attacked the English lines in a disorderly fashion. The arrows of the English archers decimated the French cavalry. As the chronicler Froissart described it, "[With their longbows] the English continued to shoot into the thickest part of the crowd, wasting none of their arrows. They impaled or wounded horses and riders, who fell to the ground in great distress, unable to get up again without the help of several men."[9] It was a stunning victory for the English and the foot soldier.

The Battle of Crécy was not decisive, however. The English simply did not possess the resources to subjugate all of France, but they continued to try. The English king, Henry V (1413–1422), was especially eager to achieve victory. At the Battle of Agincourt in 1415, the heavy, armor-plated French knights attempted to attack across a field turned to mud by heavy rain; the result was a disastrous French defeat and the death of fifteen hundred French nobles. Henry went on to forge an alliance with the duke of Burgundy, making the English masters of northern France.

The seemingly hopeless French cause fell into the hands of the dauphin Charles, the heir to the throne, who governed the southern two-thirds of French lands. Charles's cause seemed doomed until a French peasant woman quite unexpectedly saved the timid monarch. Born in 1412, the daughter of well-to-do peasants, Joan of Arc was a deeply religious person who came to believe that her favorite saints had commanded her to free France. In February 1429, Joan made her way to the dauphin's court and persuaded Charles to allow her to accompany a French army to Orléans. Apparently inspired by the faith of the peasant girl called "the Maid of Orléans," the French armies found new confidence in themselves and liberated Orléans. Within a few weeks, the entire Loire valley had been freed of the English. Joan had brought the war to a decisive turning point.

But she did not live to see the war concluded. Captured by the Burgundian allies of the English in 1430, Joan was turned over by the English to the Inquisition on charges of witchcraft. In the fifteenth century, spiritual visions were thought to be inspired by either God or the devil. Joan was condemned to death as a heretic and burned at the stake in 1431. Twenty-five years later, a new ecclesiastical court exonerated her of these charges, and five centuries later, in 1920, she was made a saint of the Roman Catholic church.

Joan of Arc's accomplishments proved decisive. Although the war dragged on for another two decades, defeats of English armies in Normandy and Aquitaine led to French victory by 1453. Important to the French success was the use of the cannon, a new weapon made possible by the invention of gunpowder. The Chinese had invented gunpower in the eleventh century and devised a simple cannon by the thirteenth century. The Mongols greatly improved this technology, developing more accurate cannons and cannonballs; both spread to the Middle East in the thirteenth century and to Europe by the fourteenth. The use of gunpowder eventually brought drastic changes to European warfare by making castles, city walls, and armored knights obsolete.

POLITICAL DISINTEGRATION

By the fourteenth century, the feudal order had begun to break down. With money from taxes, kings could now hire professional soldiers, who tended to be more reliable than feudal knights anyway. Fourteenth-century kings had their own problems as well. Many dynasties in Europe were unable to produce male heirs, while the founders of new dynasties had to fight for their positions as groups of nobles, trying to gain advantages for themselves, supported opposing candidates. Rulers encountered financial problems too. Hiring professional soldiers left them always short of cash, adding yet another element of uncertainty and confusion to fourteenth-century politics.

The Decline of the Church

The papacy of the Roman Catholic church reached the height of its power in the thirteenth century. But problems in the fourteenth century led to a serious decline for the church. By that time, the monarchies of Europe were no longer willing to accept papal claims of temporal supremacy, as is evident in the struggle between Pope Boniface VIII (1294–1303) and King Philip IV (1285–1314) of France. In his desire to acquire new revenues, Philip expressed the right to tax the clergy of France, but Boniface VIII claimed that the clergy of any state could not pay taxes to their secular ruler without the pope's consent, and he argued, popes were supreme over both the church and the state.

Philip IV refused to accept the pope's position and sent French forces to capture Boniface and bring him back to France for trial. The pope escaped but soon died from the shock of his experience. To ensure his position and avoid any future papal threat, Philip IV engineered the election of a Frenchman, Clement V (1305–1314), as pope. Using the excuse of turbulence in the city of Rome, the new pope took up residence in Avignon on the east bank of the Rhone River.

From 1305 to 1377, the popes resided in Avignon, leading to an increase in antipapal sentiment. The city of Rome was the traditional capital of the universal church. The pope was the bishop of Rome, and it was unseemly that the head of the Catholic church should reside in Avignon instead of Rome. Moreover, the splendor in which the pope and cardinals were living in Avignon led to a highly vocal criticism of both clergy and papacy in the fourteenth century. At last, Pope Gregory XI, perceiving the disastrous decline in papal prestige, returned to Rome in 1377.

Gregory XI (1370–1378) died in Rome the spring after his return. When the college of cardinals met to elect a new pope, the citizens of Rome, fearful that the French majority would choose another Frenchman who would move the papacy back to Avignon, threatened that the cardinals would not leave Rome alive unless a Roman or an Italian was elected pope. Wisely, the terrified cardinals duly elected the Italian archbishop of Bari as Pope Urban VI (1378–1389). Five months later, a group of dissenting cardinals—the French ones—declared Urban's election invalid and chose one of their number, a Frenchman, who took the title of Clement VII and promptly returned to Avignon. Because Urban remained in Rome, there were now two popes, beginning what has been called the Great Schism of the church.

The Great Schism divided Europe. France and its allies supported the pope in Avignon, whereas France's enemy England and its allies supported the pope in Rome. The Great Schism was also damaging to the faith of Christian believers. The pope was widely believed to be the true leader of Christendom; when both lines of popes denounced the other as the Antichrist, people's faith in the papacy and the church were undermined. Finally, a church council met at Constance, Switzerland, in 1417. After the competing popes resigned or were deposed, a new pope was elected who was acceptable to all parties.

By the mid-fifteenth century, as a result of these crises, the church had lost much of its temporal power. Even worse, the papacy and the church had also lost much of their moral prestige.

CONCLUSION

The collapse of the Han dynasty in China in the third century C.E. led to nearly four centuries of internal chaos. The fall of the Roman Empire in the fifth century brought a quite different result as three new civilizations emerged out of the collapse of Roman power in the Mediterranean. Islam emerged in the east. The eastern part of the old Roman Empire, increasingly Greek in culture, continued to survive as the Christian Byzantine Empire. And a new Christian European civilization was establishing its roots in the west.

The coronation of Charlemagne, the descendant of a Germanic tribe converted to Christianity, as Roman emperor in 800 symbolized the fusion of the three chief components of the new European civilization: the German tribes, the Roman legacy, and the Christian church. Charlemagne's Carolingian Empire fostered the idea of a distinct European identity. With the disintegration of that empire, power fell into the hands of many different lords, who came to constitute a powerful group of nobles that dominated the political, economic, and social life of Europe. But quietly and surely, within this world of castles and private power, kings gradually began to extend their public power and laid the foundations for the European kingdoms that in one form or another have dominated European politics ever since.

European civilization began to flourish in the High Middle Ages. The revival of trade, the expansion of towns and cities, and the development of a money economy did not mean the end of a predominantly rural European society, but they did open the door to new ways to make a living and new opportunities for people to expand and enrich their lives. At the same time, the High Middle Ages also gave birth to an intellectual and spiritual revival that transformed European society.

Fourteenth-century European was challenged by an overwhelming number of disintegrative forces, but European society proved remarkably resilient. As we shall see in the next chapter, elements of recovery would make the fifteenth century a period of significant political, economic, artistic, and intellectual change in Europe.

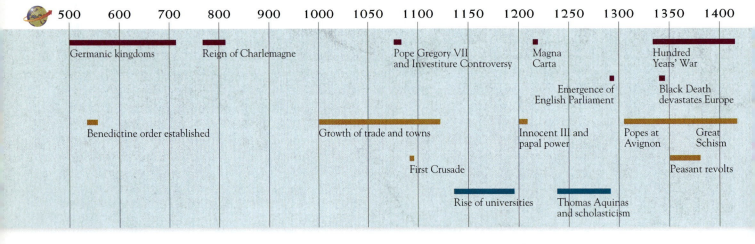

CHAPTER NOTES

1. Norman F. Cantor, ed., *The Medieval World, 300–1300* (New York, 1963), p. 104.
2. Quoted in Marvin Perry, Joseph Peden, and Theodore Von Laue, *Sources of the Western Tradition*, vol. 1(Boston, 1987), p. 218.
3. Quoted in Jean Gimpel, *The Medieval Machine* (Harmondsworth, England, 1977), p. 92.
4. Oliver J. Thatcher and Edgar H. McNeal, eds., *A Source Book for Medieval History* (New York, 1905), p. 208.

5. Quoted in R. H. C. Davis, *A History of Medieval Europe from Constantine to Saint Louis*, 2d ed. (New York, 1988), p. 252.
6. Quoted in Hans E. Mayer, *The Crusades*, trans. John Gillingham (New York, 1972), pp. 99–100.
7. Giovanni Boccaccio, *The Decameron*, trans. Frances Winwar (New York, 1955), p. xiii.
8. Jean Froissart, *Chronicles*, ed. and trans. Geoffrey Brereton (Harmondsworth, England, 1968), p. 111.
9. Ibid, p. 89.

SUGGESTED READING

Good general histories of the medieval period can be found in B. Tierney and S. Painter, *Western Europe in the Middle Ages, 300–1475* (New York, 1983); E. Peters, *Europe and the Middle Ages*, 2d ed. (Englewood Cliffs, N.J., 1989); and D. Nicholas, *The Evolution of the Medieval World: Society, Government, and Thought in Europe, 312–1500* (London, 1993). A brief history of the Early Middle Ages can be found in R. Collin, *Early Medieval Europe, 300–1000* (New York, 1991).

Surveys of Carolingian Europe include P. Riche, *The Carolingians: A Family Who Forged Europe* (Philadelphia, 1993), and R. McKitterick, *The Frankish Kingdoms Under the Carolingians, 751–987* (London, 1983). On Charlemagne, see H. R. Loyn and J. Percival, *The Reign of Charlemagne* (New York, 1976).

Two introductory works on fief-holding are J. R. Strayer, *Feudalism* (Princeton, N.J., 1985), and the classic work by M. Bloch, *Feudal Society* (London, 1961). For an important revisionist view, see S. Reynolds, *Fiefs and Vassals* (Oxford, 1994).

There are numerous works on the various medieval states. On England, see R. Frame, *The Political Development of the British Isles, 1100–1400* (Oxford, 1990). On Germany, see B. Arnold, *Princes and Territories in Medieval Germany* (Cambridge, 1991). On France, see J. Dunbabib, *France in the Making, 843–1180* (Oxford, 1985). On Italy, see D. J. Herlihy, *Cities and Society in Medieval Italy* (London, 1980). On eastern Europe, see N. Davies, *God's Playground: A History of Poland*, vol. 1 (Oxford, 1981), and S. Franklin and J. Shephard, *The Emergence of Rus, 750–1200* (New York, 1996).

On economic conditions in the Middle Ages, see N. J. G. Pounds, *An Economic History of Medieval Europe* (New York, 1974). Urban history is covered in D. Nicholas, *The Growth of the Medieval City: From Late Antiquity to the Early Fourteenth Century* (New York, 1997). On women in general, see D. J. Herlihy, *Opera Muliebria: Women and Work in Medieval Europe* (New York, 1990). On peasant life, see R. Fossier, *Peasant Life in the Medieval West* (New York, 1988).

For a general survey of church life, see R. W. Southern, *Western Society and the Church in the Middle Ages*, rev. ed. (New York, 1990). On the papacy in the High Middle Ages, see I. S. Robinson, *The Papacy* (Cambridge, 1990). The papacy of Innocent III is covered in J. E. Sayers, *Innocent III, Leader of Europe, 1198–1216* (New York, 1994). Good works on monasticism include C. H. Lawrence, *Medieval Monasticism* (London, 1984), a good general account, and H. Leyser, *Hermits and the New Monasticism* (London, 1984). On the Inquisition, see B. Hamilton, *The Medieval Inquisition* (New York, 1981). A good general study of the church in the fourteenth century is F. P. Oakley, *The Western Church in the Later Middle Ages* (Ithaca, N.Y., 1980).

The development of universities is covered in S. Ferruolo, *The Origin of the University* (Stanford, Calif., 1985), and the brief, older work by C. H. Haskins, *The Rise of Universities* (Ithaca, N.Y., 1957). On the Gothic movement, see M. Camille, *Gothic Art: Glorious Visions* (New York, 1996), and C. Wilson, *The Gothic Cathedral* (London, 1990).

On the Crusades see H. E. Mayer, *The Crusades*, 2d ed. (New York, 1988), and J. Riley-Smith, ed., *The Oxford Illustrated History of the Crusades* (New York, 1995).

On the Black Death, see P. Ziegler, *The Black Death* (New York, 1969), and D. J. Herlihy, *The Black Death and the Transformation of the West*, ed. S. K. Cohn Jr. (Cambridge, Mass., 1997).

Worthy accounts of the Hundred Years' War include A. Curry, *The Hundred Years' War* (New York, 1993), and R. H. Neillands, *The Hundred Years' War* (New York, 1990). On Joan of Arc, see M. Warner, *Joan of Arc: The Image of Female Heroism* (New York, 1981).

INFOTRAC COLLEGE EDITION

Visit the source collections at infotrac.thomsonlearning.com and use the Search function with the following key terms.

Black Death
Charlemagne
Cities and towns, medieval
Early Christianity
Feudalism or feudal
Medieval England
Middle Ages

WORLD HISTORY RESOURCES

Visit the *Essential World History* Companion Web Site for resources specific to this textbook:

http://history.wadsworth.com/duikeressentials02/

The CD in the back of this book and the World History Resource Center at **http://history.wadsworth.com/world/** offer a variety of tools to help you succeed in this course, including access to quizzes; images; documents; interactive simulations, maps, and timelines; movie explorations; and a wealth of other sources.

NEW PATTERNS OF CIVILIZATION

*I*n Part II of this book, we examined the period that followed the collapse of the civilizations of antiquity down to the end of the fourteenth century. During this period, a number of significant forces were at work in human society. The concept of civilization gradually spread from such heartland regions as the Middle East, the Mediterranean basin, the South Asian subcontinent, and China into new areas of the world—to sub-Saharan Africa, to central and western Europe, to Southeast Asia, and even to the islands of Japan, off the eastern edge of the Eurasian landmass. Across the oceans, unique but advanced civilizations began to take shape in the Americas. In the meantime, the vast migration of peoples continued, leading not only to bitter conflicts but also to increased interchanges of technology and ideas. The result was the transformation of separate and distinct cultures and civilizations into an increasingly complex and vast world system embracing not only technology and trade but also ideas and religious beliefs.

What explains this explosion in human activity? One answer is advances in technology. Improved irrigation methods, the introduction of new crops, and the increased use of the iron plow led to a substantial rise in food production, thus creating wealth that could be used for the purchase of other goods. Advances were made in ship construction and navigational techniques. Other factors were the mastery of monsoon patterns in the Indian Ocean, the domestication of the camel in North Africa and the Middle East, and increased trade. During the first millennium C.E., the great trade routes of the traditional world—the Silk Road from China to the Middle East and then on to the Mediterranean, the caravan trade across the Sahara, and the maritime network that stretched across the Indian Ocean—all reached their maturity.

As had been the case during antiquity, the Middle East was the heart of this activity. The Arab Empire, which took shape after the death of Muhammad in the early seventh century, provided the key link in the revived trade routes through the region. Muslim traders—both Arab and Berber—opened contacts with West African societies south of the Sahara, while their ships followed the monsoon winds eastward as far as the Spice Islands in Southeast Asia. Nomads from Central Asia carried goods back and forth along the Silk Road between the Middle East and China. For the next several hundred years, the great cities of the Middle East— Mecca, Damascus, and Baghdad—became among the wealthiest in the known world. The great Chinese city of Chang'an lay at the eastern extremity of the Silk Road as it snaked eastward across Central Asia.

Islam's contributions to the human experience during this period were cultural and technological as well as economic. Muslim philosophers preserved the works of the ancient Greeks for posterity, Muslim scientists and mathematicians made new discoveries about the nature of the universe and the human body, and Arab cartographers and historians mapped the known world and speculated about the fundamental forces in human society.

But the Middle East was not the only or necessarily even the primary contributor to world trade and civilization during this period. While the Arab Empire became the linchpin of trade between the Mediterranean and eastern and southern Asia, a new center of primary importance in world trade was emerging in East Asia, focused on China. China had been a major participant in regional trade during the Han dynasty, when its silks were already being transported to Rome via Central Asia, but its role had declined after the fall of the Han. Now, with the rise of the great Tang and Song dynasties, China reemerged as a major commercial power in East Asia, trading by sea with Southeast Asia and Japan and by land with the nomadic peoples of Central Asia. In general, overland trade was carried on by non-Chinese peoples in Central Asia, but the Chinese themselves became directly involved in the maritime trade with the countries in the South Seas.

By now, China was not only a regional economic power but a global one as well. The Silk Road through Turkestan became one of the most important trade routes of the era, and during the Ming dynasty, Chinese fleets briefly sailed across the Indian Ocean as far as the Red Sea and the eastern coast of Africa.

Like the Middle East, China was also a prime source of new technology. From China came paper, printing, the compass, and gunpowder. The double-hulled Chinese junks that entered the Indian Ocean during the Ming dynasty were slow and cumbersome but extremely seaworthy and capable of carrying substantial quantities of goods over long distances. Among China's other contributions were porcelain, chess, the mechanical clock, and the iron stirrup. Many such inventions arrived in Europe by way of India or the Middle East, and their Chinese origins were therefore unknown in the West.

Increasing trade on a regional or global basis also led to the exchange of ideas. Buddhism was brought to China by merchants, and Islam first arrived in sub-Saharan Africa and the Indonesian archipelago in the same manner. In their new environments, these religions initially had an impact mainly on merchants and other city-dwellers, but in some cases they gradually gained favor in the countryside.

Merchants were not the only means by which religious and cultural ideas spread, however. Sometimes migration, conquest, or relatively peaceful processes played a part. The case of the Bantu-speaking peoples in Central Africa is apparently an example of peaceful expansion; and while Islam sometimes followed the path of Arab warriors, they rarely imposed their religion by force on the local population. In some instances, as with the Mongols, the conquerors made no effort to convert others to their own religions. By contrast, Christian monks, motivated by missionary fervor, converted many of the peoples of central and eastern Europe. Roman Catholic monks brought Latin Christianity to the Ger-manic and western Slavic peoples, and monks from the Byzantine Empire largely converted the southern and eastern Slavic populations to Eastern Orthodox Christianity.

Another characteristic of the period between 500 and 1400 C.E. was the almost constant migration of nomadic and seminomadic peoples. Dynamic forces in the Gobi Desert, Central Asia, the Arabian peninsula, and Central Africa provoked vast numbers of peoples to abandon their homelands and seek their livelihood elsewhere. Sometimes the migration was peaceful. More often, however, migration produced violent conflict and sometimes invasion and subjugation. As had been the case during antiquity, the most active source of migration was Central Asia. From here, Turkic-speaking peoples spilled over the Hindu Kush into northern India, southwest into Persia, and farther west into the Balkans

TRADE AND CIVILIZATION

Between 500 and 1400, the level of interdependence among human societies began to intensify as three major trade routes—the Indian Ocean, the Silk Road, and the trans-Saharan caravan route—began to create the framework for a single world trade system. New technology, new crops, and new ideas crossed from one end of the known world to the other. Contacts occurred in the realm of technology as in that of ideas, including inventions such as paper, the compass, and gunpowder; crops such as sugar, cotton, and spices; and great religious systems such as Buddhism, Hinduism, Christianity, and Islam. One interesting aspect of this process was the close relationship between missionary activities and trade. Buddhist merchants first brought the teachings of Siddhartha Gautama to China, and Muslim traders carried the words of the prophet Muhammad to Southeast Asia and sub-Saharan Africa. At the same time, Christian missionaries may have brought the first accurate knowledge of silk manufacturing from China to the Mediterranean.

What were the major causes of the rapid expansion of trade during this period? One key factor was the introduction of new technology in the field of transportation. The development of the compass, improved techniques in mapmaking and shipbuilding, and greater knowledge of wind patterns all contributed to the expansion of maritime trade far from familiar shores. Caravan trade, once carried by wheeled chariots or on the backs of oxen, now used the camel as the preferred beast of burden through the parched deserts of Africa and the Middle East.

Another factor in the expansion of commerce during this period was the appearance of several multinational empires that created zones of stability and affluence in key areas from North Africa eastward toward the Pacific. Central to the process was the emergence of the empire of the Abbasids in the Middle East. China reached a zenith of prosperity during the Tang and Song dynasties as Europe was slowly emerging from the collapse of the Roman Empire. In the thirteenth century, the Mongol invasions brought this era to an end but then created a new era of peace and stability that lasted for over a century and fostered long-distance trade throughout the known world.

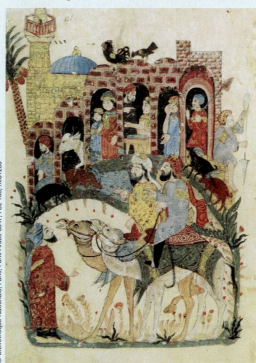

➤ **ARAB MERCHANTS IN A CARAVAN.** By land or by sea, Arab trade routes extended over half the globe. The world of Islam and the camel, both portrayed in this thirteenth-century miniature, were essential components of Muslim commercial ventures.

© Bibliotheque Nationale, Paris, Paris Arabe 5847, FOL 138, RcC1230

FEUDAL ORDERS AROUND THE WORLD

When we use the word *feudalism,* we usually think of European knights on horseback clad in iron coats and armed with sword and lance. However, between 800 and 1500, a form of social organization that a later generation of historians called feudalism developed in different parts of the world. By the term *feudalism,* these historians meant a decentralized political order in which local lords owed loyalty and provided military service to a king or more powerful lord. In Europe, a feudal order based on lords and vassals arose between 800 and 900 and flourished for the next four hundred years.

In Japan, a feudal order much like that found in Europe developed between 800 and 1500. By the end of the ninth century, powerful nobles in the countryside, while owing a loose loyalty to the Japanese emperor, began to exercise political and legal power in their own extensive lands. To protect their property and security, these nobles retained samurai, warriors who owed loyalty to the nobles and provided military service for them. Like knights in Europe, the samurai followed a warrior code and fought on horseback, clad in iron. However, they carried a sword and bow and arrow rather than a sword and lance.

➤ **A KNIGHT'S EQUIPMENT.** Pictured here is a charging European knight with his equipment. The introduction of the high saddle, stirrups, and larger horses allowed horsemen to wear heavier armor and to wield long lances. Compare the equipment of the European knight to that of the samurai warrior on page 227.

© Leiden, University Library, BPL 20, f.60r

In some respects, the political relationships among the Indian states beginning in the fifth century took on the character of the feudal system that emerged in Europe in the Middle Ages. Like medieval European lords, local Indian rajas were technically vassals of the king, but unlike in European feudalism, the relationship was not a contractual one. Still, the Indian model became highly complex, with "inner" and "outer" vassals, depending on their physical or political proximity to the king, and "greater" or "lesser" vassals, depending on their power and influence. As in Europe, the vassals themselves often had vassals.

In the Valley of Mexico, the Aztecs developed a political system between 1300 and 1500 that bore some similarities to the Japanese, Indian, and European feudal orders. Although the Aztec king was a powerful, authoritarian ruler, the local rulers of lands outside the capital city were allowed considerable freedom. However, they did pay tribute to the king and also provided him with military forces. Unlike the knights and samurai of Europe and Japan, however, Aztec warriors were armed with sharp knives made of stone and spears of wood fitted with razor-sharp blades cut from stone.

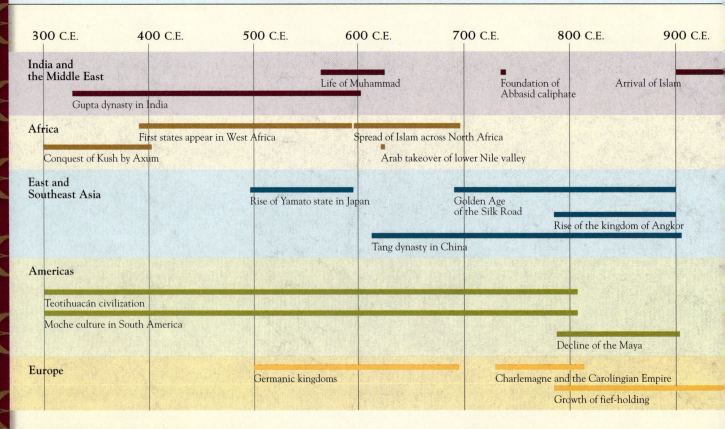

	300 C.E.	400 C.E.	500 C.E.	600 C.E.	700 C.E.	800 C.E.	900 C.E.
India and the Middle East				Life of Muhammad	Foundation of Abbasid caliphate		Arrival of Islam
	Gupta dynasty in India						
Africa		First states appear in West Africa		Spread of Islam across North Africa			
	Conquest of Kush by Axum			Arab takeover of lower Nile valley			
East and Southeast Asia			Rise of Yamato state in Japan		Golden Age of the Silk Road	Rise of the kingdom of Angkor	
				Tang dynasty in China			
Americas		Teotihuacán civilization					
	Moche culture in South America					Decline of the Maya	
Europe			Germanic kingdoms		Charlemagne and the Carolingian Empire		
					Growth of fief-holding		

in southeastern Europe. Later, Central Asia gave birth to an even more fearsome force in the form of the Mongols. Mongol expansion began with the unification of Mongol tribes in the Gobi Desert by Genghis Khan and culminated in the advance of Mongolian armies to the gates of central Europe and the conquest of China in the thirteenth century. Wherever they went, they left a train of enormous destruction and loss of life. Inadvertently, the Mongols were also the source of a new wave of epidemics that swept through much of Europe and the Middle East in the fourteenth century. The spread of the plague—known at the time as the Black Death—took much of the population of Europe to an early grave.

But there was another side to the era of nomadic expansion. Often, as historian Thomas J. Barfield has noted, the nomadic peoples had a symbiotic relationship with the sedentary societies, propping up governments like the Tang dynasty in China in order to protect their source of income. Once nomadic warriors completed their conquests, they settled down to become administrators. Often the results were constructive. German migrations and Viking incursions contributed to the creation of dynamic new societies in Europe, and Turkish invasions led to the rise of states in the Anatolian peninsula and northern India.

Even the invasions of the Mongols—the "scourge of God," as Europeans of the thirteenth and fourteenth centuries called them—had constructive as well as destructive consequences. After their initial conquests, for a brief period of three generations, the Mongols provided an avenue for trade throughout the most extensive empire (known as the Pax Mongolica) the world had yet seen. When the pope dispatched envoys to the imperial court in Mongolia in the mid-thirteenth century, it was the first time Europeans had traveled the entire distance by land to East Asia.

The millennium following the destruction of the ancient empires brought about enormous changes in human society. During the era of Mongol expansion, there was widespread death and suffering throughout the known world. At the same time, the world had witnessed a significant expansion in the technological and material capacity of human societies and in the depth of contact among them. The era of widespread peace brought about as the result of the Mongol conquests also inaugurated what one scholar has described as the "idea of the unified conceptualization of the globe," creating a "basic information circuit" that spread commodities, ideas, and inventions from one end of the Eurasian supercontinent to the other. The way was prepared for a new stage of world history.

| 900 C.E. | 1000 C.E. | 1100 C.E. | 1200 C.E. | 1300 C.E. | 1400 C.E. | 1500 C.E. |

in northern India

Conquest of Baghdad by the Mongols

Ottoman Turks seize Constantinople

Portuguese ships explore West African coast

Kingdom of Zimbabwe

Spread of Mongols across East Asia

Beginning of Ming dynasty in China

Civilization of Chimor

Kingdom of the Aztecs

Rise of European kingdoms

Black Death

THE EMERGENCE OF NEW WORLD PATTERNS
(1400–1800)

Beginning in the fifteenth century, a new force entered the world scene in the form of a revived Europe. The period of history known as the early modern era (1400–1800) was marked in Europe by an explosion of scientific knowledge and the appearance of a new secular ideology that emphasized the power of human beings to dominate nature and improve their material surroundings. After the breakdown of Christian unity in the Reformation era, Europeans engaged in a vigorous period of state building that resulted in the creation of independent monarchies in western and central Europe, which formed the basis for a new European state system.

The rise of early modern Europe had an immediate as well as a long-term impact on the rest of the world. The first stage began with the discovery of the Americas by Christopher Columbus in 1492 and the equally important voyages of Vasco da Gama and Ferdinand Magellan into the Indian and Pacific Oceans. These voyages and those that followed in this so-called Age of Discovery or Age of Exploration not only injected European sea power into new areas of the world but also vastly extended the maritime trade network until for the first time it literally encircled the globe. Some historians have characterized this period as the beginning of an era of European dominance.

Significant as it was, however, the emergence of Europe as a major player on the world stage was by no means the only important feature of this period. An excessive emphasis on the expanding European civilization tends to overlook the fact that other areas of the world were realizing impressive achievements of their own. Two great new Islamic empires, founded by the Ottomans in Turkey and the Safavids in Persia, arose in the Middle East, while a third, that of the Mughals, unified the Indian subcontinent for the first time in nearly two thousand years. Islam was now firmly established in Africa south of the Sahara and in Asia as far east as the Indonesian archipelago.

In most of Asia, the European revival had only minimal effects. Portuguese merchants reached the coast of China in the early sixteenth century and landed on the islands of Japan a generation later. Merchants and missionaries from various European countries were active in both countries by the end of the century. But the ruling authorities in China and Japan, like their counterparts in the mainland states in Southeast Asia, became increasingly wary of the impact of Europeans' activities on their own societies, and by the eighteenth century, the Western presence in the region had markedly declined.

The first thrust of European expansion, then, significantly changed the face of the world, but it did not firmly establish European dominance. China remained, in the eyes of many, the most advanced and most sophisticated civilization on earth, and its achievements were imitated by its neighbors and admired by philosophers in far-off Europe. The era of Muslim dominance over the seas had come to an end, but Islam was still a force to be reckoned with. The bulk of Africa remained essentially outside the purview of European influence.

Chapter 13

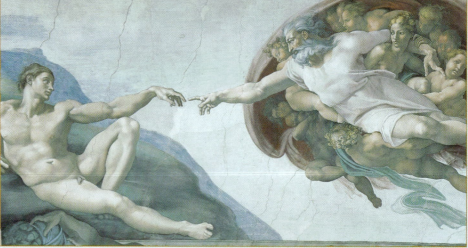

Photo Vatican Museums

RENEWAL, REFORM, AND STATE BUILDING IN EUROPE

FOCUS QUESTIONS

- What were the main features of the Renaissance, and how did it differ from the Middle Ages?
- What were the main tenets of Lutheranism and Calvinism, and how did they differ from each other and from Catholicism?
- Why is the period between 1560 and 1650 in Europe called an age of crisis, and how did the turmoil contribute to the artistic and intellectual developments of the period?
- What was absolutism, and what were the main characteristics of the absolute monarchies that merged in France, Prussia, Austria, and Russia? Why did England follow a different path?
- ➤ What did Copernicus, Kepler, Galileo, and Newton contribute to a new vision of the universe, and how did their vision differ from the Ptolemaic conception of the universe? What was the significance of this new vision?

After the disintegrative patterns of the fourteenth century, Europe began a remarkable recovery known as the Renaissance, which encompassed a revival of arts and letters in the fifteenth century, and witnessed a religious renaissance in the sixteenth century known as the Reformation. The religious division of Europe (Catholics versus Protestants) that was a result of the Reformation was instrumental in beginning a series of wars that dominated much of European history from 1560 to 1650 and exacerbated the economic and social crises that were besetting the region.

One of the responses to the crises of the seventeenth century was a search for order. The most general trend was an extension of monarchical power as a stabilizing force. This development, which historians have called absolutism or absolute monarchy, was most evident in France during the flamboyant reign of Louis XIV, regarded by some as the perfect embodiment of an absolute monarch. In his memoirs, the duc de Saint-Simon, who had first-hand experience of French court life, said that Louis was "the very figure of a hero, so imbued with a natural but most imposing majesty that it appeared even in his most insignificant gestures and movements." The king's natural grace gave him a special charm: "He was as dignified and majestic in his dressing gown as when dressed in robes of state, or on horseback at the head of his troops." He was naturally kind, and "he loved truth, justice, order, and reason." His life was orderly: "Nothing could be regulated with greater exactitude than were his days and hours." His self-control was impeccable: "He did not lose control of himself ten times in his whole life, and then only with inferior persons." But even absolute monarchs had faults, and Saint-Simon had the courage to point them out: "Louis XIV's vanity was without limit or restraint," which led to his "distaste for . . . all independence of character and sentiment in others," as well as his "mistakes of judgment in matters of importance."

The seventeenth century in Europe also witnessed the Scientific Revolution, which brought Europeans a new way of viewing the universe and their place in it. In time, the Scientific Revolution would add to Europe's growing sense of power as changes in government, the economy, and the military enabled Europeans to move out into the global stage in a dramatic fashion. •

THE RENAISSANCE

People who lived in Italy between 1350 and 1550 or so believed that they had witnessed a rebirth of classical antiquity—the world of the Greeks and Romans. To them, this marked a new age, which historians later called the Renaissance (French for "rebirth") and viewed as a distinct period of European history, which began in Italy and then spread to the rest of Europe.

Renaissance Italy was largely an urban society. The city-states became the centers of Italian political, economic, and social life. Within this new urban society, a secular spirit emerged as increasing wealth created new possibilities for the enjoyment of worldly things.

A new view of human beings emerged as people in the Italian Renaissance began to emphasize individual ability. The fifteenth-century Florentine architect Leon Battista Alberti expressed the new philosophy succinctly: "Men can do all things if they will."[1] This high regard for human worth and for individual potential gave rise to a new social ideal: the well-rounded personality or "universal person" (*l'uomo universale*) who was capable of achievements in many areas of life.

Renaissance Society

After the severe economic reversals and social upheavals of the fourteenth century, the European economy gradually recovered as manufacturing and trade increased in volume. The Italians and especially the Venetians expanded their wealthy commercial empire, rivaled only by the increasingly powerful Hanseatic League, a commercial and military alliance of north German coastal towns. Not until the sixteenth century, when overseas discoveries gave new importance to the states facing the Atlantic, did the Italian city-states begin to suffer from the competitive advantages of the more powerful national territorial states.

In the Middle Ages, society was divided into three estates: the clergy, or first estate (which will be examined later in this chapter); the nobility, or second estate; and the peasants and inhabitants of the towns and cities, the third estate. Although this social order continued into the Renaissance, some changes also became evident.

Throughout much of Europe, the landholding nobles faced declining real incomes during most of the fourteenth and fifteenth centuries. Many members of the old nobility survived, however, and new blood also infused its ranks. By 1500, the nobles, old and new, who constituted between 2 and 3 percent of the population in most countries, managed to dominate society, as they had done in the Middle Ages, holding important political posts and serving as advisers to the king.

Except in the heavily urban areas of northern Italy and Flanders, peasants made up the overwhelming mass of the third estate—they constituted 85 to 90 percent of the total European population. Serfdom decreased as the manorial system continued its decline. Increasingly, the labor dues owed by a peasant to his lord were converted into rents paid in money. By 1500, especially in western Europe, more and more peasants were becoming legally free.

The remainder of the third estate were inhabitants of towns and cities, originally merchants and artisans. But by the fifteenth century, the Renaissance town or city had become more complex. At the top of urban society were the patricians, whose wealth from capitalistic enterprises

Marriage Negotiations

Marriages were so important in maintaining families in Renaissance Italy that much energy was put into arranging them. Parents made the choices for their children, for considerations that had little to do with the modern notion of love. This selection is taken from the letters of a Florentine matron of the illustrious Strozzi family to her son Filippo in Naples. The family's considerations were complicated by the fact that the son was in exile.

ALESSANDRA STROZZI TO HER SON FILIPPO IN NAPLES

[April 20, 1464] Concerning the matter of a wife [for Filippo], it appears to me that if Francesco di Messer Tanagli wishes to give his daughter, that it would be a fine marriage. . . . Now I will speak with Marco [Parenti, Alessandra's son-in-law], to see if there are other prospects that would be better, and if there are none, then we will learn if he wishes to give her [in marriage]. . . . Francesco Tanagli has a good reputation, and he has held office, not the highest, but still he has been in office. You may ask: "Why should he give her to someone in exile?" There are three reasons. First, there aren't many young men of good family who have both virtue and property. Secondly, she has only a small dowry, 1,000 florins, which is the dowry of an artisan [although not a small sum, either—senior officials in the government bureaucracy earned 300 florins a year]. . . . Third, I believe that he will give her away, because he has a large family and he will need help to settle them. . . .

[July 26, 1465] Francesco is a good friend of Marco and he trusts him. On S. Jacopo's day, he spoke to him discreetly and persuasively, saying that for several months he had heard that we were interested in the girl and . . . that when we had made up our minds, she will come to us willingly. [He said that] you were a worthy man, and that his family had always made good marriages, but that he had only a small dowry to give her, and so he would prefer to send her outside of Florence to someone of worth, rather than to give her to someone here, from among those who were available, with little money. . . . We have information that she is affable and competent. She is responsible for a large family (there are twelve children, six boys and six girls), and the mother is always pregnant and isn't very competent. . . .

[August 31, 1465] I have recently received some very favorable information [about the Tanagli girl] from two individuals. . . . They are in agreement that whoever gets her will be content. . . . Concerning her beauty, they told me what I had already seen, that she is attractive and well-proportioned. Her face is long, but I couldn't look directly into her face, since she appeared to be aware that I was examining her . . . and so she turned away from me like the wind. . . . She reads quite well . . . and she can dance and sing. . . .

So yesterday I sent for Marco and told him what I had learned. And we talked about the matter for a while, and decided that he should say something to the father and give him a little hope, but not so much that we couldn't withdraw, and find out from him the amount of the dowry. . . . May God help us to choose what will contribute to our tranquility and to the consolation of us all. . . .

[September 13, 1465] Marco came to me and said that he had met with Francesco Tanagli, who had spoken very coldly, so that I understand that he had changed his mind.

[Filippo Strozzi eventually married Fiametta di Donato Adimari in 1466.]

---

in trade, industry, and banking enabled them to dominate their urban communities economically, socially, and politically. Below them were the petty burghers—the shopkeepers, artisans, guildmasters, and guildsmen—who were largely concerned with providing goods and services for local consumption. Below these two groups were the propertyless workers earning pitiful wages and the unemployed, living squalid and miserable lives. These poor city-dwellers constituted 30 to 40 percent of the urban population.

FAMILY AND MARRIAGE IN RENAISSANCE ITALY

The family bond was a source of great security in the urban world of Renaissance Italy. To maintain the family, parents carefully arranged marriages, often to strengthen business or family ties. Details were worked out well in advance, sometimes when children were only two or three, and reinforced by a legally binding marriage contract (see the box above).

The father-husband was the center of the Italian family. He gave it his name, managed all finances (his wife had no share in his wealth), and made the crucial decisions that determined his children's lives. A father's authority over his children was absolute until he died or formally freed his children. In Renaissance Italy, children did not become adults on reaching a certain age; adulthood came only when the father went before a judge and formally emancipated them. The age of emancipation varied from early teens to late twenties.

The wife managed the household, a position that gave women a certain degree of autonomy in their daily lives. Most wives, however, also knew that their primary function was to bear children. Upper-class wives were frequently pregnant; Alessandra Strozzi of Florence, for example, who had been married at the age of sixteen, bore eight children in ten years. For women in the Renaissance, childbirth was a fearful occasion. Not only was it painful, but it could be deadly; possibly as many as one woman in ten died in childbirth.

The Intellectual Renaissance

The emergence and growth of individualism and secularism as characteristics of the Italian Renaissance are most noticeable in the intellectual and artistic realms. The most important literary movement associated with the Renaissance is humanism.

ITALIAN RENAISSANCE HUMANISM

Renaissance humanism was an intellectual movement based on the study of the classics, the literary works of Greece and Rome. Humanists studied the liberal arts—grammar, rhetoric, poetry, moral philosophy or ethics, and history—all based on the writings of ancient Greek and Roman authors. We call these subjects the humanities.

Petrarch (1304–1374), who has often been called the father of Italian Renaissance humanism, did more than any other individual in the fourteenth century to foster the development of Renaissance humanism. Petrarch sought to find forgotten Latin manuscripts and set in motion a ransacking of monastic libraries throughout Europe. He also began the humanist emphasis on the use of pure classical Latin. Humanists used the works of Cicero as a model for prose and those of Virgil for poetry. As Petrarch said, "Christ is my God; Cicero is the prince of the language."

In Florence, the humanist movement took a new direction at the beginning of the fifteenth century. The humanists who worked as secretaries for the city council of Florence took a new interest in civic life. They came to believe that it was the duty of an intellectual to live an active life for one's state. Humanists came to believe that their study of the humanities should be put to the service of the state.

Also evident in the humanism of the first half of the fifteenth century was a growing interest in classical Greek civilization. One of the first Italian humanists to gain a thorough knowledge of Greek was Leonardo Bruni, who became an enthusiastic pupil of the Byzantine scholar Manuel Chrysoloras, who taught in Florence from 1396 to 1400.

THE IMPACT OF PRINTING

The Renaissance witnessed the development of printing, which made an immediate impact on European intellectual life and thought. Printing from hand-carved wooden blocks had been done in the West since the twelfth century and in China even before that. What was new in the fifteenth century in Europe was multiple printing with movable metal type. The development of printing with movable type was a gradual process that culminated some time between 1445 and 1450; Johannes Gutenberg of Mainz played an important role in bringing the process to completion. Gutenberg's Bible, completed in 1455 or 1456, was the first true book produced using movable type.

By 1500, there were more than a thousand printers in Europe, who collectively had published almost forty thousand titles (between eight and ten million copies). Probably 50 percent of these books were religious—Bibles and biblical commentaries, books of devotion, and sermons.

The printing of books encouraged the development of scholarly research and the desire to attain knowledge. Printing also stimulated the development of an ever-expanding lay reading public, a development that had an enormous impact on European society. Printing allowed European civilization to compete for the first time with the civilization of China.

The Artistic Renaissance

Renaissance artists sought to imitate nature in their works of art. Their search for naturalism became an end in itself: to persuade onlookers of the reality of the object or event they were portraying. At the same time, the new artistic standards reflected the new attitude of mind in which human beings became the focus of attention, the "center and measure of all things," as one artist proclaimed.

The new Renaissance style was developed by Florentine painters in the fifteenth century. Especially important were two major developments. One emphasized the technical side of painting—understanding the laws of perspective and the geometrical organization of space and light. The second development was the investigation of movement and anatomical structure. The realistic portrayal of the human nude became one of the foremost preoccupations of Italian Renaissance art. By the end of the fifteenth century, Italian painters had created a new artistic environment. Many artists had mastered the new techniques for a scientific observation of the world around them and were now ready to move into new forms of creative expression. This marked the shift to the High Renaissance.

The High Renaissance was dominated by the work of three artistic giants, Leonardo da Vinci (1452–1519), Raphael (1483–1520), and Michelangelo (1475–1564). Leonardo carried on the fifteenth-century experimental tradition by studying everything and even dissecting human bodies in order to see how nature worked. But Leonardo stressed the need to advance beyond such realism and initiated the High Renaissance's preoccupation with the idealization of nature, an attempt to generalize from realistic portrayal to an ideal form.

At twenty-five, Raphael was already regarded as one of Italy's best painters. He was acclaimed for his numerous Madonnas, in which he attempted to achieve an ideal of beauty far surpassing human standards. He is well known for his frescoes in the Vatican Palace; his School of Athens reveals a world of balance, harmony, and order—the underlying principles of the art of the classical world of Greece and Rome.

Michelangelo, an accomplished painter, sculptor, and architect, was fiercely driven by a desire to create, and he worked with great passion and energy on a remarkable number of projects. Michelangelo was influenced by Neoplatonism, especially evident in his figures on the ceiling of the Sistine Chapel. These muscular figures reveal an ideal type of human being with perfect proportions. In good Neoplatonic fashion, their beauty is meant to be a reflection of divine beauty; the more beautiful the body, the more God-like the figure.

The State in the Renaissance

In the second half of the fifteenth century, attempts were made to reestablish the centralized power of monarchical governments after the political disasters of the fourteenth century. Some historians called these states the "new monarchies," especially those of France, England, and Spain (see Map 13.1).

WESTERN EUROPE

The Hundred Years' War left France prostrate. But the war had also developed a degree of French national feeling toward a common enemy that the kings could use to reestablish monarchical power. The development of a French territorial state was greatly advanced by King Louis XI (1461–1483), known as the Spider because of his wily and devious ways. Louis strengthened the use of the *taille*—an annual direct tax usually on land or property—as a permanent tax imposed by royal authority, giving him a sound, regular source of income, which created the foundations of a strong French monarchy.

The Hundred Years' War had also strongly affected the English. The cost of the war in its final years and the losses to the labor force strained the English economy. At the end of the war, England faced even greater turmoil when a civil war, known as the War of the Roses, erupted and aristocratic factions fought over the monarchy until 1485, when Henry Tudor established a new dynasty.

As the first Tudor king, Henry VII (1485–1509) worked to establish a strong monarchical government. Henry ended the private wars of the nobility by abolishing their private armies. By not overburdening the nobility and the middle class with taxes, Henry won their favor, and they provided him with much support.

Spain, too, experienced the growth of a strong national monarchy by the end of the fifteenth century. During the Middle Ages, several independent Christian kingdoms had emerged in the course of the long reconquest of the Iberian peninsula from the Muslims. Two of the strongest were Aragon and Castile. When Isabella of Castile (1474–1504) married Ferdinand of Aragon (1479–1516) in 1469, it was a major step toward unifying Spain. The two rulers worked to strengthen royal control of the government.

Ferdinand and Isabella also pursued a policy of strict religious uniformity. Spain possessed two large religious minorities, the Jews and the Muslims, both of which had been largely tolerated in medieval Spain. Increased persecution in the fourteenth century, however, led most Spanish Jews to convert to Catholicism. In 1492, Ferdinand and Isabella took the drastic step of expelling all professed Jews from Spain. Muslims, too, were then "encouraged" to convert to Catholicism, and in 1502,

✦ **MICHELANGELO, *CREATION OF ADAM*.** In 1508, Pope Julius II recalled Michelangelo to Rome and commissioned him to decorate the ceiling of the Sistine Chapel. This colossal project was not completed until 1512. Michelangelo attempted to tell the story of the Fall of Man by depicting nine scenes from the biblical Book of Genesis. In this scene, the well-proportioned figure of Adam, meant by Michelangelo to be a reflection of divine beauty, awaits the divine spark.

MAP 13.1 Europe in the Fifteenth Century. By the second half of the fifteenth century, states in western Europe, particularly France, Spain, and England, had begun the process of modern state building. With varying success, they reined in the power of the church and nobles, increased their ability to levy taxes, and established effective government bureaucracies. ➤ *What aspects of Europe's political boundaries help explain why France and the Holy Roman Empire were often at war with each other?*

Isabella issued a decree expelling all professed Muslims from her kingdom.

CENTRAL AND EASTERN EUROPE

Unlike France, England, and Spain, the Holy Roman Empire failed to develop a strong monarchical authority. The failure of the German emperors in the thirteenth century ended any chance of centralized monarchical authority, and Germany became a land of hundreds of virtually independent states. After 1438, the position of Holy Roman Emperor was held in the hands of the Habsburg dynasty. Having gradually acquired a number of possessions along the Danube, known collectively as Austria, the house of Habsburg had become one of the wealthiest landholders in the empire and by the mid-fifteenth century had begun to play an important role in European affairs.

In eastern Europe, rulers struggled to achieve the centralization of territorial states. Religious differences troubled the area, as Roman Catholics, Eastern Orthodox Christians, and other groups, including the Mongols, confronted each other. In Poland, the nobles gained the upper hand and established the right to elect their kings, a policy that drastically weakened royal authority. In Hungary, King Matthias Corvinus (1458–1490) broke the power of the wealthy lords and created a well-organized central administration. After his death, his work was largely undone.

Since the thirteenth century, Russia had been under the domination of the Mongols. Gradually, the princes of Moscow rose to prominence by using their close relationship to the Mongol khans to increase their wealth and expand their possessions. During the reign of the great Prince Ivan III (1462–1505), a new Russian state was born.

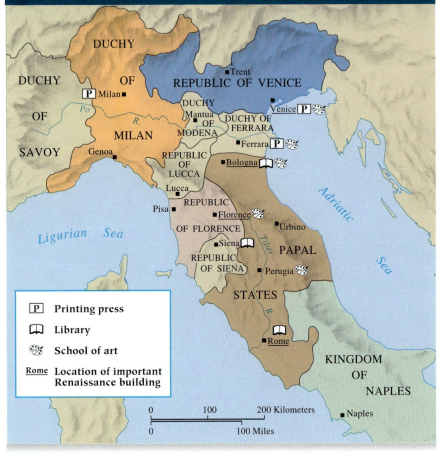

MAP 13.2 **Renaissance Italy.** Italy in the late fourteenth century was a land of five major states and numerous independent city-states. Increased prosperity and a supportive intellectual climate helped create the atmosphere for the middle and upper classes to "rediscover" Greco-Roman culture. Modern diplomacy is also a product of Renaissance Italy. ➤ *Could the presence of several other powers within easy marching distance make a ruler recognize the importance of diplomacy?*

Legend:
- P Printing press
- 📖 Library
- 🎨 School of art
- Rome Location of important Renaissance building

Milan, located at the crossroads of the main trade routes from Italian coast cities to the Alpine passes, was one of the richest city-states in Italy. In the fourteenth century, members of the Visconti family established themselves as dukes of Milan and extended their power over all of Lombardy. In 1447, a *condottiere* (leader of a mercenary band) named Francesco Sforza conquered the city and became its new duke. Both Visconti and Sforza rulers worked to create the institutions of a strongly centralized territorial state.

The other major northern Italian state was the republic of Venice, which had grown rich from trade throughout the eastern Mediterranean and into northern Europe. A small oligarchy of merchant-aristocrats, who had become extremely wealthy through their commercial activities, ran the Venetian government on behalf of their own interests. Venice's commercial empire brought in enormous revenues and gave it the status of an international power.

The republic of Florence dominated the region of Tuscany. In the course of the fourteenth century, a small but wealthy merchant oligarchy gained control of the Florentine government and established Florence as a major territorial state in northern Italy. In 1434, Cosimo de' Medici (1434–1464) took control of the ruling oligarchy. Although the wealthy Medici family maintained republican forms of government for appearance's sake, it ran the government from behind the scenes.

The growth of powerful monarchical states led to trouble for the Italians and brought an end to the independence of the Italian states. Attracted by the riches of Italy, the French king Charles VIII (1483–1498) led an army of thirty thousand men into Italy and occupied the kingdom of Naples. Other Italian states turned for help to the Spanish, who gladly complied. For the next thirty years, the French and Spanish competed to dominate Italy. The terrible sack of Rome in 1527 by the armies of the Spanish king Charles I brought a temporary end to the Italian wars. Thereafter the Spaniards dominated Italy.

Ivan III annexed other Russian principalities and took advantage of dissension among the Mongols to throw off their yoke by 1480.

THE ITALIAN STATES

During the Middle Ages, Italy had failed to develop a centralized monarchical state. Moreover, the kingdom of Naples in the south was dominated by the French house of Anjou, Sicily was ruled by the Spanish house of Aragon, and the papacy remained in shaky control of much of central Italy as rulers of the Papal States. Lack of centralized authority had enabled numerous city-states in northern and central Italy to remain independent of any political authority. Three of them—Milan, Venice, and Florence—managed to become fairly well centralized territorial states (see Map 13.2).

Chronology

THE STATE IN THE RENAISSANCE

France	
Louis XI the Spider	1461–1483
England	
Henry VII	1485–1509
Spain	
Isabella of Castile	1474–1504
Ferdinand of Aragon	1479–1516
Marriage of Ferdinand and Isabella	1469
Expulsion of the Jews	1492
Expulsion of the Muslims	1502
Eastern Europe	
Hungary: Matthias Corvinus	1458–1490
Russia: Ivan III	1462–1505
The Italian States	
Duchy of Milan	
Visconti establish themselves as rulers of Milan	1322
Sforzas	1450–1494
Florence	
Cosimo de' Medici	1434–1464
Beginning of Italian Wars— French invasion of Italy	1494
Sack of Rome	1527

MACHIAVELLI AND THE NEW STATECRAFT

No one gave better expression to the Italians' preoccupation with political power than Niccolò Machiavelli (1469–1527), who wrote *The Prince* (1513), one of the most influential works on political power in the Western world. Machiavelli's major concerns in *The Prince* were the acquisition, maintenance, and expansion of political power as the means to restore and maintain order in his time. In the Middle Ages, many political theorists stressed the ethical side of a prince's activity—how a ruler ought to behave based on Christian moral principles. Machiavelli bluntly contradicted this approach: "For the gap between how people actually behave and how they ought to behave is so great that anyone who ignores everyday reality in order to live up to an ideal will soon discover he had been taught how to destroy himself, not how to preserve himself."[2] Machiavelli considered his approach far more realistic than that of his medieval forebears. Political activity, therefore, could not be restricted by moral considerations. The prince acts on behalf of the state and for the sake of the state must be willing to let his con-

science sleep. Machiavelli was among the first to abandon morality as the basis for the analysis of political activity.

THE REFORMATION OF THE SIXTEENTH CENTURY

The Protestant Reformation is the name given to the religious reform movement that divided the western church into Catholic and Protestant groups. Although Martin Luther began the Reformation in the early sixteenth century, several earlier developments had set the stage for religious change.

Prelude to Reformation

During the second half of the fifteenth century, the new classical learning of the Italian Renaissance spread to the European countries north of the Alps and spawned a movement called Christian humanism or Northern Renaissance humanism, whose major goal was the reform of Christendom. The Christian humanists believed in the ability of human beings to reason and improve themselves and thought that through education in the sources of classical, and especially Christian, antiquity, they could instill an inner piety or an inward religious feeling that would bring about a reform of the church and society. To change society, they believed, you must first change the human beings who compose it.

The most influential of all the Christian humanists was Desiderius Erasmus (1466–1536), who formulated and popularized the reform program of Christian humanism. He called his conception of religion "the philosophy of Christ," by which he meant that Christianity should be a guiding philosophy for the direction of daily life rather than the system of dogmatic beliefs and practices that the medieval church seemed to stress. No doubt his work helped prepare the way for the Reformation; as contemporaries proclaimed, "Erasmus laid the egg that Luther hatched."

Corruption in the Catholic church was another factor that encouraged people to want reform. Between 1450 and 1520, a series of popes—called the Renaissance popes—failed to meet the church's spiritual needs. The popes were supposed to be the spiritual leaders of the Catholic church but as leaders of the Papal States were all too often involved in worldly interests. Julius II (1503–1513), the fiery "warrior-pope," personally led armies against his enemies, much to the disgust of pious Christians, who viewed the pope as a spiritual leader. As one intellectual wrote, "How, O bishop standing in the room of the Apostles, dare you teach the people the things that pertain to war?" Many high church officials were also concerned with money and used their church offices as opportunities to advance their careers and their wealth, and many ordinary parish priests seemed ignorant of their spiritual duties.

While the leaders of the church were failing to meet their responsibilities, ordinary people were clamoring for meaningful religious expression and certainty of salvation. As a result, for some, the process of salvation became almost mechanical. Collections of relics grew as more and more people sought certainty of salvation through veneration of these relics. Frederick the Wise, elector of Saxony and Martin Luther's prince, had amassed over five thousand relics to which were attached indulgences that could reduce one's time in purgatory by 1,443 years. (An indulgence is a remission, after death, of all or part of the punishment due to sin.)

Martin Luther and the Reformation in Germany

Martin Luther was a monk and a professor at the University of Wittenberg, where he lectured on the Bible. Probably sometime between 1513 and 1516, through his study of the Bible, he arrived at an answer to a problem—the assurance of salvation—that had disturbed him since his entry into the monastery.

Catholic doctrine had emphasized that both faith and good works were required of a Christian to achieve personal salvation. In Luther's eyes, human beings, weak and powerless in the sight of an almighty God, could never do enough good works to merit salvation. Through his study of the Bible, Luther came to believe that humans are not saved through their good works but through faith in the promises of God, made possible by the sacrifice of Jesus on the cross. This doctrine of salvation, or justification by grace through faith alone, became the primary doctrine of the Protestant Reformation. Because Luther had arrived at this doctrine from his study of the Bible, the Bible became for Luther, as for all other Protestants, the chief guide to religious truth.

Luther did not see himself as a rebel, but he was greatly upset by the widespread selling of indulgences. Especially offensive in his eyes was the monk Johann Tetzel, who hawked indulgences with the slogan "As soon as the coin in the coffer [money box] rings, the soul from purgatory springs." Greatly angered, in 1517, Luther issued a stunning indictment of the abuses in the sale of indulgences—the Ninety-Five Theses. Thousands of copies were printed and quickly spread to all parts of Germany.

Unable to accept Luther's ideas, the church excommunicated him in January 1521. He had also been summoned in 1520 to appear before the imperial diet or Reichstag of the Holy Roman Empire, convened by the newly elected Emperor Charles V (1519–1556). Ordered to recant the heresies he had espoused, Luther refused and made the famous reply that became the battle cry of the Reformation:

> Unless I am convicted by Scripture and plain reason—I do not accept the authority of popes and councils, for they have contradicted each other—my conscience is captive to the Word of God. I cannot and I will not recant anything, for to go against conscience is neither right nor safe. Here I stand, I cannot do otherwise. God help me. Amen.[3]

Members of the Reichstag were outraged and demanded that Luther be captured and delivered to the emperor. But Luther's ruler, Elector Frederick of Saxony, stepped in and protected him.

During the next few years, Luther's religious movement became a revolution. Luther was able to gain the support of many of the German rulers among the three hundred or so states that made up the Holy Roman Empire. These rulers quickly took control of the churches in their territories. The Lutheran churches in Germany (and later in Scandinavia) quickly became territorial or state churches in which the state supervised the affairs of the church. As part of the development of these state-dominated churches, Luther also instituted new religious services to replace the Catholic Mass. These focused on Bible reading, preaching of the word of God, and song.

From its very beginning, the fate of Luther's movement was closely tied to political affairs. In 1519, Charles I, king of Spain and the grandson of Emperor Maximilian, was elected Holy Roman Emperor as Charles V. Charles V ruled over an immense empire, consisting of Spain and its overseas possessions, the traditional Austrian Habsburg lands, Bohemia, Hungary, the Low Countries, and the kingdom of Naples in southern Italy. Politically, Charles wanted to maintain his enormous empire; religiously, he hoped to preserve the unity of his empire in the Catholic faith.

However, the internal political situation in the Holy Roman Empire was not in Charles's favor. Germany was a land of several hundred territorial states. Although all owed loyalty to the emperor, in the Middle Ages these states had become quite independent of imperial authority. By the time Charles V was able to bring military forces to Germany in 1546, Lutheranism had become well established and the Lutheran princes were well organized. Unable to defeat them, Charles was forced to negotiate a truce. An end to religious warfare in Germany came in 1555 with the Peace of Augsburg. The division of Christianity was formally acknowledged; Lutheran states were to have the same legal rights as Catholic states. Although the German states were now free to choose between Catholicism and Lutheranism, the peace settlement did not recognize the principle of religious toleration for individuals. The right of each German ruler to determine the religion of his subjects was accepted, but not the right of the subjects to choose their own religion.

The Spread of the Protestant Reformation

With the Peace of Augsburg, what had at first been merely feared was now certain: the ideal of Christian unity was forever lost. The rapid spread of new Protestant groups made this a certainty.

WOODCUT: LUTHER VERSUS THE POPE. In the 1520s, after Luther's return to Wittenberg, his teachings began to spread rapidly, ending ultimately in a reform movement supported by state authorities. Pamphlets containing picturesque woodcuts were important in the spread of Luther's ideas. In the woodcut shown here, the crucified Jesus attends Luther's service on the left, while on the right, the pope is at a table selling indulgences.

CALVIN AND CALVINISM

John Calvin (1509–1564) was educated in his native France but after his conversion to Protestantism was forced to flee for the safety of Switzerland. In 1536, he published the first edition of the *Institutes of the Christian Religion*, a masterful synthesis of Protestant thought that immediately secured Calvin's reputation as one of the new leaders of Protestantism.

On most important doctrines, Calvin stood very close to Luther. He adhered to the doctrine of justification by faith alone to explain how humans achieved salvation. But Calvin also placed much emphasis on the absolute sovereignty of God or the all-powerful nature of God—what Calvin called the "power, grace, and glory of God." One of the ideas derived from his emphasis on the absolute sovereignty of God—predestination—gave a unique cast to Calvin's teachings. This "eternal decree," as Calvin called it, meant that God had predestined some people to be saved (the elect) and others to be damned (the reprobate). According to Calvin, "He has once for all determined, both whom He would admit to salvation, and whom He would condemn to destruction."[4] Although Calvin stressed that there could be no absolute certainty of salvation, his followers did not always make this distinction. The practical psychological effect of predestination was to give later Calvinists an unshakable conviction that they were doing God's work on earth, making Calvinism a dynamic and activist faith.

In 1536, Calvin began working to reform the city of Geneva. He was able to fashion a tightly organized church order that employed both clergy and laymen in the service of the church. The Consistory, a special body for enforcing moral discipline, functioned as a court to oversee the moral life, daily behavior, and doctrinal orthodoxy of Genevans and to admonish and correct deviants. Citizens in Geneva were punished for such varied "crimes" as dancing, singing obscene songs, drunkenness, swearing, and playing cards.

Calvin's success in Geneva enabled the city to become a vibrant center of Protestantism. Following Calvin's lead, missionaries trained in Geneva were sent to all parts of Europe. Calvinism became established in France, the Netherlands, Scotland, and central and eastern Europe, and by the mid-sixteenth century, Calvin's Geneva stood as the fortress of the Reformation.

THE ENGLISH REFORMATION

The English Reformation was rooted in politics, not religion. King Henry VIII (1509–1547) had a strong desire to divorce his first wife, Catherine of Aragon, with whom the king had a daughter, Mary, but no male heir. He wanted to marry Anne Boleyn, with whom he had fallen in love. Impatient with the pope's unwillingness to grant him an annulment of his marriage, Henry turned to England's own church courts. As archbishop of Canterbury and head of the highest church court in England, Thomas Cranmer ruled in May 1533 that the king's marriage to Catherine was "absolutely void." At the beginning of June, Anne was crowned queen, and three months later, a child was born—a girl (the future queen Elizabeth I), much to the king's disappointment.

In 1534, at Henry's request, Parliament moved to finalize the break of the Church of England with Rome. The Act of Supremacy of 1534 declared that the king was "the only supreme head on earth of the Church of England," a position that gave him control of doctrine, clerical appointments, and discipline. Although Henry VIII had broken with the papacy, little change occurred in matters of doctrine, theology, and ceremony. Some of his supporters, including Archbishop Cranmer, sought a religious reformation as well as an administrative one, but Henry was unyielding. But he died in 1547 and was succeeded by his son, the underage and sickly Edward VI (1547–1553). During Edward's reign, Cranmer and others inclined toward Protestant doctrines were able to move the Church of England (or Anglican church) in a more Protestant direction. New acts of Parliament gave the clergy the right to marry and created a new Protestant church service.

Edward VI was succeeded by Mary (1553–1558), a Catholic who attempted to return England to Catholicism. Her actions aroused much anger, however, especially when "Bloody Mary" burned more than three hundred Protestant heretics. By the end of Mary's reign, England was more Protestant than it had been at the beginning.

The Catholic Reformation

By the mid-sixteenth century, Lutheranism had become established in Germany and Scandinavia and Calvinism in Switzerland, France, the Netherlands, and eastern Europe. In England, the split from Rome had resulted in the creation of a national church. The situation in Europe did not look particularly favorable to the Roman Catholic church. However, the Catholic church also underwent a revitalization in the sixteenth century, giving it new strength. There were three chief pillars of the Catholic Reformation: the Jesuits, a reformed papacy, and the Council of Trent.

The Society of Jesus, known as the Jesuits, was founded by a Spanish nobleman, Ignatius of Loyola (1491–1556). Loyola gathered together a small group of individuals who were recognized as a religious order by the pope in 1540. The new order was grounded on the principles of absolute obedience to the papacy, a strict hierarchical order for the society, the use of education to achieve its goals, and a dedication to engage in "conflict for God." A special vow of absolute obedience to the pope made the Jesuits an important instrument for papal policy. Jesuit missionaries proved singularly successful in restoring Catholicism to parts of Germany and eastern Europe.

A reformed papacy was another important factor in the development of the Catholic Reformation. The involvement of Renaissance popes in dubious financial undertakings and Italian political and military affairs had created numerous sources of corruption. It took the jolt of the Protestant Reformation to bring about serious reform. Pope Paul III (1534–1549) perceived the need for change and took the audacious step of appointing a reform commission to ascertain the church's ills. The commission's report in 1537 blamed the church's problems on the corrupt policies of popes and cardinals. It was also Paul III who formally recognized the Jesuits and began the Council of Trent.

In March 1545, a group of high church officials met in the city of Trent on the border between Germany and Italy and initiated the Council of Trent, which met intermittently from 1545 to 1563 in three major sessions. The final decrees of the Council of Trent reaffirmed traditional Catholic teachings in opposition to Protestant beliefs. Scripture and tradition were affirmed as equal authorities in religious matters; only the church could interpret Scripture. Both faith and good works were declared necessary for salvation. Belief in purgatory and in the use of indulgences was strengthened, although the selling of indulgences was prohibited.

After the Council of Trent, the Roman Catholic church possessed a clear body of doctrine and a unified church under the acknowledged supremacy of the popes. With a new spirit of confidence, the Catholic church entered a militant phase, as well prepared as the Calvinists to do battle for the Lord. An era of religious warfare was about to unfold.

EUROPE IN CRISIS, 1560–1650

Between 1560 and 1650, Europe experienced religious wars, revolutions and constitutional crises, economic and social disintegration, and a witchcraft craze. It was truly an age of crisis.

Politics and the Wars of Religion in the Sixteenth Century

By 1560, Calvinism and Catholicism had become militant religions dedicated to spreading the word of God as they interpreted it. Although their struggle for the minds and hearts of Europeans was at the heart of the religious wars of the sixteenth century, economic, social, and political forces also played an important role in these conflicts.

THE FRENCH WARS OF RELIGION (1562–1598)

Religion was central to the French civil wars of the sixteenth century. The growth of Calvinism had led to persecution by the French kings, but the latter did little to stop the spread of Calvinism. Huguenots (as the French Calvinists were called) constituted only about 7 percent of the population, but 40 to 50 percent of the French nobility became Huguenots, including the house of Bourbon, which stood next to the Valois in the royal line of succession. The conversion of so many nobles made the Huguenots a potentially dangerous political threat to monarchical power. Still, the Calvinist minority was greatly outnumbered by the Catholic majority, and the Valois monarchy was staunchly Catholic. At the same time, an extreme Catholic party, known as the ultra-Catholics, favored strict opposition to the Huguenots.

For thirty years, battles raged in France between Catholic and Calvinist parties. Finally, in 1589, Henry of Navarre, the political leader of the Huguenots and a member of the Bourbon dynasty, succeeded to the throne as Henry IV (1589–1610). Realizing, however, that he would never be accepted by Catholic France, Henry converted to Catholicism. With his coronation in 1594, the Wars of Religion finally came to an end. The Edict of Nantes in 1598 solved the religious problem by acknowledging Catholicism as the official religion of France while guaranteeing the Huguenots the right to worship and to enjoy all political privileges.

PHILIP II AND THE CAUSE OF MILITANT CATHOLICISM

The greatest advocate of militant Catholicism in the second half of the sixteenth century was King Philip II of Spain (1556–1598), the son and heir of Charles V. Philip's reign ushered in an age of Spanish greatness, both politically and culturally. Philip II had inherited from his father Spain, the Netherlands, and possessions in Italy and the New World. To strengthen his control, Philip insisted on strict conformity to Catholicism and strong monarchical authority. Achieving the latter was not an easy task, because each of the lands of his empire had its own structure of government.

Philip's attempt to strengthen his control in the Spanish Netherlands, which consisted of seventeen provinces (modern Netherlands and Belgium), soon led to a revolt. The nobles, who stood to lose the most politically, strongly opposed Philip's efforts. Religion also became a major catalyst for rebellion when Philip attempted to crush Calvinism. Violence erupted in 1566, and the revolt became organized, especially in the northern provinces, where the Dutch, under the leadership of William of Nassau, the prince of Orange, offered growing resistance. The struggle dragged on for decades until 1609, when a twelve-year truce ended the war, virtually recognizing the independence of the northern provinces. These seven northern provinces, which called themselves the United Provinces of the Netherlands, became the core of the modern Dutch state.

To most Europeans, Spain still seemed the greatest power of the age at the beginning of the seventeenth century, but the reality was quite different. The Spanish treasury was empty; the armed forces were obsolescent; and the government was inefficient. Spain continued to play the role of a great power, but real power had shifted to England.

THE ENGLAND OF ELIZABETH

When Elizabeth Tudor, the daughter of Henry VIII and Anne Boleyn, ascended the throne in 1558, England was home to fewer than four million people. Yet during her reign, the small island kingdom became leader of the Protestant nations of Europe and laid the foundations for a world empire.

Intelligent, cautious, and self-confident, Elizabeth moved quickly to solve the difficult religious problem she inherited from her half-sister, Queen Mary. Elizabeth's religious policy was based on moderation and compromise. She repealed the Catholic laws of Mary's reign, and a new Act of Supremacy designated Elizabeth as "the only supreme governor" of both church and state. The Church of England under Elizabeth was basically Protestant, but it was of a moderate bent that kept most people satisfied.

Caution and moderation also dictated Elizabeth's foreign policy. Gradually, however, Elizabeth was drawn into conflict with Spain. Having resisted for years the idea of invading England as too impractical, Philip II of Spain was finally persuaded to do so by advisers who assured him that the people of England would rise against their queen when the Spaniards arrived. A successful invasion of England would mean the overthrow of heresy and the return of England to Catholicism. Philip ordered preparations for a fleet of warships, the Armada, to spearhead the invasion of England.

The Armada was a disaster. The Spanish fleet that finally set sail had neither the ships nor the manpower that Philip had planned to send. Battered by a number of encounters with the English, the Spanish fleet sailed back to Spain by a northward route around Scotland and Ireland, where it was further pounded by storms.

Economic and Social Crises: Witchcraft Mania

The period of European history from 1560 to 1650 witnessed severe economic and social crises as well as political upheaval. Economic contraction began to be evident in some parts of Europe by the 1620s. In the 1630s and 1640s, as imports of silver from the Americas declined, economic recession intensified, especially in the Mediterranean area. Once the industrial and financial center of Europe in the age of the Renaissance, Italy was now becoming an economic backwater.

A WITCHCRAFT TRIAL IN FRANCE

Prosecutions for witchcraft reached their high point in the sixteenth and seventeenth centuries, when tens of thousands of people were brought to trial. In this excerpt from the minutes of a trial in France in 1652, we can see why the accused witch stood little chance of exonerating herself.

THE TRIAL OF SUZANNE GAUDRY

28 May, 1652. . . . Interrogation of Suzanne Gaudry, prisoner at the court of Rieux. . . . During interrogations on May 28 and May 29, the prisoner confessed to a number of activities involving the devil.

Deliberation of the Court—June 3, 1652

The undersigned advocates of the Court have seen these interrogations and answers. They say that the aforementioned Suzanne Gaudry confesses that she is a witch, that she had given herself to the devil, that she had renounced God, Lent, and baptism, that she has been marked on the shoulder, that she has cohabited with the devil and that she has been to the dances, confessing only to have cast a spell upon and caused to die a beast of Philippe Cornié. . . .

Third Interrogation, June 27

This prisoner being led into the chamber, she was examined to know if things were not as she had said and confessed at the beginning of her imprisonment.

—Answers no, and that what she has said was done so by force.

Pressed to say the truth, that otherwise she would be subjected to torture, having pointed out to her that her aunt was burned for this same subject.

—Answers that she is not a witch. . . .

She was placed in the hands of the officer in charge of torture, throwing herself on her knees, struggling to cry, uttering several exclamations, without being able, nevertheless, to shed a tear. Saying at every moment that she is not a witch.

The Torture

On this same day, being at the place of torture.

This prisoner, before being strapped down, was admonished to maintain herself in her first confessions and to renounce her lover.

—Says that she denies everything she has said, and that she has no lover. Feeling herself being strapped down, says that she is not a witch, while struggling to cry. . . . and upon being asked why she confessed to being one, said that she was forced to say it.

Told that she was not forced, that on the contrary she declared herself to be a witch without any threat.

—Says that she confessed it and that she is not a witch, and being a little stretched [on the rack] screams ceaselessly that she is not a witch.

Asked if she did not confess that she had been a witch for twenty-six years.

—Says that she said it, that she retracts it, crying that she is not a witch.

Asked if she did not make Philippe Cornié's horse die, as she confessed.

—Answers no, crying Jesus-Maria, that she is not a witch.

The mark having been probed by the officer, in the presence of Doctor Bouchain, it was adjudged by the aforesaid doctor and officer truly to be the mark of the devil.

Being more tightly stretched upon the torture rack, urged to maintain her confessions.

—Said that it was true that she is a witch and that she would maintain what she had said.

Asked how long she has been in subjugation to the devil.

—Answers that it was twenty years ago that the devil appeared to her, being in her lodgings in the form of a man dressed in a little cowhide and black breeches. . . .

Verdict

July 9, 1652. In the light of the interrogations, answers, and investigations made into the charge against Suzanne Gaudry, . . . seeing by her own confessions that she is said to have made a pact with the devil, received the mark from him, . . . and that following this, she had renounced God, Lent, and baptism and had let herself be known carnally by him, in which she received satisfaction. Also, seeing that she is said to have been a part of nocturnal carols and dances.

For expiation of which the advice of the undersigned is that the office of Rieux can legitimately condemn the aforesaid Suzanne Gaudry to death, tying her to a gallows, and strangling her to death, then burning her body and burying it here in the environs of the woods.

Population trends of the sixteenth and seventeenth centuries also reveal Europe's worsening conditions. The population of Europe increased from 60 million in 1500 to 85 million by 1600, the first major recovery of European population since the devastation of the Black Death in the mid-fourteenth century. However, records also indicate a decline of the population by 1650, especially in central and southern Europe. Europe's longtime adversaries—war, famine, and plague—continued to affect population levels. Europe's problems created social tensions, some of which became manifested in an obsession with witches.

Hysteria over witchcraft affected the lives of many Europeans in the sixteenth and seventeenth centuries. Perhaps more than 100,000 people were prosecuted throughout Europe on charges of witchcraft. As more and more people were brought to trial, the fear of witches, as well as the fear of being accused of witchcraft, escalated to frightening levels (see the box above).

Common people—usually those who were poor and without property—were more likely to be accused of witchcraft. Indeed, where lists are given, those mentioned most often are milkmaids, peasant women, and servant girls. In the witchcraft trials of the sixteenth and seventeenth centuries, more than 75 percent of the accused were women, most of them single or widowed and many over fifty years old.

That women should be the chief victims of witchcraft trials was hardly accidental. Nicholas Rémy, a witchcraft judge in France in the 1590s, found it "not unreasonable that this scum of humanity, i.e., witches, should be drawn chiefly from the feminine sex." To another judge, it came as no surprise that witches would confess to sexual experiences with Satan: "The Devil uses them so, because he knows that women love carnal pleasures, and he means to bind them to his allegiance by such agreeable provocations."[5]

By the mid-seventeenth century, the witchcraft hysteria had begun to subside. As governments grew stronger, fewer magistrates were willing to accept the unsettling and divisive conditions generated by the trials of witches. Moreover, by the end of the seventeenth and beginning of the eighteenth centuries, more and more people were questioning altogether their old attitudes toward religion and found it especially contrary to reason to believe in the old view of a world haunted by evil spirits.

Seventeenth-Century Crises

During the first half of the seventeenth century, a series of rebellions and civil wars rocked the domestic stability of many European governments. A devastating war that affected much of Europe also added to the sense of crisis.

The Thirty Years' War began in 1618 in the Germanic lands of the Holy Roman Empire as a struggle between Catholic forces, led by the Habsburg Holy Roman Emperors, and Protestant—primarily Calvinist—nobles in Bohemia who rebelled against Habsburg authority (see Map 13.3). What began as a struggle over religious issues soon became a wider conflict perpetuated by political motivations as both minor and major European powers—Denmark, Sweden, France, and Spain—entered the war. The competition for European leadership between the Bourbon dynasty of France and the Habsburg dynasties of Spain and the Holy Roman Empire was an especially important factor. Nevertheless, most of the battles were fought on German soil.

The war in Germany was officially ended in 1648 by the Peace of Westphalia, which proclaimed that all German states, including the Calvinist ones, were free to determine their own religion. The major contenders gained new territories, and France emerged as the dominant nation in Europe. The more than three hundred states that made up the Holy Roman Empire were recognized as independent states, and each was given the power to conduct its own foreign policy; this brought an end to the Holy Roman Empire as a political entity and ensured German disunity for another two hundred years. The Peace of Westphalia made it clear that political motives, not religious convictions, had become the guiding force in public affairs.

THE PRACTICE OF ABSOLUTISM

Many people responded to the crises of the seventeenth century by searching for order. An increase in monarchical power became an obvious means for achieving stability. The result was what historians have called absolutism or absolute monarchy. Absolutism meant that the sovereign power or ultimate authority in the state rested in the hands of a king who claimed to rule by divine right—the idea that kings received their power from God and were responsible to no one except God. Late sixteenth-century political theorists believed that sovereign power consisted of the authority to make laws, tax, administer justice, control the state's administrative system, and determine foreign policy.

France Under Louis XIV

France during the reign of Louis XIV (1643–1715) has traditionally been regarded as the best example of the practice of absolute monarchy in the seventeenth century. One of the keys to Louis's power was his control of the central policy-making machinery of government because it was part of his own court and household. The royal court located at Versailles served three purposes simultaneously: it was the personal household of the king, the location of central governmental machinery, and the place where powerful subjects came to find favors and offices for themselves and their clients. The greatest danger to Louis's personal rule came from the very high nobles and princes of the blood (the royal princes), who considered it their natural role to assert the policy-making role of royal ministers. Louis eliminated this threat by removing them from the royal council, the chief administrative body of the king, and enticing them to his court, where he could keep them preoccupied with court life and out of politics. Instead of the high nobility and royal princes, Louis relied for his ministers on nobles who came from relatively new aristocratic families. His ministers were expected to be subservient; "I had no intention of sharing my authority with them," Louis said.

Louis's domination of his ministers and secretaries gave him control of the central policy-making machinery of government and thus authority over the traditional areas of monarchical power: the formulation of foreign policy, the making of war and peace, the assertion of the secular power of the crown against any religious authority, and the ability to levy taxes to fulfill these functions. However, Louis had considerably less success with the internal administration of the kingdom.

The cost of building palaces, maintaining his court, and pursuing his wars made finances a crucial issue for Louis XIV. He was most fortunate in having the services of Jean-Baptiste Colbert (1619–1683) as controller general of finances. Colbert sought to increase the wealth and power of France by general adherence to mercantilism, a set of principles that dominated economic thought in the seventeenth century. According to the mercantilists, the prosperity of a nation depended on a plentiful supply of bullion (gold and silver). For this reason, it was desirable to achieve a favorable balance of trade in which goods exported were of greater value than those imported, promoting an influx of gold and silver payments that would increase the quantity of bullion. Mercantilism focused on the role of the state, believing that state intervention in the economy was desirable for the sake of the national good.

The increase in royal power that Louis pursued led the king to develop a professional army numbering 100,000 men in peacetime and 400,000 in time of war. To achieve the prestige and military glory befitting an absolute king as well as to ensure the domination of his Bourbon dynasty over European affairs, Louis waged four wars between 1667 and 1713. His ambitions roused much of Europe to form coalitions that were determined to prevent the certain

Sun Kings, West and East

At the end of the seventeenth century, two powerful rulers dominated the affairs of their regions and saw themselves as "sun kings"—the sources of light for their people. On the left, Louis XIV, who ruled France from 1643 to 1715, is seen in a portrait by Hyacinth Rigaud that captures the king's sense of royal dignity and grandeur. On the right, Kangxi, who ruled China from 1661 to 1722, is seen in a nineteenth-century portrait that shows the ruler seated in majesty on his imperial throne.

© Réunion des Musées Nationaux/Art Resource, NY

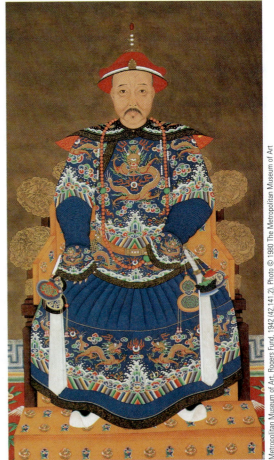

Metropolitan Museum of Art, Rogers Fund, 1942 (42.141.2). Photo © 1980 The Metropolitan Museum of Art

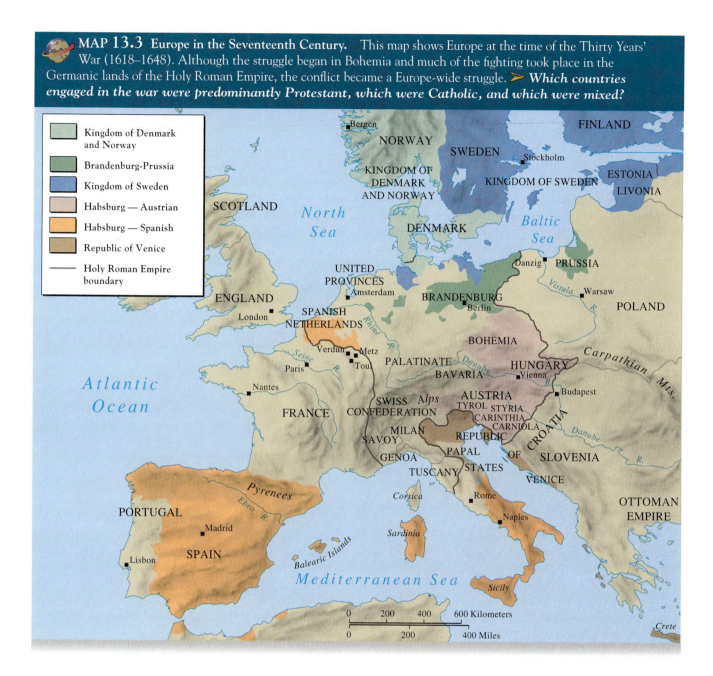

MAP 13.3 Europe in the Seventeenth Century. This map shows Europe at the time of the Thirty Years' War (1618–1648). Although the struggle began in Bohemia and much of the fighting took place in the Germanic lands of the Holy Roman Empire, the conflict became a Europe-wide struggle. ➤ *Which countries engaged in the war were predominantly Protestant, which were Catholic, and which were mixed?*

Legend:
- Kingdom of Denmark and Norway
- Brandenburg-Prussia
- Kingdom of Sweden
- Habsburg — Austrian
- Habsburg — Spanish
- Republic of Venice
- Holy Roman Empire boundary

destruction of the European balance of power by Bourbon hegemony. Louis left France impoverished and surrounded by enemies.

Absolutism in Central and Eastern Europe

During the seventeenth century, a development of great importance for the modern Western world took place with the appearance in central and eastern Europe of three new powers: Prussia, Austria, and Russia.

Frederick William the Great Elector (1640–1688) laid the foundation for the Prussian state. Realizing that the land he had inherited, known as Brandenburg-Prussia, constituted a small, open territory with no natural fron-

tiers for defense, Frederick William built an army of forty thousand men, making it the fourth largest in Europe. To sustain the army, Frederick William established the General War Commissariat to levy taxes for the army and oversee its growth. The commissariat soon evolved into an agency for civil government as well. The new bureaucratic machine became the elector's chief instrument to govern the state. Many of its officials were members of the Prussian landed aristocracy, the Junkers, who also served as officers in the all-important army.

In 1701, Frederick William's son Frederick officially gained the title of king. Elector Frederick III became King Frederick I; and Brandenburg-Prussia, simply Prussia. In the eighteenth century, Prussia emerged as a great power in Europe.

The Austrian Habsburgs had long played a significant role in European politics as Holy Roman Emperors. By the end of the Thirty Years' War, the Habsburg hopes of creating an empire in Germany had been dashed. In the seventeenth century, the house of Austria created a new empire in eastern and southeastern Europe.

The nucleus of the new Austrian Empire remained the traditional Austrian hereditary possessions: Lower and Upper Austria, Carinthia, Carniola, Styria, and Tyrol. To these had been added the kingdom of Bohemia and parts of northwestern Hungary. After the defeat of the Turks in 1687 (see Chapter 15), Austria took control of all of Hungary, Transylvania, Croatia, and Slovenia, thus establishing the Austrian Empire in southeastern Europe.

The Austrian monarchy, however, never became a highly centralized, absolutist state, primarily because it contained so many different national groups. The Austrian Empire remained a collection of territories held together by the Habsburg emperor, who was archduke of Austria, king of Bohemia, and king of Hungary. Each of these regions, however, had its own laws and political life.

A new Russian state had emerged in the fifteenth century under the leadership of the principality of Moscow and its grand dukes. In the sixteenth century, Ivan IV (1533–1584) became the first ruler to take the title of *tsar* (the Russian word for *caesar*). When Ivan's dynasty came to an end in 1598, it was followed by a period of anarchy that did not end until the Zemsky Sobor (national assembly) chose Michael Romanov as the new tsar, establishing a dynasty that lasted until 1917. One of its most prominent members was Peter the Great.

Peter the Great (1689–1725) was a towering, strong man at 6 feet 9 inches tall and enjoyed a low kind of humor—belching contests and crude jokes—and vicious punishments, including floggings, impalings, and roastings. Peter received a firsthand view of the West when he made a trip there in 1697–1698 and returned to Russia with a firm determination to westernize or Europeanize Russia. He was especially eager to borrow European technology in order to give him the army and navy he needed to make Russia a great power.

As could be expected, one of his first priorities was the reorganization of the army and the creation of a navy. Employing both Russians and Europeans as officers, he conscripted peasants for twenty-five-year stints of service to build a standing army of 210,000 men. Peter has also been given credit for forming the first Russian navy. To impose the rule of the central government more effectively throughout the land, Peter divided Russia into provinces. Although he hoped to create a "police state," by which he meant a well-ordered community governed in accordance with law, few of his bureaucrats shared his concept of duty to the state. Peter hoped for a sense of civic duty, but his own forceful personality created an atmosphere of fear that prevented it.

The object of Peter's domestic reforms was to make Russia into a great state and military power. His primary goal was to "open a window to the west," meaning an ice-free port easily accessible to Europe. This could only be achieved on the Baltic, but at that time, the Baltic coast was controlled by Sweden, the most important power in northern Europe. A long and hard-fought war with Sweden won Peter the lands he sought. In 1703, Peter began the construction of a new city, Saint Petersburg, his window to the west and a symbol that Russia was looking westward to Europe. Under Peter, Russia became a great military power and, by his death in 1725, an important European state.

ENGLAND AND THE EMERGENCE OF CONSTITUTIONAL MONARCHY

Not all states were absolutist in the seventeenth century. One of the most prominent examples of resistance to absolute monarchy came in England, where king and Parliament struggled to determine the roles each should play in governing England.

Revolution and Civil War

With the death of Queen Elizabeth I in 1603, the Tudor dynasty became extinct, and the Stuart line of rulers was inaugurated with the accession to the throne of Elizabeth's cousin, King James VI of Scotland, who became James I (1603–1625) of England. James espoused the divine right of kings, a viewpoint that alienated Parliament, which had grown accustomed under the Tudors to act on the premise that monarch and Parliament together ruled England as a "balanced polity." Then, too, the Puritans—Protestants within the Anglican church who, inspired by Calvinist theology, wished to eliminate every trace of Roman Catholicism from the Church of England—were alienated by the king's strong defense of the Anglican church. Much of England's gentry, mostly well-to-do landowners, had become Puritans, and this Puritan gentry formed an important and substantial part of the House of Commons, the lower house of Parliament. It was not wise to alienate these men.

The conflict that had begun during the reign of James came to a head during the reign of his son, Charles I (1625–1649). Charles also believed in divine-right monarchy, and religious differences also added to the hostility between Charles I and Parliament. Grievances mounted until England finally slipped into a civil war (1642–1648) won by the parliamentary forces, due largely to the New

Model Army of Oliver Cromwell, the only real military genius of the war. The New Model Army was composed primarily of more extreme Puritans known as the Independents, who, in typical Calvinist fashion, believed they were doing battle for God. As Cromwell wrote in one of his military reports, "Sir, this is none other but the hand of God; and to Him alone belongs the glory." We might give some credit to Cromwell; his soldiers were well trained in the new military tactics of the seventeenth century.

After the execution of Charles I on January 30, 1649, Parliament abolished the monarchy and the House of Lords and proclaimed England a republic or commonwealth. But Cromwell and his army, unable to work effectively with Parliament, dispersed it by force and established a military dictatorship. After Cromwell's death in 1658, the army decided that military rule was no longer feasible and restored the monarchy in the person of Charles II, the son of Charles I.

Restoration and a Glorious Revolution

Charles was sympathetic to Catholicism, and Parliament's suspicions were aroused in 1672 when Charles took the audacious step of issuing the Declaration of Indulgence, which suspended the laws that Parliament had passed against Catholics and Puritans after the restoration of the monarchy. Parliament forced the king to suspend the declaration.

The accession of James II (1685–1688) to the crown virtually guaranteed a new constitutional crisis for England. An open and devout Catholic, his attempt to further Catholic interests made religion once more a primary cause of conflict between king and Parliament. Parliamentary outcries against James's policies stopped short of rebellion because members knew that he was an old man and that his successors were his Protestant daughters Mary and Anne, born to his first wife. But on June 10, 1688, a son was born to James II's second wife, also a Catholic. Suddenly the specter of a Catholic hereditary monarchy loomed large. A group of prominent English noblemen invited the Dutch chief executive, William of Orange, husband of James's daughter Mary, to invade England. William and Mary raised an army and invaded England while James, his wife, and their infant son fled to France. With little bloodshed, England had undergone its "Glorious Revolution."

In January 1689, Parliament offered the throne to William and Mary, who accepted it along with the provisions of a bill of rights (see the box on p. 290). The Bill of Rights affirmed Parliament's right to make laws and levy taxes. The rights of citizens to keep arms and have a jury trial were also confirmed. By deposing one king and establishing another, Parliament had destroyed the divine-right theory of kingship (William was, after all, king by grace of

ABSOLUTE AND LIMITED MONARCHY

France	
Louis XIV	1643–1715
Brandenburg-Prussia	
Frederick William the Great Elector	1640–1688
Elector Frederick III (King Frederick I)	1688–1713
Russia	
Ivan IV the Terrible	1533–1584
Peter the Great	1689–1725
First trip to the West	1697–1698
Construction of Saint Petersburg begins	1703
England	
Civil wars	1642–1648
Commonwealth	1649–1653
Charles II	1660–1685
Declaration of Indulgence	1672
James II	1685–1688
Glorious Revolution	1688
Bill of Rights	1689

Parliament, not God) and asserted its right to participate in the government. Parliament did not have complete control of the government, but it now had the right to participate in affairs of state. Over the next century, it would gradually prove to be the real authority in the English system of constitutional monarchy.

EUROPEAN CULTURE

Art and intellectual activity experienced dramatic changes in the sixteenth and seventeenth centuries. Especially important in developing a new view of the world was the Scientific Revolution.

Art: The Baroque

The artistic movement known as the Baroque dominated the Western artistic world for a century and a half. The Baroque began in Italy in the last quarter of the sixteenth century and spread to the rest of Europe and Latin America. Baroque artists sought to harmonize the classical ideals of Renaissance art with the spiritual feelings of the

THE BILL OF RIGHTS

*I*n 1688, the English experienced yet another revolution, a bloodless one in which the Stuart king James II was replaced by Mary, James's daughter, and her husband, William of Orange. After William and Mary had assumed power, Parliament passed a bill of rights that specified the rights of Parliament and laid the foundation for a constitutional monarchy.

THE BILL OF RIGHTS

Whereas the said late King James II having abdicated the government, and the throne being thereby vacant, his Highness the prince of Orange (whom it hath pleased Almighty God to make the glorious instrument of delivering this kingdom from popery and arbitrary power) did (by the device of the lords spiritual and temporal, and diverse principal persons of the Commons) cause letters to be written to the lords spiritual and temporal, being Protestants, and other letters to the several counties, cities, universities, boroughs, and Cinque Ports, for the choosing of such persons to represent them, as were of right to be sent to parliament, to meet and sit at Westminster upon the two and twentieth day of January, in this year 1689, in order to such an establishment as that their religion, laws, and liberties might not again be in danger of being subverted; upon which letters elections have been accordingly made.

And thereupon the said lords spiritual and temporal and Commons, pursuant to their respective letters and elections, being now assembled in a full and free representation of this nation, taking into their most serious consideration the best means for attaining the ends aforesaid, do in the first place (as their ancestors in like case have usually done), for the vindication and assertion of their ancient rights and liberties, declare:

1. That the pretended power of suspending laws, or the execution of laws, by regal authority, without consent of parliament is illegal.

2. That the pretended power of dispensing with the laws, or the execution of law by regal authority, as it hath been assumed and exercised of late, is illegal.

3. That the commission for erecting the late court of commissioners for ecclesiastical causes, and all other commissions and courts of like nature, are illegal and pernicious.

4. That levying money for or to the use of the crown by pretense of prerogative, without grant of parliament, for longer time or in other manner than the same is or shall be granted, is illegal.

5. That it is the right of the subjects to petition the king, and all commitments and prosecutions for such petitioning are illegal.

6. That the raising or keeping a standing army within the kingdom in time of peace, unless it be with consent of parliament, is against law.

7. That the subjects which are Protestants may have arms for their defense suitable to their conditions, and as allowed by law.

8. That election of members of parliament ought to be free.

9. That the freedom of speech, and debates or proceedings in parliament, ought not to be impeached or questioned in any court or place out of parliament.

10. That excessive bail ought not to be required, nor excessive fines imposed, nor cruel and unusual punishments inflicted.

11. That jurors ought to be duly impaneled and returned, and jurors which pass upon men in trials for high treason ought to be freeholders.

12. That all grants and promises of fines and forfeitures of particular persons before conviction are illegal and void.

13. And that for redress of all grievances, and for the amending, strengthening, and preserving of the laws, parliament ought to be held frequently.

---

sixteenth-century religious revival. In large part, Baroque art and architecture reflected the search for power that was characteristic of much of the seventeenth century. Baroque churches and palaces featured richly ornamented facades, sweeping staircases, and an overall splendor meant to impress people.

Baroque painting was known for its use of dramatic effects to arouse the emotions, especially evident in the works of Peter Paul Rubens (1577–1640), a prolific artist and an important figure in the spread of the Baroque from Italy to other parts of Europe. In his artistic masterpieces, bodies in violent motion, heavily fleshed nudes, a dramatic use of light and shadow, and rich sensuous pigments converge to express intense emotions.

A Golden Age of Literature in England

In England, writing for the stage reached new heights between 1580 and 1640. The golden age of English literature is often called the Elizabethan Era because much of the English cultural flowering occurred during Elizabeth I's reign. Of all the forms of Elizabethan literature, none expressed the energy and intellectual versatility of the era better than drama. And no dramatist is more famous or more accomplished than William Shakespeare (1564–1614).

Shakespeare was a "complete man of the theater." Although best known for writing plays, he was also an actor and a shareholder in the chief acting company of the time, the Lord Chamberlain's Company, which played

PETER PAUL RUBENS, *THE LANDING OF MARIE DE'
MEDICI AT MARSEILLES.*   Peter Paul Rubens played a key role
in spreading the Baroque style from Italy to other parts of
Europe. *In The Landing of Marie de' Medici at Marseilles,* Rubens
made dramatic use of light and color, bodies in motion, and luxurious nudes to heighten the emotional intensity of the scene.
This was one of a cycle of twenty-one paintings dedicated to the
queen mother of France.

in various London theaters. Shakespeare is to this day
hailed as a genius. A master of the English language, he
imbued its words with power and majesty. And his technical proficiency was matched by incredible insight into
human psychology. Whether writing tragedies or come-
dies, Shakespeare exhibited a remarkable understanding
of the human condition (see the box on p. 292).

The Scientific Revolution

The Scientific Revolution ultimately challenged conceptions and beliefs about the nature of the external world
that had become dominant by the Late Middle Ages.
The Scientific Revolution taught Europeans to view the
universe in a new way.

TOWARD A NEW HEAVEN: A REVOLUTION IN ASTRONOMY

The philosophers of the Middle Ages had used the ideas
of Aristotle, Ptolemy (the greatest astronomer of antiquity, who lived in the second century C.E.), and Christianity to construct the Ptolemaic or geocentric
conception of the universe. In this conception, the
universe was seen as a series of concentric spheres with a
fixed or motionless earth at its center. Composed of
material substance, the earth was imperfect and constantly
changing. The spheres that surrounded the earth were
made of a crystalline, transparent substance and moved in
circular orbits around the earth. The heavenly bodies,
which numbered ten in 1500, were pure orbs of light,
embedded in the moving, concentric spheres. Working
outward from the earth, the first eight spheres contained
the Moon, Mercury, Venus, the Sun, Mars, Jupiter, Saturn,
and the fixed stars. The ninth sphere imparted to the
eighth sphere of the fixed stars its daily motion, while
the tenth sphere was frequently described as the prime
mover that moved itself and imparted motion to the other
spheres. Beyond the tenth sphere was the Empyrean
Heaven—the location of God and all the saved souls. God
and the saved souls were at one end of the universe, then,
and humans were at the center. They had power over the
earth, but their real purpose was to achieve salvation.

Nicholas Copernicus (1473–1543), a native of Poland,
was a mathematician who felt that Ptolemy's geocentric
system failed to accord with the observed motions of the
heavenly bodies and hoped that his heliocentric (sun-
centered) conception would offer a more accurate explanation. Copernicus argued that the sun was motionless
at the center of the universe. The planets revolved around
the sun in the order of Mercury, Venus, the earth, Mars,
Jupiter, and Saturn. The moon, however, revolved around
the earth. Moreover, what appeared to be the movement
of the sun around the earth was really explained by the
daily rotation of the earth on its axis and the journey of
the earth around the sun each year. But Copernicus did
not reject the idea that the heavenly spheres moved in circular orbits.

The next step in destroying the geocentric conception and supporting the Copernican system was taken by
Johannes Kepler (1571–1630). A brilliant German mathematician and astronomer, Kepler arrived at laws of planetary motion that confirmed Copernicus's heliocentric
theory. In his first law, however, he contradicted Copernicus by showing that the orbits of the planets around the
sun were not circular but elliptical, with the sun at one
focus of the ellipse rather than at the center.

Kepler's work destroyed the basic structure of the
Ptolemaic system. People could now think in new terms
of the actual paths of planets revolving around the sun
in elliptical orbits. But important questions remained

WILLIAM SHAKESPEARE: IN PRAISE OF ENGLAND

William Shakespeare is one of the most famous playwrights in the Western world. He was a universal genius, outclassing all others in his psychological insights, depth of characterization, imaginative skills, and versatility. His historical plays reflected the patriotic enthusiasm of the English in the Elizabethan Era, as this excerpt from *Richard II* illustrates.

WILLIAM SHAKESPEARE, RICHARD II

This royal throne of kings, this sceptered isle,
This earth of majesty, this seat of Mars,
This other Eden, demi-Paradise,
This fortress built by Nature for herself
Against infection and the hand of war,
This happy breed of men, this little world,
This precious stone set in the silver sea,
Which serves it in the office of a wall
Or as a moat defensive to a house
Against the envy of less happier lands—
This blessed plot, this earth, this realm, this England,

This nurse, this teeming womb of royal kings,
Feared by their breed and famous by their birth,
Renowned for their deeds as far from home,
For Christian service and true chivalry,
As is the sepulcher in stubborn Jewry [the Holy Sepulcher in
    Jerusalem]
Of the world's ransom, blessed Mary's Son—
This land of such dear souls, this dear dear land,
Dear for her reputation through the world,
Is now leased out, I die pronouncing it,
Like a tenement or pelting farm.
England, bound in with the triumphant sea,
Whose rocky shore beats back the envious siege
Of watery Neptune, is now bound in with shame,
With inky blots and rotten parchment bonds.
That England, that was wont to conquer others,
Hath made a shameful conquest of itself.
Ah, would the scandal vanish with my life,
How happy then were my ensuing death!

unanswered. For example, what were the planets made of? An Italian scientist achieved the next important breakthrough to a new cosmology by answering that question.

Galileo Galilei (1564–1642) taught mathematics and was the first European to make systematic observations of the heavens by means of a telescope, inaugurating a new age in astronomy. Galileo turned his telescope to the skies and made a remarkable series of discoveries: mountains on the moon, four moons revolving around Jupiter, and sunspots. Galileo's observations seemed to destroy yet another aspect of the traditional cosmology in that the universe seemed to be composed of material similar to that of the earth rather than a perfect and unchanging substance.

Galileo's revelations, published in *The Starry Messenger* in 1610, made Europeans aware of a new picture of the universe. But the Catholic church condemned Copernicanism and ordered Galileo to abandon the Copernican thesis. The church attacked the Copernican system because it threatened not only Scripture but also an entire conception of the universe. The heavens were no longer a spiritual world but a world of matter.

By the 1630s and 1640s, most astronomers had come to accept the new heliocentric conception of the universe. Nevertheless, the problem of explaining motion in the universe and tying together the ideas of Copernicus, Galileo, and Kepler had not yet been done. This would be the work of an Englishman who has long been considered the greatest genius of the Scientific Revolution.

Born in 1642, Isaac Newton taught at Cambridge University, where he wrote his major work, *Mathematical Principles of Natural Philosophy*, known simply as the *Principia* by the first word of its Latin title. In the first book of the *Principia*, Newton defined the three laws of motion that govern the planetary bodies, as well as objects on earth. Crucial to his whole argument was the universal law of gravitation, which explained why the planetary bodies did not go off in straight lines but continued in elliptical orbits about the sun. In mathematical terms, Newton explained that every object in the universe is attracted to every other object by a force called gravity.

Newton had demonstrated that one mathematically proven universal law could explain all motion in the universe. At the same time, the Newtonian synthesis created a new cosmology in which the universe was seen as one huge, regulated machine that operated according to natural laws in absolute time, space, and motion. Newton's world-machine concept dominated the modern worldview until the twentieth century, when Albert Einstein's concept of relativity created a new picture of the universe.

EUROPE, CHINA, AND SCIENTIFIC REVOLUTIONS

An interesting question that arises is why the Scientific Revolution occurred in Europe and not in China. In the Middle Ages, China had been the most technologically advanced civilization in the world. After 1500, that dis-

MEDIEVAL CONCEPTION OF THE UNIVERSE. As this sixteenth-century illustration shows, the medieval cosmological view placed the earth at the center of the universe, surrounded by a series of concentric spheres. The earth was imperfect and constantly changing, while the heavenly bodies that surrounded it were perfect and incorruptible. Beyond the tenth and final sphere was heaven, where God and all the saved souls were located.

THE COPERNICAN SYSTEM. The Copernican system was presented in *On the Revolutions of the Heavenly Spheres*, published shortly before Copernicus's death. As shown in this illustration from the first edition of the book, Copernicus maintained that the sun was the center of the universe while the planets, including the earth, revolved around it. Moreover, the earth rotated daily on its axis.

tinction passed to the West. Historians are not sure why. Some have contrasted the sense of order in Chinese society with the competitive spirit existing in Europe. Others have emphasized China's ideological viewpoint that favored living in harmony with nature rather than trying to dominate it. One historian has even suggested that China's civil service system drew the "best and the brightest" into government service, to the detriment of other occupations.

CONCLUSION

In the next chapter, we will examine how the movement of Europeans outside of Europe began to change the shape of world history. But what had made this development possible? After all, the religious division of Europe had led to almost a hundred years of religious warfare complicated by serious political, economic, and social issues before Europeans finally admitted that they would have to accept different ways of worshiping God.

At the same time, the concept of a united Christendom, held as an ideal since the Middle Ages, had been irrevocably destroyed by the religious wars, enabling a system of nation-states to emerge in which power politics

took on increasing significance. Within those states there slowly emerged some of the machinery that made possible a growing centralization of power. In those states called absolutist, strong monarchs with the assistance of their aristocracies provided the leadership for greater centralization. In all the major European states, a growing concern for power led to larger armies and greater conflict, stronger economies, and more powerful governments. From a global point of view, the political and economic power of Europeans was beginning to slowly outstrip that of other peoples.

The Scientific Revolution also represents a major turning point in modern civilization. With a new conception of the universe came a new conception of humankind. Europeans came to believe that by using only reason they could understand and dominate the world of nature. Combined with the eighteenth-century Enlightenment (see Chapter 17), the Scientific Revolution gave the West an intellectual boost that contributed to the increased confidence of Western civilization. Europeans—with their strong governments, prosperous economies, and strengthened military forces—began to dominate other parts of the world, leading to a growing belief in the superiority of their civilization.

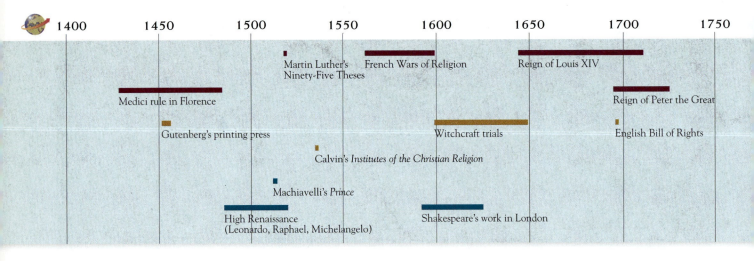

1400   1450   1500   1550   1600   1650   1700   1750

Martin Luther's
Ninety-Five Theses

French Wars of Religion

Reign of Louis XIV

Medici rule in Florence

Reign of Peter the Great

Gutenberg's printing press

Witchcraft trials

English Bill of Rights

Calvin's *Institutes of the Christian Religion*

Machiavelli's *Prince*

High Renaissance
(Leonardo, Raphael, Michelangelo)

Shakespeare's work in London

CHAPTER NOTES

1. Quoted in Jacob Burckhardt, *The Civilization of the Renaissance in Italy*, trans. S. G. C. Middlemore (London, 1960), p. 81.
2. Niccolò Machiavelli, *The Prince*, trans. David Wootton (Indianapolis, 1995), p. 48.
3. Quoted in Roland Bainton, *Here I Stand: A Life of Martin Luther* (New York, 1950), p. 144.
4. John Calvin, *Institutes of the Christian Religion,* trans. John Allen (Philadelphia, 1936), vol. 1, p. 228; vol. 2, p. 181.
5. Quoted in Joseph Klaits, *Servants of Satan: The Age of Witch Hunts* (Bloomington, Ind., 1985), p. 68.

SUGGESTED READING

General works on the Renaissance in Europe include D. L. Jensen, *Renaissance Europe*, 2d ed. (Lexington, Mass., 1991); P. Burke, *The European Renaissance: Centres and Peripheries* (Oxford, 1998); and J. R. Hale, *The Civilization of Europe in the Renaissance* (New York, 1994). For a good summary of literature on the Renaissance, see P. Burke, *The Renaissance* (New York, 1997).

Numerous facets of social life in the Renaissance are examined in J. R. Hale, *Renaissance Europe: The Individual and Society* (London, 1971). On family and marriage, see D. Herlihy, *The Family in Renaissance Italy* (St. Louis, 1974), and the valuable C. Klapisch-Zuber, *Women, Family, and Ritual in Renaissance Italy* (Chicago, 1985). Women are examined in M. L. King, *Women of the Renaissance* (Chicago, 1991).

Brief introductions to Renaissance humanism can be found in D. Kelley, *Renaissance Humanism* (Boston, 1991), and C. G. Nauert Jr., *Humanism and the Culture of Renaissance Europe* (Cambridge, 1995). The impact of printing is exhaustively examined in E. Eisenstein, *The Printing Press as an Agent of Change*, 2 vols. (New York, 1978). Good surveys of Renaissance art include R. Turner, *Renaissance Florence: The Invention of a New Art* (New York, 1997), and F. Hartt, *History of Italian Renaissance Art*, 4th ed. (Englewood Cliffs, N.J., 1994).

For a general work on the political development of Europe in the Renaissance, see J. H. Shennan, *The Origins of the Modern European State, 1450–1725* (London, 1974). The best overall study

of the Italian states is L. Martines, *Power and Imagination: City-States in Renaissance Italy* (New York, 1979). Machiavelli's life can be examined in Q. Skinner, *Machiavelli* (Oxford, 1981).

Basic surveys of the Reformation period include H. J. Grimm, *The Reformation Era, 1500–1650*, 2d ed. (New York, 1973); D. L. Jensen, *Reformation Europe*, 2d ed. (Lexington, Mass., 1990); G. R. Elton, *Reformation Europe, 1517–1559* (Cleveland, 1963); C. Lindberg, *The European Reformations* (Cambridge, Mass., 1996); and E. Cameron, *The European Reformation* (New York, 1991).

The classic account of Martin Luther's life is R. Bainton, *Here I Stand: A Life of Martin Luther* (New York, 1950). More recent works include J. M. Kittelson, *Luther the Reformer: The Story of the Man and His Career* (Minneapolis, 1986), and H. A. Oberman, *Luther: Man Between God and the Devil* (New York, 1992). Two worthwhile surveys of the English Reformation are A. G. Dickens, *The English Reformation*, 2d ed. (New York, 1989), and G. R. Elton, *Reform and Reformation: England, 1509–1558* (Cambridge, Mass., 1977). On John Calvin, see A. McGrath, *A Life of John Calvin: A Study in the Shaping of Western Culture* (Cambridge, Mass., 1990), and W. J. Bouwsma, *John Calvin* (New York, 1988). A good introduction to the Catholic Reformation can be found in M. R. O'Connell, *The Counter-Reformation, 1559–1610* (New York, 1974).

On the French Wars of Religion, see M. P. Holt, *The French Wars of Religion, 1562–1629* (New York, 1995), and R. J. Knecht, *The*

French Wars of Religion, 1559–1598, 2d ed. (New York, 1996). A good biography of Philip II is G. Parker, *Philip II*, 3d ed. (Chicago, 1995). Elizabeth's reign can be examined in C. Haigh, *Elizabeth I*, 2d ed. (New York, 1998). On the Thirty Years' War, see R. G. Asch, *The Thirty Years' War: The Holy Roman Empire and Europe, 1618–1648* (New York, 1997). A good general work on the period of the English Revolution is M. A. Kishlansky, *A Monarchy Transformed* (London, 1996). On England, see also W. A. Speck, *The Revolution of 1688* (Oxford, 1988).

Witchcraft hysteria can be examined in J. B. Russell, *A History of Witchcraft* (London, 1980), and B. P. Levack, *The Witch-Hunt in Early Modern Europe* (London, 1987).

For a brief account of seventeenth-century French history, see J. B. Collins, *The State in Early Modern France* (Cambridge, 1995). A solid and very readable biography of Louis XIV is J. B. Wolf, *Louis XIV* (New York, 1968). For a brief study, see P. R. Campbell, *Louis XIV, 1661–1715* (London, 1993). On the creation of an Austrian state, see C. Ingrao, *The Habsburg Monarchy, 1618–1815* (Cambridge, 1994). F. L. Carsten, *The Origins of Prussia* (Oxford, 1954), remains an outstanding study of early Prussian history. Works on Peter the Great include M. S. Anderson, *Peter the Great*, 2d ed. (New York, 1995), and L. Hughes, *Russia in the Age of Peter the Great* (New Haven, Conn., 1998).

For a general survey of Baroque culture, see J. S. Held, *Seventeenth and Eighteenth Century Art: Baroque Painting, Sculpture, Architecture* (New York, 1971). The literature on Shakespeare is enormous. For a biography, see A. L. Rowse, *The Life of Shakespeare* (New York, 1963).

Four general surveys of the Scientific Revolution are A. G. R. Smith, *Science and Society in the Sixteenth and Seventeenth Centuries* (London, 1972); J. R. Jacob, *The Scientific Revolution: Aspirations and Achievements, 1500–1700* (Atlantic Highlands, N.J., 1998); S. Shapin, *The Scientific Revolution* (Chicago, 1996); and J. Henry, *The Scientific Revolution and the Origins of Modern Science* (New York, 1997).

INFOTRAC COLLEGE EDITION

Visit the source collections at infotrac.thomsonlearning.com and use the Search function with the following key terms.

Louis XIV	Reformation
Machiavelli	Renaissance
Martin Luther not King	Thirty Years' War

WORLD HISTORY RESOURCES

Visit the *Essential World History* Companion Web Site for resources specific to this textbook:

http://history.wadsworth.com/duikeressentials02/

The CD in the back of this book and the World History Resource Center at http://history.wadsworth.com/world/ offer a variety of tools to help you succeed in this course, including access to quizzes; images; documents; interactive simulations, maps, and timelines; movie explorations; and a wealth of other sources.

The Art Archive, London

Chapter 14

New Encounters: The Creation of a World Market

Focus Questions

- Why did Europeans begin to embark on voyages of discovery and expansion at the end of the fifteenth century?
- How did Portugal and Spain acquire their overseas empires, and how did their empires differ?
- How and why did the Europeans expand into Africa, and what were the main consequences of their presence there?
- What were the main features of the African slave trade, and what effects did it have on Africa?
- ➤ What were the main characteristics of Southeast Asian civilization, and how was it affected by the coming of Islam and the Europeans?

W hen, in the spring of 1498, a local official asked the Portuguese explorer Vasco da Gama why he had come all the way to India from his homeland in Europe, he replied simply, "Christians and spices." Da Gama might have been more accurate if he had reversed the order of his objectives. As it turned out, God was probably much less important than gold and glory to Europeans like himself who participated in the Age of Exploration that was already under way. Still, da Gama's comments at Calicut were an accurate forecast of the future, for his voyage inaugurated an extended period of European expansion into Asia, led by merchant adventurers and missionaries, that lasted several hundred years and had effects that are still felt today. Eventually it resulted in a Western takeover of existing trade routes in the Indian Ocean and the establishment of colonies throughout Asia, Africa, and Latin America. So complete did Western dominance seem that some historians assumed that the peoples of the non-Western world were mere passive recipients in this process, absorbing and assimilating the advanced knowledge of the

West and offering nothing in return. Historians writing about the period after 1500 often talked metaphorically about the "impact of the West" and the "response" of non-Western peoples.

That image of impact and response, however, is not an entirely accurate description of what took place between the end of the fifteenth century and the end of the eighteenth. Although European rule was firmly established in Latin America and the island regions of Southeast Asia, traditional governments and institutions elsewhere remained largely intact and in some areas, notably South Asia and the Middle East, displayed considerable vitality. Moreover, although da Gama and his contemporaries are deservedly famous for their contribution to a new era of maritime commerce that circled the globe, they were not alone in extending the world trade network and transporting goods and ideas from one end of the earth to the other. Islam, too, was on the march, blazing new trails into Southeast Asia and across the Sahara to the civilizations that flourished along the banks of the Niger River. In this chapter, we turn our attention to the stunning expansion in the scope and volume of commercial and cultural contacts that took place in the generations preceding and following da Gama's historic voyage to India, as well as to the factors that brought about this expansion. •

AN AGE OF EXPLORATION AND EXPANSION

The voyage of Vasco da Gama has customarily been seen as a crucial step in the opening of trade routes to the East. In fact, however, as has been pointed out in earlier chapters, the Indian Ocean had been a busy thoroughfare for centuries. The spice trade had been carried on by sea in the region since the days of the legendary Queen of Sheba, and Chinese junks had sailed to the area in search of cloves and nutmeg since the Tang dynasty. Then, during the early fifteenth century, Chinese fleets sailed into the Indian Ocean and all the way to the coast of East Africa in search of trade and alliances (see Chapter 16).

Islam and the Spice Trade

By the fourteenth century, a growing percentage of the spice trade was being transported in Muslim ships sailing from ports in India or the Middle East. Muslims, either Arabs or Indian converts, had taken part in the Indian Ocean trade for centuries, and by the thirteenth century, Islam had established a presence in seaports on the islands of Sumatra and Java and was gradually moving inland. In 1292, the Venetian traveler Marco Polo observed that Muslims were engaging in missionary activity in northern Sumatra: "This kingdom is so much frequented by the Saracen merchants that they have converted the natives to the Law of Mahomet—I mean the townspeople only, for the hill people live for all the world like beasts, and eat human flesh, as well as other kinds of flesh, clean or unclean."[1]

But the major impact of Islam came in the early fifteenth century with the rise of the new sultanate at Malacca, whose founder was a Muslim convert. With its strategic location astride the strait of the same name (see Map 14.1), Malacca was "a city that was made for commerce; . . . the trade and commerce between the different nations for a thousand leagues on every hand must come to Malacca,"[2] said a sixteenth-century Portuguese visitor. Within a few years, Malacca become the leading power in the region.

Unfortunately for the Muslim traders who had come to Southeast Asia for the spice trade, others would also covet that trade. The arrival of Vasco da Gama's fleet was a sure sign that others would soon follow.

A New Player: Europe

For almost a millennium, Catholic Europe had been confined to one area. Its one major attempt to expand beyond those frontiers, the Crusades, had largely failed. Of course, Europe had never completely lost contact with the outside world: the goods of Asia and Africa made their way into medieval castles, the works of Muslim philosophers were read in medieval universities, and the Vikings in the ninth and tenth centuries had even explored the eastern fringes of North America. Nevertheless, Europe's contacts with non-European civilizations remained limited until the fifteenth century, when Europeans began to embark on a remarkable series of overseas journeys. What caused European seafarers to undertake such dangerous voyages to the ends of the earth?

Europeans had long been attracted to the East. In the Middle Ages, myths and legends of an exotic land of great riches and magic were widespread. The most famous medieval travelers to the East were the Polos of Venice. In 1271, Nicolò and Maffeo, merchants from Venice, accompanied by Nicolò's son Marco, undertook the lengthy journey to the court of the great Mongol ruler Khubilai Khan (see Chapter 10). As one of the Great Khan's ambassadors,

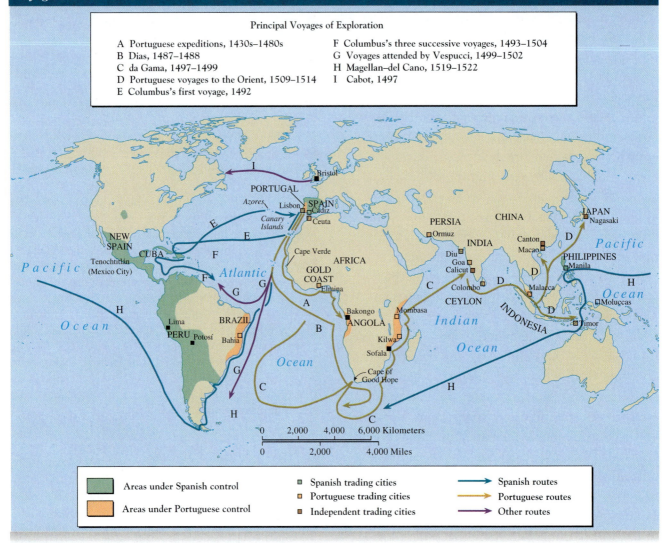

MAP 14.1 European Voyages and Possessions in the Sixteenth and Seventeenth Centuries. This map indicates the most important voyages launched by Europeans during their momentous Age of Exploration in the sixteenth and seventeenth centuries. ➤ *Why did Vasco da Gama sail so far into the South Atlantic on his voyage to Asia?*

Principal Voyages of Exploration

A Portuguese expeditions, 1430s–1480s
B Dias, 1487–1488
C da Gama, 1497–1499
D Portuguese voyages to the Orient, 1509–1514
E Columbus's first voyage, 1492

F Columbus's three successive voyages, 1493–1504
G Voyages attended by Vespucci, 1499–1502
H Magellan–del Cano, 1519–1522
I Cabot, 1497

Areas under Spanish control
Areas under Portuguese control

Spanish trading cities
Portuguese trading cities
Independent trading cities

Spanish routes
Portuguese routes
Other routes

Marco traveled to Japan as well and did not return to Italy until 1295. An account of his experiences, the *Travels*, proved to be the most informative of all the descriptions of Asia by medieval European travelers. Others, like the Franciscan friar John Plano Carpini, had preceded the Polos, but in the fourteenth century, the conquests of the Ottoman Turks and then the breakup of the Mongol Empire reduced Western traffic to the East. With the closing of the overland routes, a number of people in Europe became interested in the possibility of reaching Asia by sea.

An economic motive thus looms large in Renaissance European expansion (see Chapter 13). The rise of capitalism in Europe was undoubtedly a powerful spur to the process. Merchants, adventurers, and government officials had high hopes of finding precious metals and expanding

the areas of trade, especially for the spices of the East. Spices continued to be transported to Europe via Arab intermediaries but were outrageously expensive. Adventurous Europeans did not hesitate to express their desire to share in the wealth. As one Spanish conquistador explained, he and his kind went to the New World to "serve God and His Majesty, to give light to those who were in darkness, and to grow rich, as all men desire to do."[3]

This statement expresses another major reason for the overseas voyages—religious zeal. A crusading mentality was particularly strong in Portugal and Spain, where the Muslims had largely been driven out in the Middle Ages. Contemporaries of Prince Henry the Navigator of Portugal said that he was motivated by "his great desire to make increase in the faith of our Lord Jesus Christ and to bring him all the souls that should be saved." Although most scholars believe that the religious motive was secondary to economic considerations, it would be foolish to overlook the genuine desire on the part of both explorers and conquistadors, let alone missionaries, to convert the heathen to Christianity. Hernán Cortés, the conqueror of Mexico, asked his Spanish rulers if it was not their duty to ensure that the native Mexicans were "introduced into and instructed in the holy Catholic faith."[4] Spiritual and secular affairs were closely intertwined in the sixteenth century. No doubt, grandeur and glory as well as plain intellectual curiosity and a spirit of adventure also played some role in European expansion.

If "God, glory, and gold" were the primary motives, what made the voyages possible? First of all, the expansion of Europe was a state enterprise, tied to the growth of centralized monarchies during the Renaissance. By the second half of the fifteenth century, European monarchies had increased both their authority and their resources and were in a position to turn their energies beyond their borders. That meant the invasion of Italy for France, but for Portugal, a state not strong enough to pursue power in Europe, it meant going abroad. The Spanish scene was more complex, since the Spanish monarchy was strong enough by the sixteenth century to pursue power both on the Continent and beyond.

At the same time, by the end of the fifteenth century, European states had a level of knowledge and technology that enabled them to achieve a regular series of voyages beyond Europe. Although the highly schematic and symbolic medieval maps were of little help to sailors, the *portolani*, or detailed charts made by medieval navigators and mathematicians in the thirteenth and fourteenth centuries, were more useful. With details on coastal contours, distances between ports, and compass readings, they proved of great value for voyages in European waters. But because the *portolani* were drawn on a flat scale and took no account of the curvature of the earth, they were of little use for longer overseas voyages. Only when seafarers began to venture beyond the coasts of Europe did they begin to accumulate information about the actual shape of the earth. By the end of the fifteenth century, cartography had developed to the point that Europeans possessed fairly accurate maps of the known world.

Jomard, *Les Monuments de la Geographie*, Paris, 1862, Photo courtesy of the New York Public Library, Map Division, Stor, Lenox and Tilden Foundations

➤ **A SIXTEENTH-CENTURY MAP OF AFRICA.** Advances in mapmaking also contributed to the European Age of Exploration. Here a section of a world map by the early-sixteenth-century Spanish cartographer Juan de la Cosa shows the continent of Africa. Note the drawing of the legendary Prester John, mentioned in Chapter 10, at the right, and the Portuguese caravels with their lateen sails in the South Atlantic Ocean. In the minds of Europeans at the time, the legend of Prester John had been identified with the Christian king of Ethiopia.

In addition, Europeans had developed remarkably seaworthy ships as well as new navigational techniques. European shipbuilders had mastered the use of the stern-post rudder (an import from China) and had learned how to combine the use of lateen sails with a square rig. With these innovations, they could construct ships mobile enough to sail against the wind and engage in naval warfare and also large enough to mount heavy cannons and carry a substantial amount of goods over long distances. Previously sailors had used a quadrant and their knowledge of the position of the polestar to ascertain their latitude. Below the equator, however, this technique was useless. Only with the assistance of new navigational aids such as the compass (a Chinese invention) and the astrolabe (an astronomical instrument used to measure the altitude of the sun and the stars above the horizon) were they able to explore the high seas with confidence.

The Portuguese Maritime Empire

Portugal took the lead in exploration when it began exploring the coast of Africa under the sponsorship of Prince Henry the Navigator (1394–1460). Prince Henry's motives were a blend of seeking a Christian kingdom as an ally against the Muslims, acquiring new trade opportunities for Portugal, and extending Christianity. In 1419, he founded a school for navigators on the southwestern coast of Portugal. Shortly thereafter, Portuguese fleets began probing southward along the western coast of Africa in search of gold. In 1441, Portuguese ships reached the Senegal River, just north of Cape Verde, and brought home a cargo of black Africans, most of whom were sold as slaves to wealthy buyers elsewhere in Europe. Within a few years, an estimated thousand slaves were shipped annually from the area back to Lisbon.

Continuing southward, in 1471 the Portuguese discovered a new source of gold along the southern coast of the hump of West Africa (an area that would henceforth be known to Europeans as the Gold Coast). To facilitate trade in gold, ivory, and slaves (some slaves were brought back to Lisbon and others were bartered to local merchants for gold), the Portuguese leased land from local rulers and built stone forts along the coast.

Hearing reports of a route to India around the southern tip of Africa, Portuguese sea captains continued their probing. In 1487, Bartolomeu Dias took advantage of westerly winds in the South Atlantic to round the Cape of Good Hope, but he feared a mutiny from his crew and returned home without continuing onward. Ten years later, a fleet under the command of Vasco da Gama rounded the cape and stopped at several ports controlled by Muslim merchants along the coast of East Africa, including Sofala, Kilwa, and Mombasa. Then da Gama's fleet crossed the Arabian Sea and arrived off the port of Calicut on the southwestern coast of India, on May 18, 1498. The Por-

AN EARLY JEWISH COMMUNITY IN INDIA. When Vasco de Gama arrived in the port city of Cochin, along the western coast of India, in 1498, he was surprised to discover the presence of a Jewish community that had been in the area since as early as the first century C.E. Jewish merchants from the Middle East had settled there to take part in the trading network that stretched westward from the Indian Ocean all the way to the Mediterranean Sea. Shown here is the entrance gate to the Jewish quarter in Cochin. Inside the gates are a number of commercial establishments and a synagogue that dates back to the fourteenth century.

tuguese crown had sponsored da Gama's voyage with the clear objective of destroying the Muslim monopoly over the spice trade, a monopoly that had been intensified by the Ottoman conquest of Constantinople in 1453 (see Chapter 15). Calicut was a major entrepôt on the long route from the Spice Islands to the Mediterranean Sea, but the ill-informed Europeans believed it was the source of the spices themselves. Although he lost two ships en route, da Gama's remaining vessels returned to Europe with their holds filled with ginger and cinnamon, a cargo that earned the investors a profit of several thousand percent.

During the next years, the Portuguese set out to gain control of the spice trade. In 1510, Admiral Afonso de Albuquerque established his headquarters at Goa, on the western coast of India south of present-day Bombay. From there, the Portuguese raided Arab shippers, provoking the following comment from an Arab source: "[The

THE PORTUGUESE CONQUEST OF MALACCA

In 1511, a Portuguese fleet led by Afonso de Albuquerque attacked the Muslim sultanate at Malacca, on the west coast of the Malay peninsula. Occupation of the port gave the Portuguese control over the strategic Strait of Malacca and the route to the Spice Islands. In this passage, Albuquerque tells his men the reasons for the attack. Note that he sees control of Malacca as a way to reduce the power of the Muslim world. The relevance of economic wealth to military power continues to underlie conflicts among nations today. The Pacific War in the 1940s, for example, began as a result of a conflict over control of the rich resources of Southeast Asia.

THE COMMENTARIES OF THE GREAT AFONSO DE ALBUQUERQUE, SECOND VICEROY OF INDIA

Although there be many reasons which I could allege in favor of our taking this city and building a fortress therein to maintain possession of it, two only will I mention to you, on this occasion. . . .

The first is the great service which we shall perform to Our Lord in casting the Moors out of this country. . . . If we can only achieve the task before us, it will result in the Moors resigning India altogether to our rule, for the greater part of them—or perhaps all of them—live upon the trade of this country and are become great and rich, and lords of extensive treasures. . . . For when we were committing ourselves to the business of cruising in the Straits (of the Red Sea), where the King of Portugal had often ordered me to go (for it was there that His Highness considered we could cut down the commerce which the Moors of Cairo, of Mecca, and of Judah, carry on with these parts), Our Lord for his service thought right to lead us hither, for when Malacca is taken the places on the Straits must be shut up, and they will never more be able to introduce their spiceries into those places.

And the other reason is the additional service which we shall render to the King D. Manuel in taking this city, because it is the headquarters of all the spiceries and drugs which the Moors carry every year hence to the Straits without our being able to prevent them from so doing; but if we deprive them of this their ancient market there, there does not remain for them a single port, nor a single situation, so commodious in the whole of these parts, where they can carry on their trade in these things. . . . I hold it as very certain that if we take this trade of Malacca away out of their hands, Cairo and Mecca are entirely ruined, and to Venice will no spiceries be conveyed except that which her merchants go and buy in Portugal.

Portuguese] took about seven vessels, killing those on board and making some prisoner. This was their first action, may God curse them."[5] In 1511, Albuquerque attacked Malacca itself.

For Albuquerque, control of Malacca would serve two purposes. It could help to destroy the Arab spice trade network by blocking passage through the Strait of Malacca, and it could also provide the Portuguese with a way station en route to the Spice Islands and other points east (see the box above). After a short but bloody battle, the Portuguese seized the city and put the local Arab population to the sword. They then proceeded to erect a fort, a factory (a common term at the time for a warehouse), and a church.

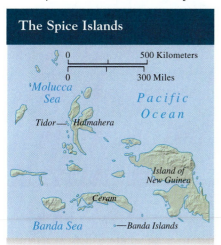

The Spice Islands

0 — 500 Kilometers
0 — 300 Miles

'Molucca Sea
Tidor — Halmahera
Pacific Ocean
Island of New Guinea
Ceram
Banda Sea — Banda Islands

From Malacca, the Portuguese launched expeditions farther east, to China and the Moluccas, then known as the Spice Islands. There they signed a treaty with a local sultan for the purchase and export of cloves to the European market. Within a few years, they had managed to seize control of the spice trade from Muslim traders and had garnered substantial profits for the Portuguese monarchy.

Why were the Portuguese so successful? Basically, their success was a matter of guns and seamanship. The first Portuguese fleet to arrive in Indian waters was relatively modest in size. It consisted of three ships and twenty guns, a force sufficient for self-defense and intimidation but not for serious military operations. Sixteenth-century Portuguese fleets were more heavily armed and were capable of inflicting severe defeats if necessary on local naval and land forces. The Portuguese by no means possessed a monopoly on the use of firearms and explosives, but they used the maneuverability of their light ships to maintain their distance while bombarding the enemy with their powerful cannons. Such tactics gave them a military superiority over lightly armed rivals that they were able to exploit until the arrival of other European forces several decades later.

Voyages to the "New World"

While the Portuguese were seeking access to the spice trade of the Indies by sailing eastward through the Indian Ocean, the Spanish attempted to reach the same destination by sailing westward across the Atlantic. Although the Spanish came to overseas discovery and exploration later than the Portuguese, their greater resources enabled them to establish a far grander overseas empire.

An important figure in the history of Spanish exploration was an Italian from Genoa, Christopher Columbus (1451–1506). Knowledgeable Europeans were aware that the world was round but had little understanding of its circumference or the extent of the continent of Asia. Convinced that the circumference of the earth was smaller than contemporaries believed and that Asia was larger, Columbus felt that Asia could be reached by sailing due west instead of eastward around Africa. After being rejected by the Portuguese, he persuaded Queen Isabella of Spain to finance his exploratory expedition, which reached the Americas in October 1492 and explored the coastline of Cuba and the northern shores of the neighboring island of Hispaniola. Columbus believed that he had reached Asia and in three subsequent voyages (1493, 1498, and 1502) sought in vain to find a route through the outer islands to the Asian mainland. In his four voyages, Columbus reached all the major islands of the Caribbean, which he called the Indies, as well as Honduras in Central America.

Although Columbus clung to his belief until his death, other explorers soon realized that he had discovered a new frontier altogether. State-sponsored explorers joined the race to the New World. A Venetian seafarer, John Cabot, explored the New England coastline of the Americas under a license from King Henry VII of England. The continent of South America was discovered accidentally by the Portuguese sea captain Pedro Cabral in 1500. Amerigo Vespucci, a Florentine, accompanied several voyages and wrote a series of letters describing the geography of the New World. The publication of these letters led to the use of the name "America" (after Amerigo) for the new lands.

The newly discovered territories were referred to as the New World, even though they possessed flourishing civilizations populated by millions of people when the Europeans arrived. But the Americas were new to the Europeans, who quickly saw opportunities for conquest and exploitation. The Spanish, in particular, were interested because in 1494 the Treaty of Tordesillas had divided the newly discovered world into separate Portuguese and Spanish spheres of influence. Thereafter the route east around the Cape of Good Hope was to be reserved for the Portuguese, while the route across the Atlantic (except for the eastern hump of South America) was assigned to Spain. The Spanish conquistadors were a hardy lot of mostly upper-class individuals motivated by a typical sixteenth-century blend of glory, greed, and religious crusading zeal. Although sanctioned by the Castilian crown, these groups were financed and outfitted privately, not by the government.

Their superior weapons, organizational skills, and determination brought the conquistadors incredible success. Beginning in 1519 with a small band of men, Hernán Cortés took three years to overthrow the mighty Aztec Empire in central Mexico, led by the chieftain Moctezuma

➤ COLUMBUS LANDS IN THE NEW WORLD.   In the log that he wrote during his first voyage to the Americas, Christopher Columbus noted that the peoples of the New World were intelligent and friendly, and relations between them and the Spanish were amicable at first. Later, however, the conquistadors began to mistreat the local people. Here is a somewhat imaginative painting of the first encounter from a European perspective. Note the upturned eyes of Columbus and several of his companions, suggesting that their motives were spiritual rather than material.

SPANISH ACTIVITIES IN THE AMERICAS

Christopher Columbus's first voyage to the Americas	1492
Last voyages of Columbus	1502–1504
Spanish conquest of Mexico	1519–1522
Francisco Pizarro's conquest of the Incas	1531–1536

(see Chapter 6). By 1550, the Spanish had gained control of northern Mexico. Between 1531 and 1536, another expedition led by a hardened and somewhat corrupt soldier, Francisco Pizarro (1470–1541), took control of the Inca Empire high in the Peruvian Andes. The Spanish conquests were undoubtedly facilitated by the previous arrival of European diseases, which had decimated the local population. Although it took another three decades before the western part of Latin America was brought under Spanish control (the Portuguese took over Brazil), already by 1535, the Spanish had created a system of colonial administration that made the New World an extension of the old—at least in European eyes.

Administration of the Spanish Empire in the New World

Spanish policy toward the inhabitants of the New World, whom the Europeans called Indians, was a combination of confusion, misguided paternalism, and cruel exploitation. Confusion arose over the nature of the Indians. Queen Isabella declared the Indians to be subjects of Castile and instituted the *encomienda* system, which permitted the conquering Spaniards to collect tribute from the natives and use them as laborers. In return, the holders of an *encomienda* were supposed to protect the Indians and supervise their spiritual and material needs. In practice, this meant that the settlers were free to implement the system as they pleased. Three thousand miles from Spain, Spanish settlers largely ignored their government and brutally used the Indians to pursue their own economic interests. Indians were put to work on sugar plantations and in the lucrative gold and silver mines. Forced labor, starvation, and especially disease took a fearful toll on Indian lives. With little or no natural resistance to European diseases, the Indians of America were ravaged by smallpox, measles, and typhus brought by the explorers and the conquistadors. Although scholarly estimates of native populations vary drastically, a reasonable guess is that at least half of the natives died of European diseases. On Hispaniola alone, out of an initial population of 100,000 natives when Columbus arrived in 1493, only 300 Indians survived by

1570. In 1542, largely in response to the publications of Bartolomé de Las Casas, a Dominican monk who championed the Indians (see the box on p. 304), the government abolished the *encomienda* system and provided more protection for the natives.

The chief organ of colonial administration was the Council of the Indies. The council nominated colonial viceroys, oversaw their activities, and kept an eye on ecclesiastical affairs in the colonies. Spanish possessions in the New World were initially divided between New Spain (Mexico, Central America, and the Caribbean islands), with its center in Mexico City, and Peru (western South America), with its capital at Lima. Each area was governed by a viceroy who served as the king's chief civil and military officer.

By papal agreement, the Catholic monarchs of Spain were given extensive rights over ecclesiastical affairs in the New World. They could nominate church officials, build churches, collect fees, and supervise the various religious orders that conducted missionary activities. Catholic monks had remarkable success converting and baptizing hundreds of thousands of Indians in the early years of the conquest. Soon after the missionaries came the establishment of dioceses, parishes, schools, and hospitals—all the trappings of a European society.

The Impact of European Expansion

The arrival of the Europeans had an enormous impact on both the conquerors and the conquered. The native American civilizations, which (as we discussed in Chapter 6) had their own unique qualities and a degree of sophistication rarely appreciated by the conquerors, were virtually destroyed, while the native populations were ravaged by diseases introduced by the Europeans. Ancient social and political structures were ripped up and replaced by European institutions, religion, language, and culture.

How does one evaluate the psychological impact of colonization on the colonizers? The relatively easy European success in dominating native peoples undoubtedly reinforced the conviction of Europeans in the inherent superiority of their civilization. The Scientific Revolution of the seventeenth century, to be followed by the era of imperialism a century later, then served to strengthen the Eurocentric perspective that has long pervaded Western civilization in its relationship with the rest of the world.

European expansion also affected the conquerors in the economic arena. Wherever they went in the Americas, Europeans sought gold and silver. One Aztec observer commented that the Spanish conquerors "longed and lusted for gold. Their bodies swelled with greed, and their hunger was ravenous; they hungered like pigs for that gold."[6] Rich silver deposits were found and exploited in Mexico and southern Peru (modern Bolivia). When the mines at Potosí in Peru were opened in 1545, the value of precious metals imported into Europe quadrupled. It has

LAS CASAS AND THE SPANISH TREATMENT OF THE AMERICAN NATIVES

artolomé de Las Casas (1474–1566) was a Dominican monk who participated in the conquest of Cuba and received land and Indians in return for his efforts. But in 1514, he underwent a radical transformation that led him to believe that the Indians had been cruelly mistreated by his fellow Spaniards. He spent the remaining years of his life (he lived to the age of ninety-two) fighting for the Indians. This section is taken from his most influential work, Brevísima Relación de la Destrucción de las Indias, *known to English readers as* The Tears of the Indians. *This work was largely responsible for the legend of the Spanish as inherently "cruel and murderous fanatics." Many scholars today feel that Las Casas may have exaggerated his account to shock his contemporaries into action.*

BARTOLOMÉ DE LAS CASAS, THE TEARS OF THE INDIANS

There is nothing more detestable or more cruel than the tyranny which the Spaniards use toward the Indians for the getting of pearl. Surely the infernal torments cannot much exceed the anguish that they endure, by reason of that way of cruelty; for they put them under water some four or five ells deep, where they are forced without any liberty of respiration, to gather up the shells wherein the Pearls are; sometimes they come up again with nets full of shells to take breath, but if they stay any while to rest themselves, immediately comes a hangman row'd in a little boat, who as soon as he hath well beaten them, drags them again to their labor. Their food is nothing but filth, and the very same that contains the Pearl, with small portion of that bread which that Country affords; in the first whereof there is little nourishment; and as for the latter, it is made with great difficulty, besides that they have not enough of that neither for sustenance; they lie upon the ground in fetters, lest they should run away; and many times they are drown'd in this labor, and are never seen again till they swim upon the top of the waves; oftentimes they also are devoured by certain sea monsters, that are frequent in those seas. Consider whether this hard usage of the poor creatures be consistent with the precepts which God commands concerning charity to our neighbor, by those that cast them so undeservedly into the dangers of a cruel death, causing them to perish without any remorse or pity, or allowing them the benefit of the Sacraments, or the knowledge of Religion; it being impossible for them to live any time under the water; and this death is so much the more painful, by reason that by the coarctation of the breast, while the lungs strive to do their office, the vital parts are so afflicted that they die vomiting the blood out of their mouths. Their hair also, which is by nature black, is hereby changed and made of the same color with that of the sea Wolves; their bodies are also so besprinkled with the froth of the sea, that they appear rather like monsters than men.

been estimated that between 1503 and 1650, some 16 million kilograms of silver and 185,000 kilograms of gold entered the port of Seville, fueling a price revolution that affected the Spanish economy.

But gold and silver were only two of the products sent to Europe from the New World. Into Seville flowed sugar, dyes, cotton, vanilla, and hides from livestock raised on the South American pampas. New agricultural products native to the Americas, such as potatoes, cacao, corn, manioc, and tobacco, were also imported. Because of its trading posts in Asia, Portugal soon challenged the Italian states as the chief entry point of the eastern trade in spices, jewels, silk, carpets, ivory, leather, and perfumes. Economic historians believe that the increase in the volume and area of European trade and the rise in fluid capital due to this expansion were crucial factors in producing a new era of commercial capitalism that represented the first step toward the world economy that has characterized the modern era.

European expansion, which was in part a product of European rivalries, also deepened those rivalries and increased the tensions among European states. Bitter conflicts arose over the cargoes coming from the New World and Asia. Although the Spanish and Portuguese were first in the competition, by the end of the sixteenth century, new competitors were entering the scene and beginning to challenge the dominance of the Iberian powers. The first to arrive were the English and the Dutch.

Why did Europeans risk their lives to explore new lands far from friendly shores? For some, expansion abroad brought hopes for land, riches, and social advancement. Although some wives accompanied their husbands abroad, many ordinary European women found new opportunities for marriage in the New World because of the lack of white women. In the violence-prone world of early Spanish America, a number of women also found themselves rich after their husbands were killed unexpectedly. In one area of Central America, women owned about 25 percent of the landed estates by 1700.

New Rivals

Portugal's efforts to dominate the trade of the Indian Ocean were never totally successful. The Portuguese lacked both the numbers and the wealth to overcome local resistance and colonize the Asian regions. Moreover, their massive investments in ships and laborers for their empire (hundreds of ships and hundreds of thousands of workers in shipyards and overseas bases) proved very costly. Disease, shipwreck, and battles took a heavy toll of life. The empire was simply too large and Portugal too small to maintain it, and by the end of the century, the Portuguese were being severely challenged by rivals.

The Spanish had established themselves in Asia in the early 1520s, when Ferdinand Magellan, seeking a western route to the Spice Islands across the Pacific Ocean, had sailed around the southern tip of South America, crossed the Pacific, and landed on the island of Cebu in the Philippine Islands. Although Magellan and some forty of his crew were killed in a skirmish with the local population, one of the two remaining ships sailed on to Tidor, in the Moluccas, and thence around the world via the Cape of Good Hope. In the words of a contemporary historian, they arrived in Cádiz "with precious cargo and fifteen men surviving out of a fleet of five sail."[7]

As it turned out, the Spanish could not follow up on Magellan's accomplishment, and in 1529, they sold their rights in Tidor to the Portuguese. But Magellan's voyage was not a total loss. In the absence of concerted resistance from the local population, the Spanish managed to consolidate their control over the Philippines, which eventually became a major Spanish base in the carrying trade across the Pacific.

The primary threat to the Portuguese toehold in Southeast Asia, however, came from the English and the Dutch. In 1591, the first English expedition to the Indies through the Indian Ocean arrived in London with a cargo of pepper. Nine years later, a private joint-stock company, the East India Company, was founded to provide a stable source of capital for future voyages. In 1608, an English fleet landed at Surat, on the northwestern coast of India. Trade with Southeast Asia soon followed.

The Dutch were quick to follow suit, and the first Dutch fleet arrived in India in 1595. In 1602, the Dutch East India Company was established under government sponsorship and was soon actively competing with the English and the Portuguese in the region.

The Dutch, the French, and the English also began to make inroads on Spanish and Portuguese possessions in the Americas. War and steady pressure from their Dutch and English rivals eroded Portuguese trade in both the West and the East, although Portugal continued to profit from its large colonial empire in Brazil. A formal administration system had been instituted in Brazil in 1549, and Portuguese migrants had established massive plantations there to produce sugar for export to the

Cape Horn and the Strait of Magellan

Old World. The Spanish also maintained an enormous South American empire, but Spain's importance as a commercial power declined rapidly in the seventeenth century because of a drop in the output of the silver mines and the poverty of the Spanish monarchy.

The Dutch formed their own Dutch West India Company in 1621 to compete with Spanish and Portuguese interests in the Americas. But although it made some inroads in Portuguese Brazil and the Caribbean (see Map 14.2), the company's profits were never large enough to compensate for the expenditures. Dutch settlements were also established on the North American continent. The mainland colony of New Netherland stretched from the mouth of the Hudson River as far north as Albany, New York. In the meantime, French colonies appeared in the Lesser Antilles, and in Louisiana, at the mouth of the Mississippi River.

In the second half of the seventeenth century, however, rivalry and years of warfare with the English and the French (who had also become active in North America) brought the decline of the Dutch commercial empire in the New World. In 1664, the English seized the colony of New Netherland and renamed it New York, and the Dutch West India Company soon went bankrupt. In 1663, Canada became the property of the French crown and was administered like a French province. But the French failed to provide adequate men or money, allowing their continental wars to take precedence over the conquest of the North American continent. By the early eighteenth century, the French began to cede some of their American possessions to their English rival.

The English, meanwhile, had proceeded to create a colonial empire in the New World along the Atlantic seaboard of North America. The desire to escape from religious oppression combined with economic interests did make successful colonization possible, as the Massachusetts Bay Company demonstrated. The Massachusetts colony had only four thousand settlers in its early years, but by 1660, their number had swelled to forty thousand.

AFRICA IN TRANSITION

Although the primary objective of the Portuguese in rounding the Cape of Good Hope was to find a sea route to the Spice Islands, they soon discovered that profits were

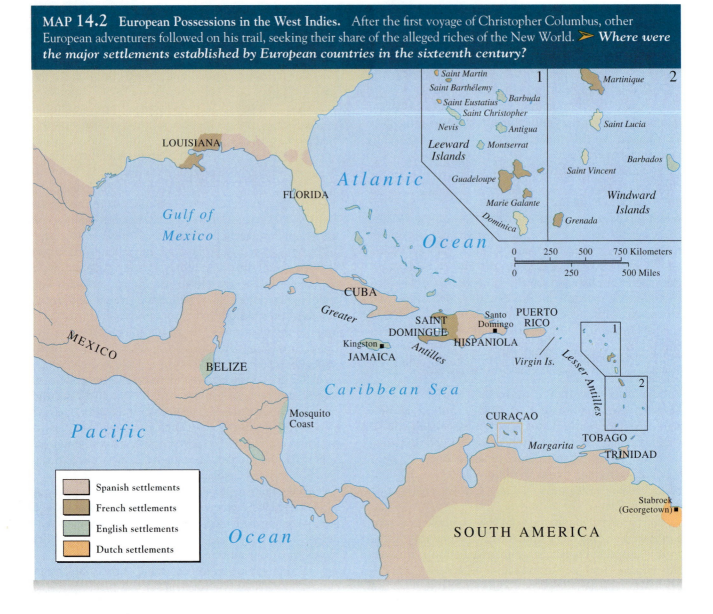

MAP 14.2 European Possessions in the West Indies. After the first voyage of Christopher Columbus, other European adventurers followed on his trail, seeking their share of the alleged riches of the New World. ➤ *Where were the major settlements established by European countries in the sixteenth century?*

Spanish settlements
French settlements
English settlements
Dutch settlements

to be made en route, along the eastern coast of Africa. In the early sixteenth century, a Portuguese fleet seized a number of East African port cities, including Kilwa, Sofala, and Mombasa, and built forts along the coast in an effort to control the trade in the area. Above all, the Portuguese wanted to monopolize the trade in gold, which was mined by Bantu workers in the hills along the upper Zambezi River and then shipped to Sofala on the coast (see Chapter 8). For centuries, the gold trade had been monopolized by local Shona peoples at Zimbabwe. In the fifteenth century, it had come under the control of a Shona dynasty known as the Mwene Metapa. The Portuguese opened treaty relations with the Mwene Metapa, and Jesuit priests were eventually posted to the court in 1561. At first, the Mwene Metapa found the Europeans useful as an ally against local rivals, but by the end of the sixteenth century, the Portuguese had established a protectorate and

forced the local ruler to grant title to large tracts of land to European officials and private individuals living in the area. The Portuguese, however, lacked the personnel, the capital, and the expertise to dominate local trade, and in the late seventeenth century, a vassal of the Mwene Metapa succeeded in driving them from the plateau; his descendants maintained control of the area for the next two hundred years.

The first Europeans to settle in southern Africa were the Dutch. After an unsuccessful attempt to seize the Portuguese settlement on the island of Mozambique off the East African coast, in 1652 the Dutch set up a way station at the Cape of Good Hope to serve as a base for their fleets en route to the East Indies. At first, the new settlement was meant simply to provide food and other provisions to Dutch ships, but eventually it developed into a permanent colony. Dutch farmers, known as Boers and speak-

FORT JESUS AT MOMBASA. Mombasa, a port city on the eastern coast of Africa, was a jumping-off point for the Portuguese as they explored the lands bordering on the Indian Ocean. Erected in the early sixteenth century atop a bluff overlooking the harbor, Fort Jesus remained an imposing symbol of European power until 1698, when the Portuguese were expelled by the Arabs. Castles built in this style are situated along the sea routes to the Spice Islands, but the European presence has now departed.

Courtesy of William J. Duiker

ing a Dutch dialect that evolved into Afrikaans, began to settle in the sparsely occupied areas outside the city of Cape Town. The temperate climate and the absence of tropical diseases made the territory near the cape practically the only land south of the Sahara that the Europeans had found suitable for habitation.

West Africa had been penetrated from across the Sahara since ancient times, and contact undoubtedly increased after the establishment of Muslim control over the Mediterranean coastal regions. Muslim traders crossed the desert carrying Islamic values, political culture, and legal traditions along with their goods. The early stage of state formation had culminated with the kingdom of Mali (see Chapter 8).

After Mali's decline, it was succeeded by the kingdom of Songhai. Under King Askia Mohammed (1493–1528), the leader of a pro-Islamic faction who had seized power from members of the original founding family, the state increasingly relied on Islamic institutions and ideology to strengthen national unity and centralize authority. Askia Mohammed himself embarked on a pilgrimage to Mecca and was recognized by the caliph of Cairo as the Muslim ruler of the Niger River valley. On his return from Mecca, he tried to revive Timbuktu as a major center of Islamic learning but had little success in converting his subjects. He did preside over a significant increase in trans-Saharan trade, which provided a steady source of income to Songhai and other kingdoms in the region. Despite the efforts of Askia Mohammed and his successors, centrifu-

gal forces within Songhai eventually led to its breakup after his death.

The period of Songhai's decline was also a time of increased contact with Europeans. The English, the French, and the Dutch all became active in the West African trade in the mid-sixteenth century. During the mid-seventeenth century, the Dutch seized a number of Portuguese forts along the West African coast while at the same time taking over the bulk of the Portuguese trade across the Indian Ocean.

The Slave Trade

The European exploration of the African coastline had little apparent significance for most peoples living in the interior of the continent, except for a few who engaged in direct or indirect trade with the foreigners. But for peoples living on or near the coast, the impact was often great indeed. As the trade in slaves increased during the sixteenth through the eighteenth centuries, thousands, and then millions, were removed from their homes and forcibly exported to plantations in the New World.

Traffic in slaves had existed for centuries before the arrival of Portuguese fleets along African shores. The primary market for African slaves was the Middle East, where most were used as domestic servants. Slavery also existed in many European countries, where a few slaves from Africa or war captives from the regions north of the Black Sea were used for domestic purposes or as agricultural workers in the lands adjacent to the Mediterranean.

At first, the Portuguese simply replaced European slaves with African ones. During the second half of the fifteenth century, about a thousand slaves were taken to Portugal each year; the vast majority were apparently destined to serve as domestic servants for affluent families throughout Europe. But the discovery of the New World in the 1490s and the subsequent planting of sugarcane in South America and the islands of the Caribbean changed the situation. Cane sugar was native to Indonesia and had first been introduced to Europeans from the Middle East during the Crusades. By the fifteenth century, it was grown (often by slaves from Africa or the region of the Black Sea) in modest amounts on Cyprus, Sicily, and southern regions of the Iberian peninsula. But when the Ottoman Empire seized much of the eastern Mediterranean (see Chapter 15), the Europeans needed to seek out new areas suitable for cultivation. Demand increased as sugar gradually replaced honey as a sweetener, especially in northern Europe.

The primary impetus to the sugar industry came from the colonization of the Americas. During the sixteenth century, plantations were established along the eastern coast of Brazil and on several islands in the Caribbean. Because the cultivation of cane sugar is an arduous process demanding both skill and large quantities of labor, the new plantations required more workers than could be provided

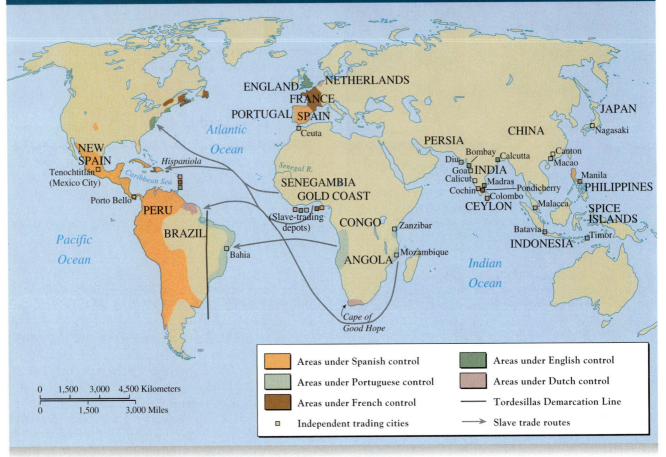

MAP 14.3 The Slave Trade. Beginning in the sixteenth century, the trade in African slaves to the New World became a major source of profit to European merchants. This map traces the routes taken by slave-trading ships, as well as the territories and ports of call of European powers in the seventeenth century. ➤ *What were the major destinations for the slave trade?*

by the Indian population in the New World, many of whom had died of diseases imported from the Old World. Since the climate and soil of much of West Africa were not especially conducive to the cultivation of sugar, African slaves began to be shipped to Brazil and the Caribbean to work on the plantations. The first were sent from Portugal, but in 1518, a Spanish ship carried the first boatload of African slaves directly from Africa to the New World.

During the next two centuries, the trade in slaves increased by massive proportions (see Map 14.3). An estimated 275,000 enslaved Africans were exported to other countries during the sixteenth century, with 2,000 going annually to the Americas alone. During the next century, the total climbed to over a million and jumped to six million in the eighteenth century, when the trade spread from West and Central Africa to East Africa. It has been estimated that altogether as many as ten million African slaves were transported to the Americas between the early sixteenth and the late nineteenth centuries. As many as two million were exported to other areas during the same period.

One reason for these astonishing numbers, of course, was the tragically high death rate. Though figures on the number of slaves who died on the journey are almost entirely speculative, a high proportion undoubtedly died on the voyage before arriving at their destination. We know that mortality rates for Europeans in the West Indies were ten to twenty times higher than in Europe, and a European arriving in the West Indies had a life expectancy of five to ten years (in Africa, where yellow fever was prevalent, the average life expectancy for an arriving European was only about one year). Ironically, African slaves who survived the brutal voyage fared somewhat better than whites: death rates for newly arrived Europeans in the West Indies averaged more than 125 per 1,000 annually, but the figure for Africans was only about 30 per 1,000.

The reason for these staggering death rates was clearly more than maltreatment, although that was certainly a factor. As we have seen, the transmission of diseases from one continent to another brought high death rates among those lacking immunity. African slaves were somewhat less

A SLAVE MARKET IN AFRICA

Traffic in slaves had been carried on in Africa since the kingdom of the pharaohs in ancient Egypt. But the slave trade increased dramatically after the arrival of European ships off the coast of West Africa. The following passage by a Dutch observer describes a slave market in Africa and the conditions on the ships that carried the slaves to the New World.

SLAVERY IN AFRICA: A FIRSTHAND REPORT

Not a few in our country fondly imagine that parents here sell their children, men their wives, and one brother the other. But those who think so deceive themselves, for this never happens on any other account but that of necessity, or some great crime; most of the slaves that are offered to us are prisoners of war, who are sold by the victors as their booty.

When these slaves come to Fida, they are put in prison all together; and when we treat concerning buying them, they are brought out into a large plain. There, by our surgeons, whose province it is, they are thoroughly examined, even to the smallest member, and that naked too, both men and women, without the least distinction or modesty. Those that are approved as good are set on one side; and the lame or faulty are set by as invalids. . . .

The invalids and the maimed being thrown out, . . . the remainder are numbered, and it is entered who delivered them. In the meanwhile, a burning iron, with the arms or name of the companies, lies in the fire, with which ours are marked on the breast. This is done that we may distinguish them from the slaves of the English, French, or others (which are also marked with their mark), and to prevent the Negroes exchanging them for worse, at which they have a good hand.

I doubt not but this trade seems very barbarous to you, but since it is followed by mere necessity, it must go on; but we take all possible care that they are not burned too hard, especially the women, who are more tender than the men.

When we have agreed with the owners of the slaves, they are returned to their prison. There from that time forward they are kept at our charge, costing us two pence a day a slave; which serves to subsist them, like our criminals, on bread and water. To save charges, we send them on board our ships at the very first opportunity, before which their masters strip them of all they have on their backs so that they come aboard stark naked, women as well as men. In this condition they are obliged to continue, if the master of the ship is not so charitable (which he commonly is) as to bestow something on them to cover their nakedness.

You would really wonder to see how these slaves live on board, for though their number sometimes amounts to six or seven hundred, yet by the careful management of our masters of ships, they are so regulated that it seems incredible. And in this particular our nation exceeds all other Europeans, for the French, Portuguese and English slave ships are always foul and stinking; on the contrary, ours are for the most part clean and neat.

The slaves are fed three times a day with indifferent good victuals, and much better than they eat in their own country. Their lodging place is divided into two parts, one of which is appointed for the men, the other for the women, each sex being kept apart. Here they lie as close together as it is possible for them to be crowded.

We are sometimes sufficiently plagued with a parcel of slaves which come from a far inland country who very innocently persuade one another that we buy them only to fatten and afterward eat them as a delicacy. When we are so unhappy as to be pestered with many of this sort, they resolve and agree together (and bring over the rest to their party) to run away from the ship, kill the Europeans, and set the vessel ashore, by which means they design to free themselves from being our food.

I have twice met with this misfortune; and the first time proved very unlucky to me, I not in the least suspecting it, but the uproar was quashed by the master of the ship and myself by causing the abettor to be shot through the head, after which all was quiet.

---

susceptible to European diseases than the American Indian populations. Indeed, they seem to have possessed a degree of immunity, perhaps because their ancestors had developed antibodies to "white people's diseases" owing to the trans-Saharan trade. The Africans would not have had immunity to native American diseases, however.

Slaves were obtained by traditional means. Before the coming of the Europeans in the fifteenth century, most slaves in Africa were prisoners or war captives or had inherited their status. Many served as domestic servants or as wageless workers for the local ruler. When Europeans first began to take part in the slave trade, they would nor-

mally purchase slaves from local African merchants at the infamous slave markets in exchange for gold, guns, or other European manufactured goods such as textiles or copper or iron utensils (see the box above). At first, local slave traders obtained their supply from immediately surrounding regions, but as demand increased, they had to move farther inland to locate their victims. In a few cases, local rulers became concerned about the impact of the slave trade on the political and social well-being of their societies. In a letter to the king of Portugal in 1526, King Affonso of Congo (Bakongo) complained that "so great, Sire, is the corruption and licentiousness that our country

THE PENETRATION OF AFRICA

is being completely depopulated."[8] As a general rule, however, local monarchs viewed the slave trade as a source of income, and many launched forays against defenseless villages in search of unsuspecting victims.

The effects of the slave trade varied from area to area. It might be assumed that apart from the tragic effects on the lives of individual victims and their families, the practice would have led to the depopulation of vast areas of the continent. This did occur in some areas, notably in modern Angola, south of the Congo River basin, and in thinly populated areas in East Africa, but it was less true in West Africa. There high birthrates were often able to counterbalance the loss of able-bodied adults, and the introduction of new crops from the New World, such as maize, peanuts, and manioc, led to an increase in food production that made it possible to support a larger population. One of the many cruel ironies of history is that while the institution of slavery was a tragedy for many, it benefited others.

Still, there is no denying the reality that from a moral point of view, the slave trade represented a tragic loss for millions of Africans, not only for the individual victims, but also for their families. One of the more poignant aspects of the trade is that as many as 20 percent of those sold to European slavers were children, a statistic that may be partly explained by the fact that many European countries had enacted regulations that permitted more children than adults to be transported aboard the ships.

How did Europeans justify cruelty of such epidemic proportions? In some cases, they rationalized that slave traders were only carrying on a tradition that had existed for centuries throughout the Mediterranean and African world.

In fact, African intermediaries were active in the process and were often able to dictate the price, volume, and availability of slaves to European purchasers. In others, they eased their consciences by noting that slaves brought from Africa would now be exposed to the Christian faith and would be able to replace American Indian workers, many of whom were considered too physically fragile for the heavy human labor involved in cutting sugarcane.

Political and Social Structures in a Changing Continent

Of course, the Western economic penetration of Africa had other dislocating effects. As in other parts of the non-Western world, the importation of manufactured goods from Europe undermined the foundations of local cottage industry and impoverished countless families. The demand for slaves and the introduction of firearms intensified political instability and civil strife. At the same time, the impact of the Europeans should not be exaggerated. Only in a few isolated areas, such as South Africa and Mozambique, were permanent European settlements established. Elsewhere, at the insistence of African rulers and merchants, European influence generally did not penetrate beyond the coastal regions.

Nevertheless, inland areas were often affected by events taking place elsewhere. In the western Sahara, for example, the diversion of trade routes toward the coast led to the weakening of the old Songhai trading empire and its eventual conquest by a vigorous new Moroccan dynasty in the late sixteenth century. In 1590, Moroccan forces defeated Songhai's army at Gao, on the Niger River, and then occupied the great caravan center of Timbuktu.

European influence had a more direct impact along the coast of West Africa, especially in the vicinity of European forts such as Dakar and Sierra Leone, but no European colonies were established there before 1800. Most of the numerous African states in the area from Cape Verde to the delta of the Niger River were sufficiently strong to resist Western encroachments, and they often allied with each other to force European purchasers to respect their monopoly over trading operations. Some, like the powerful Ashanti kingdom, established in 1680 on the Gold Coast, profited substantially from the rise in seaborne commerce. Some states, particularly along the so-called Slave Coast, in what is now Dahomey and Togo, or in the densely populated Niger River delta, took an active part in the slave trade. The demands of slavery and the temptations of economic profit, however, also contributed to the increase in conflict among the states in the area.

This was especially true in the region of the Congo River, where Portuguese activities eventually led to the splintering of the Congo Empire and two centuries of rivalry and internal strife among the successor states in the area. A similar pattern developed in East Africa, where Portuguese activities led to the decline and eventual collapse of the Mwene Metapa. Northward along the coast, in present-day Kenya and Tanzania, African rulers, assisted by Arab forces from Oman and Muscat in the Arabian peninsula, expelled the Portuguese from Mombasa in 1728. Swahili culture now regained some of the dynamism it had possessed before the arrival of Vasco da Gama and his successors. But with much shipping now diverted southward to the route around the Cape of Good Hope, the commerce of the area never completely recovered and was increasingly dependent on the export of slaves and ivory obtained through contacts with African states in the interior.

SOUTHEAST ASIA IN THE ERA OF THE SPICE TRADE

In Southeast Asia, the encounter with the West that began with the arrival of Portuguese fleets in the Indian Ocean at the end of the fifteenth century eventually resulted in the breakdown of traditional societies and the advent of colonial rule. The process was a gradual one, however.

The Arrival of the West

As we have seen, the Spanish soon followed the Portuguese into Southeast Asia. By the seventeenth century, the Dutch, English, and French had begun to join the scramble for rights to the lucrative spice trade.

Within a short time, the Dutch, through the aggressive and well-financed Dutch East India Company (Vereenigde Oost-Indische Compagnie, or VOC), had not only succeeded in elbowing their rivals out of the spice trade but had also begun to consolidate their political and military control over the area. On the island of Java, where they established a fort at Batavia (today's Jakarta) in 1619, the Dutch found that it was necessary to bring the inland regions under their control to protect their position. Rather than establishing a formal colony, however, they tried to rule as much as possible through the local landed aristocracy. On Java and the neighboring island of Sumatra, the VOC established pepper plantations, which soon became the source of massive profits for Dutch merchants in Amsterdam. Elsewhere they attempted to monopolize the clove trade by limiting cultivation of the crop to one island. By the end of the eighteenth century, the Dutch had succeeded in bringing almost the entire Indonesian archipelago under their control.

The arrival of the Europeans had somewhat less impact on mainland Southeast Asia, where cohesive monarchies in Burma, Thailand, and Vietnam resisted foreign encroachment. In addition, the coveted spices did not thrive on the mainland, so the Europeans' efforts there were far less determined than in the islands. The Portuguese did establish limited trade relations with several mainland states, including the Thai kingdom at Ayuthaya, Burma, Vietnam, and the remnants of the old Angkor kingdom in Cambodia. By the early seventeenth century, other nations had followed and had begun to compete actively for trade and missionary privileges. As was the case elsewhere, the Europeans soon became involved in local factional disputes as a means of obtaining political and economic advantages.

In Vietnam, the arrival of Western merchants and missionaries coincided with a period of internal conflict among ruling groups in the country. After their arrival in the mid-seventeenth century, the European powers characteristically began to intervene in local politics, with the Portuguese and the Dutch supporting rival factions. By the end of the century, when it became clear that economic opportunities were limited, most European states abandoned their factories (trading stations) in the area. French missionaries attempted to remain, but their efforts were hampered by the local authorities, who viewed the Catholic insistence that

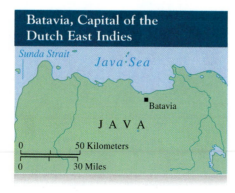

Batavia, Capital of the Dutch East Indies

Sunda Strait

Java Sea

Batavia

JAVA

0   50 Kilometers

0   30 Miles

converts give their primary loyalty to the pope as a threat to the legal status and prestige of the Vietnamese emperor (see the box on p. 313).

State and Society in Precolonial Southeast Asia

Between 1400 and 1800, Southeast Asia experienced the last flowering of traditional culture before the advent of European rule in the nineteenth century. Although the coming of the Europeans had an immediate and direct impact in some areas, notably the Philippines and parts of the Malay world, in most areas Western influence was still relatively limited.

Nevertheless, Southeast Asian societies were changing in several subtle ways—in their trade patterns, their means of livelihood, and their religious beliefs. In some ways, these changes accentuated the differences between individual states in the region. Yet beneath these differences was an underlying commonality of life for most people. Despite the diversity of cultures and religious beliefs in the area, Southeast Asians were in most respects closer to each other than they were to peoples outside the region. For the most part, the states and peoples of Southeast Asia were still in control of their own destiny.

RELIGION AND KINGSHIP

During the early modern era, both Buddhism and Islam became well established in Southeast Asia, and Christianity began to attract some converts, especially in the Philippines. Buddhism was dominant in lowland areas

---

Europe in Asia

As Europeans began to move into parts of Asia, they reproduced many of the physical surroundings of their homeland in the port cities they built there. This is evident in comparing these two scenes. Below is a seventeenth-century view of Batavia, which the Dutch built as their headquarters on the northern coast of Java in 1619. The scene at the right is from a sixteenth-century engraving of Amsterdam. This Dutch city had become the financial and commercial capital of Europe. It was also the chief port for the ships of the VOC, which brought the spices of the East to Europe.

© Private Collection/Bridgeman Art Library

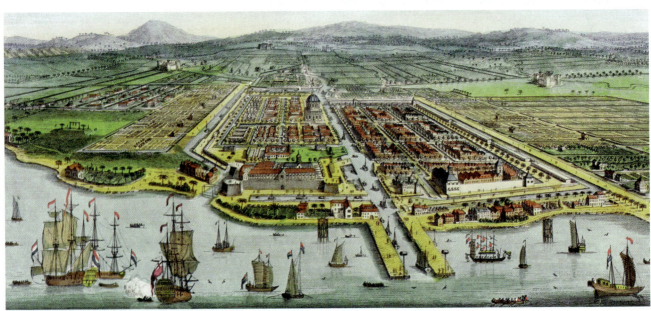

The Art Archive, London

AN EXCHANGE OF ROYAL CORRESPONDENCE

In 1681, King Louis XIV of France wrote a letter to the "king of Tonkin" (the Trinh family head, then acting as viceroy to the Vietnamese ruler) requesting permission for Christian missionaries to proselytize in Vietnam. The latter politely declined the request on the grounds that such activity was prohibited by ancient custom. In fact, Christian missionaries had been active in Vietnam for years, and their intervention in local politics had aroused the anger of the court in Hanoi.

A LETTER TO THE KING OF TONKIN FROM LOUIS XIV

Most high, most excellent, most mighty, and most magnanimous Prince, our very dear and good friend, may it please God to increase your greatness with a happy end!

We hear from our subjects who were in your Realm what protection you accorded them. We appreciate this all the more since we have for you all the esteem that one can have for a prince as illustrious through his military valor as he is commendable for the justice which he exercises in his Realm. We have even been informed that you have not been satisfied to extend this general protection to our subjects but, in particular, that you gave effective proofs of it to Messrs. Deydier and de Bourges. We would have wished that they might have been able to recognize all the favors they received from you by having presents worthy of you offered you; but since the war which we have had for several years, in which all of Europe had banded together against us, prevented our vessels from going to the Indies, at the present time, when we are at peace after having gained many victories and expanded our Realm through the conquest of several important places, we have immediately given orders to the Royal Company to establish itself in your kingdom as soon as possible, and have commanded Messrs. Deydier and de Bourges to remain with you in order to maintain a good relationship between our subjects and yours, also to warn us on occasions that might present themselves when we might be able to give you proofs of our esteem and of our wish to concur with your satisfaction as well as with your best interests.

By way of initial proof, we have given orders to have brought to you some presents which we believe might be agreeable to you. But the one thing in the world which we desire most, both for you and for your Realm, would be to obtain for your subjects who have already embraced the law of the only true God of heaven and earth, the freedom to profess it, since this law is the highest, the noblest, the most sacred, and especially the most suitable to have kings reign absolutely over the people.

We are even quite convinced that, if you knew the truths and the maxims which it teaches, you would give first of all to your subjects the glorious example of embracing it. We wish you this incomparable blessing together with a long and happy reign, and we pray God that it may please Him to augment your greatness with the happiest of endings.

Written at Saint-Germain-en-Laye, the 10th day of January, 1681,

Your very dear and good friend,
Louis

ANSWER FROM THE KING OF TONKIN TO LOUIS XIV

The King of Tonkin sends to the King of France a letter to express to him his best sentiments, saying that he was happy to learn that fidelity is a durable good of man and that justice is the most important of things. Consequently practicing of fidelity and justice cannot but yield good results. Indeed, though France and our Kingdom differ as to mountains, rivers, and boundaries, if fidelity and justice reign among our villages, our conduct will express all of our good feelings and contain precious gifts. Your communication, which comes from a country which is a thousand leagues away, and which proceeds from the heart as a testimony of your sincerity, merits repeated consideration and infinite praise. Politeness toward strangers is nothing unusual in our country. There is not a stranger who is not well received by us. How then could we refuse a man from France, which is the most celebrated among the kingdoms of the world and which for love of us wishes to frequent us and bring us merchandise? These feelings of fidelity and justice are truly worthy to be applauded. As regards your wish that we should cooperate in propagating your religion, we do not dare to permit it, for there is an ancient custom, introduced by edicts, which formally forbids it. Now, edicts are promulgated only to be carried out faithfully; without fidelity nothing is stable. How could we disdain a well-established custom to satisfy a private friendship? . . .

We beg you to understand well that this is our communication concerning our mutual acquaintance. This then is my letter. We send you herewith a modest gift, which we offer you with a glad heart.

This letter was written at the beginning of winter and on a beautiful day.

THE THAI CAPITAL AT AYUTHAYA. The Thai arrived in Southeast Asia in the thirteenth century, driven out of southern China by the Mongols. They then destroyed the Angkor empire and set up their capital at Ayuthaya, which was one of the finest cities in Asia from the fifteenth to the eighteenth century. After a Burmese invasion in 1767, most of Ayuthaya's inhabitants were killed, and all official Thai records were destroyed. Here the remains of some Buddhist stupas, erected in a ceremonial precinct in the center of the city, are a visual confirmation of the influence of Theravada Buddhism on Thai society.

on the mainland, from Burma to Vietnam. At first, Muslim influence was felt mainly on the Malay peninsula and along the northern coast of Java and Sumatra, where local merchants encountered their Muslim counterparts from foreign lands on a regular basis.

Buddhism and Islam also helped shape Southeast Asian political institutions. As the political systems began to mature, they evolved into four main types: Buddhist kings, Javanese kings, Islamic sultans, and Vietnamese emperors (for the case of Vietnam, which was strongly influenced by China, see Chapter 11). In each case, institutions and concepts imported from abroad were adapted to local circumstances.

The Buddhist style of kingship took shape between the eleventh and the fifteenth centuries. It became the predominant political system in the Buddhist states of mainland Southeast Asia—Burma, Ayuthaya, Laos, and Cambodia. Perhaps the dominant feature of the Buddhist model was the godlike character of the monarch, who was considered by virtue of his karma to be innately superior to other human beings and served as a link between human society and the cosmos.

The Javanese model was a blend of Buddhist and Islamic political traditions. Like their Buddhist counterparts, Javanese monarchs possessed a sacred quality and maintained the balance between the sacred and the material world.

The Islamic model was found mainly on the Malay peninsula and along the coast of the Indonesian archipelago. In this pattern, the head of state was a sultan, who was viewed as a mortal, although he still possessed some magical qualities.

ECONOMY AND SOCIETY

During the early period of European penetration, the economy of most Southeast Asian societies was based on agriculture, as it had been for thousands of years. Still,

by the sixteenth century, commerce was beginning to affect daily life, especially in the cities that were beginning to proliferate along the coasts or on navigable rivers. In part, this was because agriculture itself was becoming more commercialized as cash crops like sugar and spices replaced subsistence farming in rice or other cereals in some areas.

Regional and interregional trade were already expanding before the coming of the Europeans. The central geographical location of Southeast Asia enabled it to become a focal point in a widespread trading network. Spices, of course, were the mainstay of the interregional trade, but Southeast Asia exchanged other products as well. The region exported tin (mined in Malaya since the tenth century), copper, gold, tropical fruits and other agricultural products, cloth, gems, and luxury goods in exchange for manufactured goods, ceramics, and high-quality textiles such as silk from China.

In general, Southeast Asians probably enjoyed a somewhat higher living standard than most of their contemporaries elsewhere in Asia. Although most of the population was poor by modern Western standards, hunger was not a widespread problem. Several factors help explain this relative prosperity. In the first place, most of Southeast Asia has been blessed by a salubrious climate. The uniformly high temperatures and the abundant rainfall enable as many as two or even three crops to be grown each year. Second, although the soil in some areas is poor, the alluvial deltas on the mainland are fertile, and the volcanoes of Indonesia periodically spew forth rich volcanic ash that renews the mineral resources of the soil of Sumatra and Java. Finally, with some exceptions, most of Southeast Asia was relatively thinly populated.

Social institutions tended to be fairly homogeneous throughout Southeast Asia. Compared with China and India, there was little social stratification, and the nuclear family predominated. In general, women fared better in

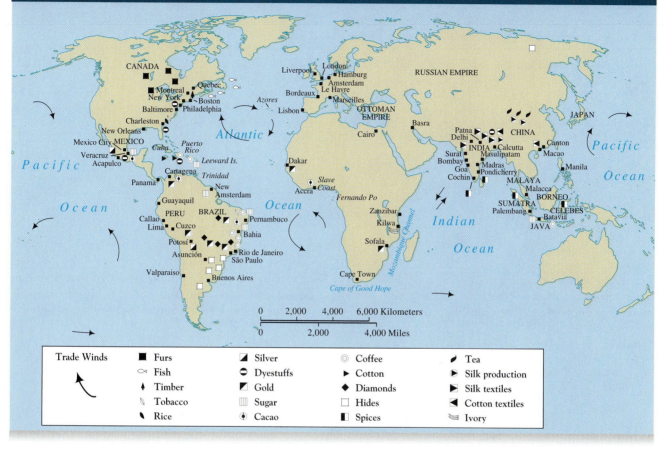

MAP 14.4 **The Pattern of World Trade from the Sixteenth to the Eighteenth Centuries.** This map shows the major products that were traded by European merchants throughout the world during the era of European exploration. Prevailing wind patterns in the oceans are shown on the map. ➤ *What were the primary sources of gold and silver, so sought after by Columbus and his successors?*

the region than anywhere else in Asia. Daughters often had the same inheritance rights as sons, and family property was held jointly between husband and wife. Wives were often permitted to divorce their husbands, and monogamy was the rule rather than the exception. Although women were usually restricted to specialized work, such as making ceramics, weaving, or transplanting the rice seedlings into the main paddy fields, and rarely possessed legal rights equal to those of men, they enjoyed a comparatively high degree of freedom and status in most societies in the region and were sometimes involved in commerce.

CONCLUSION

During the fifteenth century, Europeans burst onto the world scene. Beginning with the seemingly modest ventures of the Portuguese ships that sailed southward along the West African coast, the process accelerated with the epoch-making voyages of Christopher Columbus to the Americas and Vasco da Gama to the Indian Ocean in the

1490s. Soon a number of other European states had entered the scene, and by the end of the eighteenth century, they had created a global trade network dominated by Western ships and Western power that distributed foodstuffs, textile goods, spices, and precious minerals from one end of the globe to the other (see Map 14.4).

In less than three hundred years, the European Age of Exploration changed the face of the world. In some areas, such as the Americas and the Spice Islands, it led to the destruction of indigenous civilizations and the establishment of European colonies. In others, as in Africa, South Asia, and mainland Southeast Asia, it left native regimes intact but had a strong impact on local societies and regional trade patterns.

At the time, many European observers viewed the process in a favorable light. Not only did it expand world trade and foster the exchange of new crops and discoveries between the Old and the New Worlds (a process that will be discussed in the Reflection at the end of Part III), but it also introduced the message of Jesus Christ to "heathen peoples" around the globe. Most modern historians have been much more critical, concluding that European activities during the sixteenth and seventeenth centuries created a "tributary mode of production" based on European profits from unequal terms of trade that foreshadowed the exploitative relationship characteristic of the later colonial period. Other scholars have questioned that contention, however, and argue that although Western commercial operations had a significant impact on global trade patterns, they did not—at least not before the eighteenth century—freeze out non-European participants. Muslim merchants, for example, were long able to evade European efforts to eliminate them from the spice trade, and the trans-Saharan caravan trade was relatively unaffected by European merchant shipping along the West African coast.

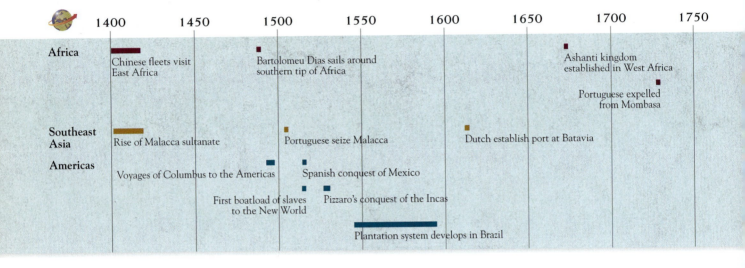

CHAPTER NOTES

1. Harry J. Benda and John A. Larkin, eds., *The World of Southeast Asia: Selected Historical Readings* (New York, 1967), p. 13.
2. J. H. Parry, *The European Reconnaissance: Selected Documents* (New York, 1968), p. 113, quoting from Armando Cortesão, *The Summa Oriental of Tomé Pires* (London, 1944), vol. 2, pp. 283–287.
3. Quoted in J. H. Parry, *The Age of Reconnaissance: Discovery, Exploration, and Settlement, 1450 to 1650* (New York, 1963), p. 33.
4. Quoted in Richard B. Reed, "The Expansion of Europe," in Richard DeMolen, ed., *The Meaning of the Renaissance and Reformation* (Boston, 1974), p. 308.
5. K. N. Chaudhuri, *Trade and Civilization in the Indian Ocean: An Economic History from the Rise of Islam to 1750* (Cambridge, 1985), p. 65.
6. Miguel Leon-Portilla, ed., *The Broken Spears: The Aztec Account of the Conquest of Mexico* (Boston, 1969), p. 51.
7. Quoted in Parry, *Age of Reconnaissance*, pp. 176–177.
8. Quoted in Basil Davidson, *Africa in History: Themes and Outlines* (London, 1968), p. 137.

SUGGESTED READING

Classic works on the period of European expansion include J. H. Parry, *The Age of Reconnaissance: Discovery, Exploration, and Settlement, 1450 to 1650* (New York, 1963); B. Penrose, *Travel and Discovery in the Renaissance, 1420–1620* (New York, 1962); and the brief work by J. H. Parry, *The Establishment of European Hegemony, 1415–1715* (New York, 1961). Also see K. M. Panikkar, *Asia and Western Dominance* (London, 1959), and H. Furber, *Rival Empires of Trade in the Orient, 1600–1800* (Minneapolis, 1976). For a more critical interpretation, see E. Wolf, *Europe and the People Without History* (Berkeley, Calif., 1982), and A. G. Frank, *World Accumulation, 1492–1789* (New York, 1978).

On the technological aspects, see C. M. Cipolla, *Guns, Sails, and Empires: Technological Innovation and the Early Phases of European Expansion, 1400–1700* (New York, 1965); F. Fernandez-Armesto, ed., *The Times Atlas of World Exploration* (New York, 1991); and R. C. Smith, *Vanguard of Empire: Ships of Exploration in the*

Age of Columbus (Oxford, 1993); also see A. Pagden, *Lords of All the World: Ideologies of Empire in Spain, Britain, and France, c. 1500–c. 1800* (New Haven, Conn., 1995). For an overview on the impact of European expansion in the Indian Ocean, see K. N. Chaudhuri, *Trade and Civilization in the Indian Ocean: An Economic History from the Rise of Islam to 1750* (Cambridge, 1985). For a series of stimulating essays reflecting modern scholarship, see J. D. Tracy, *The Rise of Merchant Empires: Long-Distance Trade in the Early Modern World, 1350–1750* (Cambridge, 1990).

For a fundamental work on Spanish colonization, see J. H. Parry, *The Spanish Seaborne Empire* (New York, 1966). A recent work on the conquistadors is H. Thomas, *Conquest: Montezuma, Cortés, and the Fall of Old Mexico* (New York, 1993). The human effects of the interaction of New and Old World cultures are examined thoughtfully in A. W. Crosby, *The Columbian Exchange: Biological and Cultural Consequences of 1492* (Westport, Conn., 1972).

On Portuguese expansion, the fundamental work is C. R. Boxer, *The Portuguese Seaborne Empire, 1415–1825* (New York, 1969). For a more recent interpretation, see W. B. Diffie and G. D. Winius, *Foundations of the Portuguese Empire, 1415–1580* (Minneapolis, 1979). On the Dutch, see J. I. Israel, *Dutch Primacy in World Trade, 1585–1740* (Oxford, 1989). The effects of European trade in Southeast Asia are discussed in A. Reid, *Southeast Asia in the Age of Commerce, 1450–1680* (New Haven, Conn., 1989).

On the African slave trade, the standard work is P. Curtin, *The African Slave Trade: A Census* (Madison, Wis., 1969). For more recent treatments, see P. Lovejoy, *Transformations in Slavery: A History of Slavery in Africa* (1983), and P. Manning, *Slavery and African Life* (Cambridge, 1990); H. Thomas, *The Slave Trade* (New York, 1997), provides a useful overview.

For a brief introduction to women's experiences during the Age of Exploration and global trade, see S. Hughes and B. Hughes, *Women in World History*, vol. 2 (Armonk, N.Y., 1997). For a more theoretical discussion of violence and gender in the early modern period, consult R. Trexler, *Sex and Conquest: Gendered Violence, Political Order, and the European Conquest of the Americas* (Ithaca, N.Y., 1995). The native American female experience with the European encounter is presented in R. Gutierrez, *When Jesus Came the Corn Mothers Went Away: Marriage, Sexuality and Power in New Mexico, 1500–1846* (Stanford, Calif., 1991), and K. Anderson, *Chain Her by One Foot: The Subjugation of Women in Seventeenth Century New France* (London, 1991).

INFOTRAC COLLEGE EDITION

Visit the source collections at **infotrac.thomsonlearning.com** and use the Search function with the following key terms.

African history	mercantilism
Christopher Columbus	Vasco da Gama

WORLD HISTORY RESOURCES

Visit the *Essential World History* Companion Web Site for resources specific to this textbook:

http://history.wadsworth.com/duikeressentials02/

The CD in the back of this book and the World History Resource Center at **http://history.wadsworth.com/world/** offer a variety of tools to help you succeed in this course, including access to quizzes; images; documents; interactive simulations, maps, and timelines; movie explorations; and a wealth of other sources.

© Sonia Halliday Photographs

THE MUSLIM EMPIRES

FOCUS QUESTIONS

- Why are the Ottoman, Safavid, and Mughal Empires sometimes called "gunpowder empires," and how accurate is that characterization?
- What were the main characteristics of each of the Muslim empires, and in what ways were they similar?
- What contact did each of the Muslim empires have with Europeans, and how was each empire affected by that contact?
- What role did women play in each of the Muslim empires?
- ➤ How did each of the great Muslim empires come into existence, and why did they ultimately decline?

One of the primary objectives of European leaders in seeking a route to the Spice Islands was to lessen the political and economic power of Islam by reducing the Muslims' strong position in the global trade network. As we saw in Chapter 14, Portuguese fleets, followed by those of the Spanish, the English, and the Dutch, had some success in wresting control over the spice trade from Muslim shippers, although the latter were never totally driven out of the business. By the eighteenth century, the Indian Ocean had ceased to be an Arab preserve and had become, in some respects, a European lake.

Thus the European dream of controlling global trade markets had become a reality. But in the broader scheme of things, the goal of crippling the power of Islam was not entirely realized, for Europe's success had not been achieved by the collapse of its great rival. To the contrary, the Muslim world, which appeared to have entered a period of decline with the collapse of the Abbasid caliphate during the era of the Mongols, managed to revive in the shadow of Europe's Age of Exploration, a period that also saw the rise of three great Muslim empires. These powerful Muslim states—those of the Ottomans, the Safavids, and the Mughals—dominated the Middle East and the South Asian subcontinent and brought stability to a region that had been in turmoil for centuries. •

THE OTTOMAN EMPIRE

The Ottoman Turks were among the various Turkic-speaking peoples who had spread westward from Central Asia in the ninth, tenth, and eleventh centuries. The first to dominate were the Seljuk Turks, who initially attempted to revive the declining Abbasid caliphate in Baghdad. Later they established themselves in the Anatolian peninsula at the expense of the Byzantine Empire. Turks served as warriors or administrators, while the peasants who tilled the farmland were mainly Greek.

In the late thirteenth century, a new group of Turks under the tribal leader Osman (1280–1326) began to consolidate their power in the northwestern corner of the Anatolian peninsula. At first, the Osman Turks were relatively peaceful and engaged in pastoral pursuits, but as the Seljuk Empire began to disintegrate in the early fourteenth century, they began to expand and founded the Osmanli (later to be known as Ottoman) dynasty.

The Ottomans gained a key advantage by seizing the Bosporus and the Dardanelles, between the Mediterranean and the Black Seas. The Byzantine Empire, of course, had controlled the area for centuries, serving as a buffer between the Muslim Middle East and the Latin West. The Byzantines, however, had been severely weakened by the sack of Constantinople in the Fourth Crusade (in 1204) and the Western occupation of much of the empire for the next half century. In 1345, Ottoman forces under their leader Orkhan I (1326–1360) crossed the Bosporus for the first time to support a usurper against the Byzantine emperor in Constantinople. Setting up their first European base at Gallipoli at the Mediterranean entrance to the Dardanelles, Turkish forces expanded gradually into the Balkans and allied with fractious Serbian and Bulgar forces against the Byzantines. In these unstable conditions, the Ottomans gradually established permanent settlements throughout the area, where Turkish beys (provincial governors in the Ottoman Empire; from the Turkish *beg*, "knight") drove out the previous landlords and collected taxes from the local Slavic peasants. The Ottoman leader now began to claim the title of sultan or sovereign of his domain.

In 1360, Orkhan was succeeded by his son Murad I, who consolidated Ottoman power in the Balkans and gradually reduced the Byzantine emperor to a vassal. Murad now began to build up a strong military administration based on the recruitment of Christians into an elite guard. Called Janissaries (from the Turkish *yeni cheri*, "new troops"), they were recruited from the local Christian population in the Balkans and then converted to Islam and trained as foot soldiers or administrators. One of the major advantages of the Janissaries was that they were directly subordinated to the sultanate and therefore owed their loyalty to the person of the sultan. Other military forces were organized by the beys and were thus loyal to their local tribal leaders.

The Janissary corps also represented a response to changes in warfare. As the knowledge of firearms spread in the late

❧ **MEHMET II, CONQUEROR OF CONSTANTINOPLE.** Identified with the seizure of Constantinople from the Byzantine Empire in 1453, Mehmet II was one of the most illustrious Ottoman sultans. This Turkish miniature portrays Mehmet II with his handkerchief, a symbol of the supreme power of the Ottoman ruler. He is also smelling a rose, representing his cultural interests, especially as patron of the arts.

fourteenth century, the Turks began to master the new technology, including siege cannons and muskets. The traditional nomadic cavalry charge was now outmoded and was superseded by infantry forces armed with muskets. Thus the Janissaries provided a well-armed infantry who served both as an elite guard to protect the palace and as a means of extending Turkish control in the Balkans. With his new forces, Murad defeated the Serbs at the famous Battle of Kosovo in 1389 and ended Serbian hegemony in the area.

Under Murad's successor, Bayazid I (1389–1402), the Ottomans advanced northward, annexed Bulgaria, and slaughtered the flower of French cavalry at a major battle on the Danube. When Mehmet II (1451–1481) succeeded to the throne, he was determined to capture Constantinople. Already in control of the Dardanelles, he ordered the construction of a major fortress on the Bosporus just north of the city, which put the Turks in a position to strangle the Byzantines.

THE FALL OF CONSTANTINOPLE

Few events in the history of the Ottoman Empire are more dramatic than the conquest of Constantinople in 1453. In this excerpt, the conquest is described by Kritovoulos, a Greek who later served in the Ottoman administration. Although the author did not witness the conquest itself, he was apparently well informed about the event and provides us with a vivid description.

KRITOVOULOS, *LIFE OF MEHMED THE CONQUEROR*

So saying, he [the Sultan] led them himself. And they, with a shout on the run and with a fearsome yell, went on ahead of the Sultan, pressing on up to the palisade. After a long and bitter struggle they hurled back the Romans [Byzantines] from there and climbed by force up the palisade. They dashed some of their foe down into the ditch between the great wall and the palisade, which was deep and hard to get out of, and they killed them there. The rest they drove back to the gate.

He had opened this gate in the great wall, so as to go easily over to the palisade. Now there was a great struggle there and great slaughter among those stationed there, for they were attacked by the heavy infantry and not a few others in irregular formation, who had been attracted from many points by the shouting. There the Emperor Constantine [Constantine XIII Paleologus], with all who were with him, fell in gallant combat.

The heavy infantry were already streaming through the little gate into the City, and others had rushed in through the breach in the great wall. Then all the rest of the army, with a rush and a roar, poured in brilliantly and scattered all over the City. And the Sultan stood before the great wall, where the standard also was and the ensigns, and watched the proceedings. The day was already breaking. . . .

The soldiers fell on them [the citizens] with anger and great wrath. For one thing, they were actuated by the hardships of the siege. For another, some foolish people had hurled taunts and curses at them from the battlements all through the siege. Now, in general they killed so as to frighten all the City, and to terrorize and enslave all by the slaughter.

When they had had enough of murder, and the City was reduced to slavery, some of the troops turned to the mansions of the mighty, by bands and companies and divisions, for plunder and spoil. Others went to the robbing of churches, and others dispersed to the simple homes of the common people, stealing, robbing, plundering, killing, insulting, taking and enslaving men, women, and children, old and young, priests, monks—in short, every age and class. . . .

After this the Sultan entered the City and looked about to see its great size, its situation, its grandeur and beauty, its teeming population, its loveliness, and the costliness of its churches and public buildings and of the private houses and community houses and those of the officials. . . . When he saw what a large number had been killed, and the ruin of the buildings, and the wholesale ruin and destruction of the City, he was filled with compassion and repented not a little at the destruction and plundering. Tears fell from his eyes as he groaned deeply and passionately: "What a city we have given over to plunder and destruction." . . .

As for the great City of Constantine, raised to a great height of glory and dominion and wealth in its own times, overshadowing to an infinite degree all the cities around it, renowned for its glory, wealth, authority, power, and greatness, and all its other qualities, it thus came to its end.

The last Byzantine emperor desperately called for help from the Europeans, but only the Genoese came to his defense. With eighty thousand troops ranged against only seven thousand defenders, Mehmet laid siege to Constantinople in 1453. In their attack on the city, the Turks made use of massive cannons with 26-foot barrels that could launch stone balls weighing up to 1,200 pounds each. The Byzantines stretched heavy chains across the Golden Horn, the inlet that forms the city's harbor, to prevent a naval attack from the north and prepared to make their final stand behind the 13-mile-long wall along the western edge of the city. But Mehmet's forces seized the tip of the peninsula north of the Golden Horn and then dragged their ships overland across the peninsula from the Bosporus and put them into the water behind the chains.

Finally, the walls were breached; the Byzantine emperor died in the final battle (see the box above).

Expansion of the Empire

With their new capital at Constantinople, renamed Istanbul, the Ottoman Turks were now a dominant force in the Balkans and the Anatolian peninsula. They now began to advance to the east against the Shi'ite kingdom of the Safavids in Persia (see "The Safavids" later in this chapter),

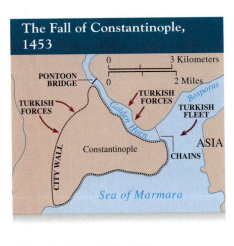

The Fall of Constantinople, 1453

MAP 15.1 **The Ottoman Empire.** This map shows the territorial growth of the Ottoman Empire from the eve of the conquest of Constantinople in 1453 to the end of the seventeenth century, when a defeat at the hands of Austria led to the loss of a substantial portion of central Europe. ➤ *Where did the Ottomans come from?*

Map legend:
- Ottoman Empire, 1451
- Ottoman gains to 1481
- Ottoman gains to 1521
- Ottoman gains to 1566
- Area lost to Austria in 1699
- Battle sites

which had been promoting rebellion among the Anatolian tribal population and disrupting Turkish trade through the Middle East. After defeating the Safavids at a major battle in 1514, Emperor Selim I (1512–1520) consolidated Turkish control over Mesopotamia and then turned his attention to the Mamluks in Egypt, who had failed to support the Ottomans in their struggle against the Safavids. The Mamluks were defeated in Syria in 1516; Cairo fell a year later. Now controlling several of the holy cities of Islam, including Jerusalem, Mecca, and Medina, Selim declared himself to be the new caliph, or successor to Muhammad. During the next few years, Turkish armies and fleets advanced westward along the African coast, occupying Tripoli, Tunis, and Algeria and eventually penetrating almost to the Strait of Gibraltar (see Map 15.1).

The impact of Turkish rule on the peoples of North Africa was relatively light. Like their predecessors, the Turks were Muslims, and they preferred where possible to administer their conquered regions through local rulers. Central government direction was achieved through appointed pashas who collected taxes (and then paid a fixed percentage as tribute to the central government), maintained law and order, and were directly responsible to Istanbul. The Turks ruled from coastal cities like Algiers, Tunis, and Tripoli and made no attempt to control the interior beyond maintaining the trade routes through the Sahara to the trading centers along the Niger River. Meanwhile, local pirates along the Barbary Coast—the northern coast of Africa from Egypt to the Atlantic Ocean—competed with their Christian rivals in raiding the shipping that passed through the Mediterranean.

By the seventeenth century, the links between the imperial court in Istanbul and its appointed representatives in the Turkish regencies in North Africa had begun to decline. Some of the pashas were dethroned by local elites, while others, such as the bey of Tunis, became

© Sonia Halliday Photographs

➤ THE SIEGE OF VIENNA. After seizing the Byzantine capital of Constantinople in 1453, Turkish forces began advancing into southern Europe to extend the borders of the Ottoman Empire. By 1529, they had reached the gates of Vienna, capital of the Habsburg Empire, which they placed under siege. In this contemporary painting from the Topkapi Palace in Istanbul, Turkish forces across the Danube River have besieged the walled city, shown in the background. Despite the use of cannons, first introduced to the West by Ottoman forces during this campaign, the siege was unsuccessful.

hereditary rulers. Even Egypt, whose agricultural wealth and control over the route to the Red Sea made it the most important country in the area to the Turks, gradually became autonomous under a new official class of Janissaries.

TURKISH EXPANSION IN EUROPE

After their conquest of Constantinople in 1453, the Ottoman Turks tried to extend their territory in Europe. Under the leadership of Suleyman I the Magnificent (1520–1566), Turkish forces advanced up the Danube,

seizing Belgrade in 1521 and winning a major victory over the Hungarians at the Battle of Mohács on the Danube in 1526. Subsequently the Turks overran most of Hungary, moved into Austria, and advanced as far as Vienna, where they were finally repulsed in 1529. At the same time, they extended their power into the western Mediterranean and threatened to turn it into a Turkish lake until a large Turkish fleet was destroyed by the Spanish at Lepanto in 1571.

Under a new line of grand vezirs in the second half of the seventeenth century, the Ottoman Empire again took the offensive. By mid-1683, the Ottomans had marched through the Hungarian plain and laid siege to Vienna. Repulsed by a mixed army of Austrians, Poles, Bavarians, and Saxons, the Turks retreated and were pushed out of Hungary by a new European coalition. Although they retained the core of their empire, the Ottoman Turks would never again be a threat to Europe. Although the Turkish empire held together for the rest of the seventeenth and the eighteenth centuries, it would be faced with new challenges from the ever-growing Austrian Empire in southeastern Europe and the new Russian giant to the north.

The Nature of Turkish Rule

Like other Muslim empires in Persia and India, the Ottoman political system was the result of the evolution of tribal institutions into a sedentary empire. At the apex of the Ottoman system was the sultan, who was the supreme authority in both a political and a military sense. The origins of this system can be traced back to the bey, who was only a tribal leader, a first among equals, who could claim loyalty from his chiefs so long as he could provide booty and grazing lands for his subordinates. Disputes were settled by tribal law, while Muslim laws were secondary. Tribal leaders collected taxes—or booty—from areas under their control and sent one-fifth on to the bey. Both administrative and military power were centralized under the bey, and the capital was wherever the bey and his administration happened to be.

But the rise of empire brought about an adaptation to Byzantine traditions of rule. The status and prestige of the sultan now increased relative to the subordinate tribal leaders, and the position took on the trappings of imperial rule. Court rituals were inherited from the Byzantines and Persians, and a centralized administrative system was adopted that increasingly isolated the sultan in his palace. The position of the sultan was hereditary, with a son, although not necessarily the eldest, always succeeding the father. This practice led to chronic succession struggles upon the death of individual sultans, and the losers were often executed (strangled with a silk bowstring) or imprisoned. Heirs to the throne were assigned as provincial governors to provide them with experience.

The heart of the sultan's power was in the Topkapi Palace in the center of Istanbul. Topkapi (meaning "cannon gate") was constructed in 1459 by Mehmet II and served as an administrative center as well as the private residence of the sultan and his family. Eventually it had a staff of twenty thousand employees. The private domain of the sultan was called the harem ("sacred place"). Here he resided with his concubines. Normally a sultan did not marry but chose several concubines as his favorites; they were accorded this status after they gave birth to sons. When a son became a sultan, his mother became known as the queen mother and served as adviser to the throne. This tradition, initiated by the influential wife of Suleyman the Magnificent, often resulted in considerable authority for the queen mother in the affairs of state.

Members of the harem, like the Janissaries, were often of slave origin and formed an elite element in Ottoman society. Since the enslavement of Muslims was forbidden, slaves were taken among non-Islamic peoples. Some concubines were prisoners selected for the position, while others were purchased or offered to the sultan as a gift. They were then trained and educated like the Janissaries in a system called *devshirme* ("collection"). *Devshirme* had originated in the practice of requiring local clan leaders to provide prisoners to the sultan as part of their tax obligation. Talented males were given special training for eventual placement in military or administrative positions, while their female counterparts were trained for service in the harem, with instruction in reading, the Koran, sewing and embroidery, and musical performance. They were ranked according to their status, and some were permitted to leave the harem to marry officials.

Unique to the Ottoman Empire from the fifteenth century onward was the exclusive use of slaves to reproduce its royal heirs. Contrary to myth, few of the women of the imperial harem were used for sexual purposes, as the majority were relatives of the sultan's extended family—sisters, daughters, widowed mothers, and in-laws, with their own personal slaves and entourage. Contemporary European observers compared the atmosphere in the Topkapi harem to a Christian nunnery, with its hierarchical organization, enforced chastity, and rule of silence.

Because of their proximity to the sultan, the women of the harem often wielded so much political power that the era has been called "the sultanate of women." Queen mothers administered the imperial household and engaged in diplomatic relations with other countries while controlling the marital alliances of their daughters with senior civilian and military officials or members of other royal families in the region. One princess was married seven separate times from the age of two after her previous husbands died either in battle or by execution.

The sultan ruled through an imperial council that met four days a week and was chaired by the chief minister known as the grand vezir (*wazir*, sometimes rendered in English as *vizier*). The sultan often attended behind a screen, whence he could privately indicate his desires to the grand vezir. The latter presided over the imperial bureaucracy. Like the palace guard, the bureaucrats were not an exclusive group but were chosen at least partly by merit from a palace school for training officials. Most officials were Muslims by birth, but some talented Janissaries became senior members of the bureaucracy, and almost all the later grand vezirs came from the *devshirme* system.

Local administration during the imperial period was a product of Turkish tribal tradition and was similar in some respects to fief-holding in Europe. The empire was divided into provinces and districts governed by officials who, like their tribal predecessors, combined both civil and military functions. Senior officials were assigned land in fief by the sultan and were then responsible for collecting taxes and supplying armies to the empire. These lands were then farmed out to the local cavalry elite called the *sipahis*, who exacted a tax from all peasants in their fiefdoms for their salary.

Religion and Society in the Ottoman World

Like most Turkic-speaking peoples in the Anatolian peninsula and throughout the Middle East, the Ottoman ruling elites were Sunni Muslims. Ottoman sultans had claimed the title of caliph ("defender of the faith") since the early sixteenth century and thus theoretically were responsible for guiding the flock and maintaining Islamic law, the *Shari'a*. In practice, the sultan assigned these duties to a supreme religious authority, who administered the law and maintained a system of schools for educating Muslims.

Islamic law and customs were applied to all Muslims in the empire. Like their rulers, most Turkic-speaking people were Sunni Muslims, but some communities were attracted to Sufism (see Chapter 7) or other heterodox doctrines. The government tolerated such activities so long as their practitioners remained loyal to the empire, but in the early sixteenth century, unrest among these groups—some of whom converted to the Shi'ite version of Islamic doctrine—outraged the conservative *ulama* and eventually led to war against the Safavids (see "The Safavids" later in this chapter).

Non-Muslims—mostly Orthodox Christians (Greeks and Slavs), Jews, and Armenian Christians—formed a significant minority within the empire, which treated them with relative tolerance. Non-Muslims were compelled to pay a head tax (because of their exemption from military service), and they were permitted to practice their religion or convert to Islam, although Muslims were prohibited from adopting another faith. Most of the population in European areas of the empire remained Christian, but in some places, such as the territory now called Bosnia, substantial numbers converted to Islam.

Technically, women in the Ottoman Empire were subject to the same restrictions that afflicted their counterparts in other Muslim societies, but their position was ameliorated to some degree by various factors. In the first place, non-Muslims were subject to the laws and customs of their own religions; thus Orthodox Christian, Jewish, and Armenian Christian women were spared some of the restrictions applied to their Muslim sisters. In the second place, Islamic laws as applied in the Ottoman Empire defined the legal position of women comparatively tolerantly. Women were permitted to own and inherit property, including their dowries. They could not be forced into marriage and in certain cases were permitted to seek a divorce. As we have seen, women often exercised considerable influence in the palace and in a few instances even served as senior officials, such as governors of provinces. The relatively tolerant attitude toward women in Ottoman-held territories has been ascribed by some to Turkish tribal traditions, which took a more egalitarian view of sex roles than the sedentary societies of the region did.

The Ottomans in Decline

By the seventeenth century, signs of internal rot had begun to appear in the empire, although the first loss of imperial territory did not occur until 1699, at the Battle of Carlowitz. Apparently, a number of factors were involved. In the first place, the administrative system inherited from the tribal period began to break down. Although the *devshirme* system of training officials continued to function,

devshirme graduates were now permitted to marry and inherit property and to enroll their sons in the palace corps. Thus they were gradually transformed from a meritocratic administrative elite into a privileged and often degenerate hereditary caste. Local administrators were corrupted and taxes rose as the central bureaucracy lost its links with rural areas. The imperial treasury was depleted by constant wars, and transport and communications were neglected. Interest in science and technology, once a hallmark of the Arab Empire, was in decline. In addition, the empire was increasingly beset by economic difficulties caused by the diversion of trade routes away from the eastern Mediterranean and the price inflation brought about by the influx of cheap American silver.

Another sign of change within the empire was the increasing degree of material affluence and the impact of Western ideas and customs. Sophisticated officials and merchants began to mimic the habits and lifestyles of their European counterparts, dressing in the European fashion, purchasing Western furniture and art objects, and ignoring Muslim strictures against the consumption of alcohol and sexual activities outside marriage. During the sixteenth and early seventeenth centuries, coffee and tobacco were introduced into polite Ottoman society, and cafés for the consumption of both began to appear in the major cities (see the box on p. 325). One sultan in the early seventeenth century issued a decree prohibiting the consumption of both coffee and tobacco, arguing (correctly, no doubt) that many cafés were nests of antigovernment intrigue. He even began to wander incognito through the streets of Istanbul at night. Any of his subjects detected in immoral or illegal acts were summarily executed and their bodies left on the streets as an example to others.

There were also signs of a decline in competence within the ruling family. Whereas the first sultans reigned twenty-seven years on average, later ones averaged only thirteen years. The throne now went to the oldest surviving male, while his rivals were kept secluded in a latticed cage and thus had no governmental experience if they succeeded to rule. Later sultans also became less involved in government, and more power flowed to the office of the grand vezir (called the Sublime Porte) or to eunuchs and members of the harem. Palace intrigue increased as a result.

Ottoman Art

The Ottoman sultans were enthusiastic patrons of the arts and maintained large ateliers of artisans and artists, primarily at the Topkapi Palace in Istanbul but also in other important cities of the vast empire. The period from Mehmet II in the fifteenth century to the early eighteenth century witnessed the flourishing of pottery, rugs, silk and other textiles, jewelry, arms and armor, and calligraphy. All adorned the palaces of the new rulers, testifying to

A Turkish Discourse on Coffee

Coffee was first introduced to Turkey from the Arabian peninsula in the mid-sixteenth century and allegedly came to Europe during the Turkish siege of Vienna in 1529. The following account was written by Katib Chelebi, a seventeenth-century Turkish author who, among other things, compiled an extensive encyclopedia and bibliography. Here, in The Balance of Truth, *he describes how coffee entered the empire and the problems it caused for public morality. (In the Muslim world, as in Europe and later in colonial America, the drinking of coffee was associated with coffeehouses, where rebellious elements often gathered to promote antigovernment activities.) Chelebi died in Istanbul in 1657, reportedly while drinking a cup of coffee.*

KATIB CHELEBI, *THE BALANCE OF TRUTH*

[Coffee] originated in Yemen and has spread, like tobacco, over the world. Certain sheikhs, who lived with their dervishes in the mountains of Yemen, used to crush and eat the berries . . . of a certain tree. Some would roast them and drink their water. Coffee is a cold dry food, suited to the ascetic life and sedative of lust. . . .

It came to Asia Minor by sea, about 1543, and met with a hostile reception, fetwas [decrees] being delivered against it. For they said, Apart from its being roasted, the fact that it is drunk in gatherings, passed from hand to hand, is suggestive of loose living. It is related of Abul-Suud Efendi that he had holes bored in the ships that brought it, plunging their cargoes of coffee into the sea. But these strictures and prohibitions availed nothing. . . . One coffeehouse was opened after another, and men would gather together, with great eagerness and enthusiasm, to drink. Drug addicts in particular, finding it a life-giving thing, which increased their pleasure, were willing to die for a cup.

Storytellers and musicians diverted the people from their employments, and working for one's living fell into disfavor. Moreover the people, from prince to beggar, amused themselves with knifing one another. Toward the end of 1633, the late Ghazi Gultan Murad, becoming aware of the situation, promulgated an edict, out of regard and compassion for the people, to this effect: Coffeehouses throughout the Guarded Domains shall be dismantled and not opened hereafter. Since then, the coffeehouses of the capital have been as desolate as the heart of the ignorant. . . . But in cities and towns outside Istanbul, they are opened just as before. As has been said above, such things do not admit of a perpetual ban.

---

their opulence and exquisite taste. The artists came from all parts of the realm and beyond.

By far the greatest contribution of the Ottoman Empire to world art was its architecture, especially the magnificent mosques of the second half of the sixteenth century. Traditionally, prayer halls in mosques were subdivided by numerous pillars that supported small individual domes, creating a private, forestlike atmosphere. The Turks, however, modeled their new mosques on the open floor plan of the Byzantine church of Hagia Sophia (completed in 537), which had been turned into a mosque by Mehmet II, and began to push the pillars toward the outer wall to create a prayer hall with an uninterrupted central area under one large dome. With this plan, large numbers of believers could worship in unison in accordance with Muslim preference. By the mid-sixteenth century, the greatest of all Ottoman architects, Sinan, began erecting the first of his eighty-one mosques with an uncluttered prayer area. Each was topped by an imposing dome, and often, as at Edirne, the entire building was framed with four towering narrow minarets. By emphasizing its vertical lines, the minarets camouflaged the massive stone bulk of the structure and gave it a feeling of incredible lightness. These four graceful minarets would find new expression sixty years later in India's white marble Taj Mahal (see "Mughal Culture" later in this chapter).

Earlier the thirteenth-century Seljuk Turks of Anatolia had created beautiful tile decorations with two-color mosaics. Now Ottoman artists invented a new glazed tile art with painted flowers and geometrical designs in brilliant blue, green, yellow, and their own secret "tomato red." Entire walls, both interior and exterior, were covered with the painted tiles, which adorned palaces as well as mosques.

The sixteenth century also witnessed the flourishing of textiles and rugs. The Byzantine emperor Justinian had introduced the cultivation of silkworms to the West in the sixth century, and the silk industry resurfaced under the Ottomans. Perhaps even more famous than Turkish silk are the rugs. But whereas silks were produced under the patronage of the sultans, rugs were a peasant industry. Each village boasted its own distinctive design and color scheme for the rugs it produced.

THE SAFAVIDS

After the collapse of the empire of Tamerlane in the early fifteenth century, the area extending from Persia into Central Asia lapsed into anarchy. The Uzbeks, Turkic-speaking peoples from Central Asia, were the chief political and military force in the area. From their capital at

THE BLUE MOSQUE, ISTANBUL. The magnificent mosques built under the patronage of Suleyman the Magnificent are a great legacy of the Ottoman Empire and a fitting supplement to the cathedral of Hagia Sophia, built by the Byzantine emperor Justinian in the sixth century C.E. Towering under a central dome, these mosques seem to defy gravity, and, like European Gothic cathedrals, convey a sense of weightlessness. The Blue Mosque, so called for the blue tiles in its interior, is one of the most impressive and most graceful in Istanbul. A far cry from the seventh-century desert mosques constructed of palm trunks, the Ottoman mosques stand among the architectural wonders of the world.

Bukhara, they maintained a semblance of control over the highly fluid tribal alignments until the emergence of the Safavid dynasty in Persia at the beginning of the sixteenth century.

The Safavid dynasty was founded by Shah Ismail (1487–1524), the descendant of a sheikh called Safi al-Din (thus the name Safavid), who traced his origins to Ali, the fourth imam of the Muslim faith. In the early fourteenth century, Safi had been the leader of a community of Turkic-speaking tribespeople in Azerbaijan, near the Caspian Sea. Safi's community was only one of many Sufi mystical religious groups throughout the area. In time, the doctrine spread among nomadic groups throughout the Middle East and was transformed into the more activist Shi'i heresy. Its adherents were known as "red heads" because of their distinctive red cap with twelve folds, meant to symbolize allegiance to the twelve imams of the Shi'i faith.

In 1501, Ismail's forces seized much of Iran and Iraq, and he called himself the shah of a new Persian state.

Baghdad was subdued in 1508 and the Uzbeks in Bukhara shortly thereafter. Ismail now sent Shi'ite preachers into Anatolia to proselytize and promote rebellion among Turkish tribal peoples in the Ottoman Empire. In retaliation, the Ottoman sultan, Selim I, advanced against the Safavids in Iran and won a major battle near Tabriz in 1514. But Selim could not maintain control of the area, and Ismail regained Tabriz a few years later.

The Ottomans returned to the attack in the 1580s and forced the new Safavid shah, Abbas I the Great (1587–1629), to sign a punitive peace in which much territory was lost. The capital was subsequently moved from Tabriz in the northwest to Isfahan in the south. Still, it was under Shah Abbas that the Safavids reached the zenith of their glory. He established a system similar to the Janissaries in Turkey to train administrators to replace the traditional warrior elite. He also used the period of peace to strengthen his army, now armed with modern weapons, and in the early seventeenth century, he attempted to regain the lost territories. Although he had some initial success, war resumed in the 1620s, and a lasting peace was not achieved until 1638 (see Map 15.2).

Abbas the Great had managed to strengthen the dynasty significantly, and for a time after his death in 1629, it remained stable and vigorous. But succession conflicts plagued the dynasty. Partly as a result, the power of the more militant Shi'ites began to increase at court and in Safavid society at large. The intellectual freedom that had characterized the empire at its height was curtailed under the pressure of religious orthodoxy, and Iranian women, who had enjoyed considerable freedom and influence during the early empire, were forced to withdraw into seclusion and behind the veil. Meanwhile, attempts to suppress the religious beliefs of minorities led to increased popular unrest. In the early eighteenth century, Afghan warriors took advantage of local revolts to seize the capital of Isfahan, forcing the remnants of the Safavid ruling family to retreat to Azerbaijan, their original homeland. The Ottomans seized territories along the western border. Eventually order was restored by the military adventurer Nadir Shah Afshar, who launched an extended series of campaigns that restored the country's borders and even occupied the Mughal capital of Delhi (see "Twilight of the Mughals" later in this chapter). After his death, the Zand dynasty ruled until the end of the eighteenth century.

Safavid Politics and Society

Like the Ottoman Empire, Iran under the Safavids was a mixed society. The Safavids had come to power with the support of nomadic Turkic-speaking tribal groups, and leading elements from those groups retained considerable influence within the empire. But the majority of the population were Iranian; most of them were farmers or townspeople, with attitudes inherited from the relatively sophisticated and urbanized culture of pre-Safavid Iran. Faced with the problem of integrating unruly Turkic-speaking tribal peoples with the sedentary Persian-speaking population of the urban areas, the Safavids used the Shi'ite faith as a unifying force. The shah himself acquired an almost divine quality and claimed to be the spiritual leader of all Islam. Shi'ism was declared the state religion.

Although there was a landed aristocracy, aristocratic power and influence were firmly controlled by strong-minded shahs, who confiscated aristocratic estates when

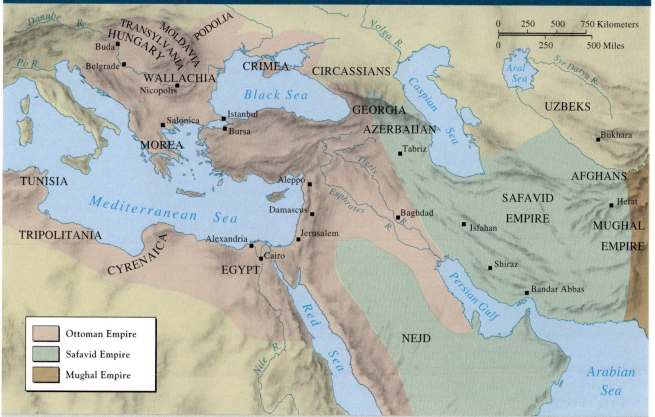

MAP 15.2   The Ottoman and Safavid Empires, c. 1683.   During the seventeenth century, the two empires contested vigorously for hegemony in the eastern Mediterranean and the Middle East. This map shows the territories controlled by each state in the late seventeenth century. ➤ *What were the key cities in the two empires?*

Ottoman Empire
Safavid Empire
Mughal Empire

possible and brought them under the control of the crown. Appointment to senior positions in the bureaucracy was by merit rather than birth.

The Safavid shahs took a direct interest in the economy and actively engaged in commercial and manufacturing activities, although there was also a large and affluent urban bourgeoisie. Like the Ottoman sultan, one shah regularly traveled the city streets incognito to check on the honesty of his subjects. When he discovered that a baker and butcher were overcharging for their products, he had the baker cooked in his own oven and the butcher roasted on a spit.

At its height, Safavid Iran was a worthy successor to the great Persian empires of the past, although it was probably not as wealthy as its Mughal and Ottoman neighbors to the east and west. Hemmed in by the sea power of the Europeans to the south and by the land power of the Ottomans to the west, the early Safavids had no navy and were forced to divert overland trade with Europe through southern Russia to avoid an Ottoman blockade. In the early seventeenth century, the situation improved when Iranian forces, in cooperation with the English, seized the island of Hormuz from Portugal and established a new seaport on the southern coast at Bandar Abbas. As a consequence, commercial ties with Europe began to increase.

Safavid Art and Literature

Persia witnessed an extraordinary flowering of the arts during the reign of Shah Abbas I. His new capital of Isfahan was a grandiose planned city with wide visual perspectives and a sense of order almost unique in the region. Shah Abbas ordered his architects to position his palaces, mosques, and bazaars around the Maydan-i-Shah, a mas-

THE ROYAL ACADEMY OF ISFAHAN. Along with institutions such as libraries and hospitals, theological schools were often included in the mosque compound. One of the most sumptuous was the Royal Academy of Isfahan, built by the shah of Iran in the early eighteenth century. This view shows the large courtyard surrounded by arcades of student rooms, reminiscent of the arrangement of monks' cells in European cloisters.

© George Holton/Photo Researchers, Inc.

THE MUGHAL CONQUEST OF NORTHERN INDIA

Babur, the founder of the great Mughal dynasty, began his career by allying with one Indian prince against another and then turned on his ally to put himself in power, a tactic that had been used by the Ottomans and the Mongols before him (see Chapter 10). In this excerpt from his memoirs, Babur describes his triumph over the powerful army of his Indian enemy, the sultan Ibrâhim.

BABUR, MEMOIRS

They made one or two very poor charges on our right and left divisions. My troops making use of their bows, plied them with arrows, and drove them in upon their center. The troops on the right and the left of their center, being huddled together in one place, such confusion ensued, that the enemy, while totally unable to advance, found also no road by which they could flee. The sun had mounted spear-high when the onset of battle began, and the combat lasted till midday, when the enemy were completely broken and routed, and my friends victorious and exulting. By the grace and mercy of Almighty God, this arduous undertaking was rendered easy for me, and this mighty army, in the space of half a day, laid in the dust. Five or six thousand men were discovered lying slain, in one spot, near Ibrâhim. We reckoned that the number lying slain, in different parts of this field of battle, amounted to fifteen or sixteen thousand men. On reaching Agra, we found, from the accounts of the natives of Hindustân, that forty or fifty thousand men had fallen in this field. After routing the enemy, we continued the pursuit, slaughtering, and making them prisoners. . . .

It was now afternoon prayers when Tahir Taberi, the younger brother of Khalîfeh, having found Ibrâhim lying dead amidst a number of slain, cut off his head, and brought it in. . . .

In consideration of my confidence in Divine aid, the Most High God did not suffer the distress and hardships that I had undergone to be thrown away, but defeated my formidable enemy, and made me the conqueror of the noble country of Hindustân. This success I do not ascribe to my own strength, nor did this good fortune flow from my own efforts, but from the fountain of the favor and mercy of God.

---

sive rectangular polo ground. Much of the original city is still in good condition and remains the gem of modern Iran. The immense mosques are richly decorated with elaborate blue tiles. The palaces are delicate structures with unusual slender wooden columns. These architectural wonders of Isfahan epitomize the grandeur, delicacy, and color that defined the Safavid golden age. To adorn the splendid buildings, Safavid artisans created imaginative metalwork, tile decorations, and original and delicate glass vessels.

The greatest area of productivity, however, was in textiles. Silk weaving based on new techniques became a national industry. The silks depicted birds, animals, and flowers in a brilliant mass of color with silver and gold threads. Above all, carpet weaving flourished, stimulated by the great demand for Persian carpets in the West.

The long tradition of Persian painting continued in the Safavid era but changed from paintings to line drawings and from landscape scenes to portraits, mostly of young ladies, boys, lovers, or dervishes. Although some Persian artists studied in Rome, Safavid art was little influenced by the West. Riza-i-Abassi, the most famous artist of this period, created exquisite works on simple naturalistic subjects, such as an ox plowing, hunters, or lovers. Soft colors, delicacy, and flowing movement were the dominant characteristics of the painting of this era.

THE GRANDEUR OF THE MUGHALS

In retrospect, the period from the sixteenth to the eighteenth centuries can be viewed as a high point of traditional culture in India. The era began with the creation of one of the subcontinent's greatest empires—that of the Mughals. For the first time since the Mauryan dynasty, the entire subcontinent was united under a single government, with a common culture that inspired admiration and envy throughout the entire region.

The Mughal Empire reached its peak in the sixteenth century under the famed Emperor Akbar and maintained its vitality under a series of strong rulers for another century (see Map 15.3). Then the dynasty began to weaken, a process that was hastened by the increasingly insistent challenge of the foreigners arriving by sea. The Portuguese, who first arrived in 1498, were little more than an irritant. Two centuries later, however, Europeans began to seize control of regional trade routes and to meddle in the internal politics of the subcontinent. By the end of the eighteenth century, nothing remained of the empire but a shell. But some historians see the seeds of decay less in the challenge from abroad than in internal weakness—in the very nature of the dynasty itself, which was always more a heterogeneous collection of semiautonomous political forces than a centralized empire in the style of neighboring China.

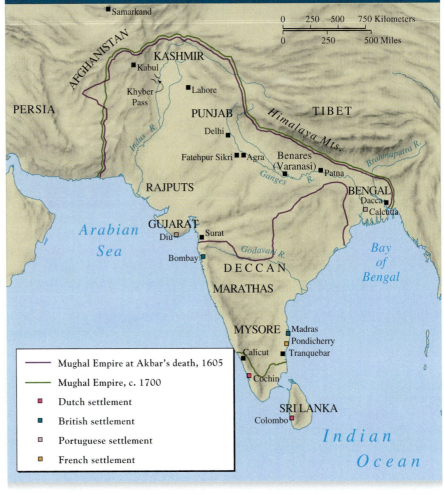

MAP 15.3 The Mughal Empire. This map indicates the expansion of the Mughal Empire from the death of Akbar in 1605 to the rule of Aurangzeb at the end of the seventeenth century. ➤ *In which cities on the map were European settlements located?*

Legend:
- Mughal Empire at Akbar's death, 1605
- Mughal Empire, c. 1700
- Dutch settlement
- British settlement
- Portuguese settlement
- French settlement

The Mughal Dynasty: A "Gunpowder Empire"?

When the Portuguese fleet led by Vasco da Gama arrived at the port of Calicut in the spring of 1498, the Indian subcontinent was still divided into a number of Hindu and Muslim kingdoms. But it was on the verge of a new era of unity that would be brought about by a foreign dynasty called the Mughals. Like so many recent rulers of northern India, the founders of the Mughal Empire were not natives of India but came from the mountainous region north of the Ganges River. The founder of the dynasty, known to history as Babur (1483–1530), had an illustrious pedigree. His father was descended from the great Asian conqueror Tamerlane, his mother from the Mongol conqueror Genghis Khan.

Babur had inherited a fragment of Tamerlane's empire in an upland valley of the Syr Darya River. Driven south by the rising power of the Uzbeks and then the Safavid dynasty in Persia, Babur and his warriors seized Kabul in 1504 and, thirteen years later, crossed the Khyber Pass to India.

Following a pattern that we have seen before, Babur began his rise to power by offering to help an ailing dynasty against its opponents. Although his own forces were far smaller than those of his adversaries, he possessed advanced weapons, including artillery, and used them to great effect. His use of mobile cavalry was particularly successful against the massed forces, supplemented by mounted elephants, of his enemy. In 1526, with only twelve thousand troops against an enemy force nearly ten times that size, Babur captured Delhi and established his power in the plains of northern India (see the box on p. 329). Over the next several years, he continued his conquests in northern India, until his early death in 1530 at the age of forty-seven.

Babur's success was due in part to his vigor and his charismatic personality, which earned him the undying loyalty of his followers. His son and successor Humayun (1530–1556) was, in the words of one British historian, "intelligent but lazy." In 1540, he was forced to flee to Persia, where he lived in exile for sixteen years. Finally, with the aid of the Safavid shah of Persia, he returned to India and reconquered Delhi in 1555 but died the following year in a household accident, reportedly from injuries suffered in a fall after smoking a pipeful of opium.

Humayun was succeeded by his son Akbar (1556–1605). Born while his father was living in exile, Akbar was only fourteen when he mounted the throne. Illiterate but highly intelligent and industrious, Akbar set out to extend his domain, then limited to Punjab and the upper Ganges River valley. "A monarch," he remarked, "should be ever intent on conquest, otherwise his neighbors rise in arms against him. The army should be exercised in warfare, lest from want of training they become self-indulgent."[1] By the end of his life, he had brought Mughal rule to most of the subcontinent, from the Himalaya Mountains to the Godavari River in central India and from Kashmir to the mouths of the Brahmaputra and the Ganges. In so doing, Akbar had created the greatest Indian empire since the Mauryan dynasty nearly two thousand years earlier. It was an empire that appeared highly centralized from the outside but was actually a collection of semiautonomous principalities ruled by provincial elites and linked together by the overarching majesty of the Mughal emperor.

Akbar and Indo-Muslim Civilization

Although Akbar was probably the greatest of the conquering Mughal monarchs, like his famous predecessor Asoka, he is best known for the humane character of his rule. Above all, he accepted the diversity of Indian society and took steps to reconcile his Muslim and Hindu subjects.

Though raised an orthodox Muslim, Akbar had been exposed to other beliefs during his childhood and had little patience with the pedantic views of Muslim scholars at court. As emperor, he displayed a keen interest in other religions, not only tolerating Hindu practices in his own domains but also welcoming the expression of Christian views by his Jesuit advisers. Akbar put his policy of religious tolerance into practice by taking a Hindu princess as one of his wives, and the success of this marriage may well have had an effect on his religious convictions. He patronized classical Indian arts and architecture and abolished many of the restrictions faced by Hindus in a Muslim-dominated society.

During his later years, Akbar became steadily more hostile to Islam. To the dismay of many Muslims at court, he sponsored a new form of worship called the Divine Faith (Din-i-Ilahi), which combined characteristics of several religions with a central belief in the infallibility of all decisions reached by the emperor. The new faith aroused deep hostility in Muslim circles and rapidly vanished after his death.

Akbar also extended his innovations to the empire's administration. Although the upper ranks of the government continued to be dominated by nonnative Muslims, a substantial proportion of lower-ranking officials were Hindus, and a few Hindus were appointed to positions of importance. At first, most officials were paid salaries, but later they were ordinarily assigned sections of agricultural land for their temporary use; they kept a portion of the taxes paid by the local peasants in lieu of a salary. These local officials, known as zamindars, were expected to forward the rest of the taxes from the lands under their control to the central government.

The same tolerance that marked Akbar's attitude toward religion and administration extended to the Mughal legal system. While Muslims were subject to the Islamic codes (the Shari'a), Hindu law applied to areas settled by Hindus, who after 1579 were no longer required to pay the hated jizya, or poll tax on non-Muslims. Punishments for crime were relatively mild, at least by the standards of the day, and justice was administered in a relatively impartial and efficient manner.

Overall, Akbar's reign was a time of peace and prosperity. Although all Indian peasants were required to pay about one-third of their annual harvest to the state through the zamindars, the system was applied fairly, and when drought struck in the 1590s, the taxes were reduced or even suspended altogether. Thanks to a long period of relative peace and political stability, commerce and manufacturing flourished. Foreign trade, in particular, thrived as Indian goods, notably textiles, tropical food products, spices, and precious stones, were exported in exchange for gold and silver. Tariffs on imports were low. Much of the foreign commerce was handled by Arab traders, since the Indians, like their Mughal rulers, did not care for travel by sea. Internal trade, however, was dominated by large merchant castes, who also were active in banking and handicrafts.

Twilight of the Mughals

Akbar died in 1605 and was succeeded by his son Jahangir (1605–1628). During the early years of his reign, Jahangir continued to strengthen central control over the vast empire. Eventually, however, his grip began to weaken (according to his memoirs, he "only wanted a bottle of wine and a piece of meat to make merry"), and the court fell under the influence of one of his wives, the Persian-born Nur Jahan (see the box on p. 332). The empress took advantage of her position to enrich her own family and arranged for her niece Mumtaz Mahal to marry her husband's third son and ultimate successor, Shah Jahan. When Shah Jahan succeeded to the throne in 1628, he quickly demonstrated the single-minded quality of his grandfather (albeit in a much more brutal manner), ordering the assassination of all of his rivals in order to secure his position.

THE POWER BEHIND THE THRONE

*D*uring his reign as Mughal emperor, Jahangir (1605–1628) was addicted to alcohol and opium. Because of his weakened condition, his Persian wife Nur Jahan began to rule on his behalf. She also groomed his young son Khurram to rule as the future emperor Shah Jahan and arranged for him to marry her own niece Mumtaz Mahal, thereby cementing her influence over two successive Mughal rulers. During this period, Nur Jahan was the de facto ruler of India, exerting her influence in both internal and foreign affairs during an era of peace and prosperity. Although the extent of her influence was often criticized at court, her performance impressed many European observers, as these remarks by two English visitors attest.

NUR JAHAN, EMPRESS OF MUGHAL INDIA

If anyone with a request to make at Court obtains an audience or is allowed to speak, the King hears him indeed, but will give no definite answer of Yes or No, referring him promptly to Asaf Khan, who in the same way will dispose of no important matter without communicating with his sister, the Queen, and who regulates his attitude in such a way that the authority of neither of them may be diminished. Anyone then who obtains a favour must thank them for it, and not the King. . . .

Her abilities were uncommon; for she rendered herself absolute, in a government in which women are thought incapable of bearing any part. Their power, it is true, is sometimes exerted in the haram; but, like the virtues of the magnet, it is silent and unperceived. Nur Jahan stood forth in public; she broke through all restraint and custom, and acquired power by her own address, more than by the weakness of Jahangir. . . .

Her former and present supporters have been well rewarded, so that now most of the men who are near the King owe their promotion to her, and are consequently under . . . obligations to her. . . . Many misunderstandings result, for the King's orders or grants of appointments, etc., are not certainties, being of no value until they have been approved by the Queen.

During a reign of three decades, Shah Jahan maintained the system established by his predecessors while expanding the boundaries of the empire by successful campaigns in the Deccan Plateau and against Samarkand, north of the Hindu Kush. But Shah Jahan's rule was marred by his failure to deal with the growing domestic problems. He had inherited a nearly empty treasury because of Empress Nur Jahan's penchant for luxury and ambitious charity projects. Though the majority of his subjects lived in grinding poverty, Shah Jahan's frequent military campaigns and expensive building projects put a heavy strain on the imperial finances and compelled him to raise taxes. At the same time, the government did little to improve rural conditions. In a country where transport was primitive (it often took three months to travel the 600 miles between Patna, in the middle of the Ganges River valley, and Delhi) and drought conditions frequent, the dynasty made few efforts to increase agricultural efficiency or to improve the roads or the irrigation network. A Dutch merchant in Gujarat described conditions during a famine in the mid-seventeenth century:

As the famine increased, men abandoned towns and villages and wandered helplessly. It was easy to recognize their condition: eyes sunk deep in head, lips pale and covered with slime, the skin hard, with the bones showing through, the belly nothing but a pouch hanging down empty, knuckles and kneecaps showing prominently. One would cry and howl for hunger, while another lay stretched on the ground dying in misery; wherever you went, you saw nothing but corpses.[2]

In 1648, Shah Jahan moved his capital from Agra to Delhi and built the famous Red Fort in his new capital city. But he is best known for the Taj Mahal in Agra, widely considered to be the most beautiful building in India, if not in the entire world. The story is a romantic one—that the Taj was built by the emperor in memory of his wife Mumtaz Mahal, who had died giving birth to her thirteenth child at the age of thirty-nine. But the story has a less attractive side: the expense of the building, which employed twenty thousand masons over twenty years, forced the government to raise agricultural taxes, further impoverishing many Indian peasants.

Succession struggles returned to haunt the dynasty in the mid-1650s when Shah Jahan's illness led to a struggle for power between his sons Dara Shikoh and Aurangzeb. Dara Shikoh was described by his contemporaries as progressive and humane, but he apparently lacked political acumen and was outmaneuvered by Aurangzeb (1658–1707), who had Dara Shikoh put to death and then imprisoned his father in the fort at Agra.

Aurangzeb is one of the most controversial individuals in the history of India. A man of high principle, he attempted to eliminate many of what he considered to be India's social evils, prohibiting the immolation of widows on their husband's funeral pyre (*sati*), the castration of eunuchs, and the exaction of illegal taxes. With less success, he tried to forbid gambling, drinking, and prostitution. But Aurangzeb, a devout and somewhat doctrinaire Muslim, also adopted a number of measures that reversed the policies of religious tolerance established by his predecessors. The building of new Hindu temples was prohibited, and the Hindu poll tax was restored. Forced conversions to Islam were resumed, and non-Muslims were driven from the court. Aurangzeb's heavy-handed religious policies led to considerable domestic unrest and to a revival of Hindu fervor during the last years of his reign. A number of revolts also broke out against imperial authority.

During the eighteenth century, Mughal power was threatened from both within and without. Fueled by the growing power and autonomy of the local gentry and merchants, rebellious groups in provinces throughout the empire, from the Deccan to the Punjab, began to reassert local authority and reduce the power of the Mughal emperor to that of a "tinsel sovereign." Increasingly divided, India was vulnerable to attack from abroad. In 1739, Delhi was sacked by the Persians, who left it in ashes.

A number of obvious reasons for the virtual collapse of the Mughal Empire can be identified, including the draining of the imperial treasury and the decline in competence of the Mughal rulers. But it should also be noted that even at its height under Akbar, the empire was a loosely knit collection of heterogeneous principalities held together by the authority of the throne, which tried to combine Persian concepts of kingship with the Indian tradition of decentralized power. Decline set in when centrifugal forces gradually began to predominate over centripetal ones.

The Impact of Western Power in India

As we have seen, the first Europeans to arrive were the Portuguese. Although they established a virtual monopoly over regional trade in the Indian Ocean, they did not aggressively seek to penetrate the interior of the subcontinent. The situation changed at the end of the sixteenth century, when the English and the Dutch entered the scene. Soon both powers were in active competition with Portugal, and with each other, for trading privileges in the region.

Penetration of the new market was not easy. When the first English fleet arrived at Surat, a thriving port on the northwestern coast of India, in 1608, their request for trading privileges was rejected by Emperor Jahangir. Needing lightweight Indian cloth to trade for spices in the East Indies, the English persisted, and in 1616, they were finally permitted to install their own ambassador at the imperial court in Agra. Three years later, the first English factory was established at Surat.

During the next several decades, the English presence in India steadily increased while Mughal power gradually waned. By midcentury, additional English factories had been established at Fort William (now the great city of Calcutta) on the Hoogly River near the Bay of Bengal and at Madras on the southeastern coast. From there, English ships carried Indian-made cotton goods to the East Indies, where they were bartered for spices, which were shipped back to England.

English success in India attracted rivals, including the Dutch and the French. The Dutch abandoned their interests to concentrate on the spice trade in the middle of the seventeenth century, but the French were more persistent

Chronology

THE MUGHAL ERA

Arrival of Vasco da Gama at Calicut	1498
Babur seizes Delhi	1526
Death of Babur	1530
Humayun recovers throne in Delhi	1555
Death of Humayun and accession of Akbar	1556
Death of Akbar and accession of Jahangir	1605
Arrival of English at Surat	1608
Reign of Emperor Shah Jahan	1628–1657
Foundation of English fort at Madras	1639
Aurangzeb succeeds to the throne	1658
Bombay ceded to England	1661
Death of Aurangzeb	1707
French capture Madras	1746
Battle of Plassey	1757

and established factories of their own. For a brief period, under the ambitious empire builder Joseph François Dupleix, the French competed successfully with the British. But the military genius of Sir Robert Clive, an aggressive British administrator and empire builder who eventually became the chief representative of the East India Company in the subcontinent, and the refusal of the French government to provide financial support for Dupleix's efforts eventually left the French with only their fort at Pondicherry and a handful of small territories on the southeastern coast.

In the meantime, Clive began to consolidate British control in Bengal, where the local ruler had attacked Fort William and imprisoned the local British population in the infamous Black Hole of Calcutta (an underground prison for holding the prisoners, many of whom died in captivity). In 1757, a small British force numbering about three thousand defeated a Mughal-led army over ten times that size in the Battle of Plassey. As part of the spoils of victory, the British East India Company exacted from the now-decrepit Mughal court the authority to collect taxes from extensive lands in the area surrounding Calcutta. Less than ten years later, British forces seized the reigning Mughal emperor in a skirmish at Buxar, and the British began to consolidate their economic and administrative control over Indian territory through the surrogate power of the now powerless Mughal court (see Map 15.4).

To officials of the East India Company, the expansion of their authority into the interior of the subcontinent

MAP 15.4 India in 1805. By the early eighteenth century, virtually all of the Indian subcontinent had fallen under British domination. The extent of British territory, with prominent cities and major geographical terms indicated, is shown here. ➤ *Where was the capital of the Mughal Empire?*

Kabul

KASHMIR

SIKHS

Lahore

Indus R.

Delhi

Himalaya Mts.

NEPAL

Benares ✕ Buxar
(Varanasi)

RAJPUTS

Jaipur

Ganges R.

SIND

BENGAL

MARATHAS

Surat

Plassey ✕

Calcutta

*Arabian
Sea*

ORISSA

Bombay (Br.)

*Bay of
Bengal*

GOA

CARNATIC

Madras

Pondicherry (Fr.)

*Indian

Ocean*

| | British territory |
| ✕ | Battle sites |

SRI LANKA

0   250   500   750 Kilometers
0   250   500 Miles

probably seemed like a simple commercial decision, a move designed to seek guaranteed revenues to pay for the increasingly expensive military operations in India. To historians, it marks a major step in the gradual transfer of all of the Indian subcontinent to the British East India Company and later, in 1858, to the British crown. The process was more haphazard than deliberate.

The company's takeover of vast landholdings, notably in the eastern Indian states of Orissa and Bengal, may have been a windfall for enterprising British officials, but it was a disaster for the Indian economy. In the first place, it resulted in the transfer of capital from the local Indian aristocracy to company officials, most of whom sent their profits back to Britain. Second, it hastened the destruction of once healthy local industries because British goods such as machine-made textiles were imported duty-free into India to compete against local products. Finally,

British expansion hurt the peasants. As the British took over the administration of the land tax, they also applied British law, which allowed the lands of those unable to pay the tax to be confiscated. In the 1770s, a series of massive famines led to the death of an estimated one-third of the population in the areas under company administration. The British government attempted to resolve the problem by assigning tax lands to the local revenue collectors (*zamindars*) in the hope of transforming them into English-style rural gentry, but many collectors themselves fell into bankruptcy and sold their lands to absentee bankers while the now landless peasants remained in abject poverty. It was hardly an auspicious beginning to "civilized" British rule.

As a result of such problems, Britain's rise to power in India did not go unchallenged. Astute Indian commanders avoided pitched battles with the well-armed British troops but harassed and ambushed them in the manner of guerrillas in our time. Haidar Ali, one of Britain's primary rivals for control in southern India, said:

> You will in time understand my mode of warfare. Shall I risk my cavalry which cost a thousand rupees each horse, against your cannon ball which cost two pice? No! I will march your troops until their legs swell to the size of their bodies. You shall not have a blade of grass, nor a drop of water. I will hear of you every time your drum beats, but you shall not know where I am once a month. I will give your army battle, but it must be when I please, and not when you choose.[3]

Unfortunately for India, not all its commanders were as astute as Haidar Ali. In the last years of the eighteenth century, the stage was set for the final consolidation of British rule over the subcontinent.

Society and Culture Under the Mughals

The Mughals were the last of the great traditional Indian dynasties. Like so many of their predecessors since the fall of the Guptas nearly a thousand years before, the Mughals were Muslims. But like the Ottoman Turks, the best Mughal rulers did not simply impose Islamic institutions and beliefs on a predominantly Hindu population; they combined Muslim with Hindu and even Persian concepts and cultural values in a unique social and cultural synthesis that still today seems to epitomize the greatness of Indian civilization.

DAILY LIFE

Whether Mughal rule had much effect on the lives of ordinary Indians seems somewhat problematic. The treatment of women is a good example. Women had traditionally played an active role in Mongol tribal society—many actually fought on the battlefield alongside the men—and Babur and his successors often relied on the women in their families for political advice. Women from aristocratic families were often awarded honorific titles, received salaries, and were permitted to own land and engage in business. Women at court sometimes received an education, and aristocratic women often expressed their creative talents by writing poetry, painting, or playing music. Women of all castes were adept at spinning thread, either for their own use or to sell to weavers to augment the family income. Weaving was carried out in home production units by all the members of the subcaste weaving families. They sold simple cloth to local villages and fine cottons, silks, and wool to the Mughal court. By Akbar's rule, in fact, the textile manufacturing was of such high quality and so well established that India sold cloth to much of the world: Arabia, the coast of East Africa, Egypt, Southeast Asia, and Europe.

To a certain degree, these Mughal attitudes toward women may have had an impact on Indian society. Women were allowed to inherit land, and some even possessed *zamindar* rights. Women from mercantile castes sometimes took an active role in business activities. At the same time, however, as Muslims, the Mughals subjected women to certain restrictions under Islamic law. On the whole, these Mughal practices coincided with and even accentuated existing tendencies in Indian society. The Muslim practice of isolating women and preventing them from associating with men outside the home (*purdah*) was adopted by many upper-class Hindus as a means of enhancing their status or protecting their women from unwelcome advances by Muslims in positions of authority. In other ways, Hindu practices were unaffected. The custom of *sati* continued to be practiced despite efforts by the Mughals to abolish it, and child marriage (most women were betrothed before the age of ten) remained common. Women were still instructed to obey their husbands without question and to remain chaste.

For their part, Hindus sometimes attempted to defend themselves and their religious practices against the efforts of some Mughal monarchs to impose the Islamic religion and Islamic mores on the indigenous population. In some cases, despite official prohibitions, Hindu men forcibly married Muslim women and then converted them to the native faith, while converts to Islam normally lost all of their inheritance rights within the Indian family. Government orders to destroy Hindu temples were often ignored by local officials, sometimes as the result of bribery or intimidation. Sometimes Indian practices had an influence on the Mughal elites, as many Mughal chieftains married Indian women and adopted Indian forms of dress.

Long-term stability led to increasing commercialization and the spread of wealth to new groups within Indian society. The Mughal era saw the emergence of an affluent landed gentry and a prosperous merchant class. Members of prestigious castes from the pre-Mughal period reaped many of the benefits of the increasing wealth, but some of these changes transcended caste boundaries and led to the emergence of new groups who achieved status and wealth on the basis of economic achievement rather than traditional kinship ties. During the late eighteenth century, this economic prosperity was shaken by the decline of the Mughal Empire and the increasing European presence. But many prominent Indians reacted by establishing commercial relationships with the foreigners.

MUGHAL CULTURE

The era of the Mughals was one of synthesis in culture as well as in politics and religion. The Mughals combined Islamic themes with Persian and indigenous motifs to produce a unique style that enriched and embellished Indian art and culture. The Mughal emperors were zealous patrons of the arts and enticed painters, poets, and artisans from as far away as the Mediterranean. Apparently, the generosity of the Mughals made it difficult to refuse a trip to India. It was said that they would reward a poet with his weight in gold.

Undoubtedly, the Mughals' most visible achievement was in architecture. Here they integrated Persian and Indian styles in a new and sometimes breathtakingly beautiful form best symbolized by the Taj Mahal, built by the emperor Shah Jahan in the mid-seventeenth century. Although the human and economic cost of the Taj tarnishes the romantic legend of its construction, there is no denying the beauty of the building. It had evolved from a style that originated several decades earlier with the tomb of Humayun.

Humayun's mausoleum had combined Persian and Islamic motifs in a square building finished in red sandstone and topped with a dome. The Taj brought the style to perfection. Working with a model created by his Persian architect, Shah Jahan raised the dome and replaced the red sandstone with brilliant white marble. The entire exterior and interior surface is decorated with cut-stone geometrical patterns, delicate black stone tracery, or intricate inlay of colored precious stones in floral and Koranic arabesques. The technique of creating dazzling floral mosaics of lapis lazuli, malachite, carnelian, turquoise, and mother of pearl may have been introduced by Italian artists at the Mughal court. Shah Jahan spent his last years imprisoned in a room in the Red Fort at Agra; from his windows, he could see the beautiful memorial to his beloved wife.

The Taj was by no means the only magnificent building erected during the Mughal era. Akbar, who, in the words of a contemporary, "[dressed] the work of his mind and heart in the garment of stone and clay," was the first of the great Mughal builders. His first palace at Agra, the Red Fort, was begun in 1565. A few years later, he ordered the construction of a new palace at Fatehpur Sikri, 26 miles west of Agra. The new palace was built in honor of a Sufi mystic who had correctly forecast the birth of a son to the emperor. In gratitude, Akbar decided to build a new capital city and palace on the site of the mystic's home in the village of Sikri. Over a period of fifteen years, from 1571 to 1586, a magnificent new city in red sandstone was constructed.

The Taj Mahal and the Vierzehnheiligen

Raised on a marble platform above the Jumma River, the Taj (shown below) is dramatically framed by contrasting twin red sandstone mosques, magnificent gardens, and a long reflecting pool that mirrors and magnifies its beauty. The effect is one of monumental size, near-blinding brilliance, and delicate lightness, a startling contrast to the heavier and more masculine Baroque style then popular in Europe. This is evident in the Vierzehnheiligen (Fourteen Saints), located in southern Germany and designed by Balthasar Neumann in the Baroque-Rococo style of eighteenth-century Europe. Although as monumental in size as the Taj Mahal, the Vierzehnheiligen possesses a sense of heaviness that differs considerably from the lightness of the Indian architectural masterpiece.

Courtesy Carol C. Coffin

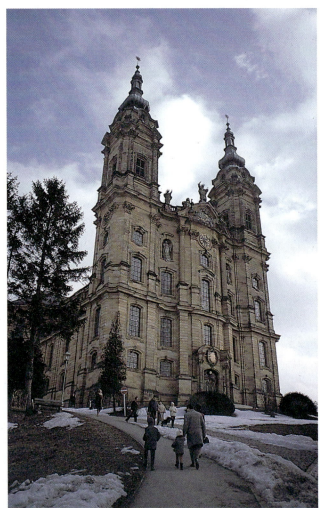

Courtesy of James R. Spencer

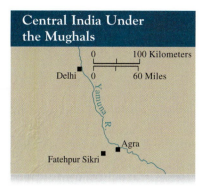

Although the city was abandoned before completion and now stands almost untouched, it is a popular destination for tourists and pilgrims.

The other major artistic achievement of the Mughal period was painting. As in so many other areas of endeavor, painting in Mughal India resulted from the blending of two cultures. While living in exile, Emperor Humayun had learned to admire Persian miniatures. On his return to India in 1555, he invited two Persian masters to live in his palace and introduce the technique to his adopted land. His successor, Akbar, appreciated the new style and popularized it with his patronage. He established a state workshop at Fatehpur Sikri for two hundred artists, mostly Hindus, who worked under the guidance of the Persian masters to create the Mughal school of painting.

The "Akbar style" combined Persian with Indian motifs, such as the use of extended space and the portrayal of physical human action, characteristics not usually seen in Persian art. Akbar also apparently encouraged the imitation of European art forms, including the portrayal of Christian subjects, the use of perspective, lifelike portraits, and the shading of colors in the Renaissance style. The depiction of the human figure in Mughal painting outraged orthodox Muslims at court, but Akbar argued that the painter, "in sketching anything that has life . . . must come to feel that he cannot bestow individuality upon his work, and is thus forced to think of God, the Giver of Life, and will thus increase in knowledge."[4]

The development of Indian literature was held back by the absence of printing, which was not introduced until the end of the Mughal era. Literary works were inscribed by calligraphers, and one historian has estimated that the library of Agra contained more than 24,000 volumes. Poetry, in particular, flourished under the Mughals, who established poet laureates at court. Poems were written in the Persian style and in the Persian language. In fact, Persian became the official language of the court until the sack of Delhi in 1739.

Another aspect of the long Mughal reign was a Hindu revival of devotional literature, much of it dedicated to Krishna and Rama. The retelling of the Ramayana in the vernacular culminated in the sixteenth-century Hindi version by the great poet Tulsidas (1532–1623). His *Ramcaritmanas* presents the devotional story with a deified Rama and Sita. Tulsidas's genius was in combining the conflicting cults of Vishnu and Siva into a unified and overwhelming love for the divine, which he expressed in some of the most moving of all Indian poetry. The *Ramcaritmanas* has eclipsed its two-thousand-year-old Sanskrit ancestor in popularity and even became the basis of an Indian television series in the late 1980s.

CONCLUSION

The three empires that we have discussed in this chapter exhibit a number of striking similarities. First of all, they were Muslim in their religious affiliation, although the Safavids were Shi'ite rather than Sunni, a distinction that often led to mutual tensions and conflict. More important, perhaps, they were all of nomadic origin, and the political and social institutions that they adopted carried the imprint of their preimperial past. Once they

THE PALACE OF THE WINDS AT JAIPUR. Built by the maharaja of Jaipur in 1799, this imposing building, part of a palace complex, is today actually only a facade. Behind the intricate pink sandstone window screens, the women of the palace were able to observe city life while at the same time remaining invisible to prying eyes. The palace, like most of the buildings in the city of Jaipur, was constructed of sandstone, a product of the nearby desert of Rajasthan.

achieved imperial power, however, all three ruling dynasties displayed an impressive capacity to administer a large empire and brought a degree of stability to peoples who had all too often lived in conditions of internal division and war.

Another similarity is that the mastery of the techniques of modern warfare, including the use of firearms, played a central role in all three empires' ability to overcome their rivals and rise to regional hegemony. Some scholars have therefore labeled them "gunpowder empires" in the belief that technical prowess in the art of warfare was a key element in their success. Although that is undoubtedly true, we should not forget that other factors, such as dynamic leadership, political acumen, and the possession of an ardent following motivated by religious zeal, were equally if not more important in their drive to power and ability to retain it. Weapons by themselves do not an empire make.

The rise of these powerful Muslim states coincided with the opening period of European expansion at the end of the fifteenth century and the beginning of the sixteenth. The military and political talents of these empires helped protect much of the Muslim world from the resurgent forces of Christianity. To the contrary, the Ottoman Turks carried their empire into the heart of Christian Europe and briefly reached the gates of the great city of Vienna. By the end of the eighteenth century, however, the Safavid dynasty had imploded, and the powerful Mughal Empire was in a state of virtual collapse. Only the Ottoman Empire was still functioning. Yet it too had lost much of its early expansionistic vigor and was showing signs of internal decay.

The reasons for the decline of these empires have inspired considerable debate among historians. One factor was undoubtedly the expansion of European power into the Indian Ocean and the Middle East. But internal causes were probably more important in the long run. All three empires experienced growing factionalism within the ruling elite, incompetence within the palace, and the emergence of divisive forces in the empire at large—factors that have marked the passing of traditional empires since early times. Paradoxically, one of the greatest strengths of these empires—their mastery of gunpowder—may have simultaneously been a serious weakness in that it allowed them to develop a complacent sense of security. With little incentive to turn their attention to new developments in science and technology, they were increasingly vulnerable to attack by the advanced nations of the West. The weakening of the gunpowder empires created a political vacuum into which the dynamic and competitive forces of European capitalism were quick to enter.

The gunpowder empires, however, were not the only states in the Old World that were able to resist the first outward thrust of European expansion. Farther to the east, the mature civilizations in China and Japan successfully faced a similar challenge from Western merchants and missionaries. Unlike their counterparts in South Asia and the Middle East, as the nineteenth century dawned, they continued to thrive.

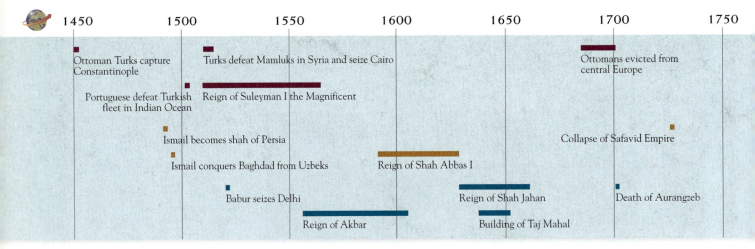

Timeline (1450–1750):

- Ottoman Turks capture Constantinople (c. 1453)
- Portuguese defeat Turkish fleet in Indian Ocean (c. 1500)
- Ismail becomes shah of Persia (c. 1500)
- Ismail conquers Baghdad from Uzbeks (c. 1510)
- Turks defeat Mamluks in Syria and seize Cairo (c. 1517)
- Reign of Suleyman I the Magnificent (c. 1520–1566)
- Babur seizes Delhi (c. 1526)
- Reign of Akbar (c. 1556–1605)
- Reign of Shah Abbas I (c. 1588–1629)
- Reign of Shah Jahan (c. 1628–1658)
- Building of Taj Mahal (c. 1632–1653)
- Ottomans evicted from central Europe (c. 1699)
- Death of Aurangzeb (c. 1707)
- Collapse of Safavid Empire (c. 1722)

CHAPTER NOTES

1. Vincent A. Smith, *The Oxford History of India* (Oxford, 1967), p. 341.
2. Quoted in Michael Edwardes, *A History of India: From the Earliest Times to the Present Day* (London, 1961), p. 188.
3. Quoted in Edwardes, *History of India*, p. 220.
4. Quoted in Roy C. Craven, *Indian Art: A Concise History* (New York, 1976), p. 205.

SUGGESTED READING

The most complete general survey of the Ottoman Empire is S. J. Shaw, *History of the Ottoman Empire and Modern Turkey* (Cambridge, 1976). Shaw is difficult reading but informative on administrative matters. A more readable albeit less definitive account is Lord Kinross, *The Ottoman Centuries: The Rise and Fall of the Ottoman Empire* (New York, 1977), which is larded with human-interest stories. Also of interest is B. Lewis, *Istanbul and the Civilization of the Ottoman Empire* (Norman, Okla., 1963), written by a veteran Arabist.

For a dramatic account of the conquest of Constantinople in 1453, see S. Runciman, *The Fall of Constantinople, 1453* (Cambridge, 1965). The life of Mehmet II is chronicled in F. Babinger, *Mehmed the Conqueror and His Time*, trans. R. Manheim (Princeton, N.J., 1979). On Suleyman the Magnificent, see R. Merriman, *Suleiman the Magnificent, 1520–1566* (Cambridge, 1944). On the Safavids, see R. M. Savory, *Iran Under the Safavids* (Cambridge, 1980), and E. B. Monshi, *History of Shah Abbas the Great*, 2 vols. (Boulder, Colo., 1978).

For a concise introduction to Ottoman art, consult D. T. Rice, *Islamic Art* (London, 1975); E. J. Grube, *The World of Islam* (New York, 1967); and J. Bloom and S. Blair, *Islamic Arts* (London, 1997).

For an overview of the Mughal era, see S. Wolpert, *New History of India* (New York, 1989). A more dramatic account for the general reader is W. Hansen, *The Peacock Throne: The Drama of Mogul India* (New York, 1972).

There are a number of specialized works on various aspects of the period. For a treatment of the Mughal era in the context of Islamic rule in India, see S. M. Ikram, *Muslim Civilization in India* (New York, 1964). The concept of "gunpowder empires" is persuasively analyzed in D. E. Streusand, *The Formation of the Mughal Empire* (Delhi, 1989). Economic issues predominate in much recent scholarship. For example, S. Subrahmanyan, *The Political Economy of Commerce: Southern India, 1500–1650* (Cambridge, 1990), focuses on the inter-action between internal and external trade in southern India during the early stages of the period. The Mughal Empire is analyzed in a broad Central Asian context in R. C. Foltz, *Mughal India and Central Asia* (Karachi, 1998). Finally, K. N. Chaudhuri, *Trade and Civilization in the Indian Ocean: An Economic History from the Rise of Islam to 1750* (Cambridge, 1985), views Indian commerce in the perspective of the regional trade network throughout the Indian Ocean.

Personal accounts of the period are numerous, although most are by European visitors. For some examples, see R. C. Temple, ed., *The Travels of Peter Mundy, in Europe and Asia, 1608–1667* (Cambridge, 1907–1936); J. B. Tavernier, *Travels in India* (London, 1925); T. Roe, *The Embassy of Sir Thomas Roe, 1615–1619* (London, 1926); and F. Bernier, *Travels in the Mogul Empire, 1656–1668* (London, 1968). For an inside look, see J. Leyden and W. Erskine, trans., *Memoirs of Zehir-ed-Din Muhammad Babur* (London, 1921).

Standard works on Mughal art and culture include A. L. Basham, *A Cultural History of India* (Oxford, 1975); R. C. Craven, *Indian Art: A Concise History* (New York, 1976); and M. C. Beach, *The Imperial Image* (Washington, D.C., 1981).

For treatments of all three Muslim empires in a comparative context, see J. J. Kissling et al., *The Last Great Muslim Empires* (Princeton, N.J., 1996), and M. G. S. Hodgson, *Rethinking World History: Essays on Europe, Islam, and World History* (Cambridge, 1993).

For an introduction to the women of the Ottoman Empire and those of the Mughal Empire, see S. Hughes and B. Hughes, *Women in World History*, vol. 2 (Armonk, N.Y., 1997). For a more detailed presentation of women in the imperial harem, consult L. P. Peirce, *The Imperial Harem: Women and Sovereignty in the Ottoman Empire* (Oxford, 1993). The fascinating story of the royal woman who played an important role behind the scenes is found in E. B. Findly, *Nur Jahan: Empress of Mughal India* (Oxford, 1993).

INFOTRAC COLLEGE EDITION

Visit the source collections at **infotrac.thomsonlearning.com** and use the Search function with the following key terms.

Islam	Ottoman Empire
Mughal	Safavid

WORLD HISTORY RESOURCES

Visit the *Essential World History* Companion Web Site for resources specific to this textbook:

http://history.wadsworth.com/duikeressentials02/

The CD in the back of this book and the World History Resource Center at **http://history.wadsworth.com/world/** offer a variety of tools to help you succeed in this course, including access to quizzes; images; documents; interactive simulations, maps, and timelines; movie explorations; and a wealth of other sources.

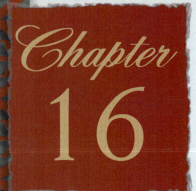

Courtesy of William J. Duiker

THE EAST ASIAN WORLD

FOCUS QUESTIONS

- Why were the Manchus so successful at establishing a foreign dynasty in China, and what were the main characteristics of their rule?
- How did China and Japan respond to the coming of the Europeans, and what impact did the Europeans have on these East Asian civilizations in the sixteenth through eighteenth centuries?
- How did the unification of Japan come about, and how did the Tokugawa rulers maintain that unity?
- How did the economy and society of Japan change during the Tokugawa era, and how did Japanese culture reflect those changes?
- ➤ How did the economy and society of China change during the Ming and Qing eras, and to what degree did these changes seem to be leading toward an industrial revolution on the Western model?

In December 1717, the emperor Kangxi returned from a hunting trip north of the Great Wall and began to suffer from dizzy spells. Conscious of his approaching date with mortality—he was now nearly seventy years of age—the emperor called together his sons and leading government officials in the imperial palace and issued the following edict:

> The rulers of the past all took reverence for Heaven's laws and reverence for their ancestors as the fundamental way in ruling the country. To be sincere in reverence for Heaven and ancestors entails the following: Be kind to men from afar and keep the able ones near, nourish the people, think of the profit of all as being the real profit and the mind of the whole country as being the real mind, be considerate to officials and act as the father to the people, protect the state before danger comes and govern well before there is any disturbance, be always diligent and always careful, and maintain the balance between leniency and strictness, between principle and expediency, so that long-range plans can be made for the country: That's all there is to it.[1]

As a primer for political leadership, the emperor's edict reflects the genius of Confucian philosophy at its best and has a timeless quality that applies to our age as well as to the golden age of the Qing dynasty.

Kangxi reigned during one of the most glorious eras in the long history of China. Under the Ming (1369–1644) and the early Qing (1644–1911) dynasties, the empire expanded its borders to a degree not seen since the Han and the Tang. Chinese culture was the envy of its neighbors and earned the admiration of many European visitors, including Jesuit priests and Enlightenment philosophers.

On the surface, China appeared to be an unchanging society patterned after the Confucian vision of a "golden age" in the remote past. Although few observers could have been aware of it at the time, however, China was changing—and rather rapidly.

A similar process was under way in neighboring Japan. A vigorous new shogunate called the Tokugawa rose to power in the early seventeenth century and managed to revitalize the traditional system in a somewhat more centralized form that enabled it to survive for another 250 years. But major structural changes were also taking place in Japanese society.

One of the many factors involved in the quickening pace of change in both countries was contact with the West, which began with the arrival of Portuguese ships in Chinese and Japanese ports in the first half of the sixteenth century. The Ming and the Tokugawa initially opened their doors to European trade and missionary activity. Later, however, Chinese and Japanese rulers became concerned about the corrosive effects of Western ideas and practices and attempted to protect their traditional societies from external intrusion. •

CHINA AT ITS APEX

In 1514, a Portuguese fleet dropped anchor off the coast of China, just south of the Pearl River estuary and present-day Hong Kong. It was the first direct contact between the Chinese Empire and the West since the arrival of the Venetian adventurer Marco Polo two centuries earlier, and it opened an era that would eventually change the face of China and, indeed, all the world.

From the Ming to the Qing

By the time the Portuguese fleet arrived off the coast of China, the Mongol Empire had long since disappeared. It had gradually weakened after the death of Khubilai Khan and was finally overthrown in 1368 by a massive peasant rebellion under the leadership of Zhu Yuanzhang, who had declared himself the founding emperor of a new Ming (Bright) dynasty and assumed the reign title of Ming Hongwu (Ming Hung Wu, or Ming Martial Emperor). The Ming inaugurated a new era of greatness in Chinese history. Under a series of strong rulers, China extended its rule into Mongolia and Central Asia. The Ming even briefly reconquered Vietnam, which, after a thousand years of Chinese rule, had reclaimed its independence following the collapse of the Tang dynasty in the tenth century. Along the northern frontier, the emperor Yongle (Yung Lo, 1402–1424) strengthened the Great Wall and pacified the nomadic tribespeople who had troubled China in previous centuries. A tributary relationship was established with the Yi dynasty in Korea.

The internal achievements of the Ming were equally impressive. When they replaced the Mongols in the fourteenth century, the Ming turned to traditional Confucian institutions as a means of ruling their vast empire. These included the six ministries at the apex of the bureaucracy, the use of the civil service examinations to select members of the bureaucracy, and the division of the empire into provinces, districts, and counties. As before, Chinese villages were relatively autonomous, and local councils of elders continued to be responsible for adjudicating disputes, initiating local construction and irrigation projects, mustering a militia, and assessing and collecting taxes.

The society that was governed by this vast hierarchy of officials was a far cry from the predominantly agrarian society that had been ruled by the Han. In the burgeoning cities near the coast and along the Yangtze River valley, factories and workshops were vastly increasing the variety and output of their manufactured goods. The population had doubled, and new crops had been introduced, greatly expanding the food output of the empire.

In 1405, in a splendid display of Chinese maritime might, Yongle sent a fleet of Chinese trading ships under the eunuch admiral Zhenghe (Cheng Ho) through the Strait of Malacca and out into the Indian Ocean; there they traveled as far west as the east coast of Africa, stopping on the way at ports in South Asia. The size of the fleet was impressive: it included nearly 28,000 sailors on sixty-two ships, some of them junks larger by far than any other oceangoing vessels the world had yet seen. China seemed about to become a direct participant in the vast trade network that

Courtesy of William J. Duiker

⚜ **THE GREAT WALL OF CHINA.** Although the Great Wall is popularly believed to be over two thousand years old, the part of the wall that is most frequently visited by tourists was a reconstruction undertaken during the early Ming dynasty as a means of protection against invasion from the north. Part of that wall, which was built to protect the imperial capital of Beijing from rampaging nomadic peoples to the north, is shown here.

extended as far west as the Atlantic Ocean, thus culminating the process of opening China to the wider world that had begun with the Tang dynasty.

Why the expeditions were undertaken has been a matter of some debate. Some historians assume that economic profit was the main reason. Others point to Yongle's native curiosity and note that the voyage—and the six others that followed it—returned not only with goods but also with a plethora of information about the outside world as well as with some items unknown in China (the emperor was especially intrigued by the giraffes and placed them in the imperial zoo).

Whatever the case, the voyages resulted in a dramatic increase in Chinese knowledge about the world and the

nature of ocean travel. They also brought massive profits for their sponsors, including individuals connected with Admiral Zhenghe at court. This aroused resentment among conservatives within the bureaucracy, some of whom viewed commercial activities with a characteristic measure of Confucian disdain.

Shortly after Yongle's death, the voyages were discontinued, never to be revived. The decision had long-term consequences and in the eyes of many modern historians marks a turning inward of the Chinese state, away from commerce and toward a more traditional emphasis on agriculture, away from the exotic lands to the south and toward the heartland of the country in the Yellow River valley. The imperial capital was moved from Nanjing, in central China, back to Beijing.

FIRST CONTACTS WITH THE WEST

Despite the Ming's retreat from active participation in the maritime trade, when the Portuguese arrived in 1514, China was in command of a vast empire that stretched from the steppes of Central Asia to the China Sea, from the Gobi Desert to the tropical rain forests of Southeast Asia. From the lofty perspective of the imperial throne in Beijing, the Europeans could only have seemed like an unusually exotic form of barbarian to be placed within the familiar framework of the tributary system, the hierarchical arrangement in which rulers of all other countries were regarded as "younger brothers" of the Son of Heaven. Indeed, the bellicose and uncultured behavior of the Portuguese so outraged Chinese officials that they expelled the Europeans, but after further negotiations, the Portuguese were permitted to occupy the tiny territory of Macao, a foothold they would retain until the end of the twentieth century.

Initially the arrival of the Europeans did not have much impact on Chinese society. Direct trade between Europe and China was limited, and Portuguese ships became involved in the regional trade network, carrying silk to Japan in return for Japanese silver.

More influential than trade, perhaps, were the ideas introduced by Christian missionaries. Among the most active and the most effective were highly educated Jesuits, who were familiar with European philosophical and scientific developments. Recognizing the Chinese pride in their own culture, the Jesuits attempted to draw parallels between Christian and Confucian concepts (for example, they identified the Western concept of God with the Chinese character for Heaven) and to show the similarities between Christian morality and Confucian ethics. European inventions such as the clock, the prism, and various astronomical and musical instruments impressed Chinese officials, hitherto deeply imbued with a sense of the superiority of Chinese civilization, and helped Western ideas win acceptance at court. An elderly Chinese scholar expressed his wonder at the miracle of eyeglasses:

THE ART OF PRINTING

Europeans obtained much of their early information about China from the Jesuits who served at the Ming court in the sixteenth and seventeenth centuries. Clerics such as the Italian Matteo Ricci (1552–1610) found much to admire in Chinese civilization. Here Ricci expresses a keen interest in Chinese printing methods, which at that time were well in advance of the techniques used in the West.

MATTEO RICCI, *THE DIARY OF MATTHEW RICCI*

The art of printing was practiced in China at a date somewhat earlier than that assigned to the beginning of printing in Europe, which was about 1405. It is quite certain that the Chinese knew the art of printing at least five centuries ago, and some of them assert that printing was known to their people before the beginning of the Christian era, about 50 B.C. Their method of printing differs widely from that employed in Europe, and our method would be quite impracticable for them because of the exceedingly large number of Chinese characters and symbols. . . .

Their method of making printed books is quite ingenious. The text is written in ink, with a brush made of very fine hair, on a sheet of paper which is inverted and pasted on a wooden tablet. When the paper has become thoroughly dry, its surface is scraped off quickly and with great skill, until nothing but a fine tissue bearing the characters remains on the wooden tablet. Then, with a steel graver, the workman cuts away the surface following the outlines of the characters until these alone stand out in low relief. From such a block a skilled printer can make copies with incredible speed, turning out as many as fifteen hundred copies in a single day. . . . This scheme of engraving wooden blocks is well adapted for the large and complex nature of the Chinese characters, but I do not think it would lend itself very aptly to our European type, which could hardly be engraved upon wood because of its small dimensions.

Their method of printing has one decided advantage, namely, that once these tablets are made, they can be preserved and used for making changes in the text as often as one wishes. Additions and subtractions can also be made as the tablets can be readily patched. . . . We have derived great benefit from this method of Chinese printing, as we employ the domestic help in our homes to strike off copies of the books on religious and scientific subjects which we translate into Chinese from the languages in which they were written originally. In truth, the whole method is so simple that one is tempted to try it for himself after once having watched the process. The simplicity of Chinese printing is what accounts for the exceedingly large numbers of books in circulation here and the ridiculously low prices at which they are sold.

White glass from across the Western Seas
Is imported through Macao:
Fashioned into lenses big as coins,
They encompass the eyes in a double frame.
I put them on—it suddenly becomes clear;
I can see the very tips of things!
And read fine print by the dim-lit window
Just like in my youth.[2]

For their part, the missionaries were much impressed with many aspects of Chinese civilization, and reports of their experiences heightened European curiosity about this great society on the other side of the world (see the box above).

THE MING BROUGHT TO EARTH

During the late sixteenth century, the Ming began to decline as a series of weak rulers led to an era of corruption, concentration of landownership, and ultimately peasant rebellions and tribal unrest along the northern frontier. The inflow of vast amounts of foreign silver led to an alarming increase in inflation. Then the arrival of the English and the Dutch disrupted the silver trade; silver imports plummeted, severely straining the Chinese economy by raising the value of the metal relative to that of copper.

Crop yields declined due to harsh weather, and the resulting scarcity reduced the ability of the government to provide food in times of imminent starvation. High taxes, provoked in part by increased official corruption, led to peasant unrest and worker violence in urban areas.

As always, internal problems were accompanied by unrest along the northern frontier. Following long precedent, the Ming had attempted to pacify the frontier tribes by forging alliances with them and granting trade privileges. One of the alliances was with the Manchus (also known as the Jurchen), the descendants of peoples who had briefly established a kingdom in northern China during the early thirteenth century. The Manchus, a mixed agricultural and hunting people, lived northeast of the Great Wall in the area known today as Manchuria.

At first, the Manchus were satisfied with consolidating their territory and made little effort to extend their rule south of the Great Wall. But during the first decades of the seventeenth century, a major epidemic devastated the population in many areas of the country. The suffering brought on by the epidemic helped spark a vast peasant revolt led by Li Zicheng (Li Tzu-ch'eng, 1604–1651), a postal worker in central China who had been dismissed from his job as part of a cost-saving measure by the imperial court. In the 1630s, Li managed to extend the revolt throughout the country and finally occupied the capital of Beijing in 1644.

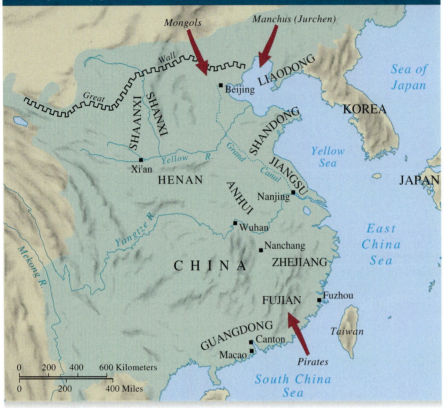

The last Ming emperor committed suicide by hanging himself from a tree in the palace gardens.

But Li was unable to hold his conquest. The overthrow of the Ming dynasty presented a great temptation to the Manchus. With the assistance of many military commanders who had deserted from the Ming, they conquered Beijing on their own (see Map 16.1). Li Zicheng's army disintegrated, and the Manchus declared the creation of a new dynasty with the reign title of the Qing (Ch'ing, or Pure). Once again, China was under foreign rule.

The Greatness of the Qing

The accession of the Manchus to power in Beijing was not universally applauded. Some Ming loyalists fled to Southeast Asia, but others continued their resistance to the new rulers from inside the country. To make it easier to identify the rebels, the government ordered all Chinese to adopt Manchu dress and hairstyles. All Chinese males were to shave their foreheads and braid their hair into a queue; those who refused were to be executed. As a popular saying put it, "Lose your hair or lose your head."[3]

But the Manchus eventually proved to be more adept at adapting to Chinese conditions than their predecessors, the Mongols. Unlike the latter, who had tried to impose their own methods of ruling, the Manchus adopted the Chinese political system (although, as we shall see, they retained their distinct position within it) and were gradually accepted by most Chinese as the legitimate rulers of the country.

Like all of China's great dynasties, the Qing was blessed with a series of strong early rulers who pacified the country, rectified many of the most obvious social and economic inequities, and restored peace and prosperity. For the Ming dynasty, these strong emperors had been Hongwu and Yongle; under the Qing, they would be Kangxi (K'ang Hsi) and Qianlong (Ch'ien Lung). The two Qing monarchs ruled China for well over a century, from the middle of the seventeenth century to the end of the eighteenth, and were responsible for much of the greatness of Manchu China.

Kangxi (1661–1722) was arguably the greatest ruler in Chinese history. Ascending to the throne at the age of seven, he was blessed with diligence, political astuteness, and a strong character and began to take charge of Qing administration while still an adolescent. During the six decades of his reign, Kangxi not only stabilized imperial rule by pacifying the restive peoples along the northern and western frontiers but also managed to make the dynasty acceptable to the general population. As an active patron of arts and letters, he cultivated the support of scholars through a number of major projects.

During Kangxi's reign, the activities of the Western missionaries, Dominicans and Franciscans as well as Jesuits, reached their height. The emperor was quite tolerant of the Christians, and several Jesuit missionaries became influential at court. Several hundred court officials converted to Christianity, as did an estimated 300,000 ordinary Chinese. But the Christian effort was ultimately undermined by squabbling among the Western religious orders over the Jesuit policy of accommodating local beliefs and practices in order to facilitate conversion. Jealous Dominicans and Franciscans complained to the pope, who issued an edict ordering all missionaries and converts to conform to the official orthodoxy set forth in Europe. At first, Kangxi attempted to resolve the problem by

SIXTEEN CONFUCIAN COMMANDMENTS

Although the Qing dynasty was of foreign origin, its rulers found Confucian maxims convenient for maintaining the social order. In 1670, the great emperor Kangxi issued the Sacred Edict to popularize Confucian values among the common people. The edict was read publicly at periodic intervals in every village in the country and set the standard for behavior throughout the empire.

KANGXI'S SACRED EDICT

1. Esteem most highly filial piety and brotherly submission, in order to give due importance to the social relations.
2. Behave with generosity toward your kindred, in order to illustrate harmony and benignity.
3. Cultivate peace and concord in your neighborhoods, in order to prevent quarrels and litigations.
4. Recognize the importance of husbandry and the culture of the mulberry tree, in order to ensure a sufficiency of clothing and food.
5. Show that you prize moderation and economy, in order to prevent the lavish waste of your means.
6. Give weight to colleges and schools, in order to make correct the practice of the scholar.
7. Extirpate strange principles, in order to exalt the correct doctrine.
8. Lecture on the laws, in order to warn the ignorant and obstinate.
9. Elucidate propriety and yielding courtesy, in order to make manners and customs good.
10. Labor diligently at your proper callings, in order to stabilize the will of the people.
11. Instruct sons and younger brothers, in order to prevent them from doing what is wrong.
12. Put a stop to false accusations, in order to preserve the honest and good.
13. Warn against sheltering deserters, in order to avoid being involved in their punishment.
14. Fully remit your taxes, in order to avoid being pressed for payment.
15. Unite in hundreds and tithing, in order to put an end to thefts and robbery.
16. Remove enmity and anger, in order to show the importance due to the person and life.

---

appealing directly to the Vatican, but the pope was uncompromising. After Kangxi's death, his successor began to suppress Christian activities throughout China.

Kangxi's achievements were carried on by his successors, Yongzheng (Yung Cheng, 1722–1736) and Qianlong (1736–1795). Like Kangxi, Qianlong was known for his diligence, tolerance, and intellectual curiosity, and he too combined vigorous military action against the unruly tribes along the frontier with active efforts to promote economic prosperity, administrative efficiency, and scholarship and artistic excellence. The result was continued growth for the Manchu Empire throughout much of the eighteenth century.

QING POLITICS

One reason for the success of the Manchus was their ability to adapt to their new environment. They retained the Ming political system with relatively few changes. They also tried to establish their legitimacy as China's rightful rulers by stressing their devotion to the principles of Confucianism. Emperor Kangxi ostentatiously studied the sacred Confucian classics and issued a "sacred edict" that proclaimed to the entire empire the importance of the moral values established by the master (see the box above).

Still, the Manchus, like the Mongols, were ethnically, linguistically, and culturally distinct from their subject population. The Qing attempted to cope with this reality by adopting a two-pronged strategy. On the one hand, the Manchus, representing less than 2 percent of the entire population, were legally defined as distinct from everyone else in China. The Manchu nobles retained their aristocratic privileges, while their economic base was protected by extensive landholdings and revenues provided from the state treasury. Other Manchus were assigned farmland and organized into military units, called banners, which were stationed as separate units in various strategic positions throughout China. These "bannermen" were the primary fighting force of the empire. Ethnic Chinese were prohibited from settling in Manchuria and were still compelled to wear their hair in a queue as a sign of submission to the ruling dynasty.

But while the Qing attempted to protect their distinct identity within an alien society, they also recognized the need to bring ethnic Chinese into the top ranks of imperial administration. Their solution was to create a system, known as dyarchy, in which all important administrative positions were shared equally by Chinese and Manchus. Meanwhile, the Manchus themselves, despite official efforts to preserve their separate language and culture, were increasingly assimilated into Chinese civilization.

CHINA ON THE EVE OF THE WESTERN ONSLAUGHT

In some ways, China was at the height of its power and glory in the mid-eighteenth century. But it was also under Qianlong that the first signs of the internal decay of the

Manchu dynasty began to appear. The clues were familiar ones. Qing military campaigns along the frontier were expensive and placed heavy demands on the imperial treasury. As the emperor aged, he became less astute in selecting his subordinates and fell under the influence of corrupt elements at court.

Corruption at the center led inevitably to unrest in rural areas, where higher taxes, bureaucratic venality, and rising pressure on the land because of the growing population had produced economic hardship. The heart of the unrest was in central China, where discontented peasants who had recently been settled on infertile land launched a revolt known as the White Lotus Rebellion (1796–1804). The revolt was eventually suppressed but at great expense.

Unfortunately for China, the decline of the Qing dynasty occurred just as China's modest relationship with the West was about to give way to a new era of military confrontation and increased pressure for trade. The first problems came in the north, where Russian traders seeking skins and furs began to penetrate the region between Siberian Russia and Manchuria. Earlier the Ming dynasty had attempted to deal with the Russians by the traditional method of placing them in a tributary relationship. But the tsar refused to play by Chinese rules. His envoys to Beijing ignored the tribute system and refused to perform the kowtow (the ritual of prostration and knocking the head on the ground performed by foreign emissaries before the emperor), the classical symbol of fealty demanded of all foreign ambassadors to the Chinese court. Formal diplomatic relations were finally established in 1689, when the Treaty of Nerchinsk settled the boundary dispute and provided for regular trade between the two countries. Through such arrangements, the Manchus were able not only to pacify the northern frontier but also to extend their rule over Xinjiang and Tibet to the west and southwest (see Map 16.2).

Dealing with the foreigners who arrived by sea was more difficult. By the end of the seventeenth century, the English had replaced the Portuguese as the dominant force in Euro-

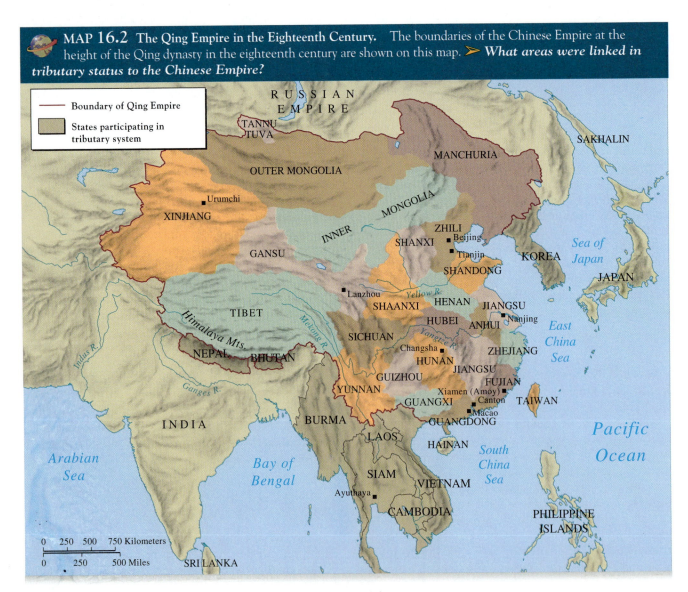

MAP 16.2 The Qing Empire in the Eighteenth Century. The boundaries of the Chinese Empire at the height of the Qing dynasty in the eighteenth century are shown on this map. ➤ **What areas were linked in tributary status to the Chinese Empire?**

The Art Archive/Marine Museum Stockholm/Dagli Orti (A)

⬥ **EUROPEAN WAREHOUSES AT CANTON.** Aggravated by the growing presence of foreigners in the eighteenth century, the Chinese court severely restricted the movement of European traders in China. They were permitted to live only in a compound near Canton during the seven months of the trading season and could go into the city only three times a month. In this painting, the Dutch and British flags fly over the warehouses and residences of the foreign community, while Chinese sampans and junks sit anchored in the river.

pean trade. Operating through the East India Company, which served as both a trading unit and the administrator of English territories in Asia, the English established their first trading post at Canton in 1699. Over the next decades, trade with China, notably the export of tea and silk to England, increased rapidly. To limit contact between Chinese and Europeans, the Qing licensed Chinese trading firms at Canton to be the exclusive conduit for trade with the West. Eventually the Qing confined the Europeans to a small island just outside the city walls and permitted them to reside there only from October through March.

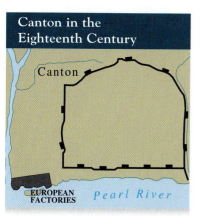

Canton in the Eighteenth Century

Canton

EUROPEAN FACTORIES *Pearl River*

For a while, the British tolerated this system, but by the end of the eighteenth century, the British government became restive at the uneven balance of trade between the two countries, which forced the British to ship vast amounts of silver bullion to China in exchange for its silks, porcelains, and teas. In 1793, a mission under Lord Macartney visited Beijing to press for liberalization of trade restrictions. A compromise was reached on the kowtow (Macartney was permitted to bend on one knee as was the British custom), but Qianlong expressed no interest in British manufactured products. An exasperated Macartney compared the Chinese Empire to "an old, crazy, first-rate man-of-war" that had once awed its neighbors "merely by her bulk and appearance" but was now destined under incompetent leadership to be "dashed to pieces on the shore."[4] With his contemptuous dismissal of the British request, the emperor had inadvertently sowed the seeds for a century of humiliation.

Changing China

During the Ming and Qing dynasties, China remained a predominantly agricultural society; nearly 85 percent of its people were farmers. But although most Chinese still lived in rural villages, the economy was undergoing a number of changes.

THE POPULATION EXPLOSION

In the first place, the center of gravity was continuing to shift steadily from the north to the south. In the early centuries of Chinese civilization, the administrative and

Chronology

CHINA DURING THE EARLY MODERN ERA

Rise of Ming dynasty	1369
Voyages of Zhenghe	1405–1433
Portuguese arrive in southern China	1514
Matteo Ricci arrives in China	1601
Li Zicheng occupies Beijing	1644
Manchus seize China	1644
Reign of Kangxi	1661–1722
Treaty of Nerchinsk	1689
First English trading post at Canton	1699
Reign of Qianlong	1736–1795
Lord Macartney's mission to China	1793
White Lotus Rebellion	1796–1804

economic center of gravity was clearly in the north. By the early Qing, the economic breadbasket of China was located along the Yangtze River and regions to the south. One concrete indication of this shift occurred during the Ming dynasty, when Emperor Yongle ordered the renovation of the Grand Canal to facilitate the shipment of rice from the Yangtze delta to the food-starved north.

Moreover, the population was beginning to increase rapidly. For centuries, China's population had remained within a range of 50 to 100 million, rising in times of peace and prosperity and falling in periods of foreign invasion and internal anarchy. During the Ming and the early Qing, however, the population increased from an estimated 70 to 80 million in 1390 to over 300 million at the end of the eighteenth century. There were probably several reasons for this population increase: the relatively long period of peace and stability under the early Qing; the introduction of new crops from the Americas, including peanuts, sweet potatoes, and maize; and the planting of a new species of faster-growing rice from Southeast Asia.

Of course, this population increase meant much greater population pressure on the land, smaller farms, and a razor-thin margin of safety in case of climatic disaster. The imperial court attempted to deal with the problem through a variety of means, most notably by preventing the concentration of land in the hands of wealthy landowners. Nevertheless, by the eighteenth century, almost all the land that could be irrigated was already under cultivation, and the problems of rural hunger and landlessness became increasingly serious.

SEEDS OF INDUSTRIALIZATION

Another change that took place during the early modern period in China was the steady growth of manufacturing and commerce. Taking advantage of the long era of peace and prosperity, merchants and manufacturers began to expand their operations beyond their immediate provinces. Commercial networks began to operate on a regional and sometimes even a national basis, as trade in silk, metal and wood products, porcelain, cotton goods, and cash crops like cotton and tobacco developed rapidly. Foreign trade also expanded as Chinese merchants set up extensive contacts with countries in Southeast Asia.

Although this rise in industrial and commercial activity resembles the changes occurring in western Europe, China and Europe differed in several key ways. In the first place, members of the bourgeoisie in China were not as independent as their European counterparts. In China, trade and manufacturing remained under the firm control of the state. In addition, political and social prejudices against commercial activity remained strong. Reflecting an ancient preference for agriculture over manufacturing and trade, the state levied heavy taxes on manufacturing and commerce while attempting to keep agricultural taxes low.

One of the consequences of these differences was a growing technological gap between China and Europe. The Chinese reaction to European clockmaking techniques provides an example. In the early seventeenth century, the Jesuit Matteo Ricci introduced advanced European clocks driven by weights or springs. The emperor was fascinated and found the clocks more reliable than Chinese methods of keeping time. Over the next decades, European timepieces became a popular novelty at court, but the Chinese expressed little curiosity about the technology involved, provoking one European to remark that playthings like cuckoo clocks "will be received here with much greater interest than scientific instruments or *objets d'art*."[5]

Daily Life in Qing China

Daily life under the Ming and early Qing dynasties continued to follow traditional patterns. As in earlier periods, Chinese society was organized around the family. The ideal family unit in Qing China was the joint family, in which as many as three or even four generations lived under the same roof. When sons married, they brought their wives to live with them in the family homestead. Unmarried daughters would also remain in the house. Aging parents and grandparents remained under the same roof and were cared for by younger members of the household until they died. This ideal did not always correspond to reality, however, since many families did not possess sufficient land to support a large household.

The family continued to be important in early Qing times for much the same reasons as in earlier times. As a labor-intensive society based primarily on the cultivation of rice, China needed large families to help with the harvest and to provide security for parents too old to work in the fields. Sons were particularly prized, not only because they had strong backs but also because they would raise their own families under the parental roof. With few opportunities for employment outside the family, sons had little choice but to remain with their parents and help on the land. Within the family, the oldest male was king, and his wishes theoretically had to be obeyed by all family members. Marriages were normally arranged for the benefit of the family, often by a go-between, and the groom and bride were usually not consulted. Frequently they did not meet until the marriage ceremony. Under such conditions, love was clearly a secondary consideration. In fact, it was often viewed as detrimental since it inevitably distracted the attention of the husband and wife from their primary responsibility to the larger family unit.

Although this emphasis on filial piety might seem to represent a blatant disregard for individual rights, the obligations were not all on the side of the children. The father was expected to provide support for his wife and children and, like the ruler, was supposed to treat those in his care with respect and compassion. All too often, however, the male head of the family was able to exact his privileges without performing his responsibilities in return.

Beyond the joint family was the clan. Sometimes called a lineage, a clan was an extended kinship unit consisting of dozens or even hundreds of joint and nuclear families linked together by a clan council of elders and a variety of other common social and religious functions. The clan served a number of useful purposes. Some clans possessed lands that could be rented out to poorer families, or richer families within the clan might provide land for the poor. Since there was no general state-supported educational system, sons of poor families might be invited to study in a school established in the home of a more prosperous relative. If the young man succeeded in becoming an official, he would be expected to provide favors and prestige for the clan as a whole.

THE ROLE OF WOMEN

In traditional China, the role of women had always been inferior to that of men. A sixteenth-century Spanish visitor to South China observed that Chinese women were "very secluded and virtuous, and it was a very rare thing for us to see a woman in the cities and large towns, unless it was an old crone." Women were more visible, he said, in rural areas, where they frequently could be seen working in the fields.[6]

The concept of female inferiority had deep roots in Chinese history. This view was embodied in the belief that only a male would carry on sacred family rituals and that men alone had the talent to govern others. Only males could aspire to a career in government or scholarship. Within the family system, the wife was clearly subordinated to the husband. Legally she could not divorce her husband or inherit property. The husband, however, could divorce his wife if she did not produce male heirs, or he could take a second wife as well as a concubine for his pleasure. A widow suffered especially, because she had to either raise her children on a single income or fight off her former husband's greedy relatives, who would coerce her to remarry since, according to the law, they would then inherit all of her previous property and her original dowry.

Female children were less desirable because of their limited physical strength and because their parents would be required to pay a dowry to the parents of their future husband. Female children normally did not receive an education, and in times of scarcity when food was in short supply, daughters might even be put to death.

Though women were clearly inferior to men in theory, this was not always the case in practice. Capable women often compensated for their legal inferiority by playing a strong role within the family. Women were often in charge of educating the children and handled the family budget. Some privileged women also received training in the Confucian classics, although their schooling was generally for a shorter time and less rigorous than that of their male counterparts. A few produced significant works of art and poetry.

Cultural Developments

During the late Ming and the early Qing dynasties, traditional culture in China reached new heights of achievement. With the rise of a wealthy urban class, the demand for art, porcelain, textiles, and literature grew significantly.

THE RISE OF THE CHINESE NOVEL

During the Ming dynasty, a new form of literature arose that eventually evolved into the modern Chinese novel. Although considered less respectable than poetry and nonfiction prose, these groundbreaking works (often written anonymously or under pseudonyms) were enormously popular, especially among well-to-do urban dwellers.

Written in a colloquial style, the new fiction was characterized by a realism that resulted in vivid portraits of Chinese society. Many of the stories sympathized with society's downtrodden—often helpless maidens—and dealt with such crucial issues as love, money, marriage, and power. Adding to the realism were sexually explicit passages that depicted the private side of Chinese life. Readers delighted in sensuous tales that, no matter how pornographic, always professed a moral lesson; the villains were punished and the virtuous rewarded.

The Dream of the Red Chamber is generally considered China's most distinguished popular novel. Published in

➤ **THE TEMPLE OF HEAVEN.**   This temple, located in the capital city of Beijing, is one of the most important historical structures in China. Built in 1420 at the order of the Ming emperor Yongle, it served as the location for the emperor's annual ceremony appealing to Heaven for a good harvest. Yongle's temple burned to the ground in 1889 but was immediately rebuilt according to the original design.

1791, it tells of the tragic love between two young people caught in the financial and moral disintegration of a powerful Chinese clan. The hero and the heroine, both sensitive and spoiled, represent the inevitable decline of the Chia family and come to an equally inevitable tragic end, she in death and he in an unhappy marriage to another.

THE ART OF THE MING AND THE QING

During the Ming and the early Qing, China produced its last outpouring of traditional artistic brilliance. Although most of the creative work was modeled on past examples, the art of this period is impressive for its technical perfection and breathtaking quantity.

In architecture, the most outstanding example is the Imperial City in Beijing. Building on the remnants of the palace of the Yuan dynasty, the Ming emperor Yongle ordered renovations when he returned the capital to Beijing in 1421. Succeeding emperors continued to add to the palace, but the basic design has not changed since the Ming era. Surrounded by high walls, the immense compound is divided into a maze of private apartments and offices and an imposing ceremonial quadrangle with a series of stately halls for imperial audiences and banquets. The grandiose scale, richly carved marble, spacious gardens, and graceful upturned roofs also contribute to the splendor of the "Forbidden City."

The decorative arts flourished in this period, especially the intricately carved lacquerware and the boldly shaped and colored cloisonné, a type of enamelwork in which colored areas are separated by thin metal bands. Silk production reached its zenith, and the best-quality silks

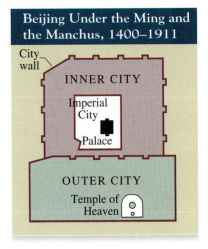

Beijing Under the Ming and the Manchus, 1400–1911

City wall

INNER CITY

Imperial City

Palace

OUTER CITY

Temple of Heaven

❧ **THE IMPERIAL CITY IN BEIJING.** During the fifteenth century, the Ming dynasty erected an immense imperial city on the remnants of the palace of Khubilai Khan in Beijing. Surrounded by $6\frac{1}{2}$ miles of walls, the enclosed compound is divided into a maze of private apartments and offices; it also includes an imposing ceremonial quadrangle with stately halls for imperial audiences and banquets. Because it was off-limits to commoners, the compound was known as the Forbidden City.

were highly prized in Europe, where chinoiserie, as Chinese art of all kinds was called, was in vogue. Perhaps the most famous of all the achievements of the Ming era was its blue-and-white porcelain, still prized by collectors throughout the world.

During the Qing dynasty, artists produced great quantities of paintings, mostly for home consumption. Inside the Forbidden City in Beijing, court painters worked alongside Jesuit artists and experimented with Western techniques. Most scholarly painters and the literati, however, totally rejected foreign techniques and became obsessed with traditional Chinese styles. As a result, Qing painting became progressively more repetitive and stale.

❧ Tokugawa Japan

At the end of the fifteenth century, the traditional Japanese system was at a point of near anarchy. With the decline in the authority of the Ashikaga shogunate at Kyoto, clan rivalries had exploded into an era of warring states. Even at the local level, power was frequently diffuse. The typical daimyo (great lord) domain had often become little more than a coalition of fief-holders held together by a loose allegiance to the manor lord. Nevertheless, Japan was on the verge of an extended era of national unification and peace under the rule of its greatest shogunate—the Tokugawa.

The Three Great Unifiers

The process began in the mid-sixteenth century with the emergence of three very powerful political figures, Oda Nobunaga (1568–1582), Toyotomi Hideyoshi (1582–1598), and Tokugawa Ieyasu (1598–1616). In 1568, Oda Nobunaga, the son of a samurai and a military commander under the Ashikaga shogunate, seized the imperial capital of Kyoto and placed the reigning shogun under his domination. During the next few years, the brutal and ambitious Nobunaga attempted to consolidate his rule throughout the central plains by defeating his rivals and suppressing the power of the Buddhist estates, but he was killed by one of his generals in 1582 before the process was complete. He was succeeded by Toyotomi Hideyoshi, a farmer's son who had worked his way up through the ranks to become a military commander. Hideyoshi located his capital at Osaka, where he built a castle to accommodate his headquarters, and gradually extended his power outward to the southern islands of Shikoku and Kyushu (see Map 16.3). By 1590, he had persuaded most of the daimyo on the Japanese islands to accept his authority and created a national currency. Then he invaded Korea in an abortive effort to export his rule to the Asian mainland.

Despite their efforts, however, neither Nobunaga nor Hideyoshi was able to eliminate the power of the local daimyo. Both were compelled to form alliances with some daimyo in order to destroy other more powerful rivals.

A PRESENT FOR LORD TOKITAKA

The Portuguese introduced firearms to Japan in the sixteenth century, and Japanese warriors were quick to explore the possibilities of these new weapons. In this passage, the daimyo of a small island off the southern tip of Japan receives an explanation of how to use the new weapons and is fascinated by the results. Note how Lord Tokitaka attempts to understand the procedures in terms of traditional Daoist beliefs.

THE JAPANESE DISCOVER FIREARMS

"There are two leaders among the traders, the one called Murashusa, and the other Christian Mota. In their hands they carried something two or three feet long, straight on the outside with a passage inside, and made of a heavy substance. The inner passage runs through it although it is closed at the end. At its side there is an aperture which is the passageway for fire. Its shape defies comparison with anything I know. To use it, fill it with powder and small lead pellets. Set up a small . . . target on a bank. Grip the object in your hand, compose your body, and closing one eye, apply fire to the aperture. Then the pellet hits the target squarely. The explosion is like lightning and the report like thunder. Bystanders must cover their ears. . . . This thing with one blow can smash a mountain of silver and a wall of iron. If one sought to do mischief in another man's domain and he was touched by it, he would lose his life instantly. Needless to say this is also true for the deer and stag that ravage the plants in the fields."

Lord Tokitaka saw it and thought it was the wonder of wonders. He did not know its name at first nor the details of its use. Then someone called it "iron-arms," although it was not known whether the Chinese called it so, or whether it was so called only on our island. Thus, one day, Tokitaka spoke to the two alien leaders through an interpreter: "Inca-pable though I am, I should like to learn about it." Whereupon, the chiefs answered, also through an interpreter: "If you wish to learn about it, we shall teach you its mysteries." Tokitaka then asked, "What is its secret?" The chief replied: "The secret is to put your mind aright and close one eye." Tokitaka said: "The ancient sages have often taught how to set one's mind aright, and I have learned something of it. If the mind is not set aright, there will be no logic for what we say or do. Thus, I understand what you say about setting our minds aright. However, will it not impair our vision for objects at a distance if we close an eye? Why should we close an eye?" To which the chiefs replied: "That is because concentration is important in everything. When one concentrates, a broad vision is not necessary. To close an eye is not to dim one's eyesight but rather to project one's concentration farther. You should know this." Delighted, Tokitaka said: "That corresponds to what Lao Tzu has said, 'Good sight means seeing what is very small.'"

That year the festival day of the Ninth Month fell on the day of the Metal and the Boar. Thus, one fine morning the weapon was filled with powder and lead pellets, a target was set up more than a hundred paces away, and fire was applied to the weapon. At first the people were astonished; then they became frightened. But in the end they all said in unison: "We should like to learn!" Disregarding the high price of the arms, Tokitaka purchased from the aliens two pieces of the firearms for his family treasure. As for the art of grinding, sifting, and mixing of the powder, Tokitaka let his retainer, Shinokawa Shoshiro, learn it. Tokitaka occupied himself, morning and night, and without rest in handling the arms. As a result, he was able to convert the misses of his early experiments into hits—a hundred hits in a hundred attempts.

At the conclusion of his conquests in 1590, Toyotomi Hideyoshi could claim to be the supreme proprietor of all registered lands in areas under his authority. But he then reassigned those lands as fiefs to the local daimyo, who declared their allegiance to him. The daimyo in turn began to pacify the countryside, carrying out extensive "sword hunts" to disarm the population and attracting samurai to their service. The Japanese tradition of decentralized rule had not been overcome.

After Hideyoshi's death in 1598, Tokugawa Ieyasu, the powerful daimyo of Edo (modern Tokyo), moved to fill the vacuum. Neither Hideyoshi nor Oda Nobunaga had claimed the title of shogun, but Ieyasu named himself shogun in 1603, initiating the most powerful and long-lasting of all Japanese shogunates. The Tokugawa rulers completed the restoration of central authority begun by Nobunaga and Hideyoshi and remained in power until 1868, when a war dismantled the entire system. As a contemporary phrased it, "Oda pounds the national rice cake, Hideyoshi kneads it, and in the end Ieyasu sits down and eats it."[7]

Opening to the West

The unification of Japan took place almost simultaneously with the coming of the Europeans. Portuguese traders sailing in a Chinese junk that may have been blown off course by a typhoon had landed on the islands in 1543. Within a few years, Portuguese ships were stopping at Japanese ports on a regular basis to take part in the regional trade between Japan, China, and Southeast Asia. The first Jesuit missionary, Francis Xavier, arrived in 1549.

Initially the visitors were welcomed. The curious Japanese were fascinated by tobacco, clocks, spectacles, and other European goods, and local daimyo were interested in purchasing all types of European weapons and armaments (see the box above). Oda Nobunaga and Toyotomi

MAP 16.3 **Tokugawa Japan.** This map shows the Japanese islands during the long era of the Tokugawa shogunate. Key cities, including the shogun's capital of Edo, are shown. ➤ *Where was the location of the imperial court?*

CHINA

Hokkaido

Hakodate

Sea of Japan

KOREA

Honshu

Lake Biwa

Nikko
Kanto Plain · Edo
Yokohama

Yellow Sea

Kobe · Nagoya
Himeji
Hiroshima
Kyoto
Osaka

Tsushima

Shimonoseki

Pacific Ocean

East China Sea

Nagasaki

Shikoku

Inland Sea

Kyushu

Kagoshima

0   100   200   300 Kilometers
0   100   200 Miles

local lords began to erect castles on the European model, many of which still exist today.

The missionaries also had some success in converting a number of local daimyo, some of whom may have been motivated in part by the desire for commercial profits. By the end of the sixteenth century, thousands of Japanese in the southernmost islands of Kyushu and Shikoku had become Christians. But papal claims to the loyalty of all Japanese Christians and the European habit of intervening in local politics soon began to arouse suspicion in official circles. Missionaries added to the problem by deliberately destroying local idols and shrines and turning some temples into Christian schools or churches.

Inevitably, the local authorities reacted. In 1587, Toyotomi Hideyoshi issued an edict prohibiting further Christian activities within his domains. Japan, he declared, was "the land of the Gods," and the destruction of shrines by the foreigners was "something unheard of in previous ages."[8] The Jesuits were ordered to leave the country within twenty days. Hideyoshi was careful to distinguish missionary from trading activities, however, and merchants were permitted to continue their operations (see the box on p. 354).

The Jesuits protested the expulsion, and eventually Hideyoshi relented, permitting them to continue proselytizing so long as they were discreet. But he refused to repeal the edicts, and when the aggressive activities of newly arrived Spanish Franciscans aroused his ire, he ordered the execution of nine missionaries and a number of their

Hideyoshi found the new firearms helpful in defeating their enemies and unifying the islands. The effect on Japanese military architecture was particularly striking as

➤ **THE PORTUGUESE ARRIVE AT NAGASAKI.** Portuguese traders landed in Japan by accident in 1543. In a few years, they arrived regularly, taking part in a regional trade network between Japan, China, and Southeast Asia. In these panels done in black lacquer and gold leaf, we see a late-sixteenth-century Japanese interpretation of the first Portuguese landing at Nagasaki.

TOYOTOMI HIDEYOSHI EXPELS THE MISSIONARIES

*W*hen Christian missionaries in sixteenth-century Japan began to interfere in local politics and criticize traditional religious practices, Toyotomi Hideyoshi issued an edict calling for their expulsion. In this letter to the Portuguese viceroy in Asia, Hideyoshi explains his decision. Note his conviction that Buddhists, Confucianists, and followers of Shinto all believe in the same God and his criticism of Christianity for rejecting all other faiths.

TOYOTOMI HIDEYOSHI, LETTER TO THE VICEROY OF THE INDIES

Ours is the land of the Gods, and God is mind. Everything in nature comes into existence because of mind. Without God there can be no spirituality. Without God there can be no way. God rules in times of prosperity as in times of decline. God is positive and negative and unfathomable. Thus, God is the root and source of all existence. This God is spoken of by Buddhism in India, Confucianism in China, and Shinto in Japan. To know Shinto is to know Buddhism as well as Confucianism.

As long as man lives in this world, Humanity will be a basic principle. Were it not for Humanity and Righteousness, the sovereign would not be a sovereign, nor a minis-ter of a state a minister. It is through the practice of Humanity and Righteousness that the foundations of our relationships between sovereign and minister, parent and child, and husband and wife are established. If you are interested in the profound philosophy of God and Buddha, request an explanation and it will be given to you. In your land one doctrine is taught to the exclusion of others, and you are not yet informed of the [Confucian] philosophy of Humanity and Righteousness. Thus there is no respect for God and Buddha and no distinction between sovereign and ministers. Through heresies you intend to destroy the righteous law. Hereafter, do not expound, in ignorance of right and wrong, unreasonable and wanton doctrines. A few years ago the so-called Fathers came to my country seeking to bewitch our men and women, both of the laity and clergy. At that time punishment was administered to them, and it will be repeated if they should return to our domain to propagate their faith. It will not matter what sect or denomination they represent—they shall be destroyed. It will then be too late to repent. If you entertain any desire of establishing amity with this land, the seas have been rid of the pirate menace, and merchants are permitted to come and go. Remember this.

Japanese converts. When the missionaries continued to interfere in local politics, Tokugawa Ieyasu ordered the eviction of all missionaries in 1612.

At first, Japanese authorities hoped to maintain commercial relations with European countries even while suppressing the Western religion, but eventually they decided to prohibit foreign trade altogether and closed the two major foreign factories on the island of Hirado and at Nagasaki. The sole remaining opening to the West was at Deshima Island in Nagasaki harbor, where a small Dutch community was permitted to engage in limited trade with Japan (the Dutch, unlike the Portuguese and the Spanish, had not allowed missionary activities to interfere with their commercial interests). Dutch ships were permitted to dock at Nagasaki harbor only once a year and, after close inspection, were allowed to remain for two or three months.

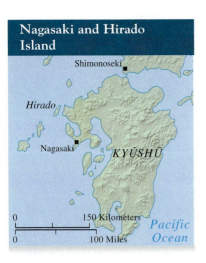

Nagasaki and Hirado Island

Shimonoseki

Hirado

Nagasaki

KYŪSHŪ

0   150 Kilometers
0   100 Miles

Pacific Ocean

Conditions on the island of Deshima itself were quite confining: the Dutch physician Engelbert Kaempfer complained that the Dutch lived in "almost perpetual imprisonment."[9] Nor were the Japanese free to engage in foreign trade. A small amount of commerce took place with China, but Japanese subjects of the shogunate were forbidden to leave the country on penalty of death.

The Tokugawa "Great Peace"

Once in power, the Tokugawa attempted to strengthen the system that had governed Japan for over three hundred years. They followed precedent in ruling through the *bakufu,* composed now of a coalition of daimyo, and a council of elders. But the system was more centralized than it had been previously. Now the shogunate government played a dual role. It set national policy on behalf of the emperor in Kyoto while simultaneously governing the shogun's own domain, which included about one-quarter of the national territory as well as the three great cities of Edo, Kyoto, and Osaka. As before, the state was divided into separate territories, called domains (*han*), which were ruled by a total of about 250 individual daimyo.

In theory, the daimyo were essentially autonomous since they were able to support themselves from taxes on their lands (the shogunate received its own revenues from its extensive landholdings). In actuality, the shogunate was able to guarantee daimyo loyalties by compelling daimyo to maintain two residences, one in their own domains and the other at Edo, and to leave their families in Edo as hostages for the daimyo's good behavior. Keeping up two residences also placed the Japanese nobility in a difficult economic position. Some were able to defray the high costs by concentrating on cash crops such as sugar, fish, and forestry products; but most were rice producers, and their revenues remained roughly the same throughout the period. The daimyo were also able to protect their economic interests by depriving their samurai retainers of their proprietary rights over the land and transforming them into salaried officials. The fief thus became a stipend, and the personal relationship between the daimyo and his retainers gradually gave way to a bureaucratic authority.

The Tokugawa also tinkered with the social system by limiting the size of the samurai class and reclassifying samurai who supported themselves by tilling the land as commoners. In fact, with the long period of peace brought about by Tokugawa rule, the samurai gradually ceased to be a warrior class and were required to live in the castle towns. As a gesture to their glorious past, samurai were still permitted to wear their two swords, and a rigid separation was maintained between persons of samurai status and the nonaristocratic segment of the population.

SEEDS OF CAPITALISM

The long period of peace under the Tokugawa shogunate made possible a dramatic rise in commerce and manufacturing, especially in the growing cities of Edo, Kyoto, and Osaka. By the mid-eighteenth century, Edo, with a population of more than one million, was one of the largest cities in the world. The growth of trade and industry was stimulated by a rising standard of living—driven in part by technological advances in agriculture and an expansion of arable land—and the voracious appetites of the aristocrats for new products.

Most of this commercial expansion took place in the major cities and the castle towns, where the merchants and artisans lived along with the samurai, who were clustered in neighborhoods surrounding the daimyo's castle. Banking flourished and paper money became the normal medium of exchange in commercial transactions. Merchants formed guilds not only to control market conditions but also to facilitate government control and the collection of taxes. Under the benign if somewhat contemptuous supervision of Japan's noble rulers, a Japanese merchant class gradually began to emerge from the shadows to play a significant role in the life of the Japanese nation. Some historians view the Tokugawa era as the first stage in the rise of an indigenous form of capitalism.

Eventually the increased pace of industrial activity spread beyond the cities into rural areas. As in Great Britain, cotton was a major factor. Cotton had been intro-

CHRONOLOGY

JAPAN AND KOREA DURING THE EARLY MODERN ERA

First phonetic alphabet in Korea	Fifteenth century
Portuguese merchants arrive in Japan	1543
Francis Xavier arrives in Japan	1549
Rule of Oda Nobunaga	1568–1582
Seizure of Kyoto	1568
Rule of Toyotomi Hideyoshi	1582–1598
Edict prohibiting Christianity in Japan	1587
Invades Korea	1592
Death of Toyotomi Hideyoshi and withdrawal of army from Korea	1598
Rule of Tokugawa Ieyasu	1598–1616
Creation of Tokugawa shogunate	1603
Dutch granted permission to trade at Nagasaki	1609
Order evicting Christian missionaries	1612
Yi dynasty of Korea declares fealty to China	1630s
Christian uprising suppressed in Japan	1637
Dutch post at Nagasaki transferred to Hirado	1641

duced to China during the Song dynasty and had spread to Korea and Japan shortly thereafter. Traditionally, however, cotton cloth had been too expensive for the common people, who instead wore clothing made of hemp. Imports increased during the sixteenth century, however, when cotton cloth began to be used for uniforms, matchlock fuses, and sails. Eventually, technological advances reduced the cost, and specialized communities for producing cotton cloth began to appear in the countryside and were gradually transformed into towns. By the eighteenth century, cotton had firmly replaced hemp as the cloth of choice for most Japanese.

Not everyone benefited from the economic changes of the seventeenth and eighteenth centuries, however; the samurai were barred by tradition and prejudice from commercial activities. Most samurai still relied on their revenues from rice lands, which were often insufficient to cover their rising expenses; consequently they fell heavily into debt. Others were released from servitude to their lord and became "masterless samurai." Occasionally these unemployed warriors (known as *ronin*, or "wave men") revolted or plotted against the local authorities.

The effects of economic developments on the rural population during the Tokugawa era are harder to estimate. Some farm families benefited by exploiting the growing demand for cash crops. But not all prospered. Most peasants continued to rely on rice cultivation and were whipsawed between declining profits and rising costs and taxes (as daimyo expenses increased, land taxes often took up to 50 percent of the annual harvest). Many were forced to become tenants or to work as wage laborers on the farms of wealthy neighbors or in village industries. When rural conditions in some areas became desperate, peasant revolts erupted. According to one estimate, nearly seven thousand disturbances took place during the Tokugawa era.

Some Japanese historians, influenced by a Marxist view of history, have interpreted such evidence as an indication that the Tokugawa economic system was highly exploitative, with feudal aristocrats oppressing powerless peasants. Recent scholars, however, have tended to adopt a more balanced view, maintaining that in addition to agriculture, manufacturing and commerce experienced extensive growth. Some point out that although the population doubled in the seventeenth century, a relatively low rate for the time period, so did the amount of cultivable land, while agricultural technology made significant advances.

The relatively low rate of population growth probably meant that Japanese peasants were spared the kind of land hunger that many of their counterparts in China faced. Recent evidence indicates that the primary reasons for the relatively low rate of population growth were late marriage, abortion, and infanticide.

Life in the Village

The changes that took place during the Tokugawa era had a major impact on the lives of ordinary Japanese. In some respects, the result was an increase in the power of the central government at the village level. The shogunate increasingly relied on Confucian maxims advocating obedience and hierarchy to enhance its authority with the general population. Decrees from the *bakufu* instructed the peasants on all aspects of their lives, including their eating habits and their behavior. At the same time, the increased power of the government led to more autonomy from the local daimyo for the peasants. Villages now had more control over their local affairs.

At the same time, the Tokugawa era saw the emergence of the nuclear family (*ie*) as the basic unit in Japanese society. In previous times, Japanese peasants had few legal rights. Most were too poor to keep their conjugal family unit intact or to pass property on to their children. Many lived at the manorial residence or worked as servants in the households of more affluent villagers. Now, with farm income on the rise, the nuclear family took on the same form as in China, although without the joint family concept. The Japanese system of inheritance was based on pri-

mogeniture. Family property was passed on to the eldest son, although younger sons often received land from their parents to set up their own families after marriage.

Another result of the changes under the Tokugawa was that women were somewhat more restricted than they had been previously. The rights of females were especially restricted in the samurai class, where Confucian values were highly influential. Male heads of households had broad authority over property, marriage, and divorce; wives were expected to obey their husbands on pain of death. Males often took concubines or homosexual partners, while females were expected to remain chaste. The male offspring of samurai parents studied the Confucian classics in schools established by the daimyo, while females were reared at home, where only the fortunate might receive a rudimentary training in reading and writing Chinese characters. Some women, however, became accomplished poets and painters since, in aristocratic circles, female literacy was prized for enhancing the refinement, social graces, and moral virtue of the home.

Women were similarly at a disadvantage among the common people. Marriages were arranged, and as in China, the new wife moved in with the family of her husband. A wife who did not meet the expectations of her spouse or his family was likely to be divorced. Still, gender relations were more egalitarian than among the nobility. Women were generally valued as childbearers and homemakers, and both sexes worked in the fields. Coeducational schools were established in villages and market towns, and about one-quarter of the students were female. Poor families, however, often put infant daughters to death or sold them into prostitution.

Such attitudes toward women operated within the context of the increasingly rigid stratification of Japanese society. Deeply conservative in their social policies, the Tokugawa rulers established strict legal distinctions between the four main classes in Japan (warriors, artisans, peasants, and merchants). Intermarriage between classes was forbidden in theory, although sometimes the prohibitions were ignored in practice. Below these classes were Japan's outcasts, the *eta*. Formerly they were permitted to escape their status, at least in theory. The Tokugawa made their status hereditary and enacted severe discriminatory laws against them, regulating their place of residence, their dress, and even their hairstyles.

Tokugawa Culture

Under the Tokugawa, a vital new set of cultural values began to appear, especially in the cities. This innovative era witnessed the rise of popular literature written by and for the townspeople. With the development of woodblock printing in the early seventeenth century, literature became available to the common people, literacy levels rose, and lending libraries increased the accessibility of the printed word.

THE LITERATURE OF
THE NEW MIDDLE CLASS

The best examples of this new urban fiction are the works of Saikaku (1642–1693), considered one of Japan's finest novelists. Saikaku's greatest novel, *Five Women Who Loved Love*, relates the amorous exploits of five women of the merchant class. Based partly on real-life experiences, it broke from the Confucian ethic of wifely fidelity to her husband and portrayed women who were willing to die for love—and all but one eventually did. Despite the tragic circumstances, the tone of the novel is upbeat and sometimes comic, and the author's wry comments prevent the reader from becoming emotionally involved with the heroines' misfortunes.

In the theater, the rise of *Kabuki* threatened the long dominance of the *No* play, replacing the somewhat restrained and elegant thematic and stylistic approach of the classical drama with a new emphasis on violence, music, and dramatic gestures. Significantly, the new drama emerged not from the rarefied world of the court but from the new world of entertainment and amusement. Its very commercial success, however, led to difficulties with the government, which periodically attempted to restrict or even suppress it. Early *Kabuki* was often performed by prostitutes, and shogunate officials, fearing that such activities could have a corrupting effect on the nation's morals, prohibited women from appearing on the stage; at the same time, they attempted to create a new professional class of male actors to impersonate female characters on stage.

In contrast to the popular literature of the Tokugawa period, poetry persevered in its more serious tradition. The most exquisite poetry was produced in the seventeenth century by the greatest of all Japanese poets, Basho (1644–1694). He was concerned with the search for the meaning of existence and the poetic expression of his experience. With his love of Daoism and Zen Buddhism, Basho found answers to his quest for the meaning of life in nature, and his poems are grounded in seasonal imagery. The following are among his most famous poems:

> *The ancient pond*
> *A frog leaps in*
> *The sound of the water.*

> *On the withered branch*
> *A crow has alighted—*
> *The end of autumn.*

His last poem, dictated to a disciple only three days prior to his death, succinctly expressed his frustration with the unfinished business of life:

> *On a journey, ailing—*
> *my dreams roam about*
> *on a withered moor.*

Like all great artists, Basho made his poems seem effortless and simple. He speaks directly to everyone, everywhere.

TOKUGAWA ART

Art also reflected the dynamism and changes in Japanese culture under the Tokugawa regime. The shogun's order that all daimyo and their families live every other year in Edo set off a burst of building as provincial rulers competed to erect the most magnificent mansion. Furthermore, the shoguns themselves constructed splendid castles adorned with sumptuous, almost ostentatious decor and furnishings. And the prosperity of the newly rising merchant class added fuel to the fire. Japanese paintings, architecture, textiles, and ceramics all flourished during this affluent era.

Although Japan was isolated from the Western world during much of the Tokugawa era, Japanese art was enriched by ideas from other cultures. Japanese pottery makers borrowed both techniques and designs from Korea to produce handsome ceramics. The passion for "Dutch learning" inspired Japanese to study Western medicine, astronomy, and languages and also led to experimentation with oil painting and Western ideas of perspective and the interplay of light and dark. Europeans desired Japanese lacquerware and metalwork, inlaid with ivory and mother-of-pearl, and especially the ceramics, which were now as highly prized as those of the Chinese.

Perhaps the most famous of all Japanese art of the Tokugawa era is the woodblock print. Genre painting, or representations of daily life, began in the sixteenth century and found its new mass-produced form in the eighteenth-century woodblock print. The now literate mercantile class was eager for illustrated texts of the amusing and bawdy tales that had circulated in oral tradition. Some prints depict entire city blocks filled with people, trades, and festivals, while others show the interiors of houses; thus they provide us with excellent visual documentation of the times. Others portray the "floating world" of the entertainment quarter, with scenes of carefree revelers enjoying the pleasures of life.

One of the most renowned of the numerous block-print artists was Utamaro (1754–1806), who painted erotic and sardonic women in everyday poses, such as walking down the street, cooking, or drying their bodies after a bath. Hokusai (1760–1849) was famous for *Thirty-Six Views of Mount Fuji*, a new and bold interpretation of the Japanese landscape.

KOREA: THE HERMIT KINGDOM

While Japan was gradually moving away from its agrarian origins, the Yi dynasty in Korea was attempting to pattern its own society on the Chinese model. The dynasty had been founded by the military commander Yi Song Gye in the late fourteenth century and immediately set out to establish close political and cultural relations with the Ming dynasty. From their new capital at Seoul, located on the Han River in the center of the peninsula, the Yi rulers accepted a tributary relationship with their powerful neighbor and engaged in the wholesale adoption of Chinese institutions and values. As in China, the civil service examinations tested candidates on their knowledge of the Confucian classics, and success was viewed as an essential step toward upward mobility.

There were differences, however. As in Japan, the dynasty continued to restrict entry into the bureaucracy to members of the aristocratic class, known in Korea as the *yangban* (or "two groups," the civilian and military). At the same time, the peasantry remained in serflike conditions, working on government estates or on the manor holdings of the landed elite. A class of slaves (*chonmin*) labored on government plantations or served in certain occupations, such as butchers and entertainers, considered beneath the dignity of other groups in the population.

Popular Culture: East and West

By the eighteenth century, a popular culture distinct from the elite culture of the nobility was beginning to emerge in the urban worlds of both the East and the West. At the top right is a scene from the "floating world," as the pleasure district in Edo, Japan, was called. Seen here are courtesans, storytellers, jesters, and various other entertainers. Below is a scene from the celebration of Carnival on the Piazza Sante Croce in Florence, Italy. Carnival was a period of festivities before Lent, mostly celebrated in Roman Catholic countries. Carnival became an occasion for indulgence in food, drink, games, and practical jokes.

Eventually Korean society began to show signs of independence from Chinese orthodoxy. In the fifteenth century, a phonetic alphabet for writing the Korean spoken language (*hangul*) was devised. Although it was initially held in contempt by the elites and used primarily as a teaching device, eventually it became the medium for private correspondence and the publishing of fiction for a popular audience. At the same time, changes were taking place in the economy, where rising agricultural production contributed to a population increase and the appearance of a small urban industrial and commercial sector, and in society, where the long domination of the

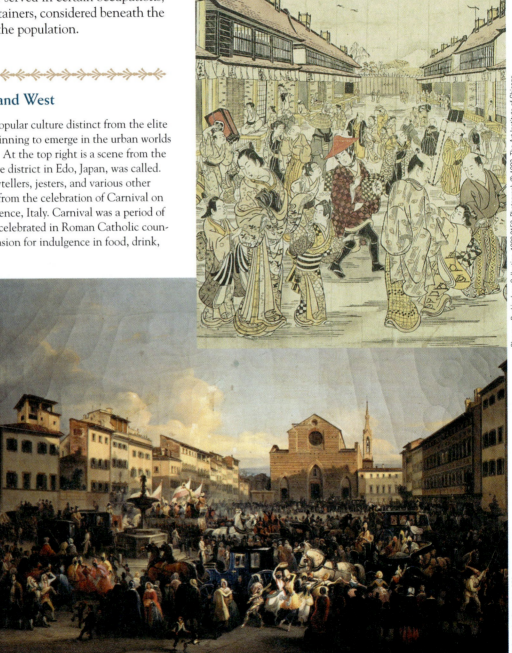

yangban class began to weaken. As their numbers increased and their power and influence declined, some *yangban* became merchants or even moved into the ranks of the peasantry, further blurring the distinction between the aristocratic class and the common people.

In general, Korean rulers tried to keep the country isolated from the outside world, but they were not always successful. The Japanese invasion under Toyotomi Hideyoshi in the late sixteenth century had a disastrous impact on Korean society. A Manchu force invaded northern Korea in the 1630s and eventually compelled the Yi dynasty to grant allegiance to the new imperial government in Beijing. Korea was relatively untouched by the arrival of European merchants and missionaries, although information about Christianity was brought to the peninsula by Koreans returning from tribute missions to China, and a small Catholic community was established there in the late eighteenth century.

 ## CONCLUSION

When Christopher Columbus sailed from southern Spain in his three ships in August 1492, he was seeking a route to China and Japan. He did not find it, but others soon did. In 1514, Portuguese ships arrived on the coast of southern China. Thirty years later, a small contingent of Portuguese merchants became the first Europeans to set foot on the islands of Japan.

At first, the new arrivals were welcomed, if only as curiosities. Eventually several European nations established trade relations with China and Japan, and Christian missionaries of various religious orders were active in both countries and in Korea as well. But their success was short-lived. Europeans eventually began to be perceived as detrimental to law and order, and during the seventeenth century, the majority of the foreign merchants

and missionaries were evicted from all three countries. From that time until the middle of the nineteenth century, China, Japan, and Korea were relatively little affected by events taking place beyond their borders.

That fact deluded many observers into the assumption that the societies of East Asia were essentially stagnant, characterized by agrarian institutions and values reminiscent of those of the feudal era in Europe. As we have seen, however, that picture is misleading, for all three countries were changing and by the early nineteenth century were quite different from what they had been three centuries earlier.

Ironically, these changes were especially marked in Tokugawa Japan, an allegedly "closed country," where traditional classes and institutions were under increasing strain, not only from the emergence of a new merchant class but also from the centralizing tendencies of the powerful Tokugawa shogunate. Some historians have seen strong parallels between Tokugawa Japan and early modern Europe, which gave birth to centralized empires and a strong merchant class during the same period. The image of the monarchy is reflected in a song sung at the shrine of Toyotomi Hideyoshi in Kyoto:

Who's that
Holding over four hundred provinces
In the palm of his hand
And entertaining at a tea-party?
It's His Highness
So mighty, so impressive![10]

By the beginning of the nineteenth century, then, powerful tensions, reflecting a growing gap between ideal and reality, were at work in both Chinese and Japanese society. Under these conditions, both countries were soon forced to face a new challenge from the aggressive power of an industrializing Europe.

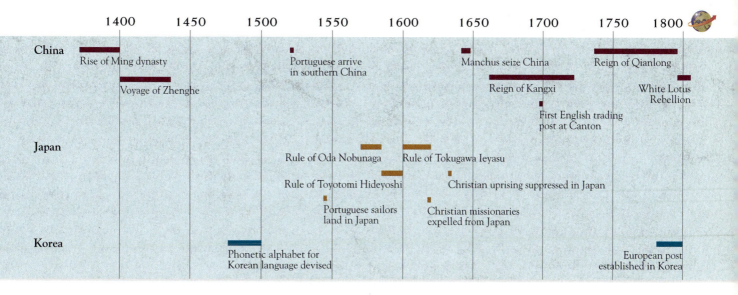

	1400	1450	1500	1550	1600	1650	1700	1750	1800

China — Rise of Ming dynasty; Voyage of Zhenghe; Portuguese arrive in southern China; Manchus seize China; Reign of Kangxi; First English trading post at Canton; Reign of Qianlong; White Lotus Rebellion

Japan — Rule of Oda Nobunaga; Rule of Toyotomi Hideyoshi; Portuguese sailors land in Japan; Rule of Tokugawa Ieyasu; Christian missionaries expelled from Japan; Christian uprising suppressed in Japan

Korea — Phonetic alphabet for Korean language devised; European post established in Korea

CHAPTER NOTES

1. From Jonathan D. Spence, *Emperor of China: Self-Portrait of K'ang Hsi* (New York, 1974), pp. 143–144.
2. Richard Strassberg, *The World of K'ang Shang-jen: A Man of Letters in Early Ch'ing China* (New York, 1983), p. 275.
3. Lynn Struve, *The Southern Ming, 1644–1662* (New Haven, Conn., 1984), p. 61.
4. J. L. Cranmer-Byng, *An Embassy to China: Lord Macartney's Journal, 1793–1794* (London, 1912), p. 340.
5. Daniel J. Boorstin, *The Discoverers: A History of Man's Search to Know His World and Himself* (New York, 1983), p. 63.
6. C. R. Boxer, ed., *South China in the Sixteenth Century* (London, 1953), p. 265.
7. Chie Nakane and Sinzaburo Oishi, eds., *Tokugawa Japan* (Tokyo, 1990), p. 14.
8. Quoted in Jurgis Elisonas, "Christianity and the Daimyo," in John Whitney Hall, ed., *The Cambridge History of Japan*, vol. 4 (Cambridge, 1991), p. 360.
9. Engelbert Kaempfer, *The History of Japan: Together with a Description of the Kingdom of Siam, 1690–1692*, vol. 2 (Glasgow, 1906), pp. 173–174.
10. Quoted in Ryusaku Tsunda et al., *Sources of Japanese Tradition* (New York, 1964), p. 313.

SUGGESTED READING

For a general overview of this period in East Asian history, see volumes 8 and 9 of F. W. Mote and D. Twitchett, eds., *The Cambridge History of China* (Cambridge, 1976), and J. W. Hall, ed., *The Cambridge History of Japan*, vol. 4 (Cambridge, 1991).

For information on Chinese voyages into the Indian Ocean, see P. Snow, *The Star Raft: China's Encounter with Africa* (Ithaca, N.Y., 1988). Also see Ma Huan, *Ying-hai Sheng-lan: The Overall Survey of the Ocean's Shores* (Bangkok, 1996), an ocean survey by a fifteenth-century Chinese cataloger.

On the late Ming, see J. D. Spence, *The Search for Modern China* (New York, 1990), and L. Struve, *The Southern Ming, 1644–1662* (New Haven, Conn., 1984). On the rise of the Qing, see F. Wakeman Jr., *The Great Enterprise: The Manchu Reconstruction of Imperial Order in Seventeenth-Century China* (Berkeley, Calif., 1985). On Kangxi, see J. D. Spence, *Emperor of China: Self-Portrait of K'ang Hsi* (New York, 1974). Social issues are discussed in S. Naquin and E. Rawski, *Chinese Society in the Eighteenth Century* (New Haven, Conn., 1987). Also see J. D. Spence and J. Wills, eds., *From Ming to Ch'ing* (New Haven, Conn., 1979). For a very interesting account of Jesuit missionary experiences in China, see L. J. Gallagher, ed. and trans., *China in the Sixteenth Century: The Journals of Matthew Ricci, 1583–1616* (New York, 1953). For brief biographies of Ming-Qing luminaries such as Wang Yangming, Zheng Chenggong, and Emperor Qianlong, see J. E. Wills Jr., *Mountains of Fame: Portraits in Chinese History* (Princeton, N.J., 1994).

The best surveys of Chinese literature are Liu Wu-chi, *An Introduction to Chinese Literature* (Bloomington, Ind., 1966); S. Owen, *An Anthology of Chinese Literature: Beginnings to 1911* (New York, 1996); and V. Mair, *The Columbia Anthology of Traditional Chinese Literature* (New York, 1994). For a concise and comprehensive introduction to the Chinese art of this period, see M. Sullivan, *The Arts of China*, 4th ed. (Berkeley, Calif., 1999); C. Clunas, *Art in China* (Oxford, 1997); and M. Tregear, *Chinese Art*, rev. ed. (London, 1997). For the best introduction to the painting of this era, see Yang Xin et al., *Three Thousand Years of Chinese Paintings* (New Haven, Conn., 1997).

On Japan before the rise of the Tokugawa, see J. W. Hall et al., eds., *Japan Before Tokugawa: Political Consolidation and Economic Growth* (Princeton, N.J., 1981). See also M. E. Berry, *Hideyoshi* (Cambridge, Mass., 1982), the first biography of this fascinating figure in Japanese history. On the first Christian activities, see G. Elison, *Deus Destroyed: The Image of Christianity in Early Modern Japan* (Cambridge, Mass., 1973), and C. R. Boxer, *The Christian Century in Japan, 1549–1650* (Berkeley, Calif., 1951).

On the Tokugawa era, see H. Bolitho, *Treasures Among Men: The Fudai Daimyo in Tokugawa Japan* (New Haven, Conn., 1974), and R. B. Toby, *State and Diplomacy in Early Modern Japan: Asia in the Development of the Tokugawa Bakufu* (Princeton, N.J., 1984). See also R. N. Bellah, *Tokugawa Religion: The Values of Pre-Industrial Japan* (New York, 1957), and C. I. Mulhern, ed., *Heroic with Grace: Legendary Women of Japan* (Armonk, N.Y., 1991). Three other worthwhile studies are S. Vlastos, *Peasant Protests and Uprisings in Tokugawa Japan* (Berkeley, Calif., 1986); H. Ooms, *Tokugawa Ideology: Early Constructs, 1570–1680* (Princeton, N.J., 1985); and C. Nakane, ed., *Tokugawa Japan: The Social and Economic Antecedents of Modern Japan* (Tokyo, 1990).

For a brief introduction to women in the Ming and Qing dynasties as well as the Tokugawa era, see S. Hughes and B. Hughes, *Women in World History*, vol. 2 (Armonk, N.Y., 1997). To witness Chinese village life in 1670, consult the classic J. D. Spence, *The Death of Woman Wang* (New York, 1978). For women's literacy in seventeenth-century China, see D. Ko, *Teachers of the Inner Chambers: Women and Culture in Seventeenth Century China* (Stanford, Calif., 1994). Most valuable is the collection of articles edited by G. L. Bernstein, *Re-Creating Japanese Women, 1600–1945* (Berkeley, Calif., 1991).

On Japanese literature of the Tokugawa era, see D. Keene, *World Within Walls: Japanese Literature of the Pre-Modern Era, 1600–1867* (New York, 1976). Of special value for the college student are D. Keene's *Anthology of Japanese Literature* (New York, 1955), *The Pleasures of Japanese Literature* (New York, 1988), and *Japanese Literature: An Introduction for Western Readers* (London, 1953). For an introduction to Basho's life, poems, and criticism, consult the stimulating *Basho and His Interpreters: Selected Hokku with Commentary* (Stanford, Calif., 1991), by M. Ueda.

For the most comprehensive and accessible overview of Japanese art, see P. Mason, *Japanese Art* (New York, 1993). For a concise introduction to Japanese art of the Tokugawa era, see J. Stanley-Baker, *Japanese Art* (London, 1984).

InfoTrac
College Edition

Visit the source collections at infotrac.thomsonlearning.com and use the Search function with the following key terms.

China history   Qing

Japan history   Tokugawa

Ming China

World History
Resources

Visit the *Essential World History* Companion Web Site for resources specific to this textbook:

http://history.wadsworth.com/duikeressentials02/

The CD in the back of this book and the World History Resource Center at http://history.wadsworth.com/world/ offer a variety of tools to help you succeed in this course, including access to quizzes; images; documents; interactive simulations, maps, and timelines; movie explorations; and a wealth of other sources.

Chapter 17

THE WEST ON THE EVE OF A NEW WORLD ORDER

CHAPTER OUTLINE

- THE ENLIGHTENMENT
- ECONOMIC CHANGES AND THE SOCIAL ORDER
- CHANGING PATTERNS OF WAR: GLOBAL CONFRONTATION
- COLONIAL EMPIRES AND REVOLUTION IN THE WESTERN HEMISPHERE
- TOWARD A NEW POLITICAL ORDER: ENLIGHTENED ABSOLUTISM
- THE FRENCH REVOLUTION
- THE AGE OF NAPOLEON
- CONCLUSION

FOCUS QUESTIONS

- Who were the leading figures of the Enlightenment, and what were their main contributions?
- What changes occurred in the European economy in the eighteenth century, and to what degree were these changes reflected in social patterns?
- How did Spain and Portugal administer their American colonies, and what were the main characteristics of Latin American society in the eighteenth century?
- What do historians mean by the term *enlightened absolutism*, and to what degree did eighteenth-century Prussia, Austria, and Russia exhibit its characteristics?
- What were the causes, the main events, and the results of the American Revolution and the French Revolution? Which aspects of the French Revolution did Napoleon preserve, and which did he destroy?
- In what ways were the American Revolution, the French Revolution, and the seventeenth-century English revolutions alike? In what ways were they different?

Historians have often portrayed the eighteenth century as the final phase of Europe's old order, before the violent upheaval and reordering of society associated with the French Revolution. The old order—still largely agrarian, dominated by kings and landed aristocrats, and grounded in privileges for nobles, clergy, towns, and provinces—seemed to continue a basic pattern that had prevailed in Europe since medieval times. However, just as a new intellectual order based on rationalism and secularism was emerging in Europe, demographic, economic, social, and political patterns were beginning to change in ways that proclaimed the emergence of a modern new order.

A key factor in the emergence of the new world order was the French Revolution. On the morning of July 14, 1789, a Parisian mob of some eight thousand men and women in search of weapons streamed toward the Bastille, a royal armory filled with arms and ammunition. The Bastille was also a state prison, and although it held only seven prisoners at the time, in the eyes of these angry Parisians, it was a glaring symbol of the government's despotic policies. It was defended by the marquis de Launay and a small garrison of 114 men. The attack on the Bastille began in earnest in the early afternoon, and after three hours of fighting, de Launay and the garrison surrendered. Angered by the loss of ninety-eight protesters, the victors beat de Launay to death, cut off his head, and carried it aloft in triumph through the streets of Paris. When King Louis XVI was told the news of the fall of the Bastille by the duc de La Rochefoucauld-Liancourt, he exclaimed, "Why, this is a revolt." "No, Sire," replied the duke. "It is a revolution."

The French Revolution has been portrayed as a major turning point in European political and social history, as a time when the institutions of the old regime were destroyed and a new order was created based on individual rights, representative institutions, and a concept of loyalty to the nation rather than the monarch. The revolutionary upheavals of the era, especially in France, did create new liberal and national political ideals, summarized in the French revolutionary slogan "Liberty, Equality, Fraternity," that transformed France and then spread to other European countries and the rest of the world. •

 THE ENLIGHTENMENT

The impetus for political and social change in the eighteenth century stemmed in part from the Enlightenment. The Enlightenment was a movement of intellectuals who were greatly impressed with the accomplishments of the Scientific Revolution. When they used the word *reason*—one of their favorite words—they were advocating the application of the scientific method to the understanding of all life. All institutions and all systems of thought were subject to the rational, scientific way of thinking if people would only free themselves from the shackles of past, worthless traditions, especially religious ones. If Isaac Newton could discover the natural laws regulating the world of nature, they too, by using reason, could find the laws that governed human society. This belief in turn led them to hope that they could make progress toward a better society than the one they had inherited. *Reason, natural law, hope, progress*—these were the buzzwords in the heady atmosphere of eighteenth-century Europe.

The Path to Enlightenment

Major sources of inspiration for the Enlightenment were two Englishmen, Isaac Newton and John Locke. Newton contended that the world and everything in it worked like a giant machine. Enchanted by the grand design of this world-machine, the intellectuals of the Enlightenment were convinced that by following Newton's rules of reasoning, they could discover the natural laws that governed politics, economics, justice, and religion.

John Locke's theory of knowledge also made a great impact. In his *Essay Concerning Human Understanding*, written in 1690, Locke denied the existence of innate ideas and argued instead that every person was born with a *tabula rasa*, a blank mind:

> Let us then suppose the mind to be, as we say, white paper, void of all characters, without any ideas. How comes it to be furnished? Whence comes it by that vast store which the busy and boundless fancy of man has painted on it with an almost endless variety? Whence has it all the materials of reason and knowledge? To this I answer, in one word, from experience. . . . Our observation, employed either about external sensible objects or about the internal operations of our minds perceived and reflected on by ourselves, is that which supplies our understanding with all the materials of thinking.[1]

By denying innate ideas, Locke's philosophy implied that people were molded by their environment, by whatever they perceived through their senses from their surrounding world. By changing the environment and subjecting people to proper influences, they could be changed and a new society created. And how should the environment be changed? Newton had paved the way: reason enabled enlightened people to discover the natural laws to which all institutions should conform.

The Philosophes and Their Ideas

The intellectuals of the Enlightenment were known by the French term *philosophes*, although they were not all French and few were philosophers in the strict sense of the term.

They were literary people, professors, journalists, economists, political scientists, and above all, social reformers. Although it was a truly international and cosmopolitan movement, the Enlightenment also enhanced the dominant role being played by French culture; Paris was its recognized capital. Most of the leaders of the Enlightenment were French. The French philosophes, in turn, affected intellectuals elsewhere and created a movement that touched the entire Western world, including the British and Spanish colonies in America.

To the philosophes, the role of philosophy was not just to discuss the world but to change it. A spirit of rational criticism was to be applied to everything, including religion and politics. Spanning almost a century, the Enlightenment evolved with each succeeding generation, becoming more radical as new thinkers built on the contributions of their predecessors. A few individuals, however, dominated the landscape so completely that we can gain insight into the core ideas of the philosophes by focusing on the three French giants—Montesquieu, Voltaire, and Diderot.

MONTESQUIEU

Charles de Secondat, the baron de Montesquieu (1689–1755), came from the French nobility. His most famous work, *The Spirit of the Laws,* was published in 1748. In this comparative study of governments, Montesquieu attempted to apply the scientific method to the social and political arena to ascertain the "natural laws" governing the social and political relationships of human beings. Montesquieu distinguished three basic kinds of government: republic, monarchy, and despotism. Montesquieu used England as an example of monarchy, and it was his analysis of England's constitution that led to his most lasting contribution to political thought—the importance of checks and balances achieved by means of a separation of powers. He believed that England's system, with its separate executive, legislative, and judicial powers that served to limit and control each other, provided the greatest freedom and security for a state. The translation of his work into English two years after publication ensured its being read by American political leaders, who eventually incorporated its principles into the U.S. Constitution.

VOLTAIRE

The greatest figure of the Enlightenment was François-Marie Arouet, known simply as Voltaire (1694–1778). Son of a prosperous middle-class family from Paris, he studied law, although he achieved his first success as a playwright. Voltaire was a prolific author and wrote an almost endless stream of pamphlets, novels, plays, letters, philosophical essays, and histories.

Voltaire was especially well known for his criticism of traditional religion and his strong attachment to the ideal of religious toleration. As he grew older, Voltaire became ever more strident in his denunciations. "Crush the infamous thing," he thundered repeatedly—the infamous thing being religious fanaticism, intolerance, and superstition.

Throughout his life, Voltaire championed not only religious tolerance but also deism, a religious outlook shared by most other philosophes. Deism was built on the Newtonian world-machine, which implied the existence of a mechanic (God) who had created the universe. To Voltaire and most other philosophes, the universe was like a clock, and God was the clockmaker who had created it, set it in motion, and allowed it to run according to its own natural laws.

DIDEROT

Denis Diderot (1713–1784) was the son of a skilled craftsman from eastern France who became a freelance writer so that he could be free to study and read in many subjects and languages. One of Diderot's favorite topics was Christianity, which he condemned as fanatical and unreasonable. As he grew older, his literary attacks on Christianity grew more vicious. Of all religions, Christianity, he averred, was the worst, "the most absurd and the most atrocious in its dogma."

Diderot's most famous contribution to the Enlightenment was the *Encyclopedia,* or *Classified Dictionary of the Sciences, Arts, and Trades,* a twenty-eight-volume compendium of knowledge that he edited and referred to as the "great work of his life." Its purpose, according to Diderot, was to "change the general way of thinking." It did precisely that in becoming a major weapon of the philosophes' crusade against the old French society. The contributors included many philosophes who attacked religious intolerance and advocated a program for social, legal, and political improvements that would lead to a society that was more cosmopolitan, more tolerant, more humane, and more reasonable. The *Encyclopedia* was sold to doctors, clergymen, teachers, lawyers, and even military officers, thus spreading the ideas of the Enlightenment.

TOWARD A NEW "SCIENCE OF MAN"

The Enlightenment belief that Newton's scientific methods could be used to discover the natural laws underlying all areas of human life led to the emergence in the eighteenth century of what the philosophes called a "science of man," or what we would call the social sciences. In a number of areas, such as economics, politics, and education, the philosophes arrived at natural laws that they believed governed human actions.

Adam Smith (1723–1790) has been viewed as one of the founders of the modern discipline of economics. Smith believed that individuals should be left free to pursue their own economic self-interest. Through the actions of these individuals, all society would ultimately benefit. Consequently the state should in no way interrupt the free play of natural economic forces by government regulations on the economy but should leave it alone, a doctrine that subsequently became known as *laissez-faire* (French for "leave it alone").

Smith gave to government only three basic functions: it should protect society from invasion (army), defend its citizens from injustice (police), and keep up certain public works, such as roads and canals, that private individuals could not afford.

THE LATER ENLIGHTENMENT

By the late 1760s, a new generation of philosophes who had grown up with the worldview of the Enlightenment began to move beyond their predecessors' beliefs. Most famous was Jean-Jacques Rousseau (1712–1778), whose political beliefs were presented in two major works. In his *Discourse on the Origins of the Inequality of Mankind*, Rousseau argued that people had adopted laws and governors in order to preserve their private property. In the process, they had become enslaved by government. What, then, should people do to regain their freedom? In his celebrated treatise *The Social Contract*, published in 1762, Rousseau found an answer in the concept of the social contract. In a social contract, an entire society agreed to be governed by its general will. Each individual might have a particular will contrary to the general will, but if the individual put his particular will (self-interest) above the general will, he should be forced to abide by the general will. "This means nothing less than that he will be forced to be free," said Rousseau, because the general will was not only political but also ethical; it represented what the entire community ought to do.

Another influential treatise by Rousseau was his novel *Émile*, one of the Enlightenment's most important works on education. Rousseau's fundamental concern was that education should foster, rather than restrict, children's natural instincts. Rousseau's own experiences had shown him the importance of the emotions. What he sought was a balance between heart and mind, between emotion and reason.

But Rousseau did not necessarily practice what he preached. His own children were sent to orphanages, where many children died at a young age. Rousseau also viewed women as "naturally" different from men. In Rousseau's *Émile*, Sophie, Émile's intended wife, was educated for her role as wife and mother by learning obedience and the nurturing skills that would enable her to provide loving care for her husband and children. Not everyone in the eighteenth century, however, agreed with Rousseau.

THE "WOMAN QUESTION" IN THE ENLIGHTENMENT

For centuries, many male intellectuals had argued that the nature of women made them inferior to men and made male domination of women necessary and right. Female thinkers in the eighteenth century, however, provided suggestions for improving the conditions of women. The strongest statement for the rights of women was advanced by the English writer Mary Wollstonecraft (1759–1797), viewed by many as the founder of modern European feminism.

In her *Vindication of the Rights of Woman*, written in 1792, Wollstonecraft pointed out two contradictions in the views of women held by some Enlightenment thinkers. To argue that women must obey men, she said, was contrary to the beliefs of the same individuals that a system based on the arbitrary power of monarchs over their subjects or slave owners over their slaves was wrong. The subjection of women to men was equally wrong. In addition, she argued that the Enlightenment was based on an ideal of reason innate in all human beings. If women have reason, then they too are entitled to the same rights that men have. Women, Wollstonecraft declared, should have equal rights with men in education and in economic and political life as well (see the box on p. 366).

Culture in an Enlightened Age

Although the Baroque style that had dominated the seventeenth century continued to be popular, by the 1730s, a new style affecting decoration and architecture known as Rococo had spread throughout Europe. Unlike the Baroque, which stressed power, grandeur, and movement, Rococo emphasized grace, charm, and gentle action. Rococo rejected strict geometrical patterns and had a fondness for curves; it liked to follow the wandering lines of natural objects, such as seashells and flowers. It made much use of interlaced designs colored in gold with delicate contours and graceful arcs. Highly secular, its lightness and charm spoke of the pursuit of pleasure, happiness, and love.

Some of Rococo's appeal is evident already in the work of Antoine Watteau (1684–1721), whose lyrical views of aristocratic life, refined, sensual, and civilized, with gentlemen and ladies in elegant dress, revealed a world of upper-class pleasure and joy. Underneath that exterior, however, was an element of sadness as the artist revealed the fragility and transitory nature of pleasure, love, and life.

HIGH CULTURE

Historians have grown accustomed to distinguishing between a civilization's high culture and its popular culture. High culture is the literary and artistic culture of the educated and wealthy ruling classes; popular culture is the written and unwritten culture of the masses, most of which has traditionally been passed down orally. By the eighteenth century, European high culture reflected the learned tastes of theologians, scientists, philosophers, intellectuals, poets, and dramatists, for all of whom Latin remained a truly international language.

Especially noticeable in the eighteenth century was an expansion of both the reading public and publishing.

THE RIGHTS OF WOMEN

*M*ary Wollstonecraft responded to an unhappy childhood in a large family by seeking to lead an independent life. Few occupations were available for middle-class women in her day, but she survived by working as a teacher, chaperone, and governess to aristocratic children. All the while, she wrote and developed her ideas on the rights of women. This excerpt was taken from her Vindication of the Rights of Woman, *written in 1792. This work led to her reputation as the foremost British feminist thinker of the eighteenth century.*

MARY WOLLSTONECRAFT, *VINDICATION OF THE RIGHTS OF WOMAN*

It is a melancholy truth—yet such is the blessed effect of civilization—the most respectable women are the most oppressed; and, unless they have understandings far superior to the common run of understandings, taking in both sexes, they must, from being treated like contemptible beings, become contemptible. How many women thus waste life away the prey of discontent, who might have practiced as physicians, regulated a farm, managed a shop, and stood erect, supported by their own industry, instead of hanging their heads surcharged with the dew of sensibility, that consumes the beauty to which it at first gave luster. . . .

Proud of their weakness, however, [women] must always be protected, guarded from care, and all the rough toils that dignify the mind. If this be the fiat of fate, if they will make themselves insignificant and contemptible, sweetly to waste "life away," let them not expect to be valued when their beauty fades, for it is the fate of the fairest flowers to be admired and pulled to pieces by the careless hand that plucked them. In how many ways do I wish, from the purest benevolence, to impress this truth on my sex; yet I fear that they will not listen to a truth that dear-bought experience has brought home to many an agitated bosom, nor willingly resign the privileges of rank and sex for the privileges of humanity, to which those have no claim who do not discharge its duties. . . .

Would men but generously snap our chains, and be content with rational fellowship instead of slavish obedience, they would find us more observant daughters, more affectionate sisters, more faithful wives, and more reasonable mothers—in a word, better citizens. We should then love them with true affection, because we should learn to respect ourselves; and the peace of mind of a worthy man would not be interrupted by the idle vanity of his wife.

Whereas French publishers issued three hundred titles in 1750, about sixteen hundred were being published yearly in the 1780s. Although many of these titles were still geared for small groups of the educated elite, many were also directed to the new reading public of the middle classes, which included women and even urban artisans.

An important aspect of the growth of publishing and reading in the eighteenth century was the development of magazines for the general public. Great Britain saw 25 different periodicals published in 1700, 103 in 1760, 158 in 1780. Along with magazines came daily newspapers. The first was printed in London in 1702, but by 1780, thirty-seven other English towns had their own newspapers.

POPULAR CULTURE

The distinguishing characteristic of popular culture is its collective nature. Group activity was especially common in the festival, a broad name used to cover a variety of celebrations: community festivals in Catholic Europe that celebrated the feast day of the local patron saint; annual festivals, such as Christmas and Easter, that go back to medieval Christianity; and Carnival, which was celebrated in the Mediterranean world of Spain, Italy, and France as well as in Germany and Austria.

Indeed, the ultimate festival was Carnival, which began after Christmas and lasted until the start of Lent,

the forty-day period of fasting and purification leading up to Easter. Because during Lent people were expected to abstain from meat, sex, and most recreations, Carnival was a time of great indulgence when heavy consumption of food and drink were the norm. It was a time of intense sexual activity as well. Songs with double meanings that would ordinarily be considered offensive could be sung publicly at this time of year. A float of Florentine "keymakers," for example, sang this ditty to the ladies: "Our tools are fine, new and useful. We always carry them with us. They are good for anything. If you want to touch them, you can."

ECONOMIC CHANGES AND THE SOCIAL ORDER

The eighteenth century in Europe witnessed the beginning of economic changes that ultimately had a strong impact on the rest of the world.

New Economic Patterns

Europe's population began to grow around 1750 and continued to increase steadily. The total European population was probably around 120 million in 1700, 140 million in

➤ **ANTOINE WATTEAU, *THE PILGRIMAGE TO CYTHERA*.** Antoine Watteau was one of the most gifted painters in eighteenth-century France. His portrayal of aristocratic life reveals a world of elegance, wealth, and pleasure. In this painting, Watteau depicts a group of aristocratic pilgrims about to depart the island of Cythera, where they have paid homage to Venus, the goddess of love.

1750, and 190 million in 1790. A falling death rate was perhaps the most important reason for this population growth. Of great significance in lowering death rates was the disappearance of bubonic plague, but so was diet. More plentiful food and better transportation of food supplies led to improved nutrition and relief from devastating famines.

More plentiful food was in part a result of improvements in agricultural practices and methods in the eighteenth century, especially in Britain, parts of France, and the Low Countries. Food production increased as more land was farmed, yields per acre increased, and climate improved. Also important to the increased yields was the cultivation of new vegetables, including two important American crops, the potato and maize (Indian corn). Both had been brought to Europe from the Americas in the sixteenth century.

In European industry in the eighteenth century, the most important product was textiles, most of which were still produced by master artisans in guild workshops. But a shift in textile production to the countryside was spreading to many rural areas of Europe by the "putting-out" or "domestic" system in which a merchant-capitalist entrepreneur bought the raw materials, mostly wool and flax, and "put them out" to rural workers who spun the raw material into yarn and then wove it into cloth on simple looms. Capitalist-entrepreneurs sold the finished product, made a profit, and used it to purchase materials to manu-

facture more. This system became known as the "cottage industry" because the spinners and weavers did their work on spinning wheels and looms in their own cottages.

In the eighteenth century, overseas trade boomed. Some historians speak of the emergence of a true global economy, pointing to the patterns of trade that interlocked Europe, Africa, the Far East, and the Americas (see Map 14.4 in Chapter 14). One such pattern involved the influx of gold and silver into Spain from its colonial American empire. Much of this gold and silver made its way to Britain, France, and the Netherlands in return for manufactured goods. British, Dutch, and French merchants in turn used their profits to buy tea, spices, silk and cotton goods from China and India to sell in Europe. Another important source of trading activity involved the plantations of the Western Hemisphere. The plantations were worked by African slaves and produced tobacco, cotton, coffee, and sugar, all products in demand by Europeans.

Commercial capitalism created enormous prosperity for some European countries. By 1700, Spain, Portugal, and the Dutch Republic, which had earlier monopolized overseas trade, found themselves increasingly overshadowed by France and England, which built enormously profitable colonial empires in the course of the eighteenth century. After the French lost the Seven Years' War in 1763, Britain emerged as the world's strongest overseas trading nation, and London became the world's greatest port.

European Society in the Eighteenth Century

The pattern of Europe's social organization, first established in the Middle Ages, continued well into the eighteenth century. Society was still divided into the traditional "orders" or "estates" determined by heredity.

Because society was still mostly rural in the eighteenth century, the peasantry constituted the largest social group, about 85 percent of Europe's population. There were rather wide differences within this group, however, especially between free peasants and serfs. In eastern Germany, eastern Europe, and Russia, serfs remained tied to the lands of their noble landlords. In contrast, peasants in Britain, northern Italy, the Low Countries, Spain, most of France, and some areas of western Germany were largely free.

The nobles, who constituted only 2 to 3 percent of the European population, played a dominating role in society. Being born a noble automatically guaranteed a place at the top of the social order, with all its attendant special privileges and rights. Nobles, for example, were exempt from many forms of taxation. Since medieval times, landed aristocrats had functioned as military officers, and eighteenth-century nobles held most of the important offices in the administrative machinery of state and controlled much of the life of their local districts.

Townspeople were still a distinct minority of the total population except in the Dutch Republic, Britain, and parts of Italy. At the end of the eighteenth century, about one-sixth of the French population lived in towns of two thousand people or more. The biggest city in Europe was London, with a million inhabitants; Paris was a little more than half that size.

Many cities in western and even central Europe had a long tradition of patrician oligarchies that continued to control their communities by dominating town and city councils. Just below the patricians stood an upper crust of the middle classes: nonnoble officeholders, financiers and bankers, merchants, wealthy *rentiers* who lived off their investments, and important professionals, including lawyers. Another large urban group was the lower middle class, made up of master artisans, shopkeepers, and small traders. Below them were the laborers or working classes and a large group of unskilled workers who served as servants, maids, and cooks at pitifully low wages.

CHANGING PATTERNS OF WAR: GLOBAL CONFRONTATION

The philosophes condemned war as a foolish waste of life and resources in stupid quarrels of no value to humankind. Despite their words, the rivalry among states that led to costly struggles remained unchanged in the European world of the eighteenth century. Europe consisted of a number of self-governing, individual states that were chiefly guided by the self-interest of the ruler. And as Frederick the Great of Prussia said, "The fundamental rule of governments is the principle of extending their territories."

In 1740, a major conflict erupted over the succession to the Austrian throne. King Frederick II of Prussia took advantage of the succession of a woman, Maria Theresa (1740–1780), to the throne of Austria by invading Austrian Silesia. The War of the Austrian Succession (1740–1748) was fought in three areas of the world. In Europe, Prussia seized Silesia from Austria while France occupied the Austrian Netherlands. In Asia, France took Madras in India from the British, and in North America, the British captured the French fortress of Louisbourg at the entrance to the Saint Lawrence River. By 1748, all parties were exhausted and agreed to a peace treaty that guaranteed the return of all occupied territories to their original owners, with the exception of Silesia.

The Seven Years' War: A Global Conflict

Maria Theresa refused to accept the loss of Silesia and prepared for its return by working diplomatically to separate Prussia from its chief ally, France. In 1756, Austria achieved a diplomatic revolution. French-Austrian rivalry had existed since the late sixteenth century. But two new rivalries now replaced the old one: the rivalry of Britain and France over colonial empires and the rivalry of Austria and Prussia over Silesia. France abandoned Prussia and allied with Austria. Russia, which saw Prussia as a major hindrance to Russian goals in central Europe, joined the new alliance. In turn, Great Britain allied with Prussia. These new alliances now led to another worldwide war.

Again there were three major areas of conflict: Europe, India, and North America. In Europe, the British and Prussians fought the Austrians, Russians, and French. With his superb army and military skill, Frederick the Great of Prussia was able for some time to defeat the Austrian, French, and Russian armies. Eventually, however, his forces were gradually worn down and faced utter defeat until a new Russian tsar, Peter III, withdrew Russian troops from the conflict. A stalemate ensued, ending the European conflict in 1763. All occupied territories were returned, and Austria officially recognized Prussia's permanent control of Silesia.

The struggle between Britain and France in the rest of the world had more decisive results. In India, the French had returned Madras to Britain after the War of the Austrian Succession, but the struggle continued. Ultimately, the British under Robert Clive won out, not because they had better forces but because they were more persistent. By the Treaty of Paris in 1763, the French withdrew and left India to the British.

By far the greatest conflicts of the Seven Years' War took place in North America. French North America (Canada and Louisiana) was thinly populated and run by the French government as a vast trading area. British North America had come to consist of thirteen colonies on the eastern coast of the present United States. They were thickly populated, containing about 1.5 million people by 1750, and were also prosperous.

British and French rivalry in North America finally led to war. Despite initial French successes, the British went on to seize Montreal, the Great Lakes area, and the Ohio valley. The French were forced to make peace. By the Treaty of Paris, they ceded Canada and the lands east of the Mississippi to England. Their ally Spain transferred Spanish Florida to British control; in return, the French gave their Louisiana territory to the Spanish. By 1763, Great Britain had become the world's greatest colonial power.

COLONIAL EMPIRES AND REVOLUTION IN THE WESTERN HEMISPHERE

The colonial empires in the Western Hemisphere were an integral part of the European economy in the eighteenth century and became entangled in the conflicts of the European states. Nevertheless, the colonies of Latin America and British North America were developing along lines that sometimes differed significantly from those of Europe.

The Society of Latin America

In the sixteenth century, Portugal came to dominate Brazil while Spain established a colonial empire in the New World that included Central America, most of South America, and parts of North America. Within the lands of Central and South America, a new civilization arose that we have come to call Latin America (see Map 17.1).

Latin America was a multiracial society. Already by 1501, Spanish rulers allowed intermarriage between Europeans and native American Indians, whose offspring became known as *mestizos*. In addition, over a period of three centuries, possibly as many as eight million African slaves were brought to Spanish and Portuguese America to work the plantations. Mulattoes—the offspring of Africans and whites—joined mestizos and descendants of whites, Africans, and native Indians to produce a unique multiracial society in Latin America.

THE ECONOMIC FOUNDATIONS

Both the Portuguese and the Spanish sought to profit from their colonies in Latin America. One source of wealth came from the abundant supplies of gold and silver. The Spaniards were especially successful, finding supplies of gold in the Caribbean and New Granada (Colombia) and silver in Mexico and the viceroyalty of Peru. Most of the gold and silver was sent to Europe, and little remained in the New World to benefit the people whose labor had produced it.

Although the pursuit of gold and silver offered prospects of fantastic financial rewards, agriculture proved to be a more abiding and more rewarding source of prosperity for Latin America. A noticeable feature of Latin American agriculture was the dominant role of the large landowner. Both Spanish and Portuguese landowners created immense estates, which left the Indians either to work as peons—native peasants permanently dependent on the landowners—on their estates or as poor farmers on marginal lands. This system of large landowners and dependent peasants has remained one of the persistent features of Latin American society. By the eighteenth century, both Spanish and Portuguese landowners were producing primarily for sale abroad.

Trade was another avenue for the economic exploitation of the American colonies. Latin American colonies became sources of raw materials for Spain and Portugal as gold, silver, sugar, tobacco, diamonds, animal hides, and a number of other natural products made their way to Europe. In turn, the mother countries supplied their colonists with manufactured goods.

THE STATE AND THE CHURCH IN COLONIAL LATIN AMERICA

Portuguese Brazil and Spanish America were colonial empires that lasted over three hundred years. The difficulties of communication and travel between the New World and Europe made the attempts of the Spanish and Portuguese monarchs to provide close regulation of their empires virtually impossible, which left colonial officials in Latin America with much autonomy in implementing imperial policies. However, the Iberians tried to keep the most important posts of colonial government in the hands of Europeans. Beginning in the mid-sixteenth century, the Portuguese monarchy began to assert its control over Brazil by establishing the position of governor-general. To rule his American empire, the king of Spain appointed a viceroy, the first of which was established for New Spain (Mexico) in 1535. Another viceroy was appointed for Peru in 1543. In the eighteenth century, two additional viceroyalties—New Granada and La Plata—were added. All of the major government positions were held by Spaniards.

From the beginning of their conquest of the New World, Spanish and Portuguese rulers were determined to Christianize the native peoples. This policy gave the Catholic church an important role to play in the New World—a role that added considerably to church power. Catholic missionaries fanned out to different parts of the Spanish Empire. To facilitate their efforts, missionaries brought Indians together into villages where the natives could be converted, taught trades, and encouraged to grow crops. Their missions enabled missionaries to control the lives of the Indians and keep them docile.

The Catholic church constructed hospitals, orphanages, and schools, which instructed Indian students in the

MAP 17.1 Latin America in the Eighteenth Century. In the eighteenth century, Latin America was largely the colonial preserve of the Spanish, although Portugal continued to dominate Brazil. The Latin American colonies supplied the Spanish and Portuguese with gold, silver, sugar, tobacco, cotton, and animal hides. ➤ *How do you explain the ability of Europeans to dominate such large areas of Latin America?*

Portuguese colonized by 1640
Portuguese colonized by 1750
Portuguese frontier lands, 1750
Spanish colonized by 1640
Spanish colonized by 1750
Spanish frontier lands, 1750
French colonies
Dutch colonies
English colonies
Jesuit mission states
Routes of colonial trade
Extent of Inca Empire in 1525

rudiments of reading, writing, and arithmetic. The church also provided outlets for women other than marriage. Nunneries were places of prayer and quiet contemplation, but women in religious orders, many of them of aristocratic background, often lived well and operated outside their establishments by running schools and hospitals. Indeed, one of these nuns, Sor Juana Inés de la Cruz (1651–1695), was one of seventeenth-century Latin America's best-known literary figures. She wrote poetry and prose and urged that women be educated.

British North America

In the eighteenth century, Spanish power in the New World was increasingly challenged by the British. (The United Kingdom of Great Britain came into existence in 1707, when the governments of England and Scotland were united; the term *British* came into use to refer to both English and Scots.) In eighteenth-century Britain, the king or queen and Parliament shared power, with Parliament gradually gaining the upper hand. The monarch

⇒ **SOR JUANA INÉS DE LA CRUZ.** Nunneries in colonial Latin America gave women—especially upper-class women— some opportunity for intellectual activity. As a woman, Juana Inés de la Cruz was denied admission to the University of Mexico. Consequently she entered a convent, where she wrote poetry and plays until her superiors forced her to focus on less worldly activities.

chose ministers who were responsible to the crown and who set policy and guided Parliament. Parliament had the power to make laws, levy taxes, pass budgets, and indirectly influence the monarch's ministers.

Growing trade and industry led to a growing middle class in Britain that favored expansion of trade and world empire. These people found a spokesman in William Pitt the Elder, who became prime minister in 1757 and expanded the British Empire by acquiring Canada and India in the Seven Years' War.

THE AMERICAN REVOLUTION

At the end of the Seven Years' War in 1763, Great Britain had become the world's greatest colonial power. In North America, Britain controlled Canada and the lands east of the Mississippi. After the Seven Years' War, British policy makers sought to obtain new revenues from the colonies to pay for British army expenses in defending the colonists. An attempt to levy new taxes by the Stamp Act of 1765 led to riots and the law's quick repeal.

The Americans and British had different conceptions of empire. The British envisioned a single empire with Parliament as the supreme authority throughout. The Americans, in contrast, had their own representative assemblies. They believed that neither king nor Parliament should interfere in their internal affairs and that no tax could be levied without the consent of their own assemblies.

Crisis followed crisis in the 1770s until 1776, when the colonists decided to declare their independence from the British Empire. On July 4, 1776, the Second Continental Congress approved a declaration of independence written by Thomas Jefferson. A stirring political document, the Declaration of Independence affirmed the Enlightenment's natural rights of "life, liberty, and the pursuit of happiness" and declared the colonies to be "free and independent states absolved from all allegiance to the British crown." The war for American independence had formally begun.

Of great importance to the colonies' cause was their support by foreign countries who were eager to gain revenge for earlier defeats at the hands of the British. French officers and soldiers served in the American Continental Army under George Washington as commander in chief. When the army of General Cornwallis was forced to surrender to a combined American and French army and French fleet under Washington at Yorktown in 1781, the British decided to call it quits. The Treaty of Paris, signed in 1783, recognized the independence of the American colonies and granted the Americans control of the territory from the Appalachians to the Mississippi River.

BIRTH OF A NEW NATION

The thirteen American colonies had gained their independence; but a fear of concentrated power and concern for their own interests caused them to have little enthusiasm for establishing a united nation with a strong central government, and so the Articles of Confederation, ratified in 1781, did not create one. A movement for a different form of national government soon arose. In the summer of 1787, fifty-five delegates attended a convention in Philadelphia to revise the Articles of Confederation. The convention's delegates—wealthy, politically experienced, and well educated—rejected revision and decided instead to devise a new constitution.

The proposed United States Constitution established a central government distinct from and superior to governments of the individual states. The central or federal government was divided into three branches, each with some power to check the functioning of the others.

A president would serve as the chief executive with the power to execute laws, veto the legislature's acts, supervise foreign affairs, and direct military forces. Legislative power was vested in the second branch of government, a bicameral legislature composed of the Senate, elected by the state legislatures, and the House of Representatives, elected directly by the people. A supreme court and other courts "as deemed necessary" by Congress provided the third branch of government. They would enforce the Constitution as the "supreme law of the land."

The Constitution was approved by the states—by a slim margin. Important to its success was a promise to add a bill of rights to the Constitution as the new government's first piece of business. Accordingly, in March 1789, the new Congress enacted the first ten amendments to the Constitution, ever since known as the Bill of Rights. These guaranteed freedom of religion, speech, press, petition, and assembly, as well as the right to bear arms, protection against unreasonable searches and arrests, trial by jury, due process of law, and protection of property rights. Many of these rights were derived from the natural rights philosophy of the eighteenth-century philosophes and the American colonists. Is it any wonder that many European intellectuals saw the American Revolution as the embodiment of the Enlightenment's political dreams?

TOWARD A NEW POLITICAL ORDER: ENLIGHTENED ABSOLUTISM

There is no doubt that Enlightenment thought had some impact on the political development of European states in the eighteenth century. The philosophes believed in natural rights, which were thought to be inalienable privileges that ought not to be withheld from any person. These natural rights included equality before the law, freedom of religious worship, freedom of speech and press, and the right to assemble, hold property, and pursue happiness.

But how were these natural rights to be established and preserved? Most philosophes believed that people needed to be ruled by an enlightened ruler. What, however, made rulers enlightened? They must allow religious toleration, freedom of speech and press, and the rights of private property. They must foster the arts, sciences, and education. Above all, they must obey the laws and enforce them fairly for all subjects. Only strong monarchs seemed capable of overcoming vested interests and effecting the reforms society needed. Reforms then should come from above (from absolute rulers) rather than from below (from the people).

Many historians once assumed that a new type of monarchy emerged in the later eighteenth century, which they called "enlightened despotism" or "enlightened abso-

lutism." Monarchs such as Frederick II of Prussia, Catherine the Great of Russia, and Joseph II of Austria supposedly followed the advice of the philosophes and ruled by enlightened principles. Recently, however, scholars have questioned the usefulness of the concept of "enlightened absolutism." We can determine the extent to which it can be applied by examining the major "enlightened absolutists" of the later eighteenth century.

Prussia

Frederick II, known as Frederick the Great (1740–1786), was one of the best-educated and most cultured monarchs in the eighteenth century. He was well versed in Enlightenment thought and even invited Voltaire to live at his court for several years. A believer in the king as the "first servant of the state," Frederick the Great was a conscientious ruler who enlarged the Prussian army (to 200,000 men) and kept a strict watch over the bureaucracy.

For a time, Frederick seemed quite willing to make enlightened reforms. He abolished the use of torture except in treason and murder cases and also granted limited freedom of speech and press, as well as complete religious toleration. However, he kept Prussia's rigid social structure and serfdom intact and avoided any additional reforms.

The Austrian Empire of the Habsburgs

The Austrian Empire had become one of the great European states by the beginning of the eighteenth century. Yet it was difficult to rule because it was a sprawling empire composed of many different nationalities, languages, religions, and cultures (see Map 17.2).

Joseph II (1780–1790) believed in the need to sweep away anything standing in the path of reason. As he said, "I have made Philosophy the lawmaker of my empire, her logical applications are going to transform Austria." Joseph's reform program was far-reaching. He abolished serfdom, abrogated the death penalty, and established the principle of equality of all before the law. Joseph produced drastic religious reforms as well, including complete religious toleration.

Joseph's reform program proved overwhelming for Austria, however. He alienated the nobility by freeing the serfs and alienated the church by his attacks on the monastic establishment. Even the serfs were unhappy, unable to comprehend the drastic changes inherent in Joseph's policies. His successors undid many of his reforms.

Russia Under Catherine the Great

Catherine II the Great (1762–1796) was an intelligent woman who was familiar with the works of the philosophes and seemed to favor enlightened reforms. She invited the French philosophe Diderot to Russia and, when he arrived, urged him to speak frankly "as man to man." He did, outlining a far-reaching program of political and financial reform. But Catherine was skeptical about impractical theories, which, she said, "would have turned everything in my kingdom upside down." She did consider the idea of a new law code that would recognize the principle of the equality of all people in the eyes of the law. But in the end, she did nothing, knowing that her success depended on the support of the Russian nobility. In 1785, she gave the nobles a charter that exempted them from taxes. Catherine's policy of favoring the landed nobility led to even worse conditions for the Russian peasants and a rebellion that soon faltered and collapsed. Catherine responded by even greater measures against the peasantry.

Above all, Catherine proved a worthy successor to Peter the Great in her policies of territorial expansion westward into Poland and southward to the Black Sea. Russia spread southward by defeating the Turks. Russian expansion westward occurred at the expense of neighboring Poland. In three partitions of Poland, Russia gained about 50 percent of Polish territory.

Of the rulers we have discussed, only Joseph II sought truly radical changes based on Enlightenment ideas. Both Frederick II and Catherine II liked to talk about enlightened reforms, and they even attempted some. But the policies of neither seemed seriously affected by Enlightenment thought. Necessities of state and maintenance of the existing system took precedence over reform. Indeed, many historians maintain that Joseph, Frederick, and Catherine were all primarily guided by a concern for the power and well-being of their states. In the final analysis, heightened state power was used to create armies and wage wars to gain more power.

It would be foolish, however, to overlook the fact that the ability of enlightened rulers to make reforms was also limited by political and social realities. Everywhere in Europe, the hereditary aristocracy was still the most powerful class in society. As the chief beneficiaries of a system based on traditional rights and privileges for their class, they were not willing to support a political ideology that trumpeted the principle of equal rights for all. The first

MAP 17.2 Europe in 1763. By the middle of the eighteenth century, five major powers dominated Europe—Prussia, Austria, Russia, Britain, and France. Each sought to enhance its power both domestically, through a bureaucracy that collected taxes and ran the military, and internationally, by capturing territory or preventing other powers from capturing territory. ➤ *Given the distribution of Prussian and Habsburg holdings, in what areas of Europe were they most likely to compete for land and power?*

serious challenge to their supremacy would come in the French Revolution, an event that blew open the door to the modern world of politics.

THE FRENCH REVOLUTION

The year 1789 witnessed two far-reaching events, the beginning of a new United States of America under its revamped Constitution and the eruption of the French Revolution. Compared to the American Revolution a decade earlier, the French Revolution was more complex, more violent, and far more radical in its attempt to reconstruct both a new political and a new social order.

Background to the French Revolution

The root causes of the French Revolution must be sought in the condition of French society. Before the Revolution, France was a society grounded in privilege and inequality. Its population of 27 million was divided, as it had been since the Middle Ages, into three orders or estates.

SOCIAL STRUCTURE OF THE OLD REGIME

The first estate consisted of the clergy and numbered about 130,000 people who owned approximately 10 percent of the land. Clergy were exempt from the *taille*, France's chief tax. Clergy were also radically divided: the higher clergy, stemming from aristocratic families, shared the interests of the nobility, while the parish priests were often poor and from the class of commoners.

The second estate was the nobility, composed of about 350,000 people who owned about 25 to 30 percent of the land. The nobility had continued to play an important and even crucial role in French society in the eighteenth century, holding many of the leading positions in the government, the military, the law courts, and the higher church offices. The nobles sought to expand their power at the expense of the monarchy and to maintain their control over positions in the military, church, and government. Common to all nobles were tax exemptions, especially from the *taille*.

The third estate, or the commoners of society, constituted the overwhelming majority of the French population. They were divided by vast differences in occupation, level of education, and wealth. The peasants, who alone constituted 75 to 80 percent of the total population, were by far the largest segment of the third estate. They owned about 35 to 40 percent of the land, although their landholdings varied from area to area and over half had little or no land on which to survive. Serfdom no longer existed on any large scale in France, but French peasants still had obligations to their local landlords that they deeply resented. These "relics of feudalism," or aristocratic privileges, were obligations that

survived from an earlier age and included the payment of fees for the use of village facilities, such as the flour mill, community oven, and winepress.

Another part of the third estate consisted of skilled craftspeople, shopkeepers, and other wage earners in the cities. In the eighteenth century, a rise in consumer prices greater than the increase in wages left these urban groups with a noticeable decline in purchasing power. Their daily struggle for survival led many of these people to play an important role in the Revolution, especially in Paris.

About 8 percent of the population, or 2.3 million people, constituted the bourgeoisie or middle class, who owned about 20 to 25 percent of the land. This group included merchants, industrialists, and bankers who controlled the resources of trade, manufacturing, and finance and benefited from the economic prosperity after 1730. The bourgeoisie also included professional people—lawyers, holders of public offices, doctors, and writers. Many members of the bourgeoisie had their own set of grievances because they were often excluded from the social and political privileges monopolized by nobles. At the same time, remarkable similarities existed at the upper levels of society between the wealthier bourgeoisie and the nobility. By obtaining public offices, wealthy middle-class individuals could enter the ranks of the nobility.

Moreover, the new political ideas of the Enlightenment proved attractive to both the aristocracy and the bourgeoisie. Both elites, long accustomed to a new socioeconomic reality based on wealth and economic achievement, were increasingly frustrated by a monarchical system resting on privileges and on an old and rigid social order based on the concept of estates. The opposition of these elites to the old order led them ultimately to drastic action against the monarchical regime. In a real sense, the Revolution had its origins in political grievances.

OTHER PROBLEMS FACING THE FRENCH MONARCHY

The inability of the French monarchy to deal with new social realities was exacerbated by specific problems in the 1780s. Although France had enjoyed fifty years of economic expansion, bad harvests in 1787 and 1788 and the beginnings of a manufacturing depression resulted in food shortages, rising prices for food and other goods, and unemployment in the cities. The number of poor, estimated at almost one-third of the population, reached crisis proportions on the eve of the Revolution.

The immediate cause of the French Revolution was the near collapse of government finances. Costly wars and royal extravagance drove French governmental expenditures ever higher. On the verge of a complete financial collapse, the government of Louis XVI (1774–1792) was finally forced to call a meeting of the Estates-General, the French parliamentary body that had not met since 1614. The Estates-General consisted of representatives from the three orders of French society. In the elections for the Estates-General, the government had ruled that the third estate should get double representation (it did, after all, constitute 97 percent of the population). Consequently, while both the first estate (the clergy) and the second estate (the nobility) had about three hundred delegates each, the third estate had almost six hundred representatives, most of whom were lawyers from French towns.

From Estates-General to National Assembly

The Estates-General opened at Versailles on May 5, 1789. It was troubled from the start with the question of whether voting should be by order or by head (each delegate having one vote). Traditionally, each order would vote as a group and have one vote. That meant that the first and second estates could outvote the third estate two to one. The third estate demanded that each deputy have one vote. With the assistance of liberal nobles and clerics, that would give the third estate a majority. When the first estate declared in favor of voting by order, the third estate responded dramatically. On June 17, 1789, the third estate declared itself the "National Assembly" and decided to draw up a constitution. This was the first step in the French Revolution because the third estate had no legal right to act as the National Assembly. But this audacious act was soon in jeopardy, as the king sided with the first estate and threatened to dissolve the Estates-General. Louis XVI now prepared to use force.

The common people, however, saved the third estate from the king's forces. On July 14, a mob of Parisians stormed the Bastille, a royal armory, and proceeded to dismantle it, brick by brick. Louis XVI was soon informed that the royal troops were unreliable. Louis's acceptance of that reality signaled the collapse of royal authority; the king could no longer enforce his will. The fall of the Bastille had saved the National Assembly.

At the same time, popular revolts broke out throughout France, both in the cities and in the countryside.

Behind the popular uprising was a growing resentment of the entire landholding system, with its fees and obligations. The fall of the Bastille and the king's apparent capitulation to the demands of the third estate now led peasants to take matters into their own hands. Peasant rebellions occurred throughout France, serving as a backdrop to the Great Fear, a vast panic that spread like wildfire through France in July and August. The greatest impact of the agrarian revolts and Great Fear was on the National Assembly meeting in Versailles.

Revolution and Revolt in France and China

Both France and China experienced revolutionary upheaval at the end of the eighteenth century and well into the nineteenth century. In both countries, common people often played an important role. At top is a scene from the storming of the Bastille in 1789. This early success ultimately led to the overthrow of the monarchy. At the bottom is a scene from one of the struggles during the Taiping Rebellion, a major peasant revolt in the mid-nineteenth century in China. An imperial Chinese army is shown recapturing the city of Nanjing from Taiping rebels in 1864.

Musée de la Revolution Francais, Vizille, France/Visual Arts Library, London/Bridgeman Art Library

The Art Archive/School of Oriental & African Studies/Eileen Tweedy

DECLARATION OF THE RIGHTS OF MAN AND THE CITIZEN

*O*ne of the important documents of the French Revolution, the Declaration of the Rights of Man and the Citizen was adopted in August 1789 by the National Assembly. The declaration affirmed that "men are born and remain free and equal in rights," that governments must protect these natural rights, and that political power is derived from the people.

DECLARATION OF THE RIGHTS OF MAN AND THE CITIZEN

The representatives of the French people, organized as a national assembly, considering that ignorance, neglect, and scorn of the rights of man are the sole causes of public misfortunes and of corruption of governments, have resolved to display in a solemn declaration the natural, inalienable, and sacred rights of man, so that this declaration, constantly in the presence of all members of society, will continually remind them of their rights and their duties. . . . Consequently, the National Assembly recognizes and declares, in the presence and under the auspices of the Supreme Being, the following rights of man and citizen:

1. Men are born and remain free and equal in rights; social distinctions can be established only for the common benefit.
2. The aim of every political association is the conservation of the natural and imprescriptible rights of man; these rights are liberty, property, security, and resistance to oppression.
3. The source of all sovereignty is located in essence in the nation; no body, no individual can exercise authority which does not emanate from it expressly.
4. Liberty consists in being able to do anything that does not harm another person. . . .
6. The law is the expression of the general will; all citizens have the right to concur personally or through their representatives in its formation; it

must be the same for all, whether it protects or punishes. All citizens being equal in its eyes are equally admissible to all honors, positions, and public employments, according to their capabilities and without other distinctions than those of their virtues and talents.

7. No man can be accused, arrested, or detained except in cases determined by the law, and according to the forms which it has prescribed. . . .
10. No one may be disturbed because of his opinions, even religious, provided that their public demonstration does not disturb the public order established by law.
11. The free communication of thoughts and opinions is one of the most precious rights of man: every citizen can therefore freely speak, write, and print. . . .
12. The guaranteeing of the rights of man and citizen necessitates a public force; this force is therefore instituted for the advantage of all, and not for the private use of those to whom it is entrusted. . . .
14. Citizens have the right to determine for themselves or through their representatives the need for taxation of the public, to consent to it freely, to investigate its use, and to determine its rate, basis, collection, and duration.
15. Society has the right to demand an accounting of his administration from every public agent.
16. Any society in which guarantees of rights are not assured nor the separation of powers determined has no constitution.
17. Property being an inviolable and sacred right, no one may be deprived of it unless public necessity, legally determined, clearly requires such action, and then only on condition of a just and prior indemnity.

Destruction of the Old Regime

One of the first acts of the National Assembly was to destroy the relics of feudalism and aristocratic privilege. On the night of August 4, 1789, the National Assembly voted to abolish the rights of landlords and the fiscal exemptions of nobles, clergy, towns, and provinces. On August 26, the National Assembly adopted the Declaration of the Rights of Man and the Citizen (see the box above). This charter of basic liberties affirmed the demise of aristocratic privileges by proclaiming an end to exemptions from taxation, freedom and equal rights for all men, and access to public office based on talent. All citizens

were to have the right to take part in the legislative process. Freedom of speech and the press were coupled with the outlawing of arbitrary arrests.

The declaration also raised another important issue. Did its ideal of equal rights for all men also include women? Many deputies insisted that it did, provided that, as one said, "women do not hope to exercise political rights and functions." Olympe de Gouges, a playwright, refused to accept this exclusion of women from political rights. Echoing the words of the official declaration, she penned the Declaration of the Rights of Woman and the Female Citizen, in which she insisted that women should have all the same rights as men. The National Assembly ignored her demands.

In the meantime, Louis XVI, who had remained inactive at Versailles, refused to accept the decrees on the abolition of feudalism and the declaration of rights. On October 5, thousands of Parisian women, described by one eyewitness as "detachments of women . . . armed with broomsticks, lances, pitchforks, swords, pistols and muskets," marched to Versailles and forced the king to accept the new decrees. The crowd now insisted that the royal family return to Paris. On October 6, the king complied. As a goodwill gesture, he brought along wagonloads of flour from the palace stores, escorted by women armed with pikes (some of which held the severed heads of the king's guards) singing, "We are bringing back the baker, the baker's wife, and the baker's boy" (the king, queen, and their son). The king became virtually a prisoner in Paris.

Because the Catholic church was seen as an important pillar of the old order, it too was reformed. Most of the lands of the church were seized. The new Civil Constitution of the Clergy was put into effect. Both bishops and priests were to be elected by the people and paid by the state. The Catholic church, still an important institution in the life of the French people, now became an enemy of the Revolution.

By 1791, the National Assembly had finally completed a new constitution that established a limited constitutional monarchy. There was still a monarch (now called "king of the French"), but the new Legislative Assembly was to make the laws. The Legislative Assembly, in which sovereign power was vested, was to sit for two years and consist of 745 representatives chosen by an indirect system of election that preserved power in the hands of the more affluent members of society. Only active citizens (men over the age of twenty-five paying in taxes the equivalent of three days' unskilled labor) could vote for electors (men paying taxes equal in value to ten days' labor). This relatively small group of fifty thousand electors then chose the deputies.

By 1791, the old order had been destroyed. However, many people—including Catholic priests, nobles, lower classes hurt by a rise in the cost of living, peasants who remained opposed to dues that had still not been abandoned, and political clubs like the Jacobins who offered more radical solutions to France's problems—opposed the new order. The king also made things difficult for the new government when he sought to flee France in June 1791 and almost succeeded before being recognized, captured, and brought back to Paris. In this unsettled situation, under a discredited and seemingly disloyal monarch, the new Legislative Assembly held its first session in October 1791. France's relations with the rest of Europe soon led to Louis's downfall.

On August 27, 1791, the monarchs of Austria and Prussia, fearing that revolution would spread to their countries, invited other European monarchs to use force to reestab-lish monarchical authority in France. Insulted by this threat, the Legislative Assembly declared war on Austria on April 20, 1792. The French fared badly in the initial fighting, and a frantic search for scapegoats began. As one observer noted, "Everywhere you hear the cry that the king is betraying us, the generals are betraying us, that nobody is to be trusted; . . . that Paris will be taken in six weeks by the Austrians. . . . We are on a volcano ready to spout flames."[2] Defeats in war coupled with economic shortages in the spring led to renewed political demonstrations, especially against the king. In August 1792, radical political groups in Paris took the king captive and forced the Legislative Assembly to suspend the monarchy and call for a national convention, chosen on the basis of universal male suffrage, to decide on the future form of government. The French Revolution was about to enter a more radical stage.

The Radical Revolution

In September 1792, the newly elected National Convention began its sessions. Dominated by lawyers and other professionals, two-thirds of its deputies were under forty-five, and almost all had gained political experience as a result of the Revolution. Almost all distrusted the king. As a result, the convention's first step on September 21 was to abolish the monarchy and establish a republic. On January 21, 1793, the king was executed, and the destruction of the old regime was complete. But the execution of the king created new enemies for the Revolution both at home and abroad while strengthening those who were already its enemies.

In Paris, the local government, known as the Commune, whose leaders came from the working classes, favored radical change and put constant pressure on the convention, pushing it to ever more radical positions. Moreover, the National Convention still did not rule all of France. Peasants in the west and inhabitants of France's major provincial cities refused to accept the authority of the convention.

A foreign crisis also loomed large. By the beginning of 1793, after the king had been executed, most of Europe—an informal coalition of Austria, Prussia, Spain, Portugal, Britain, the Dutch Republic, and even Russia—aligned militarily against France. Grossly overextended, the French armies began to experience reverses, and by late spring, France was threatened with invasion. If the invasion was successful, both the Revolution and the revolutionaries would be destroyed and the old regime reestablished.

A NATION IN ARMS

To meet these crises, the convention gave broad powers to an executive committee of twelve known as the Committee of Public Safety, which came to be dominated by Maximilien Robespierre. For a twelve-month period, from 1793 to 1794, the Committee of Public Safety took control of France. To save the Republic from its foreign foes, the committee decreed a universal mobilization of the nation on August 23, 1793:

> Young men will fight, young men are called to conquer. Married men will forge arms, transport military baggage and guns and will prepare food supplies. Women, who at long last are to take their rightful place in the revolution and follow their true destiny, will forget their futile tasks: their delicate hands will work at making clothes for soldiers; they will make tents and they will extend their tender care to shelters where the defenders of the *Patrie* [nation] will receive the help that their wounds require. Children will make lint of old cloth. It is for them that we are fighting: children, those beings destined to gather all the fruits of the revolution, will raise their pure hands toward the skies. And old men, performing their missions again, as of yore, will be guided to the public squares of the cities where they will kindle the courage of young warriors and preach the doctrines of hate for kings and the unity of the Republic.[3]

In less than a year, the French revolutionary government had raised an army of 650,000; by September 1794, it numbered 1,169,000. The Republic's army was the largest ever seen in European history. It now pushed the allies back across the Rhine and even conquered the Austrian Netherlands.

The French revolutionary army was an important step in the creation of modern nationalism. Previously wars had been fought between governments or ruling dynasties by relatively small armies of professional soldiers. The new French army was the creation of a "people's" government; its wars were now "people's" wars. The entire nation was to be involved in the war. But when dynastic wars became people's wars, warfare increased in ferocity and lack of restraint. The wars of the French revolutionary era opened the door to the total war of the modern world.

REIGN OF TERROR

To meet the domestic crisis, the National Convention and the Committee of Public Safety launched the "Reign of Terror." Revolutionary courts were instituted to protect the Republic from its internal enemies. In the course of nine months, sixteen thousand people were officially killed under the blade of the guillotine—a revolutionary device for the quick and efficient separation of heads from bodies. The Committee of Public Safety held that this bloodletting was only temporary. Once the war and the domestic emergency were over, they would be succeeded by a "republic of virtue" in which the Declaration of the Rights of Man and the Citizen would be fully implemented.

Revolutionary armies were set up to bring recalcitrant cities and districts back under the control of the National Convention. The Committee of Public Safety decided to make an example of Lyons, which had defied the authority of the National Convention. By April 1794, some 1,880 citizens of Lyons had been executed. When the guillotine proved too slow, cannon fire was used to blow condemned men into open graves. A German observed:

> Whole ranges of houses, always the most handsome, burnt. The churches, convents, and all the dwellings of the former patricians were in ruins. When I came to the guillotine, the blood of those who had been executed a few hours beforehand was still running in the street. . . . I said to a group of sansculottes [radicals] that it would be decent to clear away all this human blood. Why should it be cleared? one of them said to me. It's the blood of aristocrats and rebels. The dogs should lick it up.[4]

The National Convention also pursued a policy of dechristianization. A new calendar was instituted in which years were no longer numbered from the birth of Christ

⟡ **WOMEN PATRIOTS.** Women played a variety of roles in the events of the French Revolution. This picture shows a women's patriotic club discussing the decrees of the National Convention, an indication that some women became highly politicized by the upheavals of the Revolution.

THE FRENCH REVOLUTION

1789	
Meeting of Estates-General	May 5
Formation of National Assembly	June 17
Fall of the Bastille	July 14
Great Fear	Summer
Abolition of feudalism	August 4
Declaration of the Rights of Man and the Citizen	August 26
March to Versailles; king's return to Paris	October 5–6
1790	
Civil Constitution of the Clergy	July 12
1791	
Flight of the king	June 20–21
1792	
France declares war on Austria	April 20
Attack on the royal palace	August 10
Abolition of monarchy	September 21
1793	
Execution of the king	January 21
Levy-in-mass	August 23
1794	
Execution of Robespierre	July 28
1795	
Adoption of Constitution of 1795—the Directory	August 2

but from September 22, 1792, the first day of the French Republic. The new calendar also eliminated Sundays and church holidays. In Paris, the cathedral of Notre-Dame was designated the Temple of Reason; in November 1793, a public ceremony dedicated to the worship of reason was held in the former cathedral in which patriotic maidens adorned in white dresses paraded before a "temple of reason" where the high altar once stood.

Reaction and the Directory

By the summer of 1794, the French had been successful on the battlefield against their foreign foes, making the Terror less necessary. But the Terror continued because Robespierre, who had become a figure of power and authority, became obsessed with purifying the body politic of all the corrupt. Many deputies in the National Convention

were fearful, however, that they were not safe while Robespierre was free to act and gathered enough votes to condemn him. Robespierre was guillotined on July 28, 1794.

After the death of Robespierre, a reaction set in as more moderate middle-class leaders took control. The Reign of Terror came to a halt, and the National Convention reduced the power of the Committee of Public Safety. Churches were allowed to reopen for public worship. In addition, a new constitution was created in August 1795 that reflected the desire for a stability that did not sacrifice the ideals of 1789. Five directors—the Directory—acted as the executive authority.

The period of the Revolution under the government of the Directory (1795–1799) was an era of stagnation and corruption, a materialistic reaction to the sacrifices that had been demanded in the Reign of Terror. At the same time, the government of the Directory faced political enemies from both the left and the right of the political spectrum. On the right, royalists who wanted to restore the monarchy continued their agitation. On the left, radical hopes of power were revived by continuing economic problems. Battered from both sides, unable to solve the country's economic problems, and still carrying on the wars inherited from the Committee of Public Safety, the Directory increasingly relied on the military to maintain its power. This led to a coup d'état in 1799 in which the popular military general Napoleon Bonaparte seized power.

THE AGE OF NAPOLEON

Napoleon dominated both French and European history from 1799 to 1815. He was born in 1769 in Corsica shortly after France had annexed the island. The young Napoleon was sent to France to study in one of the new military schools and was a lieutenant when the Revolution broke out in 1789. The Revolution and the European war that followed gave him new opportunities, and Napoleon rose quickly through the ranks. In 1794, at the age of only twenty-five, he was made a brigadier general by the Committee of Public Safety. Two years later, he commanded the French armies in Italy, where he won a series of victories and returned to France as a conquering hero (see the box on p. 380). After a disastrous expedition to Egypt, Napoleon returned to Paris, where he participated in the coup that gave him control of France. He was only thirty years old.

After the coup of 1799, a new form of the Republic—called the Consulate—was proclaimed in which Napoleon, as first consul, controlled the entire executive authority of government. He had overwhelming influence over the legislature, appointed members of the administrative bureaucracy, commanded the army, and conducted foreign affairs. In 1802, Napoleon was made consul for life, and in 1804, he returned France to monarchy when he had himself crowned as Emperor Napoleon I.

NAPOLEON AND PSYCHOLOGICAL WARFARE

*I*n 1796, at the age of twenty-seven, Napoleon Bonaparte was given command of the French army in Italy,
where he won a series of stunning victories. His use of speed,
deception, and surprise to overwhelm his opponents is well known.
In this selection from a proclamation to his troops in Italy,
Napoleon also appears as a master of psychological warfare.

NAPOLEON BONAPARTE, PROCLAMATION TO FRENCH TROOPS IN ITALY (APRIL 26, 1796)

Soldiers:

In a fortnight you have won six victories, taken twenty-
one standards [flags of military units], fifty-five pieces of
artillery, several strong positions, and conquered the richest
part of Piedmont [in northern Italy]; you have captured
15,000 prisoners and killed or wounded more than 10,000
men. . . . You have won battles without cannon, crossed
rivers without bridges, made forced marches without shoes,
camped without brandy and often without bread. Soldiers
of liberty, only republican troops could have endured what
you have endured. Soldiers, you have our thanks! The
grateful Patrie [nation] will owe its prosperity to you. . . .

The two armies which but recently attacked you with
audacity are fleeing before you in terror; the wicked men
who laughed at your misery and rejoiced at the thought of
the triumphs of your enemies are confounded and trembling.

But, soldiers, as yet you have done nothing compared
with what remains to be done. . . . Undoubtedly the greatest obstacles have been overcome; but you still have battles
to fight, cities to capture, rivers to cross. Is there one among
you whose courage is abating? No. . . . All of you are consumed with a desire to extend the glory of the French people; all of you long to humiliate those arrogant kings who
dare to contemplate placing us in fetters; all of you desire to
dictate a glorious peace, one which will indemnify the
Patrie for the immense sacrifices it has made; all of you wish
to be able to say with pride as you return to your villages, "I
was with the victorious army of Italy!"

Domestic Policies

One of Napoleon's first domestic policies was to establish peace with the oldest and most implacable enemy of
the Revolution, the Catholic church. In 1801, Napoleon
arranged a concordat with the pope that recognized
Catholicism as the religion of a majority of the French
people. In return, the pope agreed not to raise the
question of the church lands confiscated in the Revolution. As a result of the concordat, the Catholic church was
no longer an enemy of the French government.

Napoleon's most enduring domestic achievement was
his codification of the laws. Before the Revolution, France
had some three hundred local legal systems. During the
Revolution, efforts were made to prepare a single code of
laws for the entire nation, but it remained for Napoleon
to bring the work to completion in the famous Civil Code.
This preserved most of the revolutionary gains by recognizing the principle of the equality of all citizens before
the law, the abolition of serfdom and feudalism, and religious toleration. Property rights were protected, and the
interests of employers were safeguarded by outlawing trade
unions and strikes.

At the same time, the Civil Code strictly curtailed
the rights of some people. During the radical phase of
the French Revolution, new laws had made divorce an
easy process for both husbands and wives and allowed sons
and daughters to inherit property equally. Napoleon's Civil
Code undid these laws. Divorce was still allowed but was
made more difficult for women to obtain. Women were
now "less equal than men" in other ways as well. When
they married, their property came under the control of
their husbands, and in lawsuits, they were treated as
minors.

Napoleon also developed a powerful, centralized administrative machine and worked hard to develop a bureaucracy of capable officials. Early on, the regime showed that
it cared little whether the expertise of officials had been
acquired in royal or revolutionary bureaucracies. Promotion, whether in civil or military offices, was to be based
not on rank or birth but on ability only. This principle of
a government career open to talent was, of course, what
many bourgeois had wanted before the Revolution.

In his domestic policies, then, Napoleon both destroyed
and preserved aspects of the Revolution. Liberty had been
replaced by an initially benevolent despotism that grew
increasingly arbitrary as the demands of war overwhelmed
Napoleon and the French. The Civil Code, however, preserved the equality of all citizens before the law. The concept of careers open to talent was also a gain of the
Revolution that Napoleon preserved.

Napoleon's Empire and the European Response

When Napoleon became consul in 1799, France was at war
with a second European coalition of Russia, Great Britain,
and Austria. Napoleon realized the need for a pause and
made a peace treaty in 1802. But war was renewed in 1803
with Britain, who was soon joined by Austria, Russia, and
Prussia in the Third Coalition. In a series of battles from

THE CORONATION OF NAPOLEON. In 1804, Napoleon restored monarchy to France when he had himself crowned as emperor. In the coronation scene painted by Jacques-Louis David, Napoleon is shown crowning his wife, the empress Josephine, while the pope looks on. The painting shows Napoleon's mother seated in the box in the background, even though she was not at the ceremony.

1805 to 1807, Napoleon's Grand Army defeated the Austrian, Prussian, and Russian armies, giving Napoleon the opportunity to create a new European order.

THE GRAND EMPIRE

From 1807 to 1812, Napoleon was the master of Europe. His Grand Empire was composed of three major parts: the French Empire, dependent states, and allied states (see Map 17.3). The French Empire, the inner core of the Grand Empire, consisted of an enlarged France extending to the Rhine in the east and including the western half of Italy north of Rome. Dependent states were kingdoms under the rule of Napoleon's relatives; these came to include Spain, the Netherlands, the kingdom of Italy, the Swiss Republic, the Grand Duchy of Warsaw, and the Confederation of the Rhine (a union of all German states except Austria and Prussia). Allied states were those defeated by Napoleon and forced to join his struggle against Britain; these included Prussia, Austria, Russia, and Sweden.

Within his empire, Napoleon sought acceptance of certain revolutionary principles, including legal equality, religious toleration, and economic freedom. As he explained to his brother Jerome after he had made him king of the new German state of Westphalia:

> What the people of Germany desire most impatiently is that talented commoners should have the same right to your esteem and to public employments as the nobles, that any trace of serfdom and of an intermediate hierarchy between the sovereign and the lowest class of the people should be completely abolished. The benefits of the Code Napoléon, the publicity of judicial procedure, the creation of juries must be so many distinguishing marks of your monarchy. . . . What nation would wish to return under the arbitrary Prussian government once it had tasted the benefits of a wise and liberal administration? The peoples of Germany, the peoples of France, of Italy, of Spain all desire equality and liberal ideas. I have guided the affairs of Europe for many years now, and I have had occasion to convince myself that the buzzing of the privileged classes is contrary to the general opinion. Be a constitutional king.[5]

MAP 17.3 Napoleon's Grand Empire. Napoleon's Grand Army won a series of victories against Britain, Austria, Prussia, and Russia that gave the French emperor full or partial control over much of Europe by 1807. ➤ **On the Continent, what is the overall relationship between distance from France and degree of French control, and how can you account for this?**

Legend:
- French Empire
- Under French control
- Allied to France
- → Napoleon's route, 1812
- ⚔ Battle site

In the inner core and dependent states of his Grand Empire, Napoleon tried to destroy the old order. Nobility and clergy everywhere in these states lost their special privileges. He decreed equality of opportunity with offices open to talent, equality before the law, and religious toleration. This spread of French revolutionary principles was an important factor in the development of liberal traditions in these countries.

Napoleon hoped that his Grand Empire would last for centuries; it collapsed almost as rapidly as it had been formed. Two major reasons explain this: Great Britain and nationalism. As long as Britain ruled the waves, it was not subject to military attack. Napoleon hoped to invade Britain, but he could not overcome the British navy's decisive defeat of a combined French-Spanish fleet at Trafal-

gar in 1805. To defeat Britain, Napoleon turned to his Continental System. Put into effect between 1806 and 1808, it attempted to prevent British goods from reaching the European continent in order to weaken Britain economically and destroy its capacity to wage war. But the Continental System failed. Allied states resented it; some began to cheat and others to resist. New markets in the Middle East and in Latin America gave Britain new outlets for its goods.

The second important factor in the defeat of Napoleon was nationalism. This political creed had arisen during the French Revolution in the French people's emphasis on solidarity against other peoples. Nationalism involved the unique cultural identity of a people based on common language and national symbols. French nationalism had made possible the mass armies of the revolutionary and Napoleonic eras. But Napoleon's conquests aroused nationalism in two ways: by making the French hated oppressors and thus arousing the patriotism of others in opposition to French nationalism and by showing the people of Europe what nationalism was and what a nation in arms could do. It was a lesson not lost on other peoples and rulers. A Spanish uprising against Napoleon's rule, aided by British support, kept a French force of 200,000 pinned down for years.

THE FALL OF NAPOLEON

The beginning of Napoleon's downfall came in 1812 with his invasion of Russia. The refusal of the Russians to remain in the Continental System left Napoleon with little choice. Although aware of the risks in invading such a huge country, he also knew that if the Russians were allowed to challenge the Continental System unopposed, others would soon follow suit. In June 1812, he led his Grand Army of more than 600,000 men into Russia. Napoleon's hopes for victory depended on quickly defeating the Russian armies, but the Russian forces retreated and refused to give battle, torching their own villages and countryside to keep Napoleon's army from finding food. When the Russians did stop to fight at Borodino, Napoleon's forces won an indecisive and costly victory. When the remaining troops of the Grand Army arrived in Moscow, they found the city ablaze. Lacking food and supplies, Napoleon abandoned Moscow late in October and made a retreat across Russia in terrible winter conditions. Only 40,000 of the original 600,000 men managed to arrive back in Poland in January 1813.

This military disaster led other European states to rise up and attack the crippled French army. Paris was captured in March 1814, and Napoleon was sent into exile on the island of Elba, off the coast of Italy. Meanwhile the Bourbon monarchy was restored in the person of Louis XVIII, the Count of Provence, brother of the executed king. Louis XVII, son of Louis XVI, had died in prison at age ten. Napoleon, bored on Elba, slipped back into France. When troops were sent to capture him, Napoleon opened his coat and addressed them: "Soldiers of the 5th regiment, I am your Emperor. . . . If there is a man among you would kill his Emperor, here I am!" No one fired a shot. Shouting "Vive l'Empereur! Vive l'Empereur," the troops went over to his side, and Napoleon entered Paris in triumph on March 20, 1815.

The powers that had defeated him pledged once more to fight him. Having decided to strike first at his enemies, Napoleon raised yet another army and moved to attack the allied forces stationed in what is now Belgium. At Waterloo on June 18, Napoleon met a combined British and Prussian army under the duke of Wellington and suffered a bloody defeat. This time, the victorious allies exiled him to Saint Helena, a small, forsaken island in the South Atlantic. Only Napoleon's memory continued to haunt French political life.

CONCLUSION

Everywhere in Europe at the beginning of the eighteenth century, the old order remained strong. Nobles, clerics, towns, and provinces all had privileges. Everywhere in the eighteenth century, monarchs sought to enlarge their bureaucracies to raise taxes to support the large standing armies that had originated in the seventeenth century. The existence of five great powers, with two of them (France and England) embattled in the East and in the Western Hemisphere, ushered in a new scale of conflict; the Seven Years' War can legitimately be viewed as the first world war. Although the wars changed little on the European continent, British victories enabled Great Britain to emerge as the world's greatest naval and colonial power. Everywhere in Europe, increased demands for taxes to support these conflicts led to attacks on the privileged orders and a desire for change not met by the ruling monarchs. At the same time, sustained population growth and dramatic changes in finance, trade, and industry created tensions that undermined the traditional foundations of the old order. The inability of that old order to deal meaningfully with these changes led to a revolutionary outburst at the end of the eighteenth century that brought the old order to an end.

The revolutionary era of the late eighteenth century was a time of dramatic political transformations. Revolutionary upheavals, beginning in North America and continuing in France, spurred movements for political liberty and equality. The documents promulgated by these revolutions, the Declaration of Independence and the Declaration of the Rights of Man and the Citizen, embodied the fundamental ideas of the Enlightenment and created a liberal political agenda based on a belief in popular sovereignty—the people as the source of political power—and the principles of liberty and equality. Liberty meant, in theory, freedom from arbitrary power as well as the freedom to think, write, and worship as one chose. Equality meant equality in rights and equality of opportunity based on talent rather than wealth or status at birth. In practice, equality remained limited; property owners had greater opportunities for voting and officeholding, and women were still not treated as the equals of men.

The French Revolution set in motion a modern revolutionary concept. No one had foreseen or consciously planned the upheaval that began in 1789, but thereafter, radicals and revolutionaries knew that mass uprisings by the common people could overthrow unwanted elitist governments. For these people, the French Revolution became a symbol of hope; for those who feared such changes, it became a symbol of dread. The French Revolution became the classical political and social model for revolution. At the same time, the liberal and national political ideals created by the Revolution dominated the political landscape for well over a century. A new era had begun, and the world would never be the same.

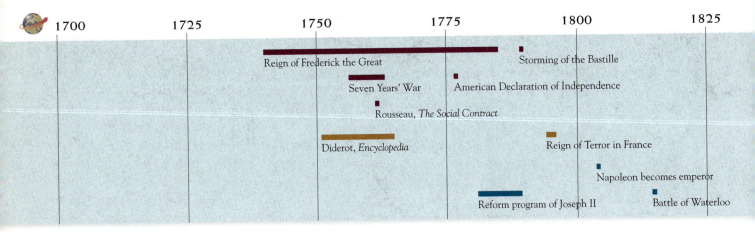

| 1700 | 1725 | 1750 | 1775 | 1800 | 1825 |

Reign of Frederick the Great

Storming of the Bastille

Seven Years' War

American Declaration of Independence

Rousseau, *The Social Contract*

Diderot, *Encyclopedia*

Reign of Terror in France

Napoleon becomes emperor

Reform program of Joseph II

Battle of Waterloo

CHAPTER NOTES

1. John Locke, *An Essay Concerning Human Understanding* (New York, 1964), pp. 89–90.
2. Quoted in William Doyle, *The Oxford History of the French Revolution* (Oxford, 1989), p. 184.
3. Quoted in Leo Gershoy, *The Era of the French Revolution* (Princeton, N.J., 1957), p. 157.

4. Quoted in Doyle, *Oxford History of the French Revolution*, p. 254.
5. Quoted in J. Christopher Herold, ed., *The Mind of Napoleon* (New York, 1955), pp. 74–75.

SUGGESTED READING

Two sound, comprehensive surveys of eighteenth-century Europe are I. Woloch, *Eighteenth-Century Europe* (New York, 1982), and M. S. Anderson, *Europe in the Eighteenth Century* (London, 1987).

Good introductions to the Enlightenment can be found in U. Im Hof, *The Enlightenment* (Oxford, 1994); D. Goodman, *The Republic of Letters: A Cultural History of the French Enlightenment* (Ithaca, N.Y., 1994); and D. Outram, *The Enlightenment* (Cambridge, 1995). A more detailed synthesis can be found in the two volumes by P. Gay, *The Enlightenment: An Interpretation* (New York, 1966–1969). For a short, popular survey on the French philosophes, see F. Artz, *The Enlightenment in France* (Kent, Ohio, 1968). On women in the eighteenth century, see N. Z. Davis and A. Farge, eds., *A History of Women: Renaissance and Enlightenment Paradoxes* (Cambridge, Mass., 1993), and O. Hufton, *The Prospect Before Her: A History of Women in Western Europe, 1500–1800* (New York, 1998).

A readable general survey on the arts and literature is M. Levy, *Rococo to Revolution* (London, 1966). An important study on popular culture is P. Burke, *Popular Culture in Early Modern Europe* (New York, 1978).

On the European nobility in the eighteenth century, see J. Dewald, *The European Nobility 1400–1800* (Cambridge, 1996), and H. M. Scott, *The European Nobility in the Seventeenth and Eighteenth Centuries* (London, 1995). On European cities, see J. de Vries, *European Urbanization, 1500–1800* (Cambridge, Mass., 1984). The

warfare of this period is examined in M. S. Anderson, *War and Society in Europe of the Old Regime, 1615–1789* (New York, 1988).

For a brief survey of Latin America, see E. B. Burns, *Latin America: A Concise Interpretative History*, 4th ed. (Englewood Cliffs, N.J., 1986). More detailed works on colonial Latin American history include S. J. Stein and B. H. Stein, *The Colonial Heritage of Latin America* (New York, 1970), and J. Lockhardt and S. B. Schwartz, *Early Latin America: A History of Colonial Spanish America and Brazil* (New York, 1983). A history of the revolutionary era in America can be found in R. Middlekauff, *The Glorious Cause: The American Revolution, 1763–1789* (New York, 1982), and C. Bonwick, *The American Revolution* (Charlottesville, Va., 1991).

On enlightened absolutism, see H. M. Scott, ed., *Enlightened Absolutism: Reform and Reformers in Late Eighteenth-Century Europe* (Ann Arbor, Mich., 1990). Good biographies of some of Europe's monarchs include R. Asprey, *Frederick the Great: The Magnificent Enigma* (New York, 1986); I. De Madariaga, *Catherine the Great: A Short History* (New Haven, Conn., 1990); and T. C. W. Blanning, *Joseph II* (New York, 1994).

A well-written introduction to the French Revolution can be found in W. Doyle, *The Oxford History of the French Revolution* (Oxford, 1989). For the entire revolutionary and Napoleonic eras, see O. Connelly, *The French Revolution and Napoleonic Era*, 3d ed. (Fort Worth, Tex., 2000), and D. M. G. Sutherland, *France, 1789–1815: Revolution and Counter-Revolution* (London, 1985). Two brief works are A. Forrest, *The French Revolution* (Oxford, 1995), and J. M. Roberts, *The French Revolution,* 2d ed. (New York, 1997).

The origins of the French Revolution are examined in W. Doyle, *Origins of the French Revolution* (Oxford, 1988). On the early years of the Revolution, see T. Tackett, *Becoming a Revolutionary* (Princeton, N.J., 1996), and N. Hampson, *Prelude to Terror* (Oxford, 1988). Important works on the radical stage of the French Revolution include N. Hampson, *The Terror in the French Revolution* (London, 1981); R. R. Palmer, *Twelve Who Ruled* (Princeton, N.J., 1941); and R. Cobb, *The People's Armies* (London, 1987). The importance of the revolutionary wars in the radical stage of the Revolution is underscored in T. C. W. Blanning, *The French*

Revolutionary Wars, 1787–1802 (New York, 1996). On the Directory, see M. Lyons, *France Under the Directory* (Cambridge, 1975). On the role of women in revolutionary France, see O. Hufton, *Women and the Limits of Citizenship in the French Revolution* (Toronto, 1992), and J. Landes, *Women and the Public Sphere in the Age of the French Revolution* (Ithaca, N.Y., 1988). The best brief biography of Napoleon is F. Markham, *Napoleon* (New York, 1963). Also valuable are M. Lyons, *Napoleon Bonaparte and the Legacy of the French Revolution* (New York, 1994); G. J. Ellis, *Napoleon* (New York, 1997); and the massive biographies by F. J. McLynn, *Napoleon: A Biography* (London, 1997), and A. Schom, *Napoleon Bonaparte* (New York, 1997).

InfoTrac College Edition

Visit the source collections at infotrac.thomsonlearning.com and use the Search function with the following key terms.

American Revolution

Enlightenment

French Revolution

John Locke

Napoleon

Napoleonic Wars

Rousseau

World History Resources

Visit the *Essential World History* Companion Web Site for resources specific to this textbook:

http://history.wadsworth.com/duikeressentials02/

The CD in the back of this book and the World History Resource Center at **http://history.wadsworth.com/world/** offer a variety of tools to help you succeed in this course, including access to quizzes; images; documents; interactive simulations, maps, and timelines; movie explorations; and a wealth of other sources.

THE EMERGENCE OF NEW WORLD PATTERNS (1400–1800)

Historians often refer to the period from the fifteenth to the eighteenth centuries as the early modern era. During these years, several factors were at work that created the conditions of our own time.

From a global perspective, perhaps the most noteworthy event of the period was the extension of the maritime trade network throughout the entire populated world. The Chinese had inaugurated the process with their groundbreaking voyages to East Africa in the early fifteenth century, but the primary instrument of that expansion was a resurgent Europe, which exploded onto the world scene with the initial explorations of the Portuguese and the Spanish at the end of the fifteenth century and then gradually came to dominate shipping on international trade routes during the next three centuries.

Some contemporary historians argue that it was this sudden burst of energy from Europe that created the first truly global economic network. According to Immanuel Wallerstein, one of the leading proponents of this theory, the Age of Exploration led to the creation of a new "world system" characterized by the emergence of global trade networks dominated by the rising force of European capitalism, which now began to scour the periphery of the system for access to markets and cheap raw materials.

In the view of other contemporary historians, however, Wallerstein's view must be qualified. Some, for example, point to the Mongol expansion beginning in the thirteenth century, or even to the rise of the Arab Empire in the Middle East a few centuries earlier, as signs of the creation of a global communications network enabling goods and ideas to travel from one end of the Eurasian supercontinent to the other.

Whatever the truth of this debate, there are still many reasons for considering the end of the fifteenth century as a crucial date in world history. In the most basic sense, it marked the end of the long isolation of the Western Hemisphere from the rest of the inhabited world. In so doing, it led to the creation of the first truly global network of ideas and commodities, which would introduce plants, ideas, and (unfortunately) many new diseases to all humanity (see the box on p. 387). Second, the period gave birth to a stunning increase in trade and manufacturing that stimulated major economic changes not only in Europe but in other parts of the world as well.

The period from 1400 to 1800, then, was an incubation period for the modern world and the launching pad for an era of Western domination that would reach fruition in the nineteenth century. To understand why the West emerged as the leading force in the world at that time, it is necessary to grasp what factors were at work in Europe and why they were absent in other major civilizations around the globe.

Historians have identified improvements in navigation, shipbuilding, and weaponry that took place in Europe in the early modern era as essential elements in the Age of Exploration. As we have seen, many of these technological advances were based on earlier discoveries that had taken place elsewhere—in China, India, and the Middle East—and had then been brought to Europe on Muslim ships or along the trade routes through Central Asia. But it was the capacity and the desire of the Europeans to enhance their wealth and power by making practical use of the discoveries of others that was the significant factor in the equation and enabled them to dominate international sea lanes and create vast colonial empires in the New World.

But technological innovations by themselves cannot provide the final answer to the question of why at this time in history Europe suddenly became the engine for rapid global change. Another factor, certainly, was the change in the European worldview, the shift from a metaphysical to a materialist perspective and the growing inclination among European intellectuals to question first principles. Whereas in China, for example, the "investigation of things" had been put to the use of analyzing and confirming principles first established by Confucius during the Chinese "golden age," in early modern Europe, empirical scientists rejected received religious ideas, developed a new conception of the universe, and sought ways to improve material conditions around them.

Why were European thinkers more interested than their counterparts elsewhere in practical applications for their discoveries? One explanation perhaps lies in the growing strength of the urban bourgeoisie in many areas of early modern Europe and the deliberate appeal that scientists made to European mercantile elites when they showed how the new scientific ideas could be applied directly to specific technological needs.

A final factor can be attributed to political changes that were beginning to take place in Europe during this period. The breakup of the world of Christendom, a consequence of the religious wars of the sixteenth and seventeenth centuries, helped give birth to independent and relatively centralized monarchies in many areas of Europe. In the eighteenth century, this process continued as most European states enlarged their bureaucratic machinery

THE COLUMBIAN EXCHANGE

*I*n the Western world, the discovery of the Americas has traditionally been viewed essentially in a positive sense, as the first step in a process that expanded the global trade network and eventually led to economic well-being and political democracy in societies throughout the world. That view has come under sharp attack from some observers, however, who claim that for the peoples of the New World, the primary legacy of the European conquest was not improved living standards but harsh colonial exploitation and the spread of pestilential diseases that decimated the local population. In recent years, the brunt of such criticism has been directed at Christopher Columbus, one of the chief initiators of the discovery and conquest of the Americas. Taking issue with the prevailing image of Columbus as a heroic figure in world history, critics view him as a symbol of Spanish colonial repression and a prime mover in the virtual extinction of the peoples and cultures of the New World.

There is no doubt that the record of the European conquistadors in the Western Hemisphere leaves much to be desired, and certainly the voyages of Columbus were not of universal benefit to his contemporaries or to the generations later to come. But to focus solely on the evils that were committed in the name of exploration and the propagation of Christianity distorts the historical realities of the era. The age of European expansion that began with Prince Henry the Navigator and Christopher Columbus was only the latest in a series of population movements that included the spread of nomadic peoples across Central Asia and the expansion of Islam from the Middle East after the death of the prophet Muhammad. In fact, the migration of peoples in search of survival and a better livelihood has been a central theme in the evolution of the human race since the dawn of prehistory.

Even more important, it seems clear that the consequences of such population movements are too complex to be summed up in moral or ideological simplifications. The European expansion into the Americas, for example, not only brought the destruction of cultures and dangerous new diseases but also initiated the exchange of plant and animal species that have ultimately been of widespread benefit to peoples throughout the globe. The introduction of the horse, cow, and various grain crops vastly increased food productivity in the New World. The cultivation of corn, manioc, and the potato have had the same effect in Asia, Africa, and Europe. Whether Christopher Columbus was a hero or a villain is a matter of debate. That he and his contemporaries played a key role in the emergence of the modern world is a matter on which there can be no doubt.

➤ **MASSACRE OF THE INDIANS.** This sixteenth-century engraving is an imaginative treatment of what was probably an all-too-common occurrence as the Spanish attempted to enslave the American peoples and convert them to Christianity.

Fototas Archive

and consolidated their governments in order to collect the revenues and amass the armies they needed to compete militarily with rivals. In this highly competitive environment, political leaders desperately sought ways to enhance their wealth and power and grasped eagerly at whatever tools were available to guarantee their survival and prosperity.

European expansion was not fueled solely by economic considerations, however. As had been the case with the rise of Islam in the seventh and eighth centuries, religion played a major role in motivating the European Age of Exploration in the early modern era. Although Christianity was by no means a new religion in the fifteenth century (as Islam had been at the moment of Arab expansion), the world of Christendom was in the midst of a major period of conflict with the forces of Islam, a rivalry that had been exacerbated by the conquest of the Byzantine Empire by the Ottoman Turks in 1453.

Although the claims of Portuguese and Spanish adventurers that their activities were motivated primarily by a desire to bring the word of God to non-Christian peoples undoubtedly included a considerable measure of self-delusion and hypocrisy, there seems no reason to doubt that religious motives played a meaningful part in the European Age of Exploration. Religious motives were perhaps less evident in the activities of the non-Catholic powers that entered the competition beginning in the seventeenth century. English and Dutch merchants and officials were more inclined to be motivated purely by the pursuit of economic profit or by the prevailing "beggar thy neighbor" mercantile philosophy of the day.

Conditions in many areas of Asia were less conducive to these economic and political developments. In China, after Yongle's brief experiment in maritime exploration was abandoned, a centralized monarchy continued to rely on a prosperous agricultural sector as the economic foundation of the empire. In Japan, power was centralized under the powerful Tokugawa shogunate, and the era of peace and stability that ensued saw an increase in manufacturing and commercial activity. But Japanese elites, after initially expressing interest in the outside world, abruptly shut the door on European trade and ideas in an effort to protect the "land of the gods" from external contamination.

In India and the Middle East, commerce and manufacturing had played a vital role in the life of societies since the emergence of the Indian Ocean trade network in the first centuries C.E. But beginning in the eleventh century, the area had suffered through an extended period of political instability, marked by invasions of nomadic peoples from Central Asia. The violence of the period and the local rulers' lack of experience in promoting maritime commerce had a severe depressing effect on urban manufacturing and commerce.

In the early modern era, then, Europe was best placed to take advantage of the technological innovations that had become increasingly available throughout the Old World. It possessed the political stability, the capital, and what today might be called the "modernizing elite" that provided the spur to active efforts to take advantage of new conditions for their own benefit. Whereas other regions were still beset by internal obstacles or had deliberately "turned inward" to seek their destiny, Europe now turned outward to seek a new and dominant position in the world. This should not blind us to the facts that significant changes were taking place in other parts of the world as well and that many of these changes had relatively little to do with the situation in the West (see the box on p. 389). As we have seen, the impact of European expansion on the rest of the world was still limited at the end of the eighteenth century. While European political authority was firmly established in a few key areas, such as the Spice Islands and Latin America, in most regions of Africa and Asia traditional societies remained relatively intact. And processes at work in these societies were often operating independently of events in Europe

and would later give birth to forces that acted to restrict or shape the Western impact.

One of these forces was the progressive emergence of centralized states, some of them built on the concept of ethnic unity. In Japan, the Tokugawa shogunate had asserted an unprecedented degree of political and cultural authority. In India, a centralized empire had been created for the first time since the fall of the Mauryas in the era of antiquity. In mainland Southeast Asia, organized states that were broadly based on rising ethnic consciousness emerged in Burma, Thailand, and Vietnam. This trend was somewhat less apparent in the Middle East, where the Ottoman Empire still laid claim to universal hegemony over the entire eastern Mediterranean and Mesopotamia, and in sub-Saharan Africa, where the forces of state building were still in an embryonic stage.

Within these centralized states, the steady growth of a commercial and manufacturing sector was beginning to create the conditions for a future industrial revolution. A number of Asian societies made technological advances during this period and witnessed the emergence of a more visible and articulate urban bourgeoisie. For the moment, however, such forces were mere portents for the future, not signs of an imminent industrial revolution. At the beginning of the nineteenth century, the primary fact of life for most Asian and African societies was the expansionist power of an industrializing and ever more aggressive Europe. The power and ambition of the West provided an immediate challenge to the independence and destiny of societies throughout the rest of the world. The nature of that challenge will be the subject of our next section.

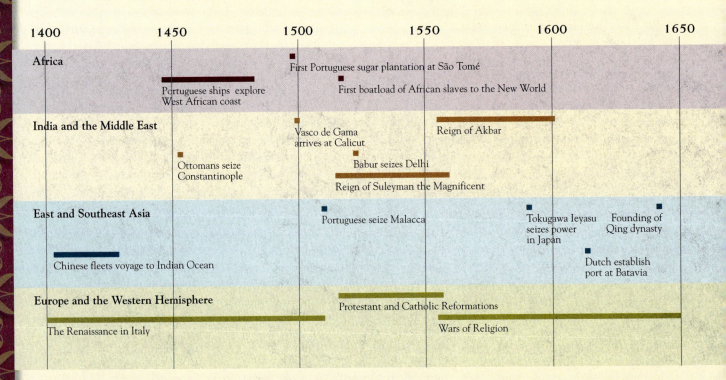

	1400	1450	1500	1550	1600	1650

Africa
First Portuguese sugar plantation at São Tomé
First boatload of African slaves to the New World
Portuguese ships explore West African coast

India and the Middle East
Vasco de Gama arrives at Calicut
Reign of Akbar
Ottomans seize Constantinople
Babur seizes Delhi
Reign of Suleyman the Magnificent

East and Southeast Asia
Portuguese seize Malacca
Tokugawa Ieyasu seizes power in Japan
Founding of Qing dynasty
Chinese fleets voyage to Indian Ocean
Dutch establish port at Batavia

Europe and the Western Hemisphere
Protestant and Catholic Reformations
The Renaissance in Italy
Wars of Religion

POPULATION EXPLOSION

Between 1700 and 1800, Europe, China, and to a lesser degree India and the Ottoman Empire experienced a dramatic growth in population. In Europe, the population grew from 120 million people to almost 200 million by 1800; China, from less than 200 million to 300 million during the same period.

Four factors were important in causing this population explosion. First, better growing conditions, made possible by an improvement in climate, affected wide areas of the world and enabled people to produce more food. Summers in both China and Europe were warmer beginning in the early eighteenth century. Second, by the eighteenth century, people had begun to develop immunities to the epidemic diseases that had caused such widespread loss of life between 1500 and 1700. The spread of people by ship after 1500 had led to devastating epidemics. For example, the arrival of Europeans in Mexico led to smallpox, measles, and chickenpox among a native population that had no immunities to European diseases. In 1500, between 11 and 20 million people lived in the area of Mexico; by 1650, only 1.5 million remained. Gradually, however, people developed immunities to these diseases.

➤ **FESTIVAL OF THE YAM.** The spread of a few major food crops made possible new sources of nutrition to feed more people. The importance of the yam to the Ashanti people of West Africa is evident in this celebration of a yam festival at harvest time in 1817.

A third factor in the population increase came from new food sources. As a result of the Columbian exchange (see the box on p. 387) American food crops—such as corn, potatoes, and sweet potatoes—were brought to other parts of the world, where they became important food sources. China had imported a new species of rice from Southeast Asia that had a shorter harvest cycle than that of existing varieties. These new foods provided additional sources of nutrition that enabled more people to live for a longer time. At the same time, land development and canal building in the eighteenth century also enabled government authorities to move food supplies to areas threatened with crop failure and famine.

Finally, the use of new weapons based on gunpowder allowed states to control larger territories and ensure a new degree of order. The early rulers of the Qing dynasty, for example, pacified the Chinese Empire and ensured a long period of peace and stability. Absolute monarchs achieved similar goals in a number of European states. Less violence led to fewer deaths at the same time that an increase in food supplies and a decrease in death from diseases were occurring, thus making possible in the eighteenth century the beginning of the world population explosion that persists to this day.

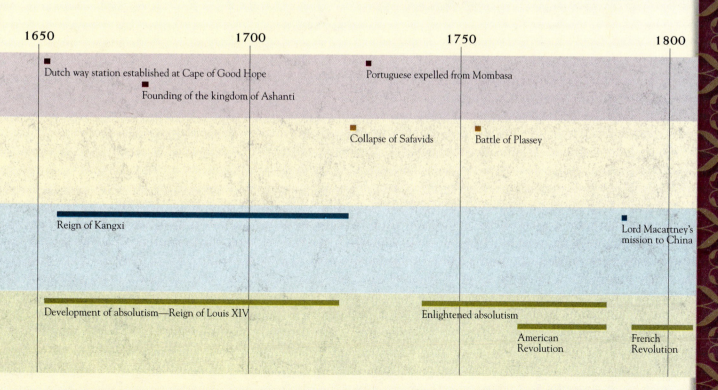

1650 — 1700 — 1750 — 1800

Dutch way station established at Cape of Good Hope

Founding of the kingdom of Ashanti

Portuguese expelled from Mombasa

Collapse of Safavids

Battle of Plassey

Reign of Kangxi

Lord Macartney's mission to China

Development of absolutism—Reign of Louis XIV

Enlightened absolutism

American Revolution

French Revolution

© The Art Archive/Eileen Tweedy

GLOSSARY

absolutism a form of government where the sovereign power or ultimate authority rested in the hands of a monarch who claimed to rule by divine right and was therefore responsible only to God.

Agricultural (Neolithic) Revolution the shift from hunting animals and gathering plants for sustenance to producing food by systematic agriculture that occurred gradually between 10,000 and 4000 B.C. (the Neolithic or "New Stone" Age).

agricultural revolution the application of new agricultural techniques that allowed for a large increase in productivity in the eighteenth century.

anarchism a political theory that holds that all governments and existing social institutions are unnecessary and advocates a society based on voluntary cooperation.

ANC the African National Congress. Founded in 1912, it was the beginning of political activity by South African blacks. Banned by politically dominant European whites in 1960, it was not officially "unbanned" until 1990. It is now the official majority party of the South African government.

Analects the body of writing containing conversations between Confucius and his disciples that preserves his worldly wisdom and pragmatic philosophies.

anti-Semitism hostility toward or discrimination against Jews.

appeasement the policy, followed by the European nations in the 1930s, of accepting Hitler's annexation of Austria and Czechoslovakia in the belief that meeting his demands would assure peace and stability.

Arianism a Christian heresy that taught that Jesus was inferior to God. Though condemned by the Council of Nicaea in 325, Arianism was adopted by many of the Germanic peoples who entered the Roman Empire over the next centuries.

aristocracy a class of hereditary nobility in medieval Europe; a warrior class who shared a distinctive lifestyle based on the institution of knighthood, although there were social divisions within the group based on extremes of wealth.

Arthasastra an early Indian political treatise that sets forth many fundamental aspects of the relationship of rulers and their subjects. It has been compared to Machiavelli's well-known book, *The Prince*, and has provided principles upon which many aspects of social organization have developed in the region.

Aryans Indo–European-speaking nomads who entered India from the Central Asian steppes between 1500 and 1000 B.C.E. and greatly affected Indian society, notably by establishing the caste system. The term was later adopted by German Nazis to describe their racial ideal.

ASEAN the Association for the Southest Asian Nations formed in 1967 to promote the prosperity and political stability of its member nations. Currently Brunei, Indonesia, Laos, Malaysia, Myanmar, the Philippines, Singapore, Thailand, and Vietnam are members. Other countries in the region participate as "observer" members.

Ausgleich the "Compromise" of 1867 that created the dual monarchy of Austria-Hungary. Austria and Hungary each had its own capital, constitution, and legislative assembly, but were united under one monarch.

authoritarian state a state that has a dictatorial government and some other trappings of a totalitarian state, but does not demand that the masses be actively involved in the regime's goals as totalitarian states do.

auxiliaries troops enlisted from the subject peoples of the Roman Empire to supplement the regular legions composed of Roman citizens.

bakufu the centralized government set up in Japan in the twelfth century. *See* shogunate system.

balance of power a distribution of power among several states such that no single nation can dominate or interfere with the interests of another.

Bao-jia system the Chinese practice, reportedly originated by the Qin dynasty in the third century B.C.E., of organizing families into groups of five or ten to exercise mutual control and surveillance and reduce loyalty to the family.

Baroque a style that dominated Western painting, sculpture, architecture and music from about 1580 to 1730, generally characterized by elaborate ornamentation and dramatic effects. Important practitioners included Bernini, Rubens, Handel, and Bach.

Bedouins nomadic tribes originally from northern Arabia, who became important traders after the domestication of the camel during the first millennium B.C.E. Early converts to Islam, their values and practices deeply affected Muhammad.

benefice in the Christian church, a position, such as a bishopric, that consisted of both a sacred office and the right of the holder to the annual revenues from the position.

bhakti in Hinduism, devotion as a means of religious observance open to all persons regardless of class.

bicameral legislature a legislature with two houses.

Black Death the outbreak of plague (mostly bubonic) in the mid-fourteenth century that killed from 25 to 50 percent of Europe's population.

Blitzkrieg "lightning war." A war conducted with great speed and force, as in Germany's advance at the beginning of World War II.

bodhisattvas in some schools of Buddhism, individuals who have achieved enlightenment but, because of their great compassion, have chosen to renounce Nirvana and to remain on earth in spirit form to help all human beings achieve release from reincarnation.

Bolsheviks a small faction of the Russian Social Democratic Party who were led by Lenin and dedicated to violent revolution; seized power in Russia in 1917 and were subsequently renamed the Communists.

boyars the Russian nobility.

Brezhnev Doctrine the doctrine, enunciated by Leonid Brezhnev, that the Soviet Union had a right to intervene if socialism was threatened in another socialist state; used to justify the use of Soviet troops in Czechoslovakia in 1968.

caliph the secular leader of the Islamic community.

calpulli in Aztec society, a kinship group, often of a thousand or more, which served as an intermediary with the central government, providing taxes and conscript labor to the state.

capital material wealth used or available for use in the production of more wealth.

cartel a combination of independent commercial enterprises that work together to control prices and limit competition.

Cartesian dualism Descartes's principle of the separation of mind and matter (and mind and body) that enabled scientists to view matter as something separate from themselves that could be investigated by reason.

caste system a system of rigid social hierarchy in which all members of that society are assigned by birth to specific "ranks," and inherit specific roles and privileges.

caudillos strong leaders in nineteenth-century Latin America, who were usually supported by the landed elites and ruled chiefly by military force, though some were popular; they included both modernizers and destructive dictators.

censorate one of the three primary Chinese ministries, originally established in the Qin dynasty, whose inspectors surveyed the efficiency of officials throughout the system.

chaebol a South Korean business structure similar to the Japanese keiretsu.

chansons de geste a form of vernacular literature in the High Middle Ages that consisted of heroic epics focusing on the deeds of warriors.

chivalry the ideal of civilized behavior that emerged among the nobility in the eleventh and twelfth centuries under the influence of the church; a code of ethics knights were expected to uphold.

Christian (northern) humanism an intellectual movement in northern Europe in the late fifteenth and early sixteenth centuries that combined the interest in the classics of the Italian Renaissance with an interest in the sources of early Christianity, including the New Testament and the writings of the church fathers.

civic humanism an intellectual movement of the Italian Renaissance that saw Cicero, who was both an intellectual and a statesman, as the ideal and held that humanists should be involved in government and use their rhetorical training in the service of the state.

civil rights the basic rights of citizens including equality before the law, freedom of speech and press, and freedom from arbitrary arrest.

civil service examination an elaborate Chinese system of selecting bureaucrats on merit, first introduced in 165 B.C.E., developed by the Tang dynasty in the seventh century C.E. and refined under the Song dynasty; later adopted in Vietnam and with less success in Japan and Korea. It contributed to efficient government, upward mobility, and cultural uniformity.

class struggle the basis of the Marxist analysis of history, which says that the owners of the means of production have always oppressed the workers and predicts an inevitable revolution. *See* Marxism.

Cold War the ideological conflict between the Soviet Union and the United States after World War II.

collective farms large farms created in the Soviet Union by Stalin by combining many small holdings into one large farm worked by the peasants under government supervision.

collective security the use of an international army raised by an association of nations to deter aggression and keep the peace.

coloni free tenant farmers who worked as sharecroppers on the large estates of the Roman Empire (singular: *colonus*).

Comintern a worldwide organization of Communist parties, founded by Lenin in 1919, dedicated to the advancement of world revolution; also known as the Third International.

common law law common to the entire kingdom of England; imposed by the king's courts beginning in the twelfth century to replace the customary law used in county and feudal courts that varied from place to place.

commune in medieval Europe, an association of townspeople bound together by a sworn oath for the purpose of obtaining basic liberties from the lord of the territory in which the town was located; also, the self-governing town after receiving its liberties.

conciliarism a movement in fourteenth- and fifteenth-century Europe that held that final authority in spiritual matters resided with a general church council, not the pope; emerged in response to the Avignon papacy and the Great Schism and used to justify the summoning of the Council of Constance (1414–1418).

condottieri leaders of bands of mercenary soldiers in Renaissance Italy who sold their services to the highest bidder.

Confucianism a system of thought based on the teachings of Confucius (551–479 B.C.E.) that developed into the ruling ideology of the Chinese state. *See* Neo-Confucianism.

conquistadors "conquerors." Leaders in the Spanish conquests in the Americas, especially Mexico and Peru, in the sixteenth century.

conscription a military draft.

conservatism an ideology based on tradition and social stability that favored the maintenance of established institutions, organized religion, and obedience to authority and resisted change, especially abrupt change.

consuls the chief executive officers of the Roman Republic. Two were chosen annually to administer the government and lead the army in battle.

consumer society a term applied to Western society after World War II as the working classes adopted the consumption patterns of the middle class and installment plans, credit cards, and easy credit made consumer goods such as appliances and automobiles widely available.

Continental System Napoleon's effort to bar British goods from the Continent in the hope of weakening Britain's economy and destroying its capacity to wage war.

cosmopolitanism the quality of being sophisticated and having wide international experience.

cottage industry a system of textile manufacturing in which spinners and weavers worked at home in their cottages using raw materials supplied to them by capitalist entrepreneurs.

cultural relativism the belief that no culture is superior to another because culture is a matter of custom, not reason, and derives its meaning from the group holding it.

cuneiform "wedge-shaped." A system of writing developed by the Sumerians that consisted of wedge-shaped impressions made by a reed stylus on clay tablets.

daimyo prominent Japanese families who provided allegiance to the local shogun in exchange for protection; similar to vassals in Europe.

decolonization the process of becoming free of colonial status and achieving statehood; occurred in most of the world's colonies between 1947 and 1962.

deism belief in God as the creator of the universe who, after setting it in motion, ceased to have any direct involvement in it and allowed it to run according to its own natural laws.

demesne the part of a manor retained under the direct control of the lord and worked by the serfs as part of their labor services.

depression a very severe, protracted economic downturn with high levels of unemployment.

destalinization the policy of denouncing and undoing the most repressive aspects of Stalin's regime; begun by Nikita Khrushchev in 1956.

détente the relaxation of tension between the Soviet Union and the United States that occurred in the 1970s.

dharma in Hinduism and Buddhism, the law that governs the universe, and specifically human behavior.

dialectic logic, one of the seven liberal arts that made up the medieval curriculum. In Marxist thought, the process by which all change occurs through the clash of antagonistic elements.

Diaspora the scattering of Jews throughout the ancient world after the Babylonian captivity in the sixth century B.C.E.

dictator in the Roman Republic, an official granted unlimited power to run the state for a short period of time, usually six months, during an emergency.

diocese the area under the jurisdiction of a Christian bishop; based originally on Roman administrative districts.

direct representation a system of choosing delegates to a representative assembly in which citizens vote directly for the delegates who will represent them.

divination the practice of seeking to foretell future events by interpreting divine signs, which could appear in various forms, such as in entrails of animals, in patterns in smoke, or in dreams.

divine-right monarchy a monarchy based on the belief that monarchs receive their power directly from God and are responsible to no one except God.

domino theory the belief that if the Communists succeeded in Vietnam, other countries in Southeast and East Asia would also fall (like dominoes) to communism; a justification for the U.S. intervention in Vietnam.

dualism the belief that the universe is dominated by two opposing forces, one good and the other evil.

dynastic state a state where the maintenance and expansion of the interests of the ruling family is the primary consideration.

economic imperialism the process in which banks and corporations from developed nations invest in underdeveloped regions and establish a major presence there in the hope of making high profits; not necessarily the same as colonial expansion in that businesses invest where they can make a profit, which may not be in their own nation's colonies.

empiricism the practice of relying on observation and experiment.

enclosure movement in the eighteenth century, the fencing in of the old open fields, combining many small holdings into larger units that could be farmed more efficiently.

encomienda system the system by which Spain first governed its American colonies. Holders of an encomienda were supposed to protect the Indians as well as using them as laborers and collecting tribute but in practice exploited them.

encyclical a letter from the pope to all the bishops of the Roman Catholic church.

enlightened absolutism an absolute monarchy where the ruler follows the principles of the Enlightenment by introducing reforms for the improvement of society, allowing freedom of speech and the press, permitting religious toleration, expanding education, and ruling in accordance with the laws.

Enlightenment an eighteenth-century intellectual movement, led by the philosophes, that stressed the application of reason and the scientific method to all aspects of life.

entrepreneur one who organizes, operates, and assumes the risk in a business venture in the expectation of making a profit.

Epicureanism a philosophy founded by Epicurus in the fourth century B.C.E. that taught that happiness (freedom from emotional turmoil) could be achieved through the pursuit of pleasure (intellectual rather than sensual pleasure).

equestrians a group of extremely wealthy men in the late Roman Republic who were effectively barred from high office, but sought political power commensurate with their wealth; called equestrians because many had gotten their start as cavalry officers (*equites*).

ethnic cleansing the policy of killing or forcibly removing people of another ethnic group; used by the Serbs against Bosnian Muslims in the 1990s.

eucharist a Christian sacrament in which consecrated bread and wine are consumed in celebration of Jesus' Last Supper; also called the Lord's Supper or communion.

evolutionary socialism a socialist doctrine espoused by Eduard Bernstein who argued that socialists should stress cooperation and evolution to attain power by democratic means rather than by conflict and revolution.

fascism an ideology or movement that exalts the nation above the individual and calls for a centralized government with a dictatorial leader, economic and social regimentation, and forcible suppression of opposition; in particular, the ideology of Mussolini's Fascist regime in Italy.

feminism the belief in the social, political, and economic equality of the sexes; also, organized activity to advance women's rights.

fief a landed estate granted to a vassal in exchange for military services.

Final Solution the physical extermination of the Jewish people by the Nazis during World War II.

five pillars of Islam the core requirements of the faith, observation of which would lead to paradise: belief in Allah and his Prophet Muhammad; prescribed prayers; observation of Ramadan; pilgrimage to Mecca; and giving alms to the poor.

folk culture the traditional arts and crafts, literature, music, and other customs of the people; something that people make, as opposed to modern popular culture, which is something people buy.

four modernizations the slogan for radical reforms of Chinese industry, agriculture, technology, and national defense, instituted by Deng Xiaoping after his accession to power in the late 1970s.

free trade the unrestricted international exchange of goods with low or no tariffs.

fundamentalism a movement that emphasizes rigid adherence to basic religious principles; coined to describe Evangelical Christianity, it is often used to characterize Islamic conservatives.

general strike a strike by all or most workers in an economy; espoused by Georges Sorel as the heroic action that could be used to inspire the workers to destroy capitalist society.

gentry well-to-do English landowners below the level of the nobility; played an important role in the English Civil War of the seventeenth century.

geocentric theory the idea that the earth is at the center of the universe and that the sun and other celestial objects revolve around the earth.

glasnost "openness." Mikhail Gorbachev's policy of encouraging Soviet citizens to openly discuss the strengths and weaknesses of the Soviet Union.

Gleichschaltung the coordination of all government institutions under Nazi control in Germany from 1933.

global civilization human society considered as a single world-wide entity, in which local differences are less important than overall similarities.

good emperors the five emperors who ruled from 96 to 180 (Nerva, Trajan, Hadrian, Antoninus Pius, and Marcus Aurelius), a period of peace and prosperity for the Roman Empire.

Great Schism the crisis in the late medieval church when there were first two and then three popes; ended by the Council of Constance (1414–1418).

guest workers foreign workers working temporarily in European countries.

guild an association of people with common interests and concerns, especially people working in the same craft. In medieval Europe, guilds came to control much of the production process and to restrict entry into various trades.

gymnasium in classical Greece, a place for athletics; in the Hellenistic Age, a secondary school with a curriculum centered on music, physical exercise, and literature.

Hegira the flight of Muhammad from Mecca to Medina in 622, which marks the first date on the official calendar of Islam.

heliocentric theory the idea that the sun (not the earth) is at the center of the universe.

Hellenistic literally, "to imitate the Greeks"; the era after the death of Alexander the Great when Greek culture spread into the Near East and blended with the culture of that region.

helots serfs in ancient Sparta, who were permanently bound to the land that they worked for their Spartan masters.

heresy the holding of religious doctrines different from the official teachings of the church.

Hermeticism an intellectual movement beginning in the fifteenth century that taught that divinity is embodied in all aspects of nature; included works on alchemy and magic as well as theology and philosophy. The tradition continued into the seventeenth century and influenced many of the leading figures of the Scientific Revolution.

hetairai highly sophisticated courtesans in ancient Athens who offered intellectual and musical entertainment as well as sex.

hieroglyphics a highly pictorial system of writing most often associated with ancient Egypt. Also used (with different "pictographs") by other ancient peoples such as the Mayans.

high culture the literary and artistic culture of the educated and wealthy ruling classes.

Hinduism the main religion in India, it emphasizes reincarnation, based on the results of the previous life, and the desirability of escaping this cycle. Its various forms feature both asceticism and the pleasures of ordinary life, and encompass a multitude of gods as different manifestations of one ultimate reality.

Holocaust the mass slaughter of European Jews by the Nazis during World War II.

Hopewell culture a Native American society that flourished from about 200 B.C.E. to 400 C.E., noted for large burial mounds and extensive manufacture. Largely based in Ohio, its traders ranged as far as the Gulf of Mexico.

hoplites heavily armed infantry soldiers used in ancient Greece in a phalanx formation.

Huguenots French Calvinists.

humanism an intellectual movement in Renaissance Italy based upon the study of the Greek and Roman classics.

Hundred Schools (of philosophy) in China around the third century B.C.E., a wide-ranging debate over the nature of human beings, society, and the universe. The Schools included Legalism and Daoism, as well as Confucianism.

iconoclasm an eighth-century Byzantine movement against the use of icons (pictures of sacred figures), which was condemned as idolatry.

ideology a political philosophy such as conservatism or liberalism.

imperialism the policy of extending one nation's power either by conquest or by establishing direct or indirect economic or cultural authority over another. Generally driven by economic self-interest, it can also be motivated by a sincere (if often misguided) sense of moral obligation.

imperium "the right to command." In the Roman Republic, the chief executive officers (consuls and praetors) possessed the *imperium*; a military commander was an *imperator*. In the Roman Empire, the title *imperator*, or emperor, came to be used for the ruler.

indirect representation a system of choosing delegates to a representative assembly in which citizens do not choose the delegates directly but instead vote for electors who choose the delegates.

individualism emphasis on and interest in the unique traits of each person.

indulgence the remission of part or all of the temporal punishment in purgatory due to sin; granted for charitable contributions and other good deeds. Indulgences became a regular practice of the Christian church in the High Middle Ages, and their abuse was instrumental in sparking Luther's reform movement in the sixteenth century.

infanticide the practice of killing infants.

inflation a sustained rise in the price level.

intendants royal officials in seventeenth-century France who were sent into the provinces to execute the orders of the central government.

intervention, principle of the idea, after the Congress of Vienna, that the great powers of Europe had the right to send armies into countries experiencing revolution to restore legitimate monarchs to their thrones.

isolationism a foreign policy in which a nation refrains from making alliances or engaging actively in international affairs.

jihad in Islam, "striving in the way of the Lord." The term is ambiguous and has been subject to varying interpretations, from the practice of conducting raids against local neighbors to the conduct of "holy war" against unbelievers.

joint-stock company a company or association that raises capital by selling shares to individuals who receive dividends on their investment while a board of directors runs the company.

joint-stock investment bank a bank created by selling shares of stock to investors. Such banks potentially have access to much more capital than do private banks owned by one or a few individuals.

Jomon the earliest known Neolithic inhabitants of Japan, named for the cord pattern of their pottery.

justification by faith the primary doctrine of the Protestant Reformation; taught that humans are saved not through good works, but by the grace of God, bestowed freely through the sacrifice of Jesus.

kami spirits who were worshiped in early Japan, and resided in trees, rivers, and streams. *See* Shinto.

keiretsu a type of powerful industrial or financial conglomerate that emerged in post–World War II Japan following the abolition of zaibatsu.

kolkhoz a collective farm in the Soviet Union, in which the great bulk of the land was held and worked communally. Between 1928 and 1934, 250,000 kolkhozes replaced 26 million family farms.

laissez-faire "to let alone." An economic doctrine that holds that an economy is best served when the government does not interfere but allows the economy to self-regulate according to the forces of supply and demand.

latifundia large landed estates in the Roman Empire (singular: *latifundium*).

lay investiture the practice in which a layperson chose a bishop and invested him with the symbols of both his temporal office and his spiritual office; led to the Investiture Controversy, which was ended by compromise in the Concordat of Worms in 1122.

Lebensraum "living space." The doctrine, adopted by Hitler, that a nation's power depends on the amount of land it occupies; thus, a nation must expand to be strong.

Legalism a Chinese philosophy that argued that human beings were by nature evil and would follow the correct path only if coerced by harsh laws and stiff punishments. Adopted as official ideology by the Qin dynasty, it was later rejected but remained influential.

legitimacy, principle of the idea that after the Napoleonic wars peace could best be reestablished in Europe by restoring legitimate monarchs who would preserve traditional institutions; guided Metternich at the Congress of Vienna.

Leninism Lenin's revision of Marxism that held that Russia need not experience a bourgeois revolution before it could move toward socialism.

liberal arts the seven areas of study that formed the basis of education in medieval and early modern Europe. Following Boethius and other late Roman authors, they consisted of grammar, rhetoric, and dialectic or logic (the *trivium*) and arithmetic, geometry, astronomy, and music (the *quadrivium*).

liberalism an ideology based on the belief that people should be as free from restraint as possible. Economic liberalism is the idea that the government should not interfere in the workings of the economy. Political liberalism is the idea that there should be restraints on the exercise of power so that people can enjoy basic civil rights in a constitutional state with a representative assembly.

limited liability the principle that shareholders in a joint-stock corporation can be held responsible for the corporation's debts only up to the amount they have invested.

limited (constitutional) monarchy a system of government in which the monarch is limited by a representative assembly and by the duty to rule in accordance with the laws of the land.

lineage group the descendants of a common ancestor; relatives, often as opposed to immediate family.

Mahayana a school of Buddhism that promotes the idea of universal salvation through the intercession of bodhisattvas; predominant in north Asia.

mandates a system established after World War I whereby a nation officially administered a territory (mandate) on behalf of the League of Nations. Thus, France administered Lebanon and Syria as mandates, and Britain administered Iraq and Palestine.

manor an agricultural estate operated by a lord and worked by peasants who performed labor services and paid various rents and fees to the lord in exchange for protection and sustenance.

Marshall Plan the European Recovery Program, under which the United States provided financial aid to European countries to help them rebuild after World War II.

Marxism the political, economic, and social theories of Karl Marx, which included the idea that history is the story of class struggle and that ultimately the proletariat will overthrow the bourgeoisie and establish a dictatorship en route to a classless society.

mass education a state-run educational system, usually free and compulsory, that aims to ensure that all children in society have at least a basic education.

mass leisure forms of leisure that appeal to large numbers of people in a society including the working classes; emerged at the end of the nineteenth century to provide workers with amusements after work and on weekends; used during the twentieth century by totalitarian states to control their populations.

mass politics a political order characterized by mass political parties and universal male and (eventually) female suffrage.

mass society a society in which the concerns of the majority—the lower classes—play a prominent role; characterized by extension of voting rights, an improved standard of living for the lower classes, and mass education.

materialism the belief that everything mental, spiritual, or ideal is an outgrowth of physical forces and that truth is found in concrete material existence, not through feeling or intuition.

megaliths large stones, widely used in Europe from around 4000 to 1500 B.C.E. to create monuments, including sophisticated astronomical observatories.

Meiji Restoration the period during the late 19th and early 20th century in which fundamental economic and cultural changes occured in Japan, tranforming it from a feudal and agrarian society to an industrial and technological society.

mercantilism an economic theory that held that a nation's prosperity depended on its supply of gold and silver and that the total volume of trade is unchangeable; therefore, advocated that the government play an active role in the economy by encouraging exports and discouraging imports, especially through the use of tariffs.

Mesolithic Age the period from 10,000 to 7000 B.C.E., characterized by a gradual transition from a food-gathering/hunting economy to a food-producing economy.

mestizos the offspring of intermarriage between Europeans, originally Spaniards, and native American Indians.

metics resident foreigners in ancient Athens; not permitted full rights of citizenship but did receive the protection of the laws.

militarism a policy of aggressive military preparedness; in particular, the large armies based on mass conscription and complex, inflexible plans for mobilization that most European nations had before World War I.

ministerial responsibility a tenet of nineteenth-century liberalism that held that ministers of the monarch should be responsible to the legislative assembly rather than to the monarch.

Modernism the new artistic and literary styles that emerged in the decades before 1914 as artists rebelled against traditional efforts to portray reality as accurately as possible (leading to Impressionism and Cubism) and writers explored new forms.

monotheistic/monotheism having only one god; the doctrine or belief that there is only one god.

mulattoes the offspring of Africans and Europeans, particularly in Latin America.

mutual deterrence the belief that nuclear war could best be prevented if both the United States and the Soviet Union had sufficient nuclear weapons so that even if one nation launched a preemptive first strike, the other could respond and devastate the attacker.

mystery religions religions that involve initiation into secret rites that promise intense emotional involvement with spiritual forces and a greater chance of individual immortality.

nationalism a sense of national consciousness based on awareness of being part of a community—a "nation"—that has common institutions, traditions, language, and customs and that becomes the focus of the individual's primary political loyalty.

nationalities problem the dilemma faced by the Austro-Hungarian Empire in trying to unite a wide variety of ethnic groups including, among others, Austrians, Hungarians, Poles, Croats, Czechs, Serbs, Slovaks, and Slovenes in an era when nationalism and calls for self-determination were coming to the fore.

nationalization the process of converting a business or industry from private ownership to government control and ownership.

nation in arms the people's army raised by universal mobilization to repel the foreign enemies of the French Revolution.

nation-state a form of political organization in which a relatively homogeneous people inhabits a sovereign state, as opposed to a state containing people of several nationalities.

NATO the North Atlantic Treaty Organization; a military alliance formed in 1949 in which the signatories (Belgium, Canada, Denmark, France, Great Britain, Iceland, Italy, Luxembourg, the Netherlands, Norway, Portugal, and the United States) agreed to provide mutual assistance if any one of them was attacked; later expanded to include other nations, including former members of the Warsaw Pact—Poland, the Czech Republic, and Hungary.

natural laws a body of laws or specific principles held to be derived from nature and binding upon all human society even in the absence of positive laws.

natural rights certain inalienable rights to which all people are entitled; include the right to life, liberty, and property, freedom of speech and religion, and equality before the law.

natural selection Darwin's idea that organisms that are most adaptable to their environment survive and pass on the variations that enabled them to survive, while other, less adaptable organisms become extinct; "survival of the fittest."

Nazi New Order the Nazis' plan for their conquered territories; included the extermination of Jews and others considered inferior, ruthless exploitation of resources, German colonization in the east, and the use of Poles, Russians, and Ukrainians as slave labor.

negritude a philosophy shared among African blacks that there exists a distinctive "African personality" that owes nothing to Western values and provides a common sense of purpose and destiny for black Africans.

Neo-Confucianism the dominant ideology of China during the second millennium C.E., it combined the metaphysical speculations of Buddhism and Daoism with the pragmatic Confucian approach to society, maintaining that the world is real, not illusory, and that fulfillment comes from participation, not withdrawal. It encouraged an intellectual environment that valued continuity over change and tradition over innovation.

Neoplatonism a revival of Platonic philosophy; in the third century C.E., a revival associated with Plotinus; in the Italian Renaissance, a revival associated with Marsilio Ficino who attempted to synthesize Christianity and Platonism.

New Course a short-lived, liberalizing change in Soviet policy to its Eastern European allies instituted after the death of Stalin in 1953.

New Culture Movement a protest launched at Peking University after the failure of the 1911 revolution, aimed at abolishing the remnants of the old system and introducing Western values and institutions into China.

New Democracy the initial program of the Chinese Communist government, from 1949 to 1955, focusing on honest government, land reform, social justice, and peace rather than on the utopian goal of a classless society.

New Economic Policy a modified version of the old capitalist system introduced in the Soviet Union by Lenin in 1921 to revive the economy after the ravages of the civil war and war communism.

new imperialism the revival of imperialism after 1880 in which European nations established colonies throughout much of Asia and Africa.

new monarchies the governments of France, England, and Spain at the end of the fifteenth century, where the rulers were successful in reestablishing or extending centralized royal authority, suppressing the nobility, controlling the church, and insisting upon the loyalty of all peoples living in their territories.

Nirvana in Buddhist thought, enlightenment, the ultimate transcendence from the illusion of the material world; release from the wheel of life.

nobiles "nobles." The small group of families from both patrician and plebeian origins who produced most of the men who were elected to office in the late Roman Republic.

Nok culture in northern Nigeria, one of the most active early iron-working societies in Africa, artifacts from which date back as far as 500 B.C.E.

nuclear family a family group consisting only of father, mother, and children.

old regime/old order the political and social system of France in the eighteenth century before the Revolution.

oligarchy rule by a few.

Open Door notes a series of letters sent in 1899 by U.S. Secretary of State John Hay to Great Britain, France, Germany, Italy, Japan and Russia, calling for equal economic access to the China market for all states and for the maintenance of the territorial and administrative integrity of the Chinese Empire.

opium trade the sale of the addictive product of the poppy, specifically by British traders to China in the 1830s. Chinese attempts to prevent it led to the Opium War of 1839–1842, which resulted in British access to Chinese ports and has traditionally been considered the beginning of modern Chinese history.

optimates "best men." Aristocratic leaders in the late Roman Republic who generally came from senatorial families and wished to retain their oligarchical privileges.

orders/estates the traditional tripartite division of European society based on heredity and quality rather than wealth or economic standing, first established in the Middle Ages and continuing into the eighteenth century; traditionally consisted of those who pray (the clergy), those who fight (the nobility), and those who work (all the rest).

organic evolution Darwin's principle that all plants and animals have evolved over a long period of time from earlier and simpler forms of life.

Organization of African Unity founded in Addis Ababa in 1963, it was intended to represent the interests of all the newly independent countries of Africa and provided a forum for the discussion of common problems until 2001, when it was replaced by the African Union.

Paleolithic Age the period of human history when humans used simple stone tools (c. 2,500,000–10,000 B.C.E.).

pan-Africanism the concept of African continental unity and solidarity in which the common interests of African countries transcend regional boundaries.

pantheism a doctrine that equates God with the universe and all that is in it.

paterfamilias the dominant male in a Roman family whose powers over his wife and children were theoretically unlimited, though they were sometimes circumvented in practice.

patriarchal/patriarchy a society in which the father is supreme in the clan or family; more generally, a society dominated by men.

patriarchal family a family in which the husband/father dominates his wife and children.

patricians great landowners who became the ruling class in the Roman Republic.

patronage the practice of awarding titles and making appointments to government and other positions to gain political support.

Pax Romana "Roman peace." A term used to refer to the stability and prosperity that Roman rule brought to the Mediterranean world and much of western Europe during the first and second centuries C.E.

peaceful coexistence the policy adopted by the Soviet Union under Khrushchev in 1955, and continued by his successors, that called for economic and ideological rivalry with the West rather than nuclear war.

Pentateuch the first five books of the Hebrew Bible (Genesis, Exodus, Leviticus, Numbers, and Deuteronomy).

peoples' democracies a term invented by the Soviet Union to define a society in the early stage of socialist transition, applied to Eastern European countries in the 1950s.

perestroika "restructuring." A term applied to Mikhail Gorbachev's economic, political, and social reforms in the Soviet Union.

permissive society a term applied to Western society after World War II to reflect the new sexual freedom and the emergence of a drug culture.

Petrine supremacy the doctrine that the bishop of Rome—the pope—as the successor of Saint Peter (traditionally considered the first bishop of Rome) should hold a preeminent position in the church.

phalanx a rectangular formation of tightly massed infantry soldiers.

philosophes intellectuals of the eighteenth-century Enlighten-ment who believed in applying a spirit of rational criticism to all things, including religion and politics, and who focused on improving and enjoying this world, rather than on the afterlife.

plebeians the class of Roman citizens who included nonpatrician landowners, craftspeople, merchants, and small farmers in the Roman Republic. Their struggle for equal rights with the patricians dominated much of the Republic's history.

pluralism the practice in which one person holds several church offices simultaneously; a problem of the late medieval church.

pogroms organized massacres of Jews.

polis an ancient Greek city-state encompassing both an urban area and its surrounding countryside; a small but autonomous political unit where all major political and social activities were carried out in a central location.

political democracy a form of government characterized by universal suffrage and mass political parties.

politiques a group who emerged during the French Wars of Religion in the sixteenth century; placed politics above religion and believed that no religious truth was worth the ravages of civil war.

polygyny the state or practice of having more than one wife at a time.

polytheistic/polytheism having many gods; belief in or the worship of more than one god.

popular culture as opposed to high culture, the unofficial, written and unwritten culture of the masses, much of which was passed down orally; centers on public and group activities such as festivals. In the twentieth century, refers to the entertainment, recreation, and pleasures that people purchase as part of mass consumer society.

populares "favoring the people." Aristocratic leaders in the late Roman Republic who tended to use the people's assemblies in an effort to break the stranglehold of the *nobiles* on political offices.

popular sovereignty the doctrine that government is created by and subject to the will of the people, who are the source of all political power.

praetorian guard the military unit that served as the personal bodyguard of the Roman emperors.

praetors the two senior Roman judges, who had executive authority when the consuls were away from the city and could also lead armies.

predestination the belief, associated with Calvinism, that God, as a consequence of his foreknowledge of all events, has predetermined those who will be saved (the elect) and those who will be damned.

price revolution the dramatic rise in prices (inflation) that occurred throughout Europe in the sixteenth and early seventeenth centuries.

primogeniture an inheritance practice in which the eldest son receives all or the largest share of the parents' estate.

principate the form of government established by Augustus for the Roman Empire; continued the constitutional forms of the Republic and consisted of the *princeps* ("first citizen") and the senate, although the *princeps* was clearly the dominant partner.

proletariat the industrial working class. In Marxism, the class who will ultimately overthrow the bourgeoisie.

purdah the Indian term for the practice among Muslims and some Hindus of isolating women and preventing them from associating with men outside the home.

Puritans English Protestants inspired by Calvinist theology who wished to remove all traces of Catholicism from the Church of England.

querelles des femmes "arguments about women." A centuries-old debate about the nature of women that continued during the Scientific Revolution as those who argued for the inferiority of women found additional support in the new anatomy and medicine.

rationalism a system of thought based on the belief that human reason and experience are the chief sources of knowledge.

realism in medieval Europe, the school of thought that, following Plato, held that the individual objects we perceive are not real but merely manifestations of universal ideas existing in the mind of God. In the nineteenth century, a school of painting that emphasized the everyday life of ordinary people, depicted with photographic realism.

Realpolitik "politics of reality." Politics based on practical concerns rather than theory or ethics.

real wages/income/prices wages/income/prices that have been adjusted for inflation.

reason of state the principle that a nation should act on the basis of its long-term interests and not merely to further the dynastic interests of its ruling family.

reincarnation the idea that the individual soul is reborn in a different form after death; in Hindu and Buddhist thought, release from this cycle is the objective of all living souls.

relativity theory Einstein's theory that holds, among other things, that (1) space and time are not absolute but are relative to the observer and interwoven into a four-dimensional space-time continuum and (2) matter is a form of energy ($E = mc^2$).

Renaissance the "rebirth" of classical culture that occurred in Italy between c. 1350 and c. 1550; also, the earlier revivals of classical culture that occurred under Charlemagne and in the twelfth century.

rentier a person who lives on income from property and is not personally involved in its operation.

reparations payments made by a defeated nation after a war to compensate another nation for damage sustained as a result of the war; required from Germany after World War I.

revisionism a socialist doctrine that rejected Marx's emphasis on class struggle and revolution and argued instead that workers should work through political parties to bring about gradual change.

revolution a fundamental change in the political and social organization of a state.

revolutionary socialism the socialist doctrine espoused by Georges Sorel who held that violent action was the only way to achieve the goals of socialism.

rhetoric the art of persuasive speaking; in the Middle Ages, one of the seven liberal arts.

Rococo a style, especially of decoration and architecture, that developed from the Baroque and spread throughout Europe by the 1730s. While still elaborate, it emphasized curves, lightness, and charm in the pursuit of pleasure, happiness, and love.

sacraments rites considered imperative for a Christian's salvation. By the thirteenth century consisted of the eucharist or Lord's Supper, baptism, marriage, penance, extreme unction, holy orders, and confirmation of children; Protestant reformers of the sixteenth century generally recognized only two—baptism and communion (the Lord's Supper).

samurai literally "retainer"; similar to European knights. Usually in service to a particular shogun, these warriors lived by a strict code of ethics and duty.

sans-culottes the common people who did not wear the fine clothes of the upper classes (sans-culottes means "without breeches") and played an important role in the radical phase of the French Revolution.

sati the Hindu ritual requiring a wife to throw herself upon her her deceased husband's funeral pyre.

satrap/satrapy a governor with both civil and military duties in the ancient Persian Empire, which was divided into satrapies, or provinces, each administered by a satrap.

scholasticism the philosophical and theological system of the medieval schools, which emphasized rigorous analysis of contradictory authorities; often used to try to reconcile faith and reason.

scientific method a method of seeking knowledge through inductive principles; uses experiments and observations to develop generalizations.

Scientific Revolution the transition from the medieval worldview to a largely secular, rational, and materialistic perspective; began in the seventeenth century and was popularized in the eighteenth.

secularization the process of becoming more concerned with material, worldly, temporal things and less with spiritual and religious things.

self-determination the doctrine that the people of a given territory or a particular nationality should have the right to determine their own government and political future.

self-strengthening a late-nineteenth-century Chinese policy, by which Western technology would be adopted while Confucian principles and institutions were maintained intact.

senate/senators the leading council of the Roman Republic; composed of about 300 men (senators) who served for life and dominated much of the political life of the Republic.

serf a peasant who is bound to the land and obliged to provide labor services and pay various rents and fees to the lord; considered unfree but not a slave because serfs could not be bought and sold.

Shinto a kind of state religion in Japan, derived from beliefs in nature spirits and until recently linked with belief in the divinity of the emperor and the sacredness of the Japanese nation.

shogunate system the system of government in Japan in which the emperor exercised only titular authority while the shogun (regional military dictators) exercised actual political power.

skepticism a doubtful or questioning attitude, especially about religion.

Social Darwinism the application of Darwin's principle of organic evolution to the social order; led to the belief that progress comes from the struggle for survival as the fittest advance and the weak decline.

socialism an ideology that calls for collective or government ownership of the means of production and the distribution of goods.

social security/social insurance government programs that provide social welfare measures such as old age pensions and sickness, accident, and disability insurance.

Socratic method a form of teaching that uses a question-and-answer format to enable students to reach conclusions by using their own reasoning.

Sophists wandering scholars and professional teachers in ancient Greece who stressed the importance of rhetoric and tended toward skepticism and relativism.

soviets councils of workers' and soldiers' deputies formed throughout Russia in 1917; played an important role in the Bolshevik Revolution.

sphere of influence a territory or region over which an outside nation exercises political or economic influence.

stateless societies the pre-Columbian communities in much of the Americas who developed substantial cultures without formal nation-states.

Stoicism a philosophy founded by Zeno in the fourth century B.C.E. that taught that happiness could be obtained by accepting one's lot and living in harmony with the will of God, thereby achieving inner peace.

subinfeudation the practice in which a lord's greatest vassals subdivided their fiefs and had vassals of their own, and those vassals, in turn, subdivided their fiefs and so on down to simple knights whose fiefs were too small to subdivide.

suffrage the right to vote.

suffragists those who advocate the extension of the right to vote (suffrage), especially to women.

surplus value in Marxism, the difference between a product's real value and the wages of the worker who produced the product.

Swahili a mixed African-Arabian culture that developed by the twelfth century along the east coast of Africa; also, the national language of Kenya and Tanzania.

syncretism the combining of different forms of belief or practice, as, for example, when two gods are regarded as different forms of the same underlying divine force and are fused together.

Taika reforms the seventh-century "great change" reforms that established the centralized Japanese state.

taille a French tax on land or property, developed by King Louis XI in the fifteenth century as the financial basis of the monarchy. It was largely paid by the peasantry; the nobility and the clergy were exempt.

tariffs duties (taxes) imposed on imported goods; usually imposed both to raise revenue and to discourage imports and protect domestic industries.

tetrarchy rule by four; the system of government established by Diocletian (284–305) in which the Roman Empire was divided into two parts, each ruled by an "Augustus" assisted by a "Caesar."

theocracy a government ruled by a divine authority.

Theravada a school of Buddhism that stresses personal behavior and the quest for understanding as a means of release from the wheel of life, rather than the intercession of bodhisattvas; predominant in Sri Lanka and Southeast Asia.

three-field system in medieval agriculture, the practice of dividing the arable land into three fields so that one could lie fallow while the others were planted in winter grains and spring crops.

three kingdoms Koguryo, Paekche, and Silla, rivals but all under varying degrees of Chinese influence, which together controlled virtually all of Korea from the fourth to the seventh centuries.

three obediences the traditional duties of Japanese women, in permanent subservience: child to father, wife to husband, and widow to son.

tithe a tenth of one's harvest or income; paid by medieval peasants to the village church.

Tongmenghui the political organization—"Revolutionary Alliance"—formed by Sun Yat-sen in 1905, which united various revolutionary factions and ultimately toppled the Manchu dynasty.

Torah the body of law in Hebrew Scripture, contained in the Pentateuch (the first five books of the Hebrew Bible).

totalitarian state a state characterized by government control over all aspects of economic, social, political, cultural, and intellectual life, the subordination of the individual to the state, and insistence that the masses be actively involved in the regime's goals.

total war warfare in which all of a nation's resources, including civilians at home as well as soldiers in the field, are mobilized for the war effort.

trade union an association of workers in the same trade, formed to help members secure better wages, benefits, and working conditions.

transubstantiation a doctrine of the Roman Catholic church that teaches that during the eucharist the substance of the bread and wine is miraculously transformed into the body and blood of Jesus.

trench warfare warfare in which the opposing forces attack and counterattack from a relatively permanent system of trenches protected by barbed wire; characteristic of World War I.

tribute system an important element of Chinese foreign policy, by which neighboring states paid for the privilege of access to Chinese markets, received legitimation and agreed not to harbor enemies of the Chinese Empire.

Truman Doctrine the doctrine, enunciated by Harry Truman in 1947, that the United States would provide economic aid to countries that said they were threatened by Communist expansion.

twice-born the males of the higher castes in traditional Indian society, who underwent an initiation ceremony at puberty.

tyrant/tyranny in an ancient Greek *polis* (or an Italian city-state during the Renaissance), a ruler who came to power in an unconstitutional way and ruled without being subject to the law.

ulama a convocation of leading Muslim scholars, the earliest of which shortly after the death of Muhammad drew up a law code, called the Shari'a, based largely on the Koran and the sayings of the Prophet, to provide believers with a set of prescriptions to regulate their daily lives.

umma the Muslim community, as a whole.

uncertainty principle a principle in quantum mechanics, posited by Heisenberg, that holds that one cannot determine the path of an electron because the very act of observing the electron would affect its location.

unconditional surrender complete, unqualified surrender of a belligerent nation.

untouchables the lowest level of Indian society, technically outside the caste system and considered less than human; renamed harijans ("children of God") by Gandhi and later dalits, they remain the object of discrimination despite affirmative action programs.

utopian socialists intellectuals and theorists in the early nineteenth century who favored equality in social and economic conditions and wished to replace private property and competition with collective ownership and cooperation; deemed impractical and "utopian" by later socialists.

varna Indian classes, or castes. *See* caste system.

vassal a person granted a fief, or landed estate, in exchange for providing military services to the lord and fulfilling certain other obligations such as appearing at the lord's court when summoned and making a payment on the knighting of the lord's eldest son.

vernacular the everyday language of a region, as distinguished from a language used for special purposes. For example, in medieval Paris, French was the vernacular, but Latin was used for academic writing and for classes at the University of Paris.

volkish thought the belief that German culture is superior and that the German people have a universal mission to save Western civilization from inferior races.

war communism Lenin's policy of nationalizing industrial and other facilities and requisitioning the peasants' produce during the civil war in Russia.

War Guilt Clause the clause in the Treaty of Versailles that declared that Germany (and Austria) were responsible for starting World War I and ordered Germany to pay reparations for the damage the Allies had suffered as a result of the war.

Warsaw Pact a military alliance, formed in 1955, in which Albania, Bulgaria, Czechoslovakia, East Germany, Hungary, Poland, Romania, and the Soviet Union agreed to provide mutual assistance. Dissolved in 1991, some former members joined NATO.

welfare state a social/political system in which the government assumes the primary responsibility for the social welfare of its citizens by providing such things as social security, unemploy-ment benefits, and health care.

wergeld "money for a man." In early Germanic law, a person's value in monetary terms, which was paid by a wrongdoer to the family of the person who had been injured or killed.

world-machine Newton's conception of the universe as one huge, regulated, and uniform machine that operated according to natural laws in absolute time, space, and motion.

Young Turks a successful Turkish reformist group in the late nineteenth and early twentieth centuries.

zaibatsu powerful business cartels formed in Japan during the Meiji era and outlawed following World War II.

zamindars Indian tax collectors, who were assigned land, from which they kept part of the revenue; the British revived the system in a misguided attempt to create a landed gentry.

Zen Buddhism (in Chinese, Chan or Ch'an) a school of Buddhism particularly important in Japan, some of whose adherents stress that enlightenment (satori) can be achieved suddenly, though others emphasize lengthy meditation.

ziggurat a massive stepped tower upon which a temple dedicated to the chief god or goddess of a Sumerian city was built.

Zionism an international movement that called for the establishment of a Jewish state or a refuge for Jews in Palestine.

Zoroastrianism a religion founded by the Persian Zoroaster in the seventh century B.C.E.; characterized by worship of a supreme god Ahuramazda who represents the good against the evil spirit, identified as Ahriman.

PRONUNCIATION GUIDE

Abbasid   AB-uh-sid or a-BA-sid
Abu Bakr   a-BOO BAH-ker
Achaemenid   a-KEE-muh-nid
Adenauer, Konrad   AD-n'our-er
Aeschylus   ESS-kuh-lus
Afrikaners   a-fri-KAH-ners
Agamemnon   ag-uh-MEM-nahn
Agincourt   AJ-in-kor
Ahuramazda   ah-HOOR-ah-MAHZ-duh
Akhenaten   ah-kuh-NAH-tun
Akkadian   a-KAY-dee-un
al-Mas'udi   al-ma-SOO-dee
Albigensian   al-bi-GEN-see-un
Albuquerque, Afonso de   AL-buh-kur-kee, ah-FON-soh d'
Allah   AH-luh or AL-uh
Allende, Salvador   ah-YEN-day, SAL-vuh-DOR
al-Ma'mun   al-MAH-moon
al-Rahman, Abd   al-RAH-mun, abd
Amenhotep   ah-mun-HOE-tep
Andropov, Yuri   an-DROP-ov, YOOR-ee
Antigonid   an-TIG-oh-nid
apella   a-PELL-uh
Apennines   A-puh-NINES
Aquinas, Thomas   uh-KWIGH-nus
Archimedes   are-kuh-MEE-deez
Aristotle   ar-i-STAH-tul
Aristophanes   ar-i-STAH-fuh-neez
Arthasastra   ar-tuh-SAHS-tra
Ashkenazic   ash-kuh-NAH-zic
Ashurnasirpal   ah-shoor-NAH-suh-pul
Asoka   a-SHOH-kuh or a-SOH-kuh
assignat   as-seen-YAH or AS-sig-nat
Assyrians   uh-SEER-ee-uns
Attalid   AT-a-lid
Augustine   AW-gus-STEEN
Auschwitz-Birkenau   OUSH-vitz-BUR-kuh-now
Ausgleich   OUS-glike
Avicenna   av-i-SEN-uh
Avignon   ah-veen-YONE
Axum   OX-oom
Bach, Johann Sebastian   BAHK, yoh-HAHN
  suh-BASS-chen
Barbarossa   bar-buh-ROH-suh
Baroque   buy-ROHK
Bastille   ba-STEEL
Beauvoir, Simone de   boh-VWAH, see-MOAN duh
Belisarius   bell-i-SAR-ee-us

benefice   BEN-uh-fiss
Bhagavadgita   bog-ah-vahd-GEE-ta
Blitzkrieg   BLITZ-kreeg
Boeotia   bee-OH-shuh
Boer   BOHR
Boleyn, Anne   BUH-lin
Bólívar, Simón   BOH-luh-VAR, see-MOAN
Bologna   buh-LOHN-yuh
Brandt, Willy   BRAHNT, VIL-ee
Brétigny   bray-tee-NYEE
Brezhnev, Leonid   BREZH-nef, lyi-on-YEET
Briand, Aristide   bree-AHN, a-ree-STEED
Bulganin, Nilolai   bul-GAN-in, nyik-uh-LYE
Bund deutscher Mädel   BUNT DOICHer MAIR-del
Burschenschaften   BOOR-shen-shaft-un
Buthelezi, Mangosuthu   boo-teh-LAY-zee, man-go-SOO-tu
Calais   ka-LAY
caliph/caliphate   KAY-lif/KAY-li-FATE
Cambyses   kam-BY-seez
Camus, Albert   kuh-MOO, al-BEAR
Canaanites   KAY-nuh-nites
Cao Cao   tsau tsau
Capet/Capetian   ka-PAY or KAY-put/kuh-PEE-shun
Carolingian   kar-oh-LIN-jun
carruca   ca-ruh-kuh
Carthage/Carthaginian   KAR-thij/KAR-thuh-JIN-ee-un
Castlereagh, Viscount   KAS-ul-RAY
Castiglione, Baldassare   kass-teel-YOHnay, bahl-dah-SAR-ay
Çatal Hüyük   CHAH-tul HOO-YOOK
Catharism   KA-tha-ri-zem
Catullus   ka-TULL-us
caudillos   kow-THEE-yohz (TH as in the)
Cavendish, Margaret   KAV-un-dish
Cavour, Camillo di   ka-VOOR, kah-MIL-oh
Chaeronea   ker-oh-NEE-uh
Chaldean   kal-DEE-un
Charlemagne   SHAR-luh-mane
Chernenko, Konstantin   cher-NYEN-koh, kon-stun-TEEN
Chiang Kai-Shek   CHANG KIGH-shek
Chirac, Jacques   SHE-RAHK, ZHAHK
Chulalongkorn   CHOO-LAH-LONG-KON
Cicero   SIS-uh-roh
Cistercians   si-STIR-shuns
Cixi   TSE-she
Cleisthenes   KLISE-thuh-neez
Clemenceau, Georges   klem-un-SOH, ZHORZH
Clovis   KLOH-vis

Colbert, Baptiste   kahl-BEHR, buh-TEEST

Comneni   kahm-NEE,nee

Concordat of Worms   kon-KOR-dat of WURMZ or VAWRMZ

condottieri   kon-dah-TEE-AIR-ee

consul   KON-sul

Copernicus, Nicolaus   koh-PURR-nuh-kus, nee-koh-LAH-us

Corinth   KOR-inth

Cortés, Hernán   kor-TEZ, er-NAHN

Courbet, Gustave   koor-BAY, guh-STAWV

Crassus   KRASS-us

Crécy   kray-SEE

Croesus   KREE-suhs

Cruz, Juana Ines de la   KROOZ, WAHN-uh ee NAYS de lah

Curie, Marie   kyoo-REE, muh-REE

d'Este, Isabella   ES-tay

Daimyo   die-AIM-yo

Dao De Jing   dow duh JING

Darius   duh-RYE-us

dauphin   DAW-fin

de Gaulle, Charles   duh GOLL, SHARL

Delacroix, Eugène   del-uh-KWAW, yoo-ZHAHN

Deng Xiaoping   DUNG shee-ow-ping

Descartes, René   day-KART, ruh-NAY

Dias, Bartholomeu   DEE-us, bar-too-loo-MAY

Diaspora   die-AS-pur-uh

Díaz, Porfirio   DEE-ahz, pah-FEER-yoh

Diderot, Denis   DEE-duh-roh, duh-NEE

Diem, Ngo Dinh   dzee-EM, NGOH Den

Diocletian   die-uh-KLEE-shun

Dorians   DOR-ee-uns

Douhet, Giulio   doo-EE, JOOL-yoh

Duma   DOO-muh

Echeverria, Luis   ah-chuh-vuh-REE-uh, loo-EES

Einsatzgruppen   INE-zats-groo-pen

encomienda   en-koh-mee-EN-dah

Engels, Friedrich   ENG-ulz, FREE-drik

Entente Cordiale   ahn-TAHNT kor-DYALL

ephor   EF-or

Epicurus/Epicureanism   EP-i-KYOOR-us/EP-i-kyoo-REE-uh-ni-zem

Erasmus, Desiderius   i-RAZZ-mus, des-i-DIR-ee-us

Erhard, Ludwig   AIR-hart

Etruscan   i-TRUSS-kuhn

Euripides   yoo-RIP-i-deez

exchequer   EX-chek-ur

Fa Xian   fa SHIEN

fasces   FASS-eez

Fascio di Combattimento   FASH-ee-oh di com-BATT-ee-men-toh

Fatimid   FAT-i-mid

Flaubert, Gustave   floh-BEAR, guh-STAWV

Friedan, Betty   fri-DAN

Friedrich, Caspar David   FREE-drik, KASS-par DAHV-eet

Frimaire   free-MARE

Fronde   FROND

Führer   FYOOR-ur

gabelle   gah-BELL

Garibaldi, Giuseppe   gar-uh-BAWL-dee, joo-ZEP-pay

Gaugamela   gaw-guh-MEE-luh

gerousia   juh-ROO-see-uh

Gierek, Edward   GYER-ek

Gilgamesh   GILL-guh-mesh

glasnost   GLAZ-nohst

Gleichschaltung   GLIKE-shalt-ung

Gomulka, Wladyslaw   goh-MOOL-kuh, vla-DIS-lawf

Gorbachev, Mikhail   GOR-buh-chof, meek-HALE

Gracchus   GRA-kus

Gropius, Walter   GROH-pee-us, VAHL-ter

Grossdeutsch   gross-DOICH

Guevara, Ernesto "Che"   gay-VAR-uh, er-NAY-stoh "CHAY"

Habsburg   HAPS-burg

Hadrian   HAY-dree-un

Hagia Sophia   HAG-ee-uh soh-FEE-uh

hajj   HAJ

Hammurabi   ham-uh-RAH-bee

Han Gaozu   HAHN GOW-ZOO

Hannibal   HAN-uh-bul

Harappan   har-RAP-an

harijans   har-uh-JAHNS

Harun al-Rashid   huh-ROON al-ra-SHEED

Hatshepsut   hat-SHEP-soot

Havel, Vaclav   HAH-vuhl, VAHT-slaf

Haydn, Franz Joseph   HIDE-n, FRAHNTS

hegemon   HEJ-uh-mon

Hegira   huh-JIGH-ruh

Hellenistic   hell-uh-NIS-tik

helots   HELL-uts

Herzl, Theodor   HERT-sul, TAY-oh-dor

Heydrich, Reinhard   HIGH-drik, RINE-hart

Hidalgo y Castilla, Miguel   hi-DAL-goh ee cahs-TEEL-yuh, mee-GEL

hieroglyph   HIGH-ur-oh-glif

Hitler Jugend   JOO-gunt

Ho Chi Minh   HOE CHEE MIN

Höch, Hannah   HOKH

Hohenstaufen   HOE-un-SHTAU-fun

Hohenzollern   HOE-un-ZAHL-lurn

Homo erectus   HOH-MOH i-RECK-tuhs

Homo habilis   HOH-MOH HAB-uh-lus

Homo sapiens   HOH-MOH SAY-pee-enz

hoplites   HOP-lites

Horace   HOR-us

Höss, Rudolf   HAHSS, roo-DAHLF

Huguenots   HYOO-guh-nots

Husak, Gustav HOO-sahk, guh-STAHV
Hydaspes high-DASS-peez
Hyksos hik-SAHS or hik-SOHS
Ibn Khaldun ib-en-kal-DOON
Ibn Sina ib-en SEE-nuh
Ieyasu, Tokugawa ee-eye-AY-soo, toe-koo-GAH-wah
Ignatius of Loyola ig-NAY-shus of loi-OH-luh
Il Duce eel DOO-chay
imperator im-puh-RAH-tor
imperium im-PIER-ee-um
intendant in-TEN-duhnt
Inukai Tsuyoshi EE-NUH-KIGH TSOO-yah-shee
Isis EYE-sis
Issus ISS-us
Jacobin JAK-uh-bin
Jagiello yah-GYELL-oh
Jaruzelski, Wojciech yahr-uh-ZEL-skee, VOI-chek
Jiang Qing JIANG CHING
jihad ji-HAHD
Jinnah, Mohammed Ali JEE-nah, moe-HA-mud a-LEE
Judaea joo-DEE-uh
Junkers YOONG-kers
Justinian juh-STIN-ee-un
Juvenal JOO-vuh-nul
Ka'aba stone KAH-BAH
Kadar, Janos KAY-dahr, YAHN-us
Kadinsky, Vassily kan-DIN-skee, vus-YEEL-yee
kamikaze kah-mi-KAH-zee
Kangxi KANG-she
Keiretsu business arrangement kai-RET-su
Kerensky, Alexander kuh-REN-skee
Keynes, John Maynard KAYNZ
Khan, Khubilai KHAN, KOO-bil-eye
Khatemi, Mohammed KHAH-tee-mee
Khayyam, Omar kigh-YAHM, oh-MAR
Khmer Rouge ka-MEHR roozh
Khoisan KOY-SAN
Khrushchev, Nikita KROOSH-chef, nuh-KEE-tuh
Khufu KOO-FOO
Kita, Ikki KEE-tah EEk-EE
Knossos NAH-sus
Koguryo ko-GOOR-yo
Kohl, Helmut KOLE, HELL-mut
Kolkhoz kahl-KAWZ
Kollantai, Alexandra kawl-un-TIE
Kosovo kah-suh-VOH
Kraft durch Freude CRAFT durch FROI-duh
Kristallnacht KRIS-tal-NAHCHT
Kshatriya kuh-SHOT-ria
Kuchuk-Kainarji koo-CHOOK-kigh-NAR-jee
kulaks koo-LAKS
kulturkampf kool-TOOR-kahmf
Kundera, Milan KOON-de-rah, MIL-ahn

Kwasniewski, Aleksander KWAHS-noo-skee, ah-lek-SAHN-der
laissez-faire les-ay-FAIR
Lao Tzu LAUW DZU
latifundia lat-uh-FUN-dee-uh
Latium LAY-shee-um
Laurier, Wilfred LOR-ee-ay
Lebensraum LAY-benz-roum
Lee Kuan-yew LEE KWAN YEW
Lévesque, René luh-VEK, ruh-NAY
Lin Zexu LIN DZUH-shoo
Livy LIV-ee
López Portillo, José LOH-pez por-TEE-yoh, hoh-ZAY
Luddites LUD-ites
Ludendorff, Erich LOOD-un-dorf
Luftwaffe LUFT-vaf-uh
l'uomo universale l'oo-OH-moh oo-nee-vehr-SAH-leh
Lycurgus ligh-KUR-gus
Machiavelli, Niccolò mak-ee-uh-VELL-ee, nee-koh-LOH
Machu Picchu MAH-CHOO PEEK-SHOO
Madero, Francisco muh-der-oh, fran-CIS-koh
Magyars MAG-yars
Mahabharata MA-HA-bah-rah-tah
Majapahit mah-ja-PAH-heet
Malleus Maleficarum mall-EE-us mal-uh-FIK-ar-um
Manchukuo man-CHOO-KWOH
Manetho MAN-uh-THOH
Mao Zedong mau zee-DONG
Marie Antoinette muh-REE an-twuh-NET
Marius MAR-ee-us
Marquez, Gabriel Garcia MAR-kays, gab-ree-ELL gar-SEE-uh
Massaccio muh-ZAHCH-ee-OH
Mbecki, Thabo mu-BEK-ee, TYE-bo
Meiji MAY-jee
Mein Kampf mine KAHMF
Menander me-NAN-der
Mendeleyev, Dmitri men-duh-LAY-ef, di-MEE-tri
Meroë mer-OH-ee
Mesopotamia mess-oh-poh-TAME-ee-uh
mestizos me-STEE-zohs
Metternich, Klemens von MET-er-nik, KLAY-mens
Michelangelo my-kell-AN-juh-loh
Mieszko MYESH-koh
Millet, Jean-François mi-LAY, ZHAHN-FRAN-swah
Milosevic, Slobodan mi-LOH-suh-vich, slaw-BAW-dahn
Miltiades mil-TIGH-uh-DEEZ
missi dominici MISS-ee doe-MIN-ee-chee
Mitterrand, Francois mee-ter-AHN, FRAN-swah
Moche MO-chay
Moctezuma mahk-tuh-ZOO-muh
Moldavia mahl-DAY-vee-uh
Monet, Claude moh-NAY, KLODE

Montesquieu   MONT-ess-skyoo

Montessori, Maria   mon-ti-SOR-ee

Morisot, Berthe   mor-ee-ZOH, BERT

Mozart, Wolfgang Amadeus   MOHT-sart, volf-GANG ah-muh-DAY-us

Muawiyah   moo-AH-wee-yah

Mughal   MOO-gahl

Muhammad   moe-HA-mud

mulattoes   muh-LA-tohs

Muslim   MUZ-lum

Mutsuhito   moo-tsoo-HEE-toe

Mwene Metapa   MWAHN-uh muh-TAH-puh

Mycenaean   my-suh-NEE-un

Nagy, Imry   NAHJD, IM-re

Nebuchadnezzar   neb-uh-kad-NWZZ-ar

Nehru, Jawaharlal   NAY-roo, jah-WAH-har-lahl

Nero   NEE-roh

Neumann, Balthasar   NOI-mahn, BAHL-tah-zar

Nevsky, Alexander   NEW-skee

Ngo Dinh Diem   NGOH din dee-EM

Ngugi Wa Thiong'o   en-GU-ji WA THIE-ong-oh

Nimwegen   NIM-vay-gun

Nkrumah, Kwame   en-KRU-may, KWA-may

Novotny, Antonin   noh-VOT-nee, AN-ton-yeen

Nyerere, Julius   nyay-RARE-ee

Nystadt   nee-STAHD

Octavian   ok-TAY-vee-un

optimates   opp-tuh-MAH-tays

Osiris   oh-SIGH-ris

Ovid   OV-id

Pachakuti   PAH-chah-koo-tee

Pahlavi dynasty   pah-LAH-vee

Palenque   pah-LENG-kay

Paleologus   pay-lee-OHL-uh-gus

Pankhurst, Emmeline   PANK-herst, em-uh-LINE

papal curia   PAY-pul KOOR-ee-uh

Parlement   par-luh-MAHN

paterfamilias   pay-ter-fuh-MILL-ee-us

Peloponnesus   pe-luh-puh-NEE-sus

Pentateuch   PEN-tuh-tuke

perestroika   pair-ess-TROY-kuh

Pericles   PER-i-kleez

Perón, Juan   pay-ROHN, WAHN

Pétain, Henri   pay-TAN, AHN-ree

Petrarch   PE-trark

philosophe   fee-luh-ZAWF

Phoenicians   fi-NISH-uns

Picasso, Pablo   pi-KAW-soh

Pinochet, Augusto   PEE-noh-shay, aw-GOO-stoh

Pisistratus   pi-SIS-truh-tus

Pissaro, Camille   pi-SARR-oh, kah-MEEYL

Pizarro, Francesco   pi-ZARR-oh, frahn-CHASE-koh

Planck, Max   PLAHNK

Plantagenet   plan-TA-juh-net

Plato   PLAY-toe

Poincaré, Raymond   pwan-kah-RAY, re-MOAN

polis   POE-lis

politiques   puh-lee-TEEKS

Polybius   poe-LIB-ee-us

Pompey   POM-pee

pontifex maximus   PON-ti-feks MAK-suh-mus

populares   POP-yoo-lar-ays

praetor   PREE-ter

princeps   PRIN-seps

procurator   PROK-yuh-ray-ter

Ptolemy/Ptolemaic   TOL-uh-mee/TOL-uh-MAY-ik

Punic   PYOO-nik

Pugachev, Emelyan   poo-guh-CHEF, em-ELL-yun

Pyrrhus/Pyrrhic   PIR-us/PIR-ik

Qadhafi, Muammar   gah-DAH-fee, myoo-am-MAR

Qianlong   chee-UN-LUNG

Qin Shi Huangdi   chin SHE hwang-DEE

Qing dynasty   CHING

Quesnay, François   kay-NAY, FRAN-swah

Quetzalcoatl   ket-SAHL-koh-AHT-ul

Quipu   KEE-poo

Quran   kuh-RAN

Rameses   RAM-i-seez

Raphael   RAFF-ee-ul

Rasputin   rass-PYOO-tin

Realpolitik   ray-AHL-poe-li-teek

Reichsrat   RIKES-raht

Ricci, Matteo   REECH-ee, mah-TAY-oh

risorgimento   ree-SOR-jee-men-toe

Robespierre, Maximilien   ROHBZ-pee-air, mak-SEE-meel-yahn

Rococo   ro-KOH-koh

Rosas, Juan Manuel de   ROH-sahs, WAHN mahn-WELL duh

Rousseau, Jean-Jacques   roo-SOH ZHAHN-ZHAHK

Sadducees   SA-juh-seez

Sadi   sah-DEE

Safavids   suh-FAH-weedz

Sakharov, Andrei   SAH-kuh-rof, ahn-DRAY

Saladin   SAL-uh-din

Sallust   SALL-ust

San Martin, José   SAN mar-TEEN, hoh-ZAY

Sartre, Jean-Paul   SAR-truh, ZHAHN-PAUL

satrap/satrapy   SAY-trap/SAY-truh-pee

Schleswig-Holstein   SCHLES-vig-HOLE-stine

Schlieffen   SHLEE-fun

Schmidt, Helmut   SHMIT, HELL-mut

Schroeder, Gerhard   SHROH-der, ger-HART

Schönberg, Arnold   SHURN-burg, ARR-nawlt

Schutzstaffel   SHOOTS-shah-ful

Seleucus/Seleucid   si-LOO-kus/si-LOO-sid

Seljuk Turks   SELL-juke

Seneca   SEN-i-kuh

Sephardic   suh-FAR-dik

sesterces   SES-ters-eez

Sforza   SFORT-zuh

Shari'a   shay-REE-uh

Shari'ya   shay-REE-uh

Sheikh   SHEEK or SHAYK

Shi'ite   SHE-ite

Shotoku Taishi   show-TOE-koo tie-ISH-ee

Siddhartha Gautama   sid-AR-tha guh-TAW-mah

Sieveking, Amalie   SEEVE-king

Sima Qian   suh-MAH chee-AHN or chee-YEN

Sjahrir Sutan   SYAH-rir, soo-TAN

Socrates   SOK-ruh-teez

Solon   SOH-lun

Solzhenitsyn, Alexander   SOLE-zhuh-NEET-sin

Somoza, Anastasio   suh-MOH-zuh, ahn-ash-TAHS-yoh

Sophocles   SOF-uh-kleez

Soyinka, Wole   shah-YIN-kuh, WAH-lay

Spartacus   SPAR-tuh-kus

Speer, Albert   SHPIER

squadristi   sqah-DREES-tee

Sri Lanka   SREE-LAHN-kuh

Srivijaya   sree-vee-JAH-ya

Stoicism   STOH-i-siz-um

Stravinsky, Igor   struh-VIN-skee, EE-gor

Stresemann, Gustav   SHTRAY-zuh-mahn, GUS-tahf

Sturmabteilung   SHTOORM-AP-ti-loong

Sudetenland   soo-DAYT-un-LAND

Suger, Abbot   soo-ZHER

Suleyman I the Magnificent   soo-lee-MAHN

Sumerian   soo-MER-ee-un

Suttner, Bertha von   ZOOT-ner

Tacitus   TASS-i-tus

taille   TAH-yuh or TIE

Tang Taizong   TANG TYE-zawng

Tanzania   tan-zah-NEE-ah

Tenochtitlán   tay-NAWCH-teet-LAHN

Teotihuacán   TAY-oh-tee-WAH-kahn

Tertullian   tur-TULL-yun

Theocritus   thee-OCK-ri-tus

Thermidor   ter-mee-DOR

Thermopylae   thur-MOP-uh-lee

Thucydides   thoo-SID-uh-deez

Thutmosis   thoot-MOH-sus

Tiberius   tie-BIR-ee-us

Tito   TEE-toh

Tlaxcala   tlah-SKAHL-uh

Torah   TOR-uh

Tordesillas   tor-duh-SEE-yus

Toussaint L'Ouverture   too-SAN loo-vur-TOOR

Trajan   TRAY-jun

Trevithick, Richard   TREV-uh-thik

Trudeau, Pierre   TROO-doh, pee-YEHR

Tutankhamen   tuh-tan-KAH-muhn

Tzara, Tristan   TSAH-rah, tri-STAN

Uighur   yu-EE-gur

ulama   oo-lah-MAH

Ulbricht, Walter   UL-brikt, VAHL-ter

Umayyads   oo-MY-ads

Unam Sanctam   OON-ahm SANK-tahm

universitas   yoo-ni-VER-si-tahs

Vaisya   VIGHSH-yuh

Valois   VAL-wah

van Eyck, Jan   van IKE

van Gogh, Vincent   van GOE

Vargas, Getúlio   VAR-gus, zhuh-TOOL-yoo

Venetia   vuh-NEE-shee-uh

Vesalius, Andreas   vi-SAY-lee-us, ahn-DRAY-us

Vespucci, Amerigo   ves-POO-chee, ahm-ay-REE-goe

Vierzenheiligen   feer-tsun-HILE-i-gun

Virgil   VUR-jul

vizier   vuy-ZEER

Volkschulen   FOLK-shool-un

Voltaire   vole-TAIR

Walesa, Lech   va-WENZ-uh, LEK

Wallachia   wah-lay-KEE-uh

Watteau, Antoine   wah-TOE, AHN-twahn

Weizsäcker, Richard von   VITS-zek-er, RIK-art

wergeld   wur-GELD

Winkelmann, Maria   VING-kul-mun

Xerxes   ZURK-seez

Xhosa   KOH-suh

Xinjiang   shin-JI-ang

Xiongnu (Hsiung-nu)   she-ONG-noo

Xuan Zang   SHYAHN ZAHNG

Yahweh   YAH-wah

Yeltsin, Boris   YELT-sun

Yi Song-gye   YEE sohn-GEE

yishuv   YISH-uv

Zapata, Emiliano   zuh-PAH-tuh, ay-mel-YAHN-oh

zemstvos   ZEMPST-voh

Zeno   ZEE-noh

Zhang Xueliang   JANG shwee-lee-ONG

Zhenge   JUNG-huh

Zhou   JOE

Zhu Xi   JOO SHEE

Zhu Yuanzhang   jew whan-JANG

ziggurat   ZIG-guh-rat

Zimbabwe   zim-BAH-bway

Zola, Emile   ZOH-luh, ay-MEEL

zollverein   TSOL-fuh-rine

Zoroaster   ZOR-oh-as-ter

INDEX

Russia (*continued*)
  religion of, 154
  Seven Years' War, 368
  Viking settlements, 250
  war with France, 380–81, 383

S

Sacred Edict (Kangxi), 345
Sacrifice, of humans, 118, 126
Sadducees, 104
Safavid Empire, 321, 325–29
Safi al-Din, 326
The Sahara, 160
Saharan civilizations, 162–63
Saikaku, 357
Saint-Denis, abbey of, 258
Saint Petersburg, 288
Saladin, 143, 260
Salamis, battle of, 76
Samarra, Great Mosque of, 149
Samnites, 91
Samudragupta, 182
Samurai, 226–27, 228, 268, 355
San people, 172, 175
Sanskrit, 41, 192, 194
Sati, 33, 188, 332
Saxons, 249
Scholasticism, 257–58
Science and technology
  Arab empire, 148
  Enlightenment Age, 364–65
  Greece, ancient, 86
  India, 43
Scientific Revolution, 291–93, 363
Scotland, 288, 370. *See also* Great Britain
Sculpture
  Africa, 174–75
  Greece, ancient, 78, 80, 86
  India, 192
  Japan, 233
Sea trade, 208
Second Punic War, 94
Selim I, 321, 326
Seljuk Turks, 143, 156, 319, 325
Senate
  of Roman Empire, 97
  of Roman Republic, 95
Sennacherib, 21
Serbs, 249, 319
Serfs. *See* Feudalism
Sermon on the Mount, 106
Seven Years' War, 368–69
Severan rulers, 103
Seville, 304
Sexual relations, 9, 34, 82
Sforza family, 278
Shadow plays, 194–95
Shah Jahan, 331–32, 336
Shakespeare, William, 290–91, 292
Shakuntala (Kalidasa), 192
Shang dynasty, 6, 47–49
Shari'a, 138, 324
Shi'ite Muslims, 141, 143, 327

Shinto, 230–31
Ships, 59, 300
Shogunate system, 227–28, 354–55
Shona peoples, 306
Shotoku Taishi, 225–26
Sicily, 93–94, 101, 151, 278
Siddhartha Gautama, 37–39, 183, 184
Sigiriya, royal palace at, 191
Sikhism, 188–89
Sikri, 336–37
Silesia, 368
Silk, 52, 151–52
"Silk Road," 52, 181, 204, 207–8, 266
Silla kingdom, 235
Silver, 283, 303–4, 343, 369
Sima Qian, 56, 57
Sinan, 325
Sind, conquest of, 185
Sitar, 193
Slavery
  Africa, 166, 173–74
  Arab Empire, 146
  Aztec civilization, 124
  Greece, ancient, 75, 81
  in Mesopotamia, 7
  Ottoman Empire, 323
  in Roman Empire, 101, 102
Slave trade, 307–10
Slavic peoples, 249–50
Slovenia, 288
Smith, Adam, 364–65
The Social Contract (Rousseau), 365
Society and social structure
  Abbasid dynasty, 141
  Africa, 172–74
  Arab Empire, 146–47
  Aryan civilization (India), 30
  Aztec civilization, 124
  China, 48–49, 59, 61–63, 208–9, 216
  Europe, early modern, 368
  Europe, medieval, 246–47, 273
  Europe, Renaissance, 273–74
  France, pre-revolution, 374
  Greece, ancient, 81
  India, 32–33, 184–85, 189
  Japan, 229, 355, 356
  Korea, 235, 358–59
  Mesopotamia, 7
  Mughal Empire, 335
  Neolithic Revolution, 6
  Olmec civilization, 118
  Roman Republic, 91, 92–93
  Southeast Asia, 194, 195–96, 314–15
  Vietnam, 238
Socrates, 79
Solomon, 18
Solomonids, 167
Solon, 75
Somalia, 167, 176
Song dynasty, 205, 206, 207, 210, 218, 237
Songhai kingdom, 307
Song Taizu, 205
Son-Jara, 177

Sophocles, 78
South America, first civilizations in, 127–30, 132
Southeast Asia
  agriculture in, 193, 196, 314
  economy of, 314
  geography of, 193
  Indian influence over, 193, 194, 196
  political structure, 314
  religion of, 196–98, 312, 314
  society and social structure, 194, 195–96, 314–15
  spice trade era, 311–15
  states of, 193–95
Southern Africa
  Dutch colonies in, 306–7
  early states of, 170–72
  exploration of, 159–60
  first civilizations, 164
Spain
  under Arab control, 142, 149
  Armada disaster, 283
  colonialism, 303, 306, 369, 370
  control of Italy, 278
  exploration, 116, 126–27, 298, 299, 302–3, 305
  in Latin America, 369, 370
  in Mexico, 303
  monarchy, 15th century, 276
  North American colonies, 369
  religious conflict, 283
  Thirty Years' War, 285
  trade, 367
Sparta, 68–69, 74, 77
Spartacus, 101
Spice Islands, 301
Spice trade, 297, 300–301
The Spirit of the Laws (Montesquieu), 364
Sports and games
  Aztec civilization, 126
  Mayan civilization, 120, 121
Spring Festival on the River, 209
Sri Lanka, 191
Srivijaya, 193–94
Stamp Act, 371
The Starry Messenger, 292
Steel, 207
Stele, 163
Stoicism, 87, 100
Stone Age, 3–6
Stonehenge, 17
Strasbourg, 262
Strozzi, Alessandra, 274
Stuart dynasty, 288
Sudras, 32
Sufism, 148
Sugar industry, 307–8
Sui dynasty, 203
Sui Yangdi, 203
Suleyman I, 322
Sumerians, 7–11
Summa Theologica (Aquinas), 257
Sunni Muslims, 141, 143, 323
Surat, English arrival at, 333